# ILLUMINATED MANUSCRIPTS AND BOOKS IN THE BODLEIAN LIBRARY

GARLAND REFERENCE LIBRARY
OF THE HUMANITIES
(VOL. 123)

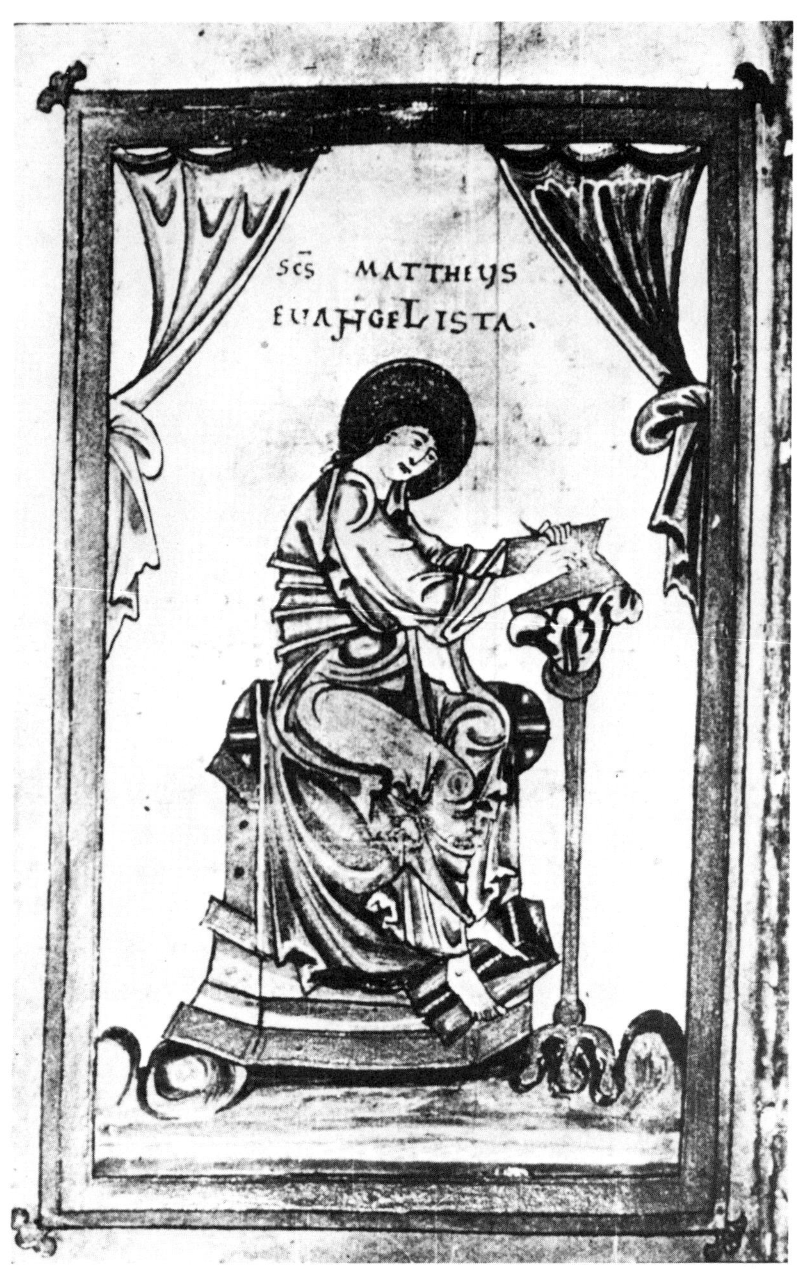
SCS MATTHEUS
EUANGELISTA.

Plate I

# ILLUMINATED MANUSCRIPTS AND BOOKS IN THE BODLEIAN LIBRARY

## *A Supplemental Index*

compiled and edited by

Thomas H. Ohlgren

*Associate Professor of English*

*Purdue University*

GARLAND PUBLISHING, INC. • NEW YORK & LONDON

1978

**Library of Congress Cataloging in Publication Data**

Oxford. University. Bodleian Library.
Illuminated manuscripts and books in the Bodleian Library.

(Garland reference library of the humanities; v. 123)
"Supplement to Illuminated manuscripts: an index to selected Bodleian Library color reproductions."
1. Illumination of books and manuscripts, Medieval—Catalogs. 2. Illumination of books and manuscripts, Medieval—Catalogs—Indexes. 3. Illumination of books and manuscripts—Slides—Indexes. 4. Illumination of books and manuscripts—England—Oxford—Catalogs. 5. Illumination of books and manuscripts—England—Oxford—Catalogs—Indexes. 6. Oxford. University. Bodleian Library—Catalogs. I. Ohlgren, Thomas H., 1941– II. Oxford. University. Bodleian Library. Illuminated manuscripts. III. Title.
ND2920.09 1977 Suppl 016.7456'7'09407402574
ISBN 0-8240-9820-X 78-14778

Printed on acid-free, 250-year-life paper
Manufactured in the United States of America

# CONTENTS

# ILLUSTRATIONS

All illustrations are from the slide sets listed in this volume. The SM (Slides Medieval) numbers refer to Purdue's shelving scheme; the first number indicates the abstract / slide set number while the second indicates the frame / slide number. The photographs are published with the kind permission of the Bodleian Library.


Plate I. *frontispiece*

MS Lat. Liturg. f. 5, f. 3$^{v}$ (SM 549–27), English, 11th/ 2nd quarter, *Gospel Book of Queen Margaret*. St. Matthew.

Plate II. *facing page 1*

a. MS Canon Ital. 280, f. 204$^{v}$ (SM 641–19), Italian/ North, 15th/ c. 1400, *Life of the Virgin and of Christ*. Harrowing of Hell. Adam and Eve watch.
b. MS Rawl. Liturg. e. 4, f. 16$^{v}$ (SM 650–4), Flemish, 15th/ 3rd quarter, *Book of Hours*. Christ in Garden of Gethsemane.
c. MS Rawl. D. 403, f. 3$^{v}$ (SM 610–2), English, 15th/ 1498. Last Judgment.
d. MS Douce 391, 3rd opening (SM 619–4), Spanish, 16th/ 2nd half, *Portolan Chart*. Map of India, Persia, Arabia.

Plate III. *following page 201*

a. MS Ashmole 789, f. 365 (SM 724–1), English, 14th/ after 1387, *Astronomical Calendar*. Blood-letting figure.
b. MS Ashmole 5, f. 34$^{v}$ (SM 724–3), English, 14th/ after 1387, *Astronomical Calendar*. Zodiacal man.
c. MS Ashmole 370, f. 27$^{v}$ (SM 724–2), English, 15th/ c. 1424, *Astronomical Calendar*. Zodiacal man.

blame sin. Genesis 3/ verses 21 & 23/ Expulsion. Genesis 4/ verses 1–2/ Adam prefers Abel to Cain. Christ prefers Christians to wicked.

c. MS Douce 366, f. 89 (SM 712–9), English/ East Anglia, 13th/ late to c. 1300, *Ormesby Psalter*. Psalm 68/69 initial S Salvum me fac/ Jonah and the whale.

d. MS Digby 223, f. 129 (SM 534–6), French/ North, 13th/ late, *The Quest of the Grail*. Gawain rides in pursuit of the quest.

Plate VII. *following page 231*

a. MS Auct. T. 2. 4, f. 58v (SM 543–6), Italian/ South?, 10th?, *Seven Greek Prophets*. Ornamental medallion/ bust of prophet.

b. MS Laud Misc. 644, f. 10v (SM 618–2), French/ Bayeux, 13th/ c. 1268–74, *Astronomical and Astrological Treatises*. Centaurus holds branch and small animal.

c. MS Rawl. Liturg. e. 27, f. 17 (SM 581–3), French, 15th/ 2nd quarter, *Book of Hours/ Use of Le Mans, Mass of St. Gregory*. Pope Gregory kneels at altar. Christ shows wounds.

d. MS Rawl. B. 214, f. 200 (SM 571–5), English, 15th/ mid, *Prologue to Ovid and Metamorphoses*. Mars and Venus embrace. Vulcan with hammer and tongs. Hercules wears cloak with lion's head. Aesculapius follows Hercules.

Plate VIII. *following page 313*

a. MS Bodley 717, f. 287v (SM 546–26), English/ Exeter, 12th/ early, St. Jerome's *Commentary on Isaiah*. Hugo Pictor/ self-portrait of illuminator.

b. MS Canon Ital. 85, f. 10v (SM 707–148), Italian/ Mantua or Ferrara, 15th/ c. 1463–64, *Filocolo* by Boccaccio. Initial S.

c. MS Laud Misc. 173, f. 115v (SM 635–2), German, 15th/ early, *Lives of Saints*. St. Brendan lands ship at Isle of Birds.

d. PR Arch. B. b. 4 (SM 637–16), Russian/ Kiev, 17th/

# PREFACE

## W. O. Hassall

*M.A., D.Phil., F.S.A., F.R.Hist. Soc.*
*Senior Assistant Librarian of the Bodleian Library*
*Librarian of the Earls of Leicester at Holkham*

Custodians of great collections of manuscripts and early-printed books have the contradictory problem of preserving treasures for posterity while also making them accessible for scholarship. They can never exhibit more than a fraction of these treasures, and books exhibited can be displayed to reveal only a single opening of two facing pages.

While centuries must elapse before any high proportion of the contents of the manuscripts can be reproduced in color, on paper, the Bodleian Library has made many, many pages available by less conventional means, such as 35mm. color microfilm.

This work has proceeded for some fifteen years.* What has been produced on film can be used as separate slides. Many of the chief pages in the chief manuscripts are now thus accessible, although the proportion of what has been reproduced, compared with what could be reproduced, is not high. The quantity reproduced is, however, sufficiently great to present problems of retrieval, especially to those who are unfamiliar with the originals and who are physically far away from them.

Among those who have sought a solution to this problem, Professor Thomas Ohlgren has completed two remarkable works. Each of the Bodleian films is normally accompanied by a brief handlist that gives information about the source and nature of its contents. After seven years' work, Professor

*See "Colour Slides," *Bodleian Library Record*, July 1973.

Ohlgren has produced two computer-generated catalogs with indices to 750 of the Bodleian color microfilms. With their aid, scholars and teachers can find many references to visual materials both in the original manuscripts and in the large collection of slides, mounted from Bodleian Library films, at Purdue University. The original manuscripts are mostly in the Bodleian Library at Oxford. The Bodleian reproductions can be available in any library of the world that chooses to buy any of them, always provided that this is not prevented by the Customs and Imports regulations of its government.

The Bodleian Library welcomes this opportunity of explaining a number of important points:

The references in Professor Ohlgren's two volumes are, of course, intended primarily as a key to the holdings at Purdue University. They are useful for identifying themes, styles, types of manuscripts, and Bodleian shelfmarks. When scholars use them for ordering material direct from the Bodleian Library, it is important to note that the "abstract" numbers in the index are not the same as the Bodleian Library roll numbers. The correct Bodleian roll numbers are listed in the abstracts under the heading **Negative Reference**. As there may be occasional ambiguities in the numbering of slides, those ordering individual slides should include the subject as well as the Bodleian reference number of each slide.

The Bodleian Library issues a printed price list of films, arranged by roll number. For historical reasons, some films record all the illuminations in one manuscript; others contain a selection of pictures with a common factor, such as subject or provenance, taken from one or more manuscripts. Often the original selections were made to meet the requirements of a particular scholar. Recently the Bodleian has produced a series of "Miscellany" filmstrips, which include omissions from earlier filmstrips together with material ordered by customers wanting only one or two slides that could not in themselves form an entire roll. Details of the earliest "Miscellany" films are available on the latest price list. It is hoped that more will be made available soon.

The Bodleian Library makes a great effort to keep a stock of every item listed. The earliest negatives, because of their age, may occasionally have faults. It is not practical, however, to rephotograph them, and the library has decided to continue to sell the originals even with such blemishes rather than to delete them from the series. The Bodleian cannot unfortunately undertake to lend, hire, or send any of its transparencies on approval.

The Bodleian Library's success in making tens of thousands of reproductions available to the world is mainly due to the assistance of a group of devoted, unpaid volunteers. As it is impossible to thank all by name, it seems invidious to name any of them. However, it would be unjust not to mention Mrs. G. Spriggs, Mrs. Stone, Mrs. L. Valentine, and the Hon. Mrs. Wilson among those who did much of the work of producing descriptions of the separate illuminations in some thousands of manuscripts. Other volunteers have made it possible for visitors to the Bodleian to have access to two series of mounted slides, from every existing roll. From these they may purchase anything required. One series is arranged in numerical order according to the handlist, the other under various broad topics. Apart from the series of slides available for sale, others are available in the Bodleian Library for consultation. One complete set is arranged by library shelfmark and page or folio number. Other select sets are arranged by date and locality of production, and by Biblical or other topic.

An obvious defect in the treasury of pictorial source material as yet available lies in the piecemeal nature of the coverage of some important manuscripts. It is hoped that this will be remedied by the production of color microfiches.

A defect of the handlists is that they have to be very brief indeed and contain inconsistencies. More leisurely and detailed descriptions of three dozen of the chief manuscripts, with some discussion of the styles, types of manuscripts, and the donors of the great collections from which they come, are assembled with reproductions in color, often of the original size, in A. G. and W. O. Hassall, *Treasures from the Bodleian Library* (Gordon Fraser, 1976).

It is important, also, to observe that no reproductions may be made from slides without prior permission from the Bodleian Library. Although all the photographs, with a few exceptions, are copyrighted by the Bodleian Library, the copyright of some of the originals belongs elsewhere.

The bulk of the reproductions are from Bodleian Western Manuscripts, but some printed material, notably of the John Johnson collection of printed ephemera, is included. Some of the manuscripts photographed belong to Oxford College Libraries and even to libraries outside Oxford, notably that at Holkham. The project, however, excludes all Oriental manuscripts in the Bodleian.

The vast accumulation of material now available presents a difficult problem of retrieval even to those familiar with it, and with the originals that it reproduces. Thomas Ohlgren has attacked this problem with great success. *Illuminated Manuscripts and Books in the Bodleian Library: A Supplemental Index* is a valuable and useful contribution to medieval and Renaissance studies. Lecturers and research workers have now a means of finding what this corpus of visual information consists of that is relevant to their immediate needs, even though they have never before seen either the slides or the original manuscripts. Many will derive benefit from Professor Ohlgren's labors without realizing their debt to his indices. For many, illustrated manuscripts and books will give a truer image of the past, thanks to the tools that Professor Ohlgren has provided for medieval research.

# GENERAL INTRODUCTION

## Thomas H. Ohlgren

This volume is a supplement to *Illuminated Manuscripts: An Index to Selected Bodleian Library Color Reproductions* (Garland, 1977). It comprises an additional 250 abstracts of and indices to the Bodleian Library filmstrips. The Bodleian contains one of the world's more comprehensive and beautiful collections of illuminated medieval manuscripts and Renaissance printed books. Although this volume provides access to a large variety of original artifacts, ranging from Roman mosaics and wall paintings to watercolors, papyri, and maps, its primary focus is upon illuminated manuscripts and early-printed books, dating in the main from the ninth century through the seventeenth century. Some of the notable manuscripts described in this volume are: *The Caedmon Genesis* (MS Junius 11), *The Ormesby Psalter* (MS Douce 366), *The Douce Apocalypse* (MS Douce 180), *The Romance of Alexander* (MS Bodley 264), *The Codex Mendoza* (MS Arch. Selden A.1), *The Bible Moralisée* (MS Bodley 270b), and *The Anglo-Saxon Chronicle E-Text* (MS Laud Misc. 636). Altogether, this volume provides access to over ten thousand folios and pages from 672 manuscripts and one hundred printed books.

Some of the thousands of topics illustrated by the Bodleian slides include: alchemy, allegory, architecture, arms and armor, astronomy and astrology, Biblical iconography from Genesis to Revelation, botanical and zoological illustration, calendars, Church history, Classical texts, costume, daily life, drama, engineering, furniture, heraldry, law, maps, mathematics, medicine, music, paleography and calligraphy, philosophy, romance, saints, science, tournaments, typology, and warfare. Indeed, the collection represents a veritable encyclopedia of knowledge known to Western civilization, very much in the tradition of Vincent of Beauvais' *Speculum majus*.

This volume should appeal to a variety of users. For teachers, it provides means to illustrate historical periods once called dark. With the resurgence of interest in medieval and Renaissance studies, teachers at all levels will find its contents invaluable. Some teachers of early periods have discovered that academic subjects, such as history, literature, art history, and philosophy, can best be taught by employing a broad cultural approach. Such courses strive to demonstrate cultural correlatives and interrelations among the arts. This volume will facilitate the location of apposite photographic materials for teaching. For scholars and archivists, this volume constitutes a reference guide to the chief illuminated manuscripts and books in the Bodleian Library. Access to these important documents is, of course, possible through other reference tools, but *Illuminated Manuscripts and Books in the Bodleian Library* is unique in giving descriptions of the iconography for each illuminated folio or page. Since each descriptor is followed by slide-set and frame numbers, individual slide retrieval is possible. For library scientists, this volume provides access to documents representing the history of the book from roll to codex. For literary scholars, it is a vivid reminder that the inspiration to illustrate written texts is almost as old as writing itself. Illustrations in the form of diagrams, marginal drawings, historiated initials, and narrative cycles were incorporated into written texts to improve readers' understanding by helping them to remember important ideas and concepts in the texts. Many illustrations were not mere decorative embellishments but had a didactic purpose: to describe and to explain through pictorial language the written word.

Each Bodleian Library slide set is represented in this volume by a structured abstract. Each abstract is divided into a maximum of fifteen fields of information. The **Library** field contains the name of the library possessing the manuscript or book. Libraries other than the Bodleian represented in the collection include those at All Souls College, Balliol College, Corpus Christi College at Oxford, Corpus Christi College at Cambridge, Hertford College, Holkham Hall, Jesus College, Keble College, Lambeth Palace, Lincoln College, Magdalen College, Merton College, New College, Oriel College, Queen's College, Trinity College, and University College. The **Slide Set Title** field indicates the title assigned to the slide set by the Bodleian or other library. The **Negative Reference** field contains the roll number assigned to each filmstrip by the Bodleian; when ordering rolls from the Bodleian Library, the purchaser must cite this number. The **Rental Fee** field indicates the fee for renting the slide set from Purdue University; for specific information on how to place a rental order, see the instructions at the end of the introduction. The **Comments** field contains descriptive information such as available printed editions, the number of illuminations, the patron, or paleographical data. The **Title of Manuscript** field indicates the name, other than the shelfmark, assigned to the manuscript or book by the library. The **Shelfmark** field indicates the cataloging scheme employed by the library in shelving the original manuscript or book. Folio numbers for most of the manuscripts described in this volume have also been included, a feature lacking in the first volume. The **Provenance** field contains the country and, if known, the city in which the document originated. The **Date Executed** field indicates the century and, if known, the year in which the manuscript or book was produced. The **Language** field indicates the language of the text of the manuscript or book. The **Artist / School** field indicates the name of the artist or school of illumination. Similarly, the **Author** field permits access to the works of specific authors. A new field, the **Scribe** field, indicates the name of the scribe who executed or copied the manuscript. The **Type of Manuscript** field classifies each manuscript and book according to dominant generic type, e.g., bestiary, chronicle, herbal, psalter, or treatise. The **Contents** field, finally, consists of at least one keyphrase description of the iconographic contents of each slide in the set. Each keyphrase is followed immediately by a numerical code. The number before the slash indicates the specific abstract in this volume as well as the slide set in the collection. The number after the slash indicates the specific slide within the set. The index generated from the **Contents** field permits individual slide retrieval.

The index comprises thirteen separate indices, one for each field of information in the 250 abstracts, except for the **Rental Fee** and **Comments** fields, which were not indexed. All indices lead users to the appropriate abstracts, which, in turn, lead users to (a) the desired slide sets at Purdue; (b) the unmounted rolls at the Bodleian Library; or (c) the original manuscripts and books in England. The following examples reveal not only the ease of using the indices but also the broad range and depth of the materials indexed. Suppose you are interested in locating all of the filmed psalters in the supplement. Turning to the **Type of Manuscript** index, you would find seventy-two entries, leading you to fifty-one slide sets containing 428 slides. Or suppose you wanted to find every filmed folio from a specific manuscript known to be in the Bodleian. The desired information can be retrieved from at least three indices. If you knew the title of the work, for example, the *Roman de la Rose*, you could find thirteen entries in the **Title of Manuscript** index, leading you to nineteen illuminated folios from the romance. If you knew the shelfmarks, MS Douce 195 or MS Douce 364, you could locate the same slides through the **Shelfmark** index. And finally, if you knew the author, Guillaume de Lorris, you could locate the sets by means of the **Author** index. Thus, depending upon the amount of information you possess, you can retrieve information about the same sets through a number of different avenues.

For many, the most useful index is the **Contents** index, containing almost 11,000 keyphrases. The range of the subjects as well as the quantity of specific types of subjects is very large: "Initial" (992 entries), "Saint" and "Saints" (468 entries), "Christ" (348 entries), "Psalm" (239 entries), "Map" (234 entries), "David" (146 entries), "Job" (118 entries), "Virgin" (78 entries), "Grotesques" (61 entries), "Knights" (57 entries), and so forth. An entry, it should be pointed out, can consist of a reference to a single slide or to an entire slide set. The ten entries for books of hours, for instance, actually lead the user to at least 250 illuminated folios from books of hours.

To place a rental order from Purdue University, supply the abstract number, the title of the slide set, the desired date of use, the shipping address, and the billing address. The fee listed under the **Rental Fee** field in each abstract is for two days of use. Shipping time is not charged. For each additional day of use, the cost is one-fifth of the base rate. In addition, you will be charged for shipping costs. Return all shipments to Purdue by the same carrier that was used to ship the slide set to you. For reservations, call the Audio-Visual Center at 1-317-749-6188 or write Purdue University, Audio-Visual Center, Stewart Center, West Lafayette, Indiana 47907.

Scholars are also welcome to use the Bodleian collection at Purdue University. Facilities for viewing the slides as well as for study and research are available in the Audio-Visual Center and Purdue University Libraries.

It is important to note that *unmounted* rolls of transparencies can be purchased directly from the Bodleian at a cost comparable to renting the mounted slide sets from Purdue University. Once mounted, the purchased slides become part of your institution's permanent collection. In addition, Oxford Microform Publications Ltd. (Blue Boar Street, Oxford OX1 4EY, England) is offering for sale a series of complete texts and colored illuminations of Bodleian manuscripts in microfiche format. Ten manuscript titles have been published to date. Still other filmstrips and microfilms of Bodleian manuscripts are available from EP Microform Ltd. (Bradford Road, East Ardsley, Wakefield, West Yorkshire WF3 2JN, England).

For this as well as the other Garland volume I owe a debt to many individuals here and abroad. My chief debt is to Dr. W.O.

Hassall and his staff, particularly Elizabeth Arkell, who created and supplied the basic data that made this project possible. The National Endowment for the Humanities awarded me in 1973–74 a Younger Humanist Fellowship that permitted me to complete the data gathering in Oxford. Robert L. Ringel, Dean of the School of Humanities, Social Science, and Education at Purdue, and Lasco Kovacs, Humanities Librarian, provided funds to acquire the 750 rolls of Bodleian filmstrips. Jacob H. Adler, Head of the Department of English, provided funds to mount the collection of 30,000 slides. John Wilshusen, Director of Purdue's Audio-Visual Center, and Kathleen Armatis aided greatly in shelving the collection. Lesley M. Bloomfield, Editor of EP Microform Ltd., kindly provided detailed descriptions of folios in MS Bodley 270b. This volume, finally, would not exist if Peter L. Jobusch, Senior Systems Analyst at Purdue, had not provided the technical expertise needed to bring this lengthy project to completion.

# CODER'S INTRODUCTION
## Subject Access to Medieval Iconography

Thomas H. Ohlgren

The coding of the iconography of the Bodleian illuminations involved a great deal more than simply translating the handlist information into machine-readable form. The coding procedures also involved verifying the existing data, finding information not included on the handlists, and creating descriptions where none existed. In addition, the data for each slide set had to be partitioned into fifteen fields of information so that a separate index could be generated from each field (except the **Rental Fee** and **Comments** fields, which were not indexed). Each field presented its own coding problems, but the greatest challenge was in the coding for the **Contents** index, the chief means of access to the subject matter or iconography of the Bodleian illuminations. My goal was not only to provide iconographic descriptions for each slide in the collection but also to formulate associational cross-references to aid users. The task was complicated by at least six problems. The following discussion is an attempt to enumerate the problems faced, the solutions developed, and the results obtained.

First, I had to make a fundamental decision regarding the nature of the classification scheme to be employed. A classification scheme is a logical system for organizing masses of data into partitioned groups so that related subjects, concepts, or persons are systematically brought together. Two approaches to the coding of the **Contents** field were available. One approach would have been to superimpose a generalized classification scheme, such as the Iconclass System or the

Santa Cruz Universal Slide Classification System, on the Bodleian data. The Iconclass System, developed for the Decimal Index of the Art of the Low Countries by H. Van De Waal and completed by L. D. Couprie, "aims at making retrieval of iconographic material easier by means of a classification of reproductions according to their subject matter." The system employs structured, hierarchical divisions and subdivisions of iconographic data. It, like the Universal Slide Classification System developed by Wendell W. Simons and Luraine C. Tansey, is essentially an a priori scheme; that is, the contents of the Bodleian slides would be searched for persons, scenes, and motifs that fit into preconceived sets of pigeonholes. The problem with this approach is that the actual contents of the Bodleian slides, which are highly specialized, may not fit the static categories offered by these schemes. In addition, the Iconclass System and Santa Cruz scheme are designed primarily as shelving and retrieval schemes for *individual* photographic reproductions. Since the Bodleian materials exist in roll and set form, they do not lend themselves to the shelving apparatus of these systems. Finally, these schemes do not lend themselves to natural-language descriptions of iconographic content. They employ elaborate numeric signatures as the means of classification. In the Iconclass System, for instance, the signature 11L46C24 is intelligible only when each element is checked in multiple volumes. Only then can the user determine that 11L = the Church, 46C = traffic and transport, and 46C24 = sailing ships. The user must then combine these elements to determine that the signature means "the Church symbolized by a sailing vessel."

The second approach, which was used in this project, could be called an a posteriori scheme; by that I mean that the descriptions of the iconography of the Bodleian slides emerge from firsthand experience with the slides themselves. The slides are then classified according to their actual contents, not according to a set of pigeonholes that may not accurately denote the specific subject matter of the illuminated folios. In addition, the content descriptions for the Bodleian slides are written in natural language. No elaborate numeric signatures have to be decoded by the user.

The second problem concerned the vocabulary of iconographic terms needed to code the Bodleian slides. Since the Bodleian handlists had been prepared by many different individuals, they were inconsistent in the use of iconographic terminology. The coder had to know, for instance, that the handlist entries "deposition," "dormition," and "pentecost" were synonyms for "descent from the cross," "death of the virgin," and "descent of the Holy Ghost." When faced with multiple synonyms, I either listed separately all the terms for the same slide or chose one term as the major entry and provided cross-references to it under the alternative entries. My task would have been greatly simplified if I had had access to a standard thesaurus of iconographic terms for Christian and secular iconography. Although several photographic archives, such as the Index of Christian Art at Princeton and the Warburg Institute in London, have developed their own classification schemes for internal use, no standard thesaurus of terms exists for general use. The Iconclass System, with its thousands of descriptors, could fill this need once the project is completed. In addition, it would be very helpful if the Index of Christian Art would publish a list of their iconographic descriptors.

Third, I recognized at once the seemingly impossible task of finding verbal equivalents for pictorial content. Verbal language is inadequate for expressing visual language. Words are only crude approximations for images. Ideally, any indexing and retrieval system should refer the user directly to the pictorial materials. The natural-language indexing terms and the verbal abstracts of the slide sets are simply intermediaries to get the user to the slides themselves. It is, of course, now technically feasible to use the computer to automatically retrieve coded microfiche cards containing the pictorial images, and to display them on a remote terminal equipped with a cathode-ray tube. The user, instead of using a printed index and manually searching for the slides in the file, enters a search request to the data base and receives a list of keyphrases containing the search term as well as the numeric code for the fiche card and frame number. The user can then request the automated retrieval system to display the desired slide on the screen. Such an on-line system, however, is very expensive, and it would be difficult to justify the expenditure for an infrequently used slide file.

Fourth, since BIRS (Basic Information Retrieval System), the indexing package used in the production of both volumes, prohibits the use of more than ten terms or sixty-five characters in each keyphrase, it was often impossible to describe fully the contents of an individual slide with one keyphrase. Some folios contain either a multiplicity of motifs or compositions of great complexity. Consequently, I decided for the supplement to list multiple entries for each slide, something that was not done consistently in the first volume. I developed what might be called the principle of progressive divisibility. For example, slide set 598 (Bodleian Roll 244a) contains thirty-nine illuminated folios from MS Douce 6, a fourteenth-century Flemish psalter. Although the major motifs are illustrations to Psalms 110 to 121, including historiated initials, the folios also contain a profusion of minor compositions. The coded entry for frame 2 is as follows:

PSALM 110/111/ INITIAL C CONFITEBOR/ LADY READING 598–2
INITIAL C CONFITEBOR/ LADY READING 598–2
FIGURE HOLDS UP INITIAL 598–2
MAN HOLDS BIRD'S BEAK WITH PINCERS 598–2
WOMAN WITH WHITE DOG AT FEET 598–2
WOMAN STABBING HERSELF/ WOMAN HOLDS PURSE 598–2
MAN WITH FLAIL LEANS DOWN TO WATER 598–2

In the above example, several points should be noted. The major composition, the historiated initial C to Psalm 110/111, is listed first, beginning with a reference to the specific Psalm, followed by the initial and the Latin word, and ending with the subject of the historiation. The next entry begins with the second term of the first entry, INITIAL C CONFITEBOR, and so on until each major element receives initial position in a keyphrase. If the various elements were not divided in this way, they would be buried in the keyphrase and hence not accessible through the alphabetically arranged keyphrase **Contents** index. Following the first three major entries are the other illuminations on the folio, including marginalia. Thus, seven entries were employed to describe the contents of one illuminated folio. A total of 167 entries was used to describe thirty-nine folios in this slide set.

Fifth, since the indices consist of alphabetically arranged keyphrases, I had to anticipate what initial keywords in each phrase would be most useful for users of the collection. The efficiency of any index is dependent upon the user's search strategy. When coding Biblical iconography, the choice of the initial term was relatively straightforward, although, as mentioned earlier, I had to be consistent in my choice of descriptors. Such conventional terms as "Agony in the Garden," "Annunciation," "Ascension," and "Crucifixion" were used as the initial terms in phrases describing events in the life of Christ. To aid the user further, I inverted the syntax of many phrases; for instance:

ASCENSION OF CHRIST
CHRIST'S ASCENSION
FEAST OF ALEXANDER
ALEXANDER'S FEAST

In addition, major cross-references were included. The references guide the user not only to synonymous terms but also to persons, concepts, and motifs sharing similar attributes.

DAILY LIFE SEE ANIMALS APE ARCHER BAKER BEES BOY
DAILY LIFE SEE CARDING-FLEECE CARPENTER CATS CHESS
DAILY LIFE SEE CHILDREN COOKING DANCING DOCTOR DOG
DAILY LIFE SEE FALCONER FEAST FIGURE GAME GIRL
DAILY LIFE SEE GROTESQUE HARE HAWKING HAYMAKING
DAILY LIFE SEE HUMAN-FIGURES HUNTING KNIGHT LADY
DAILY LIFE SEE INDIVIDUAL MONTHS AND ZODIAC SIGNS
DAILY LIFE SEE LOVER MAN-AND-WOMAN MAN MEN MUSICIANS

DAILY LIFE SEE RABBIT REAPING SHEEP SHEPHERD SHIPS
DAILY LIFE SEE SMITH SOWING SPINNING TEACHER
DAILY LIFE SEE WINEMAKING WOMAN YOUTH

The cross-references are especially important for users looking for secular iconographic motifs. Since the persons in many scenes of daily life are not identifiable by name, I had to employ generic nouns denoting rank or sex, such as "Knight," "Lady," "Man," "Woman," "Cleric," and so forth. If the major motif was an action rather than a person, I listed the verb in the initial position; for example: "Building," "Feasting," "Measuring," "Sowing." Illuminations connected with a text—literary, historical, or scientific—did not pose problems of identification, because I could consult a printed edition of the text when questions of identification arose.

Sixth, the coding operations were complicated by some shortcomings of the BIRS programs. The greatest restriction, as mentioned above, was on the length of the keyphrases. Consequently, some keyphrases are highly compressed. Furthermore, since we generated keyphrase KWOC indices where each phrase began with the most important term, we had to manipulate the syntax of many phrases. Some phrases, as a result, are awkward if not ungrammatical:

DRAGON/ TWO-HEADED WITH KNOTTED TAIL IN MARGIN 524–3
LUCIUS KING OF BRITAIN SENDS MEN TO ROME 539–6
KNIGHTS MOUNTED FIGHT AS LADY WATCHES 622–6

BIRS also prohibits the use of internal punctuation, such as commas, semicolons, dashes, and periods, which would have clarified syntactic relations among terms. Contrarieties in spelling were also a constant problem. Some of the variety of forms were due to differences between British and American spelling, such as "ploughing" and "plowing." Other irregularities were due to the deliberate inclusion of manuscript spellings, and no attempt was made to normalize them. Finally, BIRS prohibits the use of accents, diacritical marks, and other nonstandard characters.

The Bodleian project demonstrates the feasibility of a

computer-aided approach to the cataloging and indexing of photographic documents for use in teaching and research. The techniques developed for coding the Bodleian data could, of course, be emulated by other repositories of microfilms, photographs, and slides. Access to the specific contents of collections at the British Library's Department of Manuscripts, the Warburg Institute (London), the Courtauld Institute (London), the Monastic Manuscript Microfilm Library (Collegeville, Minn.), the Vatican Film Library (St. Louis University), to name a few, is severely limited by the lack of analytical catalogs with indices, including subject indices. The Bodleian data, which is stored on magnetic tape, could be combined with similarly structured data from other archives, providing an even larger data base from which to retrieve information about medieval manuscript photographic holdings.

# TECHNICAL NOTE

## Peter L. Jobusch

The data for this volume, instead of being keypunched, was keyed by Dr. Ohlgren on a Texas Instruments Silent 700 terminal. The portable terminal was connected to the CDC 6500 equipment at the Purdue University Computing Center. The data was then transferred to the IBM 370/148 at the Administrative Data Processing Center where final editing was accomplished using the ROSCOE terminal system. The final edit allowed for a higher degree of accuracy and uniformity than was possible in the previous volume.

Computer processing to produce this volume required two hours and four minutes of central processing time on the IBM 370 model 148 computer. The following table summarizes the tasks performed, the time required, and the storage needed:

| *Task* | *CPU Time* | *Partition Size* |
|---|---|---|
| 1. text processing of abstract listing | 42 minutes | 64K |
| 2. generation of **Contents** index | 24 minutes | 150K |
| 3. generation of other indices | 58 minutes | 150K |

The processing times were reduced by bypassing the preparation of a BIRS information file (IFT) and allowing the indexing program (PIP) to process the card images directly. To overcome format limitations of BIRS, the abstract listings were processed by TEXT-360.

As Gary C. Lelvis pointed out in the *Programmer's Introduction* to *Illuminated Manuscripts* (Garland, 1977), and as Dr. Ohlgren notes above, the BIRS programs contain limitations that shaped the format and structure of the catalogs and indices. Because of the expense involved, it was not possible to rectify these problems. Should BIRS be modified in the future, we would attempt to make the following improvements:

(a) allow printing of special characters in the indices. Apostrophes now print as slashes and slashes print as blanks. In addition, BIRS prohibits the use of accents, diacritical marks, and all punctuation within the keyphrase.

(b) allow longer keyphrases, both in number of terms and characters. BIRS restricts keyphrases to ten terms or sixty-five characters.

(c) improve the numbering scheme to allow the listing of both slides within an abstract and entire abstracts in the right margin.

(d) create a keyword index in which all the terms within the keyphrase would list alphabetically *with* the numerical code to allow for individual slide retrieval.

# CATALOG OF ABSTRACTS 501-750

a

b

c

d

Plate II

*$ABSTRACT 501
*LIBRARY BODLEIAN
*SLIDE SET TITLE RICHARD OF ST VICTOR
*NEGATIVE REFERENCE ROLL 283B
*RENTAL FEE $2.70
*COMMENTS EXPLANATORY DIAGRAMS CONCERN THE MEASUREMENTS OF THE TEMPLE OF JERUSALEM.
*TITLE OF MANUSCRIPT IN VISIONEM EZEKIELIS
*SHELFMARK MS BODLEY 494/ FOL 131V 501-1, MS BODLEY 494/ FOL 132 501-2, MS BODLEY 494/ FOL 133 501-3, MS BODLEY 494/ FOL 135 501-4, MS BODLEY 494/ FOL 136V 501-5, MS BODLEY 494/ FOL 137V 501-6, MS BODLEY 494/ FOL 139V 501-7, MS BODLEY 494/ FOL 154V 501-8, MS BODLEY 494/ FOL 155V 501-9, MS BODLEY 494/ FOL 156 501-10, MS BODLEY 494/ FOL 158V 501-11, MS BODLEY 494/ FOL 162V 501-12, MS BODLEY 494/ FOL 165V 501-13, MS BODLEY 494/ FOL 166V 501-14
*PROVENANCE ENGLISH
*DATE EXECUTED 12TH/ 3RD QUARTER
*LANGUAGE LATIN
*AUTHOR RICHARD OF ST VICTOR
*TYPE OF MANUSCRIPT COMMENTARY ON EZEKIEL
*CONTENTS COMMENTARY ON EZEKIEL 501/1-14, VISION OF EZEKIEL 501/1-14, DIAGRAM OF SQUARE CONTAINING TWO SQUARES 501-1, DIAGRAM OF SQUARE CONTAINING ANOTHER SQUARE 501-2, DIAGRAM OF SQUARE CONTAINING SMALLER SUBDIVISIONS 501-3, DIAGRAM OF SQUARE PLAN WITH TOWERED DOORWAYS 501-4, DIAGRAM OF SQUARE PARTITIONED INTO OBLONGS 501-5, DIAGRAM OF RECTANGULAR PLAN 501-6, DIAGRAM OF SUBDIVIDED RECTANGLES 501-7, DIAGRAM OF CIRCLE ENCLOSING TRIANGLE 501-8, DIAGRAM OF ARCHES SUPPORTED ON COLUMNS 501-9, DIAGRAM OF BUILDING 501-10, DIAGRAM OF TEMPLE PLAN/ FOUR RECTANGULAR COURTS 501-11, DIAGRAM OF TEMPLE PLAN 501-12, DIAGRAM IN RED/ BLUE AND BROWN 501-13, DIAGRAM OF PLAN 501-14

*$ABSTRACT 502
*LIBRARY BODLEIAN
*SLIDE SET TITLE CODEX MENDOZA
*NEGATIVE REFERENCE ROLL 283F
*RENTAL FEE $3.05
*COMMENTS AZTEC PICTOGRAPHIC MANUSCRIPT
*TITLE OF MANUSCRIPT CODEX MENDOZA
*SHELFMARK MS ARCH SELD A 1/ FOL 12 502-1, MS ARCH SELD A 1/ FOL 16 502-2, MS ARCH SELD A 1/ FOL 16 502-3, MS ARCH SELD A 1/ FOL 10 502-4, MS ARCH SELD A 1/ FOL 20 502/5-8, MS ARCH SELD A 1/ FOL 23 502/9-13, MS ARCH SELD A 1/ FOL 25 502-14, MS ARCH SELD A 1/ FOL 24V 502-15, MS ARCH SELD A 1/ FOL 26 502-16, MS ARCH SELD A 1/ FOL 28 502-17, MS ARCH SELD A 1/ FOL 37 502-18, MS ARCH SELD A 1/ FOL 43 502-19, MS ARCH SELD A 1/ FOL 45 502-20, MS ARCH SELD A 1/ FOL 46 502-21
*PROVENANCE MEXICO
*DATE EXECUTED 16TH/C1540
*LANGUAGE SPANISH
*AUTHOR DONE ON AUTHORITY OF DON ANTONIO MENDOZA
*TYPE OF MANUSCRIPT CHRONICLE
*CONTENTS MEXICAN ILLUMINATION 502/1-21, CODEX MENDOZA 502/1-21, CHRONICLE OF MEXICO 502/1-4, TRIBUTE DUE TO MONTEZUMA 502/5-21

*$ABSTRACT 503
*LIBRARY LINCOLN COLLEGE OXFORD
*SLIDE SET TITLE LINCOLN APOCALYPSE
*NEGATIVE REFERENCE ROLL 219A
*RENTAL FEE $5.35
*TITLE OF MANUSCRIPT LINCOLN COLLEGE APOCALYPSE
*SHELFMARK MS LINCOLN COLLEGE LAT 16/ FOL 139 503-1, MS LINCOLN COLLEGE LAT 16/ FOL 139V 503-2, MS LINCOLN COLLEGE LAT 16/ FOL 140 503-3, MS LINCOLN COLLEGE LAT 16/ FOL 140V 503-4, MS LINCOLN COLLEGE LAT 16/ FOL 141 503-5, MS LINCOLN COLLEGE LAT

16/ FOL 143V 503-6, MS LINCOLN COLLEGE LAT 16/ FOL 144 503-7, MS LINCOLN COLLEGE LAT 16/ FOL 145V 503-8, MS LINCOLN COLLEGE LAT 16/ FOL 146 503-9, MS LINCOLN COLLEGE LAT 16/ FOL 146V 503-10, MS LINCOLN COLLEGE LAT 16/ FOL 147V 503-11, MS LINCOLN COLLEGE LAT 16/ FOL 148 503/12-13, MS LINCOLN COLLEGE LAT 16/ FOL 148V 503-14, MS LINCOLN COLLEGE LAT 16/ FOL 149 503-15, MS LINCOLN COLLEGE LAT 16/ FOL 149V 503-16, MS LINCOLN COLLEGE LAT 16/ FOL 150 503-17, MS LINCOLN COLLEGE LAT 16/ FOL 150V 503-18, MS LINCOLN COLLEGE LAT 16/ FOL 151 503-19, MS LINCOLN COLLEGE LAT 16/ FOL 151V 503-20, MS LINCOLN COLLEGE LAT 16/ FOL 152 503-21, MS LINCOLN COLLEGE LAT 16/ FOL 152V 503-22, MS LINCOLN COLLEGE LAT 16/ FOL 153 503-23, MS LINCOLN COLLEGE LAT 16/ FOL 153V 503-24, MS LINCOLN COLLEGE LAT 16/ FOL 153V 503-25, MS LINCOLN COLLEGE LAT 16/ FOL 154 503-26, MS LINCOLN COLLEGE LAT 16/ FOL 155 503/27-28, MS LINCOLN COLLEGE LAT 16/ FOL 155V 503-29, MS LINCOLN COLLEGE LAT 16/ FOL 156V 503-30, MS LINCOLN COLLEGE LAT 16/ FOL 157 503-31, MS LINCOLN COLLEGE LAT 16/ FOL 157V 503-32, MS LINCOLN COLLEGE LAT 16/ FOL 158 503-33, MS LINCOLN COLLEGE LAT 16/ FOL 158V 503-34, MS LINCOLN COLLEGE LAT 16/ FOL 159 503-35, MS LINCOLN COLLEGE LAT 16/ FOL 159V 503-36, MS LINCOLN COLLEGE LAT 16/ FOL 160 503-37, MS LINCOLN COLLEGE LAT 16/ FOL 160V 503-38, MS LINCOLN COLLEGE LAT 16/ FOL 161V 503-39, MS LINCOLN COLLEGE LAT 16/ FOL 162 503-40, MS LINCOLN COLLEGE LAT 16/ FOL 163 503-41, MS LINCOLN COLLEGE LAT 16/ FOL 164 503-42, MS LINCOLN COLLEGE LAT 16/ FOL 164V 503-43, MS LINCOLN COLLEGE LAT 16/ FOL 165 503-44, MS LINCOLN COLLEGE LAT 16/ FOL 165V 503-45, MS LINCOLN COLLEGE LAT 16/ FOL 166 503-46, MS LINCOLN COLLEGE LAT 16/ FOL 166V 503-47, MS LINCOLN COLLEGE LAT 16/ FOL 167 503-48, MS LINCOLN COLLEGE LAT 16/ FOL 167V 503-49, MS LINCOLN COLLEGE LAT 16/ FOL 168 503-50, MS LINCOLN COLLEGE LAT 16/ FOL 168V 503-51, MS LINCOLN COLLEGE LAT 16/ FOL 169 503-52, MS LINCOLN COLLEGE LAT 16/ FOL 170 503-53, MS LINCOLN COLLEGE LAT 16/ FOL 171 503-54, MS LINCOLN COLLEGE LAT 16/ FOL 171V 503-55, MS LINCOLN COLLEGE LAT 16/ FOL 172V 503-56, MS LINCOLN COLLEGE LAT 16/ FOL 173 503-57, MS LINCOLN COLLEGE LAT 16/ FOL 174 503-58, MS LINCOLN COLLEGE LAT 16/ FOL 174V 503-59, MS LINCOLN COLLEGE LAT 16/ FOL 175 503-60, MS LINCOLN COLLEGE LAT 16/ FOL 175V 503-61, MS LINCOLN COLLEGE LAT 16/ FOL 176 503-62, MS LINCOLN COLLEGE LAT 16/ FOL 176V 503-63, MS LINCOLN COLLEGE LAT 16/ FOL 177V 503-64, MS LINCOLN COLLEGE LAT 16/ FOL 179V 503-65, MS LINCOLN COLLEGE LAT 16/ FOL 180V 503-66, MS LINCOLN COLLEGE LAT 16/ FOL 181 503-67

*PROVENANCE ENGLISH
*DATE EXECUTED 14TH
*LANGUAGE LATIN
*TYPE OF MANUSCRIPT APOCALYPSE
*CONTENTS LINCOLN APOCALYPSE 503/1-67, APOCALYPSE/ ENGLISH/ 13TH 503/1-67, ST PAUL PREACHING 503-1, REV 01/VERSES 4-11/ JOHN PREACHES TO CHURCHES 503-2, ST JOHN OF PATMOS PREACHES TO CHURCHES 503-2, REV 01/VERSES 12-16/ VISION OF CHRIST 503-3, ST JOHN'S VISION OF CHRIST 503-3, REV 01/VERSES 17-18/ JOHN FALLS AS IF DEAD 503-4, ST JOHN FALLS AS IF DEAD 503-4, REV 02/VERSE 1/ LETTERS TO THE CHURCHES 503-5, ST JOHN OF PATMOS WRITES TO CHURCHES 503-5, REV 04/VERSE 1/ JOHN ASCENDS TO HEAVEN 503-6, ST JOHN OF PATMOS ASCENDS TO HEAVEN 503-6, REV 04/VERSES 2-8/ VISION OF CHRIST IN MAJESTY 503-7, CHRIST IN MAJESTY 503-7, REV 04/VERSES 8-11/ VISION OF ENTHRONED CHRIST 503-8, VISION OF ENTHRONED CHRIST AND 24 ELDERS 503-8, REV 05/VERSES 1-5/ BOOK WITH SEVEN SEALS 503-9, VISION OF BOOK WITH SEVEN SEALS 503-9, REV 05/VERSES 6-8/ LAMB OPENS BOOK 503-10, LAMB OPENS THE BOOK 503-10, REV 05/VERSES 9-14/ THE NEW SONG 503-11, ELDERS AND BEASTS ADORE GOD 503-11, FOUR HORSEMEN OF THE APOCALYPSE 503/12-15, REV 06/VERSES 1-2/ FIRST HORSEMAN 503-12, HORSEMAN/ FIRST 503-12, REV 06/VERSES 3-4, SECOND HORSEMAN 503-13, HORSEMAN/ SECOND 503-13, REV 06/VERSES 5-6/ THIRD HORSEMAN 503-14, HORSEMAN/ THIRD 503-14, REV 06/VERSES 7-8/ FOURTH HORSEMAN 503-15, HORSEMAN/ FOURTH 503-15, REV 06/VERSES 9-11/ OPENING OF FIFTH SEAL 503-16,OPENING OF THE FIFTH SEAL 503-16, REV 06/VERSES 12-17/ OPENING OF SIXTH SEAL 503-17, OPENING OF THE SIXTH SEAL 503-17, EARTHQUAKE/ GREAT 503-17, REV 07/VERSES 1-3/ ANGELS

HOLD FOUR WINDS 503-18, ANGELS HOLD FOUR WINDS 503-18, WINDS/ FOUR 503-18, REV 07/VERSE 9/ GREAT MULTITUDE 503-19, MULTITUDE/ GREAT 503-19, REV 07/VERSES 13-17/ JOHN SPEAKS TO ELDER 503-20, ST JOHN OF PATMOS SPEAKS TO ELDER 503-20, REV 08/VERSES 1-5/ OPENING OF SEVENTH SEAL 503-21, OPENING OF SEVENTH SEAL 503-21, ANGELS GIVEN SEVEN TRUMPETS 503-21, REV 08/VERSE 7/ FIRST TRUMPET 503-22, TRUMPET/ FIRST 503-22, REV 08/VERSES 8-9/ SECOND TRUMPET 503-23, TRUMPET/ SECOND 503-23, REV 08/VERSES 10-11/ THIRD TRUMPET 503-24, TRUMPET/ THIRD 503-24, REV 08/VERSES 12-13/ FOURTH TRUMPET 503-25, TRUMPET/ FOURTH 503-25, REV 09/VERSE 1/ FIFTH TRUMPET 503-26, TRUMPET/ FIFTH 503-26, REV 09/VERSES 13-14/ SIXTH TRUMPET 503-27, TRUMPET/ SIXTH 503-27, REV 09/VERSES 17-19/ HORSEMEN BEAR PLAGUES 503-28, ARMY OF HORSEMEN BEAR PLAGUES 503-28, PLAGUES 503-28, REV 10/VERSE 1/ VISION OF MIGHTY ANGEL 503-29, VISION OF MIGHTY ANGEL 503-29, REV 10/VERSES 9-10/ JOHN EATS BOOK 503-30, ST JOHN OF PATMOS EATS BOOK 503-30, REV 11/VERSES 1-2/ JOHN MEASURES TEMPLE 503-31, ST JOHN OF PATMOS MEASURES TEMPLE 503-31, REV 11/VERSE 3/ TWO WITNESSES 503-32, WITNESSES/ TWO 503-32, REV 12/VERSES 4-5/ WOMAN CLOTHED WITH SUN 503-33, WOMAN CLOTHED WITH SUN BRINGS FORTH CHILD 503-33, REV 12/VERSES 7-8/ ST MICHAEL FIGHTS DRAGON 503-34, ST MICHAEL FIGHTS DRAGON 503-34, DRAGON FIGHTS ST MICHAEL 503-34, REV 12/VERSE 12/ ANGEL CRIES WOE 503-35, ANGEL CRIES WOE TO EARTH 503-35, REV 12/VERSE 14/ WOMAN FLIES TO DESERT 503-36, DRAGON MAKES WAR ON WOMAN'S SEED 503-36, REV 13/VERSES 1-3/ BEAST WITH SEVEN HEADS 503-37, BEAST WITH SEVEN HEADS AND TEN HORNS 503-37, REV 13/VERSES 4-10/ WORSHIP OF BEAST 503-38, BEAST WORSHIPPED 503-38, REV 13/VERSES 11-12/ BEAST EMERGES FROM EARTH 503-39, BEAST WITH TWO HORNS EMERGES FROM EARTH 503-39, REV 14/VERSE 1/ LAMB ON MOUNT SION 503-40, LAMB ON MOUNT SION 503-40, REV 14/VERSES 6-7/ ANGEL FLIES FROM HEAVEN 503-41, ANGEL WITH GOSPEL FLIES FROM HEAVEN 503-41, REV 14/VERSES 14-16/ HARVEST OF EARTH 503-42, HARVEST OF THE EARTH 503-42, REV 14/VERSES 17-20/ VINTAGE OF EARTH 503-43, VINTAGE OF THE EARTH 503-43, REV 15/VERSES 1-2/ ANGELS WITH PLAGUES 503-44, ANGELS WITH LAST PLAGUES 503-44, REV 15/VERSES 5-7/ ANGELS GIVEN FLASKS 503-45, ANGELS GIVEN FLASKS FILLED WITH WRATH OF GOD 503-45, REV 16/VERSES 1-2/ FIRST FLASK 503-46, ANGEL/ FIRST EMPTIES FLASK 503-46, REV 16/VERSES 3-4/ SECOND FLASK 503-47, ANGEL/ SECOND EMPTIES FLASK 503-47, REV 16/VERSES 8-9/ FOURTH FLASK 503-48, ANGEL/ FOURTH EMPTIES FLASK 503-48, REV 16/VERSES 10-12/ FIFTH AND SIXTH FLASKS 503-49, ANGELS/ FIFTH AND SIXTH EMPTY FLASKS 503-49, REV 16/VERSES 13-14/ FROGS EMERGE 503-50, FROGS EMERGE FROM BEAST/ DRAGON/ FALSE PROPHET 503-50, BEAST/ DRAGON/ FALSE PROPHET 503-50, REV 16/VERSES 17-20/ SEVENTH FLASK 503-51, ANGEL/ SEVENTH EMPTIES FLASK 503-51, REV 17/VERSES 1-4/ GREAT WHORE OF BABYLON 503-52, WHORE OF BABYLON 503-52, REV 17/VERSE 6/ WHORE DRUNK WITH BLOOD OF SAINTS 503-53, WHORE OF BABYLON DRUNK WITH BLOOD OF SAINTS 503-53, REV 18/VERSES 1-2/ FALL OF BABYLON 503-54, FALL OF BABYLON 503-54, BABYLON FALLS 503-54, REV 18/VERSES 4-20/ PEOPLE TOLD TO LEAVE BABYLON 503-55, BABYLON EXITED BY PEOPLE 503-55, REV 18/VERSE 21/ ANGEL CASTS MILLSTONE IN SEA 503-56, MILLSTONE CAST INTO THE SEA 503-56, REV 19/VERSES 1-6/ GOD ADORED BY 24 ELDERS 503-57,GOD ADORED BY 24 ELDERS AND FOUR BEASTS 503-57, REV 19/VERSES 11-16/ ARMY OF HEAVEN 503-58, ARMY OF HEAVEN LED BY RIDER ON WHITE HORSE 503-58, REV 19/VERSES 17-18/ BIRDS FEAST ON DEAD 503-59, BIRDS SUMMONED BY ANGEL TO FEAST ON DEAD 503-59, REV 19/VERSES 19-20/ BEAST DEFEATED 503-60, BEAST DEFEATED 503-60, REV 20/VERSES 1-3/ DRAGON IMPRISONED 503-61, DRAGON IMPRISONED IN BOTTOMLESS PIT 503-61, BOTTOMLESS PIT 503-61, REV 20/VERSE 4/ ANGELS GATHER SOULS 503-62, ANGELS GATHER SOULS OF THOSE BEHEADED 503-62, REV 20/VERSES 11-15/ LAST JUDGMENT 503-63, LAST JUDGMENT 503-63, REV 21/VERSES 1-2/ NEW HEAVEN AND NEW EARTH 503-64, VISION OF NEW JERUSALEM 503-64, REV 22/VERSES 1-2/ WATER AND TREE OF LIFE 503-65,WATER OF LIFE AND TREE OF LIFE 503-65, REV 22/VERSES 8-9/ JOHN FORBIDDEN TO KNEEL 503-66, ST JOHN OF PATMOS FORBIDDEN TO KNEEL 503-66, REV 20/VERSES 10-16/ JOHN HEARS CHRIST 503-67, ST JOHN OF PATMOS HEARS WORDS OF CHRIST 503-67

*$ABSTRACT 504
*LIBRARY BODLEIAN
*SLIDE SET TITLE OLD TESTAMENT ILLUSTRATIONS FROM FRANCISCAN MISSAL
*NEGATIVE REFERENCE ROLL 219C
*RENTAL FEE $2.60
*TITLE OF MANUSCRIPT FRANCISCAN MISSAL
*SHELFMARK MS DOUCE 313
*PROVENANCE FRENCH
*DATE EXECUTED 14TH/ MID
*LANGUAGE LATIN
*ARTIST/ SCHOOL FOLLOWER OF JEAN PUCELLE
*TYPE OF MANUSCRIPT MISSAL
*CONTENTS MISSAL/ FRENCH/ 14TH 504/1-12, GOD'S HOUSE ON MOUNTAIN TOP 504-1, ISAIAH 02/VERSE 2/ GOD'S HOUSE ON MOUNTAIN 504-1, SOLOMON ENTHRONED 504-2, ISAIAH 38/VERSE 1/ ISAIAH WARNS HEZEKIAH OF DEATH 504-3, ISAIAH WARNS KING HEZEKIAH OF DEATH 504-3, KINGS-III 17/VERSE 9/ ELIJAH AND WIDOW'S CURSE 504-4, ELIJAH AND THE WIDOW'S CURSE 504-4, JEREMIAH 07/VERSE 2/ JEREMIAH PREACHES AT TEMPLE 504-5, JEREMIAH PREACHES REPENTENCE AT TEMPLE DOOR 504-5, KINGS-III 01/VERSE 3/ ABISHAG BROUGHT TO DAVID 504-6, ABISHAG BROUGHT TO KING DAVID 504-6, EXODUS 12/VERSE 1/ PASSOVER INSTITUTED 504-7, PASSOVER INSTITUTED 504-7, GOD INSTRUCTS MOSES AND AARON 504-7, MOSES AND AARON INSTRUCTED BY GOD 504-7, EZEKIEL 37/VERSE 1/ VISION OF DRY BONES 504-8, EZEKIEL'S VISION OF VALLEY OF DRY BONES 504-8, JOEL 02/VERSE 28/ JOEL PROPHESYING 504-9, JOEL PROPHESYING OLD MEN SHALL DREAM 504-9, MOSES DELIVERS GOD'S WORD TO ISRAELITES 504-10, SHADRACH/ MESHACH/ ABEDNEGO IN FURNACE 504-11, FIERY FURNACE 504-11, EZEKIEL'S VISION OF GOD 504-12

*$ABSTRACT 505
*LIBRARY BODLEIAN
*SLIDE SET TITLE NEW TESTAMENT ILLUSTRATIONS FROM FRANCISCAN MISSAL
*NEGATIVE REFERENCE ROLL 219D
*RENTAL FEE $3.60
*TITLE OF MANUSCRIPT FRANCISCAN MISSAL
*SHELFMARK MS DOUCE 313
*PROVENANCE FRENCH
*DATE EXECUTED 14TH/ MID
*LANGUAGE LATIN
*ARTIST/ SCHOOL FOLLOWER OF JEAN PUCELLE
*TYPE OF MANUSCRIPT MISSAL
*CONTENTS MISSAL/ FRENCH/ 14TH 505/1-32, CHRIST CHILD SPEAKS TO DOCTORS IN TEMPLE 505-1, ST PHILIP BAPTISES ETHIOPIAN EUNUCH 505-2, TOMB OF CHRIST EMPTY 505-3, PENTECOST 505-4, APOSTLES SPEAK IN TONGUES AFTER PENTECOST 505-5, SPEAKING IN TONGUES 505-5, CHRIST ON RAINBOW 505-6, ACTS 10/VERSE 42/ CHRIST ON RAINBOW 505-6, APOSTLES HEAL AND CAST OUT DEVILS 505-7, DEVILS CAST OUT BY APOSTLES 505-7, PUBLICAN AND SINNER PRAY IN TEMPLE 505-8, CHRIST SCOURGED AND TRIAL 505-9, CRUCIFIXION 505-10, CHRIST'S DESCENT FROM CROSS 505-11, ENTOMBMENT OF CHRIST 505-12, CHRIST ENTOMBED 505-12, NATIVITY 505-13, CHRIST TEMPTED 505-14, CHRIST ENTERS JERUSALEM ON PALM SUNDAY 505-15, RESURRECTION 505-16, PENTECOST 505-17, CHRIST CALLS PETER AND ANDREW 505-18, ST PAUL CONVERTED 505-19, VIRGIN PURIFIED 505-20, ANNUNCIATION 505-21, ST ELIZABETH AND ZACHARIAS PRAY FOR CHILD 505-22, ZACHARIAS OFFERS SACRIFICE OF INCENSE 505-23, ST JOHN THE BAPTIST NAMED 505-24, CHRIST WALKS ON WATER 505-25, CHRIST APPEARS TO MARY MAGDALENE 505-26, ST MARY MAGDALENE WASHES CHRIST'S FEET 505-27, CHRIST WITH MARY AND MARTHA 505-28, ST JOHN THE BAPTIST BEHEADED 505-29, HEROD'S FEAST 505-29, CHRIST CALLS ST MATTHEW 505-30, ST MATTHEW CALLED BY CHRIST 505-30, CHRIST TEACHES ABOUT THE TRUE VINE 505-31, ZACCHEUS IN TREE LISTENS TO CHRIST 505-32

*$ABSTRACT 506
*LIBRARY BODLEIAN
*SLIDE SET TITLE THE CHURCH ILLUSTRATED FROM FRANCISCAN MISSAL
*NEGATIVE REFERENCE ROLL 219E
*RENTAL FEE $2.65
*TITLE OF MANUSCRIPT FRANCISCAN MISSAL
*SHELFMARK MS DOUCE 313
*PROVENANCE FRENCH
*DATE EXECUTED 14TH/ MID
*LANGUAGE LATIN
*ARTIST/ SCHOOL FOLLOWER OF JEAN PUCELLE
*TYPE OF MANUSCRIPT MISSAL
*CONTENTS MISSAL/ FRENCH/ 14TH 506/1-13, CHURCH CEREMONIES AND ACTIVITIES 506/1-13, PREACHING FROM PULPIT 506-1, CHRIST WITH DOCTORS IN TEMPLE 506-1, BLESSING OF PALMS ON PALM SUNDAY 506-2, PALM SUNDAY 506-2, VENERATION OF THE CROSS 506-3, PRAYERS FOR CHURCH ON GOOD FRIDAY 506-4, GOOD FRIDAY 506-4, PRAYERS DURING EASTER VIGIL 505-5, EASTER VIGIL 506-5, BLESSING OF BAPTISMAL WATERS DURING EASTER VIGIL 506-6, EASTER VIGIL 506-6, LITANY SUNG DURING EASTER VIGIL 506-7, PRIEST READS CONCLUDING PRAYERS OF MASS 506-8, EXORCISM AND BLESSING OF WATER 506-9, CANDLEMAS PROCESSION 506-10, MASS OFFERED ON ANNIVERSARY OF CHURCH DEDICATION 506-11, DEDICATION OF CHURCH/ PROCESSION 506-12, CONFESSION/ PRIEST OFFERS MASS FOR PENITENT, MASS OFFERED FOR PENITENT 506-13

*$ABSTRACT 507
*LIBRARY BODLEIAN
*SLIDE SET TITLE SAINTS FROM FRANCISCAN MISSAL
*NEGATIVE REFERENCE ROLL 219F
*RENTAL FEE $2.85
*TITLE OF MANUSCRIPT FRANCISCAN MISSAL
*SHELFMARK MS DOUCE 313
*PROVENANCE FRENCH
*DATE EXECUTED 14TH/ MID
*LANGUAGE LATIN
*ARTIST/ SCHOOL FOLLOWER OF JEAN PUCELLE
*TYPE OF MANUSCRIPT MISSAL
*CONTENTS MISSAL/ FRENCH/ 14TH 507/1-17, SAINTS FROM FRANCISCAN MISSAL 507/1-17, ST ANDREW MARTYRED 507-1, ST THOMAS TOUCHES CHRIST'S WOUNDED SIDE 507-2,CHRIST'S WOUNDED SIDE TOUCHED BY ST THOMAS 507-2, ST GEORGE AND THE DRAGON 507-3, ST PHILIP AND JAMES MARTYRED 507-4, ST HELENA FINDS THE TRUE CROSS 507-5, ST JOHN BOILED IN CAULDRON 507-6, ST ANTHONY OF PADUA 507-7, ST JAMES MARTYRED 507-8, ST LAWRENCE GIVES ALMS TO POOR 507-9, ST TIBURTIUS AND SUSANNA 507-10, ST HIPPOLYTUS AND CASSIAN 507-11, ASSUMPTION OF THE VIRGIN 507-12, ST BARTHOLOMEW MARTYRED 507-13, ST HELENA CURES MAN WITH TRUE CROSS 507-14, ST FRANCIS RECEIVES THE STIGMATA 507-15, ST CLEMENT MARTYRED 507-16, ST CATHERINE OF ALEXANDRIA MARTYRED 507-17 ST CATHERINE OF ALEXANDRIA MARTYRED 507-17

*$ABSTRACT 508
*LIBRARY BODLEIAN
*SLIDE SET TITLE PORTABLE PSALTER IV
*NEGATIVE REFERENCE ROLL 219G
*RENTAL FEE $3.55
*COMMENTS ALSO SEE ABSTRACTS 237, 456, AND 471.
*TITLE OF MANUSCRIPT PORTABLE PSALTER
*SHELFMARK MS DOUCE 5/ FOL 137V-138 508-1, MS DOUCE 5/ FOL 138V-139 508-2, MS DOUCE 5/ FOL 139V-140 508-3, MS DOUCE 5/ FOL 140V-141 508-4, MS DOUCE 5/ FOL 141V-142 508-5, MS DOUCE 5/ FOL 142V-143 508-6, MS DOUCE 5/ FOL 143V-144 508-7, MS DOUCE 5/ FOL 144V-145 508-8, MS DOUCE 5/ FOL 145V-146 508-9, MS DOUCE 5/ FOL 146V-147 508-10, MS DOUCE 5/ FOL 147V-148 508-11, MS DOUCE 5/ FOL 148V-149 508-12, MS DOUCE 5/ FOL 149V-150 508-13, MS DOUCE 5/ FOL 150V-151 508-14, MS DOUCE 5/ FOL 151V-152 508-15, MS DOUCE 5/ FOL 152V-153 508-16, MS DOUCE

5/ FOL 153V-154 508-17, MS DOUCE 5/ FOL 154V-155 508-18, MS DOUCE 5/ FOL 155V-156 508-19, MS DOUCE 5/ FOL 156V-157 508-20, MS DOUCE 5/ FOL 157V-158 508-21, MS DOUCE 5/ FOL 158V-159 508-22, MS DOUCE 5/ FOL 159V-160 508-23, MS DOUCE 5/ FOL 160V-161 508-24, MS DOUCE 5/ FOL 161V-162 508-25, MS DOUCE 5/ FOL 162V-163 508-26, MS DOUCE 5/ FOL 163V-164 508-27, MS DOUCE 5/ FOL 164V-165 508-28, MS DOUCE 5/ FOL 165V-166 508-29, MS DOUCE 5/ FOL 166V-167 508-30, MS DOUCE 5/ FOL 167V-168 508-31

*PROVENANCE FLEMISH/ GHENT

*DATE EXECUTED 14TH/C1320-30

*LANGUAGE LATIN

*TYPE OF MANUSCRIPT PSALTER/ PORTABLE

*CONTENTS PSALTER ILLUSTRATIONS 508/1-31, HUMAN FIGURES/ STAGS/ UNICORN 508-1, APES PLAYING DICE/ HUMAN FIGURES/ GROTESQUES/ UNICORN 508-2, HUMAN FIGURES/ BIRD WITH EEL 508-3, MAN WITH CLUB AND HORN/ UNICORN 508-4, BLANK FOLIO 508-5, CHRIST BEFORE PILATE 508-6, PSALM 51 ILLUMINATED Q QUID 508-6, INITIAL Q QUID 508-6, SAUL STABS HIMSELF/ DEVIL WITH HAND ON SWORD 508-6, DEVIL AND KING SAUL 508-6, HUMAN FIGURES/ ONE HOLDING BOOK AND CROSS 508-7, MAN BLOWING LONG TRUMPET 508-8, FLAGELLATION OF CHRIST 508-9, PSALM 52 ILLUMINATED D DIXIT 508-9, INITIAL D DIXIT 508-9, DAVID AND FOOL 508-9, COURT OF APES 508-9, APE ON REARING HORSE 508-9, PSALM 53 ILLUMINATED D DEUS 508-10, INITIAL D DEUS 508-10, NUDE FIGURE WALKING THROUGH WATER WITH HORSE ON SHOULDERS 508-10, FIGHTING WITH SWORD AND SPEAR 508-10, MEN WITH POLES 508-10, GOAT ON HIND LEGS 508-10, UNICORN/ TWO HARES/ SMALL BIRD 508-11, HUMAN FIGURE BLOWING TRUMPET 508-11, HUMAN FIGURE WEARING POINTED CAP 508-12, HUMAN FIGURE WITH SWORD AND SHIELD 508-13, BEAST/ STAG/ BIRD 508-13, HUMAN FIGURES/ ONE WITH TRUMPET/ OTHER WITH SWORD 508-14, PSALM 55 ILLUMINATED M MISERE INSET WITH TWO FISH 508-15, INITIAL M MISERE INSET WITH TWO FISH 508-15, DOG CHASING HARE/ MAN BLOWING TRUMPET 508-15, BLUE TITS 508-15, GROTESQUE LOOKING AT HARE 508-15, HUMAN FIGURES/ ONE WITH RAISED CLUB/ OTHER WITH TAPER 508-15, SOLDIER WITH SHIELD AND LONG SPEAR 508-16, PSALM 56 ILLUMINATED M MISERERE INSET WITH TWO HEADS 508-17, INITIAL M MISERERE INSET WITH TWO HEADS 508-17, GROTESQUE PLAYING BAGPIPES/ WOMAN LOOKS ON 508-17, HUMAN FIGURES/ ONE WITH SWORD/ ONE WITH CLUB 508-17, BIRD WITH EEL IN BEAK 508-17, HUMAN FIGURES HOLDING DICE 508-18, APE SAWING DOWN FOLIAGE BORDER 508-19, APE DRESSED AS CLERIC HOLDING SACK 508-19, HUMAN FIGURE WITH SCROLL 508-19, MAN WITH LONG TRUMPET 508-20, GROTESQUE ON HIND LEGS WITH BIRD ON TOP 508-20,MAN ON CRUTCHES 508-20, VIOLIN PLAYING 508-21, HUMAN FIGURE WITH CROWN AND STAFF 508-22, PSALM 59 ILLUMINATED D DEUS INSET WITH HEAD 508-23, INITIAL D DEUS INSET WITH HEAD 508-23, APES FIGHTING WITH DAGGER 508-23, MAN SHOOTING SMALL BIRD 508-23, HUMAN FIGURE REACHING TOWARD FEMALE GROTESQUE 508-23, APE CHOPPING DOWN FOLIAGE BORDER WITH OWL ATOP 508-24, INITIAL E/ MAN BENDING UNDER 508-24, HUMAN FIGURES/ ONE WITH SCIMITAR/ OTHER POKING BEAST 508-25, PSALM 61 ILLUMINATED N NONNE INSET WITH MAN 508-26, INITIAL N NONNE INSET WITH MAN 508-26, MAN SHOOTING HARE 508-26, THREE CAPPED HUMANS/ LONG-BILLED BIRDS 508-27, PSALM 62 ILLUMINATED D DEUS INSET WITH APE 508-28, INITIAL D DEUS INSET WITH APE 508-28, MAN PLAYING GRILL WITH TONGS 508-28, MAN PLAYING SPOON WITH STICK 508-28, PSALM 63 ILLUMINATED E EXAUDI INSET WITH BIRD 508-29, INITIAL E EXAUDI INSET WITH BIRD 508-29, HUMAN FIGURE WITH RAISED SWORD 508-30, SOLDIER-CENTAUR WITH RAISED SCIMITAR 508-31, APE EATING FROM BOWL 508-31, UNICORN/ STAG/ BIRD WITH FROG 508-31

*$ABSTRACT 509

*LIBRARY BODLEIAN

*SLIDE SET TITLE OXFORD MAPS EXHIBITION

*NEGATIVE REFERENCE ROLL 221A

*RENTAL FEE $3.20

*TITLE OF MANUSCRIPT OXONIA ANTIQUA INSTAURATA SIVE URBIS AND ACADEMIAE OXONIENSIS TOPOGRAPHICA 509-1, THE PARTICULAR DESCRIPTION OF ENGLAND/ PLATE 24 509-2, THE THEATRE OF GREAT

BRITAIN 509-3, OXFORDE 509-4, PLAN OF THE CITTIE OF OXFORD 509-5, OXFORD AS IT NOW LYETH FORTIFIED 509-6, OXONIA DEPICTA 509-7, PLAN OF THE UNIVERSITY AND CITY OF OXFORD 509-8, PLAN OF THE CITY OF OXFORD 509/9-10, A MAP OF THE COUNTY OF OXFORD 509/11-12, ORDNANCE SURVEY 509-13, PLAN OF THE CITY OF OXFORD FROM ACTUAL SURVEY 509/14-16, MAP OF OXFORD ILLUSTRATING ACLAND'S REPORT ON CHOLERA 509-17, OXFORD LOCAL BOARD/ PLAN OF MAIN AND STREET DRAINAGE 509-18, DRINK MAP OF OXFORD 509-19, ORDNANCE SURVEY SHEET/ 25 INCH MAP 509-20, ORDNANCE SURVEY/ 6 INCH MAP 509-21, LIMIT OF RESIDENCE 509-22, GEOLOGICAL SURVEY OF ENGLAND AND WALES 509-23,STADTPLAN VON OXFORD 509-24
*SHELFMARK PR GOUGH MAPS OXFORDSHIRE 2 509-1, PR GA GEN TOP 4 265 509-2, PR J MAPS 224 10 509-3, PR EC17 70 OXFORD 20 509-4, MS TOP OXON B 167 509-5
*PROVENANCE ENGLISH 509/1-23, GERMAN 509-24
*DATE EXECUTED 18TH/1728 509-1, 19TH/1879 509-2, 17TH/1610 509-3, 17TH/1643 509-4, 17TH/1644 509/5-6, 17TH/1675 509-7, 18TH/1751 509-8, 18TH/1789 509/9-10, 18TH/1797 509/11-12, 19TH/1832 509-13, 19TH/1850 509/14-16, 19TH/1855 509-17, 19TH/1872 509-18, 19TH/1883 509-19, 19TH/1876 509-20, 19TH/1887 509-21, 19TH/1888 509-22, 20TH/1908 509-23, 20TH/1941 509-24
*TYPE OF MANUSCRIPT MAPS/ 16TH-20TH CENTURY 509/1-24
*CONTENTS FACSIMILE OF EARLIEST MAP OF OXFORD 1578 509-1, FACSIMILE OF 1588 MAP OF OXFORD 509-2, CITY PLAN INSET ON OXFORDSHIRE 509-3, OXFORD EXPANDING IN 1643 509-4, FORTIFICATIONS OF ROYALISTS IN 1644 509/5-6, OXFORD AFTER THE CIVIL WAR 509-7, OXFORD IN MID 18TH CENTURY 509-8, OXFORD AFTER REDEVELOPMENT OF 1770S 509/9-10, OXFORD IMPROVEMENTS/ PRISON AND CANAL 509/11-12, OXFORD FROM 1832 ORDNANCE SURVEY 509-13, RAILROAD REACHES OXFORD 509/14-16, OXFORD MAP IN 1854 REPORT ON CHOLERA 509-17, PLAN OF MAIN AND STREET DRAINAGE 509-18, DRINK MAP SHOWING HOUSES FOR THE SALE OF INTOXICANTS 509-19, ORDNANCE SURVEY/ 25 INCH MAP 509-20, ORDNANCE SURVEY/ 6 INCH MAP 509-21, LIMIT OF RESIDENCE WITHIN UNIVERSITY 509-22, GEOLOGICAL SURVEY SHOWING LATE SAXON AND MEDIEVAL TOWN 509-23, GERMAN MAP SHOWING MORRIS MOTOR WORKS 509-24

*$ABSTRACT 510
*LIBRARY BODLEIAN
*SLIDE SET TITLE BESTIARY ILLUSTRATIONS
*NEGATIVE REFERENCE ROLL 221B
*RENTAL FEE $2.85
*SHELFMARK MS DOUCE 88/ FOL 14 510-1, MS DOUCE 88/ FOL 51 510-2, MS DOUCE 88/ FOL 78 510-3, MS DOUCE 88/ FOL 69V-70 510-4, MS DOUCE 88/ FOL 96V 510-5, MS DOUCE 88/ FOL 140 510-6, MS DOUCE 151/ FOL 3 510-7, MS DOUCE 151/ FOL 10V 510-8, MS DOUCE 151/ FOL 22V 510-9, MS DOUCE 151/ FOL 23 510-10, MS DOUCE 151/ FOL 25V 510/11-12, MS DOUCE 151/ FOL 26 510-13, MS DOUCE 151/ FOL 26V 510-14, MS DOUCE 151/ FOL 29V 510-15, MS DOUCE 151/ FOL 71V 510-16, MS DOUCE 151/ FOL 80V 510-17
*PROVENANCE ENGLISH/ ST AUGUSTINE'S CANTERBURY 510/1-6, ENGLISH 510/7-17
*DATE EXECUTED 14TH/C1300
*LANGUAGE LATIN
*TYPE OF MANUSCRIPT BESTIARY
*CONTENTS BESTIARY ILLUSTRATIONS 510/1-17, ADAM NAMING BEASTS 510-1, SHOEING A HORSE 510-2, CAMEL 510-3, MONSTERS 510-4, CROCODILE 510-5, BEAR SUCKLING CUBS 510-6, GOD CREATING BIRDS AND FISH 510-7, GENESIS 01/VERSES 20-23/ GOD CREATING BIRDS AND FISH 510-7, HUNTER AND VIRGIN KILLING UNICORN 510-8, UNICORN KILLED BY HUNTER AND VIRGIN 510-8, DOG ATTACKS MAN/ BURIAL OF MAN 510-9, DOG RETURNS TO OWN VOMIT 510-9, DOG IN WATER/ DOGS LICKING WOUNDS 510-10, COW SUCKLING CALF 510-11, BOAR 510-12, MONKEY SITTING BACKWARDS ON CAMEL 510-13, MAN/ NAKED RIDING DROMEDARY 510-14, CAT WITH MICE/ MOUSE/ WEASEL 510-15, PERINDEUS TREE WITH DOVES 510-16, DRAGONS WAIT FOR DOVES TO LEAVE PERINDEUS TREE 510-16, WHALE SWALLOWS FISH WHILE TWO SAILORS WATCH 510-17

*$ABSTRACT 511
*LIBRARY BODLEIAN
*SLIDE SET TITLE BOOK OF HOURS
*NEGATIVE REFERENCE ROLL 221C
*RENTAL FEE $2.85
*COMMENTS WRITTEN FOR A DOMINICAN
*SHELFMARK MS BUCHANAN E 18/ FOL 42 511-1, MS BUCHANAN E 18/ FOL 52 511-2, MS BUCHANAN E 18/ FOL 56 511-3, MS BUCHANAN E 18/ FOL 60 511-4, MS BUCHANAN E 18/ FOL 64 511-5, MS BUCHANAN E 18/ FOL 68 511-6, MS BUCHANAN E 18/ FOL 74 511-7, MS BUCHANAN E 18/ FOL 95 511-8, MS BUCHANAN E 18/ FOL 131 511-9, MS BUCHANAN E 18/ FOL 136V 511-10, MS BUCHANAN E 18/ FOL 139 511-11, MS BUCHANAN E 18/ FOL 139V 511-12, MS BUCHANAN E 18/ FOL 140V 511-13, MS BUCHANAN E 18/ FOL 141 511-14, MS BUCHANAN E 18/ FOL 142 511-15, MS BUCHANAN E 18/ FOL 143 511-16, MS BUCHANAN E 18/ FOL 60 511-17
*PROVENANCE FLEMISH
*DATE EXECUTED 15TH/3RD QUARTER
*LANGUAGE LATIN AND FLEMISH
*ARTIST/ SCHOOL VRELANT WILLEM
*TYPE OF MANUSCRIPT BOOK OF HOURS/ USE OF ROME
*CONTENTS BOOK OF HOURS 511/1-17, VISITATION 511-1, NATIVITY 511-2, ANNUNCIATION TO SHEPHERDS 511-3, ADORATION OF MAGI 511-4, PRESENTATION OF CHRIST IN TEMPLE 511-5, MASSACRE OF THE INNOCENTS 511-6, FLIGHT INTO EGYPT 511-7, FUNERAL SCENE 511-8, PIETA 511-9, BLESSED SACRAMENT 511-10, PANGE LINGUA GLORIOSI TEXT OF AQUINAS 511-10, ST THOMAS AQUINAS 511-11, ST VINCENT FERRIER VESTED FOR MASS 511-12, ST CATHERINE OF SIENA 511-13, ST DONATIAN OF REIMS AND BRUGES 511-14, ST ELIZABETH OF THURINGIA 511-15, ST BERNARD AS MONK 511-16, ADORATION OF MAGI/ MERMAID IN BORDER 511-17

*$ABSTRACT 512
*LIBRARY BODLEIAN
*SLIDE SET TITLE DECRETUM OF GRATIAN
*NEGATIVE REFERENCE ROLL 221D
*RENTAL FEE $2.95
*COMMENTS AN ATTEMPT TO UNIFY AND TO RECONCILE THE EXTENSIVE AND OFTEN CONTRADICTORY CORPUS OF CANON LAW. ILLUMINATED INITIALS OCCUR AT THE BEGINNINGS OF MANY TEXTUAL DIVISIONS AND THE SCENES TEND TO BE RELATED TO THE TEXT.
*TITLE OF MANUSCRIPT DECRETORUM DISCORDANTIUM CONCORDIA
*SHELFMARK MS LYELL 41/ FOL 68 512-1, MS LYELL 41/ FOL 104 512-2, MS LYELL 41/ FOL 112 512-3, MS LYELL 41/ FOL 118V 512-4, MS LYELL 41/ FOL 137V 512-5, MS LYELL 41/ FOL 142V 512-6, MS LYELL 41/ FOL 151V 512-7, MS LYELL 41/ FOL 154 512-8, MS LYELL 41/ FOL 158 512-9, MS LYELL 41/ FOL 159V 512-10, MS LYELL 41/ FOL 164V 512-11, MS LYELL 41/ FOL 187V 512-12, MS LYELL 41/ FOL 199V 512-13, MS LYELL 41/ FOL 202V 512-14, MS LYELL 41/ FOL 204 512-15, MS LYELL 41/ FOL 209V 512-16, MS LYELL 41/ FOL 231 512-17, MS LYELL 41/ FOL 231V 512-18, MS LYELL 41/ FOL 236V 512-19
*PROVENANCE FRANCE/ SOUTH-EAST?
*DATE EXECUTED 13TH
*LANGUAGE LATIN
*AUTHOR CAMADOLESE MONK
*TYPE OF MANUSCRIPT CANON LAW
*CONTENTS ABBOT RECEIVES GIFT FROM FATHER AND SON 512-1, BISHOP BLESSING 512-2, BISHOP IN BED VISITED BY PRIEST 512-3, BISHOP HOLDS ARM OF PRIEST 512-4, CANONS/ TWO 512-5, ABBOT WITH MONK 512-6, PRIEST BEDRIDDEN VISITED BY TWO MONKS 512-7, ABBOT BLESSING 512-8, ARCHBISHOP BLESSING 512-9, BISHOP GESTURING TOWARDS MAN BESIDE ALTAR 512-10, BISHOP TALKS TO TWO ARMORED KNIGHTS 512-11, BISHOP AND PRIEST 512-12, MAN AND WOMAN WITH JOINED HANDS 512-13, MAN AND WOMAN WITH JOINED HANDS 512-14, MAN HOLDS WOMAN BY ARMS 512-15, MAN AND WOMAN SEATED AND HOLDING HANDS 512-16, MAN GREETING ANOTHER COMING OUT OF PRISON 512-17, INITIAL Q DECORATED 512-18, MAN DRAWS WOMAN TO TABLE 512-19

*$ABSTRACT 513
*LIBRARY BODLEIAN
*SLIDE SET TITLE DECRETALS OF GREGORY IX
*NEGATIVE REFERENCE ROLL 221E
*RENTAL FEE $2.60
*COMMENTS ONE OF THE EARLIEST KNOWN COPIES OF THE FIRST DEFINITIVE COLLECTION OF PAPAL LETTERS AND MANDATES AND INCORPORATING THE GLOSSES OF BERNARD OF PARMA. GREGORY IX WANTED TO RECONCILE THE DIFFERENCES AND CORRECT THE ERRORS OF THE LARGE NUMBER OF EARLIER COLLECTIONS OF PAPAL RULINGS WITH THEIR EVEN GREATER NUMBER OF INTERPRETATIONS AND COMMENTARIES, AND TO PUT IN THEIR PLACE A SINGLE, AUTHORISED TEXT WITH STANDARD GLOSSES.
*TITLE OF MANUSCRIPT DECRETALS OF GREGORY IX WITH APPARATUS OF BERNARD OF PARMA
*SHELFMARK MS LAT TH B 4/ FOL 1 513-1, MS LAT TH B 4/ FOL 54 513-2, MS LAT TH B 4/ FOL 101 513-3, MS LAT TH B 4/ FOL 151 513-4, MS LAT TH B 4/ FOL 168 513-5, MS LAT TH B 4/ FOL 23V 513-6, MS LAT TH B 4/ FOL 29V 513-7, MS LAT TH B 4/ FOL 37 513-8, MS LAT TH B 4/ FOL 50V 513-9, MS LAT TH B 4/ FOL 105 513-10, MS LAT TH B 4/ FOL 113V 513-11, MS LAT TH B 4/ FOL 182 513-12
*PROVENANCE ITALIAN/ MODENA
*DATE EXECUTED 13TH/1241
*LANGUAGE LATIN
*AUTHOR DE GROPIS OF MODENA/ LEONARDUS
*TYPE OF MANUSCRIPT CANON LAW
*CONTENTS DECRETALS OF GREGORY IX 513/1-12, POPE GREGORY IX IS OFFERED A BOOK 513-1, PETITIONER READS FROM SCROLL TO SEATED MAN 513-2, PRIEST CELEBRATES MASS 513-3, BISHOP MARRIES COUPLE 513-4, BISHOP ADMONISHES TONSURED PRISONER HELD BY HUSBAND 513-5, BOAR HUNT 513-6, LION/ COW/ RAM/ GOAT 513-7, HUNTSMAN BLOWING HORN 513-8, GROTESQUE/ BIRDS/ FOX/ HERON 513-9, MONK HOLDS SCROLL 513-10, MERMAID AND MONSTER 513-11, MAN HOLDS END OF DECORATIVE MOTIF 513-12

*$ABSTRACT 514
*LIBRARY BODLEIAN
*SLIDE SET TITLE ENGLISH HUMANISTIC MSS IN THE 15TH CENTURY
*NEGATIVE REFERENCE ROLL 223A
*RENTAL FEE $3.80
*COMMENTS THE SET ILLUSTRATES THE EXHIBITION, DUKE HUMFREY AND ENGLISH HUMANISM IN THE 15TH CENTURY, HELD IN THE BODLEIAN IN 1970. A PRINTED CATALOGUE OF THE EXHIBITION IS AVAILABLE.
*TITLE OF MANUSCRIPT HUMANISTIC MISCELLANY 514/1-2, LETTERS OF LEONARDO BRUNI 514/3-5, DE VERBORUM SIGNIFICATIONE 514-6, ARISTOTLE'S ETHICS/ POLITICS/ ECONOMICS 514/7-11, GESTA REGUM BRITONUM 514/12-13, DE ORTHOGRAPHIA 514/14-15, COMEDIES OF TERENCE 514/16-20, WORKS OF POGGIO BRACCIOLINI 514/21-24, HUMANISTIC MISCELLANY 514/25-26, VIRGIL'S AENEID 514/27-29, COLLOCUTIONES AND ALLOCUTIONES 514/30-32, LETTERS OF PLINY THE YOUNGER 514-33, RAMON LULL 514/34-35, DE CESSOLIS/ JACOBUS 514-36
*SHELFMARK MS BALLIOL COLLEGE 315 514/1-2, MS BALLIOL COLLEGE 310 514/3-5, MS SAVILE 106 514-6, MS NEW COLLEGE 228 514/7-11, MS LAUD MISC 579 514/12-13, MS BALLIOL COLLEGE 290 514/14-15, MS MAGDALEN COLLEGE LAT 23 514/ 16-20, MS BODLEY 915 514/21-24, MS MAGDALEN COLLEGE LAT 39 514/ 25-26, MS NEW COLLEGE 271 514/27-29, MS NEW COLLEGE 288 514/30-32, MS LINCOLN COLLEGE LAT 77 514-33, MS MERTON COLLEGE 89 514/34-35, MS MAGDALEN COLLEGE LAT 12 514-36
*PROVENANCE ENGLISH
*DATE EXECUTED 15TH/C1442 514/1-2, 15TH/1449 514/3-5, 15TH 514-6, 15TH/1452 514/7-11, 15TH/C1450-60 514/12-15, 15TH/ MID 514/16-20, 15TH/C1450-60 514/21-24, 15TH/C1450-60 514/25-26, 15TH/C1400 514/27-29, 15TH/C1463-65 514/30-32, 15TH/BEFORE 1465 514-33, 15TH/C1470-80 514/34-35, 15TH/1456 514-36
*LANGUAGE LATIN
*AUTHOR BRUNI/ LEONARDO 514/3-5, VEGIO/ MAFFEO 514-6, ARISTOTLE 514/7-11, GEOFFREY OF MONMOUTH 514/12-13, TORTELLI/ GIOVANNI

514/14-15, TERENCE 514/16-20, BRACCIOLINI/ POGGIO 514/21-24, VIRGIL 514/27-29, CHAUNDLER/ THOMAS 514/30-32, PLINY THE YOUNGER 514-33, LULL/ RAMON 514/34-35, DE CESSOLIS/ JACOBUS 514-36
*SCRIBE THEODERICUS WERKEN 514/3-5, JO R 1452 514/7-11, THOMAS 514/16-28, FARLEY/ JOHN 514/30-32, FLEMMYNG/ ROBERT 514-33, PACY/ JOHN 514/34-35, AYLWARD/ SIMON 514-36
*TYPE OF MANUSCRIPT HUMANISTIC INITIALS AND SCRIPT
*CONTENTS INITIALS AND SCRIPT/ HUMANISTIC 514/1-36, PALEOGRAPHY 514/1-36, INITIAL S AND BORDERS 514-1, INITIAL S/ DETAIL 514-2, INITIAL L AND BORDERS 514-3, INITIAL L 514-4, COLOPHON 514-5, INITIAL A 514-6, INITIAL A/ BULL AND HAWK 514-7, BULL AND HAWK 514-7, BULL AND HAWK/ DETAIL 514-8, INITIAL O WITH MONSTER 514-9, MONSTER 514-9, INITIAL Q WITH MONSTER 514-10, MONSTER 514-10, INITIAL I WITH HEADS OF BIRD AND MAN 514-11, INITIAL C WITH BULL 514-12, INITIAL C/ DETAIL 514-13, INITIAL V WITH PUTTI 514-14, PUTTI 514-14, INITIAL Z WITH BIRDS 514-15, INITIAL P 514-16, INITIAL U/ WHOLE PAGE 514-17, INITIAL S/ DETAIL 514-18, INITIAL M WITH MERMAID 514-19, MERMAID 514-19, INITIAL Q WITH MAN 514-20, INITIAL C WITH MONSTER 514-21, MONSTER 514-21, INITIAL P 514-22, INITIAL P WITH DOG 514-23, INITIAL P WITH BIRD 514-24, INITIAL V WITH DOG 514-25, INITIAL L 514-26, INITIAL AND UNIDENTIFIED ARMS 514-27, INITIAL V WITH TWO DOGS 514-28, INITIAL M AND SCRIPT 514-29, INITIAL C 514-30, INITIAL C 514-31, INITIAL D 514-32, INITIAL P 514-33, INITIAL R WITH ARMS OF WARDEN FITZ-JAMES OF MERTON 514-34, INITIALS T AND A 514-35, COLOPHON/ WHOLE PAGE 514-36

*$ABSTRACT 515
*LIBRARY BODLEIAN
*SLIDE SET TITLE GOSPEL ILLUSTRATIONS
*NEGATIVE REFERENCE ROLL 223B
*RENTAL FEE $10.75
*COMMENTS MANY RARE GOSPEL STORIES ARE DEPICTED IN THE HISTORIATED INITIALS. MS PRESENTED BY ARCHBISHOP THOMAS ARUNDEL TO CANTERBURY.
*TITLE OF MANUSCRIPT COMMENTARY ON THE GOSPELS
*SHELFMARK MS LAUD MISC 165/ FOL 5 515-1, MS LAUD MISC 165/ FOL 13 515-2, MS LAUD MISC 165/ FOL 26V 515-3, MS LAUD MISC 165/ FOL 30 515-4, MS LAUD MISC 165/ FOL 35 515-5, MS LAUD MISC 165/ FOL 40 515-6, MS LAUD MISC 165/ FOL 44 515-7, MS LAUD MISC 165/ FOL 48V 515-8, MS LAUD MISC 165/ FOL 52 515-9, MS LAUD MISC 165/ FOL 54 515-10, MS LAUD MISC 165/ FOL 58V 515-11, MS LAUD MISC 165/ FOL 59V 515-12, MS LAUD MISC 165/ FOL 60V 515-13, MS LAUD MISC 165/ FOL 64 515-14, MS LAUD MISC 165/ FOL 68 515-15, MS LAUD MISC 165/ FOL 69 515-16, MS LAUD MISC 165/ FOL 69V 515-17, MS LAUD MISC 165/ FOL 71 515-18, MS LAUD MISC 165/ FOL 74 515-19, MS LAUD MISC 165/ FOL 77V 515-20, MS LAUD MISC 165/ FOL 82 515-21, MS LAUD MISC 165/ FOL 84V 515-22, MS LAUD MISC 165/ FOL 86 515-23, MS LAUD MISC 165/ FOL 88V 515-24, MS LAUD MISC 165/ FOL 94V 515-25, MS LAUD MISC 165/ FOL 97 515-26, MS LAUD MISC 165/ FOL 100 515-27, MS LAUD MISC 165/ FOL 102 515-28, MS LAUD MISC 165/ FOL 108 515-29, MS LAUD MISC 165/ FOL 109 515-30, MS LAUD MISC 165/ FOL 109V 515-31, MS LAUD MISC 165/ FOL 116 515-32, MS LAUD MISC 165/ FOL 116V 515-33, MS LAUD MISC 165/ FOL 118 515-34, MS LAUD MISC 165/ FOL 120 515-35, MS LAUD MISC 165/ FOL 121 515-36, MS LAUD MISC 165/ FOL 121V 515-37, MS LAUD MISC 165/ FOL 123V 515-38, MS LAUD MISC 165/ FOL 124 515-39, MS LAUD MISC 165/ FOL 125V 515-40, MS LAUD MISC 165/ FOL 127V 515-41, MS LAUD MISC 165/ FOL 133 515-42, MS LAUD MISC 165/ FOL 135V 515-43, MS LAUD MISC 165/ FOL 136 515-44, MS LAUD MISC 165/ FOL 138 515-45, MS LAUD MISC 165/ FOL 140V 515-46, MS LAUD MISC 165/ FOL 143 515-47, MS LAUD MISC 165/ FOL 149V 515/48-49, MS LAUD MISC 165/ FOL 150V 515-50, MS LAUD MISC 165/ FOL 176V 515-51, MS LAUD MISC 165/ FOL 184V 515-52, MS LAUD MISC 165/ FOL 186 515-53, MS LAUD MISC 165/ FOL 188V 515-54, MS LAUD MISC 165/ FOL 191V 515-55, MS LAUD MISC 165/ FOL 194V 515-56, MS LAUD MISC 165/ FOL 198V 515-57, MS LAUD MISC 165/ FOL 199 515-58,

MS LAUD MISC 165/ FOL 200V 515-59, MS LAUD MISC 165/ FOL 202 515-60, MS LAUD MISC 165/ FOL 205V 515-61, MS LAUD MISC 165/ FOL 211 515-62, MS LAUD MISC 165/ FOL 212V 515-63, MS LAUD MISC 165/ FOL 217 515-64, MS LAUD MISC 165/ FOL 219 515-65, MS LAUD MISC 165/ FOL 222V 515-66, MS LAUD MISC 165/ FOL 224V 515-67, MS LAUD MISC 165/ FOL 226 515-68, MS LAUD MISC 165/ FOL 228V 515-69, MS LAUD MISC 165/ FOL 232V 515-70, MS LAUD MISC 165/ FOL 234 515-71, MS LAUD MISC 165/ FOL 234V 515-72, MS LAUD MISC 165/ FOL 235V 515-73, MS LAUD MISC 165/ FOL 237 515-74, MS LAUD MISC 165/ FOL 237V 515-75, MS LAUD MISC 165/ FOL 238V 515-76, MS LAUD MISC 165/ FOL 241 515-77, MS LAUD MISC 165/ FOL 247 515-78, MS LAUD MISC 165/ FOL 250V 515-79, MS LAUD MISC 165/ FOL 252 515-80, MS LAUD MISC 165/ FOL 253V 515-81, MS LAUD MISC 165/ FOL 257 515-82, MS LAUD MISC 165/ FOL 260 515-83, MS LAUD MISC 165/ FOL 261 515-84, MS LAUD MISC 165/ FOL 261V 515-85, MS LAUD MISC 165/ FOL 262V 515-86, MS LAUD MISC 165/ FOL 263V 515-87, MS LAUD MISC 165/ FOL 264V 515-88, MS LAUD MISC 165/ FOL 265V 515-89, MS LAUD MISC 165/ FOL 267 515-90, MS LAUD MISC 165/ FOL 268V 515-91, MS LAUD MISC 165/ FOL 272 515-92, MS LAUD MISC 165/ FOL 275 515-93, MS LAUD MISC 165/ FOL 276V 515-94, MS LAUD MISC 165/ FOL 278V 515-95, MS LAUD MISC 165/ FOL 279 515-96, MS LAUD MISC 165/ FOL 280 515-97, MS LAUD MISC 165/ FOL 283V 515-98, MS LAUD MISC 165/ FOL 288 515-99, MS LAUD MISC 165/ FOL 290V 515-100, MS LAUD MISC 165/ FOL 291V 515-101, MS LAUD MISC 165/ FOL 292 515-102, MS LAUD MISC 165/ FOL 296 515-103, MS LAUD MISC 165/ FOL 296V 515-104, MS LAUD MISC 165/ FOL 298 515-105, MS LAUD MISC 165/ FOL 299 515-106, MS LAUD MISC 165/ FOL 300V 515-107, MS LAUD MISC 165/ FOL 304V 515-108, MS LAUD MISC 165/ FOL 306 515-109, MS LAUD MISC 165/ FOL 315 515-110, MS LAUD MISC 165/ FOL 319 515-111, MS LAUD MISC 165/ FOL 320 515-112, MS LAUD MISC 165/ FOL 331V 515-113, MS LAUD MISC 165/ FOL 338V 515-114, MS LAUD MISC 165/ FOL 343V 515-115, MS LAUD MISC 165/ FOL 344V 515-116, MS LAUD MISC 165/ FOL 347V 515-117, MS LAUD MISC 165/ FOL 356 515/118-119, MS LAUD MISC 165/ FOL 358V 515-120, MS LAUD MISC 165/ FOL 362AV 515-121, MS LAUD MISC 165/ FOL 363 515-122, MS LAUD MISC 165/ FOL 366V 515-123, MS LAUD MISC 165/ FOL 369 515-124, MS LAUD MISC 165/ FOL 371V 515-125, MS LAUD MISC 165/ FOL 374 515-126, MS LAUD MISC 165/ FOL 379V 515-127, MS LAUD MISC 165/ FOL 386 515-128, MS LAUD MISC 165/ FOL 391 515-129, MS LAUD MISC 165/ FOL 393 515-130, MS LAUD MISC 165/ FOL 394V 515-131, MS LAUD MISC 165/ FOL 398AV 515-132, MS LAUD MISC 165/ FOL 399V 515-133, MS LAUD MISC 165/ FOL 405 515-134, MS LAUD MISC 165/ FOL 409 515-135, MS LAUD MISC 165/ FOL 420 515-136, MS LAUD MISC 165/ FOL 425 515-137, MS LAUD MISC 165/ FOL 426 515-138, MS LAUD MISC 165/ FOL 429V 515-139, MS LAUD MISC 165/ FOL 443 515-140, MS LAUD MISC 165/ FOL 444V 515-141, MS LAUD MISC 165/ FOL 445V 515-142, MS LAUD MISC 165/ FOL 449V 515-143, MS LAUD MISC 165/ FOL 457V 515-144, MS LAUD MISC 165/ FOL 458V 515-145, MS LAUD MISC 165/ FOL 460V 515-146, MS LAUD MISC 165/ FOL 462V 515-147, MS LAUD MISC 165/ FOL 464V 515-148, MS LAUD MISC 165/ FOL 465V 515-149, MS LAUD MISC 165/ FOL 466V 515-150, MS LAUD MISC 165/ FOL 467V 515-151, MS LAUD MISC 165/ FOL 468V 515-152, MS LAUD MISC 165/ FOL 470 515-153, MS LAUD MISC 165/ FOL 470 515-153, MS LAUD MISC 165/ FOL 477V 515-154, MS LAUD MISC 165/ FOL 492 515-155, MS LAUD MISC 165/ FOL 493V 515-156, MS LAUD MISC 165/ FOL 496V 515-157, MS LAUD MISC 165/ FOL 499V 515-158, MS LAUD MISC 165/ FOL 509 515-159, MS LAUD MISC 165/ FOL 510 515-160, MS LAUD MISC 165/ FOL 514 515-161, MS LAUD MISC 165/ FOL 525 515-162, MS LAUD MISC 165/ FOL 528 515-163, MS LAUD MISC 165/ FOL 530V 515-164, MS LAUD MISC 165/ FOL 532 515-165, MS LAUD MISC 165/ FOL 533V 515-166, MS LAUD MISC 165/ FOL 534V 515-167, MS LAUD MISC 165/ FOL 539 515-168, MS LAUD MISC 165/ FOL 542V 515-169, MS LAUD MISC 165/ FOL 548 515-170, MS LAUD MISC 165/ FOL 550V 515-171, MS LAUD MISC 165/ FOL 551V 515-172, MS LAUD MISC 165/ FOL 555V 515-173, MS LAUD MISC 165/ FOL 564 515-174, MS LAUD MISC 165/ FOL 565 515-175

*PROVENANCE ENGLISH
*DATE EXECUTED 14TH/AFTER 1396
*LANGUAGE LATIN
*AUTHOR WILLIAM OF NOTTINGHAM

*TYPE OF MANUSCRIPT COMMENTARY ON THE GOSPELS
*CONTENTS GOSPEL ILLUSTRATIONS 515/1-175, ARCHBISHOP THOMAS ARUNDEL RECEIVES AND PRESENTS BOOK 515-1, PRESENTATION OF BOOK 515-1, CHRIST ENTHRONED BETWEEN SYMBOLS OF EVANGELISTS 515-2, AUTHOR LECTURES TO FOUR STUDENTS 515-2, ARCHANGEL APPEARS TO ZACHARIAS 515-3, ZACHARIAS AND ARCHANGEL 515-3, LUKE 01/VERSE 13 515-3, ANNUNCIATION 515-4, LUKE 01/VERSES 28-31/ ANNUNCIATION 515-4, VISITATION 515-5, LUKE 01/VERSES 39-41/ VISITATION 515-5, ST JOHN THE BAPTIST/ BIRTH 515-6, LUKE 01/VERSE 57/ BIRTH OF JOHN THE BAPTIST 515-6, MARY'S VIRGINITY ASSURED BY ANGEL 515-7, MATTHEW 01/VERSES 18-20/ MARY'S VIRGINITY ASSURED 515-7, JESSE TREES 515-8, MATTHEW 01/VERSE 1/ JESSE TREES 515-8, JESSE TREE SHOWING ANCESTRY OF JOSEPH AND MARY 515-9, CAESAR AUGUSTUS DECREES THAT WORLD BE TAXED 515-10, LUKE 02/VERSE 1/ CAESAR DECREES TAXES 515-10, SHEPHERD WORSHIPS INFANT CHRIST 515-11, LUKE 02/VERSES 15-16/ SHEPHERD AND INFANT CHRIST 515-11, CIRCUMCISION OF CHRIST 515-12, LUKE 02/VERSE 21/ CIRCUMCISION OF CHRIST 515-12,ADORATION OF MAGI 515-13, MATTHEW 02/VERSE 1/ ADORATION OF MAGI 515-13, PRESENTATION IN THE TEMPLE 515-14, SIMEON TAKES CHRIST CHILD IN ARMS 515-14, LUKE 02/VERSE 28/ PRESENTATION IN TEMPLE 515-14,FLIGHT INTO EGYPT 515-15, MATTHEW 02/VERSE 13/ FLIGHT INTO EGYPT 515-15, MASSACRE OF INNOCENTS 515-16, MATTHEW 02/VERSE 16/ MASSACRE OF INNOCENTS 515-16, HOLY FAMILY RETURNS FROM EGYPT 515-17, MATTHEW 02/VERSES 19-21/ RETURN FROM EGYPT 515-17, CHRIST AT AGE OF 12/ SEATED AMONG DOCTORS 515-18, LUKE 02/VERSE 46/ CHRIST AT 12 AMONG DOCTORS 515-18, ST JOHN THE BAPTIST BLESSED BY CHRIST 515-19, LUKE 03/VERSE 1/ CHRIST BLESSES JOHN THE BAPTIST 515-19, ST JOHN THE BAPTIST BAPTISES THREE MEN 515-20, MARK 01/VERSE 2/ JOHN BAPTISES THREE MEN 515-20,ST JOHN THE BAPTIST PREACHES TO CHILD AND SOLDIERS 515-21, LUKE 03/VERSE 10/ JOHN THE BAPTIST PREACHES 515-21, ST JOHN THE BAPTIST POINTS TO CHRIST 515-22, JEW LISTENS TO JOHN THE BAPTIST 515-22, MATTHEW 03/VERSE 11/ JOHN BAPTIST POINTS TO CHRIST 515-22, BAPTISM OF CHRIST 515-23, MATTHEW 03/VERSE 13/ BAPTISM OF CHRIST 515-23, CHRIST TEMPTED BY DEVIL TO MAKE BREAD FROM STONES 515-24, TEMPTATION OF CHRIST BY DEVIL 515-24, MATTHEW 04/VERSE 3/ CHRIST TEMPTED BY DEVIL 515-24, ST JOHN SAYS TO TWO DISCIPLES BEHOLD THE LAMB 515-25, JOHN 01/VERSES 35-37/ BEHOLD THE LAMB 515-25, MARRIAGE AT CANA 515-26, CHRIST TURNS WATER INTO WINE 515-26, JOHN 02/VERSE 1/ MARRIAGE AT CANA 515-26, CHRIST DRIVES MONEY-CHANGERS FROM TEMPLE 515-27, JOHN 02/VERSE 15/ MONEY-CHANGERS DRIVEN FROM TEMPLE 515-27, NICODEMUS COMES TO CHRIST BY NIGHT 515-28, JOHN 03/VERSES 1-2/ NICODEMUS COMES TO CHRIST 515-28, HEROD'S SERVANTS PUT JOHN BAPTIST INTO PRISON 515-29, MATTHEW 14/VERSE 3/ JOHN BAPTIST PUT INTO PRISON 515-29, WILLIAM NOTTINGHAM LECTURES TO EIGHT STUDENTS 515-30, CHRIST AND WOMAN OF SAMARIA AT WELL 515-31, JOHN 04/VERSE 7/ CHRIST AND WOMAN OF SAMARIA 515-31, CHRIST TEACHES IN SYNAGOGUE IN GALILEE 515-32,LUKE 04/VERSES 14-15/ CHRIST TEACHES 515-32, CHRIST PREACHES FROM SIMON'S BOAT 515-33, LUKE 05/VERSES 1-3/ CHRIST PREACHES 515-33, CHRIST HANDED BOOK OF ISAIAH 515-34, LUKE 04/VERSES 16-17/ CHRIST WITH BOOK OF ISAIAH 515-34, CHRIST ARRIVES AT CAPERNAUM 515-35, MATTHEW 04/VERSES 13-16/ CHRIST AT CAPERNAUM 515-35, CALLING OF PETER AND ANDREW 515-36, MATTHEW 04/VERSES 18-19/ CALLING OF PETER AND ANDREW 515-36, CALLING OF JAMES AND JOHN 515-37, MATTHEW 04/VERSE 21/ CALLING OF JAMES AND JOHN 515-37, CHRIST HEALS PETER'S MOTHER IN LAW 515-38, MATTHEW 08/VERSES 14-15/ CHRIST HEALS MOTHER-IN-LAW 515-38, CHRIST HEALS AND CASTS OUT SPIRITS 515-39, DEVIL DEPARTS FROM MAN'S MOUTH 515-39, MATTHEW 08/VERSE 16/ CHRIST CASTS OUT SPIRITS 515-39, CHRIST SOUGHT BY SIMON AND PETER 515-40, MARK 01/VERSES 35-36/ CHRIST IN DESERT 515-40, CHRIST AND TWO DISCIPLES IN BOAT/ CHRIST ASLEEP 515-41, CHRIST ASLEEP AS TEMPEST ARISES IN SEA 515-41, MATTHEW 08/VERSES 23-24/ CHRIST ASLEEP IN BOAT 515-41, CHRIST MEETS MAN SICK OF PALSY 515-42, MATTHEW 09/VERSES 1-2/ CHRIST AND SICK MAN 515-42, CHRIST HEALS MAN SICK OF PALSY 515-43, MATTHEW 09/VERSES 6-7/ CHRIST HEALS SICK MAN 515-43, CHRIST CALLS MATTHEW FROM CUSTOM HOUSE 515-44,MATTHEW 09/VERSE 9/ CHRIST CALLS MATTHEW 515-44, CHRIST SPEAKS ABOUT FASTING TO JOHN'S DISCIPLES 515-45, MATTHEW

09/VERSE 14/ CHRIST SPEAKS ABOUT FASTING 515-45, CHRIST ASKED TO RAISE RULER'S DAUGHTER FROM DEAD 515-46, MATTHEW 09/VERSES 18-21/ CHRIST RAISES GIRL FROM DEAD 515-47, WILLIAM NOTTINGHAM READS TO SEVEN STUDENTS 515-48, CHRIST IN GALILEE HEALS TWO LEPERS 515-49, MATTHEW 04/VERSE 23/ CHRIST HEALS LEPERS 515-49,CHRIST SPEAKS TO TWO DISCIPLES 515-50, MATTHEW 03/VERSE 13/ CHRIST AND TWO DISCIPLES 515-50, CHRIST SPEAKS ABOUT WOLVES IN SHEEP'S CLOTHING 515-51, MATTHEW 07/VERSE 15/ PARABLE OF WOLF AND SHEEP 515-51, CHRIST SAYS THAT EACH TREE IS KNOWN BY FRUIT 515-52, LUKE 06/VERSE 43/ TREE KNOWN BY ITS FRUIT 515-52,CHRIST HEALS LEPER 515-53, MATTHEW 08/VERSES 1-3/ CHRIST HEALS LEPER 515-53, CHRIST ASKED BY CENTURION TO HEAL SERVANT 515-54, MATTHEW 08/VERSES 5-6/ CHRIST ASKED TO HEAL 515-54, CHRIST GIVES DISCIPLES AUTHORITY TO HEAL 515-55, MATTHEW 10/VERSE 1/ DISCIPLES GIVEN HEALING POWERS 515-55, CHRIST SENDS DISCIPLES AS SHEEP AMONG WOLVES 515-56, MATTHEW 10/VERSE 16/ DISCIPLES AS SHEEP AMONG WOLVES 515-56, SHEEP AND WOLVES PARABLE 515-56, CHRIST'S DISCIPLES CAST OUT UNCLEAN SPIRITS 515-57, MARK 06/VERSE 13/ DISCIPLES CAST OUT SPIRITS 515-57, CHRIST RAISES WIDOW'S SON FROM DEAD 515-58, LUKE 07/VERSE 14/ CHRIST RAISES BOY FROM DEAD 515-58, ST JOHN BAPTIST IN PRISON SENDS FOR CHRIST 515-59, MATTHEW 11/VERSE 2/ JOHN BAPTIST IN PRISON 515-59, CHRIST SPEAKS TO MULTITUDE ABOUT JOHN BAPTIST 515-60, MATTHEW 11/VERSE 7/ CHRIST SPEAKS TO MULTITUDE 515-60, CHRIST IN PHARISEE'S HOUSE/ FEET WASHED 515-61, LUKE 07/VERSES 36-38/ CHRIST IN PHARISEE'S HOUSE 515-61, WILLIAM NOTTINGHAM READS TO TEN STUDENTS 515-62, CHRIST UPBRAIDS CHORAZIN AND BETHSAIDA 515-63, MATTHEW 11/VERSES 20-21 515-63, CHRIST ADMONISHES LAWYER 515-64, LUKE 10/VERSE 25/ CHRIST ADMONISHES LAWYER 515-64, CHRIST IN HOUSE OF MARY AND MARTHA 515-65, LUKE 10/VERSE 38/ CHRIST WITH MARY AND MARTHA 515-65, CHRIST AND TWO DISCIPLES IN CORNFIELD 515-66, MATTHEW 12/VERSE 1/ CHRIST IN CORNFIELD 515-66, CHRIST HEALS WITHERED HAND 515-67, MATTHEW 12/VERSE 13/ CHRIST HEALS HAND 515-67, PHARISEES TAKE COUNCIL AGAINST CHRIST 515-68, MATTHEW 12/VERSE 14/ PHARISEES AGAINST CHRIST 515-68, CHRIST HEALS MAN POSSESSED/ JEWS WATCH 515-69,JEWS WATCH CHRIST HEAL MAN 515-69, MATTHEW 12/VERSE 22/ CHRIST HEALS MAN POSSESSED 515-69, PARABLE OF TREE KNOWN BY ITS FRUIT 515-70, CHRIST PREACHES TO JEWS 515-70, MATTHEW 12/VERSE 33/ CHRIST PREACHES TO JEWS 515-70, CHRIST EXHORTS TWO MEN/ QUEEN OF SOUTH 515-71, QUEEN OF THE SOUTH 515-71, MATTHEW 12/VERSES 41-42/ CHRIST EXHORTS MEN 515-71, PARABLE OF LIGHTED CANDLE AND BUSHEL 515-72, LUKE 11/VERSE 33/ PARABLE OF LIGHTED CANDLE 515-72, CHRIST SPEAKS ABOUT UNCLEAN SPIRITS 515-73, UNCLEAN SPIRIT/ BROWN AND HAIRY 515-73, WOMAN HEARS CHRIST'S PREACHING 515-74, LUKE 11/VERSE 27/ CHRIST'S PREACHING 515-74, CHRIST HEARS THAT HIS MOTHER SEEKS HIM 515-75, MATTHEW 12/VERSE 46/ CHRIST'S MOTHER SEEKS HIM 515-75, CHRIST DINES AT HOUSE OF PHARISEE 515-76, LUKE 11/VERSE 37/ CHRIST AT HOUSE OF PHARISEE 515-76, CHRIST AMID THE MULTITUDE 515-77, LUKE 12/VERSE 1/ CHRIST AMID MULTITUDE 515-77, CHRIST SPEAKS TO PETER HOLDING KEYS 515-78, LUKE 12/VERSE 41/ CHRIST SPEAKS TO PETER 515-78, CHRIST SPEAKS OF GALILAEANS TO JEWS 515-79, LUKE 13/VERSE 1/ CHRIST SPEAKS TO JEWS 515-79, CHRIST HEALS WOMAN 515-80, LUKE 13/VERSES 10-12/ CHRIST HEALS WOMAN 515-80, CHRIST ON SHORE SPEAKS TO GROUP IN BOAT 515-81,MATTHEW 13/VERSE 2/ TEXT MISINTERPRETED IN PICTURE 515-81, CHRIST TEACHES PARABLE OF SOWER 515-82, PARABLE OF SOWER 515-82, MATTHEW 13/VERSE 18/ PARABLE OF SOWER 515-82, CHRIST TEACHES PARABLE OF LAMP UNDER BUSHEL 515-83, PARABLE OF LAMP UNDER BUSHEL 515-83, MARK 04/VERSE 21/ PARABLE OF LAMP UNDER BUSHEL 515-83, CHRIST TEACHES PARABLE OF GOOD SEED 515-84, PARABLE OF THE GOOD SEED 515-84, MATTHEW 13/VERSE 21/ PARABLE OF GOOD SEED 515-84, PARABLE OF SLEEPING SOWER 515-85, MARK 04/VERSES 26-29/ PARABLE OF SLEEPING SOWER 515-85, PARABLE OF MUSTARD SEED 515-86, MATTHEW 13/VERSES 31-32/ PARABLE OF MUSTARD SEED 515-86, PARABLE OF WOMAN WHO HID LEAVEN IN MEAL 515-87,MATTHEW 13/VERSE 33/ PARABLE OF LEAVEN IN MEAL 515-87, CHRIST TEACHES DISCIPLES 515-88, MATTHEW 13/VERSE 36/ CHRIST TEACHES DISCIPLES 515-88, PARABLE OF HEAVEN LIKE HIDDEN TREASURE 515-89,MAN DIGS IN FIELD 515-89, MATTHEW 13/VERSE 44/ PARABLE OF HEAVEN 515-89, CHRIST

AND DISCIPLES APPROACH SYNAGOGUE 515-90, MATTHEW 13/VERSE 53/ CHRIST APPROACHES SYNAGOGUE 515-90, WILLIAM NOTTINGHAM INSTRUCTS THREE STUDENTS 515-91, CHRIST HEALS AT BETHESDA 515-91, JOHN 05/VERSE 1/ CHRIST HEALS AT BETHESDA 515-91, CHRIST SAYS DEAD SHALL HEAR VOICE 515-92, JOHN 05/VERSE 25/ DEAD SHALL HEAR VOICE 515-92, HEROD'S BIRTHDAY FEAST 515-93, SALOME DANCING AT HEROD'S FEAST 515-93, ST JOHN THE BAPTIST BEHEADED 515-93, HERODIAS HOLDS ST JOHN BAPTIST'S HEAD 515-93, MARK 06/VERSES 21-28/ HEROD'S FEAST 515-93, CHRIST HEARS OF JOHN BAPTIST'S DEATH 515-94, MARK 06/VERSE 30/ CHRIST HEARS OF BAPTIST'S DEATH 515-94, FEEDING OF THE 5000 515-95, MATTHEW 14/VERSES 15-21/ FEEDING OF 5000 515-95, CHRIST OFFERS BREAD TO THREE JEWS 515-96, JOHN 06/VERSE 32/ CHRIST OFFERS BREAD TO JEWS 515-96, CHRIST MENACED BY JEWS 515-97, JOHN 06/VERSE 41/ JEWS MENACE CHRIST 515-97, CHRIST ASKED WHY DISCIPLES DO NOT WASH HANDS 515-98, MATTHEW 15/VERSES 1-2/ PHARISEES QUESTION CHRIST 515-98, CHRIST ASKED TO HEAL DAUGHTER OF CANAAN WOMAN 515-99, MATTHEW 15/VERSES 21-22/ CHRIST AND CANAAN WOMAN 515-99, CHRIST HEALS DEAF MUTE 515-100, MARK 07/VERSES 31-35/ CHRIST HEALS DEAF MUTE 515-100, CHRIST ON MOUNTAIN WITH CRIPPLED AND SICK 515-101, MATTHEW 15/VERSES 29-30/ CHRIST WITH CRIPPLED 515-101, FEEDING OF THE 4000 515-102, CHRIST SPEAKS TO DISCIPLES 515-102, PEOPLE SEATED WITH TABLE WITH FISH AND BREAD 515-102, MATTHEW 15/VERSE 32/ FEEDING OF 4000 515-102, CHRIST HEALS BLIND MAN 515-103, MARK 08/VERSES 22-25/ CHRIST HEALS BLIND MAN 515-103, HEROD SAYS CHRIST IS RISEN JOHN THE BAPTIST 515-104, ST JOHN THE BAPTIST STANDS IN OPEN SARCOPHAGUS 515-104, WILLIAM OF NOTTINGHAM LECTURES TO ELEVEN STUDENTS 515-105, CHRIST SPEAKS OF JEWISH FEAST OF TABERNACLES 515-105, JOHN 07/VERSES 2-3/ TEXT MISLABLED IN MS 515-105,CHRIST TEACHES DURING JEWISH FEAST 515-106, JOHN 07/VERSE 14/ TEXT MISLABLED IN MS 515-106, CHRIST SPEAKS TO CROWD DURING JEWISH FEAST 515-107, JOHN 07/VERSE 25/ CHRIST PREACHES DURING FEAST 515-107, PHARISEES BRING WOMAN TAKEN IN ADULTERY TO CHRIST 515-108, JOHN 08/VERSES 2-3/ ADULTEROUS WOMAN TAKEN TO CHRIST 515-108, CHRIST TELLS PHARISEES HE IS LIGHT OF WORLD 515-109, JOHN 08/VERSE 12/ CHRIST IS LIGHT OF WORLD 515-109, DISCIPLES ASK CHRIST IF BLIND MAN OR PARENTS SINNED 515-110, BLIND MAN SITS AT FEET OF CHRIST 515-110, JOHN 09/VERSES 1-3/ / BLIND MAN AT CHRIST'S FEET 515-110, CHRIST TEACHES DISCIPLES 515-111, JOHN 10/VERSE 1/ FIGURES ENTERS DOORWAY 515-111,CHRIST CONTRASTS HIMSELF WITH HIRELING 515-112, JOHN 10/VERSES 11-12/GOOD SHEPHERD AND HIRELING 515-112, TRANSFIGURATION/ WHITE DOVE DESCENDS ON CHRIST 515-113, MATTHEW 17/VERSES 1-2/ TRANSFIGURATION 515-113, CHRIST ASKED TO HEAL EPILEPTIC SON 515-114, MATTHEW 17/VERSES 14-15/ HEALING OF EPILEPTIC 515-114, PETER ASKED IF CHRIST PAYS TRIBUTE MONEY 515-115, MATTHEW 17/VERSE 24 515-115, CHRIST TELLS DISCIPLES THEY MUST ENTER HEAVEN AS CHILDREN 515-116, MATTHEW 18/VERSES 1-3/ ENTER HEAVEN AS CHILDREN 515-116, OFFENDERS PUNISHED WITH MILLSTONES 515-117, MATTHEW 18/VERSE 6/ OFFENDERS PUNISHED 515-117, WILLIAM NOTTINGHAM READS TO TEN STUDENTS 515-118, MAN LEAVES HOME TO FOLLOW CHRIST 515-119, CHRIST HEALS MAN OF DROPSY ON SABBATH 515-120, LUKE 14/VERSES 1-4/ CHRIST HEALS DROPSY 515-120, CHRIST TELLS PARABLE OF MILLSTONE 515-121, PARABLE OF MILLSTONE 515-121, LUKE 17/VERSE 2/ PARABLE OF MILLSTONE 515-121, CHRIST ASKED TO HEAL TEN LEPERS 515-122, LUKE 17/VERSES 11-13/ CHRIST HEALS LEPERS 515-122, CHRIST REMINDS DISCIPLES OF LOT'S WIFE 515-123,LOT'S WIFE AS PILLAR OF SALT 515-123, LUKE 17/VERSE 32/ CHRIST'S ALLUSION TO LOT'S WIFE 515-123, CHRIST TELLS PARABLE OF PHARISEE AND PUBLICAN 515-124, PARABLE OF PHARISEE AND PUBLICAN 515-124, LUKE 18/VERSES 9-14/ PARABLE OF PHARISEE AND PUBLICAN 515-124, CHRIST SPEAKS ABOUT DIVORCE 515-125, DIVORCE 515-125, MATTHEW 19/VERSE 3/ CHRIST SPEAKS ABOUT DIVORCE 515-125, CHRIST BLESSES LITTLE CHILDREN 515-126, MATTHEW 19/VERSES 13-15/ CHRIST AND CHILDREN 515-126, CHRIST TELLS PARABLE OF VINEYARD 515-127, HOUSEHOLDER PAYS TWO LABORERS 515-127, PARABLE OF VINEYARD 515-127, MATTHEW 20/VERSE 1/ PARABLE OF VINEYARD 515-127,LAZARUS RAISED 515-128, JOHN 11/VERSES 43-44/ LAZARUS RAISED 515-128, CAIAPHAS IN MITRE POINTS TO CHRIST 515-129, JOHN 11/VERSES

47-52/ CAIAPHAS POINTS TO CHRIST 515-129, WILLIAM NOTTINGHAM READS TO EIGHT STUDENTS 515-130, CHRIST SPEAKS TO DISCIPLES ON WAY TO JERUSALEM 515-130, MATTHEW 20/VERSE 17/ CHRIST AND DISCIPLES 515-130, CHRIST APPROACHED BY TWO SONS OF ZEBEDEE 515-131, MATTHEW 20/VERSES 21-22/ CHRIST AND SONS OF ZEBEDEE 515-131, CHRIST PASSES THROUGH JERICHO/ ZACCHAEUS IN TREE 515-132, LUKE 19/VERSE 1/ CHRIST IN JERICHO 515-132, PARABLE OF NOBLEMAN WHO GAVE MONEY TO SERVANTS 515-133, LUKE 19/VERSES 11-13/ PARABLE OF NOBLEMAN 515-133, CHRIST EATS SUPPER WITH LAZARUS/ MARTHA SERVES 515-134, MARY ANOINTS CHRIST'S FEET WITH OINTMENT 515-134, JOHN 12/VERSES 1-3/ CHRIST EATS WITH LAZARUS 515-134, CHRIST ENTERS JERUSALEM ON ASS 515-135, JOHN 12/VERSES 12-14/ CHRIST ENTERS JERUSALEM 515-135, CHRIST OVERTHROWS MONEYCHANGER'S TABLES 515-136, MATTHEW 21/VERSE 12/ CHRIST AND MONEYCHANGERS 515-136, PARABLE OF THE TWO SONS 515-137, FATHER WITH SONS 515-137, MATTHEW 21/VERSES 28-31/ PARABLE OF TWO SONS 515-137, PARABLE OF WICKED TENANTS 515-138, HOUSEHOLDER PLANTS VINE 515-138, MATTHEW 21/VERSE 33/ PARABLE OF WICKED TENANTS 515-138, PARABLE OF WEDDING FEAST 515-139, KING AND OTHERS SIT AT TABLE 515-139, MATTHEW 22/VERSE 1/ PARABLE OF WEDDING FEAST 515-139, CHRIST WARNED THAT HEROD WILL KILL HIM 515-140,HEROD HOLDS RAISED SWORD 515-140, LUKE 13/VERSE 31/ CHRIST WARNED ABOUT HEROD 515-140, CHRIST IN TREASURY POINTS TO POOR WIDOW 515-141, MARK 12/VERSES 41-44/ CHRIST IN TREASURY 515-141, CHRIST FORETELLS DESTRUCTION OF TEMPLE 515-142, MATTHEW 24/VERSES 1-2/ CHRIST FORETELLS 515-142,CHRIST FORETELLS ABOMINATION OF DESOLATION 515-143, DEVIL STANDS ON ALTAR 515-143, CHRIST SPEAKS OF NEED FOR WATCHFULNESS 515-144, HOUSEHOLDER WATCHES AT DOOR OF HOUSE 515-144, MATTHEW 24/VERSE 43/ CHRIST SPEAKS OF WATCHFULNESS 515-144, PARABLE OF WISE AND FOOLISH VIRGINS 515-145, MATTHEW 25/VERSE 1/ WISE AND FOOLISH VIRGINS 515-145, PARABLE OF THE TALENTS/ MAN STANDS BEFORE SERVANTS 515-146, MATTHEW 25/VERSE 14/ PARABLE OF TALENTS 515-146, CHRIST IN GLORY ON RAINBOW 515-147, MATTHEW 25/VERSE 31/ CHRIST ON RAINBOW 515-147, JEWS CONSPIRE AGAINST CHRIST 515-148, MATTHEW 26/VERSES 1-4/ CHRIST AND JEWS 515-148, JUDAS ISCARIOT RECEIVES SILVER FROM PRIESTS 515-149, MATTHEW 26/VERSES 14-15/ JUDAS RECEIVES SILVER 515-149, CHRIST TEACHES IN TEMPLE BY DAY 515-150, LUKE 21/VERSE 37/ CHRIST TEACHES IN TEMPLE 515-150, WILLIAM NOTTINGHAM READS TO SIX STUDENTS 515-151, CHRIST SPEAKS TO DISCIPLES BEFORE LEAVING THEM 515-151, JOHN 13/VERSE 1/ CHRIST SPEAKS TO DISCIPLES 515-151, CHRIST'S DISCIPLES PREPARE PASSOVER 515-152, MATTHEW 26/VERSES 17-19/ DISCIPLES PREPARE PASSOVER 515-152, LAST SUPPER/ ONLY FIVE DISCIPLES SHOWN 515-153, MATTHEW 26/VERSE 20/ LAST SUPPER 515-153, CHRIST WASHES DISCIPLES' FEET 515-154, JOHN 13/VERSE 5/ CHRIST WASHES DISCIPLES' FEET 515-154, CHRIST TELLS DISCIPLES HE IS TRUE VINE 515-155,JOHN 15/VERSE 1/ CHRIST AS TRUE VINE 515-155, CHRIST TELLS DISCIPLES THEIR FRUIT SHALL GLORIFY 515-156, JOHN 15/VERSE 8/ DISCIPLES' FRUIT SHALL GLORIFY 515-156, CHRIST FORETELLS COMING OF PARACLETE/ DOVE DESCENDS 515-157, JOHN 15/VERSE 26/ COMING OF PARACLETE FORETOLD 515-157, CHRIST ASCENDING TOWARD FACE OF GOD 515-158, JOHN 16/VERSE 16/ CHRIST ASCENDING TOWARD GOD 515-158, WILLIAM NOTTINGHAM LECTURES TO EIGHT STUDENTS 515-159, CHRIST AND DISCIPLES GO TO MOUNT OF OLIVES 515-159, MATTHEW 26/VERSE 30/ CHRIST GOES TO MOUNT OF OLIVES 515-159, CHRIST PRAYS IN GETHSEMANE 515-160, MATTHEW 26/VERSE 36/ CHRIST IN GETHSEMANE 515-160, CHRIST TAKEN CAPTIVE/ KISS OF JUDAS 515-161, JOHN 18/VERSE 19/ CHRIST CAPTURED 515-161, CHRIST BEFORE HIGH PRIEST/ TWO JEWS 515-162, JOHN 18/VERSE 19/ CHRIST BEFORE HIGH PRIEST 515-162, CHRIST BOUND STANDS BETWEEN ANNAS AND CAIAPHAS 515-163, JOHN 18/VERSE 24/ CHRIST BETWEEN ANNAS AND CAIAPHAS 515-163, JUDAS HANGS HIMSELF 515-164, MATTHEW 27/VERSE 5/ JUDAS HANGS HIMSELF 515-164,CHRIST BEFORE PILATE/ TWO SOLDIERS 515-165, MATTHEW 27/VERSE 11/ CHRIST BEFORE PILATE 515-165, CHRIST BEFORE PILATE/ TWO JEWS POINT 515-166, LUKE 23/VERSE 6/ CHRIST BEFORE PILATE 515-166, PILATE CALLS PRIESTS AND RULERS 515-167, LUKE 23/VERSE 13/ PILATE CALLS PRIESTS 515-167, CHRIST BEFORE PILATE ON JUDGMENT SEAT 515-168, JOHN 19/VERSE 13/ PILATE ON JUDGMENT SEAT 515-168, CHRIST NAILED TO CROSS/ STRETCHED AS IN

DRAMA 515-169, CRUCIFIXION WITH TWO ROBBERS 515-170, MATTHEW 27/VERSE 46/ CRUCIFIXION 515-170, CHRIST'S SIDE PIERCED BY SOLDIER 515-171, JOHN 19/VERSES 31-34/ CHRIST'S SIDE PIERCED 515-171, CHRIST PLACED IN SEPULCHRE 515-172, JOHN 19/VERSES 38-42/ CHRIST PLACED IN TOMB 515-172, MARYS AT EMPTY TOMB 155-173, MATTHEW 28/VERSES 1-2/ MARYS AT EMPTY TOMB 515-173, MARYS AND JOANNA TELL DISCIPLES ABOUT TOMB 515-174, LUKE 24/VERSE 10/ MARYS TELL OF TOMB 515-174, CHRIST APPEARS TO DISCIPLES ON ROAD TO EMMAUS 515-175, EMMAUS REPRESENTED AS CASTLE AS IN DRAMA 515-175, LUKE 24/VERSES 13-15/ CHRIST APPEARS TO DISCIPLES 515-175

*$ABSTRACT 516
*LIBRARY BODLEIAN
*SLIDE SET TITLE JOB FROM BIBLE MORALISEE
*NEGATIVE REFERENCE ROLL 224A
*RENTAL FEE $2.55
*COMMENTS THE COMPLETE MS CONTAINS 1785 MINIATURES ON 225 LEAVES. UNDERNEATH EACH PICTURE FROM THE OLD TESTAMENT, ANOTHER ILLUSTRATES THE LESSON A PREACHER MIGHT DRAW FROM IT. SOMETIMES IT PREFIGURES AN EVENT IN THE NEW TESTAMENT. THE INTELLECTUAL BASIS OF THIS WORK IS THE POSTILLAE IN BIBLIAM OF THE DOMINICAN, HUGH OF ST CHER, WHO DIED IN 1262.
*TITLE OF MANUSCRIPT BIBLE MORALISEE
*SHELFMARK MS BODLEY 270B/ FOL 206 516-1, MS BODLEY 270B/ FOL 208 516/2-3, MS BODLEY 270B/ FOL 213V 516-4, MS BODLEY 270B/ FOL 215V 516-5, MS BODLEY 270B/ FOL 216 516/6-7, MS BODLEY 270B/ FOL 220 516-8, MS BODLEY 270B/ FOL 222 516-9, MS BODLEY 270B/ FOL 223V 516-10, MS BODLEY 270B/ FOL 224 516-11
*PROVENANCE FRENCH
*DATE EXECUTED 13TH/ MID
*LANGUAGE LATIN
*TYPE OF MANUSCRIPT BIBLE MORALISEE
*CONTENTS JOB ILLUSTRATIONS FROM BIBLE MORALISEE 516/1-11, JOB TOLD THAT HIS SHEEP AND SERVANTS CONSUMED 516-1, JOB 01/VERSE 16/ FIRE CONSUMES SHEEP AND SERVANTS 516-1, JOB'S HEAD SHAVED/ FALLS ON GROUND 516-2, JOB 01/VERSES 20-21/ JOB'S HEAD SHAVED 516-2, JOB SMITED WITH BOILS BY SATAN 516-3, JOB 02/VERSE 7/ SATAN SMITES JOB WITH BOILS 516-3, SATAN SMITES JOB WITH BOILS 516-3, BILDAD THE SHUHITE TELLS PARABLE OF HYPOCRITE 516-4, JOB 08/VERSES 11-14/ PARABLE OF HYPOCRITE 516-4, PARABLE OF CUT DOWN TREE 516-5, JOB 14/VERSES 7-9/ PARABLE OF CUT-DOWN TREE 516-5, JOB'S SIN SEALED IN A BAG 516-6, JOB 14/VERSES 17-19/ JOB'S SIN SEALED IN BAG 516-6, PARABLE OF WICKED MAN AND HYPOCRITES 516-7, JOB 15/VERSES 33-34/ PARABLE OF WICKED MAN 516-7,PARABLE OF MURDERER 516-8, JOB 24/VERSE 14/ PARABLE OF MURDERER 516-8, JOB AS BROTHER OF DRAGONS AND COMPANION OF OSTRICHES 516-9, JOB 30/VERSES 29-31/ JOB AS BROTHER OF DRAGONS 516-9, UNICORN DRAWS HARROW 516-10, JOB 39/VERSE 10/ UNICORN DRAWS ARROW 516-10, BEHEMOTH EATS GRASS AS AN OX 516-11, JOB 40/VERSES 15-22/ BEHEMOTH 516-11,

*$ABSTRACT 517
*LIBRARY BODLEIAN
*SLIDE SET TITLE JOB
*NEGATIVE REFERENCE ROLL 224B
*RENTAL FEE $2.80
*TITLE OF MANUSCRIPT CATENA ON JOB
*SHELFMARK MS LAUD GREEK 86/ PAGE 7 517-1, MS LAUD GREEK 86/ PAGE 8 517-2, MS LAUD GREEK 86/ PAGE 11 517-3, MS LAUD GREEK 86/ PAGE 21 517-4, MS LAUD GREEK 86/ PAGE 27 517-5, MS LAUD GREEK 86/ PAGE 28 517-6, MS LAUD GREEK 86/ PAGE 32 517-7, MS LAUD GREEK 86/ PAGE 33 517-8, MS LAUD GREEK 86/ PAGE 64 517-9, MS LAUD GREEK 86/ PAGE 120 517-10, MS LAUD GREEK 86/ PAGE 143 517-11, MS LAUD GREEK 86/ PAGE 167 517-12, MS LAUD GREEK 86/ PAGE 209 517-13, MS LAUD GREEK 86/ PAGE 230 517-14, MS LAUD GREEK 86/ PAGE 307 517-15, MS LAUD GREEK 86/ PAGE 406 517-16
*PROVENANCE ITALIAN

*DATE EXECUTED 15TH
*LANGUAGE GREEK
*TYPE OF MANUSCRIPT CATENA ON JOB
*CONTENTS JOB ILLUSTRATIONS 517/1-16, JOB SURROUNDED BY FAMILY 517-1, JOB 01/VERSE 2/ JOB WITH FAMILY 517-1, JOB'S POSSESSIONS 517-2, JOB 01/VERSE 3/ JOB'S POSSESSIONS 517-2, JOB IN DAYS OF HIS PROSPERITY 517-3, JOB 01/VERSE 5/ JOB OFFERS BURNT OFFERINGS 517-3, JOB APPROACHED BY SONS OF GOD AND SATAN 517-4, JOB 01/VERSES 6-7/ JOB AND SONS OF GOD 517-4, SABEANS FALL UPON THE FLOCKS AND SLAY SERVANTS 517-5, JOB 01/VERSE 15/ SABEANS SLAY SERVANTS 517-5, FIRE OF GOD CONSUMES SHEEP AND SERVANTS 517-6, JOB 01/VERSE 16/ FIRE OF GOD 517-6, WIND SMITES FOUR CORNERS OF HOUSE 517-7, JOB 01/VERSES 18-19/ WIND DESTROYS HOUSE 517-7, JOB'S HEAD SHAVED 517-8, JOB 01/VERSE 20/ JOB SHAVES HEAD 517-8, JOB SITS ON GROUND WITH FRIENDS 517-9, JOB 02/VERSE 13/ JOB WITH FRIENDS 517-9, DRAGON APPROACHES JOB/ SEA WITH FISH 517-10, JOB 07/VERSE 12/ DRAGON APPROACHES JOB 517-10, JOB NAKED STANDS BEFORE GOD 517-11, JOB 09/VERSE 32/ JOB NAKED BEFORE GOD 517-11, CHRIST RAISES DEAD/ ANGEL BATTLES HORSEMAN 517-12, JOB 12/VERSE 20/ CHRIST RAISES DEAD 517-12, JOB/ THREE FRIENDS/ JAWS OF HELL/ BED 517-13, JOB 17/VERSES 11-16/ BED COVERED IN DARKNESS 517-13, HOUSE FALLS DOWN ON TWO MEN 517-14, JOB 19/VERSE 29/ FATE OF THE UNGODLY 517-14, MEN IN RAGS/ ONE BLIND/ TWO LAME 517-15, JOB 29/VERSES 15-16/ JOB AS EYE TO BLIND 517-15, DEVIL ON GROUND/ JORDAN FLOWS IN MOUTH 517-16, JOB 40/VERSES 18-19/ DEVIL WITH JORDAN RIVER 517-16

*$ABSTRACT 518
*LIBRARY NEW COLLEGE OXFORD
*SLIDE SET TITLE PROPHETS
*NEGATIVE REFERENCE ROLL 224C
*RENTAL FEE $3.00
*TITLE OF MANUSCRIPT BOOK OF THE PROPHETS
*SHELFMARK MS NEW COLLEGE 44/ FOL 1 518-1, MS NEW COLLEGE 44/ FOL 7 518-2, MS NEW COLLEGE 44/ FOL 11V 518-3, MS NEW COLLEGE 44/ FOL 13V 518-4, MS NEW COLLEGE 44/ FOL 17V 518-5, MS NEW COLLEGE 44/ FOL 18 518-6, MS NEW COLLEGE 44/ FOL 19V 518-7, MS NEW COLLEGE 44/ FOL 22V 518-8, MS NEW COLLEGE 44/ FOL 24 518-9, MS NEW COLLEGE 44/ FOL 26 518-10, MS NEW COLLEGE 44/ FOL 27V 518-11, MS NEW COLLEGE 44/ FOL 28V 518-12, MS NEW COLLEGE 44/ FOL 34 518-13, MS NEW COLLEGE 44/ FOL 54V 518-14, MS NEW COLLEGE 44/ FOL 68 518-15, MS NEW COLLEGE 44/ FOL 102V 518-16, MS NEW COLLEGE 44/ FOL 106 518-17, MS NEW COLLEGE 44/ FOL 108V 518-18, MS NEW COLLEGE 44/ FOL 110V 518-19, MS NEW COLLEGE 44/ FOL 158 518-20
*PROVENANCE BYZANTINE
*DATE EXECUTED 13TH-14TH
*LANGUAGE GREEK
*TYPE OF MANUSCRIPT BOOK OF THE PROPHETS
*CONTENTS PROPHETS 518/1-20, GOLD PANEL WITH FLORAL DECORATION 518-1, HOSEA 518-2, JOEL 518-3, AMOS 518-4, OBADIAH 518-5, JONAH 518-6, MICAH 518-7, NAHUM 518-8, HABAKKUK 518-9, ZEPHANIAH 518-10, HAGGAI 518-11, ZECHARIAH 518-12, MALACHI 518-13, KING CROWNED KNEELING/ DAVID? 518-14, JEREMIAH 518-15, BARUCH 518-16, BARUCH SITTING CROSSLEGGED 518-17, JEREMIAH 518-18, EZEKIEL 518-19, SUSANNA/ WIFE OF JOACHIM 518-20

*$ABSTRACT 519
*LIBRARY BODLEIAN
*SLIDE SET TITLE NORTH ITALIAN ILLUMINATION C1300 TO 1466
*NEGATIVE REFERENCE ROLL 224D
*RENTAL FEE $3.15
*TITLE OF MANUSCRIPT WORKS BY HUGO DE FOLIETO 519/1-16, DE AVILIUS 519-2, DE ROTA VERAE ET FALSAE RELIGIONIS 519-14, DE ARBORE ALTISSIMA SUPRA MONTEM POSITA 519-16, DOMINICAN PROCESSIONAL AND TROPER 519/17-22, HOMILIARY FROM ADVENT TO

EASTER SUNDAY 519-23
*SHELFMARK MS LYELL 71/ FOL 2V 519-1, MS LYELL 71/ FOL 3V 519-2, MS LYELL 71/ FOL 4 519-3, MS LYELL 71/ FOL 5 519-4, MS LYELL 71/ FOL 7V 519-5, MS LYELL 71/ FOL 9V 519-6, MS LYELL 71/ FOL 10V 519-7, MS LYELL 71/ FOL 11V 519-8, MS LYELL 71/ FOL 12 519-9, MS LYELL 71/ FOL 12V 519-10, MS LYELL 71/ FOL 14 519-11, MS LYELL 71/ FOL 16 519-12, MS LYELL 71/ FOL 24V 519-13, MS LYELL 71/ FOL 29V 519-14, MS LYELL 71/ FOL 34V 519-15, MS LYELL 71/ FOL 53V 519-16, MS LYELL 72/ FOL 9V 519-17, MS LYELL 72/ FOL 58 519-18, MS LYELL 72/ FOL 69V 519-19, MS LYELL 72/ FOL 78 519-20, MS LYELL 72/ FOL 84V 519-21, MS LYELL 72/ FOL 172 519-22, MS LYELL 77/ FOL 1 519-23
*PROVENANCE ITALIAN/ NORTH 519/1-16, ITALIAN/ NORTH-EAST? 519/17-22, ITALIAN/ PADUA 519-23
*DATE EXECUTED 12TH/C1100-C1172 519/1-16, 15TH/C1400 519/17-22, 15TH/1466 519-23
*LANGUAGE LATIN
*AUTHOR DE FOLIETO/ HUGO 519/1-16
*TYPE OF MANUSCRIPT WORKS OF HUGO DE FOLIETO 519/1-16, PROCESSIONAL AND TROPER 519/17-22, HOMILIARY 519-23
*CONTENTS ITALIAN ILLUMINATIONS 519/1-23, VIRTUES SCHEMATA 519-1, PROLOGUE TO HUGO DE FOLIETO'S DE AVIBUS 519-2, CASTLE/ MOUNTED KNIGHT/ PRIEST 519-2, WHEEL OF LIFE WITH DOVE IN CENTER 519-3, SYMBOLISM/ COLOR OF DOVE 519-3, PSALM 67/VERSE 14 519-3, DOVES/ THREE SCRIPTURAL 519-4, DOVE/ BLACK OF NOAH 519-4, DOVE OF DAVID 519-4, DOVE AT CHRIST'S BAPTISM 519-4, HAWK WITH OUTSPREAD WINGS 519-5, TURTLE DOVE 519-6, CREATOR OF HEAVEN AND EARTH WITH FOUR SPARROW NESTS 519-7, PELICAN PECKING BREAST TO FEED YOUNG 519-8, OWL/ BROWN 519-9, CROW 519-10, OSTRICH WITH KNIFE? IN BEAK 519-11, LION/ FRAGMENT OF BESTIARY 519-12, BABYLON AND JERUSALEM 519-13, WHEEL OF THE RELIGIOUS LIFE 519-14, WHEEL WITH ABBOT/ MONKS/ SIX VIRTUES 519-14, WHEEL OF FALSE RELIGION 519-15, WHEEL WITH GREEDY MONK/ IDLE MONK/ SIX VICES 519-15, ILLUSTRATION FOR DE ARBORE ALTISSIMA SUPRA MONTEM POSITA 519-16, HOMO PECCATOR ATTACKED BY GRIFFIN AND BEASTS 519-16, PALM SUNDAY ILLUSTRATION 519-17, IMAGE OF PITY/ CHRIST IN TOMB 519-18, CHRIST IN TOMB/ ANIMALS BELOW 519-18, CHRIST RISEN WALKS AWAY FROM MARY MAGDALENE 519-19, NOLI ME TANGERE 519-19, VIRGIN AND CHRIST 519-20, JONAH AND THE GOURD 519-21, ST JOHN THE BAPTIST AND AGNUS DEI 519-22, INITIAL H/ HISTORIATED WITH ST BERNARD 519-23, ST BERNARD PREACHING TO MONKS AND NUNS 519-23, ST GIUSTINA HOLDS SCROLL 519-23

*$ABSTRACT 520
*LIBRARY BODLEIAN
*SLIDE SET TITLE OLD TESTAMENT HISTORIATED INITIALS
*NEGATIVE REFERENCE ROLL 225A
*RENTAL FEE $4.10
*TITLE OF MANUSCRIPT BIBLE
*SHELFMARK MS LAUD MISC 752/ FOL 1 520-1, MS LAUD MISC 752/ FOL 4 520-2, MS LAUD MISC 752/ FOL 5V 520-3, MS LAUD MISC 752/ FOL 24 520-4, MS LAUD MISC 752/ FOL 39 520-5, MS LAUD MISC 752/ FOL 49V 520-6, MS LAUD MISC 752/ FOL 64V 520-7, MS LAUD MISC 752/ FOL 78 520-8, MS LAUD MISC 752/ FOL 78V 520-9, MS LAUD MISC 752/ FOL 87V 520-10, MS LAUD MISC 752/ FOL 97 520-11, MS LAUD MISC 752/ FOL 99V 520-12, MS LAUD MISC 752/ FOL 112 520-13, MS LAUD MISC 752/ FOL 122 520-14, MS LAUD MISC 752/ FOL 134V 520-15, MS LAUD MISC 752/ FOL 146 520-16, MS LAUD MISC 752/ FOL 163V 520-17, MS LAUD MISC 752/ FOL 186 520-18, MS LAUD MISC 752/ FOL 204 520-19, MS LAUD MISC 752/ FOL 214V 520-20, MS LAUD MISC 752/ FOL 217V 520/21-22, MS LAUD MISC 752/ FOL 227 520-23, MS LAUD MISC 752/ FOL 236V 520-24, MS LAUD MISC 752/ FOL 249 520-25, MS LAUD MISC 752/ FOL 249V 520-26, MS LAUD MISC 752/ FOL 256 520-27, MS LAUD MISC 752/ FOL 258V 520-28, MS LAUD MISC 752/ FOL 260 520-29, MS LAUD MISC 752/ FOL 265 520-30, MS LAUD MISC 752/ FOL 265V 520-31, MS LAUD MISC 752/ FOL 279 520-32, MS LAUD MISC 752/ FOL 279V 520-33, MS LAUD MISC 752/ FOL 288 520-34, MS LAUD MISC 752/ FOL 299 520-35, MS LAUD MISC 752/ FOL 299V 520-36, MS LAUD

MISC 752/ FOL 307V 520-37, MS LAUD MISC 752/ FOL 310 520-38, MS LAUD MISC 752/ FOL 314 520-39, MS LAUD MISC 752/ FOL 317V 520/40-41, MS LAUD MISC 752/ FOL 322 520-42, MS LAUD MISC 753/ FOL 332 520-43
*PROVENANCE ENGLISH
*DATE EXECUTED 12TH-13TH
*LANGUAGE LATIN
*TYPE OF MANUSCRIPT BIBLE
*CONTENTS OLD TESTAMENT HISTORIATED INITIALS 520/1-43, INITIALS/ HISTORIATED 520/1-43, INITIAL F FRATER/ FULL-PAGE INHABITED INTERLACE 520-1, MAN WRESTLING BEAR/ HARE AND TWO DOGS 520-1, ASS PLAYING HARP/ LION ATTACKING MAN/ MAN RIDING CAMEL 520-1, ST JEROME'S PREFACE 520-1, INITIAL D DESIDERII 520-2, ST JEROME IN INITIAL 520-2, ST JEROME'S PREFACE TO GENESIS 520-2, INITIAL I IN/ GENESIS SCENES 520-3, CREATION SCENES/ SIX 520-3, GENESIS 01/VERSES 1-27/ SIX SCENES 520-3, INITIAL H HEC/ MOSES AND BURNING BUSH 520-4, MOSES AND BURNING BUSH 520-4, EXODUS 03/VERSES 1-5/ MOSES AND BURNING BUSH 520-4, INITIAL V VOCAVIT/ GOD SPEAKS TO MOSES 520-5, GOD SPEAKS TO KNEELING MOSES 520-5, LEVITICUS 01/VERSE 1/ GOD SPEAKS TO MOSES 520-5, INITIAL L LOCUTUS/ MOSES BEFORE KORAH'S CONGREGATION 520-6, MOSES BEFORE KORAH'S CONGREGATION 520-6, DATHAN AND ABIRAM SWALLOWED UP BY EARTH 520-6,NUMBERS 16/VERSES 26-35/ MOSES BEFORE KORAH 520-6, INITIAL H HEC/ MOSES PREACHES TO ISRAELITES 520-7, MOSES LIES DEAD IN LAND OF MOAB 520-7, DEUTERONOMY 01/VERSE 1/ MOSES PREACHES 520-7, DEUTERONOMY 34/VERSES 1-5/ MOSES LIES DEAD 520-7, INITIAL T TANDEM/ INTERLACED FOLIAGE 520-8, ST JEROME'S PREFACE TO JUDGES 520-8, INITIAL E ET/ GOD MAKES JOSHUA NEW LEADER 520-9, JOSHUA 01/VERSE 1/ GOD MAKES JOSHUA LEADER 520-9, JOSHUA SPEARS TWO SOLDIERS WITH JAVELIN 520-9, JOSHUA 08/VERSE 26/ JOSHUA KILLS TWO SOLDIERS 520-9, INITIAL P POST/ EHUD STABS KING EGLON 520-10, JUDGES 03/VERSES 21-22/ EHUD STABS KING EGLON 520-10, INITIAL I IN/ GROTESQUE ANIMAL 520-11, INITIAL F FUIT/ HANNAH PRAYS FOR CHILD 520-12, KINGS-I 01/VERSES 10-11/ HANNAH PRAYS FOR CHILD 520-12, INITIAL F FACTUM/ AMALEKITE TELLS DAVID HE KILLED SAUL 520-13, AMALEKITE TELLS DAVID HE KILLED SAUL 520-13, DAVID AND SERVANT REND CLOTHES/ SOLDIER KILLS AMALEKITE 520-13, KINGS-II 01/VERSES 1-16 520-13, INITIAL E ET/ ANOINTING OF SOLOMON 520-14, SOLOMON ANOINTED 520-14, KINGS-I 02/VERSE 10/DEATH OF DAVID/ANOINTING OF SOLOMON 520-14, DAVID'S DEATH 520-14, KINGS-I 02/VERSE 10/ KING DAVID'S DEATH 520-14, INITIAL P PREVARICATUS/ ELIJAH IN CHARIOT OF FIRE 520-15, ELIJAH IN CHARIOT OF FIRE 520-15, ELISHA LIFTS ARMS IN AMAZEMENT 520-15, KINGS-II 02/VERSES 11-12/ ELIJAH IN CHARIOT 520-15, INITIAL N NEMO/ FOLIATED 520-16, PROLOGUE TO ISAIAH 520-16, INITIAL V VISIO/ ISAIAH SAWED IN HALF 520-16, INITIAL V VERBA/ JEREMIAH LOWERED INTO DUNGEON 520-17, JEREMIAH LOWERED INTO DUNGEON BY ROPES 520-17,JEREMIAH 38/VERSE 6/ JEREMIAH LOWERED INTO DUNGEON 520-17, INITIAL E ET/ EZEKIEL SEES HAND OF GOD 520-18, EZEKIEL SEATED BY RIVER CHEBAR SEES GOD'S HAND 520-18, EZEKIEL 01/VERSE 1/ EZEKIEL SEES GOD'S HAND 520-18, EZEKIEL HELD BY SWORDSMAN 520-18, INITIAL A ANNO/ HABAKKUK AND DANIEL 520-19, DANIEL IN LION'S DEN/ HABAKKUK FORCED TO FEED 520-19, DANIEL 14/VERSES 36-37/ DANIEL IN LION'S DEN 520-19, INITIAL V VERBUM/ JOEL AND LOCUSTS 520-20, JOEL IN WHEAT FIELD POINTS TO LOCUSTS 520-20, JOEL 01/VERSE 4/ JOEL AND LOCUSTS 520-20, INITIAL V VISIO/ GOD AND OBADIAH 520-21, OBADIAH AND GOD 520-21, INITIAL E ET/ JONAH ASLEEP 520-22, JONAH 01/VERSE 5/ JONAH ASLEEP 520-22, INITIAL V VIR/ JOB WITH THREE FRIENDS 520-23, JOB SCRAPES HIMSELF WITH POTSHERD 520-23, JOB 02/VERSES 8-13/ JOB SCRAPES HIMSELF 520-23, INITIAL B BEATUS/ KING DAVID WITH MUSICIANS 520-24, MUSICAL INSTRUMENTS/ ZITHER/ BELLS/ HARP/ TRUMPET 520-24, PSALMS/ KING DAVID WITH ZITHER 520-24, INITIAL T TRIBUS/ MAN ENTWINED IN VINES 520-25, PREFACE TO THE BOOKS OF SOLOMON 520-25, INITIAL C CROMATIO/ INTERLACED 520-25, PROLOGUE TO THE BOOKS OF SOLOMON 520-25, INITIAL P PARABOLE/ KING SOLOMON SEATED 520-26, PROVERBS/ KING SOLOMON SEATED 520-26, INITIAL V VERBA/ KING SOLOMON PREACHES 520-27,SOLOMON 520/26-27, INITIAL O OSCULETUR/ CHRIST BLESSES VIRGIN 520-28, CHRIST BLESSES CROWNED VIRGIN 520-28, SONG OF

SONGS/ CHRIST BLESSES CROWNED VIRGIN 520-28, INITIAL D DILIGITE/ KING SOLOMON WRITING 520-29, SOLOMON WRITING/ HEAD BENT TO FIT INITIAL 520-29, WISDOM OF SOLOMON/ KING SOLOMON WRITING 520-29, INITIAL M MULTORUM/ JESUS SON OF SIRACH 520-30, PROLOGUE TO ECCLESIASTICUS 520-30, JESUS SON OF SIRACH 520-30, INITIAL O OMNIS/ KING'S FEET ON LION'S HEAD 520-31, KING'S FEET ON HEADS OF LION AND DRAGON 520-31, ECCLESIASTICUS/ ENTHRONED KING 520-31, INITIAL S SI/ WINGED MONSTER WITH FOLIAGE TAIL 520-32, PREFACE TO CHRONICLES/ WINGED MONSTER 520-32, INITIAL A ADAM/ KING DAVID AND MUSICIANS 520-33, DAVID PLAYS HARP 520-33, ARK OF THE COVENANT 520-33, CHRONICLES I/ KING DAVID WITH MUSICIANS 520-33, INITIAL C CONFORTATUS/ GOD AND SOLOMON 520-34,GOD APPEARS TO SLEEPING SOLOMON 520-34, CHRONICLES II 01/VERSE 7/ GOD AND SOLOMON 520-34, INITIAL U UTRUM/ LIONS AND CRANES 520-35, PREFACE TO EZRA/ INITIAL U WITH LIONS AND CRANES 520-35, INITIAL I IN/ KING CYRUS HOLDS SCROLL 520-36, EZRA/ INITIAL I 520-36, INITIAL H HEC/ MOSES WRITES 520-37, MOSES WRITES 520-37, BARUCH/ INITIAL H WITH MOSES WRITING 520-37, INITIAL L LIBRUM/ HORNED HUMAN HEAD 520-38, PREFACE TO ESTHER/ INITIAL L 520-38, INITIAL I IN/ ESTHER STANDS BEFORE MEDALLION 520-38, ESTHER STANDS BEFORE MEDALLION WITH MAN'S HEAD 520-38, INITIAL T TOBIAS/ TOBIT GIVES TO HUNGRY 520-39, TOBIT 01/VERSE 16/ TOBIT GIVES AWAY FOOD AND CLOTHES 520-39, INITIAL A ARFAXED/ JUDITH KILLS HOLOFERNES 520/40-41, JUDITH 13/VERSE 8/ JUDITH KILLS HOLOFERNES 520/40-41, INITIAL E ET/ MATTATHIAS SLAYS JEW 520-42, MATTATHIAS SLAYS JEW AT GENTILE ALTAR 520-42, MACCABEES-I 02/VERSES 23-24/ MATTATHIAS SLAYS JEW 520-42, MATTATHIAS ON HORSEBACK SLAYS ANTIOCHUS'S MAN 520-42, INITIAL F FRATRIBUS/ KING ANTIOCHUS AND TWO SERVANTS 520-43, ANTIOCHUS COMMANDS SERVANTS WHO CUT SEVEN BROTHERS 520-43, MACCABEES-II 07/VERSE 1/ KING ANTIOCHUS AND SERVANTS 520-43

*$ABSTRACT 521
*LIBRARY BODLEIAN
*SLIDE SET TITLE NEW TESTAMENT HISTORIATED INITIALS
*NEGATIVE REFERENCE ROLL 225B
*RENTAL FEE $3.45
*TITLE OF MANUSCRIPT BIBLE
*SHELFMARK MS LAUD MISC 752/ FOL 339V 521-1, MS LAUD MISC 752/ FOL 350 521-2, MS LAUD MISC 752/ FOL 356 521-3, MS LAUD MISC 752/ FOL 357 521/4-5, MS LAUD MISC 752/ FOL 367V 521-6, MS LAUD MISC 752/ FOL 368 521-7, MS LAUD MISC 752/ FOL 376 521-8, MS LAUD MISC 752/ FOL 386 521-9, MS LAUD MISC 752/ FOL 387V 521-10, MS LAUD MISC 752/ FOL 388 521-11, MS LAUD MISC 752/ FOL 389 521-12, MS LAUD MISC 752/ FOL 389V 521-13, MS LAUD MISC 752/ FOL 390 521-14, MS LAUD MISC 752/ FOL 391V 521-15, MS LAUD MISC 752/ FOL 395V 521-16, MS LAUD MISC 752/ FOL 399V 521-17, MS LAUD MISC 752/ FOL 402 521-18, MS LAUD MISC 752/ FOL 403V 521-19, MS LAUD MISC 752/ FOL 404V 521-20, MS LAUD MISC 752/ FOL 405V 521-21, MS LAUD MISC 752/ FOL 406V 521-22, MS LAUD MISC 752/ FOL 407 521-23, MS LAUD MISC 752/ FOL 407V 521-24, MS LAUD MISC 752/ FOL 408 521-25, MS LAUD MISC 752/ FOL 409V 521-26, MS LAUD MISC 752/ FOL 410 521-27, MS LAUD MISC 752/ FOL 411 521-28, MS LAUD MISC 752/ FOL 414 521-29
*PROVENANCE ENGLISH
*DATE EXECUTED 12TH-13TH
*LANGUAGE LATIN
*TYPE OF MANUSCRIPT BIBLE
*CONTENTS NEW TESTAMENT HISTORIATED INITIALS 521/1-29, INITIALS/ HISTORIATED 521/1-29, ST MATTHEW/ LATER FAKED PORTRAIT 521-1, INITIAL I INCIPIT/ ST MARK WITH LION SYMBOL 521-2, LION/ CRANE/ CAMEL IN STEM OF INITIAL 521-2, INITIAL L LUCAS/ FOLIATED 521-3, ST LUKE WITH OX SYMBOL 521-4, INITIAL Q QUONIAM/ ARCHANGEL APPEARS TO ZACHARIAS 521-5, ZACHARIAS BURNING INCENSE IN TEMPLE 521-5, LUKE 01/VERSES 8-13/ ZACHARIAS AND ARCHANGEL 521-5, ANNUNCIATION/ GABRIEL AND MARY HOLD SCROLLS 521-5, LUKE 01/VERSE 28/ ANNUNCIATION 521-5, ST JOHN AND EAGLE SYMBOL 521-6, INITIAL I IN/ FOLIAGE AND ANIMALS 521-7, INITIAL P PRIMUM/ PENTECOST 521-8, PENTECOST/ 13 MEN

ARE SHOWN 521-8, ACTS 02/VERSES 1-4/ PENTECOST 521-8, INITIAL N NON/ DECORATIVE 521-9, INITIAL I IACOBUS/ ST JAMES HOLDS BOOK 521-9, ST JAMES HOLDS BOOK 521-9, INITIAL P PETRUS/ ST PETER HOLDS SCROLL AND KEYS 521-10, ST PETER HOLDS SCROLL AND KEYS 521-10, INITIAL Q QUOD/ ST JOHN SPEAKS OF BROTHERLY LOVE 521-11, CAIN KILLS ABEL 521-11, JOHN 03/VERSE 12/ CAIN KILLS ABEL 521-11, INITIAL S SENIOR/ FOLIATED 521-12, INITIAL S SENIOR/ TWISTING RED AND BLUE ANIMAL 521-13, INITIAL P PRIMUM/ ANIMAL INTERLACE 521-14, INITIAL P PAULUS/ ST PAUL PREACHES 521-15, INITIAL P PAULUS/ ANIMAL INTERLACE 521-16, INITIAL P PAULUS/ PAUL ON ROAD TO DAMASCUS 521-17, ST PAUL FALLS BACKWARDS 521-17, ACTS 09/VERSES 3-4/ LIGHT FROM HEAVEN HITS PAUL 521-17, INITIAL P PAULUS/ SS PAUL AND PETER CONVERSE 521-18, SS PAUL AND PETER CONVERSE 521-18, GALATIANS 01/VERSE 18/ PAUL AND PETER CONVERSE 521-18, INITIAL P PAULUS/ ST PAUL HEALS CRIPPLE 521-19, ST PAUL HEALS CRIPPLE AT LYSTRA 521-19, ACTS 14/VERSE 3/ PAUL HEALS CRIPPLE 521-19, INITIAL P PAULUS/ FOLIATED INTERLACE 521-20, INITIAL P PAULUS/ PAUL IN PRISON 521-21, ST PAUL IN PRISON HANDS SCROLL TO MESSENGER 521-21, INITIAL P PAULUS/ INTERLACED 521-22, INITIAL P PAULUS/ PAUL AND MESSENGER 521-23, ST PAUL HANDS SCROLL TO TWO MESSENGERS 521-23, INITIAL P PAULUS/ INTERLACED 521-24, INITIAL P PAULUS/ PAUL STANDS BEFORE TIMOTHY 521-25, ST PAUL STANDS BEFORE TIMOTHY BISHOP OF EPHESUS 521-25, INITIAL P PAULUS/ FOLIATED INTERLACE 521-26, INITIAL P PAULUS/ PAUL STANDS BEFORE TITUS 521-27, ST PAUL WITH SCROLL STANDS BEFORE TONSURED TITUS 521-27, INITIAL M MULTIFARIAM/ INTERLACED 521-28, INITIAL A APOCALIPSIS/ CHRIST ON RAINBOW 521-29, CHRIST ON RAINBOW WITH TWO SWORDS 521-29

*$ABSTRACT 522
*LIBRARY BODLEIAN
*SLIDE SET TITLE INITIALS FROM THE DERBY PSALTER
*NEGATIVE REFERENCE ROLL 225C
*RENTAL FEE $2.40
*COMMENTS MADE FOR STEPHEN OF DERBY, PRIOR OF CHRIST CHURCH CATHEDRAL, DUBLIN, 1349-C1382.
*TITLE OF MANUSCRIPT DERBY PSALTER
*SHELFMARK MS RAWL G 185/ FOL 1 522-1, MS RAWL G 185/ FOL 20 522-2, MS RAWL G 185/ FOL 32V 522-3, MS RAWL G 185/ FOL 43V 522-4, MS RAWL G 185/ FOL 54V 522-5, MS RAWL G 185/ FOL 68V 522-6, MS RAWL G 185/ FOL 81V 522-7, MS RAWL G 185/ FOL 97 522-8
*PROVENANCE ENGLISH
*DATE EXECUTED 14TH/ THIRD QUARTER
*LANGUAGE LATIN
*ARTIST/ SCHOOL MASTER OF THE EGERTON GENESIS
*TYPE OF MANUSCRIPT PSALTER
*CONTENTS INITIALS FROM DERBY PSALTER 522/1-8, PSALTER/ ENGLISH 522/1-8, INITIAL B BEATUS VIR/ DAVID AND GOLIATH 522-1, DAVID AND GOLIATH 522-1, JESSE TREE 522-1, INITIAL D DOMINUS ILLUMINATIO/ CHRIST BLESSES OWNER 522-2, CHRIST BLESSES THE KNEELING OWNER STEPHEN OF DERBY 522-2, INITIAL D DIXI CUSTODIAM/ DAVID POINTS TO MOUTH 522-3, DAVID PRAYS POINTING TO MOUTH 522-3, INITIAL D DIXIT INSIPIENS/ MONK AND FOOL DISPUTING 522-4, MONK DISPUTING WITH FOOL 522-4, INITIAL S SALVUM ME FAC/ GOD BLESSES DAVID 522-5, DAVID PRAYS TO BE DELIVERED FROM WATER 522-5, INITIAL E EXULTATE DEO/ GOD BLESSES MONKS 522-6, GOD BLESSES MONKS PLAYING MUSICAL INSTRUMENTS 522-6, INITIAL C CANTATE DOMINO/ MONKS SINGING 522-7, MONKS AND TWO GROTESQUES SING FROM BOOKS 522-7, INITIAL D DIXIT DOMINUS/ GOD AND CRUCIFIED CHRIST 522-8, CHRIST CRUCIFIED SUPPORTED ON GOD'S LAP 522-8

*$ABSTRACT 523
*LIBRARY BODLEIAN
*SLIDE SET TITLE OLD TESTAMENT INITIALS
*NEGATIVE REFERENCE ROLL 225D

*RENTAL FEE $6.80
*TITLE OF MANUSCRIPT BIBLE
*SHELFMARK MS CANON BIBL LAT 57/ FOL 1 523-1, MS CANON BIBL LAT 57/ FOL 3V 523-2, MS CANON BIBL LAT 57/ FOL 4 523/3-13, MS CANON BIBL LAT 57/ FOL 23 523/14-16, MS CANON BIBL LAT 57/ FOL 38 523/17-19, MS CANON BIBL LAT 57/ FOL 48V 523-20, MS CANON BIBL LAT 57/ FOL 63V 523/21-23, MS CANON BIBL LAT 57/ FOL 76V 523-24, MS CANON BIBL LAT 57/ FOL 85V 523-25, MS CANON BIBL LAT 57/ FOL 94V 523-26, MS CANON BIBL LAT 57/ FOL 95V 523-27, MS CANON BIBL LAT 57/ FOL 96V 523-28, MS CANON BIBL LAT 57/ FOL 109 523-29, MS CANON BIBL LAT 57/ FOL 119V 523-30, MS CANON BIBL LAT 57/ FOL 132 523-31, MS CANON BIBL LAT 57/ FOL 144 523-32, MS CANON BIBL LAT 57/ FOL 155 523-33, MS CANON BIBL LAT 57/ FOL 168V 523-34, MS CANON BIBL LAT 57/ FOL 172V 523-35, MS CANON BIBL LAT 57/ FOL 177V 523-36, MS CANON BIBL LAT 57/ FOL 183 523/37-38, MS CANON BIBL LAT 57/ FOL 187 523-39, MS CANON BIBL LAT 57/ FOL 192 523-40, MS CANON BIBL LAT 57/ FOL 197V 523/41-42, MS CANON BIBL LAT 57/ FOL 207 523-43, MS CANON BIBL LAT 57/ FOL 210V 523-44, MS CANON BIBL LAT 57/ FOL 212V 523-45, MS CANON BIBL LAT 57/ FOL 215 523-46, MS CANON BIBL LAT 57/ FOL 217 523/47-48, MS CANON BIBL LAT 57/ FOL 219V 523-49, MS CANON BIBL LAT 57/ FOL 222 523-50, MS CANON BIBL LAT 57/ FOL 224V 523-51, MS CANON BIBL LAT 57/ FOL 229 523-52, MS CANON BIBL LAT 57/ FOL 229V 523-53, MS CANON BIBL LAT 57/ FOL 237V 523/54-55, MS CANON BIBL LAT 57/ FOL 240 523-56, MS CANON BIBL LAT 57/ FOL 241V 523-57, MS CANON BIBL LAT 57/ FOL 247V 523/58-60, MS CANON BIBL LAT 57/ FOL 262V 523/61-62, MS CANON BIBL LAT 57/ FOL 263 523/63-64, MS CANON BIBL LAT 57/ FOL 280 523/65-69, MS CANON BIBL LAT 57/ FOL 300V 523/70-72, MS CANON BIBL LAT 57/ FOL 302V 523-73, MS CANON BIBL LAT 57/ FOL 305 523/74-76, MS CANON BIBL LAT 57/ FOL 324 523/77-79, MS CANON BIBL LAT 57/ FOL 330V 523-80, MS CANON BIBL LAT 57/ FOL 332 523-81, MS CANON BIBL LAT 57/ FOL 335 523-82, MS CANON BIBL LAT 57/ FOL 336 523-83, MS CANON BIBL LAT 57/ FOL 338 523/84-85, MS CANON BIBL LAT 57/ FOL 338V 523-86, MS CANON BIBL LAT 57/ FOL 339V 523-87, MS CANON BIBL LAT 57/ FOL 341 523/88-89, MS CANON BIBL LAT 57/ FOL 342 523-90, MS CANON BIBL LAT 57/ FOL 343 523-91, MS CANON BIBL LAT 57/ FOL 344 523-92, MS CANON BIBL LAT 57/ FOL 345 523-93, MS CANON BIBL LAT 57/ FOL 348 523-94, MS CANON BIBL LAT 57/ FOL 349 523-95, MS CANON BIBL LAT 57/ FOL 360 523-96
*PROVENANCE ITALIAN/ BOLOGNA
*DATE EXECUTED 13TH/ LATE
*LANGUAGE LATIN
*ARTIST/ SCHOOL RELATED IN STYLE TO JACOPINO DA REGGIO
*TYPE OF MANUSCRIPT BIBLE
*CONTENTS OLD TESTAMENT HISTORIATED INITIALS 523/1-96, INITIALS/ HISTORIATED 523/1-96, ST JEROME SEATED AT DESK 523-1, MEDALLIONS/ SEATED FIGURES HOLDING SCROLL AND BOOK 523-1, NEBUCHADNEZZAR SEATED IN BED 523-2, CREATION AND FALL AND REDEMPTION OF MAN 523-3,CREATION OF HEAVEN AND EARTH/ FIRST DAY 523-4,GENESIS 01/VERSE 1/ CREATION OF HEAVEN AND EARTH 523-4, CREATION OF WATERS/ SECOND DAY 523-5, GENESIS 01/VERSES 6-8/ CREATION OF WATERS 523-5, CREATION OF TREES AND PLANTS/ THIRD DAY 523-6,GENESIS 01/VERSES 11-13/ CREATION OF PLANTS 523-6, CREATION OF SUN/ MOON/ STARS/ FOURTH DAY 523-7, GENESIS 01/VERSES 14-19/ SUN/ MOON/ STARS 523-7, CREATION OF BIRDS AND ANIMALS/ FIFTH DAY 523-8, GENESIS 01/VERSES 20-23/ BIRDS AND ANIMALS 523-8, CREATION OF ADAM AND EVE/ SIXTH DAY 523-9, GENESIS 01/VERSES 26-31/ CREATION OF ADAM AND EVE 523-9, CREATOR RESTS/ SEVENTH DAY 523-10, GENESIS 02/VERSES 2-3/ CREATOR RESTS 523-10, CRUCIFIXION ON SQUARE GOLD PANEL 523-11, EXPULSION OF ADAM AND EVE 523-12, ADAM AND EVE'S EXPULSION 523-12, GENESIS 03/VERSES 23-24/ EXPULSION 523-12, ABRAHAM AND THREE ANGELS 523-13, GENESIS 18/VERSES 1-8/ ABRAHAM AND THREE ANGELS 523-13, MOSES BROUGHT TO PHARAOH'S DAUGHTER 523-14, EXODUS 02/VERSES 7-9/ MOSES AND PHARAOH'S DAUGHTER 523-14, MOSES AND EGYPTIAN 523-15, MOSES'S INTERFERENCE PROTESTED BY HEBREW 523-16, MOSES KNEELING RECEIVES INSTRUCTIONS 523-17, MOSES SPEAKS TO TWO MEN 523-18, MOSES AND OTHERS OFFER LAMBS AT ALTAR 523-19, MOSES STANDING ON DRAGON RECEIVES INSTRUCTIONS 523-20, MOSES DICTATES TO

SCRIBE HOLDING SCROLL 523-20, DEUTERONOMY/ FIRST PAGE 523-21, MOSES WITH THREE SOLDIERS 523-22, GOD SPEAKS TO MOSES AT TABERNACLE 523-23, MOSES SPEAKS TO ISRAELITES 523-23, MOSES ON DEATHBED 523-24, JOSHUA MADE NEW LEADER 523-24, CROWNED FIGURE SPEAKS TO THREE SOLDIERS 523-25, ELIMELECH AND NAOMI AND TWO SONS 523-26, NAOMI WITH HANDS ON RUTH AND BOAZ 523-26, CROWNED KING HOLDS ANOTHER CROWN 523-27, JEROME'S PROLOGUE TO KINGS 523-27, ELKANAH AND HANNA SACRIFICE LAMB 523-28, SAMUEL-I/VERSES 4-5/ ELKANAH AND HANNA 523-28, DAVID ORDERS SOLDIER TO KILL AMALEKITE 523-29,SAMUEL-II 01/VERSE 15/ DAVID ORDERS DEATH 523-29, DAVID ADVISED TO LET ABISHAG SLEEP WITH HIM 523-30, KINGS-I 01/VERSE 2/ DAVID TO SLEEP WITH ABISHAG 523-30, AHAZIAH ENQUIRES ABOUT BAALZEBUB 523-31, KINGS-II 01/VERSE 2/ AHAZIAH ENQUIRES ABOUT BAALZEBUB 523-31, TEN TRIBES OF ISRAEL 523-32, SOLOMON PRAYS FOR WISDOM 523-33, CHRONICLES-II 01/VERSE 10/ SOLOMON PRAYS FOR WISDOM 523-33, TEMPLE AT JERUSALEM REBUILT 523-34, NEHEMIAH/ AUTHOR PORTRAIT 523-35, JOSIAS HOLDING BOOK 523-36, ST JEROME PORTRAIT 523-37, TOBIT IN BED AND TOBIAS COMFORTS ANNA 523-38, JUDITH TALKS TO ELDERS AT CITY GATE 523-39, JUDITH 10/VERSES 6-9/ JUDITH WITH MAID 523-39, ESTHER/ STANDING FIGURE BLESSING 523-40, JOB SEATED ON ASHES SPEAKS TO THREE FRIENDS 523-41, JOB 02/VERSES 7-11/ JOB ON ASHHEAP 523-41, NAKED FIGURES SIT UP IN BED 523-42, JOB 07/VERSE 4?/ NAKED FIGURES IN BED 523-42, PSALM 1/ BEATUS VIR/ DAVID PLAYS REBECK 523-43,DAVID WITH REBEC 523-43, DAVID DICTATES PSALMS TO SCRIBE 523-43, PSALM 26/ DOMINUS ILLUMINATIO MEA 523-44, DAVID POINTS TO HIS EYE 523-44, PSALM 38/ DIXI CUSTODIAM 523-45, DAVID POINTS T|O HIS MOUTH 523-45, PSALM 52/ DIXIT INSIPIENS/ BALD FOOL 523-46, PSALM 68/ SALVUM ME FAC/ GOD SAVES DAVID 523-47,DAVID SAVED BY GOD FROM DEEP WATERS 523-47, NAKED FIGURES HOLD CORNUCOPIAS 523-48, CORNUCOPIAS 523-48, PSALM 80/ EXULTATE DEO/ BELL RINGING 523-49, BELLS ON ROPES RUNG BY TONSURED FIGURE 523-49, PSALM 97/ CANTATE DOMINO/ TWO FIGURES SING 523-50, PSALM 109/ DIXIT DOMINUS/ CHRIST BLESSING 523-51, CHRIST HOLDING BOOK BLESSES 523-51, ST JEROME HOLDS BOOK 523-52, PROLOGUE TO BOOKS OF SOLOMON 523-52, SOLOMON PREACHES TO NAKED FIGURE 523-53, SOLOMON ENTHRONED HOLDS ORB 523-54, MAN WITH PIG'S HEAD IN MARGIN 523-55, VIRGIN AND CHRIST CHILD 523-56, SONG OF SONGS/ VIRGIN WITH CHRIST CHILD 523-56, TONSURED FIGURE IN BLACK HABIT KNEELS 523-56, SOLOMON ENTHRONED HOLDS SCALES AND SCEPTRE 523-57, SCALES AND SCEPTRE 523-57, ARCHER DRAWS BOW AT BIRD 523-57, JESUS SON OF SIRACH RECEIVES BOOK 523-58, FIGURE WITH BOOK LECTURES 523-59, FIGURES SEATED HOLD OPEN BOOKS 523-60, SOLOMON 523-61, ST JEROME'S HEAD 523-62, ISAIAH SAWED IN HALF BY TWO MEN 523-63, ANGELS HOLD DRAPERY 523-63, ST JEROME 523-65, JEREMIAH WITH OPEN BOOK 523-66, JEREMIAH LISTENS TO VOICE OF GOD 523-67, JEREMIAH'S BOOK BROUGHT TO KING 523-68, PROPHET CAST INTO PRISON 523-69, JEREMIAH SPEAKS TO ISRAELITES BEFORE TEMPLE 523-70, FIGURE HOLDS VASE ON SHOULDER 523-70, JEREMIAH SPEAKS TO MESSENGER 523-71, MESSENGER WITH SCROLL 523-72, BARUCH STANDS BEFORE JECHONIAS AND ELDERS 523-73, BARUCH 01/VERSES 3-4/ BARUCH BEFORE JECHONIAS 523-73, EZEKIEL'S VISION 523-74, MAN IN TUNIC STANDS INSIDE MARGINAL SCROLL 523-75, MAN IN TUNIC REACHES UP TO GRASP MARGINAL SCROLL 523-76, SHADRACH/ MESHACH/ ABEDNEGO SEE COILED SERPENT 523-77, TWO PRISONERS LOOK OUT AT DANIEL 523-78, DANIEL IN LION'S DEN 523-79, DANIEL 06/VERSE 16/ DANIEL IN LION'S DEN 523-79, JOACHIM 523-80, HOSEA TAKES GOMER AS WIFE 523-81, SOLDIER ABOUT TO HURL JAVELIN AT SEATED MAN 523-81, JOEL HOLDS SCROLL 523-82, AMOS AS JEWISH PROPHET HOLDS SCROLL 523-83, JACOB 523-84, OBADIAH HOLDS SCROLL 523-85, JONAH BLESSED BY GOD 523-86, MICAH LOOKS UP TO GOD 523-87, NAHUM HOLDS BOOK WITH COVERED HANDS 523-88, ARCHER SHOOTS AT BIRD 523-89, HABAKKUK LOOKS UP AT GOD 523-90, ZEPHANIAH LOOKS UP AT GOD 523-91, MAN WITH SHIELD HURLS JAVELIN AT MONSTER 523-91, MONSTER AND MAN WITH JAVELIN 523-91, HAGGAI HOLDS SCROLL 523-92, TWO FIGURES RIDE SEA MONSTER 523-92, MONSTER/ SEA 523-92, ZECHARIAH STANDS ON NAKED FIGURE'S HANDS 523-93, MALACHI LOOKS UP AT GOD 523-94, JEW SACRIFICING AT GENTILE ALTAR KILLED 523-95, MATTATHIAS KILLS JEW AT GENTILE ALTAR 523-95, MERMAN WITH TWO TAILS 523-95, JUDAS MACCABEUS IN

JERUSALEM HANDS SCROLL 523-96, MAN HOLDING ROD FACES MAN WITH BASKET 523-96

*$ABSTRACT 524
*LIBRARY BODLEIAN
*SLIDE SET TITLE NEW TESTAMENT INITIALS
*NEGATIVE REFERENCE ROLL 225E
*RENTAL FEE $3.70
*TITLE OF MANUSCRIPT BIBLE
*SHELFMARK MS CANON BIBL LAT 57/ FOL 369 524/1-2, MS CANON BIBL LAT 57/ FOL 380 524/3-5, MS CANON BIBL LAT 57/ FOL 386V 524-6, MS CANON BIBL LAT 57/ FOL 387 524/7-9, MS CANON BIBL LAT 57/ FOL 398V 524/10-11, MS CANON BIBL LAT 57/ FOL 409 524/12-13, MS CANON BIBL LAT 57/ FOL 413V 524-14, MS CANON BIBL LAT 57/ FOL 417V 524-15, MS CANON BIBL LAT 57/ FOL 420V 524-16, MS CANON BIBL LAT 57/ FOL 422 524-17, MS CANON BIBL LAT 57/ FOL 423V 524-18, MS CANON BIBL LAT 57/ FOL 424V 524-19, MS CANON BIBL LAT 57/ FOL 425V 524-20, MS CANON BIBL LAT 57/ FOL 426V 524-21, MS CANON BIBL LAT 57/ FOL 427 524-22, MS CANON BIBL LAT 57/ FOL 428 524-23, MS CANON BIBL LAT 57/ FOL 428V 524-24, MS CANON BIBL LAT 57/ FOL 429 524-25, MS CANON BIBL LAT 57/ FOL 429V 524-26, MS CANON BIBL LAT 57/ FOL 433 534-27, MS CANON BIBL LAT 57/ FOL 444V 524-28, MS CANON BIBL LAT 57/ FOL 445V 524-29, MS CANON BIBL LAT 57/ FOL 447 524-30, MS CANON BIBL LAT 57/ FOL 447V 524-31, MS CANON BIBL LAT 57/ FOL 448V 524-32, MS CANON BIBL LAT 57/ FOL 449 524-33, MS CANON BIBL LAT 57/ FOL 449V 524-34
*PROVENANCE ITALIAN/ BOLOGNA
*DATE EXECUTED 13TH/ LATE
*LANGUAGE LATIN
*ARTIST/ SCHOOL RELATED IN STYLE TO JACOPINO DA REGGIO
*TYPE OF MANUSCRIPT BIBLE
*CONTENTS NEW TESTAMENT HISTORIATED INITIALS 524/1-34, INITIALS/ HISTORIATED 524/1-34, JESSE TREE SHOWING THREE GENERATIONS 524-1, MATTHEW 01/VERSES 1-16/ JESSE TREE 524-1, ANNUNCIATION IN MEDALLIONS 524-2, CHRIST STANDS ON PEDESTAL SUPPORTED BY GROTESQUE 524-3, DRAGON TWO HEADED WITH KNOTTED TAIL IN MARGIN 524-3, BAPTISM OF CHRIST IN MEDALLION 524-4, MARK 01/VERSES 9-11/ BAPTISM OF CHRIST 524-4, CHRIST DRIVEN INTO WILDERNESS BY SPIRIT 524-5, MARK 01/VERSE 12/ CHRIST DRIVEN INTO WILDERNESS 524-5, ST JEROME IN PROLOGUE TO LUKE 524-6, ST LUKE/ AUTHOR PORTRAIT 524-7, ZACHARIAS BURNING INCENSE IN TEMPLE 525-7, LUKE 01/VERSES 9-11/ ZACHARIAS IN TEMPLE 524-7, HEROD'S FEAST 524-8, MARK 06/VERSES 21-22/ HEROD'S FEAST 524-8, ST JOHN THE BAPTIST BEHEADED/ GIVEN TO SALOME 524-9, MARK 06/VERSES 27-28/ BEHEADING OF JOHN BAPTIST 524-9, ST JOHN STANDS ON BEAST 524-10, LAZARUS' DEATH AND RAISING 524-11, JOHN 11/VERSE 44/ RAISING OF LAZARUS 524-11, ST PAUL HANDS SCROLL TO MESSENGER 524-12, ST PAUL IN MEDALLION HOLDS OPEN BOOK 524-13, CHRIST HOLDS OPEN BOOK/ KNEELING FIGURES 524-13, ST PAUL WITH LARGE SWORD HANDS SCROLL 524-14, GROTESQUE IN MARGIN HOLDS HALBERD 524-14, ST PAUL IN II CORINTHIANS 524-15, ST PAUL HOLDS SWORD 524-16, ST PAUL HANDS SCROLL TO MESSENGER 524-17, SEATED FIGURE WITH SCROLL IN MARGIN 524-17, ST PAUL IN PHILIPPIANS TEXT 524-18, ST PAUL HOLDING BOOK IN COLOSSIANS TEXT 524-19, ST PAUL IN I THESSALONIANS TEXT 524-20, ST PAUL IN II THESSALONIANS TEXT 524-21, ST PAUL WITH SWORD IN I TIMOTHY TEXT 524-22, ST PAUL IN II TIMOTHY TEXT 524-23, ST PAUL IN TITUS TEXT 524-24, ST PAUL IN TITUS TEXT 524-25, HEBREW IN TEXT OF HEBREWS 524-26, MARY AND APOSTLES IN UPPER CHAMBER 524-27, ACTS 01/VERSES 13-14/ MARY AND APOSTLES 524-27, ST JAMES STANDS IN GOLD NICHE 524-28, TWO FIGURES SEATED ON BENCHES 524-28, ST PETER IN TEXT OF I PETER 524-29, SIMON PETER IN TEXT OF II PETER 524-30, ST JOHN IN TEXT OF I JOHN 524-31, ST JOHN IN TEXT OF II JOHN 524-32, JUDAS IN TEXT OF JUDE 524-33, CHRIST ENTHRONED SHOWING STIGMATA 524-34, TWO FIGURES WITH BOOK AND SCROLL 524-34

*$ABSTRACT 525
*LIBRARY BODLEIAN
*SLIDE SET TITLE DANCE OF DEATH
*NEGATIVE REFERENCE ROLL 225F
*RENTAL FEE $3.15
*COMMENTS SCENES FROM THE LIVES OF JOB AND ABRAHAM ARE WOVEN INTO THE RUNNING THEME THAT DEATH SHALL ALL THE WORLD SUBDUE. EACH OPENING SHOWS A SKELETON ON THE LEFT AND HIS VICTIM ON THE RIGHT.
*TITLE OF MANUSCRIPT BOOK OF HOURS/ OFFICE OF THE DEAD
*SHELFMARK MS DOUCE 135/ FOL 68 525-1, MS DOUCE 135/ FOL 68V-69 525-2, MS DOUCE 135/ FOL 69V-70 525-3, MS DOUCE 135/ FOL 70V-71 525-4, MS DOUCE 135/ FOL 71V-72 525-5, MS DOUCE 135/ FOL 72V-73 525-6, MS DOUCE 135/ FOL 73V-74 525-7, MS DOUCE 135/ FOL 74V-75 525-8, MS DOUCE 135/ FOL 75V-76 525-9, MS DOUCE 135/ FOL 76V-77 525-10, MS DOUCE 135/ FOL 77V-78 525-11, MS DOUCE 135/ FOL 78V-79 525-12, MS DOUCE 135/ FOL 79V-80 525-13, MS DOUCE 135/ FOL 80V-81 525-14, MS DOUCE 135/ FOL 81V-82 525-15, MS DOUCE 135/ FOL 82V-83 525-16, MS DOUCE 135/ FOL 83V-84 525-17, MS DOUCE 135/ FOL 84V-85 525-18, MS DOUCE 135/ FOL 85V-86 525-19, MS DOUCE 135/ FOL 86V-87 525-20, MS DOUCE 135/ FOL 87V-88 525-21, MS DOUCE 135/ FOL 88V-89 525-22, MS DOUCE 135/ FOL 89V 525-23
*PROVENANCE FRENCH
*DATE EXECUTED 16TH/ 2ND QUARTER
*LANGUAGE LATIN
*TYPE OF MANUSCRIPT BOOK OF HOURS/ USE OF ROME
*CONTENTS DANCE OF DEATH 525/1-23, DEATH/ DANCE OF 525/1-23, BOOK OF HOURS/ FRENCH 525/1-23, JOB AMONG THE ASHES 525-1, MAN AND WOMAN WITH INSTRUMENTS AND AS SKELETONS 525-2, POPE 525-2, MAN OFFERS WOMAN MIRROR WITH DEATH'S HEAD 525-3, DEATH SHOOTS A COUPLE 525-3, EMPEROR 525-3, DEATH CATCHES MAN BY ARM AND SPEARS SOLDIER 525-4, CARDINAL 525-4, TWO SKELETONS WITH TOOLS AND BASKETS 525-5, DANCE OF DEATH 525-5, KING 525-5, SKELETON RIDING BULL/ GRAVEYARD WITH ARCHBISHOP 525-6, SKELETON PLUNDERS GRAVE/ SKELETON WITH CORPSES 525-7, CONSTABLE OF A CASTLE 525-7, JOB'S BETROTHAL/ JOB IN MIDST OF FAMILY 525-8, PATRIARCH 525-8, JOB AND HIS BEASTS/ HIS HOME BURNS 525-9, KNIGHT 525-9, JOB'S SONS AND LIVESTOCK DESTROYED 525-10, BISHOP 525-10, JOB'S FAITHFULNESS/ SATAN GIVEN POWER 525-11, JOB WITH BOILS/ THREE FRIENDS VISIT 525-12, ABBOT 525-12, JOB'S WIFE URGES HIM TO RENOUNCE GOD 525-13, REEVE 525-13, GOD APPEARS TO JOB/ SHEPHERD SPEAKS TO JOB 525-14, ASTROLOGER 525-14, PROPERTY RESTORED TO JOB/ JOB AND WIFE GIVE THANKS 525-15, MERCHANT 525-15, ABRAHAM PRAYS/ GOD DEMANDS SACRIFICE OF ISAAC 525-16, FRANCISCAN FRIAR 525-16, ABRAHAM AND ISAAC CARRY WOOD/ ABRAHAM STOPPED 525-17, SERGEANT OF THE PEACE 525-17, ABRAHAM AND ISAAC PRAY/ DEATH TAKES INNKEEPER 525-18, USURER 525-18, DEATH TAKES FOOL AND OLD MAN 525-19, ADVOCATE 525-19, DEATH TAKES TRAVELLERS AND HUNCHBACK 525-20, ACTOR 525-20, DEATH TAKES BOY PLAYING WITH BALL AND BEGGAR 525-21, INFANT 525-21, DEATH POKES MAN CARRYING SACK AND PULLS LAME MAN 525-22, HERMIT 525-22, SKELETON LYING ON FLAGSTONES WITH CROWN BESIDE HIM 525-23

*$ABSTRACT 526
*LIBRARY BODLEIAN
*SLIDE SET TITLE SAINTS ETC ON MONUMENTAL BRASSES
*NEGATIVE REFERENCE ROLL 225G
*RENTAL FEE $3.90
*COMMENTS BRASS RUBBINGS FROM THE COLLECTION OF MAJOR OWEN EVANS. THE CONTENTS FIELD BEGINS WITH THE PERSON COMMEMORATED BY EACH BRASS FOLLOWED BY THE ICONOGRAPHIC SUBJECT ON EACH BRASS.
*SHELFMARK MS RUBBINGS EVANS
*PROVENANCE ENGLISH/ ELSING NORFOLK 526-1, ENGLISH/ DEERHURST GLOS 526-2, ENGLISH/ CASTLE ASHLY 526/3-7, ENGLISH/ HILDERSHAM CAMBS 526-8, ENGLISH/ KNEBWORTH HERTS 526/9-12, ENGLISH/ WIMBOURNE MINSTER DORSET 526-13, ENGLISH/ LILLINGSTONE LOVEL BUCKS 526-14, ENGLISH/ MORLEY DERBYS 526-15, ENGLISH/ BRAMPTON

NORFOLK 526-16, ENGLISH/ TATTERSHALL LINCS 526/17-22, ENGLISH/ ST MARY REDCLIFFE BRISTOL 526-23, ENGLISH/ CHILDREY BERKS 526-24, ENGLISH/ STOKE CHARITY HANTS 526-25, ENGLISH/ FOVANT WILTS 526-26, ENGLISH/ DIDDINGTON HUNTS 526/27-32, ENGLISH/ MACCLESFIELD CHESHIRE 526-33, ENGLISH/ WINDSOR BERKS 526-34, ENGLISH/ HEREFORD CATH 526-35, ENGLISH/ MORLEY DERBYS 526-36, ENGLISH/ ALL HALLOWS LONDON 526-37, ENGLISH/ BRITISH MUSEUM 526-38

*DATE EXECUTED 14TH/1347 526-1, 15TH/1400 526-2, 15TH/1401 526/3-7, 15TH/1408 526-8, 15TH/1414 526/9-12, 15TH/C1440 526-13, 15TH/1446 526-14, 15TH/1454 526-15, 15TH/1468 526-16, 15TH/C1470 526/17-22, 15TH/1475 526-23, 15TH/1477 526-24, 15TH/1482 526-25, 16TH/C1500 526-26, 16TH/1565 526/27-32, 16TH/1506 526-33, 16TH/1522 526-34, 16TH/1524 526-35, 16TH/C1525 526-36, 16TH/1533 526-37, 16TH/1547 526-38

*TYPE OF MANUSCRIPT BRASS RUBBINGS

*CONTENTS SAINTS AND OTHER RELIGIOUS SUBJECTS ON RUBBINGS 526/1-38, BRASS RUBBINGS 526/1-38, SIR HUGH HASTYNGS 526-1, VIRGIN'S CORONATION 526-1, SIR JOHN CASSY AND WIFE 526-2, SS ANNE AND JOHN THE BAPTIST 526-2, WILLIAM ERMYN/ RECTOR 526-3, SS ANNE AND PETER 526-3, WILLIAM ERMYN 526-4, SS KATHERINE AND PAUL 526-4, WILLIAM ERMYN 526-5, SS MARGARET AND ANDREW 526-5, WILLIAM ERMYN 526-6, SS MARY MAGDALENE AND NICHOLAS 526-6, WILLIAM ERMYN 526-7, SS HELEN AND LAURENCE 526-7, ROBERT PARYS 526-8, TRINITY/ MERCY SEAT 526-8, SIMON BACHE/ CANON OF ST PAUL'S 526-9, VIRGIN AND CHILD AND JOHN THE BAPTIST 526-9, SIMON BACHE 526-10, SS PETER AND PAUL 526-10, SIMON BACHE 526-11, BISHOP SAINTS/ AUGUSTINE AND THOMAS OF CANTERBURY 526-11, SIMON BACHE 526-12, SS ANDREW AND JAMES THE GREAT 526-12, ST ETHELRED/ KING OF WESSEX 526-13, ST ETHELRED 526-13, JOHN MERSTUN/ RECTOR 526-14, SACRED HEART 526-14, JOHN STATHUM AND WIFE 526-15, ST CHRISTOPHER 526-15, ROBERT BRAMPTON AND WIFE 526-16, VIRGIN AND CHILD 526-16, JOAN/ LADY CROMWELL 526-17, VIRGIN AND CHILD 526-17, JOAN/ LADY CROMWELL 526-18, ST ANNE 526-18, JOAN/ LADY CROMWELL 526-19, ST CHRISTOPHER 526-19, JOAN/ LADY CROMWELL 526-20, ST GEORGE 526-20, JOAN/ LADY CROMWELL 526-21, ST DOROTHY 526-21, JOAN/ LADY CROMWELL 526-22, ST EDMUND 526-22, PHILIP MEDO AND TWO WIVES 526-23, CHRIST BLESSING FROM CLOUD 526-23, JOAN/ WIFE OF ROBERT STRANGBON 526-24, TRINITY/ MERCY SEAT 526-24, THOMAS WAYTE 526-25, CHRIST OF PITY 526-25, GEORGE REDE/ RECTOR 526-26, ANNUNCIATION 526-26, WILLIAM TAYLARD AND WIFE 526-27, CHRIST BLESSING 526-27, WILLIAM TAYLARD AND WIFE 526-28, VIRGIN AND CHILD 526-28, WILLIAM TAYLARD AND WIFE 526-29, ST JOHN THE BAPTIST 526-29, WILLIAM TAYLARD AND WIFE 526-30, ST MARY MAGDALENE 526-30, WILLIAM TAYLARD AND WIFE 526-31, ST JOHN THE EVANGELIST 526-31, WILLIAM TAYLARD AND WIFE 526-32, ST CATHERINE 526-32, ROGER LEGH AND WIFE 526-33, ST GREGORY'S MASS 526-33, ROBERT HONYWO/ CANON OF WINDSOR 526-34, VIRGIN AND CHILD/ ST KATHERINE AND OWNER 526-34, WILLIAM PORTER/ WARDEN OF NEW COLLEGE OXFORD 526-35, ANNUNCIATION 526-35, JOHN SACHEVERELL 526-36, ST CHRISTOPHER 526-36, ANDREW EVYNGAR AND WIFE 526-37, PIETA 526-37, NICHOLAS LE BRUN 526-38, CRUCIFIXION WITH SAINTS 526-38

*$ABSTRACT 527

*LIBRARY BODLEIAN

*SLIDE SET TITLE PORTABLE PSALTER V

*NEGATIVE REFERENCE ROLL 225H

*RENTAL FEE $3.35

*COMMENTS SEE ALSO ABSTRACTS 237, 456, 471, AND 508.

*TITLE OF MANUSCRIPT PORTABLE PSALTER

*SHELFMARK MS DOUCE 5/ FOL 168V-169 527-1, MS DOUCE 5/ FOL 169V 527-2, MS DOUCE 5/ FOL 176 527-3, MS DOUCE 5/ FOL 176V-177 527-4, MS DOUCE 5/ FOL 177V-178 527-5, MS DOUCE 5/ FOL 178V-179 527-6, MS DOUCE 5/ FOL 179V-180 527-7, MS DOUCE 5/ FOL 180V-181 527-8, MS DOUCE 5/ FOL 181V-182 527-9, MS DOUCE 5/ FOL 182V-183 527-10, MS DOUCE 5/ FOL 183V-184 527-11, MS DOUCE 5/ FOL 184V-185 527-12, MS DOUCE 5/ FOL 185V-186 527-13, MS DOUCE 5/ FOL 186V-187 527-14, MS DOUCE 5/ FOL 187V-188

527/15-16, MS DOUCE 5/ FOL 188V-189 527-17, MS DOUCE 5/ FOL 189V-190 527-18, MS DOUCE 5/ FOL 190V-191 527-19, MS DOUCE 5/ FOL 191V-192 527-20, MS DOUCE 5/ FOL 192V-193 527-21, MS DOUCE 5/ FOL 193V-194 527-22, MS DOUCE 5/ FOL 194V-195 527-23, MS DOUCE 5/ FOL 195V-196 527-24, MS DOUCE 5/ FOL 196V-197 527-25, MS DOUCE 5/ FOL 197V-198 527-26, MS DOUCE 5/ FOL 198V-199 527-27
*PROVENANCE FLEMISH/ GHENT
*DATE EXECUTED 14TH/C1320-30
*LANGUAGE LATIN
*TYPE OF MANUSCRIPT PSALTER PORTABLE
*CONTENTS PSALTER ILLUSTRATIONS 527/1-27, MAN WITH FALCON/ HUMAN HEADS/ BIRD/ UNICORN 527-1, MAN HOLDS TRUMPET/ BIRDS/ HARE/ ANIMALS 527-2, MEN WITH TRUMPET AND ANIMAL SKULL/ GROTESQUE/ BEASTS 527-3, PSALM 66/67 ILLUMINATED DEUS WITH SEATED MAN 527-4, INITIAL D DEUS/ SEATED MAN 527-4, MAN AND WOMAN KISSING/MAN BEHIND WITH CLUB 527-4, HOUND CARRYING HARE TIED TO STICK 527-4, UNICORN AND APE 527-4, APE JABBING GROTESQUE WITH STICK 527-5, OWL/ HARE/ SMALL BIRD 527-5, MEN WITH AXE AND SWORD AND SHIELD 527-5, MAN WITH OPEN BOOK/ STAGS/ HEADS 527-6, WOMAN WITH RAISED SWORD/ ARMOURED MAN/ BIRDS 527-7, DOG HOODED WITH HAND-BELLS 527-8, MAN WITH AXE CHOPPING DOWN BORDER 527-8, GROTESQUE PLAYS PSALTERY/ OWL/ LION 527-8, MAN PREPARING TO CLUB LION 527-8, MAN HOLDS TRUMPET/ MAN WITH HAND IN BIRD'S BEAK 527-9, MAN HOLDS TRUMPET/ HEADS/ BEAST HOLDS SPEAR 527-10, BLANK FOLIOS EXCEPT FOR TWO LINES OF TEXT 527-11, CHRIST CARRYING CROSS 527-12, PSALM 68/69/ ILLUMINATED SALVUM 527-12, INITIAL S SALVUM WITH GOD ABOVE 527-12, DAVID IN WATER 527-12, MONK PAINTS TERMINAL HEAD/ LADY SPINS 527-12, TERMINAL HEADS/ STAGS/ UNICORN/ BIRD/ BEAST 527-13, TERMINAL HEADS/ UNICORN/ BIRD/ BEAST 527-14, MAN WITH RAISED SWORD/ BIRD HEADS/ UNICORN 527-15, DUPLICATE OF FRAME 15 527-16, MAN WITH RAISED SWORD/ BIRDS/ UNICORN 527-17, TERMINAL HEADS/ STAGS/ UNICORN/ BEAST 527-18, PSALM 69/70/ ILLUMINATED DEUS WITH MAN'S HEAD 527-19, INITIAL D DEUS/ MAN'S HEAD 527-19, MAN ON STILTS 527-19, GROTESQUE WEARING POINTED CAP WITH BELL 527-19, PSALM 70/71/ ILLUMINATED INTE WITH STANDING FIGURE 527-20, INITIAL I INTE WITH STANDING FIGURE 527-20, APE WATCHES MAN PUT ON BOOTS 527-20, LION EATS SMALLER ANIMAL 527-20, GROTESQUE/ HORNED MONSTER/ UNICORN/ STAG 527-21, TERMINAL HEADS/ BIRD/ UNICORN 527-22, MAN HOLDING HEAD OF BEAST 527-23, PSALM 71/72/ ILLUMINATED DEUS WITH MOTHER AND CHILD 527-24, INITIAL D DEUS/ MOTHER HOLDS SWADDLED CHILD 527-24, MEN CAPTURING APES 527-24, MAN BLOWS TRUMPET/ BIRD HEAD/ UNICORN 527-25, MONSTER WITH BIRD'S HEAD/ HORNED BEAST 527-26, PSALM 72/73/ ILLUMINATED QUAM WITH MAN'S HEAD 527-27, INITIAL Q QUAM WITH MAN'S HEAD 527-27, BISHOP POINTS AT BEAR/ GROTESQUE/ DOG/ BIRD 527-27

*$ABSTRACT 528
*LIBRARY BODLEIAN
*SLIDE SET TITLE PORTABLE PSALTER VI
*NEGATIVE REFERENCE ROLL 2251
*RENTAL FEE $3.35
*COMMENTS SEE ALSO ABSTRACTS 237, 456, 471, 508, AND 527.
*TITLE OF MANUSCRIPT PORTABLE PSALTER
*SHELFMARK MS DOUCE 5/ VOLUME 1
*PROVENANCE FLEMISH/ GHENT
*DATE EXECUTED 14TH/C1320-30
*LANGUAGE LATIN
*TYPE OF MANUSCRIPT PSALTER PORTABLE
*CONTENTS PSALTER ILLUSTRATIONS 528/1-27, BISHOP BLESSING/ BOY WITH BOWL OF FRUIT 528-1,MAN BLOWING TRUMPET/ HOODED MEN/ UNICORN 528-2, PSALM 73/74/ ILLUMINATED UT QUID WITH CROWNED HEAD 528-3, INITIAL U UT QUID/ CROWNED HEAD 528-3, APE CLIMBING TREE TO REACH NEST 528-4, MAN WITH SHIELD AND SWORD/ MAN WITH STICK 528-5, HUMAN HEADS/ BIRD/ ANIMALS 528-6, PSALM 74/75/ ILLUMINATED CONFITEBIMUR WITH MONSTER 528-7, INITIAL C CONFITEBIMUR WITH MONSTER 528-7, MAN HAMMERING INITIAL C INTO PLACE 528-7, MAN KILLING ANIMAL WITH SPEAR 528-7, RAM CHARGING

FIGURE WHO USES BASKET AS SHIELD 528-7, PSALM 75/76/ ILLUMINATED NOTUS WITH SEATED NUN 528-8, INITIAL N NOTUS WITH SEATED NUN 528-8, APE PULLING DOG'S TAIL 528-8, MAN HOLDS TRUMPET/ HUMAN HEADS/ ANIMALS 528-9, PSALM 76/77/ ILLUMINATED VOCE WITH HOODED HEAD 528-10, INITIAL V VOCE WITH HOODED HEAD 528-10, DOG PERFORMING AS MAN PLAYS TRUMPET 528-10, HUMAN AND ANIMAL HEADS 528-11, MAN WITH WEAPON AND SHIELD 528-12, APE RIDING CRANE/ BIRD WITH SPEAR/ DOG/ MONSTERS 528-13, MAN ARMORED WITH SHIELD AND SPEAR 528-14, MAN HOLDS TRUMPET/ BIRD/ UNICORN/ STAG 528-15,MAN HOLDS BOWL OF FRUIT/ BIRD/ UNICORN 528-16, MAN PLAYS BAGPIPES WHILE MAN DANCES 528-18, WOMAN HOLDS JUG/ MAN PREACHING 528-19, MAN BLOWING TRUMPET/ HEADS/ BIRD 528-20, HUMAN HEADS/ HORNED DEVIL/ UNICORN/ STAG 528-21, BEAST CATCHING OBJECTS IN MOUTH 528-22, PSALM 78/79/ ILLUMINATED DEUS WITH SEATED NUN 528-23, CRANE CATCHING FRUIT/ HORSE/ OWL/ GROTESQUE 528-23, HUMAN HEADS/ UNICORN 528-24, MAN SEATED ON LION HOLDING JAW 528-25, DOG CHASING HARE/ TWO GROTESQUES 528-25, WOMAN HOLDS BOOK/ STAG/ BIRD 528-26, HUMAN HEADS/ BIRDS/ DOG/ UNICORN 528-27

*$ABSTRACT 529
*LIBRARY BODLEIAN
*SLIDE SET TITLE EVANGELISTS FROM GOSPELS
*NEGATIVE REFERENCE ROLL 225J
*RENTAL FEE $2.20
*TITLE OF MANUSCRIPT GOSPELS
*SHELFMARK MS BAROCCI 31/ FOL 6V 529-1, MS BAROCCI 31/ FOL 118V 529-2, MS BAROCCI 31/ FOL 190V 529-3, MS BAROCCI 31/ FOL 314 529-4
*PROVENANCE BYZANTINE
*DATE EXECUTED 13TH
*TYPE OF MANUSCRIPT GOSPELS
*CONTENTS EVANGELISTS FROM BYZANTINE GOSPELS 529/1-4, ST MATTHEW 529-1, ST MARK 529-2, ST LUKE 529-3, ST JOHN 529-4

*$ABSTRACT 530
*LIBRARY BODLEIAN
*SLIDE SET TITLE FACSIMILES BY D M CALLARD OF ROMANESQUE INITIALS.
*SHELFMARK MS BODLEY 210 530-1, MS LAUD MISC 123 530/2-3, MS JESUS COLLEGE OXFORD 43 530/4-6, MS JESUS COLLEGE OXFORD 65 530/7-8, MS DOUCE 368 530/9-14, MS JESUS COLLEGE OXFORD B 102 530/15-24, MS LAUD LAT 17 530/25-26, MS JESUS COLLEGE OXFORD 34 530/27-29, MS JESUS COLLEGE OXFORD 48 530-30, MS JESUS COLLEGE OXFORD 52 530-31, MS JESUS COLLEGE OXFORD 53 530-32, MS JESUS COLLEGE OXFORD 62 530/33-35, MS JESUS COLLEGE OXFORD 63 530/36-37, MS JESUS COLLEGE OXFORD 67 530/38-39, MS JESUS COLLEGE OXFORD 68 530-40, MS JESUS COLLEGE OXFORD 70 530-41, MS JESUS COLLEGE OXFORD 54 530-42, MS JESUS COLLEGE OXFORD 51 530-43, MS JESUS COLLEGE OXFORD 92 530/44-50, MS MAGDALEN COLLEGE OXFORD 22 530-51, MS AUCT D 2 1 530/52-56, MS RAWL A 374 530-57, MS CORPUS CHRISTI COLLEGE OXFORD 139 530-58, MS CORPUS CHRISTI COLLEGE OXFORD 194 530-59, MS TRINITY COLLEGE 33 530-60, MS TRINITY COLLEGE OXFORD 39 530/61-62, MS TRINITY COLLEGE OXFORD 40 530-63, MS TRINITY COLLEGE OXFORD 21 530-64, MS TRINITY COLLEGE OXFORD 55 530-65, MS TRINITY COLLEGE OXFORD 69 530/66-67, MS LAMBETH PALACE 195 530-68, MS LAMBETH PALACE 63 530-69
*PROVENANCE ENGLISH/ GLOUCESTER 530/1-8, ENGLISH/ WINCHCOMB 530/9-24, ENGLISH/ CIRENCESTER 530/25-41, ENGLISH/ EVESHAM 530/42-51, ENGLISH/ LANTHONY GLOUCS 530/52-69
*CONTENTS INITIALS/ ROMANESQUE 530/1-69, ROMANESQUE INITIALS 530/1-69

*$ABSTRACT 531
*LIBRARY BODLEIAN

*SLIDE SET TITLE HERBAL
*NEGATIVE REFERENCE ROLL 227A
*RENTAL FEE $3.75
*TITLE OF MANUSCRIPT HERBAL OF APULEIUS PLATONICUS
*SHELFMARK MS ASHMOLE 1431/ FOL 3V 531-1, MS ASHMOLE 1431/ FOL 5 531-2, MS ASHMOLE 1431/ FOL 6 531-6, MS ASHMOLE 1431/ FOL 6V-7 531-4, MS ASHMOLE 1431/ FOL 7V-8 531-5, MS ASHMOLE 1431/ FOL 8V-9 531-6, MS ASHMOLE 1431/ FOL 9V-10 531-7, MS ASHMOLE 1431/ FOL 10V-11 531-8, MS ASHMOLE 1431/ FOL 11V-12 531-9, MS ASHMOLE 1431/ FOL 12V-13 531-10, MS ASHMOLE 1431/ FOL 13V-14 531-11, MS ASHMOLE 1431/ FOL 14V-15 531-12, MS ASHMOLE 1431/ FOL 15V-16 531-13, MS ASHMOLE 1431/ FOL 16V-17 531-14, MS ASHMOLE 1431/ FOL 17V-18 531-15, MS ASHMOLE 1431/ FOL 18V-19 531-16, MS ASHMOLE 1431/ FOL 19V-20 531-17, MS ASHMOLE 1431/ FOL 20V-21 531-18, MS ASHMOLE 1431/ FOL 21V-22 531-19, MS ASHMOLE 1431/ FOL 22V-23 531-20, MS ASHMOLE 1431/ FOL 23V-24 531-21, MS ASHMOLE 1431/ FOL 24V-25 531-22, MS ASHMOLE 1431/ FOL 25V-26 531-23, MS ASHMOLE 1431/ FOL 26V-27 531-24, MS ASHMOLE 1431/ FOL 27V-28 531-25, MS ASHMOLE 1431/ FOL 28V-29 531-26, MS ASHMOLE 1431/ FOL 29V-30 531-27, MS ASHMOLE 1431/ FOL 31 531-28, MS ASHMOLE 1431/ FOL 31V-32 531-29, MS ASHMOLE 1431/ FOL 32V-33 531-30, MS ASHMOLE 1431/ FOL 33V-34 531-31, MS ASHMOLE 1431/ FOL 34 531-32, MS ASHMOLE 1431/ FOL 34V-35 531-33, MS ASHMOLE 1431/ FOL 35V-36 531-34, MS ASHMOLE 1431/ FOL 36V-37 531-35
*PROVENANCE ENGLISH/ ST AUGUSTINE'S CANTERBURY
*DATE EXECUTED 11TH/C1070-1100
*LANGUAGE LATIN
*AUTHOR APULEIUS PLATONICUS
*TYPE OF MANUSCRIPT HERBAL
*CONTENTS HERBAL 531/1-35, BOTANICAL MS 531/1-35, BETONICE/ BETONY 531-1, ARRNOGLOSSE/ PLANTAIN 531-2, PENTAFILLOS/ FIVE-LEAVED GRASS 531-3, COLUMBARIS/ VERVAIN 531-3, SIMPHONIACE/ HENBANE 531-4, VIPINE/ SNAKEWEED 531-4, ACHORUM/ YELLOW FLAG 531-4, LENTOPODION/ LADY'S FLAG 531-5, SCELERATA/ RANUNCULUS SCELERATUS 531-5, BUTRACION STRATICEUM/ BUTTERWORT 531-5, ARTEMESIAE/ MUGWORT 531-5, ARTHEMISIAE TAGANTES 531-6, ARTHEMESIE LEPTAFILLOS 531-6, LAPATIUM/ WATER DOCK 531-6, DRACONTEAE/ DRAGONS 531-6, SATYRION/ RAGWORT 531-7, GENTIANAE/ AUTUM GENTIAN 531-7, CICLAMINOS/ ARISTOLOCHIA PALLIDA 531-7, PSERPINATIAE/ KNOTGRASS 531-7, ARISTOLOGIE ROUNDAE/ SMEARWORT 531-8, NASTURCIUM 5531-8, ERIBULUUS 531-8, APOLLINARIS/ GLOVEWORT 531-8, CHAMOMELUM/ CHAMOMILE 531-8, CAMEDRIS 531-9, CHAMELEAE/ TEASEL OR WOLF'S COMB 531-9, PERSOPES/ BEET 531-9, FRAGA/ STRAWBERRY 531-9, IBISCUS/ MARSH MALLOW 531-9, YPERUM/ HORSETAIL 531-10, MALVE SILVATICA TERRATICA/ MALVA SYLVESTRIS 531-10, LINGUA BOVIS/ BUGLOSS 531-10, SCILLITICI/ SQUILL 531-10, COTILIDON/ LADY'S NAVEL 531-11, GALLITRICUS/ DIGITARIA SANGUINALIS 531-11, MARRUBIUM/ HOREHOUND 531-11, EXIFION/ FOX'S FOOT 531-11, GALLITRICUM 531-11, MUOLUTA/ HOUSE LEEK 531-12, ELIOTROPION 531-12, GRIAS/ MADDER 531-12, POLLITRICUM/ HOP TREFOIL 531-12, ASTULA REGIA/ WOODRUFF 531-12, SPLENION/ HARTSTONGUE 531-12, PAPAVERIS SILVATICI/ OPIUM POPPY 531-13, YNANTES/ DROPWORT 531-13, NARCISSOS/ NARCISSUS POETICUS 531-13, POLION/ TEUCRIUM POLIUM 531-13, VICTORIOLA/ BUTCHER'S BROOM 531-14, SIMPHITUM/ COMFREY 531-14, ASTERION 531-14, LEPORIS PES/ HARE'S FOOT 531-14, DIPTANNUM/ DITTANY 531-15, SOLAGO MAIOR/ HELIOTROPIUM EUROPAEUM 531-15, SOLAGO MINOR/ AFRICAN MARIGOLD 531-15, PEONIA/ PEONY 531-15, PERISTEREON/ VERVAIN 531-16, BRIONIA/ BLACK BRYONY 531-16, NIMPHEA/ WATER LILY 531-16, CHRISION/ RED CLOVER 531-16, ISATIS/ WOAD 531-16, SCORDEON/ ALLIUM VINEALE 531-17, UMBASCUM/ MULLEIN 531-17, ERACLEA 531-17, CELIDONIA/ CELANDINE 531-17, STRIGNOS/ NIGHTSHADE 531-17, SENECION/ GROUNDSEL 531-18, FILIX/ ASPLENIUM 531-18, GRAMEN/ TWITCH GRASS 531-18, GLADIOLUS/ FLAG 531-18, ROSMARINUS/ ROSEMARY 531-18, PASTINACA/ CARROT 531-19, PERDICALIS/ PELLITORY 531-19, MERCURIALIS/ CHEADLE 531-19, RADIOLUS/ EVERFERN 531-19, ASPARAGI/ ASPARAGUS OFFICINALIS 531-20, SAVINA/ SAVIN 531-20, CANIS CAPUT/ HOUND'S HEAD 531-20, ERUSCI/ BRAMBLE 531-20, ACHILLEA/ YARROW 531-21, RUTA HORTENSIS/ RUE 531-21, MENTASTRUM/ HORSE MINT 531-21, EBULUM/ DANEWORT 531-21, PULERUM/ PENNYROYAL 531-22, NEPITA/ CATMINT

531-22, PEUCIDONUM/ CAMMOCK 531-22, INNULE CAPANAE/ ELECAMPANE 531-22, CINOGLOSSA/ HOUND'S TONGUE 531-23, SAXIFRAGA/ SUNDCORN 531-23, HEDERANIGRA/ GROUND IVY 531-23, SERPULLUM/ ORGANY 531-23, ABSINTHIUM/ WORMWOOD 531-23, SALVIA/ SAGE 531-24, CORIANDRUM/ CORIANDER 531-24, PORTULACA/ PURSLANE 531-24, CEREFOLIUM/ CHERVIL 531-24, SISIMBRIUM/ WATER MINT 531-24, OLEASTRUM/ ALEXANDERS 531-24, LILIUM/ LILY 531-24, TYTIMALLUM/ SPURGE 531-24, SILVATICUM/ SONCHUS 531-25, LUPINUM/ LUPIN 531-25, LACTERIDEUM/ DAPHNE GNIDIUM 531-25, LACTUCA LEPORICA/ LETTUCE 531-25, SCICIDEAGRIA/ CUCUMBER 531-25, CANAPUS SILVATICUS/ HEMP 531-25, RUTA MONTANA 531-25, EPTAFILLOS 531-26, OCIMUM/ WILD BASIL 531-26, APPIUM/ APIUM 531-26, CROSOCANTIS/ IVY 531-26, MENTA/ CORNMINT 531-26, ANETUM/ DILL 531-26, ORIGANUM/ MARJORAM 531-26, SEMPERVIVA 531-26, FENICULUM/ PURPLERED 531-27, ERISIFION 531-27, SIMPHITUM 531-27, PETROSILINUM/ PARSLEY 531-27, SILVATICA 531-27, BASILISCA 531-27, MANDRAGORE/ MALE MANDRAKE 531-28, BOOK OF EXTRACTS FROM DIOSCORIDES 531/29-35, SEPHRAM 531-29, BUGLOSOS 531-29, ACHANTUM/ CNICUS ERIOFOROS 531-29, ELILISFACU/ WILD SAGE 531-29, CIMINUM/ CUMINUM CYMINUM 531-29, CAMELEON ALBA/ WILD TEASEL 531-29, SERPILLOS/ THYME 531-30, CAMEDRUM 531-30, POLIGONOS 531-30, CESTRIOS 531-30, ARISTOLOGIUM/ BIRTHWORT 531-30, STICAS 531-31, POLITRICOS 531-31, SAMSACU/ ELDER 531-31, MANDRAGORA/ FEMALE MANDRAKE 531-31, THIASPIS 531-31, SISIMBRIUM/ WATER MINT 531-31, CELIDONIA/ HYPERICUM OLYMPICUM 531-31, MANDRAGORA/ DETAIL OF FEMALE MANDRAKE 531-32, CAMEMELOS/ CAMOMILE 531-33, SIDERITIS 531-33, FLAMINOS/ GREAT MULLEIN 531-33, LINOZOSTIS/ DOG'S MERCURY 531-33, ANTIRENUM/ SNAPDRAGON 531-33, BRITTANNICA 531-34, PSILLIOS 531-34, MELENA 531-34, TRIBULOSA 531-34, CONITA/ INULA VISCOSA 531-34, STRIGNOS/ NIGHTS 531-34, BUOTTHALMON/ ANTHEMIS VALENTINA 531-34, SPERITIS/ PIMPERNEL 531-35

*$ABSTRACT 532
*LIBRARY BODLEIAN
*SLIDE SET TITLE OVID
*NEGATIVE REFERENCE ROLL 227B
*RENTAL FEE $2.80
*TITLE OF MANUSCRIPT METAMORPHOSES/ BOOK I
*SHELFMARK MS DOUCE 117/ FOL 3V 532-1, MS DOUCE 117/ FOL 6 532-2, MS DOUCE 117/ FOL 7V 532-3, MS DOUCE 117/ FOL 9 532-4, MS DOUCE 117/ FOL 10 532/5-9, MS DOUCE 117/ FOL 13V 532-10, MS DOUCE 117/ FOL 18 532-11, MS DOUCE 117/ FOL 26 532-12, MS DOUCE 117/ FOL 28V 532-13, MS DOUCE 117/ FOL 34 532-14, MS DOUCE 117/ FOL 39 532-15, MS DOUCE 117/ FOL 42 532-16
*PROVENANCE FRENCH
*DATE EXECUTED 16TH/ AFTER 1531
*LANGUAGE FRENCH
*AUTHOR OVID/ TRANSLATED BY CLEMENT MAROT
*TYPE OF MANUSCRIPT LITERATURE/ CLASSICAL
*CONTENTS LITERATURE/ CLASSICAL 532/1-16, METAMORPHOSES BY OVID 532/1-16, GOD TRANSFORMS CHAOS INTO FOUR ELEMENTS 532-1, GOD STANDS AMIDST BIRDS AND ANIMALS 532-1, DIAGRAM OF EARTH AS FIVE ZONES 532-2, EARTH/ FIVE ZONES 523-2, WINDS/ FOUR BLOW ON FOUR CASTLES 532-3, FOUR WINDS/ EURUS/ ZEPHYRUS/ BOREAS/ AUSTER 532-3, PROMETHEUS CREATES MAN FROM EARTH 532-4, FOUR AGES OF MAN 532-5, AGES OF MAN 532-5, GOLDEN AGE/ MEN AND WOMEN GATHER FRUITS 532-6,SILVER AGE/ MAN PLOUGHS/ MAN IN HOUSE/ MAN CONVERSES 532-7, BRONZE AGE/ MEN TAKE UP ARMS AGAINST EACH OTHER 532-8, IRON AGE/ JUSTICE LEAVES EARTH AND MEN FIGHT 532-9, JUPITER OFFERED HUMAN FLESH 532-10, LYCAON TRANSFORMED INTO WOLF 532-10, GIANTS TRY TO ASCEND PELION 532-10, DELUGE/ DEUCALION AND PYRRA SEEK ADVICE FROM THEMIS 532-11, DEUCALION AND PYRRA THROW STONES 532-11, APOLLO SLAYS PYTHON WITH BOW 532-12, CUPID AIMS BOW AT APOLLO 532-12, PHOEBUS-APOLLO PURSUES DAPHNE WHO CHANGES INTO LAUREL 532-13, CUPID ON HILL HOLDING ARROWS 532-13, JUPITER EMBRACES IO WHO TRANSFORMS INTO HEIFER 532-14, JUNO IN HER CHARIOT 532-14, JUPITER SENDS MERCURY TO EARTH TO SLAY ARGUS 532-15, MERCURY ON EARTH WITH SLEEP-PRODUCING WAND 532-15, MERCURY SEATED WITH

ARGUS WHO FALLS ASLEEP 532-15, MERCURY CUTS OFF ARGUS'S HEAD 532-15, JUNO PLACES ARGUS'S EYES ON TAIL OF PEACOCK 532-15, PAN SEEKS SYRINX WHO HAS BEEN TRANSFORMED INTO REEDS 532-15, IO SHOWN AS HEIFER AND NYMPH 532-16, JUPITER AND JUNO CONVERSE IN CLOUDS 532-16, PHAETON AND EPAPHUS ARGUING 532-16, PHAETON ASKS FOR PROOF OF HIS HIGH BIRTH 532-16

*$ABSTRACT 533
*LIBRARY BODLEIAN
*SLIDE SET TITLE ENGLISH ROMANCES
*NEGATIVE REFERENCE ROLL 227C
*RENTAL FEE $3.20
*COMMENTS FOUR INCOMPLETE MIDDLE ENGLISH ROMANCES.
*TITLE OF MANUSCRIPT SIR ISENBRAS 533/1-6, JEST OF SIR GAWAIN 533/7-13, SIR EGLAMOUR OF ARTOIS 533/14-24
*SHELFMARK MS DOUCE 261/ FOL 1 533-1, MS DOUCE 261/ FOL 2V 533-2, MS DOUCE 261/ FOL 5V 533-3, MS DOUCE 261/ FOL 9V 533-4, MS DOUCE 261/ FOL 11V 533-5, MS DOUCE 261/ FOL 13V 533-6, MS DOUCE 261/ FOL 15V 533-7, MS DOUCE 261/ FOL 17V 533-8, MS DOUCE 261/ FOL 20 533-9, MS DOUCE 261/ FOL 21V 533-10, MS DOUCE 261/ FOL 23V 533-11, MS DOUCE 261/ FOL 24V 533-12, MS DOUCE 261/ FOL 25V 533-13, MS DOUCE 261/ FOL 26V 533-14, MS DOUCE 261/ FOL 28 533-15, MS DOUCE 261/ FOL 31 533-16, MS DOUCE 261/ FOL 32V 533-17, MS DOUCE 261/ FOL 35V 533-18, MS DOUCE 261/ FOL 38 533-19, MS DOUCE 261/ FOL 39V 533-20, MS DOUCE 261/ FOL 40 533-21, MS DOUCE 261/ FOL 44 533-22, MS DOUCE 261/ FOL 46 533-23, MS DOUCE 261/ FOL 48V 533-24
*PROVENANCE ENGLISH
*DATE EXECUTED 16TH/1564
*LANGUAGE ENGLISH/ MIDDLE ENGLISH
*AUTHOR WRITTEN BY OR FOR E B
*TYPE OF MANUSCRIPT ROMANCE
*CONTENTS ROMANCES/ MIDDLE ENGLISH 533/1-24, LITERATURE/ MIDDLE ENGLISH ROMANCES 533/1-24, ISENBRAS MOUNTED ON WHITE HORSE 533-1, ISENBRAS PRAYS FOR ADVERSITY IN YOUTH 533-2, ISENBRAS WITH WIFE AND SON KNELL BEFORE SULTAN 533-3, DEGORE UNKNOWINGLY MARRIES HIS MOTHER 533-4, DEGORE FIGHTS WITH GIANT WHILE LADY WATCHES 533-5, DEGORE AND FATHER REUNITED AFTER FIGHT 533-6, GAWAYNE LANCES SIR GILBERT'S SHOULDER 533-7, GAWAYNE UNHORSES SIR GYAMOUR 533-8, GAWAYNE UNHORSES SIR TERRY 533-9, BRANDLES FINDS FATHER AND BROTHERS DISCONSOLATE 533-10, GAWAYNE AND SIR BRANDLES DUEL ON FOOT 533-11, BRANDLES BEATS HIS SISTER 533-12, COLOPHON OF JEST OF SIR GAWAYNE/ INITIALS E B 533-13 EGLAMOUR CONFESSES LOVE FOR CHRISTABELL 533-14, CHRISTABELL AND MAIDS VISIT EGLAMOUR IN CHAMBER 533-15, EGLAMOUR SLAYS THE GIANT MARROCKE 533-16, EGLAMOUR SLAYS THE GIANT BOAR 533-17, EGLAMOUR SLAYS GIANT OUTSIDE CITY-WALL 533-18, EGLAMOUR SLAYS THE DRAGON OUTSIDE ROME 533-19, CHRISTABELL AND INFANT ARE CAST ADRIFT IN BOAT 533-20, GRIFFON STEALS CHRISTABELL'S SON 533-21, DEGRABELL MARRIES HIS MOTHER CHRISTABELL 533-22, EGLAMOUR JOUSTS AGAINST HIS SON DEGRABELL 533-23, COLOPHON OF SIR EGLAMOUR OF ARTOIS/ DATED 1564 533-24

*$ABSTRACT 534
*LIBRARY BODLEIAN
*SLIDE SET TITLE ARTHURIAN ROMANCES
*NEGATIVE REFERENCE ROLL 227D
*RENTAL FEE $2.60
*COMMENTS LANCELOT CYCLE, BRANCHES 3,4, AND 5. REFERENCES BELOW ARE TO H. O. SOMMER, THE VULGATE VERSION OF THE ARTHURIAN ROMANCES V AND VI.
*TITLE OF MANUSCRIPT ROMANCE OF LANCELOT DU LAC 534/1-2, QUEST OF THE GRAIL 534/3-6, LA MORT ARTUS 534/7-12
*SHELFMARK MS DIGBY 223/ FOL 25V 534-1, MS DIGBY 223/ FOL 48V 534-2, MS DIGBY 223/ FOL 77 534-3, MS DIGBY 223/ FOL 94V 534-4, MS DIGBY 223/ FOL 118 534-5, MS DIGBY 223/ FOL 129 534-6, MS DIGBY 223/ FOL 146 534-7, MS DIGBY 223/ FOL 161V

534-8, MS DIGBY 223/ FOL 173 534-9, MS DIGBY 223/ FOL 189V 534-10, MS DIGBY 223/ FOL 212V 534-11, MS DIGBY 223/ FOL 227 534-12
*PROVENANCE FRENCH/ NORTH
*DATE EXECUTED 13TH/ LATE
*LANGUAGE FRENCH
*ARTIST/ SCHOOL RELATED TO THE STYLE OF LANCELOT MS/ PARIS BIBL NAT FR 342
*TYPE OF MANUSCRIPT ROMANCE/ ARTHURIAN
*CONTENTS ARTHURIAN ROMANCES 534/1-12, LITERATURE/ ARTHURIAN ROMANCES 534/1-12, INVASION OF FLANDERS/ V336 534-1, YWAIN'S SQUIRE MEETS ARTHUR NEAR CAMELOT/ V369 534-2, DAMSEL COMES FOR LANCELOT/ VI3 534-3, GALAHAD TAKES LEAVE OF WOUNDED MELIAN/ VI37 534-4, LANCELOT EXHORTED BY HERMIT/ VI83 534-5, GAWAIN RIDES IN PURSUIT OF QUEST/ VI105 534-6, GALAHAD RIDES THROUGH FOREST/ VI140 534-7, GALAHAD AND PERCIVAL PRAY FOR BOHORT/ VI173 534-8, ARTHUR TOLD OF DEATH OF GALAHAD AND PERCIVAL/ VI203 534-9, ARTHUR AND GUINEVERE ARRIVE AT TAUROC CASTLE/ VI234 534-10, ARTHUR TOLD OF LANCELOT'S ABDUCTION OF QUEEN/ VI316 534-11, ARTHUR ADVISED BY GAWAIN TO ATTACK LANCELOT/ VI316 534-12

*$ABSTRACT 535
*LIBRARY BODLEIAN
*SLIDE SET TITLE BOOK OF CHESS
*NEGATIVE REFERENCE ROLL 227E
*RENTAL FEE $2.65
*COMMENTS A TRANSLATION INTO THE VENETIAN DIALECT OF THE LIBER DE SCACCHIS, A MORAL TREATISE BY JACOBUS DE CASSOLINA OF THE LATE 13TH OR EARLY 14TH CENTURY. USING THE FRAME OF THE GAME OF CHESS, PLUS HEAVY BORROWINGS FROM THE CLASSICS AND CONTEMPORARY WRITERS, HE EVOLVES A GUIDE TO THE GOOD LIFE FOR EVERY CLASS OF SOCIETY.
*TITLE OF MANUSCRIPT LIBER DE SCACCHIS
*SHELFMARK MS CANON ITAL 4/ FOL 3V 535-1, MS CANON ITAL 4/ FOL 7V 535-2, MS CANON ITAL 4/ FOL 11 535-3, MS CANON ITAL 4/ FOL 13 535-4, MS CANON ITAL 4/ FOL 19 535-5, MS CANON ITAL 4/ FOL 27V 535-6, MS CANON ITAL 4/ FOL 30V 535-7, MS CANON ITAL 4/ FOL 33 535-8, MS CANON ITAL 4/ FOL 37 535-9, MS CANON ITAL 4/ FOL 39V 535-10, MS CANON ITAL 4/ FOL 42V 535-11, MS CANON ITAL 4/ FOL 45 535-12, MS CANON ITAL 4/ FOL 47V 535-13
*PROVENANCE ITALIAN/ VENICE
*DATE EXECUTED 15TH/1459
*LANGUAGE ITALIAN/ VENETIAN DIALECT
*AUTHOR DE CESSOLIS/ JACOBUS
*SCRIBE MARINUS GALAZI?
*TYPE OF MANUSCRIPT MORAL TREATISE
*CONTENTS BOOK OF CHESS 535/1-13, CHESS AS FRAME FOR MORAL TREATISE 535/1-13, KING SITS IN CHAYER CLOTHED IN PURPLE 535-1, QUENE OUGHT TO BE CHASTE/ WISE/ HONEST 535-2, BISHOP/ ALPHYNE IS FOR TO COUNCEYLL THE KYNGE 535-3, KNYGHTES SHOLDE LEDE A NEWE LYF AND NEWE MANERS 535-4, ROOKS BEN VICAIRES AND LEGATS OF THE KYNGE 535-5, FYRST PAWNE SIGNEFIETH MAN OF THE COMYN PEPLE 535-6, SECONDE PAWNE HATH FIGURE OF A SMYTH 535-7, THIRDE PAWNE AS CLERK 535-8, FOURTH PAWN SIGNEFIED THE MARCHANS 535-9, PAWON SIGNEFYETH THE PHISICYEN SPICER AND APOTYQUAIRE 535-10, SIXTHE PAWN RESEMBLETH TAVENERS/ HOSTELERS/ SELLERS 535-11, VII PAWN ARE GARDES AND KEPARS OF CYTEES 535-12, THYS PAWN IS RYBAULDES/ PLAYERS OF DYSE/ MESSANGERS 535-13

*$ABSTRACT 536
*LIBRARY BODLEIAN
*SLIDE SET TITLE BARTOLOMEO FONZIO
*NEGATIVE REFERENCE ROLL 227F
*RENTAL FEE $3.25
*COMMENTS A FRAGMENTARY COLLECTION OF EPIGRAPHS AND COPIES OF DRAWINGS, MOSTLY OF CLASSICAL MONUMENTS BY CIRIACO D'ANCONA.

*SHELFMARK MS LAT MISC D 35/ FOL 63 536-1, MS LAT MISC D 35/ FOL 72V 536-2, MS LAT MISC D 35/ FOL 73 536/3-4, MS LAT MISC D 35/ FOL 132V-133 536-5, MS LAT MISC D 35/ FOL 133V 536-6, MS LAT MISC D 35/ FOL 134 536-7, MS LAT MISC D 35/ FOL 134V 536-8, MS LAT MISC D 35/ FOL 135 536-9, MS LAT MISC D 35/ FOL 135V 536-10, MS LAT MISC D 35/ FOL 136 536-11, MS LAT MISC D 35/ FOL 136V 536-12, MS LAT MISC D 35/ FOL 137 536-13, MS LAT MISC D 35/ FOL 137V 536-14, MS LAT MISC D 35/ FOL 138 536-15, MS LAT MISC D 35/ FOL 138V 536-16, MS LAT MISC D 35/ FOL 139 536-17, MS LAT MISC D 35/ FOL 139V 536-18, MS LAT MISC D 35/ FOL 140 536-19, MS LAT MISC D 35/ FOL 140V 536-20, MS LAT MISC D 35/ FOL 141 536-21, MS LAT MISC D 35/ FOL 141V 536-22, MS LAT MISC D 35/ FOL 152V 536-23, MS LAT MISC D 35/ FOL 153 536-24, MS LAT MISC D 35/ FOL 161V 536-25
*PROVENANCE ITALIAN/ FLORENCE
*DATE EXECUTED 15TH
*ARTIST/ SCHOOL CIRIACO D'ANCONA
*AUTHOR BARTOLOMEO FONZIO
*TYPE OF MANUSCRIPT COLLECTION OF EPIGRAPHS AND DRAWINGS
*CONTENTS HADRIAN'S TOMB IN ROME 536-1, ETHIOPIAN WHITE ELEPHANT 536-2, EGYPTIAN GIRAFFE AND LONG-HAIRED DOG 536-3, DUPLICATE OF FRAME 3 536-3, HADRIAN'S TEMPLE AT CYZICUS 536/5-12, CORINTHIAN COLUMNS SUPPORT ARCHITRAVE 536-5, MAIN DOORWAY 536-6, MEDUSA'S HEAD AND SCULPTED FRIEZE AND ENTABLATURE 536-7, CORINTHIAN COLUMN/ SCULPTED FRIEZE/ FRAGMENTS 536-8, CORINTHIAN COLUMN/ SCULPTED FRIEZE 536-9, CORINTHIAN COLUMN/ SCULPTED FRIEZE/ FRAGMENT 536-10, CORINTHIAN COLUMN/ SCULPTED FRIEZE 536-11, MEDUSA'S HEAD ON CAPITAL/ ACANTHUS LEAVES 536-12, BASE WITH INSCRIPTIONS 536-13, NYMPHS LABELLED AS MUSES 536-14, NYMPHS LABELLED AS MUSES 536-15, NYMPHS/ ONE HOLDS TAMBORINE 536-16, PAN AND ANIMALS FROM TOMB OF POLIDORUS 536-17, STATUE 536-18, ALTAR OF MYSTERY CULT DECORATED WITH SNAKES 536-19, MEDUSA'S HEAD/ DRAWING FROM BRONZE ORIGINAL 536-20, ARISTOTLE BUST 536-21, SACRIFICE TO JUPITER FROM ALTAR 536-22, STELE OF MULE KILLED BY WOLVES 536-23, MULE ATTACKED BY WOLVES 536-24, SARCOPHAGUS AND BODY OF ROMAN GIRL 536-25

*$ABSTRACT 537
*LIBRARY BODLEIAN
*SLIDE SET TITLE TROILUS AND CRISEYDE
*NEGATIVE REFERENCE ROLL 227H
*RENTAL FEE $2.50
*COMMENTS TRANSLATED INTO FRENCH BY PIERRE DE BEAUVEAU.
*TITLE OF MANUSCRIPT LE ROMAN DE TROYLE ET DE LA BELLE CRISEIDA
*SHELFMARK MS DOUCE 331/ FOL 2V 537-1, MS DOUCE 331/ FOL 8 537-2, MS DOUCE 331/ FOL 15 537-3, MS DOUCE 331/ FOL 19V 537-4, MS DOUCE 331/ FOL 26 537-5, MS DOUCE 331/ FOL 35 537-6, MS DOUCE 331/ FOL 43 537-7, MS DOUCE 331/ FOL 52 537-8, MS DOUCE 331/ FOL 55V 537-9, MS DOUCE 331/ FOL 62V 537-10
*PROVENANCE FRENCH/ WEST
*DATE EXECUTED 15TH/ 3RD QUARTER
*LANGUAGE FRENCH
*ARTIST/ SCHOOL IMITATION OF THE STYLE OF RENE D'ANJOU
*AUTHOR BOCCACCIO/ FILOSTRATO
*TYPE OF MANUSCRIPT ROMANCE
*CONTENTS LITERATURE/ TRANSLATION OF FILOSTRATO 537/1-10, LE ROMAN DE TROYLE 537/1-10, FEAST OF PALLAS 537-1, CRISEYDE IN WIDOW'S HABIT 537-1, PANDARUS TALKS TO TROILUS WHO IS IN BED 537-2, PANDARUS TALKS TO CRISEYDE AT WINDOW 537-3, CRISEYDE READS LETTER 537-4, TROILUS AND CRISEYDE GO TO BED 537-5, PRIAM EXCHANGES CRISEYDE FOR ANTENOR 537-6, PANDARUS TALKS TO LAMENTING CRISEYDE 537-7, CRISEYDE LEAVES TROY 537-8, TROILUS RETURNS HOME 537-9, TROILUS AND PANDARUS LOOK AT GREEK CAMP 537-10

*$ABSTRACT 538
*LIBRARY BODLEIAN

*SLIDE SET TITLE PSALTER ILLUSTRATIONS
*NEGATIVE REFERENCE ROLL 227I
*RENTAL FEE $2.45
*COMMENTS BELONGS TO A LARGE AND IMPORTANT GROUP OF NEAPOLITAN MSS.
*TITLE OF MANUSCRIPT PORTABLE FERIAL PSALTER
*SHELFMARK MS CANON LITURG 151/ FOL 7 538-1, MS CANON LITURG 151/ FOL 45V 538-2, MS CANON LITURG 151/ FOL 70 538-3, MS CANON LITURG 151/ FOL 94 538-4, MS CANON LITURG 151/ FOL 118 538-5, MS CANON LITURG 151/ FOL 146V 538-6, MS CANON LITURG 151/ FOL 173 538-7, MS CANON LITURG 151/ FOL 200 538-8, MS CANON LITURG 151/ FOL 279 538-9
*PROVENANCE ITALIAN/ NAPLES
*DATE EXECUTED 14TH/ 3RD QUARTER
*LANGUAGE LATIN
*ARTIST/ SCHOOL USED TO BE ASSOCIATED WITH CRISTOFORO ORIMINA
*TYPE OF MANUSCRIPT PSALTER/ PORTABLE
*CONTENTS PSALTER/ ITALIAN 14TH 538/1-9, PSALM 1/ ILLUMINATED BEATUS/ DAVID WITH PSALTERY 538-1, INITIAL B BEATUS/ DAVID WITH PSALTERY 538-1, PSALM 26/27/ ILLUMINATED DOMINUS/ DAVID POINTS TO EYE 538-2, INITIAL D DOMINUS/ DAVID POINTS TO EYE 538-2, PSALM 38/39/ ILLUMINATED DIXI/ DAVID KNEELS 538-3, INITIAL D DIXI/ DAVID KNEELS WITH TWO FEMALES 538-3, PSALM 52/53/ ILLUMINATED DIXIT/ MAN WITH SERPENT 538-4, INITIAL D DIXIT/ MAN WITH SERPENT WALKS THROUGH WILDERNESS 538-4, PSALM 68/69/ ILLUMINATED SALVUM/ DAVID BLESSED 538-5, INITIAL S SALVUM/ DAVID IN WATER BLESSED BY GOD 538-5, PSALM 80/81/ ILLUMINATED EXULTATE/ DAVID WITH INSTRUMENT 538-6, INITIAL E EXULTATE/ DAVID PLAYS INSTRUMENT IN WILDERNESS 538-6, PSALM 97/98/ ILLUMINATED CANTATE/ MONKS SING 538-7, INITIAL C CANTATE/ MONKS SING BEFORE LECTERN 538-7, ANGELS HARASS AN APE 538-7, PSALM 109/110/ ILLUMINATED DIXIT/ MONKS KNEEL 538-8, INITIAL D DIXIT/ MONKS KNEEL BEFORE CHRIST AND VIRGIN 538-8, CHRIST AND VIRGIN/ MONKS KNEEL BEFORE 538-8, LITANY/ ILLUMINATED KYRIE/ BISHOP KNEELS 538-9, INITIAL K KYRIE/ MITRED BISHOP BEFORE ALTAR 538-9

*$ABSTRACT 539
*LIBRARY BODLEIAN
*SLIDE SET TITLE ANGLO-SAXON CHRONICLE E-TEXT
*NEGATIVE REFERENCE ROLL 228A
*RENTAL FEE $9.10
*COMMENTS THE FIRST ORIGINAL NARRATIVE PROSE IN ANY WESTERN VERNACULAR. IT COVERS THE PERIOD BEGINNING WITH THE INVASION OF BRITAIN BY JULIUS CAESAR DOWN TO THE YEAR 891, AND WAS CONTINUED IN A NUMBER OF MONASTERIES UP TO THE NORMAN CONQUEST. THE LAST VERSION, THE PETERBOROUGH CHRONICLE, WAS MAINTAINED AT PETERBOROUGH UNTIL THE DEATH OF KING STEPHEN IN 1154. THE CONTENTS FIELD CONSISTS OF THE MAIN HISTORICAL EVENTS IN THE TEXT.
*TITLE OF MANUSCRIPT PETERBOROUGH CHRONICLE
*SHELFMARK MS LAUD MISC 636
*PROVENANCE ENGLISH/ PETERBOROUGH
*DATE EXECUTED 12TH/C1121
*LANGUAGE ENGLISH/ OLD ENGLISH AND LATIN
*TYPE OF MANUSCRIPT CHRONICLE IN OLD ENGLISH AND LATIN
*CONTENTS CHRONICLE IN OLD ENGLISH 539/1-182, LITERATURE/ ANGLO-SAXON CHRONICLE 539/1-182, ANGLO-SAXON CHRONICLE E-TEXT 539/1-182, PREFACE 539-1, ANNALS AD 1-26 539-2, CHRIST'S BAPTISM AND CRUCIFIXION AD30-47 539-3, CLAUDIUS INVADES BRITAIN 539-3, MARTYRDOMS OF VARIOUS APOSTLES AD62-87 539-4, APOCALYPSE WRITTEN BY ST JOHN ON PATMOS 539-4, POPE CLEMENT DIES AD100-134 539-5, POPE SIXTUS AND TELESPHORUS DEFINE TEXT OF MASS 539-5, MARCUS ANTONIUS AND AURELIANUS BEGIN TO REIGN AD155-189 539-6, LUCIUS KING OF BRITAIN SENDS MEN TO ROME 539-6, SEVERUS CONQUERS BRITAIN AD189-202 539-7, MARTYRDOM OF ST ALBAN AD254-286 539-8, ST ALBAN MARTYRDOM 539-8, COUNCIL OF NICAEA HELD AD311 539-9, REIGN OF GRATIAN/ COUNCIL OF CONSTANTINOPLE AD379-380 539-10, REIGN OF MAXIMUS/ PALAGIAN HERESY AD380-418 539-11, ROME SACKED BY GOTHS/ ROMANS LEAVE

BRITAIN 539-11, ST PATRICK SENT TO PREACH TO SCOTS AD423-443 539-12, BRITONS SEEK FOREIGN AID AGAINST PICTS 539-12, COUNCIL OF CHALCEDON AD449-455 539-13, SAXONS COME TO BRITAIN/ HENGEST AND HORSA 539-13, BATTLE OF AEGELESTHREP/ HORSA KILLED AD455-477 539-14, HENGEST RULES/ BRITONS FLEE TO LONDON 539-14, AELLE AND CISSA BESIEGE ANDERIDA AD485-507 539-15, PORTSMOUTH/ NETLEY/ CHARFORD AD501-519 539-16, CERDIC AND CYNRIC CAPTURE ISLE OF WIGHT AD527-540 539-17, NORTHUMBRIA/ BAMBURGH/ BARBURY AD544-565 539-18, ETHELBERT OF KENT'S REIGN 539-18, COLUMBA'S MISSION AD565-571 539-19, CUTHWULF CAPTURES BIEDCANFORD/ LENBURY/ ETC 539-19, BATTLE OF DYRHAM AD577-593 539-20, CUTHWINE AND CEAWLIN CAPTURE GLOUCESTER/ BATH/ ETC 539-20, GREGORY MADE POPE 539-20, POPE GREGORY SENDS AUGUSTINE TO BRITAIN AD593-604 539-21, EAST SAXONS RECEIVE CHRISTIANITY 539-21, POPE GREGORY DIES/ BATTLE AT BEANDUNE AD604-616 539-22, DEATHS OF KING ETHELBERT/ ARCHBISHOP LAURENTIUS AD616-625 539-23, KING EDWIN CONVERTED TO CHRISTIANITY AD626-628 539-24, KING CYNEGILS OF WEST SAXONS CONVERTED AD632-639 539-25, KING OSWALD'S DEATH/ CHURCH AT WINCHESTER BUILT AD639-645 539-26, KING PENDA CONVERTED/ PETERBOROUGH BUILT AD648-654 539-27, DEUSDEDIT CONSECRATED TO SEE OF CANTERBURY AD655-656 539-28, KING PENDA KILLED 539-28, PETERBOROUGH ABBEY AD656 539-29, THEODORE MADE ARCHBISHOP OF CANTERBURY AD656-658 539-32, SYNOD OF HERTFORD 539-32, WULFHERE GIVES ISLE OF WIGHT TO ETHELWALD AD660-668 539-33, CHAD AND WILFRID CONSECRATED 539-33, POPE VITALIAN SENDS THEODORE TO BRITAIN 539-33, RECULVER MINSTER AD669-675 539-34, THEODORE CONSECRATES BISHOP OF WINCHESTER 539-34, SYNOD OF HERTFORD 539-34, ETHELDRIDA BUILDS ELY 539-34, PETERBOROUGH CLAIMS TO BE UNDER JURISDICTION OF ROME AD675 539/35-36, KING ETHELRED OF MERCIA RAVAGES KENT AD675-681 539-37, WILFRED DRIVEN FROM HIS SEE 539-37, COLDINGHAM BURNT 539-37, SYNOD OF HEATHFIELD 539-37, ST HILDA DIES 539-37, ST CUTHBERT CONSECRATED BISHOP BY THEODORE AD681-687 539-38, CEADWALLA RAVAGES KENT AND ISLE OF WIGHT 539-38, POPE SERGIUS BAPTIZES CEADWALLA IN ROME AD688-699 539-39, BRIHTWOLD ELECTED ARCHBISHOP 539-39, ETHELRED'S QUEEN KILLED BY SOUTHUMBRIANS 539-39, ETHELRED OF MERCIA BECOME MONK AD702-710 539-40, CENRED SUCCEEDS ETHELRED AS KING 539-40, ALDHELM DIES 539-40, GUTHLAC DIES AD714-22 539-41, MONKS OF IONA ADOPT ROMAN OBSERVANCE OF EASTER 539-41, INE GOES TO ROME/ AETHELBALD REIGNS AD725-736 539-42, BRIHTWOLD DIES/ TATWINE SUCCEEDS HIM 539-42, KING CEOLWULF RECEIVES TONSURE AD736-748 539-43, CUTHBERT CONSECRATED ARCHBISHOP 539-43, YORK BURNED 539-43, BATTLE AT BURFORD/ CANTERBURY BURNED AD750-735 539-44, SIGEBERT DEPRIVED OF WESSEX BY WITAN 539-44, KING CYNEWULF KILLED AT MERTON AD755 539-45, AETHELBALD OF MERCIA KILLED AT SECKINGTON AD755-765 539-46, CUTHBERT'S DEATH 539-47, BATTLE OF OTFORD/ CRUCIFIX IN SKY AD766-777 539-47, OFFA CAPTURES TOWN OF BENSON 539-47, BATTLE OF OLD-SAXONS AND FRANKS AD777-779 539-48, ALCUIN/ SYNOD AT ACLEA/ SYNOD AT CHALK-HYTHE AD779-787 539-49, POPE ADRIAN SENDS MISSION TO ENGLAND 539-49, VIKING INVASION AD787-793 539-50, OFFA ORDERS EXECUTION OF KING ETHELBERT 539-50, LINDISFARNE DESTROYED BY DANES AD793-796 539-51, CENWULF OF MERCIA RAVAGES KENT AD796-802 539-52, POPE LEO III 539-52, CHARLEMAGNE'S DEATH/ ECLIPSES OF SUN AND MOON AD802-815 539-53, SYNOD AT CLOVESHO/ BATTLE OF GALFORD AD819-827 539-54, EGBERT BECOMES BRETWALDA AD827-836 539-55, NORTHUMBRIANS SUBMIT TO EGBERT AT DORE 539-55, BATTLE OF CHARMOUTH AND HINGSTON DOWN 539-55, WULFHEARD OVERCOMES DANES AD836-845 539-56, AETHELHELM KILLED BY DANES AT PORTLAND 539-56, DANES RAVISH LONDON/ KENT/ ROCHESTER/ DORSET 539-56, DANES DEFEATED AT WICGANBEORG AND SANDWICH 539-57, DANES WINTER ON THANET/ OCCUPY LONDON AND CANTERBURY 539-57, ETHELWULF GOES TO ROME/ MARRIES AND DIES AD852-860 539-58, DANES BREAK THE PEACE AD865-868 539-59, KING ALFRED BATTLES DANES AD868-871 539-60, BATTLE OF ASHDOWN 539-60, ST EDMUND'S DEATH 539-60, ETHELRED'S DEATH AD871-872 539-61, ALFRED MADE KING OF WESSEX 539-61, BATTLE OF WILTON 539-61, DANES AT TORKSEY AD872-876 539-62, ALFRED FIGHTS DANES AT SEA 539-62, DANES UNDER HEALFDENE SETTLE IN NORTHUMBRIA AD876-878 539-63, ROLLO OVERRUNS NORMANDY 539-63, ALFRED AT ATHELNEY 539-63,

ALFRED DEFEATS DANES AT CHIPPENHAM AD878-882 539-64, GUTHRUM BAPTIZED 539-64, ALFRED FIGHTS SEA BATTLE AD882-885 539-65, ALFRED SENT RELIC OF CROSS 539-65, CHARLES THE BALD'S DEATH 539-65, DANES AT PARIS/ ALFRED REPAIRS LONDON AD885-887 539-66, GUTHRUM'S DEATH 539-67, PLEGMUND ELECTED ARCHBISHOP OF CANTERBURY 539-67, ALFRED'S DEATH AD892-910 539-68, EDWARD TAKES POSSESSION OF LONDON AD910-928 539-69, WILLIAM REIGNS IN NORMANDY 539-69, BATTLE OF BRUNANBURH AD933-949 539-70, AETHELSTAN'S DEATH 539-70, EDGAR'S REIGN AD952-959 539-71, ETHELWOLD OF WINCHESTER RESTORES MONASTERIES AD959-963 539-72, PETERBOROUGH RESTORED 539-72, PETERBOROUGH'S POSSESSIONS CONFIRMED BY EDGAR 539/73-74, WINCHESTER CANONS REPLACED BY MONKS AD963-975 539-75, EDGAR CONSECRATED KING AT BATH 539-75, EDGAR'S DEATH 539-75, EDWARD'S REIGN/ COMET/ EDWARD MURDERED AD975-979 539-76, EDWIN MADE ABBOT OF ABINGDON AD979-988 539-77, ETHELRED RAVAGES DIOCESE OF ROCHESTER 539-77, DUNSTAN'S DEATH 539-77, ETHELGAR SUCCEEDS DUNSTAN AS ARCHBISHOP AD988-992 539-78, BATTLE OF MALDON 539-78, DANES ATTACK BAMBURGH/ LINSEY/ NORTHUMBRIA AD993-994 539-79, OLAF AND SWEIN ATTACK LONDON 539-79, ETHELRED MEETS OLAF AT ANDOVER AD994-999 539-80, DANES PLUNDER THE WEST COUNTRY 539-80, DANES RAVAGE KENT AND DEFEAT ENGLISH AD999-1001 539-81, MASSACRE OF ST BRICE'S DAY AD1001-1003 539-82, DANES DESTROY EXETER AND PLUNDER WEST COUNTRY 539-82, DANES DESTROY NORWICH AD1003-1005 539-83, FAMINE THROUGHOUT ENGLAND AD1005-1006 539-84, DANES ATTACK READING/ WALLINGFORD IN WINTER 539-84, ENGLISH PAY TRIBUTE TO DANES AD1006-1009 539-85, SHIPS BUILT IN PREPARATION FOR DANISH INVASION 539-85, DANES LED BY THORKEL LAND AT SANDWICH 539-86, DANES RAID AS FAR AS OXFORD AD1009-1010 539-87, ATHELSTAN KILLED NEAR CAMBRIDGE 539-87, DANISH RAIDS AD1010-1011 539-88, DANES CAPTURE CANTERBURY AD1011-1012 539-89, ST ALPHEGE'S MARTYRDOM AD1012-1013 539-90, OXFORD AND WINCHESTER GIVE SWEIN HOSTAGES AD1013 539-91, ETHELRED GOES INTO EXILE/ SWEIN REGARDED KING AD1013 539-92, CANUTE RAVAGES WESSEX/ GREAT MOOT AT OXFORD AD1015 539-93, EADRIC BETRAYS KING AND JOINS CANUTE AD1015 539-94, ETHELRED'S DEATH AD1016 539-95, BATTLE OF ASHINGDON AD1016 539-96, CANUTE BECOMES KING OF ENGLAND AD1016 539-97, DANES PAID TRIBUTE AD1018 539-98, CANUTE CONQUERS OLAF OF NORWAY AD1024-1033 539-99, CANUTE'S DEATH AD1034-1038 539-100, HAROLD BECOMES KING 539-100, HAROLD DIES AT OXFORD AD1039-1041 539-101, EDWARD BECOMES KING AD1042 539-102, BATTLE OF VAL-ES-DUNES AD1044-1046 539-103, EDWARD MAKES PEACE WITH SWEIN AD1046 539-104, ROBERT OF JUMIEGES RECEIVES PALLIUM AD1046-1048 539-105, POPE REFUSES TO CONSECRATE BISHOP OF LONDON AD1048 539-106, WELSH RAVAGE IN HERFORDSHIRE/ SWEIN OUTLAWED AD1048 539-107, SWEIN AND GODWINE SEEK BALDWIN'S PROTECTION AD1048 539-108, GODWINE ATTACKS ISLE OF WIGHT AD1052 539-109, EDWARD MAKES PEACE WITH GODWINE AD1052 539-110, GODWINE DIES/ TOSTY MADE EARL AD1052-1056 539-111, LISTS OF SUCCESSIONS OF VARIOUS BISHOPS AD1057-1061 539-112, HAROLD AND TOSTY SUBDUE WALES AD1062-1065 539-113, WESTMINSTER CONSECRATED AD1065-1066 539-114, KING EDWARD DIES/ HAROLD SUCCEEDS 539-114, BATTLE OF STAMFORD BRIDGE 539-114, HAROLD KILLED AT HASTINGS/ WILLIAM MADE KING 539-114, WILLIAM RETURNS TO ENGLAND AD1066-1069 539-115, WILLIAM SACKS YORK AND SUBDUES REVOLT 539-115, SWEIN'S SONS RAID YORK AD1068-1070 539-116, PETERBOROUGH RAVAGED BY HEREWARD 539-116, RAID ON PETERBOROUGH/ DANES ATTACK ELY 539-117, WILLIAM AND SWEIN MAKE PEACE AD1070-1071 539-118, EDWIN MURDERED/ WILLIAM ATTACKS ELY AD1071-1073 539-119, WILLIAM INVADES SCOTLAND/ KING MALCOLM MAKES PEACE 539-119, WILLIAM GOES TO NORMANDY AD1073-1075 539-120, CANUTE ATTACKS YORK AD1075-1079 539-121, LONDON BURNS IN GREAT FIRE 539-121, MALCOLM INVADES ENGLAND/ WILLIAM INVADES WALES AD1079-1083 539-122, GLASTONBURY MONKS KILLED/ MATILDA DIES AD1083-1085 539-123, WILLIAM BILLETS HIS ARMY AD1085 539-124, DOOMSDAY BOOK IS COMPILED 539-124, EDGAR LEAVES WILLIAM'S COURT AD1085-86 539-125, SICKNESS AND FAMINE IN ENGLAND AD1086 539-126, WILLIAM MAKES WAR ON PHILIP OF FRANCE AD1086 539-127, WILLIAM DIES OF A FEVER 539-127, WORKS DONE BY WILLIAM THE CONQUEROR AD1086 539-128, WILLIAM'S REIGN AND HIS DEEDS AD1086 539-129, CANUTE MURDERED BY HIS SUBJECTS AD1086 539-130,

WILLIAM II CROWNED AD1086-1087 539-131, WULSTAN ROUTS REBELS AT WORCESTER AD1087 539-132, ROBERT EARL OF NORMANDY INVADES ENGLAND AD1087 539-133, LANFRANC DIES AD1089-1091 539-134, WILLIAM AND ROBERT OF NORMANDY MAKE PEACE AD1091 539-135, WILLIAM'S ILLNESS AND PROMISES HE MADE AD1091-1093 539-136, MALCOLM AND SON EDWARD KILLED BY ROBERT AD1093 539-137, WILLIAM CHARGED WITH PURJURY/ BATTLES IN NORMANDY AD1093 539-138, WELSH ATTACK FRENCH IN WALES/ SCOTS KILL DUNCAN AD1094 539-139, WILLIAM FIGHTS ROBERT OF NORMANDY AD1095 539-140, WILLIAM DEFEATS ROBERT OF NORTHUMBERLAND AD1095 539-141, FIRST CRUSADE/ WILLIAM EXECUTES REBELS AD1095-96 539-142, HARD WINTER IN ENGLAND/ HEAVY TAXES AD1096-97 539-143, MALCOLM'S SON WINS SCOTTISH THRONE AD1097-98 539-144, WILLIAM SHOT BY OWN MAN WHILE HUNTING AD1098-1100 539-145, HENRY ELECTED KING/ MARRIES MAUD AD1100 539-146, CRUSADERS RETURN FROM JERUSALEM AD1100-1101 539-147, PEACE BETWEEN ROBERT AND HENRY AD1101-1102 539-148, POOR CROPS AND DISEASE OF CATTLE AD1102-04 539-149, HENRY CAPTURES CAEN AND BAYEUX AD1104-05 539-150, HENRY REFUSES TO RETURN LANDS AD1105-06 539-151, HENRY CAPTURES ROBERT OF NORMANDY AD1106-07 539-152, EDGAR OF SCOTLAND DIES/ PHILIP OF FRANCE DIES AD1107-1110 539-153, HENRY'S DAUGHTER MARRIES AD1110-1111 539-154, ROBERT OF FLANDERS DIES AD1111-1114 539-155, ERNULF BECOMES BISHOP OF ROCHESTER AD1114-15 539-156, CAMPAIGN IN NORMANDY AD1115-17 539-157, DISASTERS AND BAD WEATHER AD1117-18 539-158, HENRY'S SON MARRIES DAUGHTER OF COUNT OF ANJOU AD1118-19 539-159, PEACE MADE WITH FRANCE AD1119-21 539-160, HENRY MARRIES DAUGHTER OF DUKE OF LOUVAIN 539-160, FIRE AT GLOUCESTER/ STRANGE PORTENTS AD1121-22 539-161, DEATH OF BISHOP OF LINCOLN AD1122-23 539-162, WILLIAM OF CURBOIL ELECTED ARCHBISHOP OF CANTERBURY AD1123 539-163, ARCHBISHOPS GO TO ROME AD1123 539-164, HENRY GOES TO NORMANDY/ FIRE AT LINCOLN AD1123-24 539-165, POOR HARVEST/ DEBASED COINAGE AD1124 539-166, HONORIUS SUCCEEDS CALIXTUS AS POPE AD1124-25 539-167, JOHN OF CREMA SURVEYS ENGLISH CHURCH AD1125-26 539-168, DAVID OF SCOTLAND AT ENGLISH COURT AD1126-27 539-169, ABBACY OF PETERBOROUGH GIVEN TO HENRY OF POITOU AD1127 539-170, HENRY OF POITOU LIVES AT PETERBOROUGH AD1127 539-171, HUGH OF TEMPLE COLLECTS MONEY FOR CRUSADE AD1127-28 539-172, FRENCH CHRONICLE OF ENGLAND IN MARGINS 539-172, HENRY DOES NOT OBJECT TO CLERGY KEEPING WIVES AD1129 539-173, POPE HONORIUS DIES/ SPLIT IN CHURCH AD1129-30 539-174, ABBOT HENRY DRIVEN OUT OF PETERBOROUGH AD1131 539-175, HENRY DIES/ ECLIPSE OF SUN AD1131-35 539-176, STEPHEN BECOMES KING AD1135-37 539-177, TORTURES USED TO LEVY TAXES AD1137 539-178, NEW MONASTERY AT PETERBOROUGH AD1137-38 539-179, DAVID OF SCOTLAND INVADES ENGLAND 539-179, SIEGES AND INTRIGUES AD1140 539-180, ENGLAND MUCH DIVIDED AD1140 539-181, STEPHEN DIES/ HENRY II CONSECRATED AD1140 539-182

*$ABSTRACT 540
*LIBRARY BODLEIAN
*SLIDE SET TITLE BOOK OF HOURS
*NEGATIVE REFERENCE ROLL 228B
*RENTAL FEE $4.10
*COMMENTS BORDERS CONTAIN REALISTIC FLOWERS
*TITLE OF MANUSCRIPT BOOK OF HOURS
*SHELFMARK MS DOUCE 311/ FOL 1V 540-1, MS DOUCE 311/ FOL 8V 540-2, MS DOUCE 311/ FOL 14 540-3, MS DOUCE 311/ FOL 14V 540-4, MS DOUCE 311/ FOL 16V 540-5, MS DOUCE 311/ FOL 21V 540-6, MS DOUCE 311/ FOL 25V 540-7, MS DOUCE 311/ FOL 29V 540-8, MS DOUCE 311/ FOL 30 540-9, MS DOUCE 311/ FOL 39 540-10, MS DOUCE 311/ FOL 44 540-11, MS DOUCE 311/ FOL 46V 540-12, MS DOUCE 311/ FOL 55V 540-13, MS DOUCE 311/ FOL 56V 540-14, MS DOUCE 311/ FOL 57 540-15, MS DOUCE 311/ FOL 58 540-16, MS DOUCE 311/ FOL 59V 540-17, MS DOUCE 311/ FOL 73V 540-18, MS DOUCE 311/ FOL 87V 540-19, MS DOUCE 311/ FOL 91 540-20, MS DOUCE 311/ FOL 95V 540-21, MS DOUCE 311/ FOL 98 540-22, MS DOUCE 311/ FOL 99V 540-23, MS DOUCE 311/ FOL 100 540-24, MS DOUCE 311/ FOL 101 540-25, MS DOUCE 311/ FOL 101V

540-26, MS DOUCE 311/ FOL 102V 540-27, MS DOUCE 311/ FOL 112V
540-28, MS DOUCE 311/ FOL 113 540-29, MS DOUCE 311/ FOL 113V
540-30, MS DOUCE 311/ FOL 114 540-31, MS DOUCE 311/ FOL 114V
540-32, MS DOUCE 311/ FOL 115 540-33, MS DOUCE 311/ FOL 115V
540-34, MS DOUCE 311/ FOL 116V 540-35, MS DOUCE 311/ FOL 118
540-36, MS DOUCE 311/ FOL 118V 540-37, MS DOUCE 311/ FOL 119
540-38, MS DOUCE 311/ FOL 119V 540-39, MS DOUCE 311/ FOL 122
540-40, MS DOUCE 311/ FOL 125V 540-41, MS DOUCE 311/ FOL 126
540-42
*PROVENANCE FLEMISH
*DATE EXECUTED 15TH/ AFTER 1488
*LANGUAGE LATIN
*ARTIST/ SCHOOL MASTER OF THE PRAYER BOOK OF MAXIMILIAN
*TYPE OF MANUSCRIPT BOOK OF HOURS/ USE OF ROME
*CONTENTS BOOK OF HOURS/ FLEMISH/ 15TH 540/1-42DIAGRAM OF DOMINATION OF SEASONS OVER MAN 540-1, FIVE SENSES 540-1, TRINITY 540-2, GOD IN MAJESTY 540-3, CHRIST/ PRAYER TO SON 540-4, DOVE/ PRAYER TO HOLY SPIRIT 540-4, LAZARUS RAISED 540-5, PENTECOST/ VIRGIN AND APOSTLES IN CHAPEL 540-6, ALL SAINTS/ SAINTS ADORE TRINITY 540-7, LAST SUPPER/ CHRIST GIVES SOP TO JUDAS 540-8, CHILDREN OF ISRAEL GATHER MANNA 540-9, MAYING SCENE WITH YOUNG PEOPLE IN BARGES 540-9, CHRIST BETRAYED 540-10, CRUCIFIXION/ DEVOTION OF SEVEN WORDS 540-11, VIRGIN AND CHILD WITH ANGELS 540-12, ST JOHN WITH EAGLE 540-13, ST LUKE WITH OX 540-14, ST MATTHEW WITH ANGEL 540-15, ST MARK WITH LION 540-16, ANNUNCIATION 540-17, NATIVITY/ TWO SHEPHERDS AND OX AND ASS 540-18, DORMITION OF VIRGIN 540-19, ENTRY INTO JERUSALEM 540-20, VIRGIN AND CHILD 540-21, CHILDREN WITH WHIP TOPS 540-22, VIRGIN AND CHILD 540-23, ST ANNE WITH VIRGIN AND CHILD 540-24, INITIAL O WITH INSTRUMENTS OF PASSION 540-25, PASSION INSTRUMENTS 540-25, CRUCIFIXION/ WORDS HELI HELI LAMA SABAT 540-26, DAVID PRAYS TO GOD WHO HOLDS THREE ARROWS 540-27, ST MICHAEL AS ARCHANGEL 540-28, ST JOHN THE BAPTIST HOLDS AGNUS DEI 540-29, ST JOHN THE EVANGELIST 540-29, ST PETER AND ST PAUL 540-30, ST JAMES DRESSED AS PILGRIM 540-31, ST STEPHEN BEING STONED 540-31, ST NICHOLAS 540-32, ST CLAUDE 540-32, ST ANTHONY WITH CRUTCH AND PIG 540-33, ST ANDREW 540-34, ST CHRISTOPHER CARRIES CHRIST CHILD 540-34, ST SEBASTIAN PIERCED WITH SIX ARROWS 540-35, MARY MAGDALENE WITH OINTMENT POT 540-36, ST MARTHA HOLDS LADLE 540-36, ST CATHERINE HOLDS BROKEN WHEEL 540-37, ST BARBARA MARTYRED 540-38, ST APPOLLONIA HOLDS TOOTH IN PINCERS 540-39, CHRIST HOLDS ORB AND BLESSES 540-40, REQUIEM MASS/ MOURNERS NEXT TO COFFIN 540-41, VIGIL OF THE DEAD/ SKULL AND CROSS-BONES 540-42

*$ABSTRACT 541
*LIBRARY BODLEIAN
*SLIDE SET TITLE CAEDMON GENESIS
*NEGATIVE REFERENCE ROLL 228F
*RENTAL FEE $2.50
*COMMENTS REPHOTOGRAPHED FROM PRINTS TAKEN UNDER ULTRA-VIOLET LIGHT TO REVEAL HARD-POINT PRELIMINARY SKETCHES OF UNCERTAIN DATES. EACH ULTRA-VIOLET PHOTOGRAPH IS FOLLOWED BY A PHOTOGRAPH OF THE FOLIO WITHOUT ULTRA-VIOLET LIGHT.
*TITLE OF MANUSCRIPT CAEDMON GENESIS
*SHELFMARK MS JUNIUS 11/ PAGE 12 541/1-2, MS JUNIUS 11/ PAGE 55 541/3-4, MS JUNIUS 11/ PAGE 54 541/5-6, MS JUNIUS 11/ PAGE 70 541/7-8, MS JUNIUS 11/ PAGE 99 541/9-10
*PROVENANCE ENGLISH/ WINCHESTER OR CANTERBURY
*DATE EXECUTED 11TH/C1000
*LANGUAGE ENGLISH/ OLD ENGLISH
*ARTIST/ SCHOOL WINCHESTER OR CANTERBURY
*TYPE OF MANUSCRIPT LITERATURE/ ANGLO-SAXON
*CONTENTS LITERATURE/ CAEDMON GENESIS 541/1-10, CAEDMON GENESIS/ FIVE NEW DRAWINGS 541/1-10, GENESIS/ PARAPHRASE IN OLD ENGLISH 541/1-10, ST MICHAEL?/ MAN WITH SHIELD 541-1, ST MICHAEL?/ ONLY TEXT VISIBLE 541-2, JUBAL AND THE HARP/ FRAGMENT 541-3, JUBAL AND THE HARP/ ONLY TEXT VISIBLE 541-4, JUBAL AND TUBAL CAIN/ HARD-POINT UNDERDRAWING VISIBLE 541-5, JUBAL AND TUBAL CAIN 541-6, NOAH'S ARK/ ABOVE AND BELOW 541-7,

NOAH'S ARK/ ONLY TEXT VISIBLE 541-8, BIRD'S PARTIALLY-COMPLETED HEAD AND BODY 541-9, BIRD/ ONLY TEXT VISIBLE 541-10

*$ABSTRACT 542
*LIBRARY BODLEIAN
*SLIDE SET TITLE ASHMOLE'S DIARY
*NEGATIVE REFERENCE ROLL 228G
*RENTAL FEE $2.85
*COMMENTS EXTRACTS OF AUTOBIOGRAPHICAL NOTES OF THE MAJOR EVENTS IN THE LIFE OF ELIAS ASHMOLE, 1617-1692.
*TITLE OF MANUSCRIPT ASHMOLE'S DIARY
*SHELFMARK MS ASHMOLE 1136
*PROVENANCE ENGLISH
*DATE EXECUTED 17TH/1617-1692
*AUTHOR ASHMOLE/ ELIAS
*TYPE OF MANUSCRIPT DIARY
*CONTENTS DIARY OF ELIAS ASHMOLE 542/1-17, ASHMOLE'S DIARY 542/1-17, I WAS THE SON OF SIMON ASHMOLE 542-1, I WAS BAPTISED THE 2ND OF JUNE 542-2, I CAME TO ASK TO MARRY MR MAINWARING'S DAUGHTER 542-3, I CAME TO LONDON 542-4, MY WIFE BROUGHT TO BED OF A FEMALE CHILD 542-5,I HEARD OF MY WIFE'S DEATH 542-6, KING WAS BEHEADED 542-7, I MARRIED LADY MAINWARING 542-8, VISITATIONS OF STAFFORDSHIRE AND DERBYSHIRE 542-9, I MARRIED MRS ELIZA DUGDALE 542-10, I FIRST CAME TO MR DUGDALES AT BLYTH HALL 542-11, THE DREADFULL FIRE OF LONDON BEGAN 542-12, DOCTOR WILKINS AND MR WRENN VISIT ME 542-13, I HAD THE HONOUR TO DISCOURSE WITH THE KING 542-14, SIR ROBERT MURREY DIED 542-15, MY STRENGTH WAS RESTORED TO ME 542-16, DOCTOR PLOT PRESENTED ME WITH HIS BOOK 542-17

$ABSTRACT 543
*LIBRARY BODLEIAN
*SLIDE SET TITLE GREEK MS
*NEGATIVE REFERENCE ROLL 228H
*RENTAL FEE $2.60
*COMMENTS DRAWINGS ARE IN BROWN INK WITH RED, GREEN, AND ORANGE WASH.
*TITLE OF MANUSCRIPT WISDOM OF SOLOMON 543-1, PROLOGUE TO ECCLESIASTICUS 543-2, ECCLESIASTICUS 543/3-5, SEVEN GREEK PROPHETS 543/6-10, INSTITUTIO CATHOLICA 543-11, INSTITUTIO CATHOLICA/ BOOK FOUR 543-12
*SHELFMARK MS AUCT T 2 4/ FOL 9V 543-1, MS AUCT T 2 4/ FOL 17 543-2, MS AUCT T 2 4/ FOL 18 543-3, MS AUCT T 2 4/ FOL 31 543-4, MS AUCT T 2 4/ FOL 37 543-5, MS AUCT T 2 4/ FOL 58V 543-6, MS AUCT T 2 4/ FOL 71V 543-7, MS AUCT T 2 4/ FOL 78 543-8, MS AUCT T 2 4/ FOL 81V 543-9, MS AUCT T 2 4/ FOL 83V 543-10, MS AUCT T 2 4/ FOL 91 543-11, MS AUCT T 2 4/ FOL 147V 543-12
*PROVENANCE ITALIAN/ SOUTH?
*DATE EXECUTED 10TH
*LANGUAGE GREEK
*TYPE OF MANUSCRIPT APOCRYPHA AND LIVES OF PROPHETS
*CONTENTS SOLOMON IN MEDALLION 543-1, ANIMALS/ BIRDS/ INTERLACE 543-1, SOLOMON IN MEDALLION 543-2, INITIAL FORMED BY SPIRAL PILLARS 543-2, INITIAL COMPOSED OF BEARDED MEN IN TALL HATS 543-3, INTERLACE BAND TERMINATING IN TWO FISH 543-3, SOLOMON IN MEDALLION 543-4, INITIALS COMPOSED OF BIRDS AND SPIRAL PILLARS 543-5, ORNAMENTAL MEDALLION/ BUST OF PROPHET 543-6, INITIALS/ ZOOMORPHIC 543-6, INITIALS/ ZOOMORPHIC 543-7, GROTESQUE BIRD AND BIRD PREYING ON ANIMAL 543-7, INITIALS/ DECORATED WITH FOX CHASING HARES 543-8, INITIALS/ BIRD AND ANIMAL 543-9, INITIALS/ DECORATIVE 543-10, ORNAMENTAL MEDALLION WITH TWO LIONS 543-11, INTERLACE BRAID WITH PIG HEADS 543-12

*$ABSTRACT 544
*LIBRARY BODLEIAN
*SLIDE SET TITLE DOUCE PLINY I
*NEGATIVE REFERENCE ROLL 228I
*RENTAL FEE $3.45
*COMMENTS PRINTED BY NICHOLAS JENSON. FLORENTINE MINIATURES, HISTORIATED BORDERS, AND INITIALS.
*TITLE OF MANUSCRIPT NATURAL HISTORY
*SHELFMARK PR DOUCE 310
*PROVENANCE ITALIAN/ FLORENCE
*DATE EXECUTED 15TH/1476
*LANGUAGE LATIN
*ARTIST/ SCHOOL GHERARDO AND MONTE DI GIOVANNI DI MINIATO
*AUTHOR PLINY
*TYPE OF MANUSCRIPT NATURAL HISTORY
*CONTENTS PLINY'S NATURAL HISTORY 544/1-29, BINDING/ FRONT COVER 544-1, BINDING/ BACK COVER 544-2, BINDING/ NIELLO BOSS WITH EAGLE INSIGNIA 544-3, BINDING/ NIELLO BOSS WITH LAMB AND MOTTO 544-4, BINDING/ NIELLO BOSS WITH LAMB AND MOTTO 544-5, BINDING/ NIELLO BOSS WITH EAGLE INSIGNIA 544-6, INITIAL D WITH PLINY IN HIS STUDY 544-7, PLINY IN HIS STUDY 544-7, PREFACE, ELABORATE BORDERS 544-8, INITIAL S WITH BIRDS 544-9, BORDER WITH COATS OF ARMS/ FLOWERS/ OWL 544-9,UPPER BORDER WITH PUTTI/ COAT OF ARMS/ LAMB 544-10, CHRISTOFORO LANDINO PORTRAIT 544-11, DUOMO OF FLORENCE 544-11, MAN BOUND TO TREE/ CHILD CLINGING TO FIGURE 544-12, UPPER BORDER WITH PUTTI/ LION, FOUNTAIN/ GEMSTONE 544-13, UPPER BORDER/ FOUR PUTTI AROUND FOUNTAIN 544-14, RIGHT BORDER WITH PUTTI/ CHARIOT DRAWN BY VICTORIES 544-15, RIGHT BORDER WITH PUTTI 544-16, LOWER BORDER/ MEDALLION PORTRAIT 544-17, FILIPPO STROZZI AND SON 544-17, LOWER BORDER WITH EAGLE BITING ITS WING 544-18, COAT OF ARMS OF STROZZI 544-18, LOWER BORDER/ PORTRAIT OF KING FERDINAND II OF NAPLES 544-19, KING FERDINAND II OF NAPLES 544-19, LEFT BORDER/ AESCULAPIUS 544-20, AESCULAPIUS HOLDS STAFF ENTWINED WITH SERPENT 544-20, KING FERDINAND II PORTRAIT 544-21, KING FERDINAND II PORTRAIT 544-22, COAT OF ARMS WITH THREE FLAMING BALLS 544-23, COAT OF ARMS/ THREE CRESCENTS, STROZZI 544-24,KING FERDINAND II PORTRAITS 544/25-26, FIGURE WEARING LAUREL WREATH 544-27, COAT OF ARMS WITH THREE FLAMING BALLS 544-28, MEDALLION WITH LAMB AND BLANK SCROLL 544-29

*$ABSTRACT 545
*LIBRARY BODLEIAN
*SLIDE SET TITLE DOUCE PLINY II
*NEGATIVE REFERENCE ROLL 228J
*RENTAL FEE $3.85
*COMMENTS PRINTED BY NICHOLAS JENSON, VENICE, 1476. FLORENTINE HISTORIATED INITIALS FROM THE BEGINNING OF EACH BOOK.
*TITLE OF MANUSCRIPT NATURAL HISTORY
*SHELFMARK PR DOUCE 310
*PROVENANCE ITALIAN/ FLORENCE
*DATE EXECUTED 15TH/1476
*LANGUAGE LATIN
*ARTIST/ SCHOOL GHERARDO AND MONTE DI GIOVANNI DI MINIATO
*AUTHOR PLINY
*TYPE OF MANUSCRIPT NATURAL HISTORY
*CONTENTS PLINY'S NATURAL HISTORY 545/1-37, PLINY SEATED IN HIS STUDY 545-1, EARTH/ SUN/ MOON/ STARS 545-2, MAP OF THE MEDITERRANEAN 545-3, MAP OF SPAIN 545-4, MAP OF AFRICA 545-5, MAP OF THE BLACK SEA 545-6, CHILDBIRTH/ LADY LIES IN BED, OTHERS WITH INFANTS 545-7, ELEPHANT WITH THREE-TOED FEET 545-8, SEA OF FISHES/ MOUNTAINS IN BACKGROUND 545-9, BIRDS, PEACOCK/ OSTRICH/ SWANS/ LAPWING 545-10, BEES AND BEEHIVE 545-11, TREES 545-12, PALM TREE 545-13, GRAPE ARBOUR 545-14, ORCHARD/ MAN KNOCKS DOWN FRUIT WITH STICK 545-15, FRUIT TREE 545-16, MEN PLANT STOCKS WHICH PUT FORTH NEW SHOOTS 545-17, SOWER SPREADS SEEDS FROM BASKET 545-18, GARDEN/ FORMAL 545-19, GARDEN 545-20, MAIDEN MAKES GARLANDS IN MEADOW 545-21, FIELD WITH TREES AND MOUNTAINS IN BACKGROUND 545-22, DOCTOR HOLDS MEDICINAL PLANT 545-23, DOCTOR HOLDS MEDICINAL PLANT 545-24

DOCTOR STANDS IN LANDSCAPE 545-25, DOCTOR STANDS BEFORE WINDOW 545-26, FIELD WITH TREES AND CITY IN BACKGROUND 545-27, DOCTOR AT DESK WITH OPEN BOOKS 545-28, DOCTOR FEELS HIS PULSE 545-29, MAGICIAN STANDS BEFORE DOORWAY 545-30, DOCTOR HOLDS FISH 545-31, DOCTOR HOLDS TURTLE 545-32, MEN SIT BEFORE TABLE WITH GOLD/ SILVER/ JEWELS 545-33, MAN MAKES BRASS POTS BEFORE FIREPLACE 545-34, ARTIST PAINTS PORTRAIT 545-35, SCULPTOR CHISELS CAPITAL FROM MARBLE 545-36, INITIAL FILLED WITH GEMSTONES AND PEARLS 545-37

*$ABSTRACT 546
*LIBRARY BODLEIAN
*SLIDE SET TITLE EUROPEAN CULTURE
*NEGATIVE REFERENCE ROLL 229A
*RENTAL FEE $3.85
*TITLE OF MANUSCRIPT NOTITIA DIGNITATUM 546-1, BIBLE 546-2, GOLDEN LEGEND 546-3, LAUDIAN ACTS 546-4, DE CONSOLATIONE PHILOSOPHIAE 546-5, JUSTINIAN PANEL 546-6, THEODORA PANEL 546-7, SOUTH ENGLISH LEGENDARY 546-8, RULE OF ST BENEDICT 546-9, SOUTH ENGLISH LEGENDARY 546-10, HISTORIA ECCLESIASTICA 546-11, SOUTH ENGLISH LEGENDARY 546-12, GOSPELS OF ST AUGUSTINE 546-13, LIFE OF ST CUTHBERT 546-14, MACREGOL GOSPELS 546-15, LIFE OF ST CUTHBERT 546-16, GRANDES CHRONIQUES DE FRANCE 546-17, CHRISTUS SUPER ASPIDEM BOOK COVER 546-18, LIFE OF ST CUTHBERT 546/19-20, ST DUNSTAN'S CLASSBOOK 546-21, CAEDMON GENESIS 546-22, ST MARGARET'S GOSPELS 546-23, LITTLEMORE ANSELM 546-24, ON THE SONG OF SONGS 546-25, ST JEROME'S COMMENTARY ON ISAIAH 546-26, TREATISE ON IMPERIAL HERALDRY 546-28, HISTORIA MAJOR/ VOL I 546/29-30, RELIGIOUS ORDERS 546-31, LEGENDARY OF DOMINICAN NUNS OF THE HOLY CROSS 546-32, HISTORIA MAJOR/ VOL II 546-33, WORKS BY ROBERT GROSSETESTE 546-34, SUMMA/ BOOK I 546-35, ON THE RETARDATION OF OLD AGE 546-36, DIVINE COMEDY 546-37
*SHELFMARK MS CANON MISC 378/ FOL 2 546-1, MS CANON BIBL LAT 56/ FOL 3 546-2, MS QUEEN'S COLLEGE OXFORD 305/ FOL 126 546-3, MS LAUD GREEK 35/ FOL 77V-78 546-4, MS AUCT F 6 5/ FOL 1V 546-5, MS TANNER 17/ FOL 43V 546-8, MS HATTON 48/ FOL 24V-25 546-9, MS TANNER 17/ FOL 29 546-10, MS TANNER 10/ FOL 57V-58 546-11, MS TANNER 17/ FOL 111 546-12, MS CORPUS CHRISTI COLLEGE CAMBRIDGE 286 / FOL 125 546-13, MS UNIVERSITY COLLEGE 165/ PAGE II 546-14, MS AUCT D 2 19/ FOL 1 546-15, MS UNIVERSITY COLLEGE 165/ PAGE 50 546-16, MS DOUCE 217/ FOL 77V 546-17 546-17, MS DOUCE 176/ IVORY BOOK COVER 546-18, MS UNIVERSITY COLLEGE 165/ PAGE 135 546-19, MS CORPUS CHRISTI COLLEGE CAMBRIDGE 183/ FOL 1V 546-20, MS AUCT F 4 32/ FOL 1 546-21, MS JUNIUS 11/ PAGE 66 546-22, MS LAT LITURG F 5/ FOL 4 546-23, MS AUCT D 2 6/ FOL 156 546-24, MS CANON PAT LAT 156/ FOL 1 546-25, MS BODLEY 717/ FOL 287V 546-26, MS LINCOLN COLLEGE GREEK 35/ FOL 1V 546-27, MS DOUCE 278/ FOL 72V 546-28, MS CORPUS CHRISTI COLLEGE CAMBRIDGE 26/ FOL IIIV-IV 546-29, MS CORPUS CHRISTI COLLEGE CAMBRIDGE 26/ FOL 279 546-30, MS BODLEY 39/ FOL 117 546-31, MS KEBLE COLLEGE 49/ FOL 130 546-32, MS CORPUS CHRISTI COLLEGE CAMBRIDGE 16/ FOL 66 546-33, MS MERTON COLLEGE H 3 10/ FOL 1 546-34, MS MERTON COLLEGE I 12/ FOL 1 546-35, MS BODLEY 211/ FOL 5 546-36, MS CANON ITAL 108/ FOL 4 546-37
*PROVENANCE ITALIAN/ PADUA 546-1, ITALIAN/ CREMONA 546-2, FRENCH 546-3, SARDINIA 546-4, ENGLISH/ WINCHESTER OR HEREFORD 546-5, ITALIAN/ SAN VITALE RAVENNA 546/6-7, ENGLISH 546-8, ENGLISH 546-9, ENGLISH 546-10, ENGLISH 546-11, ENGLISH 546-12, ITALIAN 546-13, ENGLISH/ DURHAM? 546-14, IRISH/ BIRR 546-15, ENGLISH/ DURHAM? 546-16, FRENCH 546-17, FRENCH/ CHELLES 546-18, ENGLISH/ DURHAM? 546-19, ENGLISH/ WINCHESTER? 546-20, ENGLISH/ GLASTONBURY? 546-21, ENGLISH/ WINCHESTER OR CANTERBURY 546-22, ENGLISH 546-23, ENGLISH/ OXFORD REGION? 546-24, ITALIAN/ FLORENCE 546-25, FRENCH/ NORMANDY 546-26, CONSTANTINOPLE 546-27, FRENCH 546-28, ENGLISH 546-29, ENGLISH 546-30, ENGLISH/ NORTH 546-31, GERMANY/ REGENSBURG 546-32, ENGLISH 546-33, ENGLISH? 546-34, ENGLISH 546-35, ITALIAN 546-36, ITALIAN 546-37

*DATE EXECUTED 15TH/1436 546-1, 13TH/1265 546-2, 15TH 546-3, 06TH 546-4, 12TH/ MID 546-5, 06TH/ 2ND QUARTER 546-6, 06TH/ END QUARTER 546-7, 15TH 546-8, 08TH/C700 546-9, 15TH 546-10, 10TH 546-11, 15TH 546-12, 06TH/ LATE 546-13, 12TH/C1150 546-14, 09TH/C800 546-15, 12TH/C1150 546-16, 09TH/800 546-17, 09TH/C800 546-18, 12TH/C1150 546-19, 10TH/C930 546-20, 10TH/ MID 546-21, 11TH/C1000 546-22, 11TH 546-23, 12TH/C1150 546-24, 15TH/ EARLY 546-25, 11TH/ LATE 546-26, 14TH/ AFTER 1310 546-27, 15TH/ 2ND QUARTER 546-28, 13TH/ BEFORE 1253 546/29-30, 13TH 546-31, 13TH/ AFTER 1271 546-32, 13TH/ BEFORE 1253 546-33, 14TH/ 2ND HALF 546-34, 13TH-14TH 546-35, 15TH 546-36, 14TH 546-37

*LANGUAGE LATIN 546-1, LATIN 546-2 LATIN 546-3, GREEK AND LATIN 546-4, LATIN 546-5, ENGLISH 546-8, LATIN 546-9, ENGLISH 546-10, ENGLISH/ OLD ENGLISH 546-11, ENGLISH 546-12, LATIN 546-13, LATIN 546-14, LATIN 546-15, LATIN 546-16, FRENCH 546-17, LATIN 546-19, LATIN 546-20, LATIN 546-21, ENGLISH/ OLD ENGLISH 546-22, LATIN 546-23, LATIN 546-24, LATIN 546-25, LATIN 546-26, GREEK 546-27, FRENCH 546-28, LATIN 546-29, LATIN 546-30, LATIN 546-31, LATIN 546-32, LATIN 546-33, LATIN 546-34, LATIN 546-35, LATIN 546-36, ITALIAN 546-37

*ARTIST/ SCHOOL PERONET LAMY 546-1, MACREGOL 546-15, ADA SCHOOL 546-18, ST DUNSTAN 546-21, SCHOOL OF THE CONVENT OF S MARIA DEGLI ANGELI 546-25, HUGO PICTOR 546-26, PARIS/ MATTHEW 546/29-30 AND 33

*AUTHOR ST JEROME 546-2, BOETHIUS 546-5, GREGORY 546-10, BEDE 546-11, AUGUSTINE OF CANTERBURY 546-12, AUGUSTINE OF HIPPO 546-13, BEDE 546-14, MACREGOL 546-15, BEDE 546-16 AND 19 AND 20, BERNARD 546-25, JEROME 546-26, ROBERT GROSSETESTE 546-34, AQUINAS/ THOMAS 546-35, PSEUDO-ROGER BACON 546-36, DANTE 546-37

*TYPE OF MANUSCRIPT MILITARY TREATISE 546-1, BIBLE 546-2, GOLDEN LEGEND 546-3, ACTS 546-4, PHILOSOPHY 546-5, PANEL 546/6-7, SAINT'S LIFE 546-8, RULE 546-9, SAINT'S LIFE 546-10, LETTER 546-11, SAINT'S LIFE 546-12, GOSPELS 546-13, SAINT'S LIFE 546-14, GOSPELS 546-15, SAINT'S LIFE 546-16, CHRONICLE 546-17, BOOK COVER 546-18, SAINT'S LIFE 546-19, SAINT'S LIFE 546-20, CLASSBOOK 546-21, POETRY ON GENESIS 546-22, GOSPELS 546-23, ANSELM MS 546-24, COMMENTARY 546-25, COMMENTARY 546-26, TREATISE 546-28, HISTORY 546/29-30, RELIGIOUS ORDERS 546/31-33, SUMMA 546-35, POETRY 546-37

*CONTENTS CULTURE/ EUROPEAN 546/1-37, ROMAN EAGLE FROM NOTITIA DIGNITATUM 546-1, ST JEROME WRITING VULGATE 546-2, CONSTANTINE BAPTIZED BY POPE SYLVESTER AD323 546-3, PARALLEL COLUMNS OF GREEK AND LATIN TEXTS 546-4, BOETHIUS IN PRISON WITH PHILOSOPHY 546-5, JUSTINIAN PANEL 546-6, THEODORA PANEL 546-7, ST BENEDICT 546-8, ST BENEDICT'S RULE/ OLDEST EXTANT COPY 546-9, ST GREGORY 546-10, LETTER FROM GREGORY TO AUGUSTINE 546-11, ST AUGUSTINE OF CANTERBURY 546-12, GOSPELS OF ST AUGUSTINE 546-13, BEDE GIVES LIFE OF CUTHBERT TO BISHOP OF LINDISFARNE 546-14, MATTHEW/ OPENING TEXT FROM MACREGOL GOSPELS 546-15, LIFE AND LEARNING AT LINDISFARNE 546-16, CHARLEMAGNE'S CORONATION 546-17, CHRISTUS SUPER ASPIDEM, CAROLINGIAN BOOK COVER 546-18, ST CUTHBERT APPEARS TO KING ALFRED 546-19, ATHELSTAN AD924-939 GIVES BOOK TO ST CUTHBERT 546-20, ST DUNSTAN AT FEET OF CHRIST 546-21, CHRIST AND ST DUNSTAN 546-21, NOAH'S ARK SHOWING VIKING INFLUENCE 546-22, MATTHEW/ OPENING PAGE FROM ST MARGARET'S GOSPELS 546-23, ST ANSELM'S SERMONS 546-24, ST BERNARD TEACHING GROUP OF MONKS 546-25, SELF-PORTRAIT OF HUGO PICTOR 546-26, PORTRAIT OF FOUNDER OF NUNNERY 546-27, EMPEROR CHOSEN AND CROWNED BY ELECTORS 546-28, MAP OF THE HOLY LAND 546-29, HOLY LAND/ MAP 546-29, SALADIN DEFEATS CHRISTIANS AND CAPTURES TRUE CROSS 546-30, BENEDICTINE MONKS OF ST MARY'S ABBEY 546-31, ST DOMINIC AD1170-1221/ FOUNDER OF ORDER OF PREACHERS 546-32, ST FRANCIS OF ASSISI 546-33, WORKS BY ROBERT GROSSETESTE 546-34, SUMMA BOOK I BY AQUINAS 546-35, PSEUDO-ROGER BACON 546-36, DANTE AND VIRGIL MEET CLASSICAL AUTHORS 546-37

*$ABSTRACT 547
*LIBRARY BODLEIAN
*SLIDE SET TITLE TEXTILES
*NEGATIVE REFERENCE ROLL 229B
*RENTAL FEE $3.00
*TITLE OF MANUSCRIPT LE BESTIAIRE D'ARMOUR 547-2, ROMAN DE LA ROSE 547-3, LIFE OF ST CUTHBERT 547-5, LI LIVRES DU GRAUNT CAAM 547-9, DE BELLO GALLICO OF CAESAR 547-10, SPECULUM HUMANAE SALVATIONIS 547-13, ROMAN DE LA ROSE 547-14, PEDIGREE OF THE KINGS OF ENGLAND 547-15, GESTA INFANTIAE SALVATORIS 547-16, METAMORPHOSES OF OVID 547-18, GESTA INFANTIAE SALVATORIS 547-19, ROMAN DE LA ROSE 547-20
*SHELFMARK MS GOUGH LITURG 2/ FOL 14 547-1, MS DOUCE 308/ FOL 89 547-2, MS DOUCE 195/ FOL 144V 547-3, MS ASTOR A 24/ FOL 7 547-4, MS UNIVERSITY COLLEGE 165/ PAGE 8 547-5, MS AUCT D 2 6/ FOL 4 547-6, MS ASTOR A 24/ FOL 10 547-7, MS ASTOR A 24/ FOL 10V 547-8, MS BODLEY 264/ FOL 245V 547-9, MS DOUCE 208/ FOL 120V 547-10, MS BODLEY 401/ FOL 55V 547-11, MS DOUCE 6/ FOL 101V 547-12, MS CORPUS CHRISTI COLLEGE 161/ PAGE 7 547-13, MS DOUCE 195/ FOL 67V 547-14, MS LAT MISC B 2 ROLL 547-15, MS DOUCE 237/ FOL 8V 547-16, MS DOUCE 144/ FOL 19 547-17, MS HOLKHAM 324/ FOL 62V 547-18, MS SELDEN SUPRA 38/ FOL 27 547-19, MS DOUCE 332/ FOL 2V 547-20
*PROVENANCE ENGLISH/ NORTH 547-1, FRENCH/ LORRAINE 547-2, FRENCH 547-3, FLEMISH/ BRUGES 547-4, ENGLISH/ DURHAM? 547-5, ENGLISH/ ST ALBANS 547-6, FLEMISH/ BRUGES 547/7-8, ENGLISH 547-9, FLEMISH 547-10, ENGLISH 547-11, FLEMISH/ GHENT 547-12, ENGLISH 547-13, FRENCH 547-14, ENGLISH/ TEWKESBURY 547-15, FRENCH 547-16, FRENCH/ PARIS 547-17, FLEMISH 547-18, ENGLISH 547-19, FRENCH 547-20
*DATE EXECUTED 13TH/C1200 547-1, 14TH/ 1ST QUARTER 547-2, 15TH 547-3, 16TH/C1525 547-4, 12TH/C1150 547-5, 12TH/C1140-1158 547-6, 16TH/C1525 547-7, 16TH/C1525 547-8, 15TH/C1400 547-9, 15TH/ AFTER 1474 547-10, 14TH 547-11, 14TH/C1320-30 547-12, 15TH/ EARLY 547-13, 15TH 547-14, 15TH/C1435 547-15, 15TH/C1470-80 547-16, 15TH/1407 547-17, 15TH/C1497 547-18, 14TH/C1320-30 547-19, 14TH/ LATE 547-20
*LANGUAGE LATIN 547-1, FRENCH 547-2, FRENCH 547-3, LATIN 547-4, LATIN 547-5, LATIN 547-6, LATIN 547-7, LATIN 547-8, FRENCH 547-9, FRENCH 547-10, FRENCH 547-11, LATIN 547-12, LATIN 547-13, FRENCH 547-14, LATIN 547-15, FRENCH 547-16, FRENCH AND LATIN 547-17, LATIN 547-18, FRENCH 547-19, FRENCH 547-20
*ARTIST/ SCHOOL TESTARD/ ROBINET 547-3 AND 14, MASTER OF THE LAMBETH BIBLE 547-6
*AUTHOR DE LORRIS/ GUILLAUME AND JEAN DE MEUNG 547-3/14/20, BEDE 547-5, POLO/ MARCO 547-9, CAESAR 547-10, OVID 547-18
*TYPE OF MANUSCRIPT PSALTER 547-1, BESTIAIRE D'AMOUR 547-2, ROMANCE 547-3, BOOK OF HOURS 547-4, SAINT'S LIFE 547-5, CALENDAR 547-6, CALENDAR 547-7, CALENDAR 547-8, TRAVELOGUE 547-9, LITERATURE/ CLASSICAL 547-10, APOCALYPSE WITH COMMENTARY 547-11, PSALTER 547-12, MORAL TREATISE 547-13, ROMANCE 547-14, PEDIGREE 547-15, APOCRYPHAL CHILDHOOD OF CHRIST 547-19, BOOK OF HOURS 547-17, LITERATURE/ CLASSICAL 547-18, APOCRYPHAL CHILDHOOD OF CHRIST 547-19, ROMANCE 547-20
*CONTENTS TEXTILES AND THE WOOL TRADE 547/1-20, ANGEL APPEARS TO SHEPHERDS WITH FLOCK/ GOATS/ DOG 547-1, WOLF OUTSIDE SHEEP-PEN BITES ITS OWN LEG 547-2, SHEPHERD WATCHES OVER FLOCK IN WATTLE-PEN 547-3, SHEEP TURNED-OUT TO GRAZE 547-4, SHEPHERD'S CROOKS USED IN GAME OF SHINTY 547-5, SHEEP SHEARING 547-6, SHEEP SHEARING 547-7, SHEEP SHEARING 547-8, TRANSPORT/ PACKHORSE AND DRIVER APPROACH INN 547-9, TRANSPORT/ BARGE LOADED BY WATER-GATE 547-10, TRANSPORT/ MERCHANTS WATCH CARGOES ARRIVE 547-11, CARDING FLEECE 547-12, EVE WITH DISTAFF AND SPINDLE 547-13, SPINNING/ WOMAN WITH DISTAFF AND SPINDLE 547-14, SPINNING WHEEL 547-15, NAAMAH/ INVENTOR OF SPINNING WHEEL 547-15, WEAVING 547/16-18, VIRGIN MARY WEAVING 547-16, VIRGIN MARY WEAVING 547-17, ARACHNE AND PALLAS WEAVING 547-18, DYEING 547-19, DYER TO WHOM JESUS WAS APPRENTICED 547-19, SHEEPSKIN/ AVARICE WITH BLACK LAMBSKIN MANTLE 547-20, AVARICE WITH BAGS OF MONEY 547-20

*$ABSTRACT 548
*LIBRARY BODLEIAN
*SLIDE SET TITLE DRAMA/ THE PASSION
*NEGATIVE REFERENCE ROLL 229C
*RENTAL FEE $2.40
*COMMENTS THE PASSION AS PORTRAYED IN MEDIEVAL DRAMA.
*TITLE OF MANUSCRIPT SUMMA SUMMARUM 548-6
*SHELFMARK MS CANON LITURG 276 548-1, MS AUCT D INF 2 11 548-2, MS CANON LITURG 276 548-3, MS GOUGH LITURG 6 548-4, MS DOUCE 62 548-5, MS DOUCE 293 548-6, MS DIGBY 227 548-7, MS LITURG 59 548-8
*PROVENANCE FLEMISH 548-1, FRENCH/ NORMANDY 548-2, FLEMISH 548-3, ENGLISH 548-4, FRENCH 548-5, ENGLISH 548-6, ENGLISH/ ABINGDON 548-7, FRENCH 548-8
*DATE EXECUTED 15TH 548-1, 15TH/C1440-50 548-2, 15TH 548-3, 15TH 548-4, 15TH/C1400 548-5, 14TH/ 3RD QUARTER 548-6, 15TH/C1461 548-7, 15TH/ 3RD QUARTER 548-8
*LANGUAGE LATIN 548-1, FRENCH AND LATIN 548-2, LATIN 548-3, LATIN 548-4, FRENCH AND LATIN 548-5, LATIN 548-6, LATIN 548-7, FRENCH AND LATIN 548-8
*ARTIST/ SCHOOL MASTER OF SIR JOHN FASTOLF 548-2, SCHEERRE/ HERMANN OR A CLOSE FOLLOWER 548-4, ZENOBI DA FIRENZE 548-5, ABELL/ WILLIAM 548-7,
*AUTHOR WILLIAM OF PAGULA 548-6
*TYPE OF MANUSCRIPT BOOK OF HOURS/ USE OF ROME 548-1, BOOK OF HOURS/ USE OF SARUM 548-2, BOOK OF HOURS/ USE OF ROME 548-3, BOOK OF HOURS/ USE OF SARUM 548-4, BOOK OF HOURS/ USE OF PARIS 548-5, SUMMA 548-6, MISSAL/ BENEDICTINE USE 548-7, BOOK OF HOURS/ USE OF EVREUX 548-8
*CONTENTS PASSION AS PORTRAYED IN MEDIEVAL DRAMA 548/1-8, BETRAYAL OF CHRIST/ MALCHUS WITH LANTERN 548-1, MALCHUS WITH LANTERN AS IN YORK/ TOWNELEY PLAYS 548-1, CHRIST CROWNED WITH THORNS 548-2, TORMENTORS PRESS-DOWN THORNS WITH CLOTH TWISTS 548-2, ROAD TO CALVARY/ CHRIST LED WITH ROPE 548-3, CHRIST LED WITH ROPE AS IN LUDUS COVENTRIAE 548-3, ROAD TO CALVARY/ CHRIST LED BY ROPE 548-4, CHRIST BOUND AND NAILED TO CROSS ON GROUND 548-5, CHRIST NAILED TO CROSS AS IN CYCLE PLAYS 548-5, CRUCIFIXION/ NAILS DRIVEN ABOVE CHRIST'S HANDS 548-6 CRUCIFIXION/ CHRIST GRIPS NAILS AS ACTOR WOULD 548-7, CRUCIFIXION/ ST JOHN SITS BEFORE CROSS 548-8, ST JOHN SITS BEFORE CROSS AS IN LUDUS COVENTRIAE 548-8, LONGINUS CURED OF BLINDNESS AS IN ACTS OF PILATE 548-8

*$ABSTRACT 549
*LIBRARY BODLEIAN
*SLIDE SET TITLE ENGLISH HISTORY II
*NEGATIVE REFERENCE ROLL 229D
*RENTAL FEE $3.40
*TITLE OF MANUSCRIPT GENEALOGY OF THE KINGS OF ENGLAND TO EDWARD I 549-1, LIFE OF ST CUTHBERT 549-2, GENEALOGY OF THE KINGS OF ENGLAND TO EDWARD I 549-3, HISTORIA MAJOR/ VOL I 549-4, LIFE OF ST CUTHBERT 549-5, HISTORIA MAJOR/ VOL I 549-6, MAGNA CARTA 549-8, FORTY-TWO LINE BIBLE 549-9, MAGNA CARTA 549-10, MIROIR OR GLASSE OF THE SYNNEFUL SOULE 549/12-13, PROCESSION OF THE LORDS TO PARLIAMENT 549-14, STATUTES OF ENGLAND 549-15, PRAYERS AND HYMN TO THE VIRGIN 549-16, HOURS OF ANNE OF BOHEMIA 549-17, CHARTER OF CROYLAND ABBEY 549-18, CHRONICLE OF THE COUNTS OF FLANDERS 549/19-20, DOUCE APOCALYPSE 549-21, HISTORIA MAJOR/ VOL II 549-23, CHRONICLE OF JOHN OF WORCESTER 549/24-25, HISTORIA MAJOR/ VOL I 549-26, GOSPEL BOOK OF QUEEN MARGARET 549-27, MIROUER HISTORIALE ABREGIE 549-28
*SHELFMARK MS BODLEY ROLLS 3 549-1, MS UNIVERSITY COLLEGE 165 549-2, MS BODLEY ROLLS 3 549-3, MS CORPUS CHRISTI COLLEGE CAMBRIDGE 26 549-4, MS CORPUS CHRISTI COLLEGE CAMBRIDGE 183 549-5, MS CORPUS CHRISTI COLLEGE CAMBRIDGE 26 549-6, MS DOUCE 231 549-7, MS CH GLOUCS 8 549-8 AND 10 , PR DOUCE BIB ENG 1583 B 1 549-11, MS CHERRY 36 549/12-13, MS ASHMOLE ROLLS 45 549-14, MS HATTON 10 549-15, MS JESUS COLLEGE 126 ROLL 549-16, MS LAT LITURG F 3 549-17, MS ASHMOLE 1831 549-18, MS HOLKHAM

659 549/19-20, MS DOUCE 180 549-21, MS HOLKHAM 514 549-22, MS CORPUS CHRISTI COLLEGE CAMBRIDGE 16 549-23, MS CORPUS CHRISTI COLLEGE OXFORD 157 549/24-25, MS CORPUS CHRISTI COLLEGE CAMBRIDGE 26 549-26, MS LAT LITURG F 5 549-27, MS BODLEY 968 549-28

*PROVENANCE ENGLISH 549/1-4, ENGLISH/ WINCHESTER? 549-5, ENGLISH 549/6-8, GERMAN/ MAINZ 549-9, ENGLISH 549/10-16, FLEMISH 549-17, ENGLISH 549-18, FLEMISH 549/19-20, ENGLISH 549-21, ITALIAN 549-22, ENGLISH 549/23-27, FRENCH/ WEST 549-28

*DATE EXECUTED 13TH 549-1, 12TH 549-2, 13TH/ LAST QUARTER 549-3, 13TH/ BEFORE 1253 549-4 AND 6, 10TH/C930 549-5, 14TH 549-7, 13TH/1217 549-8 AND 10, 15TH/C1454-55 549-9, 16TH/1558-1603 549-11, 16TH/1544 549/12-13, 17TH/ 2ND HALF 549-14, 16TH/C1500 549-15, 15TH/ MID 549-16, 14TH/1382-94 549-17, 14TH/1386 549-18, 15TH/1476 549/19-20, 13TH/ BEFORE 1272 549-21, 14TH/ LATE 549-22, 13TH/ BEFORE 1253 549-23 AND 26, 12TH/C1118-40 549-24, 12TH/C1118-40 549-25, 11TH/ 2ND QUARTER 549-27, 15TH/ BEFORE 1472 549-28

*LANGUAGE LATIN 549/1-10, ENGLISH 549-12, LATIN 549-14, LATIN/ FRENCH/ ENGLISH 549-15, LATIN 549/16-18, FRENCH 549/19-20, FRENCH AND LATIN 549-21, ITALIAN 549-22, LATIN 549/23-27, FRENCH AND LATIN 549-28

*AUTHOR BEDE 549/1 AND 5, PARIS/ MATTHEW 549/4 AND 6 AND 23 AND 26 , DANTE 549-22, JOHN OF WORCESTER 549/24-25,

*TYPE OF MANUSCRIPT GENEALOGY 549-1, SAINT'S LIFE 549-2, GENEALOGY 549-3, HISTORY 549-4, SAINT'S LIFE 549-5, HISTORY 549-6, BOOK OF HOURS 549-7, MAGNA CARTA 549/ 8 AND 10, BIBLE 549-9, BINDING 549-11, MORAL TREATISE 549-12, BINDING 549-13, PARLIAMENT ROLL 549-14, STATUTES 549-15, PRAYERS AND HYMN 549-16, BOOK OF HOURS 549-17, CHARTER 549-18, CHRONICLE 549/19-20, APOCALYPSE WITH COMMENTARY 549-21, POETRY 549-22, HISTORY 549-23, CHRONICLE 549/24-25, HISTORY 549-26, GOSPEL BOOK 549-27, HISTORY 549-28

*CONTENTS ENGLISH HISTORY 549/1-28, HISTORY/ ENGLISH 549/1-28, KINGS OF ENGLAND FROM ETHELWULF TO HENRY II 549-1, ST CUTHBERT APPEARS TO KING ALFRED 549-2, KING ALFRED AND ST CUTHBERT 549-2, WILLIAM THE CONQUEROR/ PORTRAIT 549-3, EDMUND IRONSIDE AND CNUT DUEL AT DEERHURST 549-4, ATHELSTAN GIVES BEDE'S BOOK TO ST CUTHBERT 549-5, ST CUTHBERT RECEIVES BOOK FROM ATHELSTAN 549-5, KING ALFRED AD871-899/ PORTRAIT 549-6, ST GEORGE OF ENGLAND AND EARL OF LANCASTER 549-7, MAGNA CARTA/ OPENING TEXT 549-8, FORTY-TWO LINE BIBLE/ TEXT 549-9, MAGNA CARTA/ TEXT 549-10, BINDING/ EMBROIDERED OF BIBLE PRESENTED TO ELIZABETH 549-11, MIROIR OR GLASS OF THE SYNNEFUL SOULE/ DEDICATION PAGE 549-12, BINDING OF 549-12 EMBROIDERED BY ELIZABETH 549-13, KING HENRY VIII WITH ATTENDANTS 549-14, KING EDWARD IV WITH CLERGY AND COURTIERS 549-15, MARGARET OF ANJOU/ WIFE OF HENRY VI 549-16, ANNE OF BOHEMIA KNEELS BEFORE VIRGIN AND CHILD 549-17, VIRGIN AND CHILD AND ANNE OF BOHEMIA 549-17, KING RICHARD II PRESENTS CHARTER TO CROYLAND ABBEY 549-18, CHARTER OF CROYLAND ABBEY 549-18, EDWARD III DOES HOMAGE TO KING PHILIP VI 549-19, QUEEN ISABELLA/ WIFE OF EDWARD II WITH MOUNTED HOST 549-20, OXFORD UNIVERSITY GATES WITH QUEEN ISABELLA 549-20, TRINITY ADORED BY LORD EDWARD/ LATER EDWARD I 549-21, ST JOHN OF PATMOS WRITES AND PREACHES 549-21, KING HENRY III AS SLACK RULER 549-22, SORDELLO BOWS TO VIRGIL 549-22, KING HENRY III RETURNS TO FRANCE IN SHIP 549-23, VISIONS OF KING HENRY I 549-24, LORDS SPIRITUAL/ ABBOTS AND BISHOPS 549-24, KING HENRY I RETURNS TO ENGLAND BY SHIP 549-24,SHIP SCENE WITH KING HENRY I 549-24, VISIONS OF KING HENRY I/ PEASANTS AND KNIGHTS 549-25, KNIGHTS AND PEASANTS 549-25, TEMPLARS SHARE A HORSE 549-26, MATILDA FOUNDS HOSPITAL IN LONDON 549-26, ST MATTHEW PAGE FROM QUEEN MARGARET'S GOSPELS 549-27, BATTLE OF HASTINGS 549-28

*$ABSTRACT 550
*LIBRARY BODLEIAN
*SLIDE SET TITLE IRISH ILLUMINATION
*NEGATIVE REFERENCE ROLL 230A
*RENTAL FEE $2.65

*COMMENTS SELECTION OF 5 MSS OF 8TH-16TH CENTURIES.
*TITLE OF MANUSCRIPT GOSPELS OF ST LUKE AND ST JOHN 550/1-2, ANNALS OF TIGERNACH 550/3-4, PSALTER NA RANN 550/5-6, SEX AETATES MUNDI 550-7, DALLAN'S POEM IN PRAISE OF ST COLUMBA 550-8, ANNALS OF TIGERNACH 550-9, LIFE OF ST COLUMB-KILL 550-10, SERMON ON THE ASSUMPTION OF THE VIRGIN 550-12, FELIRE OENGUSSO CELI DE 550-13
*SHELFMARK MS RAWL G 167/ FOL 1 550-1, MS RAWL G 167/ FOL 60V 550-2, MS RAWL B 502/ FOL 3 550-3, MS RAWL B 502/ FOL 10V 550-4, MS RAWL B 502/ FOL 19 550-5, MS RAWL B 502/ FOL 32V-33 550-6, MS RAWL B 502/ FOL 41 550-7, MS RAWL B 502/ FOL 56 550-8, MS RAWL B 488/ FOL 2V 550-9, MS RAWL B 514/ FOL 1 550-10, MS LAUD MISC 610/ FOL 32V 550-11, MS LAUD MISC 610/ FOL 34 550-12, MS LAUD MISC 610/ FOL 59 550-13
*PROVENANCE IRISH
*DATE EXECUTED 08TH 550/1-2, 11TH 550/3-4, 12TH 550/5-8, 13TH 550-9, 16TH/ MID 550-10, 15TH/1453-54 550/11-12, 12TH 550-13
*LANGUAGE LATIN 550/1-2, IRISH 550/3-8, LATIN 550-9, IRISH 550/10-13
*ARTIST/ SCHOOL RELATED IN STYLE TO ST CHAD GOSPELS 550/1-2,
*AUTHOR O'DONNELL MAGNUS 550-10,
*TYPE OF MANUSCRIPT GOSPELS 550/1-2, ANNALS 550/3-4, PSALTER 550-5, POETRY/ IRISH 550-8, ANNALS 550-9, SAINT'S LIFE 550-10, HISTORICAL AND RELIGIOUS TEXTS 550/11-13
*CONTENTS IRISH ILLUMINATION 550/1-13, IRISH LITERATURE 550/1-13, LITERATURE/ IRISH 550/1-13, LUKE/ OPENING PAGE WITH INTERLACE 550-1, INITIAL Q QUONIAM QUIDEM 550-1, LUKE/ CHAPTER 24 WITH COLORED CAPITALS 550-2, INITIAL U UNA AUTEM 550-2, INITIAL Q IN YELLOW/ ORANGE AND BROWN 550-3, CROSS IN MARGIN OUTLINED IN ORANGE 550-4, INITIAL M ENTWINED WITH INTERLACE 550-5, INITIALS/ ZOOMORPHIC INTERLACE 550-6, INITIAL S WITH ZOOMORPHIC INTERLACE 550-7, INITIAL D IN RED/ GREEN/ PURPLE INTERLACE 550-8, INITIAL P WITH INHABITED INTERLACE 550-9, ST COLUMB-KILL WITH MITRE AND CROZIER 550-10, CANDLESTICK/ SEVEN-BRANCHED 550-11, INITIAL WITH ZOOMORPHIC INTERLACE 550-12, INITIAL FILLED WITH SCALLOPED DESIGN 550-13

*$ABSTRACT 551
*LIBRARY BODLEIAN
*SLIDE SET TITLE MANUSCRIPTS BEFORE AD1000
*NEGATIVE REFERENCE ROLL 230B
*RENTAL FEE $4.25
*TITLE OF MANUSCRIPT EXPOSITION ON JOB 551/3-12, COMMENTARY ON MINOR PROPHETS 551/13-14, GREGORIAN SACRAMENTARY 551/15-18, CODEX AUREUS PURPUREUS 551/19-39
*SHELFMARK MS AUCT D 2 14/ FOL 130 551-1, MS AUCT D 2 14/ FOL 149V 551-2, MS BODLEY 426/ FOL 1 551-3, MS BODLEY 426/ FOL 2V 551-4, MS BODLEY 426/ FOL 34V 551-5, MS BODLEY 426/ FOL 48V 551-6, MS BODLEY 426/ FOL 53V 551-7, MS BODLEY 426/ FOL 67 551-8, MS BODLEY 426/ FOL 84V 551-9, MS BODLEY 426/ FOL 85 551-10, MS BODLEY 426/ FOL 89V 551-11, MS BODLEY 426/ FOL 107V 551-12, MS LAUD MISC 148/ FOL 1 551-13, MS LAUD MISC 148/ FOL 33V 551-14, MS AUCT D 1 20/ FOL 30 551-15, MS AUCT D 1 20/ FOL 34V 551-16, MS AUCT D 1 20/ FOL 36V 551-17, MS AUCT D 1 20/ FOL 37V 551-18, MS DOUCE 59/ FOL 4 551-19, MS DOUCE 59/ FOL 25V 551-20, MS DOUCE 59/ FOL 39V 551-21, MS DOUCE 59/ FOL 51 551-22, MS DOUCE 59/ FOL 51V 551-23, MS DOUCE 59/ FOL 52 551-24, MS DOUCE 59/ FOL 66 551-25, MS DOUCE 59/ FOL 82V 551-26, MS DOUCE 59/ FOL 98 551-27, MS DOUCE 59/ FOL 100V 551-28, MS DOUCE 59/ FOL 100 551-29, MS DOUCE 59/ FOL 101 551-30, MS DOUCE 59/ FOL 115V 551-31, MS DOUCE 59/ FOL 119 551-32, MS DOUCE 59/ FOL 121V 551-33, MS DOUCE 59/ FOL 133 551-34, MS DOUCE 59/ FOL 138V 551-35, MS DOUCE 59/ FOL 143V 551-36, MS DOUCE 59/ FOL 149V 551-37, MS DOUCE 59/ FOL 161 551-38, MS DOUCE 59/ FOL 161V 551-39, MS ADD C 153/ FOL 1 551-40, MS ADD C 153/ FOL 85 551-41, MS LAUD LAT 27/ FOL 17V-18 551-42, MS LAUD LAT 27/ FOL 73V-74 551-43, MS LAUD LAT 27/ FOL 115V-116 551-44, MS LAUD LAT 27/ FOL 176V-177 551-45
*PROVENANCE ITALIAN 551/1-2, ENGLISH/ WESSEX? 551/3-12, GERMAN/ SOUTH 551/13-14, GERMAN/ ST GALL 551/15-18, FRENCH/

RHEIMS 551/19-39, FLEMISH 551/40-41, GERMAN/ LOWER SAXONY/ CORVEY? 551/42-45
*DATE EXECUTED 07TH 551/1-2, 08TH/ LATE 551/3-12, 09TH/ 1ST HALF 551/13-14, 09TH/ 2ND HALF 551/15-18, 09TH/ MID 551/19-39, 10TH/ 1ST HALF 551/40-41, 10TH/ 2ND HALF 551/42-45
*LANGUAGE LATIN
*AUTHOR PHILIPPUS PRESBITER 551/3-12, ST JEROME 551/13-14
*TYPE OF MANUSCRIPT GOSPELS 551/1-2, COMMENTARY 551/3-12, COMMENTARY 551/13-14, SACRAMENTARY 551/15-18, PSALTER 551/19-39, GOSPELS 551/40-41, GOSPELS 551/42-45
*CONTENTS MANUSCRIPTS BEFORE AD1000 551/1-45, GOSPEL OF ST JOHN/ BEGINNING 551-1, TEXT PAGE/ INVOCATION TO ST CHAD IN MARGIN 551-2, ST CHAD INVOCATION IN MARGIN 551-2, INITIAL A ADHORTANTE WITH INTERLACE TAIL 551-3, INITIAL V VIR WITH INTERLACE AND DOTS 551-4, INITIALS V AND E IN YELLOW AND ORANGE 551-5, INITIAL N NUMQUID 551-6, INITIAL A 551-7, INITIAL I 551-8, INITIAL P 551-9, INITIAL C 551-10, INITIAL A 551-11, INITIAL Y 551-12, EXPOSITION ON DANIEL 551-13, INITIAL I IN COMPOSED OF INTERLACE 551-13, INITIAL C CONTRA OF INTERLACE AND BANDS 551-13, INITIAL A ANNO/ ZOOMORPHIC 551-14, INITIAL E EXULTET 551-15, INITIAL V VERE 551-15, INITIAL I IN NOMINE IN RED AND GOLD INTERLACE 551-16, INITIALS V VERE AND D DIGNUM FORMING CROSS 551-17, INITIAL T TE IGITUR/ FULL PAGE 551-18, GOLD LETTERS ON PURPLE PARCHMENT 551/19-36, PSALM 1/ INITIAL B BEATUS/ FULL PAGE 551-19, INITIAL B BEATUS IN GOLD INTERLACE 551-19, PSALM 26/27/ INITIAL D DOMINUS 551-20, INITIAL D DOMINUS DECORATED WITH FLOWERS 551-20, PSALM 38/39/ INITIAL DIXI 551-21, INITIAL D DIXI 551-21, PSALM 51/52/ FULL-PAGE HEADING 551-22, PSALM 52/ SAUL ENTHRONED WITH DAVID 551-23, DAVID STANDS BEFORE SAUL 551-23, PSALM 51/52/ INITIAL Q QUID 551-24, INITIAL Q QUID 551-24, PSALM 68/69/ INITIAL S SALVUM 551-25, INITIAL S SALVUM DECORATED WITH FLOWERS 551-25, PSALM 80/81/ INITIAL E EXULTATE 551-26, INITIAL E EXULTATE 551-26, PSALM 97/98/ INITIAL C CANTATE 551-27, INITIAL C CANTATE 551-27, PSALM 101/102/ POOR MAN WITH BOWL 551-28, POOR MAN WITH BOWL RAISES HAND TOWARD GOD 551-28, PSALM 101/102/ FULL-PAGE HEADING 551-29, PSALM 101/102/ INITIAL D DOMINE EXAUDI 551-30, INITIAL D DOMINE EXAUDI/ FULL PAGE 551-30, PSALM 109/110/ INITIAL D DIXIT DOMINUS 551-31, INITIAL D DIXIT DOMINUS DECORATED WITH FLOWERS 551-31, PSALM 114/116/ INITIAL D DILEXI QUONIAM 551-32, INITIAL D DILEXI QUONIAM 551-32, PSALM 118/119/ INITIAL B BEATI IMMACULATI 551-33,INITIAL B BEATI IMMACULATI 551-33, PSALM 126/127/ INITIAL N NISI DOMINUS 551-34, INITIAL N NISI DOMINUS 551-34, PSALM 137/138/ INITIAL C CONFITEBOR TIBI 551-35, INITIAL C CONFITEBOR TIBI 551-35, PSALM 143/144/ INITIAL B BENEDICTUS DOMINUS 551-36, INITIAL B BENEDICTUS DOMINUS 551-36, GOLD LETTERS ON PURPLE PARCHMENT 551/37-39, INITIAL C CONFITEBOR DECORATED WITH FLOWERS 551-37, LORD'S PRAYER DECORATED WITH FLOWERS 551-38, APOSTLES CREED DECORATED WITH FLOWERS 551-39, INITIAL L LIBER/ FULL-PAGE 551-40, INITIAL Q QUONIAM/ ZOOMORPHIC INTERLACE 551-41, INITIAL L LIBER IN BANDED INTERLACE 551-42, INITIAL I INITIUM IN BANDED INTERLACE 551-43, INITIAL Q QUONIAM QUIDEM COMPOSED OF SERPENTS AND BIRDS 551-44, INITIAL I IN PRINCIPIO ERAT VERBUM IN INTERLACE 551-45

*$ABSTRACT 552
*LIBRARY BODLEIAN
*SLIDE SET TITLE ELEVENTH CENTURY MANUSCRIPTS
*NEGATIVE REFERENCE ROLL 230C
*RENTAL FEE $3.35
*TITLE OF MANUSCRIPT COMMENTARY ON BOOKS OF KINGS 552/1-4, MARTYROLOGY 552/5-7, COMMENTARY ON THE PAULINE EPISTLES 552/8-12, HOMILIARY 552/13-27
*SHELFMARK MS BODLEY 796/ FOL 4 552-1, MS BODLEY 796/ FOL 68V 552-2, MS BODLEY 796/ FOL 130V 552-3, MS BODLEY 796/ FOL 169V 552-4, MS CANON MISC 560/ FOL 3 552-5, MS CANON MISC 560/ FOL 23 552-6, MS CANON MISC 560/ FOL 23V 552-7, MS ADD D 104/ FOL 2 552-8, MS ADD D 104/ FOL 43V 552-9, MS ADD D 104/ FOL 52V 552-10, MS ADD D 104/ FOL 144 552-11, MS ADD D 104/ FOL 150

552-12, MS LAT LITURG B 2/ FOL 35V 552-13, MS LAT LITURG B 2/ FOL 38V 552-14, MS LAT LITURG B 2/ FOL 43V 552-15, MS LAT LITURG B 2/ FOL 59V 552-16, MS LAT LITURG B 2/ FOL 88V 552-17, MS LAT LITURG B 2/ FOL 103V 552-18, MS LAT LITURG B 2/ FOL 125V 552-19, MS LAT LITURG B 2/ FOL 138 552-20, MS LAT LITURG B 2/ FOL 140 552-21, MS LAT LITURG B 2/ FOL 142V 552-22, MS LAT LITURG B 2/ FOL 149V 552-23, MS LAT LITURG B 2/ FOL 166 552-24, MS LAT LITURG B 2/ FOL 167V 552-25, MS LAT LITURG B 2/ FOL 189V 552-26, MS LAT LITURG B 2/ FOL 221 552-27
*PROVENANCE ITALIAN/ NORTH 552/1-4, ITALIAN/ MILAN 552/5-7, ITALIAN/ ST CECILIA'S ROME 552/8-12, FLEMISH/ STAVELOT 552/13-27
*DATE EXECUTED 11TH/EARLY 552/1-4, 11TH/ MID 552/5-7, 11TH/1067 552/8-12, 11TH/ LATE 552/13-27
*LANGUAGE LATIN
*AUTHOR RHABANUS MAURUS 552/1-4, HAIMO 552/8-12
*TYPE OF MANUSCRIPT COMMENTARY 552/1-4, ASTRONOMICAL AND COMPUTISTICAL TREATISE 552/5-7, COMMENTARY 552/8-12, HOMILIARY 552/13-27
*CONTENTS ELEVENTH CENTURY MANUSCRIPTS 552/1-27, INITIAL F FUIT WITH ACANTHUS INFILLING 552-1, INITIAL F FACTUM/ FOLIATED AND INTERLACED 552-2, INITIAL E ET WITH BEAST HEADS AND FOLIAGE 552-3, ST PAUL?/ MARGINAL SKETCH 552-4, MAP OF THE WORLD/ ASIA AT TOP 552-5, DIAGRAM OF SOLAR SYSTEM FLANKED BY FOUR ANGELS 552-6, DIAGRAM SHOWING POSITIONS OF RISING AND SETTING SUN 552-7, CHRIST IN MANDORLA WITH ANGELS AND ST PAUL 552-8, ST PAUL WITH CHRIST AND ANGELS 552-8, INITIAL H HOC/ FORMED BY HAIRY MONSTERS 552-9,DEVIL'S HEAD 552-9, INITIAL P PRECEPTO WITH INTERLACED MONSTER 552-10, INITIAL P PAULUS WITH INHABITED HUMAN 552-11, INITIAL D DECETEREOR WITH STEM-MONSTER 552-12, SOLDIER 552-13, ST MARY MAGDALENE 552-14, INITIAL F FRACTUS/ INTERLACE 552-14, SAMSON AND THE LION 552-15, ST JOHN 552-16, LUKE 16/VERSES 19-21/ LAZARUS AND DIVES 552-17, LAZARUS WITH SORES RAISES ARM TOWARD DIVES 552-17, CHRIST HOLDS SCROLL AND BLESSES 552-18, INITIAL H HOC 552-18, LUKE 17/VERSES 11-13/ TEN LEPERS 552-19, LEPERS/ TEN 552-19, INITIAL L LEPROSI 552-19, MAN STANDS ON SACK 552-20, INITIAL E ET 552-20, LUKE 20/VERSES 29-32/ CRIPPLE STANDS WITH CRUTCH 552-21, INITIAL A ACCESSERUNT 552-21, CHRIST HOLDS BOOK AND BLESSES 552-22, MAN/ NAKED ENTWINED IN INTERLACED INITIAL S 552-22, INITIAL S SEXTUS WITH NAKED MAN 552-22, RULER WHO ASKED CHRIST TO HEAL SON 552-23, INITIAL L LECTIO INTERLACED 552-23, LUKE 19/VERSES 1-4/ ZACCHAEUS IN SYCAMORE TREE 552-24, ZACCHAEUS IN SYCAMORE TREE 552-24, ZACHARIAS AS PRIEST 552-25, ST PAUL STANDS AND HOLDS BOOK 552-26, INITIAL T TUNC INHABITED BY ROBED MAN 552-26, JOHN 15/VERSE 1/ TWO MEN HOLD VINES 552-27

*$ABSTRACT 553
*LIBRARY BODLEIAN
*SLIDE SET TITLE MAP OF PALESTINE
*NEGATIVE REFERENCE ROLL 230D
*RENTAL FEE $2.15
*COMMENTS THOUGHT TO BE THE MAPPA MEA DE TERRA SANCTA OF WILLIAM WEY, BUT NO FIRM EVIDENCE.
*TITLE OF MANUSCRIPT MAPPA MEA DE TERRA SANCTA?
*SHELFMARK MS DOUCE 389
*PROVENANCE ENGLISH
*DATE EXECUTED 15TH/C1400
*ARTIST/ SCHOOL WEY/ WILLIAM?
*TYPE OF MANUSCRIPT MAP OF PALESTINE
*CONTENTS MAP OF PALESTINE 553/1-3, JERUSALEM AND THE DEAD SEA 553-1, SEA OF GALILEE AND LAND AROUND RIVER JORDAN 553-2, DAMASCUS/ SIDON/ SEA OF GALILEE 553-3

*$ABSTRACT 554
*LIBRARY ALL SOULS COLLEGE OXFORD
*SLIDE SET TITLE ALL SOULS COLLEGE MSS

*NEGATIVE REFERENCE ROLL 232A
*RENTAL FEE $5.05
*COMMENTS MAINLY BIBLE INITIALS.
*TITLE OF MANUSCRIPT COMMENTARY ON PSALTER 554/15-16,
*SHELFMARK MS ALL SOULS COLLEGE 10/ FOL 2V 554-1, MS ALL SOULS COLLEGE 10/ FOL 49 554-2, MS ALL SOULS COLLEGE 10/ FOL 130V 554-3, MS ALL SOULS COLLEGE 10/ FOL 134 554-4, MS ALL SOULS COLLEGE 10/ FOL 140V 554-5, MS ALL SOULS COLLEGE 10/ FOL 145V 554-6, MS ALL SOULS COLLEGE 10/ FOL 147V 554-7, MS ALL SOULS COLLEGE 10/ FOL 156 554-8, MS ALL SOULS COLLEGE 10/ FOL 181V 554-9, MS ALL SOULS COLLEGE 10/ FOL 184 554-10, MS ALL SOULS COLLEGE 10/ FOL 186V 554-11, MS ALL SOULS COLLEGE 10/ FOL 188V 554-12, MS ALL SOULS COLLEGE 10/ FOL 191V 554-13, MS ALL SOULS COLLEGE 10/ FOL 193 554-14, MS ALL SOULS COLLEGE 15/ FOL 1 554-15, MS ALL SOULS COLLEGE 15/ FOL 3 554-16, MS ALL SOULS COLLEGE 4/ FOL 3 554-17, MS ALL SOULS COLLEGE 4/ FOL 46 554-18, MS ALL SOULS COLLEGE 4/ FOL 60 554-19, MS ALL SOULS COLLEGE 4/ FOL 76 554-20, MS ALL SOULS COLLEGE 4/ FOL 93 554-21, MS ALL SOULS COLLEGE 4/ FOL 94 554-22, MS ALL SOULS COLLEGE 4/ FOL 106 554-23, MS ALL SOULS COLLEGE 4/ FOL 119V 554-24, MS ALL SOULS COLLEGE 4/ FOL 121V 554-25, MS ALL SOULS COLLEGE 4/ FOL 123 554-26, MS ALL SOULS COLLEGE 4/ FOL 156 554-27, MS ALL SOULS COLLEGE 4/ FOL 174 554-28, MS ALL SOULS COLLEGE 4/ FOL 190V 554-29, MS ALL SOULS COLLEGE 2/ FOL 6 554-30, MS ALL SOULS COLLEGE 2/ FOL 104V 554-31, MS ALL SOULS COLLEGE 2/ FOL 113 554-32, MS ALL SOULS COLLEGE 2/ FOL 113V 554-33, MS ALL SOULS COLLEGE 2/ FOL 150V 554-34, MS ALL SOULS COLLEGE 2/ FOL 153 554-35, MS ALL SOULS COLLEGE 2/ FOL 168V 554/36-37, MS ALL SOULS COLLEGE 2/ FOL 173V 554/38-39, MS ALL SOULS COLLEGE 2/ FOL 177 554/40-41, MS ALL SOULS COLLEGE 2/ FOL 180 554-42, MS ALL SOULS COLLEGE 2/ FOL 183 554/43-44, MS ALL SOULS COLLEGE 2/ FOL 187 554-45, MS ALL SOULS COLLEGE 2/ FOL 190V 554/46-47, MS ALL SOULS COLLEGE 2/ FOL 194V 554/48-49, MS ALL SOULS COLLEGE 2/ FOL 198 554-50, MS ALL SOULS COLLEGE 2/ FOL 202 554-51, MS ALL SOULS COLLEGE 2/ FOL 215V 554-52, MS ALL SOULS COLLEGE 2/ FOL 226V 554-53, MS ALL SOULS COLLEGE 2/ FOL 239 554-54, MS ALL SOULS COLLEGE 2/ FOL 257 554-55, MS ALL SOULS COLLEGE 2/ FOL 271 554-56, MS ALL SOULS COLLEGE 2/ FOL 342 554-57, MS ALL SOULS COLLEGE 2/ FOL 343 554-58, MS ALL SOULS COLLEGE 2/ FOL 343V 554-59, MS ALL SOULS COLLEGE 2/ FOL 346 554-60, MS ALL SOULS COLLEGE 2/ FOL 357 554-61
*PROVENANCE ENGLISH 554/1-14, FRENCH/ WEST 554/17-29, ENGLISH 554/30-61
*DATE EXECUTED 15TH/ 2ND QUARTER 554/1-14, 15TH/1463 554/15-16, 12TH/ 1ST HALF 554/17-29, 13TH/ 3RD QUARTER 554/30-61
*LANGUAGE LATIN
*AUTHOR DE TURRECREMETA/ JOHANNES 554/15-16
*SCRIBE HOWELL/ AP 554/15-16
*TYPE OF MANUSCRIPT BIBLE/ NEW TESTAMENT 554/1-14, COMMENTARY 554/15-16, BIBLE 554/17-29, BIBLE 554/30-61
*CONTENTS INITIALS/ BIBLE 554/1-61, PALEOGRAPHY 554/1-61, ST MARK SITS WRITING/ WINGED LION 554-1, ST LUKE AS OLD MAN/ WINGED OX 554-2, ST PAUL HOLDS SWORD BY TIP OF BLADE 554-3, ST PAUL READS TO SEATED MAN 554-4, ST PAUL HOLDS SWORD BY BLADE 554-5, ST PAUL SEATED READS FROM BOOK 554-6, ST PAUL PREACHES FROM PULPIT TO HEBREWS 554-7,VIRGIN STANDS AMID EIGHT APOSTLES 554-8, ST JAMES WITH COCKLE SHELL PREACHES 554-9, ST PETER HOLDING CROZIER BLESSES 554-10, ST PETER SEATED ON MARBLE BENCH 554-11, ST JOHN GESTURES/ EAGLE 554-12, ST JOHN OF PATMOS WRITES 554-13, CHRIST WITH SEVEN CANDLESTICKS 554-14, INITIAL B IN PINK AND BLUE WITH ACANTHUS INFILLING 554-15, BORDER WITH FLOWERS AND LEAVES 554-15, INITIAL B WITH INFILLING OF TWO ROSES 554-16, INITIAL D ON GOLD SQUARE 554-17, INITIAL V VOCAVIT IN FLORAL INTERLACE 554-18, INITIAL L LOCUTUS FORMED BY WINGED DRAGON 554-19, INITIAL H HAEC FORMED BY TWISTED DRAGON 554-20, INITIAL T TANDEM INTERLACED 554-21, INITIAL E ET FORMED BY BEARDED GROTESQUE 554-22, INITIAL P POST WITH FOLIAGE INTERLACE 554-23, INITIAL I IN WITH TWISTED FOLIAGE STEM 554-24, INITIAL V VIGINTI WITH ACANTHUS INTERLACE 554-25, INITIAL F FUIT WITH ACANTHUS INTERLACE 554-26,INITIAL E ET WITH ACANTHUS INTERLACE 554-27,

INITIAL P PREVARICATUS WITH ACANTHUS INTERLACE, INITIAL N NEMO WITH ACANTHUS INTERLACE 554-29, INITIAL I IN WITH 10 PANELS OF BIBLE SCENES 554-30, CREATION/ SEVEN DAYS 554-30, ADAM AND EVE 554-30, CRUCIFIXION 554-30, RESURRECTION 554-30, INITIAL C CECIDIT/ AHAZIAH IN BED 554-31, AHAZIAH INQUIRES ABOUT BAALZEBUB'S HEALTH 554-31, INITIAL S SI FLORIATED 554-32, INITIAL A ADAM/ ADAM SEATED WITH DESCENDANTS 554-33, ADAM SEATED WITH HIS DESCENDANTS 554-33, INITIAL T TOBIAS/ TOBIT HOLDS EYE 554-34, TOBIT HOLDS EYE AS BIRD FLIES AWAY 554-34, JUDITH ABOUT TO BEHEAD HOLOFERNES 554-35, HOLOFERNES AND JUDITH 554-35, PSALM 1/ INITIAL B BEATUS/ DAVID AND GOLIATH 554-36, INITIAL B BEATUS 554-36, DAVID AND GOLIATH 554-36, PSALM 1/ INITIAL B BEATUS/ DAVID PLAYS HARP 554-37, INITIAL B BEATUS 554-37, DAVID PLAYS HARP 554-37, PSALM 26/27/ INITIAL D DOMINUS/ DAVID SEATED 554-38, INITIAL D DOMINUS 554-38, DAVID SEATED ON BLUE AND GOLD THRONE 554-38, PSALM 26/27/ INITIAL D DOMINUS/ SAMUEL ANOINTS DAVID 554-39, INITIAL D DOMINUS 554-39, DAVID ANOINTED BY SAMUEL 554-39, PSALM 38/39/ INITIAL D DIXI/ DAVID POINTS TO MOUTH 554-40, INITIAL D DIXI 554-40, DAVID POINTS TO HIS MOUTH 554-40, PSALM 38/39/ INITIAL D DIXI/ DAVID ENTHRONED 554-41, INITIAL D DIXI 554-41, DAVID ENTHRONED 554-41, PSALM 52/53/ INITIAL D DIXIT/ DAVID AND FOOL 554-42, INITIAL D DIXIT 554-42, DAVID SPEAKS TO BALD FOOL 554-42, PSALM 68/69/ INITIAL S SALVUM/ GOD BLESSING 554-43, INITIAL S SALVUM 554-43, GOD BLESSING 554-43, COOKING-POT/ THREE-LEGGED 554-43, PSALM 68/69/ INITIAL S SALVUM/ JONAH AND WHALE 554-44, INITIAL S SALVUM 554-44, JONAH EMERGES FROM MOUTH OF WHALE AND CLUTCHES TREE 554-44, PSALM 80/81/ INITIAL E EXULTATE/ DAVID PLAYS HARP 554-45, INITIAL E EXULTATE 554-45, PSALM 95/96/ INITIAL C CANTATE/ MONKS SING 554-46, INITIAL C CANTATE 554-46, MONKS STAND SINGING BEFORE LECTERN 554-46, PSALM 95/96/ INITIAL C CANTATE/ ANGEL AND SHEPHERD 554-47, INITIAL C CANTATE 554-47, ANGEL SPEAKS TO SHEPHERD WITH TWO SHEEP 554-47, PSALM 109/110/ INITIAL D DIXIT/ GOD SUPPORTS CHRIST 554-48, INITIAL D DIXIT 554-48, GOD SUPPORTS CRUCIFIED CHRIST ON CROSS 554-48,PSALM 109/110/ INITIAL D DIXIT/ TRINITY 554-49, INITIAL D DIXIT 554-49, GOD AND CHRIST WITH DOVE BETWEEN THEM 554-49, PSALM 119/120/ INITIAL A AD/ DAVID PRAYS 554-50, INITIAL A AD 554-50, DAVID KNEELS IN PRAYER 554-50, INITIAL P PARABOLE/ SOLOMON AND NAKED MAN 554-51, SOLOMON HOLDING SWITCH ADMONISHES NAKED FIGURE 554-51, INITIAL O OMNIS/ KING INSTRUCTS CROWD 554-52, KING INSTRUCTS A CROWD/ GOD WATCHES 554-52, INITIAL V VISIO/ ISAIAH SAWN IN HALF 554-53, ISAIAH SAWN IN HALF FROM CROTCH UPWARD 554-53, INITIAL V VERBA/ JEREMIAH AND MAN WITH STONES 554-54, JEREMIAH FOLLOWED BY MAN WITH STONES 554-54, INITIAL E ET/ EZEKIEL AT RIVER CHEBAR 554-55, EZEKIEL BY THE RIVER CHEBAR 554-55, INITIAL A ANNO/ DANIEL TALKS TO LIONS 554-56, DANIEL IN LION'S DEN 554-56, INITIAL P PAULUS/ PAUL IN PRISON 554-57, ST PAUL IN PRISON HANDS SCROLL TO MESSENGER 554-57, INITIAL P PAULUS/ PAUL HOLDS SWORD 554-58, ST PAUL HOLDS SWORD 554-58, GROTESQUE BITES STEM OF INITIAL 554-58, INITIAL P PAULUS/ PAUL WRITES 554-59, ST PAUL TURNS TO MAN BEHIND HIM 554-59, INITIAL P PAULUS/ PAUL WRITES 554-60, ST PAUL WRITES IN BOOK 554-60, INITIAL I IACOBUS/ JAMES THROWN FROM CASTLE 554-61, ST JAMES THROWN FROM CASTLE 554-61

*$ABSTRACT 555
*LIBRARY ALL SOULS COLLEGE OXFORD
*SLIDE SET TITLE MEDICAL MSS IN ALL SOULS COLLEGE
*NEGATIVE REFERENCE ROLL 232B
*RENTAL FEE $2.35
*TITLE OF MANUSCRIPT ARS MEDICINAE 555/1-5, ANTIDOTARIUM 555-6, APHORISMS 555-7
*SHELFMARK MS ALL SOULS COLLEGE 71/ FOL 1 555-1,MS ALL SOULS COLLEGE 71/ FOL 6 555-2, MS ALL SOULS COLLEGE 71/ FOL 13 555-3, MS ALL SOULS COLLEGE 71/ FOL 64V 555-4, MS ALL SOULS COLLEGE 71/ FOL 113V 555-5, MS ALL SOULS COLLEGE 72/ FOL 1 555-6, MS ALL SOULS COLLEGE 72/ FOL 67 555-7
*PROVENANCE FRENCH 555/1-5, ENGLISH 555-6, FRENCH 555-7

*DATE EXECUTED 13TH/ 2ND HALF 555/1-5, 14TH/ 2ND HALF 555-6, 14TH/C1300 555-7
*LANGUAGE LATIN
*AUTHOR NICOLAUS 555-6, JOHN OF DAMASCUS 555-7
*TYPE OF MANUSCRIPT MEDICAL TREATISES 555/1-7
*CONTENTS MEDICAL TREATISES 555/1-7, TEACHER SPEAKS TO TWO TONSURED STUDENTS 555-1, TEACHER HOLDS UP FLASK BEFORE STUDENTS 555-2, CLERICS STAND CONVERSING 555-3, DOCTOR VISITS SICK PATIENT IN BED 555-4, DOCTOR INSTRUCTS APOTHECARY HOLDING SCALES 555-5, APOTHECARY HOLDS PAIR OF SCALES 555-5, DOCTOR HOLDS UP FLASK 555-6, MORTAR AND PESTLE 555-6, DOCTOR HOLDS UP FLASK/ STUDENT POINTS TO POT 555-7

*$ABSTRACT 556
*LIBRARY ALL SOULS COLLEGE OXFORD
*SLIDE SET TITLE LEGAL MSS IN ALL SOULS COLLEGE
*NEGATIVE REFERENCE ROLL 232C
*RENTAL FEE $3.40
*TITLE OF MANUSCRIPT DIGESTUM VETUS 556/1-6, INFORTIATUM 556/15-16, DIGESTUM NOVUM 556/17-23, SUMMA 556/24-28
*SHELFMARK MS ALL SOULS COLLEGE 49/ FOL 1 556-1, MS ALL SOULS COLLEGE 49/ FOL 19 556-2, MS ALL SOULS COLLEGE 49/ FOL 108 556-3, MS ALL SOULS COLLEGE 49/ FOL 286V 556-4, MS ALL SOULS COLLEGE 49/ FOL 294 556-5, MS ALL SOULS COLLEGE 49/ FOL 306 556-6, MS ALL SOULS COLLEGE 50/ FOL 7 556-7, MS ALL SOULS COLLEGE 50/ FOL 8V 556-8, MS ALL SOULS COLLEGE 50/ FOL 42 556-9, MS ALL SOULS COLLEGE 50/ FOL 64V 556-10, MS ALL SOULS COLLEGE 50/ FOL 89V 556-11, MS ALL SOULS COLLEGE 50/ FOL 129 556-12, MS ALL SOULS COLLEGE 50/ FOL 164V 556-13, MS ALL SOULS COLLEGE 50/ FOL 212 556-14, MS ALL SOULS COLLEGE 51/ FOL 1 556/15-16, MS ALL SOULS COLLEGE 52/ FOL 21 556-17, MS ALL SOULS COLLEGE 52/ FOL 112V 556-18, MS ALL SOULS COLLEGE 52/ FOL 114 556-19, MS ALL SOULS COLLEGE 52/ FOL 114V 556-20, MS ALL SOULS COLLEGE 52/ FOL 206V 556-21, MS ALL SOULS COLLEGE 52/ FOL 238V 556-22, MS ALL SOULS COLLEGE 52/ FOL 256 556-23, MS ALL SOULS COLLEGE 55/ FOL 159V 556-24, MS ALL SOULS COLLEGE 55/ FOL 163 556-25, MS ALL SOULS COLLEGE 55/ FOL 165 556-26, MS ALL SOULS COLLEGE 55/ FOL 166 556-27, MS ALL SOULS COLLEGE 55/ FOL 168 556-28 MS ALL SOULS COLLEGE 55/ FOL 168 556-28
*PROVENANCE FRENCH 556/1-6, ENGLISH 556/7-14, FRENCH/ PARIS 556/15-16, ITALIAN/ BOLOGNA 556/17-23, ITALIAN 556/24-28
*DATE EXECUTED 14TH/C1300 556/1-6, 14TH/ 2ND HALF 556/7-14, 14TH/ MID 556/15-16, 14TH/ 1ST QUARTER 556/17-23, 13TH/ 2ND QUARTER 556/24-28
*LANGUAGE LATIN
*AUTHOR AZZO 556/24-28
*TYPE OF MANUSCRIPT LEGAL
*CONTENTS LEGAL MSS 556/1-28, JUSTINIAN WATCHES CLERICS BURN BOOKS 556-1, BOOK-BURNING BY CLERICS 556-1, JUSTINIAN RECEIVES BOOKS FROM CLERICS 556-2, PEASANTS REAP WHEAT/ COLLECT FRUIT 556-3, JUSTINIAN RECEIVES SCROLL FROM CLERICS 556-4,MARRIAGE/ CLERIC STANDS BETWEEN BRIDE AND GROOM 556-5, FOUR FIGURES STAND AT CHURCH DOOR 556-6, TEACHER SPEAKS TO THREE MEN 556-7, GOD ENTHRONED HOLDING GLOBE IN QUATREFOIL MANDORLA 556-8, TEACHER EXPOUNDS TO FOUR STUDENTS 556-9, KING ENTHRONED WITH TALL CROWN 556-10, TEACHER EXPOUNDS FROM BOOK ON LAP TO TWO MEN 556-11, MAN AND WOMAN CLASP HAND WHILE WOMAN WATCHES 556-12, TEACHER SPEAKS TO TWO MEN/ ONE HOLDS BATTLE-AXE 556-13, KING HOLDS STAFF OR SWORD ON HEAD OF MAN 556-14, UPPER HALF OF FOLIO 556-15, BISHOP WITH MITRE AND STAFF/ BIRD/ MAN AND WOMAN 556-15, LOWER HALF OF FOLIO 556-16, MAN AND WOMAN PLAY GAME WITH LARGE RING 556-16,INITIAL INHABITED WITH FIGURE HOLDING SCROLL 556-17, INITIALS/ THREE 556-18, INITIALS/ THREE 556-19, INITIAL WITH ABSTRACT FOLIAGE PATTERN 556-19, INITIAL WITH MAN'S HEAD WITH FUR COLLAR 556-19,INITIAL WITH FIGURE WITH HELMET AND SHIELD 556-19, INITIAL WITH MAN BENDING DOWN 556-20, INITIALS/ ABSTRACT FOLIAGE/ MEN'S HEADS 556-21, INITIALS WITH MAN'S HEAD AND BIRD WEARING CLOAK 556-22, MEDALLIONS WITH CLOAKED MEN 556-23, GROTESQUE MAN IN POINTED CAP 556-24, BIRD WITH HUMAN HEAD AND POINTED CAP 556-25, MAN

WITH CAP/ PEN-LINES ISSUE FROM MOUTH 556-26, BIRD/ HORNED 556-27, INITIALS/ FOLIATED AND INTERLACED 556-28

*$ABSTRACT 557
*LIBRARY ALL SOULS COLLEGE OXFORD
*SLIDE SET TITLE AZZO/ SUMMA
*NEGATIVE REFERENCE ROLL 232D
*RENTAL FEE $3.75
*COMMENTS CALLIGRAPHIC FIGURES IN RED AND BLUE FROM LOWER MARGINS, MOST OF THEM WITH ELABORATE PEN-LINE PATTERNS ISSUING FROM MOUTHS OF FIGURES.
*TITLE OF MANUSCRIPT SUMMA OF AZZO
*SHELFMARK MS ALL SOULS COLLEGE 55/ FOL 1 557-1, MS ALL SOULS COLLEGE 55/ FOL 7 557-2, MS ALL SOULS COLLEGE 55/ FOL 8 557-3, MS ALL SOULS COLLEGE 55/ FOL 10 557-4, MS ALL SOULS COLLEGE 55/ FOL 13 557-5, MS ALL SOULS COLLEGE 55/ FOL 13V 557-6, MS ALL SOULS COLLEGE 55/ FOL 14 557-7, MS ALL SOULS COLLEGE 55/ FOL 20 557-8, MS ALL SOULS COLLEGE 55/ FOL 22 557-9, MS ALL SOULS COLLEGE 55/ FOL 23 557-10, MS ALL SOULS COLLEGE 55/ FOL 23V 557-11, MS ALL SOULS COLLEGE 55/ FOL 29 557-12, MS ALL SOULS COLLEGE 55/ FOL 30 557-13, MS ALL SOULS COLLEGE 55/ FOL 33 557-14, MS ALL SOULS COLLEGE 55/ FOL 53V 557-15, MS ALL SOULS COLLEGE 55/ FOL 54 557-16, MS ALL SOULS COLLEGE 55/ FOL 63 557-17, MS ALL SOULS COLLEGE 55/ FOL 72V 557-18, MS ALL SOULS COLLEGE 55/ FOL 73 557-19, MS ALL SOULS COLLEGE 55/ FOL 83 557-20, MS ALL SOULS COLLEGE 55/ FOL 92V 557-21, MS ALL SOULS COLLEGE 55/ FOL 93 557-22, MS ALL SOULS COLLEGE 55/ FOL 102 557-23, MS ALL SOULS COLLEGE 55/ FOL 113V 557-24, MS ALL SOULS COLLEGE 55/ FOL 140V 557-25, MS ALL SOULS COLLEGE 55/ FOL 142 557-26, MS ALL SOULS COLLEGE 55/ FOL 144 557-27, MS ALL SOULS COLLEGE 55/ FOL 154 557-28, MS ALL SOULS COLLEGE 55/ FOL 157 557-29, MS ALL SOULS COLLEGE 55/ FOL 158 557-30, MS ALL SOULS COLLEGE 55/ FOL 159V 557-31, MS ALL SOULS COLLEGE 55/ FOL 161 557-32, MS ALL SOULS COLLEGE 55/ FOL 163 557-33, MS ALL SOULS COLLEGE 55/ FOL 164 557-34, MS ALL SOULS COLLEGE 55/ FOL 167 557-35
*PROVENANCE ITALIAN
*DATE EXECUTED 13TH/ 2ND QUARTER
*LANGUAGE LATIN
*AUTHOR AZZO
*TYPE OF MANUSCRIPT SUMMA
*CONTENTS SUMMA OF AZZO 557/1-35, DRAGON BITES NECK OF BEAST 557-1, BIRD/ HORNED 557-2, BIRD/ HORNED 557-3, GROTESQUE BEARDED MAN WITH TAIL AND BIRD'S FEET 557-4, BIRD/ HORNED BITES A LETTER OF THE TEXT 557-5, BIRD WITH POINTED EARS 557-6, MAN IN ROUND HAT 557-7, GROTESQUE MAN IN TALL POINTED HAT 557-8, BEAR SITTING ON HIND LEGS 557-9, WOMAN HOLDS OBJECTS IN HANDS 557-10, MERMAN HOLDS TORCH AND PEN-LINES 557-11, GROTESQUE WITH CAT'S EARS/ WHISKERS AND PAW 557-12, BIRD WITH LONG BEAK BITES TEXT 557-13, GROTESQUE MAN HOLDS CLUB 557-14, GROTESQUE MAN WITH FACE ON CHEST 557-15, STAG 557-16, MAN CROWNED GESTURES WITH HANDS 557-17, ANGEL WITH LEGS BENT BACKWARD AND TALL HAT 557-18, BIRD/ HORNED 557-19, HORIZONTAL ROWS OF ANIMALS/ GROTESQUES AND PEN-WORK 557-20, BIRD/ HORNED WITH LONG LEGS 557-21, BIRD BITES MAN ON ARM 557-22, MAN HOLDS OBJECT RESEMBLING KITE 557-23, GROTESQUE MAN IN POINTED CAP 557-24, TWO-HEADED BIRD WITH HUMAN ARMS AND ANIMAL LEGS 557-25, BIRD/ HORNED WITH OUTSTRETCHED WINGS AND LEGS 557-26, STAG STANDING ON HIND LEGS 557-27, BIRD/ HORNED WITH HUMAN ARM HOLDS SWORD 557-28, SERPENT 557-29, GROTESQUE 557-30, MAN IN POINTED CAP 557-31, BIRD/ HORNED 557-32, BIRD WITH HUMAN HEAD AND POINTED CAP 557-33, GROTESQUE 557-34, BIRD/ HORNED 557-35

*$ABSTRACT 558
*LIBRARY ALL SOULS COLLEGE OXFORD
*SLIDE SET TITLE AMESBURY PSALTER
*NEGATIVE REFERENCE ROLL 232E

*RENTAL FEE $4.00
*TITLE OF MANUSCRIPT AMESBURY PSALTER
*SHELFMARK MS ALL SOULS COLLEGE 6/ FOL 3 558-1, MS ALL SOULS COLLEGE 6/ FOL 4 558-2, MS ALL SOULS COLLEGE 6/ FOL 5 558-3, MS ALL SOULS COLLEGE 6/ FOL 6 558-4, MS ALL SOULS COLLEGE 6/ FOL 13 558-5, MS ALL SOULS COLLEGE 6/ FOL 16 558-6, MS ALL SOULS COLLEGE 6/ FOL 18 558-7, MS ALL SOULS COLLEGE 6/ GOL 25V 558-8, MS ALL SOULS COLLEGE 6/ FOL 31 558-9, MS ALL SOULS COLLEGE 6/ FOL 35V 558-10, MS ALL SOULS COLLEGE 6/ FOL 50V 558-11, MS ALL SOULS COLLEGE 6/ FOL 55V 558-12, MS ALL SOULS COLLEGE 6/ FOL 58 558-13, MS ALL SOULS COLLEGE 6/ FOL 58V 558-14, MS ALL SOULS COLLEGE 6/ FOL 64 558-15, MS ALL SOULS COLLEGE 6/ FOL 64V 558-16, MS ALL SOULS COLLEGE 6/ FOL 71 558-17, MS ALL SOULS COLLEGE 6/ FOL 76 558-18, MS ALL SOULS COLLEGE 6/ FOL 76V 558-19, MS ALL SOULS COLLEGE 6/ FOL 79 558-20, MS ALL SOULS COLLEGE 6/ FOL 81V 558/21-22, MS ALL SOULS COLLEGE 6/ FOL 88V 558-23, MS ALL SOULS COLLEGE 6/ FOL 96 558-24, MS ALL SOULS COLLEGE 6/ FOL 97 558-25, MS ALL SOULS COLLEGE 6/ FOL 108 558-26, MS ALL SOULS COLLEGE 6/ FOL 109V 558-27, MS ALL SOULS COLLEGE 6/ FOL 112 558-28, MS ALL SOULS COLLEGE 6/ FOL 114 558-29, MS ALL SOULS COLLEGE 6/ FOL 113V 558-30, MS ALL SOULS COLLEGE 6/ FOL 119 558-31, MS ALL SOULS COLLEGE 6/ FOL 126V 558-32, MS ALL SOULS COLLEGE 6/ FOL 128 558-33, MS ALL SOULS COLLEGE 6/ FOL 143 558/34-35, MS ALL SOULS COLLEGE 6/ FOL 143V 558-36, MS ALL SOULS COLLEGE 6/ FOL 155 558-37, MS ALL SOULS COLLEGE 6/ FOL 160V 558-38, MS ALL SOULS COLLEGE 6/ FOL 161 558-39, MS ALL SOULS COLLEGE 6/ FOL 187V 558-40
*PROVENANCE ENGLISH/ SALISBURY
*DATE EXECUTED 13TH/C1250
*LANGUAGE LATIN
*TYPE OF MANUSCRIPT PSALTER/ USE OF SARUM
*CONTENTS PSALTER/ ENGLISH/ 13TH 558/1-40, ANNUNCIATION 558-1, VIRGIN MARY NURSING CHRIST 558-2, VIRGIN'S FEET REST ON LION AND DRAGON 558-2, CRUCIFIXION/ FULL-PAGE MINIATURE 558-3, MARY AND JOHN STAND ON EITHER SIDE OF CROSS 558-3, GOD AND DOVE FLANKED BY ANGEL IN DEMI-QUATREFOIL 558-3, ADAM RISES FROM TOMB AS BLOOD OF CHRIST FLOWS 558-3, CHURCH TRIUMPHANT REPRESENTED AS CROWNED WOMAN 558-3, SYNAGOGUE REPRESENTED AS FALLING WOMAN 558-3,CHRIST IN MAJESTY IN MULTIFOIL MANDORLA 558-4, PSALM 1/ INITIAL B BEATUS VIR/ JESSE TREE 558-5, INITIAL B BEATUS VIR/ JESSE TREE 558-5, JESSE TREE/ JESSE LIES SLEEPING 558-5, KING DAVID/ VIRGIN/ CHRIST IN MAJESTY 558-5, SAMSON AND LION IN ROUNDEL 558-5, MOSES BEFORE ISRAELITES IN ROUNDEL 558-5, CAIN KILLS ABEL WITH JAWBONE IN ROUNDEL 558-5,CAIN AND ABEL MAKE OFFERINGS IN ROUNDEL 558-5, ABRAHAM SACRIFICES RAM IN PLACE OF ISAAC 558-5, NOAH'S ARK IN ROUNDEL 558-5, INITIAL/ GOAT PLAYS FIDDLE 558-6, INITIAL/ APE PLAYS HARP 558-7, INITIAL/ PERFORMING BEAR 558-8, INITIAL/ TRISKELE OF BEARDED FACES 558-9, PSALM 26/27/ INITIAL D DOMINUS ILLUMINATION 558-10, INITIAL D DOMINUS ILLUMINATIO/ SAMUEL ANOINTS DAVID 558-10, SAMUEL ANOINTS DAVID 558-10, PSALM 38/39/ INITIAL D DIXI CUSTODIAM/ MASSACRE OF INNOCENTS 558-11, INITIAL D DIXI CUSTODIAM/ MASSACRE OF INNOCENTS 558-11, MASSACRE OF INNOCENTS/ HEROD ORDERS SOLDIER TO KILL CHILD 558-11, HEROD ORDERS SOLDIER TO KILL CHILD 558-11, INITIAL/ TONSURED MAN PLAYS RIBIBE 558-12, INITIAL/ CENTAUR DRAWING BOW 558-13, INITIAL/ RABBIT PLAYING DRUM 558-14, PSALM 51/52/ INITIAL Q QUID GLORIARIS/ DOEG THE EDOMITE 558-15, INITIAL Q QUID GLORIARIS/ DOEG THE EDOMITE 558-15, DOEG THE EDOMITE BEHEADS SEVEN PRIESTS 558-15,PSALM 52/53/ INITIAL D DIXIT INSIPIENS/ TEMPTATION 558-16, INITIAL D DIXIT INSIPIENS/ TEMPTATION OF CHRIST 558-16, CHRIST TEMPTED BY HORNED DEVIL HOLDING SCROLL 558-16, INITIAL/ MERMAID SUCKLING HER YOUNG 558-17, MERMAID SUCKLING HER YOUNG 558-17, INITIAL/ PELICAN PECKING BREAST TO FEED YOUNG 558-18, PELICAN PECKING BREAST TO FEED YOUNG 558-18, INITIAL/ HARE AND DOG 558-19, HARE AND DOG 558-19, PSALM 68/69/ INITIAL S SALVUM ME FAC/ JONAH 558-20, INITIAL S SALVUM ME FAC 558-20, JONAH CAST INTO MOUTH OF WHALE 558-20, INITIAL/ EAGLE WITH SPREAD WINGS 558-21, EAGLE WITH SPREAD WINGS 558-21, INITIAL/ MONSTER SEEN FROM ABOVE 558-22, MONSTER 558-22, INITIAL/ SQUIRREL EATING NUT 558-23, SQUIRREL

EATING NUT 558-23, PSALM 80/81/ INITIAL E EXULTATE DEO/ JACOB AND ANGEL 558-24, INITIAL E EXULTATE DEO/ JACOB WRESTLES WITH ANGEL 558-24, JACOB WRESTLES WITH ANGEL 558-24, JACOB LIES ON GROUND WITH EYES OPEN 558-24, ANGEL ASCENDS LADDER 558-24, INITIAL/ NAKED MAN WITH SPEAR RIDES BIRD 558-25, MAN/ NAKED WITH SPEAR AND SHIELD RIDES BIRD 558-25, INITIAL/ ELEPHANT WITH CASTLE ON BACK 558-26, ELEPHANT WITH CASTLE ON BACK 558-26, INITIAL/ MERMAID PLAYS VIOLIN 558-27, MERMAID PLAYS VIOLIN 558-27, PSALM 97/98/ INITIAL C CANTATE DOMINO/ ANNUNCIATION 558-28, INITIAL C CANTATE DOMINO/ ANNUNCIATION TO SHEPHERDS 558-28, ANGEL BEFORE SHEPHERD POINTS TO STAR 558-28, PSALM 101/102/ INITIAL D DOMINE EXAUDI/ CHRIST'S TOMB 558-29, INITIAL D DOMINE EXAUDI/ CHRIST STEPS FROM TOMB 558-29, CHRIST FLANKED BY ANGELS STEPS FROM OPEN TOMB 558-29, INITIAL/ TWO BIRDS 558-30, INITIAL/ TRISKELE OF FISHES 558-31, INITIAL/ MERMAID PLAYS HARP 558-32, MERMAID PLAYS HARP 558-32, PSALM 109/110/ INITIAL D DIXIT DOMINUS/ TRINITY 558-33, INITIAL D DIXIT DOMINUS/ TRINITY 558-33, TRINITY/ GOD CLASPS WRIST OF CHRIST 558-33, INITIAL/ CHRIST HOLDS BOOK AND BLESSES 558-34,CHRIST HOLDS BOOK AND BLESSES 558-34, DUPLICATE OF FRAME 34 558-35, INITIAL/ OWL AND BIRD 558-36, OWL AND BIRD 558-36, INITIAL/ SCIAPOD 558-37, SCIAPOD 558-37, INITIAL/ ROOSTER 558-38, ROOSTER 558-38, INITIAL/ SEATED MONK WITH BIRCH ADMONISHES MONK 558-39, MONK/ SEATED ADMONISHES MONK WITH BIRCH 558-39, INITIAL/ MONSTER 558-40, MONSTER 558-40

*$ABSTRACT 559
*LIBRARY ALL SOULS COLLEGE OXFORD
*SLIDE SET TITLE PSALTER OF SARUM USE
*NEGATIVE REFERENCE ROLL 232F
*RENTAL FEE $3.15
*SHELFMARK MS ALL SOULS COLLEGE 7/ FOL 7 559/1-2, MS ALL SOULS COLLEGE 7/ FOL 8 559-3, MS ALL SOULS COLLEGE 7/ FOL 11 558-4, MS ALL SOULS COLLEGE 7/ FOL 21 559-5, MS ALL SOULS COLLEGE 7/ FOL 24 559-6, MS ALL SOULS COLLEGE 7/ FOL 25 559-7, MS ALL SOULS COLLEGE 7/ FOL 26 559-8, MS ALL SOULS COLLEGE 7/ FOL 28 559-9, MS ALL SOULS COLLEGE 7/ FOL 29 559-10, MS ALL SOULS COLLEGE 7/ FOL 38V 559-11, MS ALL SOULS COLLEGE 7/ FOL 49 559-12, MS ALL SOULS COLLEGE 7/ FOL 49V 559-13, MS ALL SOULS COLLEGE 7/ FOL 61 558-14, MS ALL SOULS COLLEGE 7/ FOL 75V 559-15, MS ALL SOULS COLLEGE 7/ FOL 89 559-16, MS ALL SOULS COLLEGE 7/ FOL 91 559-17, MS ALL SOULS COLLEGE 7/ FOL 103 559-18, MS ALL SOULS COLLEGE 7/ FOL 113V 559-19, MS ALL SOULS COLLEGE 7/ FOL 116 559-20, MS ALL SOULS COLLEGE 7/ FOL 124V 559-21, MS ALL SOULS COLLEGE 7/ FOL 132 559-22, MS ALL SOULS COLLEGE 7/ FOL 148V 559-23
*PROVENANCE ENGLISH/ ELY?
*DATE EXECUTED 14TH/C1320
*LANGUAGE LATIN
*TYPE OF MANUSCRIPT PSALTER/ USE OF SARUM
*CONTENTS PSALTER/ ENGLISH/ 14TH 559/1-23, PSALM 1/ INITIAL B BEATUS VIR/ DAVID PLAYS HARP 559-1, INITIAL B BEATUS VIR/ DAVID PLAYS HARP 559-1, DAVID PLAYS HARP/ MAN BLOWS TRUMPET 559-1, GITTERN PLAYED BY WOMAN 559-2, DOG CHASES HARE BENEATH THREE TREES 559-2, GROTESQUE MAN HOLDS SWORD AND SHIELD 559-3, INITIAL/ DEAD MAN RISES FROM GRAVE 559-4, DEAD MAN RISES FROM GRAVE 559-4, INITIAL/ HOODED AND WINGED GROTESQUE 559-5, GROTESQUE/ HOODED AND WINGED 559-5, INITIAL/ HOODED GROTESQUE 559-6, GROTESQUE/ HOODED 559-6, GROTESQUES WITH NECKS TWISTED TOGETHER 559-7,PSALM 26/27/ INITIAL D DOMINUS ILLUMINATIO/ DAVID 559-8, INITIAL D DOMINUS ILLUMINATIO/ DAVID POINTS TO EYE 559-8, DAVID POINTS TO HIS EYE/ GOD LEANS DOWN 559-8, MAN HOLDING CLUB CRAWLS AMONG VINES 559-9, DOG CROUCHES 559-10, PSALM 38/39/ INITIAL DIXI CUSTODIAM/ DAVID POINTS TO MOUTH 559-11, INITIAL D DIXI CUSTODIAM/ DAVID POINTS TO MOUTH 559-11, DAVID POINTS TO HIS MOUTH/ GOD IN CLOUDS 559-11, PSALM 51/52/ INITIAL Q QUID GLORIARIS/ DAVID AND GOLIATH 559-12, INITIAL Q QUID GLORIARIS/ DAVID AND GOLIATH 559-12, DAVID STANDS OVER FALLEN GOLIATH 559-12, PSALM 52/53/ INITIAL D DIXIT INSIPIENS/ DAVID AND FOOL 559-13, INITIAL D DIXIT

INSIPIENS/ DAVID ADMONISHES FOOL 559-13, DAVID ADMONISHES THE FOOL 559-13, PSALM 68/69/ INITIAL S SALVUM ME FAC/ JONAH AND WHALE 559-14, INITIAL S SALVUM ME FAC/ JONAH AND WHALE 559-14, JONAH SITS ASTRIDE WHALE 559-14, PSALM 80/81/ INITIAL E EXULTATE DEO/ DAVID WITH BELLS 559-15, INITIAL E EXULTATE DEO/ DAVID PLAYS HANDBELLS 559-15, DAVID SITS PLAYING SIX HANDBELLS WITH HAMMERS 559-15, PSALM 97/98/ INITIAL C CANTATE DOMINO/ MONKS SING 559-16, INITIAL C CANTATE DOMINO/ MONKS SING BEFORE LECTERN 559-16, MONKS STAND SINGING BEFORE LECTERN 559-16, PSALM 101/102/ INITIAL D DOMINE EXAUDI/ CHRIST IN MAJESTY 559-17, INITIAL D DOMINE EXAUDI/ CHRIST IN MAJESTY 559-17, CHRIST IN MAJESTY 559-17, PSALM 109/110/ INITIAL D DIXIT DOMINUS/ TRINITY 559-18, INITIAL D DIXIT DOMINUS/ TRINITY 559-18, TRINITY/ GOD AND CHRIST AS YOUTHFUL FIGURES 559-18, INITIAL/ TWO BEARDED FACES 559-19, PSALM 119/120/ INITIAL A AD DOMINUM/ MONK IN PRAYER 559-20, INITIAL A AD DOMINUM/ MONK KNEELS IN PRAYER 559-20, GROTESQUE MAN WITH GREEN LEGS 559-21, INITIAL/ FIGURE KNEELS BEFORE ALTAR 559-22, FIGURE KNEELS BEFORE ALTAR 559-22, INITIAL/ CLERICS CHANT BEFORE BIER 559-23, CLERICS CHANT BEFORE BIER WITH DRAPED FIGURE 559-23

*$ABSTRACT 560
*LIBRARY BODLEIAN
*SLIDE SET TITLE BOETHIUS/ DE CONSOLATIONE PHILOSOPHIAE
*NEGATIVE REFERENCE ROLL 234A
*RENTAL FEE $2.50
*TITLE OF MANUSCRIPT DE CONSOLATIONE PHILOSOPHIAE
*SHELFMARK MS DOUCE 298/ FOL 1 560-1, MS DOUCE 298/ FOL 13V 560-2, MS DOUCE 298/ FOL 33 560-3, MS DOUCE 298/ FOL 53V 560-4, MS DOUCE 298/ FOL 74V 560-5, MS DOUCE 352/ FOL 4 560-6, MS DOUCE 352/ FOL 18 560-7, MS DOUCE 352/ FOL 30 560-8, MS DOUCE 352/ FOL 43V 560-9, MS DOUCE 353/ FOL 66 560-10
*PROVENANCE FRENCH
*DATE EXECUTED 15TH/C1400 560/1-5, 15TH/C1460 560/6-10
*LANGUAGE FRENCH TRANSLATION IN VERSE 560/1-5, FRENCH TRANSLATION IN PROSE 560/6-10
*AUTHOR BOETHIUS
*TYPE OF MANUSCRIPT CONSOLATION
*CONTENTS BOETHIUS/ DE CONSOLATIONE PHILOSOPHIAE 560/1-10, FRENCH TRANSLATIONS OF BOETHIUS 560/1-10, BOETHIUS IN BED/ TWO MUSES/ LADY PHILOSOPHY 560-1, FORTUNE/ BLINDFOLDED TURNS HER WHEEL 560-2, KING AT TOP OF FORTUNE'S WHEEL 560-2, PHILOSOPHY SPEAKS TO BOETHIUS ABOUT TRUE HAPPINESS 560-3, BOETHIUS SPEAKS TO PHILOSOPHY 560-4, PHILOSOPHY SPEAKS TO BOETHIUS ABOUT DIVINE FOREKNOWLEDGE 560-5, JEHAN DE MEHUN PRESENTS TRANSLATION TO PHILIP IV 560-6, PHILIP IV RECEIVES TRANSLATION FROM JEHAN DE MEHUN 560-6, PHILOSOPHY STANDS BEFORE BOETHIUS 560-7, PHILOSOPHY STANDS WITH HANDMAIDEN BEFORE BOETHIUS 560-8, BOETHIUS AND PHILOSOPHY CONVERSE 560-9, BOETHIUS REACHING FOR BOOK SPEAKS TO PHILOSOPHY 560-10

*$ABSTRACT 561
*LIBRARY BODLEIAN
*SLIDE SET TITLE PIERS PLOWMAN C-TEXT
*NEGATIVE REFERENCE ROLL 234B
*RENTAL FEE $4.10
*COMMENTS LINE REFERENCES ARE TO SKEAT'S EDITION. THIS SET SUPPLEMENTS ROLL 168I/ABSTRACT 97.
*TITLE OF MANUSCRIPT PIERS PLOWMAN C-TEXT
*SHELFMARK MS DOUCE 104/ FOL 8 561-1, MS DOUCE 104/ FOL 9 561-2, MS DOUCE 104/ FOL 11 561-3, MS DOUCE 104/ FOL 15 561-4, MS DOUCE 104/ FOL 18 561-5, MS DOUCE 104/ FOL 19 561-6, MS DOUCE 104/ FOL 23 561-7, MS DOUCE 104/ FOL 34 561-8, MS DOUCE 104/ FOL 35 561-9, MS DOUCE 104/ FOL 35V 561-10, MS DOUCE 104/ FOL 39 561-11, MS DOUCE 104/ FOL 40 561-12, MS DOUCE 104/ FOL 41 561-13, MS DOUCE 104/ FOL 42 561-14, MS DOUCE 104/ FOL 43 561-15, MS DOUCE 104/ FOL 46 561-16, MS DOUCE 104/ FOL 47 561-17, MS DOUCE 104/ FOL 48V-49 561-18, MS DOUCE 104/ FOL 51

561-19, MS DOUCE 104/ FOL 52 561-20, MS DOUCE 104/ FOL 52V 561-21, MS DOUCE 104/ FOL 54 561-22, MS DOUCE 104/ FOL 55 561-23, MS DOUCE 104/ FOL 56 561-24, MS DOUCE 104/ FOL 60V-61 561-25, MS DOUCE 104/ FOL 63 561-26, MS DOUCE 104/ FOL 65 561-27, MS DOUCE 104/ FOL 67V 561-28, MS DOUCE 104/ FOL 69 561-29, MS DOUCE 104/ FOL 71 561-30, MS DOUCE 104/ FOL 72 561-31, MS DOUCE 104/ FOL 74 561-32, MS DOUCE 104/ FOL 79 561-33, MS DOUCE 104/ FOL 94 561-34, MS DOUCE 104/ FOL 96 561-35, MS DOUCE 104/ FOL 101 561-36, MS DOUCE 104/ FOL 102V-103 561-37, MS DOUCE 104/ FOL 105 561-38, MS DOUCE 104/ FOL 107 561-39, MS DOUCE 104/ FOL 109 561-40, MS DOUCE 104/ FOL 109V 561-41, MS DOUCE 104/ FOL 111V 561-42
*DATE EXECUTED 15TH/1427
*LANGUAGE ENGLISH/ MIDDLE ENGLISH
*AUTHOR LANGLAND/ WILLIAM
*TYPE OF MANUSCRIPT POETRY/ MIDDLE ENGLISH
*CONTENTS LITERATURE/ PIERS PLOWMAN 561/1-42, ENGLISH LITERATURE/ PIERS PLOWMAN 561/1-42, PIERS PLOWMAN C-TEXT 561/1-42, LADY MEDE RICHLY DRESSED IN RED PASSUS III 561-1, LIAR HOLDS MARRIAGE CHARTER/ PASSUS III 561-2, LADY MEDE AT WESTMINSTER/ PASSUS IV 561-3, CONSCIENCE IN BLUE MANTLE /PASSUS IV 561-4, KING ENTHRONED WITH CROWN AND SCEPTRE/ PASSUS V 561-5, REASON WEARS RED ROBE AND GREY HAT/ PASSUS V 561-6, TOM STOWE HOLDS TWO STAVES/ PASSUS VI 561-7, CASTLE OF TRUTH/ PASSUS VIII 561-8, PILGRIM WITH STAFF AND GLOVES/ PASSUS IX 561-9, FIGURE IN CLOAK AND CHAPERON/ PASSUS IX 561-10, LABOURER DIGS WITH METAL-TIPPED SPADE/ PASSUS IX 561-11, SHIP IN ROUGH WATER/ PASSUS IX 561-12, LAWYER IN GREY ROBE PLEADS/ PASSUS X 561-13, LUNATIC NAKED/ PASSUS X 561-14, BLIND MAN FEELS WAY WITH STAFF/ PASSUS X 561-15, FRIAR STANDS TALKING/ PASSUS XI 561-16, DO-BETTER TONSURED IN WHITE HABIT/ PASSUS XI 561-17, FIGURE HOLDS HANDS OVER EARS/ PASSUS XI 561-18, RAM AND PINK CALF/ PASSUS XI 561-18, MAN/ POOR HOLDS STAFF/ PASSUS XII 561-19, TEACHER BIRCHES SCHOOLBOY/ PASSUS XII 561-20, ST AUGUSTINE SITS WRITING/ PASSUS XII 561-21, CLERK/ HEAD AND SHOULDERS/ PASSUS XII 561-22, OLD AGE RESTS HEAD ON HAND/ PASSUS XIII 561-23,EMPEROR TRAJAN /PASSUS XIII 561-24, PRIEST POINTS DISAPPROVINGLY TO MONEY/ PASSUS XIV 561-25, IMAGINATION SITS IN THOUGHT/ PASSUS XV 561-26,THIEF PENITENT IN WHITE ROBE/ PASSUS XV 561-27, FRIAR/ FALSE IN WHITE HABIT/ PASSUS XVI 561-28, ACTIVA-VITA IN WORN SHOES/ PASSUS XVI 561-29, DEATH REPRESENTED AS SKELETON/ PASSUS XVI 561-30, POOR MAN BEGGING/ PASSUS XVII 561-31, FREE-WILL AS YOUTH HOLDS RING/ PASSUS XVII 561-32, HANGED MAN/ PASSUS XVIII 561-33, MERCY OR TRUTH/ PASSUS XXI 561-34, DEMON/ PASSUS XXI 561-35, CAIAPHAS THE HIGH PRIEST/ PASSUS XXII 561-36, MERCHANT HOLDS COINS/ PASSUS XXII 561-37, PIERS PLOWMAN'S TEAM OF FOUR OXEN/ PASSUS XXII 561-37, VICAR/ TONSURED/ PASSUS XXII 561-38, ANTICHRIST?/ PASSUS XXIII 561-39, TWO-TONGUED TOM POINTS TO TEXT/ PASSUS XXIII 561-40, PHYSICIAN IN FURRED HOOD/ PASSUS XXIII 561-40,PROUD PRIEST CARRIES SWORD/ PASSUS XXIII 561-41, FLATTERY DRESSED AS FRIAR HOLDS MEDICINE/ PASSUS XXIII 561-42

*$ABSTRACT 562
*LIBRARY BODLEIAN
*SLIDE SET TITLE PROGNOSTICATIONS FROM ENGLISH CALENDAR
*NEGATIVE REFERENCE ROLL 234C
*RENTAL FEE $2.30
*COMMENTS CONTAINS PREDICTIONS FOR SEVEN YEARS, LABELLED WITH LETTERS OF THE ALPHABET AND ILLUSTRATED WITH HORIZONTAL ROWS OF PICTURES. EACH YEAR BEGINS WITH WINTER AND SUMMER WEATHER REPRESENTED BY MEN'S HEADS AND AUTUMN REPRESENTED BY CORN. BELOW THE PROGNOSTICATIONS IS A ROW OF PICTURES ILLUSTRATING TWELVE FAST DAYS. THE CAPTION STATES THAT WHOEVER FASTS ON THESE DAYS AND HAS CONFESSED IS ASSURED OF A PLACE IN HEAVEN. TO FOLLOW THE HORIZONTAL SEQUENCE OF THE MANUSCRIPT, THE FRAMES SHOULD BE VIEWED IN THE FOLLOWING ORDER: 1, 3, 5, 2, 4, 6.
*TITLE OF MANUSCRIPT ASTROLOGICAL AND ECCLESIASTICAL CALENDAR IN SIX PIECES

*SHELFMARK MS RAWL D 939/ PART 4
*PROVENANCE ENGLISH
*DATE EXECUTED 14TH/ 2ND HALF
*LANGUAGE ENGLISH AND LATIN
*TYPE OF MANUSCRIPT CALENDAR
*CONTENTS CALENDAR/ ENGLISH/ 14TH 562/1-6, PROGNOSTICATIONS FROM ENGLISH CALENDAR 562/1-6, WINTERS/ WARM/ MILD/ DARK 562-1, SUMMERS/ STORMY/ RAINY/ WINDY/ GOOD 562-1, AUTUMNS/ HUMID/ GOOD 562-1, CORN COSTLY 562-1, HARVESTS GOOD/ SIEVES 562-1, FRUIT TREES 562-1, HONEY ABUNDANT/ BEE-HIVES 562-1, THUNDERSTORM/ CORPSE BENEATH CLOUDS 562-1, WINTERS/ SUMMERS/ AUTUMNS 562-2, FRUIT ABUNDANT/ TREE WITH FRUIT ON GROUND 562-2, OIL ABUNDANT/ JARS 562-2, VINTAGE GOOD/ CASK 562-2, GREAT FIRE 562-2, FAST DAY FOR FIRST FRIDAY IN MARCH/ KNIFE 562-2, FAST DAY BEFORE ANNUNCIATION/ FLEUR DE LYS 562-2, FAST DAY BEFORE PASSION/ CHRIST ON CROSS 562-2, FAST DAY FOR THE ASCENSION/ CHRIST'S ASCENSION 562-2, YOUNG MEN WILL DIE/ THREE MEN IN BED 562-3, FLOCKS WILL DIE/ SHEEP ON BACKS 562-3, WAR/ TWO MEN FIGHTING 562-3, VINTAGE GOOD/ CASKS 562-3, PEACE AND QUIET/ TWO CLASPED HANDS 562-3, KINGS WILL DIE/ DEAD KING 562-3, YOUNG GIRLS WILL DIE/ TWO DEAD GIRLS 562-3, FLOCKS KILLED BY THUNDER/ SHEEP STRUCK BY ARROWS 562-3, GREAT FIRE 562-3, WOMEN WILL DIE IN CHILDBIRTH/ DEAD WOMAN WITH CHILD 562-3, HONEY ABUNDANT/ BEE-HIVES 562-4, MEAT COSTLY/ AXE ON TABLE 562-4, FLOCKS WILL DIE/ COW AND SHEEP ON BACKS 562-4, INFLAMMATION OF EYES/ DETACHED EYEBALLS 562-4, CHILDREN WILL DIE/ TWO CHILDREN IN BED 562-4, FEVER WILL PREVAIL/ WOMAN IN BED 562-4, FLAX SCARCE AND COSTLY/ BUNDLES OF FLAX 562-4, FAST DAY BEFORE PENTECOST/ CHURCH AND HAND 562-4, FAST DAY BEFORE NATIVITY OF JOHN BAPTIST/ LAMB 562-4, FAST DAY BEFORE FEAST OF SS PETER AND PAUL 562-4, FAST DAY BEFORE ASSUMPTION OF VIRGIN/ FLEUR-DE-LYS 562-4, ROBBERY/ CASTLE WITH HEADS PEERING OVER WALLS 562-5, ROYALTY NEW/ THREE CROWNED KINGS 562-5, BEES WILL DIE/ BEE-HIVE ON SIDE 562-5, INFLAMMATION OF EYES/ DETACHED EYEBALLS 562-5, ARMIES WILL FIGHT/ CROSSED LANCES 562-5, DEMONS MANY/ THREE BLUE DEVILS 562-5, SHIPPING DANGEROUS/ THREE SHIPS IN STORM 562-5, VINTAGE DIFFICULT/ THREE WINE CASKS 562-5, DANGER TO HAY/ HAYSTACKS IN RAIN 562-5, ROYALTY 562-5, HARVEST VARIED/ SIEVE 562-6, FLAX COSTLY/ TWO BUNDLES 562-6, PEACE/ ALTAR 562-6, RIVER OVERFLOWING 562-6, FAMINE/ ARROWS 562-6, EARTHQUAKE 562-6, OLD PEOPLE WILL DIE/ OLD MAN IN BED 562-6, HAY MUCH/ FOUR GREEN HAYSTACKS 562-6, FAST DAY BEFORE NATIVITY OF VIRGIN 562-6, FAST DAY BEFORE FEAST OF ST ANDREW/ GREEN CROSS 562-6, FAST DAY BEFORE NATIVITY OF CHRIST/ BABE IN MANGER 562-6

*$ABSTRACT 563
*LIBRARY BODLEIAN
*SLIDE SET TITLE BINDINGS
*NEGATIVE REFERENCE ROLL 234D
*RENTAL FEE $2.45
*TITLE OF MANUSCRIPT PRAYERBOOK 563-1, JOHN HAUKYN'S ACCOUNTS 563-5, ALBUM OF A DUTCH LADY 563-6, COMMISSIO OF DOGE GIROLAMO PRIULI 563-7, BIBLE FROM LIBRARY AT DEENE PARK 563-9
*SHELFMARK PR ARCH A F 100 563-1, MS ASHMOLE 6 563-2, MS CANON LITURG 237 563-2, MS DOUCE 19 563/3-4, MS RAWL A 203 563-5, MS RAWL B 4 563-6, MS SELDEN SUPRA 68 563-7, MS TANNER 83 563-8
*PROVENANCE ENGLISH 563/1-2, FRENCH 563/3-4, ENGLISH 563-5, DUTCH 563-6, ITALIAN/ VENICE 563-7, PORTUGUESE 563-8, ENGLISH 563-9
*DATE EXECUTED 17TH/ ABOUT 1627 563-1, 15TH 563-2, 18TH/ EARLY 563/3-4, 16TH 563-5, 17TH/C1612-18 563-6, 16TH/1563 563-7, 17TH 563-8, 17TH/C1634-35 563-9
*TYPE OF MANUSCRIPT PRAYERBOOK 563-1, CALENDAR 563-2, BOOK OF HOURS 563/3-4, ACCOUNTS 563-5, ALBUM 563-6, COMMISSIO 563-7, BIBLE/ NEW TESTAMENT 563-8, BIBLE 563-9
*CONTENTS BINDINGS/ 15TH-18TH 563/1-9, PRESENTATION BINDING EMBROIDERED SILVER ON VELVET 563-1, GIRDLE BOOKS 563-2, FRENCH MOSAIC DOUBLURE BINDING 563/3-4, ELIZABETHAN LEDGER BINDING 563-5, VELLUM CUTWORK BINDING 563-6, GOLD-TOOLED BINDING

563-7, PRESENTATION BINDING TO CATHERINE OF BRAGANZA 563-8, EMBROIDERED SILVER ON GREEN VELVET BINDING 563-9

*$ABSTRACT 564
*LIBRARY BODLEIAN
*SLIDE SET TITLE ENGLISH 15TH CENTURY ILLUMINATION
*NEGATIVE REFERENCE ROLL 234F
*RENTAL FEE $2.30
*TITLE OF MANUSCRIPT COMPENDIUM HISTORIAE IN GENEALOGIA CHRISTI 564-1, GENEALOGY OF KINGS OF ENGLAND TO RICHARD III 564/2-3, GENEALOGY OF KINGS OF ENGLAND TO HENRY V 564-4, GENERAL PROLOGUE TO CANTERBURY TALES 564-5, TREATISE ON HERALDRY AND ORDER OF GARDER 564-6
*SHELFMARK MS BARLOW 53 ROLL 564-1, MS BODLEY ROLLS 5/ MEMBRANE 5 564-2, MS BODLEY ROLLS 5/ MEMBRANE 9 564-3, MS BODLEY ROLLS 10 564-4, MS BODLEY 686 564-5, MS DOUCE 271 564-6
*PROVENANCE ENGLISH
*DATE EXECUTED 15TH/C1420-30 564-1, 15TH/ AFTER 1485 564/2-3, 15TH/ 2ND QUARTER 564-4, 15TH/C1430-40 564-5, 15TH/ 3RD QUARTER 564-6
*LANGUAGE ENGLISH 564-1, LATIN 564/2-3, LATIN 564-4, ENGLISH/ MIDDLE ENGLISH 564-5, ENGLISH AND FRENCH 564-6
*AUTHOR PETER OF POITIERS 564-1, CHAUCER 564-5
*TYPE OF MANUSCRIPT CHURCH HISTORY 564-1, GENEALOGY 564/2-4, POETRY/ MIDDLE ENGLISH 564-5, HERALDRY 564-6
*CONTENTS FIFTEENTH CENTURY ENGLISH ILLUMINATION 564/1-6, ENGLISH ILLUMINATION 564/1-6, ADAM AND EVE/ HUMAN-FACED SERPENT IN TREE 564-1, MEDALLION WITH WORDS MORVIDUS A QUIET MAN 564-2, MEDALLIONS WITH PORTRAITS OF HIS FIVE SONS 564-2, ALFRED/ KING ENTHRONED WITH ORB AND SCEPTRE 564-3, NATIVITY/ JOSEPH AND MARY/ OX AND ASS 564-4, INITIAL W WHEN/ YOUNG MAN POINTS 564-5, EMPEROR WITH SCEPTRE AND ORB/ UNFINISHED 564-6 EMPEROR WITH SCEPTRE AND ORB/ UNFINISHED 564-6

*$ABSTRACT 565
*LIBRARY BODLEIAN
*SLIDE SET TITLE EARLY BIBLES II
*NEGATIVE REFERENCE ROLL 235A
*RENTAL FEE $2.55
*TITLE OF MANUSCRIPT LAUDIAN ACTS 565-3, TYNDALE BIBLE 565/8-9, MATTHEW BIBLE 565/10-11
*SHELFMARK MS GREEK BIBL G 4P 565-1, MS GREEK BIBL D 6P 565-2, MS LAUD GREEK 35 565-3, MS AUCT D 2 14 565-4, MS AUCT T INF 2 2 565-5, MS BODLEY 270B 565-6, MS AUCT D 5 17 565-7, PR DENYER BIBLE ENG D 1549 565/8-9
*PROVENANCE EGYPTIAN 565-1, GREEK 565-2, GREEK/ SARDINIA 565-3, ITALIAN 565-4, BYZANTINE 565-5, FRENCH 565-6, FRENCH/ PARIS 565-7, ENGLISH/ LONDON 565/8-9, FLEMISH/ ANTWERP? 565/10-11
*DATE EXECUTED 03RD-4TH 565-1, 05TH 565-2, 06TH 565-3, 07TH 565-4, 09TH 565-5, 13TH/ MID 565-6, 16TH/1536-58 565-7, 16TH/1549 565/8-9, 16TH/1537 565/10-11
*LANGUAGE GREEK 565/1-2, GREEK AND LATIN 565-3, LATIN 565-4, GREEK 565-5, LATIN 565-6, LATIN 565-7, ENGLISH/ EARLY MODERN 565/8-9, ENGLISH/ EARLY MODERN 565/10-11
*TYPE OF MANUSCRIPT BIBLES
*CONTENTS BIBLES/ EARLY 565/1-11, ACTS 26/VERSES 7-8/ WESTERN TEXT 565-1, MATTHEW 10/VERSES 32-40/ GREEK TEXT 565-2, ACTS 08/VERSES 36-40 WITH EXTRA/VERSE 37 565-3, MATTHEW 24/VERSE 29 TO 25/VERSE 16 565-4, LUKE/ BEGINNING OF TEXT/ LECTIONS MARKED 565-5, GENESIS 05/VERSE 22 TO 09/VERSE 23/ NOAH 565-6, NOAH AND PARALLELS IN BIBLE MORALISEE 565-6, MATTHEW/ BEGINNING OF TEXT 565-7, INITIAL L LIBER/ JESSE TREE 565-7, JESSE TREE 565-7, EVE CREATION 565-8, ISRAELITES CROSSING JORDAN 565-8, ABRAHAM AND ISAAC 565-8, WORSHIP OF GOLDEN CALF 565-8, PREFACE/ WILLIAM TYNDALE UNTO THE CHRISTIAN READER 565-9, ADAM AND EVE 565-10, MOSES RECEIVING THE LAW 565-10, CRUCIFIXION AND RESURRECTION 565-10, MATTHEW BIBLE/ LETTER TO KING HENRY VIII 565-11

*$ABSTRACT 566
*LIBRARY BODLEIAN
*SLIDE SET TITLE PRISCIAN
*NEGATIVE REFERENCE ROLL 235C
*RENTAL FEE $2.30
*COMMENTS MADE FOR RAPHAEL DE MARCATELLIS.
*SHELFMARK MS HOLKHAM 406/ FOL 1 566-1, MS HOLKHAM 406/ FOL 3 566/2-4, MS HOLKHAM 406/ FOL 32 566-5, MS HOLKHAM 406/ FOL 90 566-6,
*PROVENANCE FLEMISH
*DATE EXECUTED 15TH/ LATE
*LANGUAGE LATIN
*AUTHOR PRISCIAN
*TYPE OF MANUSCRIPT CLASSICAL TEXT
*CONTENTS PRISCIAN 566/1-6, INITIAL C CUM/ RED AND BLUE INTERLACE 566-1, BORDER OF FLORAL DECORATIONS AND SCROLLS 566-1, INITIAL P PHILOSOPHI/ RED AND BLUE INTERLACE 566-2, WIDE FLORAL BORDER WITH MARCATELLIS ARMS 566-2, COAT OF ARMS OF MARCATELLIS 566-2, DETAIL/ INITIALS AND FLORAL BORDER 566-3, DETAIL/ MARCATELLIS COAT OF ARMS 566-4, INITIAL S SYLLABA/ RED/ BLUE AND GOLD 566-5, LOWER BORDER OF FLORAL DECORATIONS AND SCROLLS 566-5, LOWER BORDER DECORATED WITH BAND OF FLOWERS 566-6

*$ABSTRACT 567
*LIBRARY BODLEIAN
*SLIDE SET TITLE BODLEIAN EXHIBITION II
*NEGATIVE REFERENCE ROLL 235F
*RENTAL FEE $2.40
*COMMENTS MAINLY TEXTS
*TITLE OF MANUSCRIPT AELFRIC'S HOMILIES 567-1, VERSE LETTER TO LADY CAREY 567/2-3, LETTER TO SIR THOMAS DALE 567-4, THE BOOK OF PLAIES 567-5, AN ESSAY CONCERNING HUMANE UNDERSTANDING 567-6, CRAB CANON TO HAYDN'S CAMMANDMENT 567-7, MAP OF NARNIA 567-8
*SHELFMARK MS BODLEY 340/ FOL 169V 567-1, MS ENG POET D 197 567/2-3, MS ASHMOLE 830/ FOL 118 567-4, MS ASHMOLE 208/ FOL 201V-202 567-5, MS LOCKE F 26/ FOL 3 567-6, MS MUS E 35/ FOL 108 567-7, MS ENG LETT C 220/ FOL 160 567-8
*PROVENANCE ENGLISH
*DATE EXECUTED 12TH 567-1, 17TH/1611-12 567/2-3, 17TH/1613? 567-4, 17TH/1641 567-5, 17TH/1671 567-6, 18TH/1792 567-7, 20TH/ ABOUT 1950 567-8
*ARTIST/ SCHOOL LEWIS CS 567-8
*AUTHOR DONNE/ JOHN 567/2-3, ROLFE/ JOHN 567-4, FORMAN/ SIMON 567-5, LOCKE/ JOHN 567-6, LEWIS CS 567-8
*TYPE OF MANUSCRIPT PRAYER 567-1, LETTER 567/2-4, NOTES ON PLAYS 567-5, PHILOSOPHY 567-6, MUSIC 567-7, MAP 567-8
*CONTENTS BODLEIAN EXHIBITION II 567/1-8, EARLIEST DUTCH FRAGMENT/ PRAYER TO ST NICHOLAS 567-1, DONNE'S VERSE LETTER TO LADY CAREY 567/2-3, LETTER ABOUT AMERICAN INDIAN POCAHONTAS 567-4, NOTES ON SHAKESPEARE'S RICHARD II AND WINTER'S TALE 567-5, EARLY DRAFT OF AN ESSAY CONCERNING HUMANE UNDERSTANDING 567-6, CRAB CANON TO HAYDN'S FIRST COMMANDMENT 567-7,MAP OF NARNIA/ LOCALE OF LEWIS' FAIRY-STORIES 567-8

*$ABSTRACT 568
*LIBRARY BODLEIAN
*SLIDE SET TITLE MONUMENTS OF PRINTING 1644-1906
*NEGATIVE REFERENCE ROLL 235G
*RENTAL FEE $2.70
*TITLE OF MANUSCRIPT AREOPAGITICA 568-1, HISTORIA ET ANTIQUITATES UNIVERSITATIS OXONIENSIS 568-2, ANATOMY OF THE HORSE 568-3, SELECT FABLES OF ESOP 568-4, POEMS BY GOLDSMITH AND PARNELL 568-5, ITALY 568-6, OLD WEDGWOOD 568-7, RAPE OF THE LOCK 568-8, HISTORY OF BRITISH BIRDS/ VOL 2, PARADISE LOST/ 1833 EDITION 568-10, L'ALLEGRO AND IL PENSEROSO/ 1855 EDITION 568-11, PETER PAN IN KENSINGTON GARDENS 568-12,

ILLUSTRATED LONDON NEWS DIAMOND JUBILEE 568-13, COUNTRY SEATS OF THE NOBLEMEN OF GREAT BRITIAN 568-14 AND IRELAND 568-14
*SHELFMARK PR ARCH G E 44 568-1, PR WOOD 430 568-2, PR VET A 5 A 5 568-3, PR VET A 5 E 1615 568-4, PR VET A 5 C 36/ PAGE 3 568-5, PR 280 F 2453/ PAGE 32 568-6, PR 1754 A 1/ PLATE XXVI 568-7, PR 2799 D 42/ PAGE 20 568-8, PR 189611 D 48/ PAGE 244 568-9, PR 2799 D 248/ PLATE AFTER PAGE 138 568-10, PR 17156 D 62/ PAGE 20 568-11, PR 2538 D 76/ PAGE 16 568-12, PR 2288 B 43/ PLATE VIII 568-13, PR G A GEN TOP 4 52 568-14
*PROVENANCE ENGLISH
*DATE EXECUTED 17TH/1644 568-1, 17TH/1674 568-2, 18TH/1766 568-3, 18TH/1761 568-4, 18TH/1795 568-5, 19TH/1830 568-6, 19TH/1898 568-7, 19TH/1896 568-8, 19TH/1804 568-9, 19TH/1833 568-10, 19TH/1855 568-11, 20TH/1906 568-12, 19TH/1897 568-13, 19TH/1866-81? 568-14
*ARTIST/ SCHOOL GRIGGS W 568-7, BEARDSLEY A 568-8, MARTIN J 568-10, FOSTER B 568-11, RACKHAM A 568-12, FAWCETT B 568-14
*AUTHOR MILTON/ JOHN 568-1, WOOD A 568-2, STUBBS G 568-3, DODSLEY R AND J 568-4, GOLDSMITH AND PARNELL 568-5, ROGERS S 568-6, RATHBONE F 568-7, POPE/ ALEXANDER 568-8, BEWICK T 568-9, MILTON/ JOHN 568/10-11, BARRIE JM 568-12, MORRIS F O 568-14
*CONTENTS PRINTING 1644-1906 568/1-14, TITLE PAGE OF MILTON'S AREOPAGITICA 568-1, BEGINNING OF BOOK ONE OF HISTORIA ET ANTIQUITATES 568-2, PLATE I FROM STUBBS'S ANATOMY OF THE HORSE 568-3, FRONTISPIECE FROM SELECT FABLES OF ESOP 568-4, OPENING OF THE TRAVELLER WITH VIGNETTE 568-5, OPENING OF LAKE COMO WITH VIGNETTE 568-6, THE WINE VASE--JASPER/ COLORED PLATE XXVI 568-7, ILLUSTRATION FROM RAPE OF THE LOCK 568-8, TEXT AND VIGNETTE 568-9, MEZZOTINT OF BOOK 5 LINE 308 OF PARADISE LOST 568-10, ETCHING FROM L'ALLEGRO AND IL PENSEROSO 568-11, OLD MR SALFORD WAS A CRAB-APPLE 568-12, BRITISH VICTORIES BY LAND AND SEA 568-13, WINDSOR CASTLE/ COLOR PLATE 568-14

*$ABSTRACT 569
*LIBRARY BODLEIAN
*SLIDE SET TITLE BELIAL
*NEGATIVE REFERENCE ROLL 235H
*RENTAL FEE $2.60
*TITLE OF MANUSCRIPT BELIAL BY JACOBUS DE THERAMO
*SHELFMARK PR AUCT 2 Q INFRA 2 34
*PROVENANCE GERMAN/ AUGSBURG
*DATE EXECUTED 15TH/1473
*LANGUAGE GERMAN
*AUTHOR DE THERAMO/ JACOBUS
*TYPE OF MANUSCRIPT RELIGIOUS TREATICE
*CONTENTS BELIAL 569/1-12, BELIAL BEFORE MOUTH OF HELL 569-1, HELL MOUTH WITH BELIAL 569-1, MOSES AND BELIAL BEFORE SOLOMON 569-2, BELIAL/ MOSES/ SOLOMON 569-2, BELIAL APPROACHES SOLOMON IN PRESENCE OF MOSES 569-3, BELIAL SHOWS SOLOMON ADAM AND EVE 569-4, ADAM AND EVE BY TREE OF LIFE 569-4, BELIAL KNEELS BEFORE SOLOMON IN PRESENCE OF MOSES 569-5, DESCENT INTO HELL 569-6, HELL/ DESCENT 569-6, BELIAL SHOUTS ALOUD BEFORE SOLOMON 569-7, BELIAL RECEIVES LETTER FROM GOD 569-8, WITNESS SPEAKS BEFORE TRIBUNAL 569-9, BELIAL BRINGS LETTER TO MOUTH OF HELL 569-10, HELL MOUTH/ BELIAL WITH LETTER 569-10, MOSES BRINGS LETTER TO CHRIST 569-11, DEVILS ANGRY BEFORE GOD 569-12

*$ABSTRACT 570
*LIBRARY BODLEIAN
*SLIDE SET TITLE CONQUEST OF CONSTANTINOPLE
*NEGATIVE REFERENCE ROLL 235I
*RENTAL FEE $2.25
*COMMENTS CHRONICLE OF THE FOURTH CRUSADE 1199-1207
*TITLE OF MANUSCRIPT LA CONQUETE DE CONSTANTINOPLE
*SHELFMARK MS LAUD MISC 587/ FOL 1 570/1-3, MS LAUD MISC 587/ FOL 59 570/4-5
*PROVENANCE ITALIAN/ VENICE

*DATE EXECUTED 14TH/C1330
*LANGUAGE FRENCH WITH LATIN SUPPLEMENT
*AUTHOR DE VILLEHARDOUIN/ GEOFFROI
*TYPE OF MANUSCRIPT CHRONICLE
*CONTENTS CONQUEST OF CONSTANTINOPLE 570/1-5, CRUSADE/ FOURTH 570/1-5, OPENING PAGE OF TEXT WITH BORDER DECORATIONS 570-1, INITIAL S/ FOULQUES OF NEUILLY 570-2, FOULQUES OF NEUILLY PREACHES FOURTH CRUSADE 570-2, CRUSADERS ARRIVE AT CONSTANTINOPLE 570-3, SHIP WITH TWO TOWERS AND MANGONEL 570-3, FULL PAGE WITH HISTORIATED INITIAL/ ACANTHUS BORDERS 570-4, INITIAL E WITH POPE ALEXANDER III 570-5, POPE ALEXANDER III SEATED 570-5, EMPEROR FREDERICK BARBAROSSA AND WIFE 570-5

*$ABSTRACT 571
*LIBRARY BODLEIAN
*SLIDE SET TITLE PROLOGUE TO OVID AND OTHER TEXTS
*NEGATIVE REFERENCE ROLL 235J
*RENTAL FEE $2.35
*COMMENTS INSERTED AS FOLIOS 195-201 IN MS OF DICTYS CRETENSIS. ILLUSTRATIONS OF MYTHOLOGICAL SUBJECTS.
*TITLE OF MANUSCRIPT PROLOGUE TO OVID AND METAMORPHOSES
*SHELFMARK MS RAWL B 214/ FOL 196 571-1, MS RAWL B 214/ FOL 197 571-2, MS RAWL B 214/ FOL 199 571-3, MS RAWL B 214/ FOL 199V 571-4, MS RAWL B 214/ FOL 200 571-5, MS RAWL B 214/ FOL 202 571-6, MS RAWL B 214/ FOL 202V 571-7
*PROVENANCE ENGLISH
*DATE EXECUTED 15TH/ MID
*LANGUAGE LATIN
*AUTHOR OVID
*TYPE OF MANUSCRIPT LITERATURE
*CONTENTS OVID'S PROLOGUE AND METAMORPHOSES 571/1-7, MYTHOLOGICAL SUBJECTS 571/1-7, ELEMENTS/ FOUR REPRESENTED AS INTERCONNECTED CIRCLES 571-1, MAP OF THE WORLD WITH ASIA/ EUROPE/ AFRICA 571-2, DIANA WITH TEN NYMPHS AIMS BOW AT THREE DEER 571-3, MINERVA IN ARMOR HOLDS SPEAR AND SHIELD 571-3, JUNO HOLDS SCEPTRE/ RAINBOW AND PEACOCKS 571-4, CYBELE RIDES IN CART DRAWN BY LIONS 571-4, MARS AND VENUS EMBRACING 571-5, VULCAN WITH HAMMER AND TONGS 571-5, HERCULES WEARS CLOAK WITH LION'S HEAD 571-5, AESCULAPIUS FOLLOWS HERCULES 571-5, MAP OF GREECE WITH NAMES OF MOUNTAINS 571-6, DIAGRAM OF CONCENTRIC CIRCLES WITH PEGASUS IN CENTER 571-7, PEGASUS IN CENTER OF DIAGRAM 571-7, MUSES AROUND MIDDLE CIRCLE WITH LATIN POETS 571-7

*$ABSTRACT 572
*LIBRARY BODLEIAN
*SLIDE SET TITLE CALENDAR FROM A PSALTER
*NEGATIVE REFERENCE ROLL 235K
*RENTAL FEE $2.60
*TITLE OF MANUSCRIPT PSALTER WITH CALENDAR
*SHELFMARK MS DOUCE 49/ FOL 4 572-1, MS DOUCE 49/ FOL 4V 572-2, MS DOUCE 49/ FOL 5 572-3, MS DOUCE 49/ FOL 5V 572-4, MS DOUCE 49/ FOL 6 572-5, MS DOUCE 49/ FOL 6V 572-6, MS DOUCE 49/ FOL 7 572-7, MS DOUCE 49/ FOL 7V 572-8, MS DOUCE 49/ FOL 8 572-9, MS DOUCE 49/ FOL 8V 572-10, MS DOUCE 49/ FOL 9 572-11, MS DOUCE 49/ FOL 9V 572-12
*PROVENANCE FLEMISH/ ST OMER REGION
*DATE EXECUTED 13TH/ LATE
*LANGUAGE LATIN
*TYPE OF MANUSCRIPT PSALTER WITH CALENDAR
*CONTENTS PSALTER/ FLEMISH/ 13TH 572/1-12, CALENDAR/ FLEMISH/ 13TH 572/1-12, OCCUPATIONS OF THE MONTHS 572/1-12, JANUARY/ MAN SEATED BEFORE FIRE 572-1, FEBRUARY/ WOMAN HOLDS TAPER 572-2, MARCH/ MAN DIGGING WITH SPADE 572-3, APRIL/ MAN HOLDS GLOVE 572-4, MAY/ MAN WITH FALCON 572-5, JUNE/ MAN BALANCES BUNDLE OF REEDS ON BACK 572-6, JULY/ MAN CUTS GRASS WITH SCYTHE 572-7, AUGUST/ MAN CUTS WHEAT WITH SICKLE 572-8, SEPTEMBER/ MAN COLLECTS GRAPES 572-9, OCTOBER/ MAN SOWS SEED

572-10, NOVEMBER/ MAN KNOCKS DOWN ACORNS FOR PIGS 572-11, DECEMBER/ BAKER USES SHOVEL AT BRICK OVEN 572-12

*$ABSTRACT 573
*LIBRARY BODLEIAN
*SLIDE SET TITLE MEDICAL TREATISE
*NEGATIVE REFERENCE ROLL 236A
*RENTAL FEE $2.20
*SHELFMARK MS BODLEY 362/ FOL 1 573/1-3, MS BODLEY 362/ FOL 216V 573-4
*PROVENANCE ENGLISH/ OXFORD OR SALISBURY
*DATE EXECUTED 15TH/C1448-55
*LANGUAGE LATIN
*AUTHOR HERMAN ZURKE OF GREIFSWALD
*TYPE OF MANUSCRIPT MEDICAL TREATISE
*CONTENTS MEDICAL TREATISE 573/1-4, ROSA ANGLICA OF JOHN OF GADDESDEN 573-1, INITIAL G AND ACANTHUS BORDERS 573-1, INITIAL G GALIENUS IN RED/ BLUE AND GREEN 573-2, LOWER HALF OF PAGE WITH DECORATIVE FOLIAGE 573-3, INITIAL E ET WITH TWO FACES 573-4

*$ABSTRACT 574
*LIBRARY BODLEIAN
*SLIDE SET TITLE CODEX MENDOZA
*NEGATIVE REFERENCE ROLL 236B
*RENTAL FEE $2.55
*COMMENTS AN AZTEC PICTOGRAPHIC MS WITH A SPANISH TEXT. DONE ON AUTHORITY OF DON ANTONIO DE MENDOZA, FIRST VICEROY OF NEW SPAIN, AS A PRESENT FOR EMPEROPR CHARLES V. IT CONSISTS OF THREE PARTS - HISTORY OF TENOCHTITLAN OR MEXICO CITY, TRIBUTE ROLL OF MONTEZUMA, AND MEXICAN SOCIAL CUSTOMS.
*TITLE OF MANUSCRIPT CODEX MENDOZA
*SHELFMARK MS ARCH SELD A 1/ FOL 2 574-1, MS ARCH SELD A 1/ FOL 12 574/2-3, MS ARCH SELD A 1/ FOL 38 574-4, MS ARCH SELD A 1/ FOL 57 574/5-6, MS ARCH SELD A 1/ FOL 58 574-7, MS ARCH SELD A 1/ FOL 59 574-8, MS ARCH SELD A 1/ FOL 60 574-9, MS ARCH SELD A 1/ FOL 61 574/10-11
*PROVENANCE MEXICAN
*DATE EXECUTED 16TH/ 2ND QUARTER
*LANGUAGE SPANISH AND MEXICAN
*TYPE OF MANUSCRIPT MEXICAN RECORDS
*CONTENTS CODEX MENDOZA 574/1-11, CHRONICLE/ MEXICAN/ 16TH 574/1-11, MEXICAN CHRONICLE 1324-1520 574-1, MEXICANS ARRIVE AT SITE OF MEXICO CITY IN AD1324 574-1, REIGN OF TICOCICATZIN/ BURNING TEMPLE OF CILAN 574-2, REIGN OF TECOTZICATZIN/ BURNING TEMPLE OF TAMAPACHO 574-3, TRIBUTE ROLL OF MONTEZUMA/ RED BIVALVE SHELLS 574-4, MEXICAN CUSTOMS AFTER BIRTH OF CHILD 574-5, MOTHER WITH CHILD IN CRADLE 574-5, CEREMONY OF NAMING CHILD 574-5, MIDWIFE BATHES INFANT 574-5, CHILD IN CRADLE PRESENTED IN TEMPLE 574-6, INSTRUCTION OF MEXICAN CHILDREN 574-7, BOYS WITH FATHER/ GIRLS WITH MOTHER 574-7, CHILDREN TAUGHT QUIET WORDS AT AGE THREE 574-7, BOY CARRIES WATER/ GIRL AND WORK BASKET 574-7,BOYS CARRY WOOD/ GIRL WITH SPINDLE AT AGE FIVE 574-7, BOYS SENT TO MARKET/ GIRL SPINS AT AGE SIX 574-7, INSTRUCTION AND DISCIPLINE OF MEXICAN CHILDREN 574-8, BOYS USES FISHING NET/ GIRL SPINS AT AGE SEVEN 574-8, DISOBEDIENT CHILDREN PUNISHED WITH MAGUEY SPIKES 574-8, DISOBEDIENT CHILDREN BEATEN WITH STICK AT AGE TEN 574-8, IDLE CHILDREN FORCED TO INHALE AXI SMOKE AT ELEVEN 574-9, BOY LAID ON DAMP GROUND ALL DAY AT AGE TWELVE 574-9, GIRL FORCED TO SWEEP HOUSE AND STREET AT AGE TWELVE 574-9, BOY GOES BY CANOE TO CUT RUSHES 574-9, GIRL GRINDS MAIZE AND COOKS AT AGE THIRTEEN 574-9, BOY FISHES AND GIRL WEAVES AT AGE FOURTEEN 574-9, FATHER HANDS SON AT AGE FIFTEEN TO CHIEF PRIEST 574-10, WEDDING CEREMONY/ BRIDE CARRIED TO BRIDEGROOM'S HOUSE 574-11, BRIDAL COUPLE SIT WITH CLOTHES KNOTTED TOGETHER 574-11

*$ABSTRACT 575
*LIBRARY BODLEIAN
*SLIDE SET TITLE SCOTTISH LIBRARIES
*NEGATIVE REFERENCE ROLL 236C
*RENTAL FEE $2.35
*COMMENTS TEXTS FROM TWO MSS AND TWO PRINTED BOOKS IN THE BODLEIAN AND ONE PRINTED BOOK IN JESUS COLLEGE, OXFORD. ALL FORMERLY BELONGED TO SCOTTISH LIBRARIES.
*TITLE OF MANUSCRIPT ETHICA ARISTOTLIS 575-1, CONSOLATORIUM THEOLOGICUM 575-2, DE PROPRIETATIBUS RERUM 575/3-5, FIVE TREATISES ON ST JEROME 575-6, HUGH OF ST VICTOR ON SACRAMENTS 575-6, VOLUMEN CUM CASIBUS 575-7
*SHELFMARK PR JESUS COLLEGE K 14 15 / TITLE PAGE 575-1, PR INC F F 1 1493/ FOL 2 575-2, MS ASHMOLE 1474/ FOL 1 575-3, MS ASHMOLE 1474/ FOL 239 575-4, MS ASHMOLE 1474/ FOL 247V 575-5, MS FAIRFAX 5/ FOL 9V 575-6, PR INC B F 2 1500-1/ FOL 1 575-7
*PROVENANCE FRENCH/ PARIS 575/1-2, ENGLISH 575-6
*DATE EXECUTED 16TH/1530 575-1, 15TH/1493 575-2, 13TH-14TH 575/3-5, 12TH 575-6, 16TH/1500 575-7
*LANGUAGE LATIN
*AUTHOR MAJOR/ JOHN 575-1, DE TAMBACO/ JOHANNES 575-2, ANGLICUS/ BARTHOLOMEUS 575/3-5, JEROME 575-6, HUGH OF ST VICTOR 575-6, BARTOLUS 575-7
*TYPE OF MANUSCRIPT ETHICS 575-1, RELIGIOUS TREATISE 575-2, RELIGIOUS TREATISE 575/3-5, RELIGIOUS TREATISE 575-6, RELIGIOUS TREATISE 575-7
*CONTENTS SCOTTISH LIBRARIES/ TEXTS 575/1-7, LIBRARIES/ SCOTTISH 575/1-7, LIBRARY OF ALEXANDER MYLNE/ ABBOT OF CAMBUSKENNETH 575-1, TITLE PAGE OF ETHICA ARISTOTELIS 575-1, LIBRARY OF THE CISTERCIAN ABBEY OF COUPAR ANGUS 575-2, FIRST PAGE OF TEXT WITH INSCRIPTION 575-2, LIBRARY OF THE CATHEDRAL CHURCH OF BVM ABERDEEN 575-3, PAGE OF TEXT WITH INSCRIPTION 575-3, FOLIO 239 WITH NOTE WRITTEN C1600 575-4, FOLIO 247V WITH NOTE 575-5, LIBRARY OF THE CISTERCIAN ABBEY OF BVM SWEETHEART 575-6, FOLIO 9V WITH 13TH-CENTURY TABLE OF CONTENTS 575-6, LIBRARY OF ROBERT REID/ BISHOP OF ORKNEY 575-7, TITLE PAGE WITH PRINTED EX LIBRIS 575-7

*$ABSTRACT 576
*LIBRARY QUEEN'S COLLEGE
*SLIDE SET TITLE OLD TESTAMENT INITIALS FROM A VULGATE
*NEGATIVE REFERENCE ROLL 237A
*RENTAL FEE $4.75
*SHELFMARK MS QUEEN'S COLLEGE 299/ PAGE 1 576-1, MS QUEEN'S COLLEGE 299/ PAGE 6 576/2-6, MS QUEEN'S COLLEGE 299/ PAGE 65 576-7, MS QUEEN'S COLLEGE 299/ PAGE 84 576-8, MS QUEEN'S COLLEGE 299/ PAGE 112 576-9, MS QUEEN'S COLLEGE 299/ PAGE 137 576-10, MS QUEEN'S COLLEGE 299/ PAGE 154 576-11, MS QUEEN'S COLLEGE 299/ PAGE 172 576-12, MS QUEEN'S COLLEGE 299/ PAGE 200 576-13, MS QUEEN'S COLLEGE 299/ PAGE 221 576-14, MS QUEEN'S COLLEGE 299/ PAGE 240 576-15, MS QUEEN'S COLLEGE 299/ PAGE 261 576-16, MS QUEEN'S COLLEGE 299/ PAGE 279 576-17, MS QUEEN'S COLLEGE 299/ PAGE 304 576-18, MS QUEEN'S COLLEGE 299/ PAGE 310 576-19, MS QUEEN'S COLLEGE 299/ PAGE 319 576-20, MS QUEEN'S COLLEGE 299/ PAGE 326 576-21, MS QUEEN'S COLLEGE 299/ PAGE 335 576-22, MS QUEEN'S COLLEGE 299/ PAGE 343 576-23, MS QUEEN'S COLLEGE 299/ PAGE 361 576-24, MS QUEEN'S COLLEGE 299/ PAGE 365 576-25, MS QUEEN'S COLLEGE 299/ PAGE 369 576-26, MS QUEEN'S COLLEGE 299/ PAGE 373 576-27, MS QUEEN'S COLLEGE 299/ PAGE 377 576-28, MS QUEEN'S COLLEGE 299/ PAGE 381 576-29, MS QUEEN'S COLLEGE 299/ PAGE 385 576-30, MS QUEEN'S COLLEGE 299/ PAGE 390 576-31, MS QUEEN'S COLLEGE 299/ PAGE 399 576-32, MS QUEEN'S COLLEGE 299/ PAGE 412 576-33, MS QUEEN'S COLLEGE 299/ PAGE 416 576-34, MS QUEEN'S COLLEGE 299/ PAGE 419 576-35, MS QUEEN'S COLLEGE 299/ PAGE 428 576-36, MS QUEEN'S COLLEGE 299/ PAGE 452 576-37, MS QUEEN'S COLLEGE 299/ PAGE 483 576-38, MS QUEEN'S COLLEGE 299/ PAGE 524 576-39, MS QUEEN'S COLLEGE 299/ PAGE 529 576-40, MS QUEEN'S COLLEGE 299/ PAGE 565 576-41, MS QUEEN'S COLLEGE 299/ PAGE 579 576-42, MS QUEEN'S COLLEGE 299/ PAGE 584 576-43, MS QUEEN'S COLLEGE 299/ PAGE 587 576-44, MS QUEEN'S

COLLEGE 299/ PAGE 591 576-45, MS QUEEN'S COLLEGE 299/ PAGE 592 576-46, MS QUEEN'S COLLEGE 299/ PAGE 593 576-47, MS QUEEN'S COLLEGE 299/ PAGE 596 576-48, MS QUEEN'S COLLEGE 299/ PAGE 598 576-49, MS QUEEN'S COLLEGE 299/ PAGE 600 576-50, MS QUEEN'S COLLEGE 299/ PAGE 601 576-51, MS QUEEN'S COLLEGE 299/ PAGE 603 576-52, MS QUEEN'S COLLEGE 299/ PAGE 608 576-53, MS QUEEN'S COLLEGE 299/ PAGE 611 576-54, MS QUEEN'S COLLEGE 299/ PAGE 631 576-55

*PROVENANCE FRENCH/ PARIS

*DATE EXECUTED 13TH/C1270-80

*LANGUAGE LATIN

*TYPE OF MANUSCRIPT BIBLE/ OLD TESTAMENT

*CONTENTS INITIALS/ OLD TESTAMENT 576/1-55, OLD TESTAMENT INITIALS 576/1-55, PROLOGUE/ INITIAL F FRATER/ ST JEROME WRITES 576-1, INITIAL F FRATER/ ST JEROME WRITES 576-1, ST JEROME SITS WRITING A SCROLL 576-1, GENESIS/ INITIAL I IN/ CREATION SCENES, INITIAL I IN/ CREATION SCENES 576-2, CREATION OF EARTH 576-3, CREATION OF WATERS 576-4, CREATION OF SUN AND MOON 576-4, CREATION OF BIRDS AND ANIMALS 576-5, CREATION OF TREES AND PLANTS 576-5, CREATION OF ADAM AND EVE/ CREATOR RESTS 576-6,ADAM AND EVE CREATED 576-6, LEVITICUS/ INITIAL V VOCAVIT/ MOSES AND AARON 576-7, INITIAL V VOCAVIT/ MOSES AND AARON 576-7, MOSES AND AARON OFFER RAM AT ALTAR 576-7, NUMBERS/ INITIAL L LOCUTUS/ MOSES KNEELS BEFORE GOD 576-8, INITIAL L LOCUTUS/ MOSES KNEELS BEFORE GOD 576-8, MOSES KNEELS BEFORE GOD 576-8, DEUTERONOMY/ INITIAL H HEC/ MOSES AND AARON 576-9, INITIAL H HEC/ MOSES AND AARON 576-9, MOSES SHOWS AARON THE TABLETS OF LAW 576-9, JOSHUA/ INITIAL E ET/ JOSHUA KNEELS BEFORE GOD 576-10, INITIAL E ET/ JOSHUA KNEELS BEFORE GOD 576-10, JOSHUA KNEELS BEFORE GOD 576-10, JUDGES/ INITIAL P POST/ ISRAELITES KNEEL 576-11, INITIAL P POST/ ISRAELITES KNEEL 576-11, ISRAELITES KNEEL BEFORE GOD 576-11, RUTH/ INITIAL I IN/ ELIMELECH AND NAOMI 576-12, INITIAL I IN/ ELIMELECH AND NAOMI 576-12, ELIMELECH AND NAOMI WITH TWO SONS 576-12, KINGS-II/ II SAMUEL/ INITIAL F FACTUM/ DAVID 576-13, INITIAL F FACTUM/ DAVID ORDERS SOLDIER TO KILL AMALEKITE 576-13, DAVID ORDERS DEATH OF AMALEKITE WHO KILLED SAUL 576-13, KINGS-III/ I KINGS AV/ INITIAL E ET/ DAVID IN BED 576-14, INITIAL E ET/ DAVID ADVISED TO ADMIT ABISHAG 576-14, DAVID IN BED ADVISED TO ADMIT ABISHAG 576-14, KINGS-IV/ II KINGS AV/ INITIAL P PREVARICATUS/ AHAZIAH 576-15, INITIAL P PREVARICATUS/ AHAZIAH FALLS FROM ROOF 576-15, AHAZIAH FALLS FROM ROOF OF CASTLE 576-15, CHRONICLES I/ INITIAL A ADAM/ ADAM WITH DESCENDANTS 576-16, INITIAL A ADAM/ ADAM SEATED WITH DESCENDANTS 576-16, ADAM SEATED WITH DESCENDANTS 576-16, CHRONICLES II/ INITIAL C CONFORTATUS/ SOLOMON 576-17, INITIAL C CONFORTATUS/ SOLOMON OFFERS RAM 576-17, SOLOMON OFFERS RAM AT ALTAR 576-17, ESDRAS/ EZRA AV/ INITIAL I IN/ TEMPLE REBUILT 576-18, INITIAL I IN/ TEMPLE AT JERUSALEM REBUILT 576-18, TEMPLE AT JERUSALEM REBUILT 576-18, NEHEMIAH/ INITIAL V VERBA/ NEHEMIAH AND ARTAXERXES 576-19, INITIAL V VERBA/ NEHEMIAH AND KING ARTAXERXES 576-19, NEHEMIAH OFFERS CHALICE TO KING ARTAXERXES 576-19, TOBIT/ INITIAL T TOBIAS/ BLIND TOBIT IN BED 576-20, INITIAL T TOBIAS/ BLIND TOBIT IN BED 576-20, TOBIT/ BLIND LIES IN BED/ SPARROW FLIES AWAY 576-20, JUDITH/ INITIAL A ARPHAXAD/ JUDITH BEHEADS HOLOFERNES 576-21, INITIAL A ARPHAXAD/ JUDITH BEHEADS HOLOFERNES 576-21, JUDITH DECAPITATES THE SLEEPING HOLOFERNES 576-21, ESTHER/ INITIAL I IN/ ESTHER AT FEET OF AHASUERUS 576-22, INITIAL I IN/ ESTHER AT FEET OF AHASUERUS 576-22, ESTHER KNEELS AT FEET OF AHASUERUS 576-22, JOB/ INITIAL V VIR/ JOB ON ASHES 576-23, INITIAL V VIR/ JOB ON ASHES SPEAKS TO WIFE 576-23, JOB ON ASHES SPEAKS TO WIFE AND COMFORTER 576-23, PSALMS/ INITIAL B BEATUS VIR/ DAVID AND HARP 576-24, INITIAL B BEATUS VIR/ DAVID PLAYS HARP 576-24, DAVID PLAYS HARP 576-24, PSALM 26/27/ INITIAL D DOMINUS ILLUMINATIO/ SAMUEL ANOINTS 576-25, INITIAL D DOMINUS ILLUMINATIO/ SAMUEL ANOINTS DAVID 576-25, SAMUEL ANOINTS DAVID 576-25, PSALM 38/39/ INITIAL D DIXI CUSTODIAM/ DAVID 576-26, INITIAL D DIXI CUSTODIAM/ DAVID POINTS TO MOUTH 576-26, DAVID POINTS TO HIS MOUTH 576-26, PSALM 52/53/ INITIAL D DIXIT INSIPIENS/ FOOL 576-27, INITIAL D DIXIT INSIPIENS/ FOOL WITH BAT AND BALL 576-27, FOOL WITH BAT AND BALL 576-27, PSALM 68/69/ INITIAL S

SALVUM ME FAC/ DAVID IN WATER 576-28, INITIAL S SALVUM ME FAC/ DAVID STANDS IN WATER 576-28, DAVID WITH OUTSTRETCHED ARMS STANDS IN WATER 576-28, GOD IN STARRY SKY HOLDS ORB 576-28, PSALM 80/81/ INITIAL E EXULTATE DEO/ DAVID PLAYS BELLS 576-29, INITIAL E EXULTATE DEO/ DAVID PLAYS BELLS 576-29, DAVID PLAYS FOUR BELLS WITH HAMMERS/ HARP AT FEET 576-29, PSALM 95/96/ INITIAL C CANTATE DOMINO/ MONKS SING 576-30, INITIAL C CANTATE DOMINO/ TWO MONKS SING 576-30, MONKS SING BEFORE LECTERN WITH OPEN BOOK 576-30, PSALM 109/110/ INITIAL DIXIT DOMINUS/ TRINITY 576-31, INITIAL D DIXIT DOMINUS/ TRINITY 576-31, TRINITY/ GOD AND CHRIST SIT ON BENCH 576-31, PROVERBS/ INITIAL P PARABOLE/ SOLOMON WITH SWITCH 576-32, INITIAL P PARABOLE/ SOLOMON ADMONISHES MAN 576-32, SOLOMON WITH SWITCH ADMONISHES MAN WITH BOOK 576-32, ECCLESIASTES/ INITIAL V VERBA/ SOLOMON ADMONISHES WOMAN 576-33, INITIAL V VERBA/ SOLOMON ADMONISHES WOMAN 576-33, SOLOMON ADMONISHES A WOMAN 576-33, SONG OF SOLOMON/ INITIAL O OSCULETUR/ VIRGIN AND CHILD 576-34, INITIAL O OSCULETUR/ VIRGIN AND CHILD 576-34, VIRGIN EMBRACES CHRIST CHILD ON LAP 576-34, WISDOM OF SOLOMON/ INITIAL D DILIGITE/ SOLOMON 576-35, INITIAL D DILIGITE/ SOLOMON SPEAKS TO SOLDIER 576-35, SOLOMON SPEAKS TO KNEELING SOLDIER WITH SWORD 576-35, ECCLESIASTICUS/ INITIAL O OMNIS/ KING WITH CHURCH 576-36, INITIAL O OMNIS/ KING WITH CHURCH AND CHALICE 576-36, KING SITS HOLDING CHURCH AND CHALICE 576-36, ISAIAH/ INITIAL V VISIO/ ISAIAH SAWN IN HALF 576-37, INITIAL V VISIO/ ISAIAH SAWN IN HALF 576-37, ISAIAH TIED TO PILLAR SAWN IN HALF 576-37, JEREMIAH/ INITIAL H HEC/ JEREMIAH STONED 576-38, INITIAL H HEC/ JEREMIAH STONED 576-38, JEREMIAH STONED BY MAN 576-38, BARUCH/ INITIAL E ET/ BARUCH WRITES 576-39, INITIAL E ET/ BARUCH WRITES 576-39, BARUCH WRITES A SCROLL 576-39, EZEKIEL/ INITIAL E ET/ EZEKIEL'S VISION 576-40, INITIAL E ET/ EZEKIEL'S VISION 576-40, EZEKIEL'S VISION OF FOUR CREATURES 576-40, DANIEL/ INITIAL A ANNO/ DANIEL STROKES LIONS 576-41, INITIAL A ANNO/ DANIEL STROKES TWO LIONS 576-41, DANIEL STROKES TWO LIONS IN CAVE 576-41, HOSEA/ INITIAL V VERBUM/ HOSEA EMBRACES GOMER 576-42, INITIAL V VERBUM/ HOSEA EMBRACES GOMER 576-42,HOSEA EMBRACES HIS WIFE GOMER 576-42, JOEL/ INITIAL V VERBUM/ JOEL HOLDS SCROLL 576-43, INITIAL V VERBUM/ JOEL HOLDS SCROLL 576-43, JOEL HOLDS SCROLL 576-43, AMOS/ INITIAL V VERBA/ AMOS TENDS FLOCK 576-44, INITIAL V VERBA/ AMOS TENDS FLOCK 576-44, AMOS TENDS FLOCK OF SHEEP 576-44, OBADIAH/ INITIAL V VISIO/ OBADIAH'S VISION 576-45, INITIAL V VISIO/ OBADIAH'S VISION 576-45, OBADIAH'S VISION OF GOD 576-45, JONAH/ INITIAL E ET/ JONAH EMERGES FROM WHALE 576-46, INITIAL E ET/ JONAH EMERGES FROM WHALE 576-46, JONAH EMERGES FROM MOUTH OF WHALE 576-46, NINEVEH AS BATTLEMENTED BUILDING 576-46, MICAH/ INITIAL V VERBUM/ MICAH HOLDS SCROLL 576-47, INITIAL V VERBUM/ MICAH HOLDS SCROLL 576-47, MICAH HOLDS SCROLL 576-47, NAHUM/ INITIAL O ONUS/ NAHUM PREDICTION 576-48, INITIAL O ONUS/ NAHUM PREDICTS FALL OF NINEVEH 576-48, NAHUM PREDICTS FALL OF NINEVEH 576-48, HABAKKUK/ INITIAL O ONUS/ HABAKKUK AND DANIEL 576-49, INITIAL O ONUS/ HABAKKUK TAKES FOOD TO DANIEL 576-49, HABAKKUK FORCED TO TAKE FOOD TO DANIEL 576-49, ZEPHANIAH/ INITIAL V VERBUM/ ZEPHANIAH HOLDS SCROLL 576-50, INITIAL V VERBUM/ ZEPHANIAH HOLDS SCROLL 576-50, ZEPHANIAH HOLDS SCROLL 576-50, HAGGAI/ INITIAL I IN/ HAGGAI HOLDS SCROLL 576-51, INITIAL I IN/ HAGGAI HOLDS SCROLL 576-51, HAGGAI HOLDS SCROLL 576-51, ZECHARIAH/ INITIAL I IN/ ZECHARIAH HOLDS SCROLL 576-52, INITIAL I IN/ ZECHARIAH HOLDS SCROLL 576-52, ZECHARIAH HOLDS SCROLL 576-52, MALACHI/ INITIAL O ONUS/ MALACHI HOLDS SCROLL 576-53, INITIAL O ONUS/ MALACHI HOLDS SCROLL 576-53, MALACHI HOLDS SCROLL 576-53, MACCABEES-I/ INITIAL E ET/ MATTATHIAS SLAYS JEW 576-54, INITIAL E ET/ MATTATHIAS SLAYS JEW AT GENTILE ALTAR 576-54, MATTATHIAS SLAYS JEW SACRIFICING AT GENTILE ALTAR 576-54, MACCABEES-II/ INITIAL F FRATRIBUS/ JEWISH MESSENGER 576-55, INITIAL F FRATRIBUS/ JEWISH MESSENGER 576-55, JEW IN JERUSALEM HANDS BOOK TO MESSENGER 576-55

*$ABSTRACT 577
*LIBRARY QUEEN'S COLLEGE
*SLIDE SET TITLE NEW TESTAMENT INITIALS FROM A VULGATE
*NEGATIVE REFERENCE ROLL 237B
*RENTAL FEE $3.10
*SHELFMARK MS QUEEN'S COLLEGE 299/ PAGE 645 577-1, MS QUEEN'S
COLLEGE 299/ PAGE 666 577-2, MS QUEEN'S COLLEGE 299/ PAGE 669B
577-3, MS QUEEN'S COLLEGE 299/ PAGE 689 577-4, MS QUEEN'S
COLLEGE 299/ PAGE 721 577-5, MS QUEEN'S COLLEGE 299/ PAGE 726
577-6, MS QUEEN'S COLLEGE 299/ PAGE 729 577-7, MS QUEEN'S
COLLEGE 299/ PAGE 732 577-8, MS QUEEN'S COLLEGE 299/ PAGE 734
577-9, MS QUEEN'S COLLEGE 299/ PAGE 739 577-10, MS QUEEN'S
COLLEGE 299/ PAGE 742 577-11, MS QUEEN'S COLLEGE 299/ PAGE 743
577-12, MS QUEEN'S COLLEGE 299/ PAGE 744 577/13-14, MS QUEEN'S
COLLEGE 299/ PAGE 750 577-15, MS QUEEN'S COLLEGE 299/ PAGE 77
577-16, MS QUEEN'S COLLEGE 299/ PAGE 773 577-17, MS QUEEN'S
COLLEGE 299/ PAGE 775 577-18, MS QUEEN'S COLLEGE 299/ PAGE 77
577-19, MS QUEEN'S COLLEGE 299/ PAGE 779 577/20-21, MS QUEEN'S
COLLEGE 299/ PAGE 781 577-22
*PROVENANCE FRENCH/ PARIS
*DATE EXECUTED 13TH/C1270-80
*LANGUAGE LATIN
*TYPE OF MANUSCRIPT BIBLE/ NEW TESTAMENT
*CONTENTS INITIALS/ NEW TESTAMENT 577/1-22, NEW TESTAMEN
INITIALS 577/1-22, MATTHEW/ INITIAL L LIBER/ JESSE TREE 577-1,
INITIAL L LIBER/ JESSE TREE 577-1, JESSE TREE 577-1, MARK/
INITIAL F FUIT/ ST MARK WITH BOOK 577-2, INITIAL F FUIT/ S
MARK WITH BOOK 577-2, ST MARK HOLDS BOOK 577-2, LUKE/ INITIA
F FUIT/ ST LUKE KNEELS AT ALTAR 577-3, INITIAL F FUIT/ ST LUK
KNEELS AT ALTAR 577-3, ST LUKE KNEELS AT ALTAR/ ANGE
INSTRUCTS 577-3, JOHN/ INITIAL I IN/ ST JOHN HOLDS BOOK 577-4,
INITIAL I IN/ ST JOHN HOLDS BOOK 577-4, ST JOHN HOLDS BOO
577-4, CORINTHIANS II/ INITIAL P PAULUS/ ST PAUL 577-5,
INITIAL P PAULUS/ ST PAUL HOLDS SCROLL AND SWORD 577-5, S
PAUL HOLDS SCROLL AND SWORD 577-5, GALATIANS/ INITIAL
PAULUS/ ST PAUL HOLDS SCROLL 577-6, INITIAL P PAULUS/ ST PAU
HOLDS SCROLL AND SWORD 577-6, ST PAUL HOLDS SCROLL AND SWOR
577-6, EPHESIANS/ INITIAL P PAULUS/ ST PAUL 577-7, INITIAL
PAULUS/ ST PAUL HANDS SCROLL TO MESSENGER 577-7, ST PAUL HAND
SCROLL TO MESSENGER 577-7, PHILIPPIANS/ INITIAL P PAULUS/ S
PAUL HOLDS SCROLL 577-8, INITIAL P PAULUS/ ST PAUL HOLD
SCROLL 577-8, ST PAUL HOLDS SCROLL AND SWORD 577-8,
COLOSSIANS/ INITIAL P PAULUS/ ST PAUL HOLDS SCROLL 577-9,
INITIAL P PAULUS/ ST PAUL HOLDS SCROLL 577-9, ST PAUL HOLD
SCROLL AND SWORD 577-9, TIMOTHY I/ INITIAL P PAULUS/ ST PAU
HOLDS SCROLL 577-10, INITIAL P PAULUS/ ST PAUL HOLDS SCROL
577-10, ST PAUL HOLDS SCROLL WITH BOTH HANDS 577-10, TIMOTH
II/ INITIAL P PAULUS/ ST PAUL HOLDS SWORD 577-11, INITIAL
PAULUS/ ST PAUL HOLDS SWORD AND BOOK 577-11, ST PAUL HOLD
SWORD AND GOLD BOOK 577-11, TITUS/ INITIAL P PAULUS/ ST PAU
HOLDS SCROLL 577-12, INITIAL P PAULUS/ ST PAUL HOLDS SCROL
577-12, ST PAUL HOLDS SCROLL WITH BOTH HANDS 577-12, PHILEMON,
INITIAL P PAULUS/ PAUL IN PULPIT 577-13, INITIAL P PAULUS/ S
PAUL IN PULPIT 577-13, ST PAUL IN PULPIT HANDS SCROLL T
MESSENGER 577-13, HEBREWS/ INITIAL M MULTIPHARIE/ ST PAUL AN
JEW 577-14, INITIAL M MULTIPHARIE/ ST PAUL AND JEW 577-14, S
PAUL WITH SWORD AND BOOK FACES JEW 577-14, ACTS/ INITIAL
PRIMUM/ VIRGIN AND FOUR DISCIPLES 577-15, INITIAL P PRIMUM,
VIRGIN WITH FOUR DISCIPLES 577-15, VIRGIN STANDS WITH FOU
DISCIPLES 577-15, JAMES/ INITIAL I IACOBUS/ ST JAMES WITH BOO
577-16, INITIAL I IACOBUS/ ST JAMES WITH BOOK 577-16, ST JAME
WITH BOOK 577-16, PETER-I/ INITIAL P PETRUS/ ST PETER WITH KE
577-17, INITIAL P PETRUS/ ST PETER WITH LARGE KEY 577-17, S
PETER HOLDS LARGE KEY 577-17, PETER-II/ INITIAL S SYMON/ S
PETER HOLDS BOOK 577-18, INITIAL S SYMON/ ST PETER HOLDS BOO
577-18, ST PETER HOLDS AND POINTS TO BOOK 577-18, JOHN-I,
INITIAL Q QUOD/ ST JOHN WRITES 577-19, INITIAL Q QUOD/ ST JOH
WRITES 577-19, ST JOHN WRITES 577-19, JOHN-II/ INITIAL
SENIOR/ ST JOHN HOLDS BOOK 577-20, INITIAL S SENIOR/ ST JOH
HOLDS BOOK 577-20, ST JOHN HOLDS BOOK 577-20, JOHN-III
INITIAL S SENIOR/ ST JOHN HOLDS SCROLL 577-21, INITIAL
SENIOR/ ST JOHN HOLDS SCROLL 577-21, ST JOHN HOLDS SCROL

577-21, APOCALYPSE/ INITIAL A APOCALIPSIS/ ST JOHN WRITES 577-22, INITIAL A APOCALIPSIS/ ST JOHN WRITES 577-22, ST JOHN OF PATMOS WRITES 577-22

*$ABSTRACT 578
*LIBRARY QUEEN'S COLLEGE
*SLIDE SET TITLE CALENDAR AND MINIATURES FROM BOOK OF HOURS
*NEGATIVE REFERENCE ROLL 237C
*RENTAL FEE $4.75
*SHELFMARK MS QUEEN'S COLLEGE 349/ FOL 3 578-1, MS QUEEN'S COLLEGE 349/ FOL 4 578-2, MS QUEEN'S COLLEGE 349/ FOL 5 578-3, MS QUEEN'S COLLEGE 349/ FOL 6 578-4, MS QUEEN'S COLLEGE 349/ FOL 7 578-5, MS QUEEN'S COLLEGE 349/ FOL 10 578-6, MS QUEEN'S COLLEGE 349/ FOL 11 578-7, MS QUEEN'S COLLEGE 349/ FOL 12 578-8, MS QUEEN'S COLLEGE 349/ FOL 16V 578-9, MS QUEEN'S COLLEGE 349/ FOL 32V 578-10, MS QUEEN'S COLLEGE 349/ FOL 36V 578-11, MS QUEEN'S COLLEGE 349/ FOL 40V 578-12, MS QUEEN'S COLLEGE 349/ FOL 49V 578-13, MS QUEEN'S COLLEGE 349/ FOL 50V 578-14, MS QUEEN'S COLLEGE 349/ FOL 51V 578-15, MS QUEEN'S COLLEGE 349/ FOL 52V 578-16, MS QUEEN'S COLLEGE 349/ FOL 53V 578-17, MS QUEEN'S COLLEGE 349/ FOL 54V 578-18, MS QUEEN'S COLLEGE 349/ FOL 55V 578-19, MS QUEEN'S COLLEGE 349/ FOL 56V 578-20, MS QUEEN'S COLLEGE 349/ FOL 58V-59 578-21, MS QUEEN'S COLLEGE 349/ FOL 78 578-22, MS QUEEN'S COLLEGE 349/ FOL 79V 578-23, MS QUEEN'S COLLEGE 349/ FOL 80V 578-24, MS QUEEN'S COLLEGE 349/ FOL 81 578-25, MS QUEEN'S COLLEGE 349/ FOL 81V 578-26, MS QUEEN'S COLLEGE 349/ FOL 82 578-27, MS QUEEN'S COLLEGE 349/ FOL 83 578-28, MS QUEEN'S COLLEGE 349/ FOL 87V 578-29, MS QUEEN'S COLLEGE 349/ FOL 93V-94 578-30, MS QUEEN'S COLLEGE 349/ FOL 110V 578-31, MS QUEEN'S COLLEGE 349/ FOL 116 578-32, MS QUEEN'S COLLEGE 349/ FOL 117 578-33, MS QUEEN'S COLLEGE 349/ FOL 119 578-34, MS QUEEN'S COLLEGE 349/ FOL 121V 578-35, MS QUEEN'S COLLEGE 349/ FOL 126 578-36, MS QUEEN'S COLLEGE 349/ FOL 126V 578-37, MS QUEEN'S COLLEGE 349/ FOL 127 578-38, MS QUEEN'S COLLEGE 349/ FOL 128 578-39, MS QUEEN'S COLLEGE 349/ FOL 128V 578-40, MS QUEEN'S COLLEGE 349/ FOL 129 578-41, MS QUEEN'S COLLEGE 349/ FOL 131 578-42, MS QUEEN'S COLLEGE 349/ FOL 131V 578-43, MS QUEEN'S COLLEGE 349/ FOL 132 578-44, MS QUEEN'S COLLEGE 349/ FOL 131V 578-45, MS QUEEN'S COLLEGE 349/ FOL 132 578-46, MS QUEEN'S COLLEGE 349/ FOL 132V 578-47, MS QUEEN'S COLLEGE 349/ FOL 133 578-48, MS QUEEN'S COLLEGE 349/ FOL 133V 578-49, MS QUEEN'S COLLEGE 349/ FOL 134 578-50, MS QUEEN'S COLLEGE 349/ FOL 134V 578-51, MS QUEEN'S COLLEGE 349/ FOL 139 578-52, MS QUEEN'S COLLEGE 349/ FOL 143V 578-53, MS QUEEN'S COLLEGE 349/ FOL 169V 578-54, MS QUEEN'S COLLEGE 349/ FOL 246 578-55
*PROVENANCE FLEMISH
*DATE EXECUTED 15TH/C1480-90
*LANGUAGE LATIN
*TYPE OF MANUSCRIPT CALENDAR AND BOOK OF HOURS
*CONTENTS CALENDAR AND BOOK OF HOURS 578/1-55, MARCH/ ARIES/ MAN DIGS IN THE EARTH 578-1, APRIL/ TAURUS/ MAN AND WOMAN WALK IN LANDSCAPE 578-2, MAY/ GEMINI/ NAKED COUPLE EMBRACE 578-3, JUNE/ CANCER/ MAN RAKES HAY 578-4, JULY/ LEO/ MAN CUTS WHEAT WITH SCYTHE 578-5, OCTOBER/ SCORPIO/ MAN SOWING SEED 578-6, NOVEMBER/ SAGITTARIUS/ MAN COLLECTS ACORNS 578-7, DECEMBER/ CAPRICORN/ SLAUGHTER OF CALF 578-8,ST GEORGE SLAYS DRAGON/ PRINCESS WITH LAMB 578-9, TRINITY/ GOD SUPPORTS LIMP BODY OF CHRIST 578-10, ANIMAL IN MARGIN PLAYS PORTATIVE ORGAN 578-10,ST JOHN THE BAPTIST HOLDS AGNUS DEI 578-11, AGNUS DEI WITH JOHN THE BAPTIST 578-11, ST GILES PIERCED BY ARROW/ LEAPING STAG 578-12, ST SYTHA HOLDS OPEN BOOK 578-13, ST CATHERINE HOLDS SWORD/ LARGE WHEEL AT SIDE 578-14, ST BARBARA STANDS BEFORE TOWER 578-15, ST DOROTHY WITH SMALL BASKET 578-16, ST MILDRED DRESSED AS NUN WITH BOOK AND CROZIER 578-17, ST MARGARET STANDS ON DRAGON 578-18, ST URSULA WITH 11000 VIRGINS 578-19, ST PETRONILLA HOLDS SPOONS AND READS BOOK 578-20, CHRIST PRAYS IN ROCKY GETHSEMANE 578-21, ANNUNCIATION 578-21, DOVE IN GOLD AUREOLE 578-22, ST MICHAEL RAISES SWORD TO SLAY DRAGON 578-23, SS PETER AND PAUL WITH KEY

AND SWORD 578-24, ST ANDREW HOLDS WOODEN CROSS SALTIRE 578-25, ST LAURENCE HOLDS GRIDIRON 578-26, ST STEPHEN WITH STONE ON BLEEDING HEAD 578-27, ST NICHOLAS BLESSES BOYS IN PICKLING TUB 578-28, CHRIST MOCKED AND CROWNED WITH THORNS 578-29, PILATE PRESENTS CHRIST TO THE PEOPLE 578-30, PILATE WASHING HIS HANDS 578-30, ANGEL APPEARS TO THREE SHEPHERDS 578-30, VIRGIN HOLDING CHILD STANDS ON CRESCENT MOON 578-31, VIRGIN AND CHILD IN GOLD AUREOLE 578-32, ANNUNCIATION 578-33, VIRGIN AND ST JOHN KNEEL IN PRAYER 578-34, PIETA/ ROCKY LANDSCAPE 578-35, NATIVITY/ MARY AND JOSEPH KNEEL/ OX AND ASS 578-36, ADORATION OF MAGI/ ONE IS BLACK 578-37, RESURRECTION/ CHRIST BLESSES SOLDIERS 578-38,ASCENSION/ CHRIST'S FEET DISAPPEAR AT TOP 578-39, PENTECOST/ VIRGIN AND APOSTLES KNEEL IN PRAYER 578-40, VIRGIN ON CRESCENT MOON 578-41, CHRIST/ BLOOD POURS FROM CROWN OF THORNS 578-42, CHRIST'S BLEEDING RIGHT HAND 578-43, CHRIST'S BLEEDING LEFT HAND 578-44, DUPLICATE OF FRAME 43 578-45, DUPLICATE OF FRAME 44 578-46, CHRIST'S BLEEDING HEART 578-47, CHRIST'S BLEEDING RIGHT FOOT 578-48, CHRIST'S BLEEDING LEFT FOOT 578-49, VIRGIN PRAYS IN ROCKY LANDSCAPE 578-50, ST JOHN STANDS IN ROCKY LANDSCAPE 578-51, EUCHARIST/ PRIEST ELEVATES HOST 578-52, DAVID KNEELS BEFORE CASTLE/ HAT/ MACE AND HARP 578-53, LAZARUS RAISED/ DISCIPLES/ MARTHA 578-54, ST JOHN OF PATMOS WRITES SCROLL/ EAGLE AT FEET 578-55

*$ABSTRACT 579
*LIBRARY QUEEN'S COLLEGE
*SLIDE SET TITLE TREASURES OF QUEEN'S COLLEGE
*NEGATIVE REFERENCE ROLL 237D
*RENTAL FEE $3.45
*COMMENTS INITIALS AND MINIATURES FROM SIX MSS.
*TITLE OF MANUSCRIPT HISTORY 579/23-29
*SHELFMARK MS QUEEN'S COLLEGE 52/ FOL 37 579-1, MS QUEEN'S COLLEGE 52/ FOL 174 579/2-3, MS QUEEN'S COLLEGE 52/ FOL 179V 579-4, MS QUEEN'S COLLEGE 308/ FOL 1 579-5, MS QUEEN'S COLLEGE 308/ FOL 9 579-6, MS QUEEN'S COLLEGE 308/ FOL 10V 579-7, MS QUEEN'S COLLEGE 316/ FOL 1 579-8, MS QUEEN'S COLLEGE 210/ FOL 18 579-9, MS QUEEN'S COLLEGE 210/ FOL 33 579-10, MS QUEEN'S COLLEGE 210/ FOL 35V 579-11, MS QUEEN'S COLLEGE 210/ FOL 58V 579-12, MS QUEEN'S COLLEGE 210/ FOL 66V 579-13, MS QUEEN'S COLLEGE 210/ FOL 84V 579-14, MS QUEEN'S COLLEGE 357/ FOL 2V 579/15-16, MS QUEEN'S COLLEGE 357/ FOL 8V 579-17, MS QUEEN'S COLLEGE 357/ FOL 45V 579-18, MS QUEEN'S COLLEGE 357/ FOL 69V 579-19, MS QUEEN'S COLLEGE 357/ FOL 72V 579-20, MS QUEEN'S COLLEGE 357/ FOL 92 579-21, MS QUEEN'S COLLEGE 357/ FOL 95V 579-22, MS QUEEN'S COLLEGE 304/ FOL 1 579-23, MS QUEEN'S COLLEGE 304/ FOL 49 579-24, MS QUEEN'S COLLEGE 304/ FOL 58 579-25, MS QUEEN'S COLLEGE 304/ FOL 67 579-26, MS QUEEN'S COLLEGE 304/ FOL 144V 579-27, MS QUEEN'S COLLEGE 304/ FOL 151V 579-28, MS QUEEN'S COLLEGE 304/ FOL 163V 579-29
*PROVENANCE ENGLISH 579/1-4, ENGLISH 579/5-7, FRENCH 579-8, FLEMISH/ INSERTED LEAVES 579/9-14, ENGLISH/ BORDERS AND INITIALS 579/9-14, ENGLISH 579/15-22, ENGLISH/ GLASTONBURY 579/23-29
*DATE EXECUTED 13TH/ EARLY 579/1-4, 14TH/C1370-80 579/5-7, 12TH/ LATE 579-8, 15TH/C1420-30/ INSERTED SINGLE LEAVES 579/9-14, 15TH/ 2ND QUARTER/ BORDERS AND INITIALS 579/9-14, 15TH/ LATE 579/15-22, 15TH/C1420? 579/23-29
*LANGUAGE LATIN
*AUTHOR ICKHAM/ PETER 579/23-29
*TYPE OF MANUSCRIPT BIBLE/ OLD TESTAMENT 579/1-4, BIBLE/ OLD TESTAMENT 579/5-7, BIBLE/ DEUTERONOMY 579-8, CALENDAR AND BOOK OF HOURS 579/9-14, RELIGIOUS TEXTS 579/15-22, HISTORY SHOWING DESCENT OF KINGS 579/23-29
*CONTENTS QUEEN'S COLLEGE TREASURES 579/1-29, LEVITICUS/ INITIAL V VOCAVIT/ GOD AND MOSES 579-1, INITIAL V VOCAVIT/ GOD AND MOSES 579-1, MOSES AND GOD BEFORE ALTAR WITH CALF 579-1, JUDITH/ INITIAL A APUD FORMED BY BIRD 579-2, INITIAL A APUD FORMED BY BIRD 579-2, INITIAL A ARFAXAD COMPOSED OF BIRDS/ FOLIAGE/ BEAST 579-3, ESTHER/ INITIAL I IN DIEBUS/ BIRDS/ GROTESQUE/ MASK 579-4, ST JEROME TAKES BOOK FROM BOOK-SHELF

579-5, PROLOGUE TO GENESIS/ ST JEROME HANDS BOOK TO MONK 579-6, ST JEROME HANDS BOOK TO KNEELING MONK 579-6, GENESIS/ INITIAL I IN/ GARDEN OF EDEN 579-7, GARDEN OF EDEN/ SERPENT/ ADAM AND EVE 579-7, MOSES HOLDS BOOK 579-7, MONK KNEELING WITH SCROLL 579-7, DEUTERONOMY/ INITIAL H HEC WITH ANIMAL INTERLACE 579-8, INITIAL H HEC WITH ANIMAL INTERLACE 579-8, INITIAL D DOMINE/ ELABORATE FOLIAGE BORDERS 579-9, ST MICHAEL RAISES SWORD OVER BLACK DEMON 579-10, ST CATHERINE HOLDS BROKEN WHEEL/ SWORD ON GROUND 579-11, CRUCIFIXION/ VIRGIN AND ST JOHN 579-12, LAST JUDGMENT/ CHRIST IN GLORY WITH SWORDS 579-13, DEAD RISE FROM GRAVES 579-13, BURIAL SERVICE/ TOMB/ PRIEST/ MOURNERS 579-14, ANNUNCIATION IN LANDSCAPE WITH STARRY SKY 579-15, DUPLICATE OF FRAME 15 579-16, JERUSALEM AS MEDIEVAL WALLED-CITY 579-17, NATIVITY/ MARY AND JOSEPH KNEEL/ OX AND ASS 579-18, CRUCIFIXION/ WALLED-CITY IN BACKGROUND 579-19, CHURCH OF THE HOLY SEPULCHRE/ CHRIST IN GOLD 579-20, ASCENSION/ CHRIST ASCENDS FROM MOUNTAIN TOP 579-21, CHRIST SHOWS WOUNDS 579-22, PETER OF ICKHAM SITS WRITING AT DESK 579-23, PETER OF ICKHAM SITS READING ON BED 579-24, PETER OF ICKHAM TAKES BOOK FROM CUPBOARD 579-25, PETER OF ICKHAM SITS ON BENCH 579-26, PETER OF ICKHAM READS 579-27, PETER OF ICKHAM DICTATES TO SCRIBE 579-28, PETER OF ICKHAM SITS ON CANOPIED CHAIR 579-29

*$ABSTRACT 580
*LIBRARY BODLEIAN
*SLIDE SET TITLE ENGLISH DRAWINGS
*NEGATIVE REFERENCE ROLL 238A
*RENTAL FEE $2.50
*TITLE OF MANUSCRIPT CAEDMON GENESIS 580/1-9, CHRONICLE OF FLORENCE OF WORCESTER 580-10
*SHELFMARK MS JUNIUS 11/ PAGE 53 580-1, MS JUNIUS 11/ PAGE 57 580-2, MS JUNIUS 11/ PAGE 58 580-3, MS JUNIUS 11/ PAGE 60 580-4, MS JUNIUS 11/ PAGE 62 580-5, MS JUNIUS 11/ PAGE 84 580-6, MS JUNIUS 11/ PAGE 87 580-7, MS JUNIUS 11/ PAGE 88 580-8, MS JUNIUS 11/ PAGE 96 580-9, MS CORPUS CHRISTI COLLEGE OXFORD 157/ FOL 76 580-10
*PROVENANCE ENGLISH/ WINCHESTER OR CANTERBURY 580/1-9, ENGLISH 580-10
*DATE EXECUTED 11TH/C1000 580/1-9, 12TH/C1130-40 580-10
*LANGUAGE ENGLISH/ OLD ENGLISH 580/1-9
*AUTHOR FLORENCE OF WORCESTER 580-10
*TYPE OF MANUSCRIPT LITERATURE/ CAEDMON GENESIS 580/1-9, CHRONICLE 580-10
*CONTENTS GENESIS/ CAEDMON GENESIS 580/1-9, GENERATIONS OF CAIN 580-1, IRAD SEATED 580-1, BIRTH OF MEHUJAEL 580-1, MEHUJAEL WITH HIS WIFE AND SON METHUSAEL 580-1, LAMECH WITH TWO WIVES 580-1, GENESIS 04/VERSES 18-19/ GENERATIONS OF CAIN 580-1, CAINAN RULES HIS PEOPLE 580-2, CAINAN'S WIFE HOLDS INFANT SON MAHALALEEL 580-2, GENESIS 05/VERSE 12/ CAINAN 580-2, MAHALALEEL STANDS BEFORE ALTAR 580-3, ENOCH TRAMPLES ON DRAGON/ ANGEL ADDRESSES HIM 580-4, METHUSELAH SITS WITH HANDS RAISED 580-5, BIRTH OF LAMECH/ TWO MIDWIVES 580-5, GENESIS 05/VERSE 25/ METHUSELAH 580-5, ABRAHAM'S CALL 580-6, SARAH AND LOT IN ABRAHAM'S HOUSE 580-6, ABRAHAM'S DEPARTURE TO CANAAN 580-6, ABRAHAM AND GOD 580-6, GENESIS 12/VERSES 1-7/ CALL OF ABRAHAM 580-6, ABRAHAM STANDS BETWEEN BETHEL AND HAI 580-7, ABRAHAM MAKES OFFERING/ GOD APPEARS 580-7, GENESIS 12/VERSE 8/ ABRAHAM MAKES OFFERING 580-7, ABRAHAM APPROACHES EGYPT ACCOMPANIED BY SARAH 580-8, GENESIS 13/VERSE 11/ ABRAHAM AND SARAH APPROACH EGYPT 580-8, ABRAHAM TOLD OF LOT'S CAPTIVITY 580-9, GENESIS 14/VERSE 13/ ABRAHAM TOLD OF LOT'S CAPTIVITY 580-9, CHRONICLE OF FLORENCE OF WORCESTER/ FOL 76 580-10, CRUCIFIXION/ SIBYL STANDS ON CLOUD 580-10, JONAH STANDS ON WHALE 580-10 JONAH STANDS ON WHALE 580-10

*$ABSTRACT 581
*LIBRARY BODLEIAN

*SLIDE SET TITLE MASS OF ST GREGORY
*NEGATIVE REFERENCE ROLL 238B
*RENTAL FEE $2.60
*SHELFMARK MS RAWL LITURG F 38/ FOL 87V-88 581-1, MS CANON LITURG 148/ FOL 83 581-2, MS RAWL LITURG E 27/ FOL 17 581-3, MS DOUCE 152/ FOL 85V 581-4, MS RAWL LITURG E 11/ FOL 107 581-5, MS RAWL LITURG F 32/ FOL 83V 581-6, MS RAWL LITURG F 36/ FOL 114 581-7, MS AUCT D INF 2 13/ FOL 199V-200 581-8, MS LAT LITURG G 5/ PP 302-303 581-9, MS DOUCE A 1/ FOL 148 581-10, MS CANON LITURG 76/ FOL 5 581-11, MS CANON LITURG 178/ FOL 104 581-12
*PROVENANCE FLEMISH/ GHENT 581-1, DUTCH 581-2, FRENCH 581-3, FRENCH 581-4, FRENCH/ NORMANDY 581-5, FRENCH/ WEST 581-6, FRENCH 581-7, ENGLISH 581-8, ENGLISH 581-9, ITALIAN/ VENICE 581-10, ITALIAN/ ASTI 581-11, FRENCH/ ANJOU 581-12
*DATE EXECUTED 16TH/1503 581-1, 16TH/C1500 581-2, 15TH/ 2ND QUARTER 581-3, 15TH/ LATE 581-4, 15TH/ LATE 581-5, 15TH/ LATE 581-6, 16TH/ 1ST QUARTER 581-7, 15TH/ 3RD QUARTER 581-8, 16TH/C1500 581-9, 15TH/ 2ND QUARTER 581-10, 15TH/ AFTER 147? 581-11, 16TH/ EARLY 581-12
*LANGUAGE DUTCH AND LATIN 581-1, DUTCH 581-2, FRENCH AND LATIN 581-3, FRENCH AND LATIN 581-4, FRENCH AND LATIN 581-5, LATIN 581-6, FRENCH AND LATIN 581-7, LATIN 581-8, ENGLISH AND LATIN 581-9, LATIN 581-10, FRENCH AND LATIN 581-11, LATIN 581-12
*TYPE OF MANUSCRIPT BOOK OF HOURS/ USE OF BRUSSELS 581-1, PRAYERS AND MEDITATIONS 581-2, BOOK OF HOURS/ USE OF LE MANS 581-3, BOOK OF HOURS/ USE OF AMIENS 581-4, BOOK OF HOURS/ USE OF AVRANCHES 581-5, BOOK OF HOURS/ USE OF LE MANS 581-6, BOOK OF HOURS/ USE OF ROME 581-7, BOOK OF HOURS/ USE OF SARUM 581-8, PRAYERS AND DEVOTIONS 581-9, ANTIPHONAL 581-10, BOOK OF HOURS/ USE OF ROME 581-11, BOOK OF HOURS/ USE OF ROME-ANGERS 581-12
*CONTENTS MASS OF ST GREGORY 581/1-12, POPE GREGORY AND TWO PRIESTS KNELL AT ALTAR 581-1, CHRIST STANDS ABOVE ALTAR 581-1, BORDER WITH REALISTIC FLOWERS 581-1, POPE GREGORY WITH HALO KNEELS BEFORE ALTAR 581-2, CHRIST/ NAKED RISES FROM GRAVE 581-2, POPE GREGORY KNEELS AT ALTAR 581-3, CHRIST SHOWING WOUNDS/ CROWN OF THORNS 581-3, POPE GREGORY HALOED AND TONSURED KNEELS AT ALTAR 581-4, CHRIST ABOVE WITH INSTRUMENTS OF PASSION 581-4, GROTESQUES IN BORDER 581-4, POPE GREGORY WITH GOLD HALO KNEELS AT ALTAR 581-5, CHRIST ABOVE WITH INSTRUMENTS OF PASSION 581-5, BORDER WITH FLORAL DESIGNS 581-5, POPE GREGORY KNEELS AT ALTAR 581-6, CHRIST ABOVE WITH INSTRUMENTS OF PASSION 581-6, POPE GREGORY KNEELS AT ALTAR 581-7, CHRIST WITH INSTRUMENTS OF PASSION 581-7, CARDINALS/ ROOSTER/ VEIL OF CHRIST 581-7, POPE GREGORY KNEELS AT ALTAR 581-8, CHRIST SHOWING WOUNDS STANDS ON CHALICE 581-8, BORDER WITH FLORAL DESIGNS 581-8, POPE GREGORY KNEELS AT ALTAR 581-9, CHRIST STANDS NEXT TO CROSS 581-9, BORDER WITH FLORAL DESIGNS 581-9, INITIAL O/ POPE GREGORY KNEELS AT ALTAR 581-10, POPE GREGORY KNEELS AT ALTAR 581-11, CHRIST WITH WOUNDS AND CROWN OF THORNS 581-11, POPE GREGORY KNEELS AT ALTAR 581-12, CHRIST WITH INSTRUMENTS OF PASSION 581-12

*$ABSTRACT 582
*LIBRARY BODLEIAN
*SLIDE SET TITLE INITIALS TO MACCABEES
*NEGATIVE REFERENCE ROLL 238C
*RENTAL FEE $2.40
*SHELFMARK MS AUCT D 5 9/ FOL 476 582-1, MS AUCT D 5 9/ FOL 492V 582-2, MS CANON BIBL LAT 41/ FOL 359V 582-3, MS CANON BIBL LAT 41/ FOL 371V 582-4, MS CANON BIBL LAT 11/ FOL 417 582-5, MS CANON BIBL LAT 11/ FOL 432V 582-6, MS RAWL G 6/ FOL 329 582-7, MS RAWL G 6/ FOL 340 582-8
*PROVENANCE ENGLISH 582/1-2, FRENCH 582/3-4, FRENCH 582/5-6, FRENCH/ NORTH? 582/7-8,
*DATE EXECUTED 13TH/ 2ND HALF 582/1-2, 13TH/ LATE 582/3-4, 13TH/ 3RD QUARTER 582/5-6, 13TH/ 3RD QUARTER 582/7-8
*LANGUAGE LATIN
*TYPE OF MANUSCRIPT BIBLE WITH ST JEROME'S PROLOGUE 582/1-2,

BIBLE WITH ST JEROME'S PROLOGUE 582/3-4, BIBLE 582/5-6, BIBLE 582/7-8
*CONTENTS INITIALS TO MACCABEES 582/1-8, MACCABEES-I/ INITIAL E ET/ SOLDIER KILLS JEW 582-1, INITIAL E ET/ SOLDIER OF ANTIOCHUS KILLS JEW 582-1, ANTIOCHUS'S SOLDIER KILLS JEW WHO REFUSES TO EAT PORK 582-1, MACCABEES-II/ INITIAL F FRATRIBUS/ KING RECEIVES BOOK 582-2, INITIAL F FRATRIBUS/ KING RECEIVES BOOK 582-2, KING RECEIVES BOOK FROM MESSENGER 582-2, MACCABEES-I/ INITIAL E ET/ SOLDIER KILLS JEW 582-3, INITIAL E ET/ SOLDIER KILLS JEW 582-3, ANTIOCHUS'S SOLDIER KILLS JEW WHO REFUSES TO EAT PORK 582-3, MACCABEES-II/ INITIAL F FRATRIBUS/ KING CONVERSES 582-4, KING CONVERSES WITH FIGURE BEFORE HIM 582-4, PROLOGUE/ INITIAL M MACHABEORUM 582-5, MACCABEES-I/ INITIAL E ET/ SOLDIER KILLS JEW 582-5, INITIAL E ET/ SOLDIER KILLS JEW 582-5, ANTIOCHUS'S SOLDIER KILLS JEW WHO REFUSES TO EAT PORK 582-5, MACCABEES-II/ INITIAL F FRATRIBUS/ TWO JEWS GREET 582-6, INITIAL F FRATRIBUS/ TWO JEWS GREET 582-6, JEWS RAISE HANDS IN GREETING 582-6, PROLOGUE/ INITIAL M MACHABEORI 582-7, MACCABEES-I/ INITIAL E ET/ SOLDIER KILLS JEW 582-7, INITIAL E ET/ SOLDIER KILLS JEW 582-7, ANTIOCHUS'S SOLDIER KILLS JEW WHO REFUSES TO EAT PORK 582-7, MACCABEES-II/ INITIAL F FRATRIBUS/ MAN HANDS BOOK 582-8, INITIAL F FRATRIBUS/ MAN HANDS BOOK TO MESSENGER 582-8, MAN/ ROBED HANDS BOOK TO MESSENGER 582-8

*$ABSTRACT 583
*LIBRARY BODLEIAN
*SLIDE SET TITLE STRINGED INSTRUMENTS 1
*NEGATIVE REFERENCE ROLL 238D
*RENTAL FEE $3.20
*TITLE OF MANUSCRIPT PETER LOMBARD ON THE PSALTER 583-1, DE CIVITATE DEI 583/2-3, ROMANCE OF LANCELOT DU LAC 583-12, LIFE OF THE VIRGIN AND OF CHRIST 538-19, MEMORABILIA 583-20
*SHELFMARK MS CANON PAT LAT 217/ FOL 3 583-1, MS BODLEY 691/ FOL 1 583-2, MS BODLEY 691/ FOL 1V 583-3, MS RAWL LITURG D 3/ FOL 1 583-4, MS BAROCCI 201/ FOL 146V 583-5, MS AUCT D 5 9/ FOL 279 583-6, MS DOUCE 24/ FOL 117 583-7, MS DOUCE 118/ FOL 17 583-8, MS DOUCE 118/ FOL 101 583-9, MS DOUCE 118/ FOL 160V 583-10, MS UNIVERSITY COLLEGE 100/ FOL 18V 583-11, MS DOUCE 215/ FOL 1 583-12, MS CANON LITURG 126/ FOL 6 583-13, MS CANON LITURG 126/ FOL 142 583-14, MS DOUCE D 19B/ FOL 3 583-15, MS LITURG 198/ FOL 91V 583-16, MS LAUD MISC 188/ FOL 1 583-17, MS CANON LITURG 352/ FOL 204V 583-18, MS CANON ITAL 280/ FOL 241 583-19, MS DOUCE 202/ FOL 2 583/20-21, MS RAWL LITURG E 32/ FOL 41 583-22, MS DOUCE 268/ FOL 11 583-23, MS DOUCE 267/ FOL 5A 583-24
*PROVENANCE FRENCH 583-1, FRENCH/ NORMANDY 583/2-3, ENGLISH 583-4, BYZANTINE 583-5, ENGLISH 583-6, FRENCH/ FLANDERS 583-7, FRENCH/ ARTOIS 583/8-10, ENGLISH 583-11, FRENCH 583-12, FLEMISH/ LIEGE 583/13-14, ENGLISH/ PETERBOROUGH 583-15, ENGLISH 583-16, ENGLISH 583-17, ITALIAN/ TODI 583-18, ITALIAN/ NORTH? 583-19, FRENCH 583/20-21, FLEMISH 583-22, FRENCH/ BAYEUX 583-23, FRENCH/ NORTH 583-24
*DATE EXECUTED 12TH/ LATE 583-1, 11TH/ LATE WITH 14TH ADDITIONS 583/2-3, 13TH/ LATE 583-4, 13TH/ EARLY 583-5, 13TH/ LATE 583-6, 14TH/C1300 583-7, 13TH/ LATE 583/8-10, 14TH 583-11, 14TH/C1300 583-12, 14TH/C1300 583/13-14, 14TH/ EARLY 583-15, 14TH/ 3RD QUARTER 583-16, 14TH/C1380 583-17, 14TH/ 3RD QUARTER 583-18, 15TH/C1400 583-19, 15TH/ AFTER 1401 583/20-21, 15TH/ EARLY 583-22, 15TH/1450-60 583-23, 16TH 583-24
*LANGUAGE LATIN 583/1-18, ITALIAN 583-19, FRENCH 583/20-21, LATIN 583-22, FRENCH AND LATIN 583-23, LATIN 583-24
*ARTIST/ SCHOOL MASTER OF THE GASTON PHEBUS 583/20-21, MASTER OF BEAUFORT SAINTS 583-22
*AUTHOR LOMBARD/ PETER 583-1, VALERIUS MAXIMUS 583/20-21
*TYPE OF MANUSCRIPT CATENA ON PSALTER 583-1, RELIGIOUS TREATISE 583/2-3, GRADUAL/ USE OF SARUM 583-4, CATENA ON JOB 583-5, BIBLE 583-6, PSALTER 583-7, PSALTER 583/8-10, APOCALYPSE 583-11, ROMANCE 583-12, PSALTER 583/13-14, FRAGMENT 583-15, PSALTER 583-16, BOOK OF HOURS 583-17, MISSAL/ USE OF ROME

583-18, LIFE OF THE VIRGIN AND CHRIST 583-19, MEMORABILI 583/20-21, BOOK OF HOURS 583-22, BOOK OF HOURS 583-23, BOOK O HOURS 583-24
*CONTENTS MUSICAL INSTRUMENTS/ STRINGED 583/1-24, INITIAL B, VIOL AND HARP 583-1, DAVID PLAYS HARP 583-1, FIDDLE PLAYED B GROTESQUE 583-2, ANGEL WITH GITTERN AMONG MUSICAL ANGEL 583-3, MADONNA OF MERCY HOLDS CLOAK AROUND NAKED FIGURE 583-3, FIDDLE PLAYED BY MAN 583-4, RESURRECTION IN MARGI 583-4, REBEC PLAYED BY ONE OF JOB'S COMFORTERS 583-5, JOB' COMFORTER PLAYS REBEC 583-5, INITIAL B BEATUS/ FIDDLE 583-6 DAVID PLAYS HARP 583-6 FIDDLE PLAYED BY CENTAUR 583-7, CENTAU PLAYS FIDDLE 583-7, FIDDLE PLAYED BY GROTESQUE 583-8, FIDDL PLAYED BY MAN IN JESTER'S CAP 583-9, FIDDLE PLAYED BY CROWNE LADY 583-10, FIDDLE PLAYED BY FIGURE WITH ELDERS 583-11 FIDDLE PLAYED BY GROTESQUE/ APE BALANCES 583-12, FIDDLE PLAYE BY MAN 583-13, FIDDLE PLAYED BY ANGEL 583-14, FIDDLE PLAYED B ANGEL 583-15, FIDDLE PLAYED BY MAN IN TUNIC 583-16, MANDOR AND FIDDLE PLAYED BY ANGELS 583-17, FIDDLE PLAYED BY CROWNE GROTESQUE 583-18, FIDDLE PLAYED BY ANGEL IN RESURRECTION SCEN 583-19, RESURRECTION 583-19, FIDDLE PLAYED BY WOMAN AMI FOLIAGE 583-20, MANDORE PLAYED BY WOMAN AMID FOLIAGE 583-21 FIDDLE PLAYED BY BEARDED MAN 583-22, REBEC PLAYED BY ANGE BESIDE GOD ENTHRONED 583-23, GOD ENTHRONED 583-23, REBE PLAYED BY WINGED GROTESQUE 583-24

*$ABSTRACT 584
*LIBRARY BODLEIAN
*SLIDE SET TITLE ANIMALS FROM HERBAL AND BOOK OF MEDICINE
*NEGATIVE REFERENCE ROLL 242A
*RENTAL FEE $3.30
*COMMENTS SEE ALSO ABSTRACT 139/ BODLEIAN ROLL 175K
*TITLE OF MANUSCRIPT DE VIRTUTIBUS BESTIARUM IN ARTE MEDICINAE
*SHELFMARK MS BODLEY 130/ FOL 68 584-1, MS BODLEY 130/ FOL 7 584-2, MS BODLEY 130/ FOL 77 584-3, MS BODLEY 130/ FOL 7 584-4, MS BODLEY 130/ FOL 79 584-5, MS BODLEY 130/ FOL 8 584-6, MS BODLEY 130/ FOL 81 584-7, MS BODLEY 130/ FOL 8 584-8, MS BODLEY 130/ FOL 83 584-9, MS BODLEY 130/ FOL 8 584-10, MS BODLEY 130/ FOL 85 584-11, MS BODLEY 130/ FOL 8 584-12, MS BODLEY 130/ FOL 87 584-13, MS BODLEY 130/ FOL 8 584-14, MS BODLEY 130/ FOL 89 584-15, MS BODLEY 130/ FOL 90 584-16, MS BODLEY 130/ FOL 91 584/17-18, MS BODLEY 130/ FO 91V 584-19, MS BODLEY 130/ FOL 92 584-20, MS BODLEY 130/ FO 93 584-21, MS BODLEY 130/ FOL 93V 584-22, MS BODLEY 130/ FO 94 584-23, MS BODLEY 130/ FOL 94V 584-25, MS BODLEY 130/ FO 95V 584-26
*PROVENANCE ENGLISH/ BURY ST EDMUNDS
*DATE EXECUTED 11TH/ LATE
*LANGUAGE LATIN
*AUTHOR PSEUDO APULEIUS
*TYPE OF MANUSCRIPT HERBAL AND BOOK OF MEDICINE
*CONTENTS ANIMALS FROM HERBAL AND BOOK OF HOURS 584/1-26 MEDICINE/ BOOK OF 584/1-26, MAN AND WOMAN EMBRACING 584-1 HORSE 584-2, LION 584-3, BELUA 584-4, MULE 584-5, ASS 584-6 RAM 584-7, HART 584-8, BOAR 584-9, BULL 584-10, BADGER 584-11 WOLF 584-12, DOG 584-13, HARE 584-14, GOAT 584-15, CAT 584-16 WEASEL 584-17, MOUSE 584-18, EAGLE HOLDS FISH 584-19, COC 584-20, VULTURE 584-21, HAWK WITH SMALL BIRD 584-22, CRAN 584-23, PARTRIDGE 584-24, CROW 584-25, DOVE 584-26

*$ABSTRACT 585
*LIBRARY BODLEIAN
*SLIDE SET TITLE SERMOLOGIUM
*NEGATIVE REFERENCE ROLL 242B
*RENTAL FEE $3.90
*COMMENTS MADE FOR A COMMUNITY OF CISTERCIAN NUNS IN TH DIOCESE OF CONSTANCE.
*TITLE OF MANUSCRIPT SERMOLOGIUM
*SHELFMARK MS DOUCE 185/ FOL 1V-2 585-1, MS DOUCE 185/ FOL 2V-

585-2, MS DOUCE 185/ FOL 3V-4 585-3, MS DOUCE 185/ FOL 4V-5 585-4, MS DOUCE 185/ FOL 5V-6 585-5, MS DOUCE 185/ FOL 6V-7 585-6, MS DOUCE 185/ FOL 7V-8 585-7, MS DOUCE 185/ FOL 12V-13 585-8, MS DOUCE 185/ FOL 14V-15 585-9, MS DOUCE 185/ FOL 17V 585-10, MS DOUCE 185/ FOL 23V 585-11, MS DOUCE 185/ FOL 31V 585-12, MS DOUCE 185/ FOL 33 585-13, MS DOUCE 185/ FOL 35V 585-14, MS DOUCE 185/ FOL 38 585-16, MS DOUCE 185/ FOL 39 585-17, MS DOUCE 185/ FOL 39V 585-18, MS DOUCE 185/ FOL 42 585-19, MS DOUCE 185/ FOL 44V 585-20, MS DOUCE 185/ FOL 49V 585-21, MS DOUCE 185/ FOL 51V 585-22, MS DOUCE 185/ FOL 56V 585-23, MS DOUCE 185/ FOL 64 585-24, MS DOUCE 185/ FOL 65V 585-25, MS DOUCE 185/ FOL 67V 585-26, MS DOUCE 185/ FOL 88 585-27, MS DOUCE 185/ FOL 93V 585-28, MS DOUCE 185/ FOL 103 585-29, MS DOUCE 185/ FOL 106 585-30, MS DOUCE 185/ FOL 110V 585-31, MS DOUCE 185/ FOL 143V 585-32, MS DOUCE 185/ FOL 150 585-33, MS DOUCE 185/ FOL 163 585-34, MS DOUCE 185/ FOL 182 585-35, MS DOUCE 185/ FOL 190V 585-36, MS DOUCE 185/ FOL 193 585-37, MS DOUCE 185/ FOL 195 585-38
*PROVENANCE GERMAN/ SWISS/ CONSTANCE?
*DATE EXECUTED 14TH/ 2ND HALF AND END
*LANGUAGE LATIN
*TYPE OF MANUSCRIPT SERMOLOGIUM
*CONTENTS SERMOLOGIUM 585/1-38, JESSE TREE 585-1, HUNTING SCENE IN LOWER MARGIN 585-1, DOUBLE ARCH SUPPORTED BY DOGS AND WIVERNS 585-1, ARCH SURMOUNTED BY CRANES WITH APES PLAYING DRUM 585-1, DOUBLE ARCH SUPPORTED BY DOGS AND WIVERNS 585-2, ARCH SURMOUNTED BY CRANES/ BIRD/ OWLS 585-2, MAN PLAYS HANDBELLS/ APES WITH INSTRUMENTS 585-2, DOUBLE ARCHES SUPPORTED BY DOGS AND WIVERNS 585-3, ARCH SURMOUNTED BY CRANES/ BIRDS/ OWL/ SQUIRREL 585-3, MAN PLAYS HANDBELLS/ APES WITH TRUMPETS 585-3, ARCHES AS ABOVE WITH CRANES AND APES 585-4, CRANES AND APES PLAY TRUMPET AND FIDDLE 585-4,ARCHES SURMOUNTED BY CRANES/ BIRDS/ COCK/ OWL 585-5, MAN WITH BOW AND ARROW/ APES PLAY INSTRUMENTS 585-5, ARCHES SURMOUNTED BY BIRDS AND SQUIRREL 585-6, APE JUGGLING/ MAN BATTLE WITH ROCK AND CLUB 585-6, ARCH SURMOUNTED BY CRANES/ VINE-SCROLL 585-7,ANNUNCIATION/ LIONS SUPPORT PILLARS 585-8, MUSICIANS WITH FIDDLE/ FLUTE/ PORTATIVE ORGAN 585-8, DECORATIVE FRAMES 585-9, PROPHET WRITING/ ANGEL HOLDS SCROLL 585-10, MONK AT LECTERN 585-11, MONK AT ALTAR HOLDS WAFER TOWARD GOD'S HAND 585-12, VISITATION/ MARY AND ELIZABETH EMBRACE 585-13, NATIVITY/ MARY HOLDS MATURE CHILD 585-14, JOSEPH WATERS ASS FROM PAIL 585-14, VIRGIN AT SCHOOL/ COMPANIONS HOLD BOOKS 585-14, ANNUNCIATION TO THE SHEPHERDS 585-14, ANGELS WITH FIDDLE/ PSALTERY/ PORTATIVE ORGAN 585-14, ADORATION OF THE MAGI/ BEASTS AT CORNERS 585-15, ISAIAH POINTS TO OPEN BOOK/ BEASTS AT CORNERS 585-16, INITIAL I FORMED BY CONTORTED GROTESQUE 585-17, INITIAL E EXIIT WITH ENTHRONED KING 585-17, PRESENTATION IN THE TEMPLE 585-18, CHRIST DISPUTING WITH THE DOCTORS 585-18, ANGELS WITH SCROLLS 585-19, VIRGIN AND CHILD SURROUNDED BY ANGELS 585-20, ANGELS WITH MUSICAL INSTRUMENTS 585-20, DOG HUNTING RABBIT IN MARGIN 585-20, NATIVITY/ VIRGIN NURSES SWADDLED CHILD 585-21, BIRTH OF THE VIRGIN/ FOOD OFFERED TO ST ANNE 585-22, ST ANNE OFFERED FOOD AFTER BIRTH OF VIRGIN 585-22, RABBIT PLAYS TRUMPET IN MARGIN 585-22, KING ENTHRONED/ THREE CHALICES AT FEET 585-23,FIGURES KNEEL BELOW VISION OF HALOED HEADS 585-24, NATIVITY/ JOSEPH HANDS CHILD TO VIRGIN 585-25,INITIAL Q IN GOLD INTERLACE 585-26, ADORATION OF THE MAGI 585-27, ADORATION OF THE MAGI 585-28, VIRGIN AND CHILD/ VISION OF PROPHET 585-29, FLOWER AND VINE SCROLL MOTIF 585-30, PROPHET WITH SCROLL/ TWO DOGS 585-31, INITIAL S FORMED BY GROTESQUE BIRD 585-32, VIRGIN NURSES CHILD 585-33, BISHOP WITH CROZIER 585-34, PROPHET'S VISION OF ANGEL HOLDING SCROLL 585-35, KING ENTHRONED/ GROUP OF NUNS 585-36, ANGEL HOLDS SCROLL 585-37, DEATH AND ASSUMPTION OF VIRGIN 585-38, VIRGIN'S DEATH AND ASSUMPTION 585-38

$ABSTRACT 586
*LIBRARY BODLEIAN
*SLIDE SET TITLE CALENDAR AND BORDER DETAILS FROM BOOK OF HOURS

*NEGATIVE REFERENCE ROLL 242C
*RENTAL FEE $3.35
*SHELFMARK MS DOUCE 62/ FOL 3 586-1, MS DOUCE 62/ FOL 3V-4 586-2, MS DOUCE 62/ FOL 4V-5 586-3, MS DOUCE 62/ FOL 5V-6 586-4, MS DOUCE 62/ FOL 6V-7 586-5, MS DOUCE 62/ FOL 7V-8 586-6, MS DOUCE 62/ FOL 8V-9586-7, MS DOUCE 62/ FOL 9V-10 586-8, MS DOUCE 62/ FOL 10V-11 586-9, MS DOUCE 62/ FOL 11V-12 586-10, MS DOUCE 62/ FOL 12V-13 586-11, MS DOUCE 62/ FOL 13V-14 586-12, MS DOUCE 62/ FOL 14V-15 586-13, MS DOUCE 62/ FOL 21V 586-14, MS DOUCE 62/ FOL 39V 586-15, MS DOUCE 62/ FOL 60 586-16, MS DOUCE 62/ FOL 62 586-17, MS DOUCE 62/ FOL 67V 586-18, MS DOUCE 62/ FOL 76V 586-19, MS DOUCE 62/ FOL 82 586-20, MS DOUCE 62/ FOL 102 586-21, MS DOUCE 62/ FOL 105V 586-22, MS DOUCE 62/ FOL 133 586-23, MS DOUCE 62/ FOL 135 586-24, MS DOUCE 62/ FOL 138 586-25, MS DOUCE 62/ FOL 139 586-26, MS DOUCE 62/ FOL 180 586-27
*PROVENANCE FRENCH
*DATE EXECUTED 15TH/C1400
*LANGUAGE FRENCH AND LATIN
*ARTIST/ SCHOOL ZENOBI DA FIRENZE
*TYPE OF MANUSCRIPT BOOK OF HOURS/ USE OF PARIS
*CONTENTS BOOK OF HOURS/ FRENCH/ 15TH 586/1-27, CALENDAR AND BORDER DETAILS FROM BOOK OF HOURS 586/1-27, JANUARY/ MAN WARMS FEET BEFORE FIRE 586-1, AQUARIUS/ HAND POURS WATER FROM PITCHER 586-1, MAN CARRIES BUCKETS/ BIRDS/ GROTESQUE IN MARGIN 586-1, FEBRUARY/ MAN FISHES WITH BASKET FOR CATCH BESIDE HIM 586-2, PISCES 586-2, WOMEN WITH BASKETS OF FISH IN MARGIN 586-2, MARCH/ MAN BLOWS DOUBLE HORN 586-3, ARIES/ RAM 586-3, SHEPHERD WITH FLOCK/ WOMAN PICKS FLOWERS 586-3, APRIL/ MAN KNEELS IN GRASS 586-4, TAURUS/ BULL WALKS TOWARD MAN 586-4, LADY WITH FLOWERS AND APE IN MARGINS 586-4, MAY/ FALCONER WITH DOG AND HORSE 586-5, GEMINI/ TWINS 586-5, MAN PLAYS HARP AND WOMAN WITH BOUQUETS 586-5, JUNE/ MAN SCYTHING 586-6, CANCER/ CRAB 586-6, GROTESQUE WITH NAKERS 586-6, LADY HOLDS FRUIT BASKET AND SCALES 586-6, JULY/ MAN CUTTING GRAIN WITH SICKLE 586-7, LEO/ LION 586-7, GROTESQUES WITH LUTE/ BOW/ TRUMPET 586-7, AUGUST/ MAN THRESHING 586-8, VIRGO/ MAIDEN 586-8, MAN PUSHING CASK IN WHEELBARROW 586-8, SEPTEMBER/ MAN CUTTING GRAPES 586-9, LIBRA/ SCALES 586-9, MAN WITH GRAPES/ CRANE/ TRUMPET 586-9, OCTOBER/ MAN SOWING SEEDS 586-10, SCORPIO/ SCORPION 586-10, MAN CARRIES BASKET ON BACK 586-10, NOVEMBER/ MAN FEEDING PIGS 586-11, CAPRICORN/ UNICORN 586-11, MAN WITH HORN/ LADY WITH PEARS 586-11, DECEMBER/ MAN KILLS PIG 586-12, SAGITTARIUS/ CENTAUR WITH DRAWN BOW 586-12, MAN WITH HANDBELLS/ LADY SELLING FROM TRAY 586-12, MAN CARRIES BASKET 586-13, BEGINNING OF BOOK OF ST JOHN 586-13, ST JOHN WRITING/ HALOED EAGLE 586-13, GROTESQUE PLAYS FIDDLE IN MARGIN 586-14, MAN TILTS AT QUINTAIN FROM ROWBOAT 586-15, DOG DRESSED A CLERIC PREACHES TO BIRDS 586-16, MAN PICKS FLOWERS FOR LAD 586-17, MEN WRESTLE/ GROTESQUE IN MARGIN 586-18, MAN FISHE FROM BOAT/ GROTESQUE IN MARGIN 586-19, WOMAN CHASES FOX WIT CHICKEN IN MOUTH 586-20, GROTESQUE WITH TRUMPET IN MARGI 586-20, GAME WITH SHUTTLECOCK AND PADDLES 586-21, GROTESQU HERMIT READS BENEATH LANTERN 586-22, MAN SNARES BIRDS WIT CLAPNET 586-23, MAN LURES HAWK/ DUCK IN WATER 586-24 GROTESQUE BIRD IN MARGIN 586-24, LADY AND DONKEY APPROAC WINDMILL 586-25, CAT WITH BACK RAISED AND CROUCHING DO 586-26, ANGELS WITH CANDLES BEFORE ALTAR 586-27

*$ABSTRACT 587
*LIBRARY BODLEIAN
*SLIDE SET TITLE BOOK OF HOURS
*NEGATIVE REFERENCE ROLL 242D
*RENTAL FEE $2.60
*SHELFMARK MS DOUCE 248/ FOL 24 587-1, MS DOUCE 248/ FOL 3 587-2, MS DOUCE 248/ FOL 66 587-3, MS DOUCE 248/ FOL 74 587-4, MS DOUCE 248/ FOL 75 587-5, MS DOUCE 248/ FOL 94V-9 587-6, MS DOUCE 248/ FOL 100V 587-7, MS DOUCE 248/ FOL 104 587-8, MS DOUCE 248/ FOL 109V 587-9, MS DOUCE 248/ FO 114V-115 587-10, MS DOUCE 248/ FOL 121V 587-11, MS DOUCE 248

FOL 127V-128 587-12, MS DOUCE 248/ FOL 142 587-13, MS DOUCE 248/ FOL 163V 587-14, MS DOUCE 248/ FOL 206V-207 587-15, MS DOUCE 248/ FOL 212 587-16
*PROVENANCE DUTCH/ DELFT
*DATE EXECUTED 15TH/ MID
*LANGUAGE DUTCH
*TYPE OF MANUSCRIPT BOOK OF HOURS
*CONTENTS BOOK OF HOURS/ DUTCH/ 15TH 587/1-16, GROTESQUE PLAYS REBEC IN MARGIN 587-1, PELICAN PIERCES ITS BREAST TO FEED YOUNG 587-2, RAMS EAT GRAPES FROM VINE 587-2, INITIAL WITH FIVE WOUNDS OF CHRIST 587-3, CHRIST'S FIVE WOUNDS/ INSTRUMENTS OF PASSION 587-3, CROWN OF THORNS INSET WITH AGNUS DEI 587-3, ANNUNCIATION TO THE VIRGIN 587-4, BIRDS AND SQIRREL IN MARGIN 587-4, VIRGIN AND CHILD ON CRESCENT MOON 587-5, ANGEL KNEELS ON FLOWER IN MARGIN 587-5, VISITATION/ STRAWBERRIES AND HARE IN BORDER 587-6, GROTESQUE PLAYS REBEC 586-6, NATIVITY/ JOSEPH HOLDS CANDLE 587-7, DOVE AND COLUMBINE IN BORDER 587-7, CIRCUMCISION OF CHRIST 587-8, CHRIST'S CIRCUMCISION 587-8, BIRD AND MONSTER IN BORDER 587-8, ADORATION OF THE MAGI/ JOSEPH HOLDS CHEST 587-9, PEACOCK AND MONSTER IN BORDER 587-9, PRESENTATION IN THE TEMPLE/ DOVES IN BASKET 587-10, DOG CHASES RABBIT INTO HOLE 587-10, MASSACRE OF THE INNOCENTS/ MOTHERS STRUGGLE 587-11, HEROD WATCHES AS MOTHERS STRUGGLE WITH SOLDIERS 587-11, FLIGHT INTO EGYPT 587-12, UNICORN IN VIRGIN'S LAP 587-12, DAVID PLAYS HARP/ TWO COCKS FIGHT 587-13, INITIAL FILLED WITH COCKLE SHELLS 587-13, INITIAL INSET WITH MONSTRANCE/ ANGEL WITH LUTE 587-14, ADAM AND EVE HOLD DISTAFF/ SPINDLES/ WINDER 587-15, NUN WITH BOOK EMERGES FROM FLOWER 587-15, JESTER PLAYS JAWBONE WITH COMB 587-16

*$ABSTRACT 588
*LIBRARY BODLEIAN
*SLIDE SET TITLE MS LITURG 41/ PART I
*NEGATIVE REFERENCE ROLL 242E
*RENTAL FEE $3.20
*SHELFMARK MS LITURG 41/ FOL 1 588-1, MS LITURG 41/ FOL 1V 588-2, MS LITURG 41/ FOL 2 588-3, MS LITURG 41/ FOL 2V 588-4, MS LITURG 41/ FOL 3 588-5, MS LITURG 41/ FOL 3V 588-6, MS LITURG 41/ FOL 4 588-7, MS LITURG 41/ FOL 4V 588-8, MS LITURG 41/ FOL 5 588-9, MS LITURG 41/ FOL 5V 588-10, MS LITURG 41/ FOL 6 588-11, MS LITURG 41/ FOL 6V 588-12, MS LITURG 41/ FOL 7 588-13, MS LITURG 41/ FOL 7V 588-14, MS LITURG 41/ FOL 8 588-15, MS LITURG 41/ FOL 8V 588-16, MS LITURG 41/ FOL 9 588-17, MS LITURG 41/ FOL 9V 588-18, MS LITURG 41/ FOL 10 588-19, MS LITURG 41/ FOL 10V 588-20, MS LITURG 41/ FOL 11 588-21, MS LITURG 41/ FOL 11V 588-22, MS LITURG 41/ FOL 12 588-23, MS LITURG 41/ FOL 12V 588-24
*PROVENANCE FRENCH/ CALENDAR POINTS TO PARIS
*DATE EXECUTED 15TH/C1470-80
*LANGUAGE FRENCH AND LATIN
*ARTIST/ SCHOOL MAITRE FRANCOIS
*TYPE OF MANUSCRIPT BOOK OF HOURS/ USE OF ROME
*CONTENTS BOOK OF HOURS/ FRENCH/ 15TH 588/1-24, OCCUPATIONS OF THE MONTHS 588/1-24, ZODIAC SIGNS 588/1-24, JANUARY/ MAN SITS AT TABLE 588-1, AQUARIUS/ NAKED BOYS POURS WATER FROM JUG 588-2, FEBRUARY/ MAN WARMS FEET BY FIRE 588-3, PISCES/ TWO FISH BEFORE GREEN LANDSCAPE 588-4, MARCH/ MAN PRUNES TREES 588-5, ARIES/ RAM STANDS ON PATH 588-6, APRIL/ LADIES PICK FLOWERS AND MAKE WREATH 588-7, TAURUS/ BULL IN GREEN LANDSCAPE 588-8, MAY/ MEN CARRY BRANCHES OVER SHOULDERS 588-9, GEMINI/ NUDE MALE AND FEMALE MERGE 588-10, JUNE/ MEN SCYTHE AND RAKE HAY 588-11, CANCER/ CRAB BEFORE WALLED CITY 588-12, JULY/ COUPLE CUTS AND BINDS WHEAT 588-13, LEO/ SMILING LION 588-14, AUGUST/ MAN FLAILS WHEAT 588-15, VIRGO/ MAIDEN BEFORE SHEAVES OF WHEAT 588-16, SEPTEMBER/ MAN TREADS GRAPES IN TUB 588-17, LIBRA/ WOMAN HOLDS SCALES 588-18, OCTOBER/ MAN SOWS SEEDS 588-19, SCORPIO/ SCORPION ON PATH BEFORE LANDSCAPE 588-20, NOVEMBER/ MAN KNOCKS ACORNS FROM TREES 588-21,SAGITTARIUS/ CENTAUR WITH DRAWN BOW 588-22, DECEMBER/ COUPLE SLAUGHTERS PIG 588-23, CAPRICORN/ GOAT EMERGES FROM CORNUCOPIA 588-24

*$ABSTRACT 589
*LIBRARY BODLEIAN
*SLIDE SET TITLE MS LITURG 41/ PART II
*NEGATIVE REFERENCE ROLL 242F
*RENTAL FEE $3.85
*SHELFMARK MS LITURG 41/ FOL 13 589-1, MS LITURG 41/ FOL 15V 589-2, MS LITURG 41/ FOL 17V 589-3, MS LITURG 41/ FOL 19V 589-4, MS LITURG 41/ FOL 21 589-5, MS LITURG 41/ FOL 25V 589-6, MS LITURG 41/ FOL 30 589-7, MS LITURG 41/ FOL 51 589-8, MS LITURG 41/ FOL 64V 589-9, MS LITURG 41/ FOL 66 589-10, MS LITURG 41/ FOL 67V 589-11, MS LITURG 41/ FOL 73 589-12, MS LITURG 41/ FOL 74V 589-13, MS LITURG 41/ FOL 76 589-14, MS LITURG 41/ FOL 81V 589-15, MS LITURG 41/ FOL 83 589-16, MS LITURG 41/ FOL 84V 589-17, MS LITURG 41/ FOL 89V 589-18, MS LITURG 41/ FOL 91 589-19, MS LITURG 41/ FOL 92V 589-20, MS LITURG 41/ FOL 97V 589-21, MS LITURG 41/ FOL 99 589-22, MS LITURG 41/ FOL 100 589-23, MS LITURG 41/ FOL 108V 589-24, MS LITURG 41/ FOL 110 589-25, MS LITURG 41/ FOL 111 589-26, MS LITURG 41/ FOL 116 589-27, MS LITURG 41/ FOL 117V 589-28, MS LITURG 41/ FOL 126 589-29, MS LITURG 41/ FOL 147 589-30, MS LITURG 41/ FOL 197V 589-31, MS LITURG 41/ FOL 198V 589-32, MS LITURG 41/ FOL 199V 589-33, MS LITURG 41/ FOL 200V 589-34, MS LITURG 41/ FOL 201V 589-35, MS LITURG 41/ FOL 202V 589-36, MS LITURG 41/ FOL 203V 589-37
*PROVENANCE FRENCH/ CALENDAR POINTS TO PARIS
*DATE EXECUTED 15TH/C1470-80
*LANGUAGE FRENCH AND LATIN
*ARTIST/ SCHOOL MAITRE FRANCOIS
*TYPE OF MANUSCRIPT BOOK OF HOURS/ USE OF ROME
*CONTENTS BOOK OF HOURS/ FRENCH/ 15TH 589/1-37, PERICOPE FROM ST JOHN 589-1, ST JOHN STANDS IN TUB OF BOILING OIL 589-1, ST JOHN WRITES ON PATMOS/ EAGLE HOLDS PENCASE 589-1, PERICOPE FROM ST LUKE 589-2, ST LUKE SITS WRITING/ WINGED OX 589-2, PERICOPE FROM ST MATTHEW 589-3, ST MATTHEW SITS WRITING/ ANGEL HOLDS INKPOT 589-3, PERICOPE FROM ST MARK 589-4, ST MARK SITS WRITING/ WINGED LION 589-4, PRAYER TO THE VIRGIN/ OBSECRO TE 589-5, VIRGIN AND CHILD WITH TWO ANGELS 589-5, PRAYER TO THE VIRGIN/ O INTEMERATA 589-6, PIETA/ ST JOHN AND MARY MAGDALENE ARE PRESENT 589-6, OFFICE OF THE VIRGIN/ MATINS 589-7, ANNUNCIATION 589-7, OFFICE OF THE VIRGIN/ LAUDS 589-8, VISITATION/ ZACHARIAS STANDS BEHIND VIRGIN 589-8, OFFICE OF THE CROSS/ MATINS 589-9, AGONY IN THE GARDEN/ CHRIST PRAYS BENEATH MOUNTAIN 589-9, JUDAS/ SOLDIERS/ HIGH PRIEST IN NICHES 589-9, OFFICE OF THE HOLY GHOST/ MATINS OR LAUDS 589-10, BAPTISM OF CHRIST/ ANGEL HOLDS CLOAK 589-10, CHRIST'S BAPTISM 589-10, OFFICE OF THE VIRGIN/ PRIME 589-11, NATIVITY/ MARY AND JOSEPH KNEEL 589-11, OFFICE OF THE CROSS/ PRIME 589-12, BETRAYAL OF CHRIST/ JUDAS KISSES CHRIST 589-12, CHRIST BETRAYED/ JUDAS KISSES 589-12, OFFICE OF THE HOLY GHOST/ PRIME 589-13, PENTECOST/ GOLD AND RED TONGUES OF FIRE 589-13, ST JOHN KNEELS BEFORE VIRGIN 589-13, OFFICE OF THE VIRGIN/ TIERCE 589-14, SHEPHERDS LOOK UP AT ANGEL WITH SCROLL 589-14, OFFICE OF THE HOLY GHOST/ TIERCE 589-15, CHRIST HELD BY SOLDIERS BEFORE PILATE 589-15, PILATE WASHES HIS HANDS 589-15, OFFICE OF THE HOLY GHOST/ TIERCE 589-16, DISCIPLES GO FORTH TO PREACH 589-16, OFFICE OF THE VIRGIN/ SEXT 589-17, ADORATION OF THE MAGI/ MUSICAL ANGELS 589-17, MUSICAL INSTRUMENTS/ LUTE/ HARP/ FIDDLE/ RECORDER 589-17, OFFICE OF THE CROSS/ SEXT 589-18, CHRIST CARRIES CROSS/ LED BY ROPE 589-18, OFFICE OF THE HOLY GHOST/ SEXT 589-19, ST PETER PREACHING/ DOVE IN SKY 589-19, OFFICE OF THE VIRGIN/ NONES 589-20, PRESENTATION IN THE TEMPLE 589-20, OFFICE OF THE CROSS/ NONES 589-21, CRUCIFIXION/ MARY/ JOHN AND SOLDIERS 589-21, OFFICE OF THE HOLY GHOST/ NONES 589-22, ST PETER BAPTISES THE PEOPLE 589-22, OFFICE OF THE VIRGIN/ VESPERS 589-23, FLIGHT INTO EGYPT/ VIRGIN HOLDS FRUIT 589-23, SALOME WALKS BESIDE HOLY FAMILY 589-23, IDOL FALLS FROM COLUMN ON HILL 589-23, OFFICE OF THE CROSS/ VESPERS 589-24, DESCENT FROM THE CROSS/ JOSEPH OF ARIMATHEA AND NICODEMUS 589-24, JOSEPH OF ARIMATHEA AND NICODEMUS LOWER BODY OF CHRIST 589-24, OFFICE OF THE HOLY GHOST/ VESPERS 589-25, ST PETER AND ST JOHN CONFIRM A MULTITUDE 589-25, OFFICE OF THE VIRGIN/ COMPLINE 589-26, CORONATION OF THE VIRGIN/ GOD BLESSES

VIRGIN 589-26, OFFICE OF THE CROSS/ COMPLINE 589-27, ENTOMBMENT OF CHRIST 589-27, CHRIST'S ENTOMBMENT 589-27, JOSEPH OF ARIMATHEA AND NICODEMUS AT TOMB 589-27, OFFICE OF THE HOLY GHOST/ COMPLINE 589-28, JOEL'S PROPHECY 589-28, PSALM 6/ DOMINE NE IN FURORE/ DAVID AND GOLIATH 589-29, DAVID KILLS GOLIATH WHO FALLS BACKWARDS 589-29, OFFICE OF THE DEAD/ LAST SACRAMENT 589-30, PRIEST ASPERGES DYING MAN 589-30, ANGEL CARRIES NAKED SOUL PAST DEMON TO GOD 589-30, MEMORIA/ TRINITY 589-31, TRINITY/ GOD/ CHRIST/ DOVE/ SERAPHIM 589-31, MEMORIA/ ST MICHAEL STANDS ON BELLY OF DEMON 589-32, ST MICHAEL STANDS ON BELLY OF DEMON 589-32, MEMORIA/ ST JAMES THE GREATER READS TO PILGRIMS 589-33, ST JAMES AS PILGRIM READS TO TWO PILGRIMS 589-33, MEMORIA/ ST CHRISTOPHER CROSSES WATER WITH CHRIST 589-34, ST CHRISTOPHER CROSSES WATER WITH CHRIST ON BACK 589-34, MEMORIA/ BEHEADING OF ST JOHN THE BAPTIST 589-35, ST JOHN THE BAPTIST BEHEADED/ SALOME WITH PLATTER 589-35, MEMORIA/ ST PAUL AND ST PETER 589-36, SS PAUL AND PETER 589-36, MEMORIA/ ST CATHERINE AND EXECUTIONER 589-37, ST CATHERINE KNEELS BEFORE EXECUTIONER 589-37

*$ABSTRACT 590
*LIBRARY BODLEIAN
*SLIDE SET TITLE STRINGED INSTRUMENTS II
*NEGATIVE REFERENCE ROLL 242G
*RENTAL FEE $3.30
*COMMENTS SELECTION FROM 11 MSS OF THE 14TH-18TH CENTURIES.
*TITLE OF MANUSCRIPT BOOK OF HOURS OF THE HOLY CROSS 590-19, CHANSON D'AMOUR 590-24, RECUEIL D'ARMOIRIES ET DE DEVISES 590-25, DISSERTATION ON THE TARANTULA 590-26
*SHELFMARK MS BARLOW 22/ FOL 114V 590-1, MS LAUD LAT 84/ FOL 40V 590-2, MS LAUD LAT 84/ FOL 138 590-3, MS LAUD LAT 84/ FOL 235V 590-4, MS LAUD LAT 84/ FOL 307V 590-5, MS LAUD LAT 84/ FOL 361V 590-6, MS LAUD LAT 84/ FOL 366V 590-7, MS DOUCE 77/ FOL 49 590-8, MS DOUCE 77/ FOL 49V 590-9, MS DOUCE 77/ FOL 50 590-10, MS DOUCE 77/ FOL 50V 590-11, MS DOUCE 77/ FOL 58 590-12, MS DOUCE 77/ FOL 58V 590-13, MS DOUCE 267/ FOL 5AV 590-14, MS DOUCE 267/ FOL 124 590-15, MS DOUCE 267/ FOL 130 590-16, MS LAT LITURG F 6/ FOL 17 590-17, MS LAT LITURG F 6/ FOL 119 590-18, MS GERM G 1/ FOL 70V 590-19, MS DOUCE 135/ FOL 41V 590-20, MS DOUCE 135/ FOL 48 590-21, MS DOUCE 135/ FOL 80 590-22, MS DOUCE 135/ FOL 87 590-23, MS DOUCE 375/ FOL 30 590-24, MS GOUGH DRAWINGS GAIGNIERES 16/ FOL 45 590-25, MS DOUCE 123/ FOL VI 590-26
*PROVENANCE ENGLISH 590-1, FRENCH/ FLANDERS 590/2-7, FRENCH 590/8-13, FRENCH/ BESANCON 590-14, FRENCH/ NORTH 590/15-16, FRENCH/ CENTRAL 590/17-18, FLEMISH 590-19, FRENCH 590/20-25, ITALIAN 590-26
*DATE EXECUTED 14TH/ EARLY 590-1, 14TH/ 1ST QUARTER 590/2-7, 15TH/C1450-70 590/8-13, 15TH/C1470 590-14, 16TH/ EARLY 590/15-16, 15TH/ 3RD QUARTER 590/17-18, 15TH/1495 590-19, 16TH/ 2ND QUARTER 590/20-23, 17TH/ MID 590-24, 18TH/ EARLY 590-25, 18TH/1734 590-26
*LANGUAGE LATIN 590/1-7, FRENCH AND LATIN 590/8-18, GERMAN/ LOW 590-19, LATIN 590/20-23, FRENCH 590/24-25
*ARTIST/ SCHOOL SENAULT/ LOUIS/ RELATED TO 590-24, GAIGNIERES 590-25
*TYPE OF MANUSCRIPT PSALTER 590/1-7, BOOK OF HOURS 590/8-13, BOOK OF HOURS/ USE OF BESANCON 590/14-16, BOOK OF HOURS/ USE OF ROME 590/17-18, BOOK OF HOURS 590-19, BOOK OF HOURS/ USE OF ROME 590/20-23, CHANSONS D'AMOUR 590-24
*CONTENTS MUSICAL INSTRUMENTS/ STRINGED 590/1-26, FIDDLE PLAYED BY GROTESQUE 590-1, FIDDLE PLAYED BY MAN 590-2, FIDDLE PLAYED BY APE WITH RAKE 590-3, FIDDLE PLAYED BY APE 590/4-5, FIDDLE PLAYED BY NUN 590-6, FIDDLE PLAYED BY WOMAN 590-7, FIDDLE AND BOW PLAYED BY GROTESQUE 590/8-9, REBEC PLAYED BY GROTESQUE 590/10-11, FIDDLE PLAYED BY GROTESQUE 590/12-13, REBEC PLAYED BY GROTESQUE 590-14, REBEC PLAYED BY GROTESQUE WITH ASS'S HEAD 590-15, MUSICIANS INCLUDING FIDDLER AND DRUMMER 590-16, MUSICAL ANGELS WITH LUTE/ RECORDERS/ PSALTERY/ REBEC 590-17, MANDORE AND RECORDER HELD BY PUTTO AND GROTESQUE 590-18, REBEC

AND HARP HELD BY ANGELS BESIDE VIRGIN 590-19, VIRGIN AND CHILD WITH MUSICAL ANGELS 590-19, FIDDLE PLAYED BY MAN/ NUDE LADIES BATHE 590-20, BATHING SCENE WITH NUDE LADIES 590-20, FIDDLE PLAYED BY MAN 590-21, SHAWN AND FIDDLE PLAYED BY JOB'S COMFORTERS 590-22, JOB SEATED IN ASHES/ COMFORTERS PLAY SHAWN AND FIDDLE 590-22, FIDDLE AT FEET OF MAN WITH HORN 590-23, LUTE AND FIDDLE PLAYED BY MAN 590-24, FIDDLE AND DRUM/ PRODIGAL SON 590-25, PRODIGAL SON 590-25, MUSICIANS WITH FIDDLES/ VIOLS/ BAGPIPES/ TAMBOURINE 590-26, VIOLS 590-26, BAGPIPES 590-26, TAMBOURINE 590-26

*$ABSTRACT 591
*LIBRARY BODLEIAN
*SLIDE SET TITLE VENETIAN DOGALI
*NEGATIVE REFERENCE ROLL 243A
*RENTAL FEE $2.40
*TITLE OF MANUSCRIPT COMMISSIO OF DOGE NICOLO TRON 591-1, COMMISSIO OF THE PROCURATORS OF SAN MARCO 591-2, COMMISSIO FROM DOGE ANDREA GRITTI 591-3, COMMISSIO FROM DOGE FRANCESCO DONATO 591-4, COMMISSIO OF DOGE GIROLAMO PRIULI 591-5, COMMISSIO OF DOGE ALVISE MOCENIGO 591/6-7, COMMISSIO OF DOGE DA PONTE 591-8
*SHELFMARK MS SELDEN SUPRA 67/ FOL 2 591-1, MS ASHMOLE 811/ FOL 2 591-2, MS LAUD MISC 533/ FOL 1 591-3, MS ADD C 23/ FOL 1 591-4, MS SELDEN SUPRA 68/ FOL 1 591-5, MS ADD A 189/ FOL 1V 591-6, MS ADD A 189/ FOL 2 591-7, MS BUCHANAN D 5/ FOL 1 591-8
*PROVENANCE ITALIAN/ VENICE
*DATE EXECUTED 15TH/1472 591-1, 15TH/ AFTER 1473 591-2, 16TH/1533 591-3, 16TH/1548 591-4, 16TH/1563 591-5, 16TH/1573? 591/6-7, 16TH 591-8
*LANGUAGE ITALIAN AND LATIN 591/1-2, LATIN 591/3-4 AND 8, ITALIAN AND LATIN 591/5-7
*TYPE OF MANUSCRIPT DOGALI
*CONTENTS VENETIAN DOGALI 591/1-8, INITIAL N WITH ST NICHOLAS/ FLORAL BORDER 591-1, ST NICHOLAS 591-1, TABLE OF CONTENTS 591-2, FRONTISPIECE WITH VIRGIN AND CHILD 591-3, VIRGIN AND CHILD 591-3, ST FRANCIS ADORED BY FRANCESCO MALIPIERO 591-4, GOD BLESSES GIROLAMO VENIER 591-5, ST MARK PRESENTS BOOK TO THE DOGE 591-6, CHRIST APPEARS IN CLOUD WITH BANNER 591-6, VENICE ACCOMPANIED BY JUSTICE AND TRUTH 591-7, JUSTICE AND TRUTH 591-7, ST MARK AS LION ON DECORATIVE PAGE 591-8

*$ABSTRACT 592
*LIBRARY BODLEIAN
*SLIDE SET TITLE FIFTEENTH CENTURY ILLUMINATION
*NEGATIVE REFERENCE ROLL 243B
*RENTAL FEE $2.50
*TITLE OF MANUSCRIPT CHRONICLE 592/5-6, DESCENT OF KINGS OF ENGLAND TO EDWARD IV 592-7, GENEALOGY OF THE KINGS OF ENGLAND 592/8-9, GENEALOGICAL TABLES OF KINGS OF ENGLAND TO EDWARD IV 592-10
*SHELFMARK MS GOUGH LITURG 9/ FOL 127 592-1, MS GOUGH LITURG 9/ FOL 146V 592-2, MS GOUGH LITURG 9/ FOL 176V 592-3, MS GOUGH LITURG 9/ FOL 242 592-4, MS LAUD MISC 730/ FOL 9 592-5, MS LAUD MISC 730/ FOL 10 592-6, MS BRASENOSE COLLEGE 17/ FOL 2V 592-7, MS E MUS 42/ FOL 1V 592-8, MS LYELL 33/ FOL 1V 592-9, MS CORPUS CHRISTI COLLEGE 207/ FOL 3V 592-10
*PROVENANCE ENGLISH
*DATE EXECUTED 15TH/C1430 592/1-4, 15TH/ 3RD QUARTER 592/5-6, 15TH 592-7, 15TH/C1467-69 592-8, 15TH/C1469-70 592-9, 15TH 592-10
*LANGUAGE LATIN 592/1-7 AND 10, ENGLISH 592/8-9
*AUTHOR ICKHAM/ PETER 592/5-6
*TYPE OF MANUSCRIPT BOOK OF HOURS/ USE OF SARUM 592/1-4, CHRONICLE 592/5-6, GENEALOGY 592/7-10
*CONTENTS ENGLISH ILLUMINATION/ 15TH CENTURY 592/1-10, ANGELS CARRY NAKED SOUL TO HEAVEN IN SHROUD 592-1, SOUL CARRIED TO HEAVEN 592-1, ST JEROME DRESSED AS CARDINAL WRITES 592-2,

TRINITY/ GOD HOLDS CRUCIFIED CHRIST 592-3, PASSION INSTRUMENTS 592-4, KING HOLDS SWORD 592-5, CASTLE AND WALLED CITIES 592-6, ADAM AND EVE STAND ON EITHER SIDE OF TREE 592/7-10

*$ABSTRACT 593
*LIBRARY BODLEIAN
*SLIDE SET TITLE INITIALS FROM LANFRANC
*NEGATIVE REFERENCE ROLL 243E
*RENTAL FEE $2.30
*TITLE OF MANUSCRIPT DE CORPORE ET SANGUINE DOMINI 593-1, DE CORPORE ET SANGUINE DOMINE 593/2-4, DE INCARNATIONE VERBI 593-5, DE CORPORE ET SANGUINE DOMINI 593-6
*SHELFMARK MS BODLEY 569/ FOL 1 593-1, MS BODLEY 569/ FOL 28 593-2, MS BODLEY 569/ FOL 42 593-3, MS BODLEY 569/ FOL 58V 593-4, MS BODLEY 569/ FOL 78 593-5, MS BODLEY 569/ FOL 92V 593-6
*PROVENANCE FRENCH/ NORMANDY
*DATE EXECUTED 12TH/C1100
*LANGUAGE LATIN
*ARTIST/ SCHOOL RELATED TO JUMIEGES STYLE
*AUTHOR LANFRANC 593-1, GUIMUNDUS AVERSANUS EPISCOPUS 593/2-4, ANSELM 593-5, ARNULFUS MONACHUS 593-6
*TYPE OF MANUSCRIPT RELIGIOUS TREATISE ON THE EUCHARIST
*CONTENTS EUCHARIST/ RELIGIOUS TREATISES 593/1-6, INITIALS FROM LANFRANC AND OTHER TEXTS 593/1-6, INITIAL L LANFRANCUS/ LANFRANC HOLDS CROZIER 593-1, LANFRANC HOLDS CROZIER 593-1, INITIAL A AD COMPOSED OF ANIMAL INTERLACE 593-2, INITIAL D DUM/ VOID INTERLACE 593-3, INITIAL H HACTENUS COMPOSED OF ANIMAL INTERLACE 593-4, INITIAL D DOMINO/ VOID INTERLACE 593-5, INITIAL V VENERABILI/ FOLIATED AND ANIMAL INTERLACE 593-6

*$ABSTRACT 594
*LIBRARY BODLEIAN
*SLIDE SET TITLE PSALTER/ FLEMISH
*NEGATIVE REFERENCE ROLL 243F
*RENTAL FEE $3.25
*COMMENTS ALL THE CALENDAR ILLUSTRATIONS, MINIATURES, AND HISTORIATED INITIALS.
*SHELFMARK MS DOUCE 38/ FOL 1 594-1, MS DOUCE 38/ FOL 1V 594-2, MS DOUCE 38/ FOL 2 594-3, MS DOUCE 38/ FOL 2V 594-4, MS DOUCE 38/ FOL 3 594-5, MS DOUCE 38/ FOL 3V 594-6, MS DOUCE 38/ FOL 4 594-7, MS DOUCE 38/ FOL 4V 594-8, MS DOUCE 38/ FOL 5 594-9, MS DOUCE 38/ FOL 5V 594-10, MS DOUCE 38/ FOL 6 594-11, MS DOUCE 38/ FOL 6V 594-12, MS DOUCE 38/ FOL 7V 594-13, MS DOUCE 38/ FOL 8V 594-14, MS DOUCE 38/ FOL 9V 594-15, MS DOUCE 38/ FOL 38 594-16, MS DOUCE 38/ FOL 58V 594-17, MS DOUCE 38/ FOL 59 594-18, MS DOUCE 38/ FOL 95V 594-19, MS DOUCE 38/ FOL 96 594-20, MS DOUCE 38/ FOL 119V 594-21, MS DOUCE 38/ FOL 120 594-22, MS DOUCE 38/ FOL 142V 594-23, MS DOUCE 38/ FOL 143 594-24, MS DOUCE 38/ FOL 166 594-25
*PROVENANCE FLEMISH
*DATE EXECUTED 14TH/C1300
*LANGUAGE LATIN
*ARTIST/ SCHOOL RELATED TO MISSAL OF ST BLANDIN GHENT
*TYPE OF MANUSCRIPT PSALTER
*CONTENTS PSALTER/ FLEMISH/ 14TH 594/1-25, CALENDAR/ FLEMISH 594/1-12, JANUARY/ MAN SEATED BY TABLE WITH JUG 594-1, FEBRUARY/ PURIFICATION/ VIRGIN AT ALTAR 594-2, VIRGIN AT ALTAR WITH CANDLE 594-2, MARCH/ MAN CUTTING WOOD 594-3, APRIL/ WOMAN BEFORE FLORAL BACKGROUND 594-4, MAY/ FALCONER OFFERS LURE TO HAWK 594-5, FALCONER OFFERS LURE TO HAWK 594-5, JUNE/ MAN CARRIES BUNDLE OF REEDS 594-6, JULY/ MAN CUTS GRASS WITH SCYTHE 594-7, SCYTHE 594-7, AUGUST/ MAN CUTS WHEAT WITH SICKLE 594-8, SICKLE 594-8, SEPTEMBER/ MAN CUTS GRAPES 594-9, GRAPE GATHERING 594-9, OCTOBER/ SOWING/ MAN HOLDS SEEDS IN TUNIC 594-10, SOWING/ MAN HOLDS SEEDS IN HIS TUNIC 594-10, NOVEMBER/ MAN SLAUGHTERS CALF 594-11, SLAUGHTERING OF CALF 594-11,

DECEMBER/ BAKER BEFORE BRICK OVEN 594-12, BAKER STANDS BEFORE BRICK OVEN 594-12, ANNUNCIATION TO MARY 594-13, ANNUNCIATION TO TWO SHEPHERDS/ ONE WITH BAGPIPES 594-14, PSALM 1/ INITIAL B BEATUS VIR/ KING DAVID 594-15, INITIAL B BEATUS VIR/ KING DAVID PLAYS HARP 594-15, DAVID PLAYS HARP 594-15, DAVID KILLS GOLIATH 594-15, PSALM 26/27/ INITIAL D DOMINUS ILLUMINATIO/ LAST SUPPER 594-16, INITIAL D DOMINUS ILLUMINATIO/ LAST SUPPER 594-16, LAST SUPPER/ CHRIST GIVES BREAD TO JUDAS 594-16, ST JOHN SLEEPS IN CHRIST'S LAP 594-16, BETRAYAL OF CHRIST/ JUDAS KISSES CHRIST 594-17, ST PETER STRIKES OFF MALCHUS' EAR 594-17, PSALM 38/39/ INITIAL D DIXI CUSTODIAM/ FLAGELLATION 594-18, INITIAL D DIXI CUSTODIAM/ FLAGELLATION 594-18, FLAGELLATION OF CHRIST 594-18, CHRIST'S FLAGELLATION 594-18, CHRIST'S BODY ANOINTED BY NICODEMUS 594-19, PSALM 68/69/ INITIAL S SALVUM ME FAC/ RESURRECTION 594-20, INITIAL S SALVUM ME FAC/ RESURRECTION 594-20, RESURRECTION/ ANGEL REMOVES COVER AND CHRIST STEPS OUT 594-20, NOLI ME TANGERE/ MARY MAGDALENE KNEELS BEFORE CHRIST 594-21, PSALM 80/81/ INITIAL E EXULTATE DEO/ DOUBTING THOMAS 594-22, INITIAL E EXULTATE DEO/ DOUBTING THOMAS 594-22, DOUBTING THOMAS TOUCHES CHRIST'S WOUND 594-22,ASCENSION/ CHRIST'S FEET AT TOP OF FRAME 594-23, PSALM 97/98/ INITIAL C CANTATE DOMINO/ PENTECOST 594-24, INITIAL C CANTATE DOMINO/ PENTECOST 594-24, PENTECOST/ MARY WITH DISCIPLES/ DOVE DESCENDS 594-24, PSALM 109/110/ CORONATION OF VIRGIN 594-25, CORONATION OF THE VIRGIN/ GOD CROWNS VIRGIN 594-25

*$ABSTRACT 595
*LIBRARY BODLEIAN
*SLIDE SET TITLE ADAM TO ABRAHAM
*NEGATIVE REFERENCE ROLL 243G
*RENTAL FEE $3.75
*COMMENTS ILLUSTRATIONS OF GENESIS 2 VERSE 15 TO GENESIS 12 VERSE 16 AND GENESIS 22 VERSE 9 TO GENESIS 24 VERSE 67, ACCOMPANIED BY ILLUSTRATIONS OF THE MORAL MEANINGS OF THE BIBLICAL PASSAGES. EACH PAGE OF EIGHT MEDALLIONS IS PHOTOGRAPHED AS A WHOLE AND IN FOUR PARTS.
*TITLE OF MANUSCRIPT BIBLE MORALISEE
*SHELFMARK MS BODLEY 270B/ FOL 6 595/1-5, MS BODLEY 270B/ FOL 7V 595/6-10, MS BODLEY 270B/ FOL 8 595/11-15, MS BODLEY 270B/ FOL 9V 595/16-20, MS BODLEY 270B/ FOL 10 595/21-25, MS BODLEY 270B/ FOL 11V 595/26-30, MS BODLEY 270B/ FOL 16 595/31-35
*PROVENANCE FRENCH
*DATE EXECUTED 13TH/ MID
*LANGUAGE LATIN
*TYPE OF MANUSCRIPT BIBLE MORALISEE
*CONTENTS GENESIS/ ADAM TO ABRAHAM 595/1-35, BIBLE MORALISEE/ FRENCH/ 13TH 595/1-35, GENESIS 02/VERSES 15-24/ WHOLE PAGE 595-1, GENESIS 02/VERSE 15/ GOD PUTS MAN IN PARADISE 595-2, GOD PUTS MAN IN PARADISE 595-2, CHURCH IS PARADISE INTO WHICH MAN IS PUT 595-2, GENESIS 02/VERSES 16-17/ GOD SHOWS ADAM FORBIDDEN TREE 595-3, GOD SHOWS ADAM THE FORBIDDEN TREE 595-3, GOD FORBIDS WORLDLY WISDOM 595-3, CHRIST HOLDS CROSS BETWEEN GOOD AND BAD 595-3,GENESIS 02/VERSES 21-23/ CREATION OF EVE 595-4, CREATION OF EVE FROM SLEEPING ADAM 595-4, ADAM SLEEPING SIGNIFIES CHRIST DYING 595-4, GOD DRAWS THE CHURCH FROM CHRIST'S BODY 595-4, GENESIS 02/VERSE 24/ GOD GIVES EVE TO ADAM 595-5, MARRIAGE OF CHRIST AND THE CHURCH IN VIRGIN'S WOMB 595-5, GENESIS 03/VERSE 1 TO GENESIS 04/VERSE 2 595-6, GENESIS 03/VERSES 1-6/ TEMPTATION OF ADAM AND EVE 595-7, TEMPTATION OF ADAM AND EVE 595-7, ADAM AND EVE TEMPTED 595-7, GOD'S WORD TRANSGRESSED BY OBEYING DEVIL 595-7, GENESIS 03/VERSES 9 AND 11/ GOD THREATENS ADAM 595-8, GOD THREATENS ADAM WHO BLAMES EVE 595-8, GOD THREATENS SINNERS WHO BLAME OTHERS 595-8, GENESIS 03/VERSES 21 AND 23/ EXPULSION 595-9, ADAM AND EVE EXPELLED FROM EDEN 595-9, CHRIST REPELS EVIL FROM THE CHURCH 595-9, GENESIS 04/VERSES 1-2/ ADAM PREFERS ABEL 595-10,ADAM PREFERS ABEL TO CAIN 595-10, CHRIST PREFERS CHRISTIANS TO WICKED 595-10, GENESIS 04/VERSES 2-11/ WHOLE PAGE 595-11, GENESIS 04/VERSES 2-5/ CAIN AND ABEL 595-12, CAIN AND ABEL

MAKE OFFERINGS 595-12, CHRISTIANS OFFER GOOD WORKS/ WICKED OFFER MONEY 595-12, GENESIS 04/VERSE 8/ CAIN ADDRESSES ABEL 595-13, CAIN ADDRESSES ABEL TREACHEROUSLY 595-13, JUDAS BETRAYS CHRIST 595-13, GENESIS 04/VERSE 8/ CAIN SLAYS ABEL 595-14, CAIN SLAYS ABEL WITH SCYTHE 595-14, WICKED CRUCIFY CHRIST 595-14, GENESIS 04/VERSE 11/ GOD CURSES CAIN 595-15, CAIN CURSED BY GOD 595-15, CHRIST CURSES THE WICKED HOLDING MONEY BAGS 595-15, GENESIS 05/VERSE 22 TO GENESIS 08/VERSE 9 595-16, GENESIS 05/VERSES 22-24/ ASCENSION OF ENOCH 595-17, GOD TAKES ENOCH TO HEAVEN 595-17, CHRIST TAKES THE GOOD TO HEAVEN 595-17, GENESIS 06/VERSE 14/ NOAH TOLD TO BUILD ARK 595-18, NOAH TOLD TO BUILD ARK OF WOOD AND PITCH 595-18, CHRIST BUILDS CHURCH OF SAINTS AND CHARITY 595-18, GENESIS 07/VERSES 1-7/ NOAH ENTERS ARK 595-19, NOAH AND FAMILY ENTERS ARK 595-19, CHRIST AND APOSTLES SAVED BY THE CHURCH 595-19, GENESIS 08/VERSES 6-9/ NOAH SENDS RAVEN 595-20, NOAH SENDS RAVEN WHICH DOES NOT RETURN 595-20, MONK AND WOMAN EMBRACING VERSUS CLERGY BLESSED BY CHRIST 595-20, GENESIS 08/VERSE 13 TO GENESIS 09/VERSE 23 595-21, GENESIS 08/VERSE 13/ NOAH'S DOVE RETURNS 595-22, NOAH'S DOVE RETURNS WITH OLIVE BRANCH 595-22, GOOD ARE RECONCILED TO GOD AND RETIRE FROM WORLD 595-22, GENESIS 08/VERSES 15-16/ NOAH LEAVES ARK 595-23, NOAH LEAVES ARK WITH FAMILY AND ANIMALS 595-23, GOD SAVES THE GOOD FROM PERIL 595-23, GENESIS 09/VERSES 20-21/ NOAH DRINKS 595-24, NOAH DRINKS/ MAN DIGS VINE 595-24, CHRIST DRINKS HIS CUP OF PUNISHMENT 595-24, GENESIS 09/VERSES 22-23/ NOAH'S NAKEDNESS 595-25, NOAH'S NAKEDNESS 595-25, HAM SIGNIFIES THE WICKED HUMILIATING CHRIST 595-25, MODEST SONS ARE CONVERTED GENTILES PREACHING GLORY 595-25, GENESIS 11/VERSE 4 TO 12/VERSE 16 595-26, GENESIS 11/VERSE 4/ BUILDING BABEL 595-27, BABEL BUILT 595-27, VAINGLORY OF ASTRONOMERS AND PHILOSOPHERS 595-27, GENESIS 11/VERSE 26/ ABRAHAM LEAVES FATHER'S HOUSE 595-28, GOOD CHRISTIAN DISMISSES PARENTS FOR GOD 595-28, GENESIS 12/VERSES 11-AND-13/ ABRAHAM TO EGYPT 595-29, ABRAHAM ASKES SARAH TO BE HIS SISTER 595-29, CHRIST ENTERS THE WORLD/ CHURCH IS HIS WIFE-AND-SISTER 595-29, GENESIS 12/VERSES 14-16/ PHARAOH PAYS FOR SARAH 595-30, PHARAOH PAYS ABRAHAM FOR SARAH 595-30, WORLDLY RULERS CORRUPT THE CHURCH 595-30, GENESIS 22/VERSE 9 TO GENESIS 24/VERSE 67 595-31, GENESIS 22/VERSES 9-13/ ABRAHAM AND ISAAC 595-32, ABRAHAM AND ISAAC AT ALTAR/ GOD INTERVENES 595-32, CHRIST CRUCIFIED IS LAMB AMONG THORNS 595-32, GENESIS 23/VERSES 2-10/ ABRAHAM 595-33, ABRAHAM BUYS BURIAL GROUND FOR SARAH 595-33, GOD GIVES GOSPELS TO THE APOSTLES 595-33, GENESIS 24/VERSE 11/ REBEKAH AT WELL 595-34, ABRAHAM'S SERVANT FINDS REBEKAH AT WELL 595-34, REBEKAH AT WELL 595-34, DISCIPLES FIND GENTILES GENTLE OF HEART 595-34, GENESIS 24/VERSES 51/61/67/ ISAAC MARRIES REBEKAH 595-35, ISAAC MARRIES REBEKAH 595-35, CHRIST MARRIES THE CHURCH 595-35

*$ABSTRACT 596
*LIBRARY BODLEIAN
*SLIDE SET TITLE JACOB IN EGYPT
*NEGATIVE REFERENCE ROLL 243H
*RENTAL FEE $3.00
*COMMENTS ILLUSTRATIONS OF GENESIS 45 VERSE 16 TO GENESIS 50 VERSE 25, ACCOMPANIED BY ILLUSTRATIONS OF THE MORAL MEANINGS OF THE BIBLICAL PASSAGES. EACH PAGE OF EIGHT MEDALLIONS IS PHOTOGRAPHED AS A WHOLE AND IN FOUR PARTS.
*TITLE OF MANUSCRIPT BIBLE MORALISEE
*SHELFMARK MS BODLEY 270B/ FOL 32 596/1-5, MS BODLEY 270B/ FOL 33V 596/6-10, MS BODLEY 270B/ FOL 34 596/11-15, MS BODLEY 270B/ FOL 35V 596/16-20
*PROVENANCE FRENCH
*DATE EXECUTED 13TH/ MID
*LANGUAGE LATIN
*TYPE OF MANUSCRIPT BIBLE MORALISEE
*CONTENTS GENESIS/ JACOB IN EGYPT 596/1-20, BIBLE MORALISEE/ FRENCH/ 13TH 596/1-20, GENESIS 45/VERSE 16 TO GENESIS 47/VERSE 11 596-1, GENESIS 45/VERSES 16-18/ JACOB BROUGHT TO EGYPT 596-2, JACOB BROUGHT TO EGYPT BY SONS 596-2, PHARAOH MEANS THE

WORLD/ JOSEPH MEANS CHRIST 596-2, GENESIS 46/VERSES 6-AND-29/ JACOB REUNITED WITH JOSEPH 596-3, JOSEPH'S BROTHERS MEAN THE APOSTLES LEAVING ALL FOR CHRIST 596-3, GENESIS 47/VERSE 7/ JOSEPH BRINGS JACOB TO PHARAOH 596-4, ST PETER SHOWS THE WORD TO CONSTANTINE 596-4, CONSTANTINE/ ST PETER SHOWS THE WORD 596-4, GENESIS 47/VERSE 11/ JOSEPH GIVES LANDS TO JACOB 596-5, ST PETER GIVEN CARE OF SOULS BY CHRIST 596-5, GENESIS 47/VERSES 15-29/ WHOLE PAGE 596-6, GENESIS 47/VERSE 15/ JOSEPH DEMANDS CATTLE 596-7, JOSEPH DEMANDS CATTLE DURING FAMINE 596-7, MARRIED COUPLES GAIN SPIRITUAL FOOD 596-7, GENESIS 47/VERSE 18/ EGYPTIANS OFFER LANDS FOR BREAD 596-8, EGYPTIANS ARE FAITHFUL GIVING UP WORLDLY JOYS 596-8, GENESIS 47/VERSES 20-24/ JOSEPH BUYS LAND OF EGYPT 596-9, JOSEPH BUYS FOR PHARAOH ALL LANDS OF EGYPT 596-9, EGYPTIANS ARE MARTYRS GIVING SOULS TO SERVE GOD 596-9, GENESIS 47/VERSE 29/ JACOB IS ILL 596-10, JACOB ASKS NOT TO BE BURIED IN EGYPT 596-10, JOSEPH IS CHRIST BEFORE WICKED 596-10, GENESIS 48/VERSE 14 TO GENESIS 50/VERSE 12 596-11, GENESIS 48/VERSE 14/ JACOB BLESSES SONS OF JOSEPH 596-12, JACOB BLESSES SONS OF JOSEPH 596-12, BLESSING SIGNIFIES GOD GIVING CHRIST TO PASSION 596-12, GENESIS 49/VERSE 1/ JACOB'S SONS HEAR PROPHECY 596-13, JACOB'S SONS HEAR PROPHECY CONCERNING THEM 596-13, JACOB IS CHRIST APPEARING TO APOSTLES 596-13, GENESIS 49/VERSE 29/ JACOB ASKS TO BE BURIED 596-14, JACOB ASKS TO BE BURIED IN CANAAN 596-14, JACOB'S DEATH SIGNIFIES DEATH OF ANCIENT JEWS 596-14, GENESIS 50/VERSES 3-12/ JACOB'S DEATH MOURNED 596-15, JACOB'S DEATH MOURNED BY EGYPTIANS AND CANAANITES 596-15, MOURNING SIGNIFIES GRIEF OF APOSTLES AT PASSION 596-15, GENESIS 50/VERSES 12-25/ WHOLE PAGE 596-16, GENESIS 50/VERSES 12-13/ JACOB BURIED 596-17, JACOB CARRIED INTO SEPULCHRE BY SONS 596-17, BURIAL SIGNIFIES APOSTLES KEEPING NEW LAW TO GRAVE 596-17, GENESIS 50/VERSE 14/ JOSEPH RETURNS TO EGYPT 596-18, JOSEPH AND HIS FOLLOWERS RETURN TO EGYPT 596-18, SIGNIFIES CHRIST LEADING APOSTLES TO PASSION 596-18, GENESIS 50/VERSE 21/ JOSEPH COMFORTS BROTHERS 596-19, SIGNIFIES CHRIST COMFORTING APOSTLES 596-19, GENESIS 50/VERSE 25/ JOSEPH DIES 596-20, JOSEPH DIES 596-20, SIGNIFIES THE BURIAL OF CHRIST 596-20

*$ABSTRACT 597
*LIBRARY BODLEIAN
*SLIDE SET TITLE MINIATURES FROM A PSALTER
*NEGATIVE REFERENCE ROLL 243J
*RENTAL FEE $2.45
*TITLE OF MANUSCRIPT PSALTER WITH CALENDAR
*SHELFMARK MS DOUCE 49/ FOL 30V 597-1, MS DOUCE 49/ FOL 48V 597-2, MS DOUCE 49/ FOL 64V 597-3, MS DOUCE 49/ FOL 65V 597-4, MS DOUCE 49/ FOL 82V 597-5, MS DOUCE 49/ FOL 103 597-6, MS DOUCE 49/ FOL 123V 597-7, MS DOUCE 49/ FOL 126V 597-8, MS DOUCE 49/ FOL 144V 597-9
*PROVENANCE FLEMISH/ ST OMER REGION
*DATE EXECUTED 13TH/ LATE
*LANGUAGE LATIN
*TYPE OF MANUSCRIPT PSALTER
*CONTENTS PSALTER/ FLEMISH/ 13TH 597/1-9, PSALM 26/27/ INITIAL D DOMINUS ILLUMINATIO/ BETRAYAL 597-1, INITIAL D DOMINUS ILLUMINATIO/ BETRAYAL OF CHRIST 597-1, BETRAYAL OF CHRIST/ KISS OF JUDAS/ PETER WITH SWORD 597-1, CHRIST RESTORES MALCHUS' EAR 597-1, PSALM 38/39/ INITIAL D DIXI CUSTODIAM/ CHRIST BEFORE PILATE 597-2, INITIAL D DIXI CUSTODIAM/ CHRIST BEFORE PILATE 597-2, CHRIST BROUGHT BEFORE PILATE BY SOLDIERS 597-2, PSALM 51/52/ INITIAL Q QUID GLORIARIS/ ST FRANCIS 597-3, INITIAL Q QUID GLORIARIS/ ST FRANCIS PREACHES TO BIRDS 597-3, ST FRANCIS PREACHES TO THE BIRDS 597-3, PSALM 52/53/ INITIAL D DIXIT INSIPIENS/ FLAGELLATION 597-4, INITIAL D DIXI INSIPIENS/ FLAGELLATION OF CHRIST 597-4, FLAGELLATION OF CHRIST 597-4, CHRIST FLAGELLATED 597-4, APE WITH HAMMER AND SHIELD 597-4, PSALM 68/69/ INITIAL S SALVUM ME FAC/ CALVARY 597-5, INITIAL S SALVUM ME FAC/ ROAD TO CALVARY 597-5, ROAD TO CALVARY/ CHRIST CARRIES GREEN CROSS 597-5, CHRIST CARRIES CROSS/ MAN CARRIES HAMMER 597-5, PSALM 80/81/ INITIAL E

EXULTATE DEO/ CRUCIFIXION 597-6, INITIAL E EXULTATE DEO/ CRUCIFIXION 597-6, CRUCIFIXION/ SPONGE OF VINEGAR/ LONGINUS 597-6, LONGINUS PIERCES CHRIST'S SIDE 597-6, APE BLOWS TRUMPET 597-6, PSALM 97/98/ INITIAL C CANTATE DOMINO/ DESCENT FROM CROSS 597-7, INITIAL C CANTATE DOMINO/ DESCENT FROM CROSS 597-7, JOSEPH OF ARIMATHEA LOWERS CHRIST'S BODY 597-7, NICODEMUS REMOVES NAIL FROM CHRIST'S FEET 597-7, MARY HOLDS CHRIST'S HAND TO HER FACE 597-7, PSALM 101/102/ INITIAL D DOMINE EXAUDI/ ST CLARE 597-8, INITIAL D DOMINE EXAUDI/ ST CLARE 597-8, ST CLARE HANDS BOOTS TO BAREFOOT BEGGAR 597-8,PSALM 109/110/ INITIAL D DIXIT DOMINUS/ CHRIST ANOINTED 597-9, INITIAL D DIXIT DOMINUS/ CHRIST'S BODY ANOINTED 597-9, CHRIST'S BODY ANOINTED BY DISCIPLES 597-9

*$ABSTRACT 598
*LIBRARY BODLEIAN
*SLIDE SET TITLE MS DOUCE 6/ PART 3
*NEGATIVE REFERENCE ROLL 244A
*RENTAL FEE $3.95
*COMMENTS ALMOST EVERY PAGE HAS TERMINAL HEADS AND ANIMAL HEADS AS WELL AS BIRDS, RABBITS, AND GROTESQUES.
*SHELFMARK MS DOUCE 6/ FOL 78-79V-80 598-1, MS DOUCE 6/ FOL 80V-81 598-2, MS DOUCE 6/ FOL 81V-82 598-3, MS DOUCE 6/ FOL 82V-83 598-4, MS DOUCE 6/ FOL 83V-84 598-5, MS DOUCE 6/ FOL 84V-85 598-6, MS DOUCE 6/ FOL 85V-86 598-7, MS DOUCE 6/ FOL 86V-87 598-8, MS DOUCE 6/ FOL 87V-88 598-9, MS DOUCE 6/ FOL 88V-89 598-10, MS DOUCE 6/ FOL 89V-90 598-11, MS DOUCE 6/ FOL 90V-91 598-12, MS DOUCE 6/ FOL 91V-92 598-13, MS DOUCE 6/ FOL 92V-93 598-14, MS DOUCE 6/ FOL 93AV-93B 598-15, MS DOUCE 6/ FOL 93BV-94 598-16, MS DOUCE 6/ FOL 94V-95 598-17, MS DOUCE 6/ FOL 95V-96 598-18, MS DOUCE 6/ FOL 96V-97 598-19, MS DOUCE 6/ FOL 97V-98 598-20, MS DOUCE 6/ FOL 98V-99 598-21, MS DOUCE 6/ FOL 99V-100 598-22, MS DOUCE 6/ FOL 100V-101 598-23, MS DOUCE 6/ FOL 101V-102 598-24, MS DOUCE 6/ FOL 102V-103-4 598-25, MS DOUCE 6/ FOL 103-4V-105 598-26, MS DOUCE 6/ FOL 105V-106 598-27, MS DOUCE 6/ FOL 106V-107 598-28, MS DOUCE 6/ FOL 107V-108 598-29, MS DOUCE 6/ FOL 108V-109 598-30, MS DOUCE 6/ FOL 109V-110 598-31, MS DOUCE 6/ FOL 110V-111 598-32, MS DOUCE 6/ FOL 111V-112 598-33, MS DOUCE 6/ FOL 112V-113 598-34, MS DOUCE 6/ FOL 113V-114 598-35, MS DOUCE 6/ FOL 114V-115 598-36, MS DOUCE 6/ FOL 115V-116 598-37, MS DOUCE 6/ FOL 116V-117 598-38, MS DOUCE 6/ FOL 117V-118 598-39
*PROVENANCE FLEMISH/ GHENT
*DATE EXECUTED 14TH/C1320-30
*LANGUAGE LATIN
*TYPE OF MANUSCRIPT PSALTER/ PORTABLE
*CONTENTS PSALTER/ FLEMISH/ 14TH 598/1-39, CHRIST RISEN SHOWING WOUNDS/ MARY AND JOHN KNEEL 598-1, RESURRECTION OF THE DEAD BELOW 598-1, DEVIL WITH HOOK AND ANGEL AT RESURRECTION 598-1, PSALM 109/110/ INITIAL D DIXIT/ TRINITY 598-1, INITIAL D DIXIT/ TRINITY 598-1, TRINITY 598-1, ANGEL HOLDS WREATH ABOVE COUPLE EMBRACING 598-1, MAN LIES WITH HEAD IN WOMAN'S LAP 598-1, PSALM 110/111/ INITIAL C CONFITEBOR/ LADY READING 598-2, INITIAL C CONFITEBOR/ LADY READING 598-2, FIGURE HOLDS UP INITIAL 598-2, MAN HOLDS BIRD'S BEAK WITH PINCERS 598-2, WOMAN WITH WHITE DOG AT FEET 598-2, WOMAN STABBING HERSELF/ WOMAN HOLDS PURSE 598-2, MAN WITH FLAIL LEANS DOWN TO WATER 598-2, MAN HOLDS FLASK HALF-FILLED WITH LIQUID 598-3, APE WITH PURSE HOLDS UP COIN 598-3, PSALM 111/112/ INITIAL B BEATUS/ BOYS PLAY GAME 598-4, INITIAL B BEATUS/ BOYS PLAY GAME 598-4, BOYS PLAY GAME OF STRIKE THE POT 598-4, GAME OF STRIKE THE POT 598-4, MERMAID WITH MIRROR 598-4, PSALM 112/113/ INITIAL L LAUDATE/ FALCONER 598-5, INITIAL L LAUDATE/ FALCONER 598-5, FALCONER 598-5, WOMAN TRAPS MAN IN NET 598-5, FIGURES WITH JUGS 598-5, MAN STRANGLES BIRD'S HEAD 598-5, PSALM 113/114/ INITIAL I IN/ WOMAN HOLDS DOG 598-6, INITIAL I IN/ WOMAN HOLDS DOG 598-6, MAN WORKS WITH TOOL ON TOP OF INITIAL 598-6, FIGURE HOLDS UP INITIAL 598-6, APE HOLDS SLATE LECTURES TO BIRD 598-6, MAN HOLDS TOY WINDMILL 598-6, ARMOURED MAN HOLDS SHIELD AND SPEAR 598-7, APE FEEDING BIRD FROM BOWL WITH SPOON 598-8,

ANGEL HOLDS MILLSTONE 598-8, PSALM 114/116A/ INITIAL D DILEXI/ MOTHER APE 598-9, INITIAL D DILEXI/ MOTHER APE HOLDS YOUNG 598-9, MAN ATTACKS BIRD'S HEAD WITH SWORD 598-9, PSALM 115/116B/ INITIAL C CREDIDI/ HEAD IN CIRCLET 598-10, INITIAL C CREDIDI/ HEAD IN CIRCLET OF LEAVES 598-10, MAN WITH TUBE AND BOWL BLOWS SOAP-BUBBLES 598-10, STORK EATS FROG 598-10, MAN HOLDS TREFOIL POINTED ARCH 598-10, WOMAN MAKES WREATH 598-10, MAN KNEELS BEFORE BARKING DOG 598-10, PSALM 116/117/ INITIAL L LAUDATE 598-11, INITIAL L LAUDATE 598-11, PSALM 117/118/ INITIAL C CONITEMINI INSET WITH HEAD 598-11, INITIAL C CONITEMINI INSET WITH HEAD 598-11, APE WITH KNIFE STANDS BESIDE BIRD 598-11, FOX TIED TO STAKE UNDER TREE 598-11, COOKING CHICKEN ON SPIT OVER FIRE 598-12, FALCONER/ STORK WITH BEAK IN CHURN 598-13, TOP/ SPINNING 598-14, PSALM 118/119/ INITIAL B BEATI 598-15, INITIAL B BEATI 598-15, MAN SEATED IN BASKET WITH EGGS 598-15, JUGGLING KNIVES OVER BLACK POT 598-16, SCULPTING OF PANEL WITH PICTURES OF STANDING FIGURE 598-16, SCOURGING OF MAN TIED TO STAKE 598-17, BUILDING OF CHURCH TOWER 598-17, STORK PECKS UNICORN 598-17, APE BISHOP WITH ASPERGE/ TONSURED APE WITH BOOK 598-18, GAME WITH CLUB AND BALL/ APES PLAY 598-19, PSALM 118/119/ INITIAL E ET/ TWO BEASTS 598-20, INITIAL E ET/ TWO BEASTS 598-20, GAME OF LEAP-FROG/ TWO BOYS PLAY 598-20, WOMAN HOLDS UP MIRROR 598-20, CHRIST BLESSING 598-21, BLIND MAN WITH GUIDE DOG 598-21, TOP/ SPINNING 598-21, PSALM 118/119/ INITIAL P PORTIO INSET WITH HEAD 598-22, INITIAL P PORTIO INSET WITH HEAD 598-22, APES CLIMB LADDER TO REACH NEST 598-22, HOST ADMINISTERED TO KNEELING WOMAN 598-22, MEN CARRY SACK TOWARD BUILDING 598-23, UNICORN CHARGES THE BORDER VINE 598-23, CARDING FLEECE 598-24, GROTESQUE CARRIES BUNDLE ON BACK 598-24, PSALM 118/119/ INITIAL D DEFICIT INSET WITH HEAD 598-25, INITIAL D DEFICIT INSET WITH HEAD 598-25, GROTESQUE BLOWS ON FIRE 598-25, BIRD PECKS HINDQUARTERS OF APE BEFORE BISHOP 598-25, UNICORN CHARGES ARMOURED MAN 598-26, MAN ABOUT TO STRIKE STAG WITH BIRCH 598-26, PSALM 118/119/ INITIAL Q QUOMODO INSET WITH HEAD 598-27, INITIAL Q QUOMODO INSET WITH HEAD 598-27, SCRIBE WORKING AT ELABORATE DESK 598-27, WOMAN REACHES INTO GOLD PURSE 598-27, MAN AND WOMAN SIT CONVERSING 598-28, MAN TRAINING DOG WITH STICK 598-29, PSALM 118/119/ INITIAL F FECI INSET WITH HEAD 598-30, INITIAL F FECI INSET WITH HEAD 598-30, RABBIT NIBBLES ON BORDER VINE 598-30, APE VOMITING INTO BOWL 598-31, APE HOLDS STORK'S BEAK WITH PINCERS 598-31, PSALM 118/119/ INITIAL CLAMAVI INSET WITH HEAD 598-32, INITIAL C CLAMAVI INSET WITH HEAD 598-32, ST PETER WITH KEY AND CROSS 598-32, MAN WITH FEET CUT OFF CRAWLS WITH BOWL 598-32, PSALM 118/119/ INITIAL V VIDE INSET WITH HEAD 598-33, INITIAL V VIDE INSET WITH HEAD 598-33, BOY WITH HORN AND CLUB 598-33, DOG CHASING HARE 598-33, UNICORN CHARGES BORDER VINE 598-33, PSALM 118/119/ INITIAL P PRINCIPES/ KNIGHT TILTING 598-34, INITIAL P PRINCIPES/ KNIGHT TILTING 598-34, KNIGHT TILTING AT QUINTAIN 598-34, CHRIST BETWEEN ANTLERS OF STAG 598-34, BOY POKING STICK INTO KEG 598-35, PSALM 119/120/ INITIAL A AD/ KNEELING FIGURE 598-36, INITIAL A AD/ KNEELING FIGURE 598-36, APE WITH OPEN BOOK/ TONSURED APE BEFORE HIM 598-36, UNICORN CHARGES THE BORDER VINE 598-36, PSALM 120/121/ INITIAL L LEVAVI/ FISHING SCENE 598-37, INITIAL L LEVAVI/ FISHING SCENE 598-37, APES KNOCK EGGS TOGETHER 598-37, PSALM 121/122/ INITIAL L LAETATUS INSET WITH HEAD 598-38, INITIAL L LAETATUS INSET WITH HEAD 598-38, APES HOLD UP LEGS 598-38, FIGURE WITH LONG TRUMPET/ FIGURE HOLDS STORK'S BEAK 598-39

*$ABSTRACT 599
*LIBRARY BODLEIAN
*SLIDE SET TITLE MS DOUCE 6/ PART 2
*NEGATIVE REFERENCE ROLL 244B
*RENTAL FEE $4.10
*SHELFMARK MS DOUCE 6/ FOL 37V-38 599-1, MS DOUCE 6/ FOL 38V-39 599-2, MS DOUCE 6/ FOL 39V-40 599-3, MS DOUCE 6/ FOL 40V-41 599-4, MS DOUCE 6/ FOL 41V-42 599-5, MS DOUCE 6/ FOL 42V-43 599-6, MS DOUCE 6/ FOL 43V-44 599-7, MS DOUCE 6/ FOL 44V-45

599-8, MS DOUCE 6/ FOL 45V-46 599-9, MS DOUCE 6/ FOL 46V-47 599-10, MS DOUCE 6/ FOL 47V-48 599-11, MS DOUCE 6/ FOL 48V-49 599-12, MS DOUCE 6/ FOL 49V-50 599-13, MS DOUCE 6/ FOL 50V-51 599-14, MS DOUCE 6/ FOL 51V-52 599-15, MS DOUCE 6/ FOL 52V-52A 599-16, MS DOUCE 6/ FOL 52AV-53 599-17, MS DOUCE 6/ FOL 53V-54 599-18, MS DOUCE 6/ FOL 54V-55 599-19, MS DOUCE 6/ FOL 55V-56 599-20, MS DOUCE 6/ FOL 56V-57 599-21, MS DOUCE 6/ FOL 57V-58 599-22, MS DOUCE 6/ FOL 58V-59 599-23, MS DOUCE 6/ FOL 59V-60 599-24, MS DOUCE 6/ FOL 60V-61 599-25, MS DOUCE 6/ FOL 61V-62 599-26, MS DOUCE 6/ FOL 62V-63 599-27, MS DOUCE 6/ FOL 63V-64 599-28, MS DOUCE 6/ FOL 64V-65 599-29, MS DOUCE 6/ FOL 65V-66 599-30, MS DOUCE 6/ FOL 66V-67 599-31, MS DOUCE 6/ FOL 67V-68 599-32, MS DOUCE 6/ FOL 68V-69 599-33, MS DOUCE 6/ FOL 69V-70 599-34, MS DOUCE 6/ FOL 70V-71 599-35, MS DOUCE 6/ FOL 71V-72 599-36, MS DOUCE 6/ FOL 72V-73 599-37, MS DOUCE 6/ FOL 73V-74 599-38, MS DOUCE 6/ FOL 74V-75 599-39, MS DOUCE 6/ FOL 75V-76 599-40, MS DOUCE 6/ FOL 76V-77 599-41, MS DOUCE 6/ FOL 77V-78-79 599-42

*PROVENANCE FLEMISH/ GHENT

*DATE EXECUTED 14TH/C1320-30

*LANGUAGE LATIN

*TYPE OF MANUSCRIPT PSALTER/ PORTABLE

*CONTENTS PSALTER/ FLEMISH/ 14TH 599/1-42, DESCENT FROM THE CROSS 599-1, PSALM 97/98/ INITIAL C CANTATE/ MONKS SINGING 599-1, INITIAL C CANTATE/ MONKS SINGING 599-1, MAN DRESSED AS SHEEP 599-1, PSALM 98/99/ INITIAL D DOMINUS INSET WITH HEAD 599-2, INITIAL D DOMINUS INSET WITH HEAD 599-2, UNICORN IN VIRGIN'S LAP SHOT WITH ARROW 599-2, FIGURE WITH LONG SPEAR 599-3, PSALM 99/100/ INITIAL I IUBILATE/ STANDING FIGURES 599-4, INITIAL I IUBILATE/ STANDING FIGURES 599-4, FIGURES HOLD EDGE OF INITIAL 599-4, PSALM 100/101/ INITIAL M MISERICORDIAM INSET WITH HEADS 599-5, INITIAL M MISERICORDIAM INSET WITH HEADS 599-5, SNARING BIRD WITH NET AND DECOY 599-5, FIGURE BLOWS TRUMPET 599-6, ENTOMBMENT OF CHRIST 599-7, CHRIST'S ENTOMBMENT 599-7, PSALM 101/102/ INITIAL D DOMINE/ KING KNEELING 599-7, INITIAL D DOMINE/ KING KNEELING BEFORE ALTAR 599-7, KING KNEELING BEFORE ALTAR WITH CRUCIFIX 599-7, BATTLE BETWEEN MOUNTED KNIGHTS 599-7, ARMOURED MAN WITH SHIELD AND SWORD 599-7, MONSTER SHOT WITH ARROW 599-7, FIGURES HOLD BOOK AND BLOW TRUMPET 599-8, FIGURES HOLD STAFF AND WHITE OBJECT 599-9, FIGURE WITH SHIELD AND SWORD 599-10, PSALM 102/103/ INITIAL B BENEDIC 599-11, INITIAL B BENEDIC 599-11, WEAVING/ WOMAN WITH DISTAFF AND SPINDLE 599-11, APE HOLDS SPINDLE AND WINDER 599-11, APE PICKS FRUIT FROM BORDER VINE 599-11, ARMOURED FIGURE WITH SHIELD AND SPEAR 599-12, APE KNEELS BEFORE APE WITH CROZIER 599-13, PSALM 103/104/ INITIAL B BENEDIC 599-14, INITIAL B BENEDIC 599-14, SNARING BIRD WITH DECOY AND BIRDCAGE 599-14, FALCONER 599-14, CRANE PECKING HINDQUARTERS OF APE 599-14, JAWBONE PLAYED WITH RAKE 599-15, ARMOURED FIGURE HOLDS HEAD AND SWORD/ BLOOD DRIPS 599-16, APES HOLD SWAN IN DISH AND RAM'S HEAD 599-17, FIGURES BLOW HORN AND HOLD BROOM 599-18, PSALM 104/105/ INITIAL C CONFITEMINI INSET WITH HEAD 599-19, INITIAL C CONFITEMINI INSET WITH HEAD 599-19, BELLS RUNG BY GROTESQUE 599-19, ARMOURED GROTESQUE WAVES SWORD AT GROTESQUE 599-19, HUMAN AND ANIMAL HEADS 599-20, BIRD SLAUGHTERED WITH LARGE CURVED KNIFE 599-21, FIGURE HOLDS ROD WITH FOUR OVAL OBJECTS ATTACHED 599-22, JUGGLING AND PLAYING PIPE AND TABOR 599-23, PIPE AND TABOR 599-23, PSALM 105/106/ INITIAL C CONFITEMINI/ LADY MAKES WREATH 599-24, INITIAL C CONFITEMINI/ LADY MAKES WREATH 599-24, LADY MAKES WREATH 599-24, MAN HOLDS BUNS ON STICK 599-24, MAN FILLING JUGS AT TABLE 599-24, QUILL AND KNIFE 599-25, FIGURE RELEASES BIRD FROM SACK OR HAT 599-26, FIGURE WITH TRIANGLE 599-27, PIPE AND TABOR/ LADY DANCING 599-28, FIGURE POUNDS CONTENTS OF BLACK POT 599-29, FIGURES HOLD FUR AND SACHEL 599-30, PSALM 106/107/ INITIAL C CONFITEMINI INSET WITH HEAD 599-31, INITIAL C CONFITEMINI INSET WITH HEAD 599-31, MAN AT DINING TABLE REACHES FOR FRUIT 599-31, MAN IN ARMOUR STANDS ON MONSTER 599-31, RABBIT HELD BY EARS/ DOGS BITE IT 599-31, BIRD ON BORDER VINE/ DOG KISSES MAN 599-32, FIGURE HOLDS LONG TRUMPET 599-33, FIGURE HOLDS HARP 599-34, PSALTERY 599-35, PSALM 107/108/ INITIAL P PARATUM INSET WITH

HEAD 599-36, INITIAL P PARATUM INSET WITH HEAD 599-36, APES TILTING/ READING BOOK/ EATING FRUIT 599-36, GITTERN 599-36, BAGPIPES PLAYED BY FIGURE/ DOG CONDUCTS 599-37, PSALM 108/109/ INITIAL D DEUS/ GOD HOLDS ORB 599-38, INITIAL D DEUS/ GOD HOLDS ORB 599-38, GOD HOLDS ORB 599-38, APE STIRRING POT OFFERS BOWL TO APE 599-38, STORK SITS ON TOP OF CHIMNEY 599-38, GROTESQUE HAMMERS ON BORDER DECORATION 599-38, RABBIT STRUCK WITH DISTAFF 599-39, MONSTER VOMITS INTO BOWL 599-39, FIDDLE PLAYED BY FIGURE/ APE MIMICS 599-40, FIGURE USES CLEAVER ON FISH 599-41, FIGURE VOMITS INTO BOWL HELD BY BIRD 599-41, LEPER WITH BOWL AND RATTLE 599-42

*$ABSTRACT 600
*LIBRARY BODLEIAN
*SLIDE SET TITLE MS DOUCE 6/ PART 1
*NEGATIVE REFERENCE ROLL 244C
*RENTAL FEE $3.85
*SHELFMARK MS DOUCE 6/ FOL 1 600-1, MS DOUCE 6/ FOL 1V-2 600-2, MS DOUCE 6/ FOL 2V-3 600-3, MS DOUCE 6/ FOL 3V-4 600-4, MS DOUCE 6/ FOL 4V-5 600-5, MS DOUCE 6/ FOL 5V-6 600-6, MS DOUCE 6/ FOL 6V-7 600-7, MS DOUCE 6/ FOL 7V-8 600-8, MS DOUCE 6/ FOL 8V-9 600-9, MS DOUCE 6/ FOL 9V-10 600-10, MS DOUCE 6/ FOL 10V-11 600-11, MS DOUCE 6/ FOL 11V-12 600-12, MS DOUCE 6/ FOL 12V-13 600-13, MS DOUCE 6/ FOL 13V-14 600-14, MS DOUCE 6/ FOL 14V-15 600-15, MS DOUCE 6/ FOL 15V-16 600-16, MS DOUCE 6/ FOL 16V-17 600-17, MS DOUCE 6/ FOL 17V-18 600-18, MS DOUCE 6/ FOL 18V-19600-19, MS DOUCE 6/ FOL 19V-20 600-20, MS DOUCE 6/ FOL 20V-21 600-21, MS DOUCE 6/ FOL 21V-22 600-22, MS DOUCE 6/ FOL 22V-23 600-23, MS DOUCE 6/ FOL 23V-24 600-24, MS DOUCE 6/ FOL 24V-25 600-25, MS DOUCE 6/ FOL 25V-26 600-26, MS DOUCE 6/ FOL 26V-27 600-27, MS DOUCE 6/ FOL 27V-28 600-28, MS DOUCE 6/ FOL 28V-29 600-29, MS DOUCE 6/ FOL 29V-30 600-30, MS DOUCE 6/ FOL 30V-31 600-31, MS DOUCE 6/ FOL 31V-32 600-32, MS DOUCE 6/ FOL 32V-33 600-33, MS DOUCE 6/ FOL 33V-34 600-34, MS DOUCE 6/ FOL 34V-35 600-35, MS DOUCE 6/ FOL 35V-36 600-36, MS DOUCE 6/ FOL 36V-37 600-37
*PROVENANCE FLEMISH/ GHENT
*DATE EXECUTED 14TH/C1320-30
*LANGUAGE LATIN
*TYPE OF MANUSCRIPT PSALTER/ PORTABLE
*CONTENTS PSALTER/ FLEMISH/ 14TH 600/1-37, PSALM 80/81/ INITIAL E EXULTATE/ DAVID PLAYS BELLS 600-1, INITIAL E EXULTATE/ DAVID PLAYS BELLS 600-1, DAVID PLAYS BELLS 600-1, MUSICIANS PLAY FLUTE/ ORGAN/ FIDDLE/ LADY DANCES 600-1, TERMINALS/ DOUBLE-HEADED BIRD/ FIGURE WITH BOW 600-2, PSALM 81/82/ INITIAL D DEUS INSET WITH FACE 600-3, INITIAL D DEUS INSET WITH FACE 600-3, UNICORN CHARGING MAN WITH SHIELD AND SPEAR 600-3, FIGURE HOLDS SCOOP OR SIEVE AND PICKS FRUIT 600-3, PSALM 82/83/ INITIAL D DOMINE INSET WITH HEAD 600-4, INITIAL D DOMINE INSET WITH HEAD 600-4, MEN FIGHTING WITH SWORDS AND SHIELDS 600-4, PEACOCK SHOWS ITS PLUMAGE 600-4, FALCON STANDS ON GLOVED HAND 600-5, PSALM 83/84/ INITIAL Q QUAM INSET WITH HEAD 600-6, INITIAL Q QUAM INSET WITH HEAD 600-6, FIGURE CLIMBS OVER INITIAL TO REACH GROTESQUE 600-6, MERMAID STRANGLES BIRD 600-6, FIGURE VOMITS INTO BOWL 600-7, BAGPIPES 600-7, PSALM 84/85/ INITIAL B BENEDIXISTI 600-8, INITIAL B BENEDIXISTI 600-8, MAN SITS WITH HANDS ON KNEES 600-8, GROTESQUE/ HAWK/ RABBIT/ BIRD 600-8, TERMINAL HEADS AND FIGURE HOLDING ROD 600-9, APE DRESSED AS BISHOP RIDES ON DEVIL 600-10, MAN HOLDS CHICKEN ON LONG SPIT 600-10, TERMINAL HEADS AND FIGURE DRINKING FROM JUG 600-11, PSALM 86/87/ INITIAL F FUNDAMENTA/ FIGURE PRAYING 600-12, INITIAL F FUNDAMENTA INSET WITH PRAYING FIGURE 600-12, DOG CHASING HARE 600-12, PSALM 87/88 INITIAL D DOMINE/ WOMAN HOLDS CHILD 600-13, INITIAL D DOMINE/ WOMAN HOLDS SWADDLED CHILD 600-13, FALCONER ON WHITE HORSE 600-13, HUNTER WITH CLUB AND HORN 600-13, DOGS CHASE RABBITS INTO HOLES 600-13, FIGURES WITH HORN/ BOOK/ BAGPIPES 600-14, FIGURE WITH LONG STICK/ DOGS/ SQUIRREL AND HARE 600-15, TERMINAL HEADS AND FIGURE WITH TRUMPET 600-16,TERMINAL HEADS/ FIGURE GESTURES/ FIGURE WITH ROCK 600-17, TERMINAL

HEADS/ NUN PRAYING/ FIGURE WITH BIRCH 600-18, TERMINAL HEADS/ FIGURE WITH STAFF 600-19, TERMINAL HEADS/ CROWNED LADY 600-20, TERMINAL HEADS/ FIGURES WITH WEAPONS 600-21, PSALM 89/90/ INITIAL D DOMINE INSET WITH HEAD 600-22, INITIAL D DOMINE INSET WITH HEAD 600-22, WOMAN STIRS LARGE COOKING POT 600-22, WOMAN CARRIES BASKET OF WOOD 600-22, TERMINAL HUMAN AND ANIMAL HEADS 600-23, TERMINAL HEADS/ BIRD WITH FROG/ ARMOURED FIGURE 600-24, PSALM 90/91/ INITIAL Q QUI HABITAT/ SEATED FIGURE 600-25, INITIAL Q QUI HABITAT/ SEATED FIGURE 600-25, HUNTER WITH HORN AND CLUB 600-25, DOG CHASES A RABBIT 600-25, APE WITH BASKET OF EGGS 600-25, TERMINAL HEADS/ FIGURE HOLDS FRUIT BOWL 600-26, PSALM 91/92/ INITIAL B BONUM 600-27, INITIAL B BONUM 600-27, ARCHER SHOOTS BIRD 600-27, MAN GESTURES TO CROUCHING DOG 600-27, TERMINAL HEADS/ FIGURE GESTURES 600-28, PSALM 92/93/ INITIAL D DOMINUS INSET WITH HEAD 600-29, INITIAL D DOMINUS INSET WITH HEAD 600-29, FIGURE CHOPS DOWN BORDER VINE 600-29, TERMINAL HEADS/ FIGURES WITH KNIFE AND TAPER 600-30, TERMINAL HUMAN AND ANIMAL HEADS 600-31, PSALM 94/95/ INITIAL V VENITE INSET WITH HEAD 600-32, INITIAL V VENITE INSET WITH HEAD 600-32, APE/ GROTESQUE/ WINGED FIGURE 600-32, TERMINAL HUMAN HEADS 600-33, PSALM 96/96/ INITIAL C CANTATE INSET WITH GROTESQUE 600-34, INITIAL C CANTATE INSET WITH GROTESQUE 600-34,FIGURES KISSING/ WOMAN WITH DOG/ RABBIT WITH BAGPIPES 600-34, STAG GRITTING ,TEETH/ GROTESQUE KISSES TERMINAL 600-34, PSALM 96/97/ INITIAL D DOMINUS INSET WITH GROTESQUE 600-35, INITIAL D DOMINUS INSET WITH GROTESQUE 600-35,GAME WITH BAT AND BALL/ APES PLAY 600-35, TERMINAL HUMAN AND ANIMAL HEADS 600/36-37

*$ABSTRACT 601
*LIBRARY BODLEIAN
*SLIDE SET TITLE LE CHEVALIER DELIBERE
*NEGATIVE REFERENCE ROLL 244D
*RENTAL FEE $2.75
*TITLE OF MANUSCRIPT LE CHEVALIER DELIBERE
*SHELFMARK MS DOUCE 168/ FOL 1 601-1, MS DOUCE 168/ FOL 3V 601-2, MS DOUCE 168/ FOL 5V 601-3, MS DOUCE 168/ FOL 7 601-4, MS DOUCE 168/ FOL 8V 601-5, MS DOUCE 168/ FOL 12 601-6, MS DOUCE 168/ FOL 17 601-7, MS DOUCE 168/ FOL 19V 601-8, MS DOUCE 168/ FOL 24 601-9, MS DOUCE 168/ FOL 32 601-10, MS DOUCE 168/ FOL 42V 601-11, MS DOUCE 168/ FOL 46 601-12, MS DOUCE 168/ FOL 50 601-13, MS DOUCE 168/ FOL 53 601-14, MS DOUCE 168/ FOL 55V 601-15
*PROVENANCE FLEMISH
*DATE EXECUTED 16TH/ MID
*LANGUAGE FRENCH
*AUTHOR OLIVIER DE LA MARCHE
*TYPE OF MANUSCRIPT LITERATURE
*CONTENTS LE CHEVALIER DELIBERE 601/1-15, AUTHOR AND THOUGHT DEPART ON HORSEBACK 601-1, AUTHOR MOUNTS HORSE/ OPEN TRUNK ON GROUND 601-2, AUTHOR COMBATS WITH HUTIN 601-3, AUTHOR SAVED BY RELICS OF YOUTH 601-3, AUTHOR MEETS HERMIT UNDERSTANDING 601-4, UNDERSTANDING AND AUTHOR STAND IN HERMIT'S CHAPEL 601-5, ALTAR CONTAINS RELICS OF THE VICTORIES OF ACCIDENT 601-5, AUTHOR RECEIVES THE LANCE GOVERNANCE FROM HERMIT 601-6, BATTLE WITH KNIGHT AGE ON PLAIN OF TIME 601-7, AGE TAKES AUTHOR PRISONER 601-8, DESIRE TRIES TO LURE AUTHOR INTO PALACE OF LOVE 601-9, PALACE OF LOVE 601-9, DECEPTION HOLDS KEY TO PALACE OF LOVE 601-9, REMEMBRANCE HOLDS UP MIRROR TO AUTHOR 601-9, FRESH MEMORY TAKES AUTHOR TO TOMBS 601-10, BATTLE BETWEEN DUKE PHILIP AND WEAKNESS 601-11, ATROPOS/ GODDESS OF DEATH IS JUDGE 601-11, BATTLE BETWEEN DUKE CHARLES AND ACCIDENT 601-12, AUTHOR VOLUNTEERS TO COMBAT WEAKNESS 601-13, AUTHOR AND FRESH MEMORY RETURN FROM COMBATS 601-14, HERMIT UNDERSTANDING COUNSELS AUTHOR ON DEATH 601-15

*$ABSTRACT 602
*LIBRARY BODLEIAN

*SLIDE SET TITLE MEDICAL MANUSCRIPTS
*NEGATIVE REFERENCE ROLL 244E
*RENTAL FEE $3.00
*TITLE OF MANUSCRIPT CIRURGIA OF ALBUCASIS AND OTHER TREATISES 602/1-7, BREVIARIUM JOHANNIS FILII SERAPIONIS MEDICI 602-8, CANON OF AVICENNA 602/9-12, LIBER SECRETUM SECRETORUM 602/13-15, LIBER MAGISTRI ARNALDI DE VILLANOVA 602-16, PRACTICA CIRURGIE 602/17-20
*SHELFMARK MS BODLEY 360/ FOL 4 602-1, MS BODLEY 360/ FOL 5V-6 602-2, MS BODLEY 360/ FOL 11V-12 602-3, MS BODLEY 360/ FOL 14V-15 602-4, MS BODLEY 360/ FOL 21V 602-5, MS BODLEY 360/ FOL 26 602-6, MS BODLEY 360/ FOL 26V 602-7, MS BODLEY 360/ FOL 47 602-8, MS CANON MISC 473/ FOL 2 602-9, MS CANON MISC 473/ FOL 3V 602-10, MS CANON MISC 473/ FOL 69 602-11, MS CANON MISC 473/ FOL 84 602-12, MS DOUCE 2/ FOL 1 602-13, MS DOUCE 2/ FOL 16V 602-14, MS DOUCE 2/ FOL 58V 602-15, MS DOUCE 2/ FOL 108 602-16, MS BARLOW 34/ FOL 1 602-17, MS BARLOW 34/ FOL 2V 602-18, MS BARLOW 34/ FOL 5 602-19, MS BARLOW 34/ FOL 49 602-20
*PROVENANCE ITALIAN 602/1-8, ITALIAN/ NORTH? 602/9-12, FRENCH 602/13-16, ENGLISH 602/17-20
*DATE EXECUTED 13TH/ 1ST HALF 602/1-8, 13TH/ END 602/9-12, 14TH/ EARLY 602/13-16, 15TH 602/17-20
*LANGUAGE LATIN
*AUTHOR ALBUCASIS 602/1-7, JOHANNIS FILII SERAPIONIS 602-8, AVICENNA 602/9-12, ARNALDI DE VILLANOVA 602-16, JOHN DE ARDERNE OF NEWARK 602/17-20
*TYPE OF MANUSCRIPT MEDICAL TREATISES
*CONTENTS MEDICAL TREATISES 602/1-20, SURGICAL INSTRUMENTS/ MAINLY PROBES 602/1-4, SURGICAL INSTRUMENTS/ FORCEPS/ BLADES/ HOOKS 602-5, SURGICAL INSTRUMENTS 602-6, SURGICAL INSTRUMENTS/ MAINLY CUTTING TOOLS 602-7, AUTHOR PORTRAIT/ DOCTOR HOLDS URINE FLASK 602-8, DOCTOR HOLDS URINE FLASK 602-8, AVICENNA 602-9, AUTHOR PORTRAIT/ ARCHER AND BIRD IN BORDER 602-9, DOCTOR HOLDS BOOK 602-10, DOCTOR IN BIRETTA HOLDING BOOK 602-11, DOCTOR HOLDS BOOK 602-12, ARISTOTLE AND ALEXANDER 602-13, INITIAL/ DECORATED WITH LARGE BIRD IN MARGIN 602-14, INITIAL CONTAINING GROTESQUE BIRD 602-15, AUTHOR PORTRAIT/ ARNOLD OF VILLANOVA HOLDS FLASK 602-16, ARNOLD OF VILLANOVA HOLDS SPECIMEN FLASK 602-16, MAN/ NAKED 602-17, SURGICAL INSTRUMENTS 602-18, ANATOMICAL DRAWINGS SHOWING TREATMENT AREAS 602-19, SURGICAL INSTRUMENTS AND PORTIONS OF BODIES 602-20 SURGICAL INSTRUMENTS AND PORTIONS OF BODIES 602-20

*$ABSTRACT 603
*LIBRARY BODLEIAN
*SLIDE SET TITLE ROMANCE OF ALEXANDER PART 3
*NEGATIVE REFERENCE ROLL 244F
*RENTAL FEE $5.20
*COMMENTS THIS SET, TOGETHER WITH 604-608, REPRODUCES EVERY PAGE IN MS BODLEY 264. THE ILLUMINATIONS CONSIST OF HISTORIATED INITIALS, OFTEN CONTAINING HUMAN FACES, OF PICTORIAL PANELS, AND OF DECORATED MARGINS DEPICTING SCENES OF EVERY-DAY LIFE, SPORTS AND PASTIMES, MUSICAL INSTRUMENTS AND NUMEROUS BIRDS, HARES, AND GROTESQUES.
*TITLE OF MANUSCRIPT ROMANCE OF ALEXANDER
*SHELFMARK MS BODLEY 264/ FOL 110 603-1, MS BODLEY 264/ FOL 110V 603-2, MS BODLEY 264/ FOL 111 603-3, MS BODLEY 264/ FOL 111V 603-4, MS BODLEY 264/ FOL 112 603-5, MS BODLEY 264/ FOL 112V 603-6, MS BODLEY 264/ FOL 113 603-7, MS BODLEY 264/ FOL 113V 603-8, MS BODLEY 264/ FOL 114 603-9, MS BODLEY 264/ FOL 114V 603-10, MS BODLEY 264/ FOL 115 603-11, MS BODLEY 264/ FOL 115V 603-12, MS BODLEY 264/ FOL 116 603-13, MS BODLEY 264/ FOL 116V 603-14, MS BODLEY 264/ FOL 117 603-15, MS BODLEY 264/ FOL 117V 603-16, MS BODLEY 264/ FOL 118 603-17, MS BODLEY 264/ FOL 118V 603-18, MS BODLEY 264/ FOL 119 603-19, MS BODLEY 264/ FOL 119V 603-20, MS BODLEY 264/ FOL 120 603-21, MS BODLEY 264/ FOL 120V 603-22, MS BODLEY 264/ FOL 121 603-23, MS BODLEY 264/ FOL 121V 603-24, MS BODLEY 264/ FOL 122 603-25, MS BODLEY 264/ FOL 122V 603-26, MS BODLEY 264/ FOL 123 603-27, MS BODLEY 264/ FOL

123V 603-28, MS BODLEY 264/ FOL 124 603-29, MS BODLEY 264/ FOL 124V 603-30, MS BODLEY 264/ FOL 125 603-31, MS BODLEY 264/ FOL 125V 603-32, MS BODLEY 264/ FOL 126 603-33, MS BODLEY 264/ FOL 126V 603-34, MS BODLEY 264/ FOL 127 603-35, MS BODLEY 264/ FOL 127V 603-36, MS BODLEY 264/ FOL 128 603-37, MS BODLEY 264/ FOL 128V 603-38, MS BODLEY 264/ FOL 129 603-39, MS BODLEY 264/ FOL 129V 603-40, MS BODLEY 264/ FOL 130 603-41, MS BODLEY 264/ FOL 130V 603-42, MS BODLEY 264/ FOL 131 603-43, MS BODLEY 264/ FOL 131V 603-44, MS BODLEY 264/ FOL 132 603-45, MS BODLEY 264/ FOL 132V 603-46, MS BODLEY 264/ FOL 133 603-47, MS BODLEY 264/ FOL 133V 603-48, MS BODLEY 264/ FOL 134 603-49, MS BODLEY 264/ FOL 134V 603-50, MS BODLEY 264/ FOL 135 603-51, MS BODLEY 264/ FOL 135V 603-52, MS BODLEY 264/ FOL 136 603-53, MS BODLEY 264/ FOL 136V 603-54, MS BODLEY 264/ FOL 137 603-55, MS BODLEY 264/ FOL 137V 603-56, MS BODLEY 264/ FOL 138 603-57, MS BODLEY 264/ FOL 138V 603-58, MS BODLEY 264/ FOL 139 603-59, MS BODLEY 264/ FOL 139V 603-60, MS BODLEY 264/ FOL 140 603-61, MS BODLEY 264/ FOL 140V 603-62, MS BODLEY 264/ FOL 141 603-63, MS BODLEY 264/ FOL 141V 603-64, MS BODLEY 264/ FOL 142 603-65, MS BODLEY 264/ FOL 142V 603-66, MS BODLEY 264/ FOL 143 603-67, MS BODLEY 264/ FOL 143V 603-68, MS BODLEY 264/ FOL 144 603-69, MS BODLEY 264/ FOL 144V 603-70, MS BODLEY 264/ FOL 145 603-71, MS BODLEY 264/ FOL 145V 603-72, MS BODLEY 264/ FOL 146 603-73, MS BODLEY 264/ FOL 146V 603-74, MS BODLEY 264/ FOL 147 603-75, MS BODLEY 264/ FOL 147V 603-76, MS BODLEY 264/ FOL 148 603-77, MS BODLEY 264/ FOL 148V 603-78, MS BODLEY 264/ FOL 149 603-79, MS BODLEY 264/ FOL 149V 603-80, MS BODLEY 264/ FOL 150 603-81, MS BODLEY 264/ FOL 150V 603-82, MS BODLEY 264/ FOL 151 603-83, MS BODLEY 264/ FOL 151V 603-84, MS BODLEY 264/ FOL 152 603-85, MS BODLEY 264/ FOL 152V 603-86, MS BODLEY 264/ FOL 153 603-87, MS BODLEY 264/ FOL 153V 603-88, MS BODLEY 264/ FOL 154 603-89, MS BODLEY 264/ FOL 154V 603-90, MS BODLEY 264/ FOL 155 603-91, MS BODLEY 264/ FOL 157V 603-92, MS BODLEY 264/ FOL 158 603-93, MS BODLEY 264/ FOL 158V 603-94, MS BODLEY 264/ FOL 159 603-95, MS BODLEY 264/ FOL 159V 603-96, MS BODLEY 264/ FOL 160 603-97, MS BODLEY 264/ FOL 160V 603-98, MS BODLEY 264/ FOL 161 603-99, MS BODLEY 264/ FOL 161V 603-100, MS BODLEY 264/ FOL 162 603-101, MS BODLEY 264/ FOL 162V 603-102, MS BODLEY 264/ FOL 163 603-103, MS BODLEY 264/ FOL 163V 603-104

*PROVENANCE FLEMISH
*DATE EXECUTED 14TH/1338-44
*LANGUAGE FRENCH
*ARTIST/ SCHOOL DE GRISE/ JEHAN
*TYPE OF MANUSCRIPT ROMANCE
*CONTENTS ROMANCE OF ALEXANDER PART 3 603/1-104, LITERATURE/ ROMANCE OF ALEXANDER 603/1-104, ALEXANDER/ ROMANCE 603/1-104, ALEXANDER MOUNTED IN HISTORIATED INITIAL 603-1, HOUND CHASING HARE 603-1, MAN WITH TWO BELLS 603-1, DANCE OF FOUR MONKEYS WITH FOUR WOMEN 603-1, TEXT PAGE WITH BIRDS 603-2, TEXT PAGE WITH BIRDS 603-3, TEXT PAGE WITH BIRDS 603-4, LADIES AND MEN IN RECTANGULAR PANEL 603-5, CHESS GAME 603-5, GAME PLAYED ON BOARD 603-5, APE SINGING 603-5, TEXT PAGE 603-6, CITY GATE FROM WHICH EMERGE TROOP OF MOUNTED KNIGHTS 603-7, KNIGHTS/ MOUNTED 603-7, KNIGHTS TILT ON HORSEBACK 603-7, CLARUS COMES TO MEET ALEXANDER FOR BATTLE 603-8, CARPENTERS ASTRIDE A BOARD 603-8, GRINDSTONE USED TO SHARPEN SWORD 603-8, SWORDMAKING 603-8, TEXT PAGE WITH BIRDS 603-9, GADIFER AND BETEIS FIGHT WITH CLARUS' MEN 603-10, BATTLE SCENE 603-10, MAN CARRIES THREE SWORDS AND ROUND CASE 603-10, SOLDIER DRAWS SWORD FROM SHEATH 603-10, CASTLE ON RIGHT 603-10, TEXT PAGE WITH BIRDS 603-11, TEXT PAGE WITH BIRDS 603-12, TEXT PAGE WITH BIRDS 603-13, TEXT PAGE WITH BIRD 603-14, ARMIES MOUNTED FACE EACH OTHER 603-15, BIRD CATCHING IN LOWER MARGIN 603-15, MARCIENS FIGHTS GADIFER 603-16, BULL PLAYS PIPE 603-16, BOY WITH HAND BELLS 603-16, GROTESQUE MAN WITH GOAT HEAD AND TAIL 603-16, BOY BEATS DRUM/ BOY DANCES WITH BEAR 603-16, TEXT PAGE 603-17, TEXT PAGE WITH BIRD 603-18, TROOP OF HORSES WITH CASSAMUS AND CASSIANS 603-19, CASSAMUS AND CASSIANS 603-19, HAWKING IN LOWER MARGIN 603-19, TEXT PAGE WITH MINIATURE 603-20, CASSAMUS STANDS SPEAKING TO LADY 603-21, YOUTH AND MAID KNEELING IN LOWER MARGIN 603-21, BAUDRAIN AND EDEA SIT CONVERSING 603-22, MUSICIANS IN LOWER MARGIN 603-22, ALEXANDER WITH THREE LADIES

AND YOUTH 603-23, KNIGHTS TILTING IN LOWER MARGIN 603-23, LADY STANDING BEFORE SEATED COUPLE 603-24, CHESS GAME IN LOWER MARGIN 603-24, TEXT PAGE WITH BIRDS 603-25, KING SEATED BY TENTS AND PAVILLION 603-26, HUNTING SCENE IN LOWER MARGIN 603-26, CASSAMUS SPEAKS TO MESSENGER 603-27, MUSICIANS 603-27, YOUTHS ON STILTS 603-27, COOKING SCENE IN LOWER MARGIN 603-28, TEACHER AND PUPILS 603-28, ALEXANDER'S TENT/ CASSAMUS AND GADIFER APPROACH 603-29, ALEXANDER BETWEEN CASSAMUS AND GADIFER 603-29, MAN HOLDS GOOSE IN PINCERS 603-30, MAN SHOEING WITH HAMMER 603-30, BOY BEATS DRUM 603-30, TEXT PAGE WITH BIRDS 603-31, EMENIDUS SURRENDERS SWORD TO ALEXANDER 603-32, BOY WITH CAULDRON/ MAN WITH LADLE 603-32, ALEXANDER SITS BETWEEN CASSAMUS AND GADIFER 603-33, CHESS GAME IN LOWER MARGIN 603-33, BIRD CATCHING IN LOWER MARGIN 603-34, CASSAMUS/ BAUDRAIN/ GROUP OF LADIES 603-35, CASSAMUS AND LADY 603-36, BAGPIPER 603-36, TAMBOURINE PLAYED BY MAN 603-36, HURDYGURDY PLAYED BY MAN 603-36, CHESS GAME 603-36, BOY CARRIES POLE WITH THREE HAWKS 603-37, HAWKING 603-37, CASSAMUS WITH GROUP OF MEN AND LADIES 603-38, CHESS GAME 603-38, DANCING IN LOWER MARGIN 603-39, FUNERAL PROCESSION 603-39, PORUS AND FLORIDAS JOUST 603-40, JOUSTING 603-40, CASTLE/ MOATED 603-40, ARMIES ENGAGE IN BATTLE 603-41, BATTLE SCENE 603-41, GAME OF BLINDMAN'S BLUFF IN LOWER MARGIN 603-41, FLORIDAS AND PORUS FIGHT WITH SWORDS 603-42, KNIGHTS/ MOUNTED FIGHT WITH SWORDS 603-42, GAME OF BLINDMAN'S BLUFF 603-42, TEXT PAGE WITH BIRDS 603-43, TEXT PAGE WITH BIRDS 603-44, TEXT PAGE WITH BIRDS 603-45, PORUS STRIKES SOLDIERS IN POINTED HELMETS 603-46, BUTTERFLY CATCHING IN LOWER MARGIN 603-46, PORUS STANDS IN THE MIDDLE OF GROUP OF KNIGHTS 603-47, WINEMAKING IN LOWER MARGIN 603-47, PORUS SITS AMONG GROUP OF PEOPLE 603-48, MONKEY PUSHES WHEELBARROW 603-48, WHEELBARROW 603-48, TEXT PAGE WITH BIRDS 603-49, TEXT PAGE WITH BIRDS 603-50, HOUND CHASES HARES IN UPPER MARGIN 603-51, BUTTERFLY CATCHING IN LOWER MARGIN 603-51, HOUND CHASES HARE IN LOWER MARGIN 603-52, TEXT PAGE WITH LION AND BIRDS 603-53, TEXT PAGE WITH BIRDS 603-54, TEXT PAGE WITH BIRDS 603-55, LYONES MOUNTED EMERGES FROM CASTLE 603-56, CASTLE WITH DRAWBRIDGE 603-56, KNIGHT WITH PAGE LEADING ARMOURED HORSE 603-56, GROTESQUE WITH GITTERN 603-57, GITTERN 603-57, HAWKING 603-57, DANCING COUPLES 603-57, ALEXANDER SEATED WITH KNEELING MESSENGER 603-58, MUSICIANS WITH TAMBOURINES AND TRUMPETS 603-58, ALEXANDER SEATED IN TENT WITH KNEELING MESSENGER 603-58, KNIGHTS WITH VISORS DOWN TILT 603-59, KNIGHTS LYING ON GROUND/ BROKEN SPEARS 603-60, KNIGHT WITH LION SHIELD IN LOWER MARGIN 603-60, TEXT PAGE WITH BIRDS 603-61, CASSAMUS TALKS WITH MARCIENS ABOUT HOSTAGES 603-62, CASTLE WITH MEN OUTSIDE IN LOWER MARGIN 603-62, MARCIENS LED TO VENUS' ROOM 603-63, GROTESQUE WITH BAGPIPES 603-63, BAGPIPER 603-63, TEXT PAGE WITH BIRD 603-64, TEXT PAGE WITH BIRDS 603-65, PAVILION WITH EAGLE SHIELDS 603-66, MUSICIANS IN BATTLEMENTS 603-66, FOUR COUPLES IN LOWER MARGIN 603-67, CLARUS SEATED ON DOG-HEADED CHAIR 603-68, MUSICIANS SIT ON CASTELLATED TOP 603-68, CLARUS LAYS HAND ON KNIGHT'S SHOULDER 603-69, KING AND TWO OARSMEN IN LOWER MARGIN 603-69, ALEXANDER WITH TWO KNIGHTS OUTSIDE CASTLE 603-70, CASTLE WITH THREE LADIES OUTSIDE DOOR 603-70, ALEXANDER TALKING TO THREE LADIES 603-71, CHESS GAME IN LOWER MARGIN 603-72, KING SPEAKS TO KNEELING MAN OUTSIDE CHURCH 603-73, FEAST SCENE WITH ALEXANDER AND OTHERS 603-74, ALEXANDER'S FEAST 603-74, KNIGHTS BEFORE LARGE TENT 603-75, TEXT PAGE WITH BOYS/ BIRDS/ HOUNDS 603-76, TEXT PAGE WITH BIRDS/ CHILDREN/ KING 603-77, EUMENIDUS SPEAKS TO SEATED ALEXANDER 603-78, TEXT PAGE WITH BIRDS 603-79, ALEXANDER WITH MOUNTED TROOP 603-80, MUSICIANS WITH TRUMPETS/ BAGPIPES/ DRUMS 603-80, EUMENIDES AND PORUS PREPARE TO MOUNT THEIR HORSES 603-81, KING AND BEARDED MAN TALK TO SOLDIERS 603-81, TEXT PAGE WITH BIRDS 603-82, TEXT PAGE WITH BIRDS 603-83, TEXT PAGE WITH HARE AND BIRDS 603-84, BATTLE SCENE/ KING FIGHTS ON FOOT 603-85, HORSES TRAMPLE ON FALLEN PEOPLE IN LOWER MARGIN 603-85, BAUDRAIN CLUTCHES ALEXANDER'S SWORD 603-86, BODIES/ HEADS/ WEAPONS LIE ABOUT 603-86, CART WITH TWO WHEELS DRAWN BY HORSE 603-86, KNIGHTS WOUNDED IN LOWER MARGIN 603-86, CASSIUS AND CAULUS FIGHT WHILE LADIES WATCH 603-87, CASTLE WITH TWO LADIES IN TOWERS 603-87, KING/ DOG/ KNIGHTS/

LADIES IN LOWER MARGIN 603-87, BATTLE SCENE/ SKIRMISH OF HORSE 603-88, KING SMITE ON VISOR WITH SWORD 603-88, SOLDIERS IN ARMOUR IN LOWER MARGIN 603-88, BATTLE SCENE/ HEADS AND SWORDS LIE ABOUT 603-89, SOLDIERS FIGHT IN LOWER MARGIN 603-89, TEXT PAGE WITH BIRDS IN FAINT OUTLINE 603-90, TEXT PAGE WITH BIRDS 603-91, MUSICIANS WITH TRUMPETS/ DRUMS/ BAGPIPES/HARP/ FLAGEOLET 603-92, BATTLE SCENE/ NINE KNIGHTS HORSED/ THREE DEAD 603-93, HORSE/ RIDERLESS WITH BOAR ON HOUSINGS 603-93,PORUS PLUNGES SWORD INTO HORSE 603-94, KING FALLS 603-94, WHEELBARROW WITH COGGED WHEEL 603-94, INN WITH SALTIRE-SHAPED SIGN 603-94, TEXT PAGE WITH BIRD 603-95, TEXT PAGE WITH BIRDS 603-96, TEXT PAGE WITH BIRDS 603-97, TEXT PAGE WITH BIRDS 603-98, KNIGHTS SHAKE HANDS IN LOWER MARGIN 603-99, PORUS' HEAD BANDAGED WHILE KING HOLDS HAND 603-100, TEXT PAGE WITH BIRDS 603-101, TEXT PAGE WITH BIRDS 603-102, TEXT PAGE WITH BIRDS 603-103, ALEXANDER PROMISES PHEZONA SHE WILL MARRY PORUS 603-104, FEAST SCENE WITH LADEN TABLE 603-104

*$ABSTRACT 604
*LIBRARY BODLEIAN
*SLIDE SET TITLE ROMANCE OF ALEXANDER PART 4
*NEGATIVE REFERENCE ROLL 244G
*RENTAL FEE $5.05
*COMMENTS THIS SET, TOGETHER WITH 603 AND 605-608, REPRODUCES EVERY PAGE IN MS BODLEY 264. THE ILLUMINATIONS CONSIST OF HISTORIATED INITIALS, OFTEN CONTAINING HUMAN FACES, OF PICTORIAL PANELS, AND OF DECORATED MARGINS DEPICTING SCENES OF EVERY-DAY LIFE, SPORTS AND PASTIMES, MUSICAL INSTRUMENTS AND NUMEROUS BIRDS/ HARES, AND GROTESQUES.
*TITLE OF MANUSCRIPT ROMANCE OF ALEXANDER
*SHELFMARK MS BODLEY 264/ FOL 164V 604-1, MS BODLEY 264/ FOL 165 604-2, MS BODLEY 264/ FOL 165V 604-3, MS BODLEY 264/ FOL 166 604-4, MS BODLEY 264/ FOL 166V 604-5, MS BODLEY 264/ FOL 167 604-6, MS BODLEY 264/ FOL 167V 604-7, MS BODLEY 264/ FOL 168 604-8, MS BODLEY 264/ FOL 168V 604-9, MS BODLEY 264/ FOL 169 604-10, MS BODLEY 264/ FOL 169V 604-11, MS BODLEY 264/ FOL 170 604-12, MS BODLEY 264/ FOL 170V 604-13, MS BODLEY 264/ FOL 171 604-14, MS BODLEY 264/ FOL 171V 604-15, MS BODLEY 264/ FOL 172 604-16, MS BODLEY 264/ FOL 174 604-17, MS BODLEY 264/ FOL 174V 604-18, MS BODLEY 264/ FOL 175 604-19, MS BODLEY 264/ FOL 175V 604-20, MS BODLEY 264/ FOL 176 604-21, MS BODLEY 264/ FOL 176V 604-22, MS BODLEY 264/ FOL 177 604-23, MS BODLEY 264/ FOL 177V 604-24, MS BODLEY 264/ FOL 178 604-25, MS BODLEY 264/ FOL 178V 604-26, MS BODLEY 264/ FOL 179 604-27, MS BODLEY 264/ FOL 179V 604-28, MS BODLEY 264/ FOL 180 604-29, MS BODLEY 264/ FOL 180V 604-30, MS BODLEY 264/ FOL 181 604-31, MS BODLEY 264/ FOL 181V 604-32, MS BODLEY 264/ FOL 182 604-33, MS BODLEY 264/ FOL 182V 604-34, MS BODLEY 264/ FOL 183 604-35, MS BODLEY 264/ FOL 183V 604-36, MS BODLEY 264/ FOL 184 604-37, MS BODLEY 264/ FOL 184V 604-38, MS BODLEY 264/ FOL 185 604-39, MS BODLEY 264/ FOL 185V 604-40, MS BODLEY 264/ FOL 186 604-41, MS BODLEY 264/ FOL 186V 604-42, MS BODLEY 264/ FOL 187 604-43, MS BODLEY 264/ FOL 187V 604-44, MS BODLEY 264/ FOL 188 604-45, MS BODLEY 264/ FOL 188V 604-46, MS BODLEY 264/ FOL 189 604-47, MS BODLEY 264/ FOL 189V 604-48, MS BODLEY 264/ FOL 190 604-49, MS BODLEY 264/ FOL 190V 604-50, MS BODLEY 264/ FOL 191 604-51, MS BODLEY 264/ FOL 191V 604-52, MS BODLEY 264/ FOL 192V 604-53, MS BODLEY 264/ FOL 192V 604-54, MS BODLEY 264/ FOL 193 604-55, MS BODLEY 264/ FOL 193V 604-56, MS BODLEY 264/ FOL 194 604-57, MS BODLEY 264/ FOL 194V 604-58, MS BODLEY 264/ FOL 195 604-59, MS BODLEY 264/ FOL 195V 604-60, MS BODLEY 264/ FOL 196 604-61
*PROVENANCE FLEMISH
*DATE EXECUTED 14TH/1388-44
*LANGUAGE FRENCH
*ARTIST/ SCHOOL DE GRISE/ JEHAN
*TYPE OF MANUSCRIPT ROMANCE
*CONTENTS ROMANCE OF ALEXANDER PART 4 604/1-61,LITERATURE/ ROMANCE OF ALEXANDER 604/1-61, ALEXANDER/ ROMANCE 604/1-61, FRONTISPIECE TO RESTOR DU PAON/ FOUR PANELS 604-1, KNIGHTS RIDE TO DOORWAY OF CASTLE 604-1, KING WEARING CROWN WALKS INTO

CASTLE DOOR 604-1, KING GREETS LADY COMING OUT OF DOOR 604-1, ALEXANDER AND TWO LADIES BEFORE GATE 604-1, SMITHY SCENE IN LOWER MARGIN 604-2, FORGE/ BELLOWS/ HEATING TONGS 604-2, SMITH AT TABLE WORKING ON WINGED HELMET 604-2,SMITH WORKING ON PIECE OF SCALE ARMOUR 604-2, HARES CHASED BY HOUNDS IN UPPER MARGIN 604-2, TEXT PAGE WITH BIRDS 604-3, TEXT PAGE WITH BIRDS 604-4, TEXT PAGE 604-5, KING RECEIVES LETTER FROM KNEELING MESSENGER 604-6, CASTLE AND TWO MESSENGERS IN LOWER MARGIN 604-6, CASTLE/ YOUTH AND MAID WALK AWAY 604-7, MESSENGERS WITH JAVELINS MEET IN LOWER MARGIN 604-7, AYMES RESCUES DAMSEL AND KILLS ROBBER 604-8, MONKEY WITH BOTTLE IN LOWER MARGIN 604-8, GROTESQUE APE/ PEACOCK AND OWL IN RIGHT MARGIN 604-8, AYMES RETURNS SWORD TO SHEATH AFTER BEHEADING ROBBER 604-9, AYMES AND MAID WALK TOGETHER OUTSIDE CASTLE WALL 604-9, GIRL LIES WITH HEAD IN BOY'S LAP 604-9, KING LED BY DAMSEL TO TREASURE CHESTS 604-10, GIRL OPENS CHEST IN LOWER MARGIN 604-10, AYMES RECEIVES PRESENT FROM HIS LADY 604-11, AYMES HOLDS CHEST AND SHOWS IT TO MEN 604-12, KING SEATED BEFORE KNEELING DAMSEL 604-12, CASTLE AND MEN WITH JAVELINS IN LOWER MARGIN 604-12, BISHOP JOINS HANDS OF KING AND QUEEN 604-13, MARRIAGE OF KING AND QUEEN 604-13, DOMESTIC SCENES 604-13, CAKEMAKING 604-13, MORTAR AND PESTLE 604-13, COOKING BIRDS OVER SPITS 604-13, LADY AND TWO MOUNTED MEN RIDE AWAY FROM CASTLE 604-14, MAN HELPS LADY DISMOUNT FROM HORSE 604-14, SMITHY SCENE/ SMITH WITH ANVIL AND HAMMER 604-15, MERMAID AND BIRDS IN LEFT MARGIN 604-15, KING WITH COUPLE BEFORE CASTLE GATE 604-16, CASTLE WITH BATTLEMENTED TOP 604-16, QUEEN AND THREE PAIRS OF LADIES IN LOWER MARGIN 603-16, MUSICIANS WITH FIDDLE/ ORGAN/ BAGPIPE AND DRUM 604-16, PORUS/ BAUDRAIN/ MARCIENS/ GADIFER/ CAULUS/ EDEA 604-17, PEACOCK PERCHED ON TABLE 604-17, TEXT PAGE 604-18, DRUMMER/ SEVEN YOUTHS IN A ROW/ SIX GIRLS 604-19, TEXT PAGE WITH BIRD 604-20, TEXT PAGE WITH BIRD 604-21, TEXT PAGE WITH BIRDS 604-22, TEXT PAGES WITH BIRDS 604/23-29, ELIOS AND FOUR YOUTHS 604-30, BLIND MAN WITH HURDY GURDY AND DOG ON LEAD 604-30, HURDYGURDY 604-30, MUSICIANS/ FLUTE/ ORGAN/ DRUMS/ GITTERN/ VIOL/ HARP/ PSALTERY 604-30, TEXT PAGE 604-31, DANCING/ NINE MEN AND WOMEN IN A RING 604-32, GROUP OF YOUTHS AND LADIES 604-32, MEN WITH ANIMALS' HEADS/ SIX MAIDS HAND-IN-HAND 604-32, MEN AND LADIES STAND BY PEACOCK 604-33, MUSICIANS/ TRUMPETS/ HARP/ PSALTERY/ ORGAN/ DRUM 604-33, TEXT PAGE WITH BIRD 604-34, KING AND YOUNG KNIGHTS ON HORSEBACK 604-35, KING WITH GROUP OF MEN 604-36, KING BEARDED WITH TWO YOUNG MEN 604-36, KING IN BOAT IN LOWER MARGIN 604-36, TENTS AND CASTLE 604-37, KING EMBRACED BY CANDACE 604-38, HORSEMEN AND DOG IN LOWER MARGIN 604-38, ALEXANDER EXAMINES LARGE LEAF 604-39, TENT AND PAVILION 604-39, GROUP OF MEN WITH DAGGERS 604-40, CASTLE WITH ONLOOKERS FROM BATTLEMENTS 604-40, BUILDINGS IN LOWER MARGIN 604-40, EMENIDUS HOLDS APPLE TO TWO YOUNG MEN 604-41, COUPLES KNEELING UNDER TREES/ LION/ CUCKOO 604-41, EMENIDUS SPEAKS TO ALEXANDER WHO HOLDS APPLE 604-41, TEXT PAGE WITH BIRDS 604/42-45, ALEXANDER'S DEATH PRESAGED 604-46, ALEXANDER WITH HANDS RAISED BEFORE CHURCH 604-46, MUSICIANS/ DRUMS/ CYMBALS/ HANDBELLS/ TRUMPETS/ VIOL 604-46, INITIAL N HISTORIATED WITH KING CROWNED 604-47, KING CROWNED 604-47, HARES CHASED BY DOGS IN UPPER MARGIN 604-47, BOYS WITH THREE DOGS IN LOWER MARGIN 604-47, TEXT PAGE WITH BIRDS 604-48, ALEXANDER ON HIS DEATH BED 604-49, MOURNERS FOR ALEXANDER IN LOWER MARGIN 604-49,TEXT PAGE WITH BIRDS 604-50, ALEXANDER IN BED WITH FOUR COURTIERS 604-51, MOURNERS IN LOWER MARGIN 604-51, ALEXANDER IN DEATH BED WITH EYES CLOSED 604-52, MOURNERS IN LOWER MARGIN 604-52, TEXT PAGE WITH BIRDS 604/53-54, ALEXANDER'S COFFIN UNDER COPED HEARSE 604-55, MOURNERS/ SIX HOODED MEN WEEP 604-55, TEXT PAGES WITH BIRDS 604/56-61

*$ABSTRACT 605
*LIBRARY BODLEIAN
*SLIDE SET TITLE ROMANCE OF ALEXANDER PART 5
*NEGATIVE REFERENCE ROLL 244H
*RENTAL FEE $3.20

*COMMENTS THIS SET, TOGETHER WITH 603-604 AND 606-608, REPRODUCES EVERY PAGE IN MS BODLEY 264. THE ILLUMINATIONS CONSIST OF HISTORIATED INITIALS, OFTEN CONTAINING HUMAN FACES, OF PICTORIAL PANELS, AND OF DECORATED MARGINS DEPICTING SCENES OF EVERY-DAY LIFE, SPORTS AND PASTIMES, MUSICAL INSTRUMENTS AND NUMEROUS BIRDS, HARES, AND GROTESQUES.
*TITLE OF MANUSCRIPT ROMANCE OF ALEXANDER
*SHELFMARK MS BODLEY 264/ FOL 196V 605-1, MS BODLEY 264/ FOL 197 605-2, MS BODLEY 264/ FOL 197V 605-3, MS BODLEY 264/ FOL 198 605-4, MS BODLEY 264/ FOL 198V 605-5, MS BODLEY 264/ FOL 199 605-6, MS BODLEY 264/ FOL 199V 605-7, MS BODLEY 264/ FOL 200 605-8, MS BODLEY 264/ FOL 200V 605-9, MS BODLEY 264/ FOL 201 605-10, MS BODLEY 264/ FOL 201V 605-11, MS BODLEY 264/ FOL 202 605-12, MS BODLEY 264/ FOL 202V 605-13, MS BODLEY 264/ FOL 203 605-14, MS BODLEY 264/ FOL 203V 605-15, MS BODLEY 264/ FOL 204 605-16, MS BODLEY 264/ FOL 204V 605-17, MS BODLEY 264/ FOL 205 605-18, MS BODLEY 264/ FOL 205V 605-19, MS BODLEY 264/ FOL 206 605-20, MS BODLEY 264/ FOL 206V 605-21, MS BODLEY 264/ FOL 207 605-22, MS BODLEY 264/ FOL 207V 605-23, MS BODLEY 264/ COLYPHON 605-24
*PROVENANCE FLEMISH
*DATE EXECUTED 14TH/1338-44
*LANGUAGE FRENCH
*ARTIST/ SCHOOL DE GRISE/ JEHAN
*TYPE OF MANUSCRIPT ROMANCE
*CONTENTS ROMANCE OF ALEXANDER PART 5 605/1-24,LITERATURE/ ROMANCE OF ALEXANDER 605/1-24, ALEXANDER/ ROMANCE 605/1-24, BATTLEMENTS AND TURRETS 605-1, QUEEN ON THRONE SPEAKS TO BOY 605-1, QUEEN LEADS BOY TO BUILDING 605-1, GROUP OF COURTIERS 605-1, QUEEN SEATED WITH BOY BEFORE HER 605-1, CASTLES AND MEN WITH JAVELINS IN LOWER MARGIN 605-1, INITIAL S HISTORIATED WITH QUEEN IN BED 605-2,HARES CHASED BY DOGS IN UPPER MARGIN 605-2, CASTLE/ MEN AND BOYS IN LOWER MARGIN 605-2, QUEEN WITH RAISED HAND 605-3, MAN KNEELING GIVES LETTER TO YOUTH 605-3, CASTLE/ MEN WITH SPEARS IN LOWER MARGIN 605-3,TEXT PAGE WITH BIRDS 605-4, THOLOME RECEIVES LETTER FROM MESSENGER 605-5,TENTS AND PAVILIONS IN LOWER MARGIN 605-5, TEXT PAGES WITH BIRDS 605/6-9, TROOP OF ARMED KNIGHTS RIDE INTO TOWN 605-10, ALIOR GOES TO AVENGE HIS FATHER'S DEATH 605-10,CATAPULT AND BALISTA IN LOWER MARGIN 605-10, TEXT PAGES WITH BIRDS 605/11-15, TROOP CHASES ANTIPATER AND DIVINUS PATER 605-16, COOKING SCENE IN LOWER MARGIN 605-16, TEXT PAGES WITH BIRDS 605/17-24

*$ABSTRACT 606
*LIBRARY BODLEIAN
*SLIDE SET TITLE ROMANCE OF ALEXANDER PART 6
*NEGATIVE REFERENCE ROLL 244I
*RENTAL FEE $2.70
*COMMENTS THIS SET, TOGETHER WITH 603-605 AND 607-608, REPRODUCES EVERY PAGE IN MS BODLEY 264. THE ILLUMINATIONS CONSIST OF HISTORIATED INITIALS, OFTEN CONTAINING HUMAN FACES, OF PICTORIAL PANELS, AND OF DECORATED MARGINS DEPICTING SCENES OF EVERY-DAY LIFE, SPORTS AND PASTIMES, MUSICAL INSTRUMENTS AND NUMEROUS BIRDS, HARES, AND GROTESQUES.
*TITLE OF MANUSCRIPT ROMANCE OF ALEXANDER
*SHELFMARK MS BODLEY 264/ FOL 209 606-1, MS BODLEY 264/ FOL 209V 606-2, MS BODLEY 264/ FOL 210 606-3, MS BODLEY 264/ FOL 210V 606-4, MS BODLEY 264/ FOL 211 606-5, MS BODLEY 264/ FOL 211V 606-6, MS BODLEY 264/ FOL 212 606-7, MS BODLEY 264/ FOL 212V 606-8, MS BODLEY 264/ FOL 213 606-9, MS BODLEY 264/ FOL 213V 606-10, MS BODLEY 264/ FOL 214 606-11, MS BODLEY 264/ FOL 214V 606-12, MS BODLEY 264/ FOL 215 606-13, MS BODLEY 264/ FOL 215V 606-14
*PROVENANCE ENGLISH
*DATE EXECUTED 15TH/C1400
*LANGUAGE ENGLISH
*TYPE OF MANUSCRIPT ROMANCE
*CONTENTS ROMANCE OF ALEXANDER PART 6 606/1-14,LITERATURE/ ROMANCE OF ALEXANDER 606/1-14, ALEXANDER/ ROMANCE 606/1-14,

OPENING PAGE OF ENGLISH VERSE ROMANCE OF ALEXANDER 606-1, ALEXANDER ADDRESSES THREE NAKED BRAHMANS 606-2, BRAHMAN CROSSES RIVER IN ROWBOAT 606-2, HOUND-FISH IN WATER 606-2, DRAGONS ON RIVER BANK 606-2, ALEXANDER RECEIVES LETTER FROM DINDIMUS 603-3, TEXT PAGE 606-4, DINDIMUS WRITES LETTER TO ALEXANDER 606-5, TEXT PAGE 606-5, ALEXANDER STANDS BEFORE STRIPED TENT 606-7, DINDIMUS WITH FOUR NAKED MEN 606-7, TEXT PAGE 606-8, DINDIMUS NAKED SPEAKS TO ALEXANDER 606-9, CUPID RULES THE STOMACH 606-9, ALEXANDER'S COURTIER GIVES LETTER TO DINDIMUS 606-10, TEXT PAGE 606-11, ALEXANDER RECEIVES LETTER FROM DINDIMUS 606-12, ALEXANDER'S COURTIER BRINGS LETTER TO DINDIMUS 606-13, ALEXANDER PLACES MARBLE PILLAR 606-14

*$ABSTRACT 607
*LIBRARY BODLEIAN
*SLIDE SET TITLE ROMANCE OF ALEXANDER PART 1
*NEGATIVE REFERENCE ROLL 244J
*RENTAL FEE $11.80
*COMMENTS THIS SET, TOGETHER WITH 603-606 AND 608, REPRODUCES EVERY PAGE IN MS BODLEY 264. THE ILLUMINATIONS CONSIST OF HISTORIATED INITIALS, OFTEN CONTAINING HUMAN FACES, OF PICTORIAL PANELS, AND OF DECORATED MARGINS DEPICTING SCENES OF EVERY-DAY LIFE, SPORTS AND PASTIMES, MUSICAL INSTRUMENTS AND NUMEROUS BIRDS, HARES AND GROTESQUES.
*TITLE OF MANUSCRIPT ROMANCE OF ALEXANDER
*SHELFMARK MS BODLEY 264/ FOL 1 607-1, MS BODLEY 264/ FOL 2
607-2, MS BODLEY 264/ FOL 3 607-3, MS BODLEY 264/ FOL 3V
607-4, MS BODLEY 264/ FOL 4 607-5, MS BODLEY 264/ FOL 4V
607-6, MS BODLEY 264/ FOL 5 607-7, MS BODLEY 264/ FOL 5V
607-8, MS BODLEY 264/ FOL 6 607-9, MS BODLEY 264/ FOL 6V
607-10, MS BODLEY 264/ FOL 7 607-11, MS BODLEY 264/ FOL 7V
607-12, MS BODLEY 264/ FOL 8 607-13, MS BODLEY 264/ FOL 8V
607-14, MS BODLEY 264/ FOL 9 607-15, MS BODLEY 264/ FOL 9V
607-16, MS BODLEY 264/ FOL 10 607-17, MS BODLEY 264/ FOL 10V
607-18, MS BODLEY 264/ FOL 11 607-19, MS BODLEY 264/ FOL 11V
607-20, MS BODLEY 264/ FOL 12 607-21, MS BODLEY 264/ FOL 12V
607-22, MS BODLEY 264/ FOL 13 607-23, MS BODLEY 264/ FOL 13V
607-24, MS BODLEY 264/ FOL 14 607-25, MS BODLEY 264/ FOL 14V
607-26, MS BODLEY 264/ FOL 15 607-27, MS BODLEY 264/ FOL 15V
607-28, MS BODLEY 264/ FOL 16 607-29, MS BODLEY 264/ FOL 16V
607-30, MS BODLEY 264/ FOL 17 607-31, MS BODLEY 264/ FOL 17V
607-32, MS BODLEY 264/ FOL 18 607-33, MS BODLEY 264/ FOL 18V
607-34, MS BODLEY 264/ FOL 19 607-35, MS BODLEY 264/ FOL 19V
607-36, MS BODLEY 264/ FOL 20 607-37, MS BODLEY 264/ FOL 20V
607-38, MS BODLEY 264/ FOL 21V 607-39, MS BODLEY 264/ FOL 2
607-40, MS BODLEY 264/ FOL 22V 607-41, MS BODLEY 264/ FOL 2
607-42, MS BODLEY 264/ FOL 23V 607-43, MS BODLEY 264/ FOL 2
607-44, MS BODLEY 264/ FOL 24V 607-45, MS BODLEY 264/ FOL 2
607-46, MS BODLEY 264/ FOL 25V 607-47, MS BODLEY 264/ FOL 2
607-48, MS BODLEY 264/ FOL 26V 607-49, MS BODLEY 264/ FOL 2
607-50, MS BODLEY 264/ FOL 27V 607-51, MS BODLEY 264/ FOL 2
607-52, MS BODLEY 264/ FOL 28V 607-53, MS BODLEY 264/ FOL 2
607-54, MS BODLEY 264/ FOL 29V 607-55, MS BODLEY 264/ FOL 3
607-56, MS BODLEY 264/ FOL 30V 607-57, MS BODLEY 264/ FOL 3
607-58, MS BODLEY 264/ FOL 31V 607-59, MS BODLEY 264/ FOL 3
607-60, MS BODLEY 264/ FOL 32V 607-61, MS BODLEY 264/ FOL 3
607-62, MS BODLEY 264/ FOL 33V 607-63, MS BODLEY 264/ FOL 3
607-64, MS BODLEY 264/ FOL 34V 607-65, MS BODLEY 264/ FOL 3
607-66, MS BODLEY 264/ FOL 35V 607-67, MS BODLEY 264/ FOL 3
607-68, MS BODLEY 264/ FOL 36V 607-69, MS BODLEY 264/ FOL 3
607-70, MS BODLEY 264/ FOL 37V 607-71, MS BODLEY 264/ FOL 3
607-72, MS BODLEY 264/ FOL 38V 607-73, MS BODLEY 264/ FOL 3
607-74, MS BODLEY 264/ FOL 39V 607-75, MS BODLEY 264/ FOL 4
607-76, MS BODLEY 264/ FOL 40V 607-77, MS BODLEY 264/ FOL 4
607-78, MS BODLEY 264/ FOL 41V 607-79, MS BODLEY 264/ FOL 4
607-80, MS BODLEY 264/ FOL 42V 607-81, MS BODLEY 264/ FOL 43
607-82, MS BODLEY 264/ FOL 44 607-83, MS BODLEY 264/ FOL 44
607-84, MS BODLEY 264/ FOL 45 607-85, MS BODLEY 264/ FOL 45
607-86, MS BODLEY 264/ FOL 46 607-87, MS BODLEY 264/ FOL 46
607-88, MS BODLEY 264/ FOL 47 607-89, MS BODLEY 264/ FOL 47

607-90, MS BODLEY 264/ FOL 48 607-91, MS BODLEY 264/ FOL 48V 607-92, MS BODLEY 264/ FOL 49 607-93, MS BODLEY 264/ FOL 49V 607-94, MS BODLEY 264/ FOL 50 607-95, MS BODLEY 264/ FOL 50V 607-96, MS BODLEY 264/ FOL 51 607-97, MS BODLEY 264/ FOL 51V 607-98, MS BODLEY 264/ FOL 52 607-99, MS BODLEY 264/ FOL 52V 607-100, MS BODLEY 264/ FOL 53 607-101, MS BODLEY 264/ FOL 53V 607-102, MS BODLEY 264/ FOL 54 607-103, MS BODLEY 264/ FOL 54V 607-104, MS BODLEY 264/ FOL 55 607-105, MS BODLEY 264/ FOL 55V 607-106, MS BODLEY 264/ FOL 56 607-107, MS BODLET 264/ FOL 56V 607-108, MS BODLEY 264/ FOL 57 607-109, MS BODLEY 264/ FOL 57V 607-110, MS BODLEY 264/ FOL 58 607-111, MS BODLEY 264/ FOL 58V 607-112, MS BODLEY 264/ FOL 59 607-113, MS BODLEY 264/ FOL 59V 607-114, MS BODLEY 264/ FOL 60 607-115, MS BODLEY 264/ FOL 60V 607-116, MS BODLEY 264/ FOL 61 607-117, MS BODLEY 264/ FOL 61V 607-118, MS BODLEY 264/ FOL 62 607-119, MS BODLEY 264/ FOL 62V 607-120, MS BODLEY 264/ FOL 63 607-121, MS BODLEY 264/ FOL 63V 607-122, MS BODLEY 264/ FOL 64 607-123, MS BODLEY 264/ FOL 64V 607-124, MS BODLEY 264/ FOL 65 607-125, MS BODLEY 264/ FOL 65V 607-126, MS BODLEY 264/ FOL 66 607-127, MS BODLEY 264/ FOL 66V 607-128, MS BODLEY 264/ FOL 67 607-129, MS BODLEY 264/ FOL 67V 607-130, MS BODLEY 264/ FOL 68 607-131, MS BODLEY 264/ FOL 68V 607-132, MS BODLEY 264/ FOL 69 607-133, MS BODLEY 264/ FOL 69V 607-134, MS BODLEY 264/ FOL 70 607-135, MS BODLEY 264/ FOL 70V 607-136, MS BODLEY 264/ FOL 71 607-137, MS BODLEY 264/ FOL 71V 607-138, MS BODLEY 264/ FOL 72 607-139, MS BODLEY 264/ FOL 72V 607-140, MS BODLEY 264/ FOL 73 607-141, MS BODLEY 264/ FOL 73V 607-142, MS BODLEY 264/ FOL 74 607-143, MS BODLEY 264/ FOL 74V 607-144, MS BODLEY 264/ FOL 75 607-145, MS BODLEY 264/ FOL 75V 607-146, MS BODLEY 264/ FOL 76 607-147, MS BODLEY 264/ FOL 76V 607-148, MS BODLEY 264/ FOL 77 607-149, MS BODLEY 264/ FOL 77V 607-150, MS BODLEY 264/ FOL 78 607-151, MS BODLEY 264/ FOL 78V 607-152, MS BODLEY 264/ FOL 79 607-153, MS BODLEY 264/ FOL 79V 607-154, MS BODLEY 264/ FOL 80 607-155, MS BODLEY 264/ FOL 80V 607-156, MS BODLEY 264/ FOL 81 607-157, MS BODLEY 264/ FOL 81V 607-158, MS BODLEY 264/ FOL 82 607-159, MS BODLEY 264/ FOL 82V 607-160, MS BODLEY 264/ FOL 83 607-161, MS BODLEY 264/ FOL 83V 607-162, MS BODLEY 264/ FOL 84 607-163, MS BODLEY 264/ FOL 84V 607-164, MS BODLEY 264/ FOL 85 607-165, MS BODLEY 264/ FOL 85V 607-166, MS BODLEY 264/ FOL 86 607-167, MS BODLEY 264/ FOL 86V 607-168, MS BODLEY 264/ FOL 87 607-169, MS BODLEY 264/ FOL 87V 607-170, MS BODLEY 264/ FOL 88 607-171, MS BODLEY 264/ FOL 88V 607-172, MS BODLEY 264/ FOL 89 607-173, MS BODLEY 264/ FOL 89V 607-174, MS BODLEY 264/ FOL 90 607-175, MS BODLEY 264/ FOL 90V 607-176, MS BODLEY 264/ FOL 91 607-177, MS BODLEY 264/ FOL 91V 607-178, MS BODLEY 264/ FOL 92 607-179, MS BODLEY 264/ FOL 92V 607-180, MS BODLEY 264/ FOL 93 607-181, MS BODLEY 264/ FOL 93V 607-182, MS BODLEY 264/ FOL 94 607-183, MS BODLEY 264/ FOL 94V 607-184, MS BODLEY 264/ FOL 95 607-185, MS BODLEY 264/ FOL 95V 607-186, MS BODLEY 264/ FOL 96 607-187, MS BODLEY 264/ FOL 96V 607-188, MS BODLEY 264/ FOL 97 607-189, MS BODLEY 264/ FOL 97V 607-190, MS BODLEY 264/ FOL 98 607-191, MS BODLEY 264/ FOL 98V 607-192, MS BODLEY 264/ FOL 99 607-193, MS BODLEY 264/ FOL 99V 607-194, MS BODLEY 264/ FOL 100 607-195, MS BODLEY 264/ FOL 100V 607-196

*PROVENANCE FLEMISH

*DATE EXECUTED 14TH/1338-44

*LANGUAGE FRENCH

*ARTIST/ SCHOOL DE GRISE/ JEHAN

*TYPE OF MANUSCRIPT ROMANCE

*CONTENTS ROMANCE OF ALEXANDER PART 1 607/1-196, LITERATURE/ ROMANCE OF ALEXANDER 607/1-196, ALEXANDER/ ROMANCE 607/1-196, PALACE OF NECTANEBUS 607-1, WATER MILL 607-1, SHIPS ANCHORED IN RIVER 607-1, FOX PULLS GOOSE INTO LAIR 607-1, ALEXANDER'S LIFE/ FOUR SCENES 607-2, ALEXANDER'S BIRTH 607-2, PRESENTATION OF ALEXANDER 607-2, ALEXANDER'S DREAM 607-2, ALEXANDER TAMES BUCEPHALUS 607-2, INITIAL HISTORIATED WITH DESK AND GROTESQUE 607-3, MUSICIAN/ BOY PLAYS STRINGED INSTRUMENT 607-3, CROSSBOWMAN SHOOTS BOY 607-3, CHURN 607-3, LADY AND TONSURED MAN HOLD HANDS 607-3, BOXING GROTESQUES 607-3, TEXT PAGE WITH INITIAL 607-4, TEXT PAGES WITH BIRDS 607/5-11, TEXT PAGE WITH INITIALS 607-12, TEXT PAGES WITH BIRDS AND HARES 607/13-21, BAGPIPES PLAYED BY BOY 607-22, FLUTE HELD BY GROTESQUE 607-22,

TEXT PAGES WITH BIRDS AND HARES 607/23-37, ALEXANDER IN TENT
WITH TWO KNIGHTS 607-38, FORT ON BOATS ERECTED BY ALEXANDER
607-38, SIEGE OF TYRE 607-38, SHAWM PLAYED BY HARE IN LOWER
MARGIN 607-38, TABOR AND SHAWM HELD BY APE 607-38, ALEXANDER
IN TENT 607-39, BATTLE BETWEEN GREEKS AND GEZITES 607-39,
EUMENIDES IN DESPAIR 607-39, ALEXANDER NOT TOLD HELP IS NEEDED
607-39, BIRD CATCHING IN LOWER MARGIN 607-39, DANCERS WITH
ANIMAL HEADS 607-39, INITIAL D ILLUMINATED 607-40, HARE
JUMPING IN LOWER MARGIN 607-40, NUNS PUSHED IN BARROW BY BOY
607-40, TEXT PAGES WITH BIRDS AND HARES 607/41-80, MANDORA
PLAYED BY BOY 607-43, BAGPIPES PLAYED BY GROTESQUE 607-48, BOY
HOLDS MIRROR 607-52, REBEC PLAYED BY BOY 607-54, BAGPIPER
BETWEEN COLUMNS 607-57, TABOR HELD BY BOY 607-59, GOAT AND
BIRD IN LEFT MARGIN 607-60, HAWKING IN LEFT MARGIN 607-61,
PSALTERY AND TRUMPET 607-65, TRUMPET/ DOUBLE 607-66, ORGAN/
PORTATIVE 607-67, BAGPIPER 607-69, SWORD POINT BALANCED ON
BOY'S CHIN 607-76, DOG AND CROUCHING LION 607-79, SOLDIERS
MOUNTED AT CASTLE DOOR 607-81, KING LEADS SOLDIERS 607-81,
BRUNHILDE OR BESSUS TORN APART BY HORSES 607-81, HORSES TEAR
BRUNHILDE ASUNDER 607-81, ALEXANDER AT JERUSALEM 607-82,
VIRGIN AND CHILD ON BANNER 607-82, PRIEST IN CHASUBLE HOLDS
CHARTER WITH SEALS 607-82, ALEXANDER IN TENT WITH SEVEN BARONS
607-82, ALEXANDER AND SOLDIERS FACE PERSIAN HORSEMEN 607-82,
DARIUS IN TENT WITH KNEELING MESSENGER 607-82,TRUMPETER AN
DANCING BOY IN LOWER MARGIN 607-82, BAGPIPER 607-83, PIPE AN
TABOR 607-83, PLOW DRAWN BY HORSE IN LOWER MARGIN 607-83, TEXT
PAGES WITH BIRDS/ HARES/ MONKEYS 607/84-92, ALEXANDER STANDS
BEFORE DARIUS LYING ON BED 607-93, INITIAL INSET WITH DARIUS
STABBED 607-93, DARIUS STABBED BY TWO MEN 607-93, WINDMILL/
BOY CARRIES SACK 607-93, TEXT PAGE WITH BIRDS AND HARE 607-94,
ALEXANDER IN GLASS DIVING BELL 607-95, DIVING BELL 607-95,
BAGPIPER 607-95, TILTING/ TWO BOYS ON DOG AND DONKEY 607-95,
COCK FIGHT 607-95, TEXT PAGES WITH BIRDS AND INITIALS
607/96-97, ALEXANDER AND PORUS FACING TROOP OF HORSEME
607-98, ASSAULT ON CITY OF PORUS 607-98, ALEXANDER CLIMBS
LADDER INTO CASTLE 607-98, DANCING/ FIVE BOYS IN HOODS I
LOWER MARGIN 607-98, PORUS ENTRUSTING HIS DAUGHTER TO CANDAC
607-99, BAGPIPER AND BIRD BETWEEN COLUMNS 607-99, TRUMPE
BLOWN BY BOY 607-99, FOX WITH LAMB IN LOWER MARGIN 607-99
TEXT PAGES WITH BIRDS/ HARES/ MONKEYS 607/100-103, ALEXANDE
FACES SIX BLACK BEASTS 607-104, STAG CHASED BY DOG IN LOWE
MARGIN 607-104, PUPPET SHOW WATCHED BY THREE GIRLS 607-104
ALEXANDER MAKES SIGN TO MEN IN BOAT 607-105, BOYS/ NAKED I
LOWER MARGIN 607-105, ALEXANDER AND MEN DEFEND THEMSELVE
AGAINST LIONS 607-106, SWORD AND TARGE HELD BY GROTESQU
607-106, ALEXANDER DRIVES SPEAR INTO MOUTH OF DRAGON 607-107
DRAGON/ ALEXANDER KILLS 607-107, NUN HOLDS HANDS OUT AGAINS
NAKED BOY 607-107, ALEXANDER AMONG FLAMING FAGGOTS AND BEAST
607-108, BEASTS WITH FEMALE HEADS AND KERCHIEFS 607-108
ALEXANDER BY CITY OF PORUS 607-109, PORUS' CITY DECLARE
TWENTY DAY TRUCE 607-109, MONKEY SCRATCHING IN UPPER MARGI
607-109, ALEXANDER IN DISGUISE 607-109, PORUS AT CITY GAT
607-109, PORUS THRONED 607-110, ALEXANDER IN DISGUISE HOLD
REINS OF HORSE 607-110, ALEXANDER FACES PORUS WHO ATTACKS HI
607-111, CASTLE SUPPORTED ON ELEPHANTS 607-111, ELEPHANT
SUPPORT CASTLE 607-111, MUSICIANS WITH MANDORA AND BAGPIPE
607-111, TEXT PAGE WITH INITIALS 607-112, BATTLE BETWEE
ALEXANDER AND PORUS 607-113, GROTESQUES FIGHT IN UPPER MARGI
607-113, LADY HOLDS OUT HEART TO YOUTH IN LOWER MARGI
607-113, TEXT PAGE WITH BIRDS 607-114, BATTLE SCENE/ ENCOUNTE
OF HORSEMEN 607-115, GAME OF DRAUGHTS 607-115, GAME ON MORRI
BOARD 607-115, TEXT PAGE WITH INITIALS 607-116, ALEXANDER AN
THREE INDIANS 607-117, LADY HOLDS OUT BAG TO YOUTH 607-118
ALEXANDER REFUSES TO SACRIFICE TO GOLD IDOLS 607-119, IDOLS
GOLD IN STONE ALTAR 607-119, SCYTHE AND SICKLE 607-119
ALEXANDER WOUNDS ELEPHANT 607-120, ARCHER SHOOTS AT HARES I
LOWER MARGIN 607-120,SOLDIERS ATTACK DRAGON 607-121, GAME O
BOWLS 607-121, ALEXANDER MEETS HAIRY BEARDED MEN WHO RETREA
607-122, CROSS SAW USED BY GIRL AND YOUTH 607-122, ALEXANDE
TOUCHES INSCRIPTION ON ALTAR 607-123, GAME OF DICE 607-123
GAME OF WHIPPING TOPS 607-123, MONKEY JUGGLING WITH PLATE AN
STICKS 607-123, ALEXANDER ADDRESSES FOUR KNIGHTS 607-124, GAM

OF HOOP JUMPING 607-124, ALEXANDER'S DREAM/ FIVE DRAGONS DSECEND 607-125, DRAGONS DESCEND FROM CLOUDS 607-125, BUCEPHALUS HIDES HEAD UNDER ALEXANDER'S MANTLE 607-125, GAME OF STILTS 607-125, TEXT PAGE WITH BIRDS AND HARE 607-126, MONKEY JUGGLING IN RIGHT MARGIN 607-127, ALEXANDER MOUNTED WITH SHIELD 607-127, ALEXANDER READS INSCRIPTION 607-127, BUCEPHALUS WITH LION SHIELD ON SADDLE 607-127, ALEXANDER LIFTS LID OF TOMB AND DEVIL EMERGES 607-127, DEVIL EMERGES FROM TOMB 607-127, ARMY WITH LION BANNERS AND CART 607-127, ALEXANDER'S MEN WITH WOMEN WHO LIVE IN WATER 607-128, ALEXANDER'S MEN ATTACK HAIRY HORNED MEN 607-128, INITIAL HISTORIATED WITH ALEXANDER AND HAIRY MEN 607-129, ALEXANDER AND HAIRY MEN 607-129, TOURNAMENT SCENE 607-129, KNIGHT RAISES HAND TO LADY HOLDING HELMET 607-129, KNIGHTS WITH CLOSED VISORS TILT 607-129, MONKEY CHASES BUTTERFLY IN RIGHT MARGIN 607-129, ALEXANDER AT FEAST 607-130, MEN CARRY BANNERS AND SHIELDS 607-130, MASONS BUILD HEXAGONAL TOWER 607-130, ENOCH BATHES IN FOUNTAIN AGAINST ALEXANDER'S ORDERS 607-130, FOUNTAINS/ EACH WITH A CANOPY 607-130, ALEXANDER LEADS THREE MOUNTED FIGURES TO TOWER 607-130, DEVIL WITH HOOFED HANDS AND FEET DRAGGED INTO TOWER 607-131, ALEXANDER ENTHRONED WITH TWO BEARDED MEN 607-132, FIERY BRANDS FALL FROM CLOUDS ON FIVE KNIGHTS 607-132, ALEXANDER AND MOUNTED KNIGHTS IN LOWER MARGIN 607-133, LABORERS BURY SEVEN MEN KILLED BY FIRE 607-133,ALEXANDER AT WELL-HEAD AND KNEELING MESSENGER 607-134, KING CHASES GROTESQUE CARRYING OFF LADY 607-134, ALEXANDER WITH TWO OLD MEN 607-135, PIPE AND DRUM 607-135, ALEXANDER MOUNTS BRIDGE GUARDED BY NAKED MEN 607-136, GAME OF HOODMAN BLIND IN LOWER MARGIN 607-136, TEXT PAGE WITH BIRD 607-137, ALEXANDER MEETS TWO LADIES WHO LIVE IN WOODS 607-138, LADIES LIVE IN GROUND ALL WINTER 607-138, ALEXANDER/ OLD MAN/ KNIGHT BY FOUNTAIN 607-139, HUNTING SCENE IN LOWER MARGIN 607-139, JOURNEY TO TREES OF SUN AND MOON 607-140, TREES OF SUN AND MOON 607-140, ALEXANDER AT FEAST 607-140, FEAST SCENE 607-140, ALEXANDER'S DEATH PROPHESIED 607-141, FEAST SCENE WITH KING PORUS 607-142, BATTLE BETWEEN ALEXANDER AND PORUS 607-143, PORUS LIES AT ALEXANDER'S FEET 607-143, ALEXANDER STANDS OVER DEAD BUCEPHALUS 607-144,MASON CLIMBS LADDER CARRYING HOD 607-144, BLIND MEN LED BY BOY IN LOWER MARGIN 607-144, ALEXANDER AND PORUS JOUST 607-145, BATH HOUSE SCENE/ NUDE BATHERS 607-145, PORUS DIES 607-146, PORUS' FUNERAL 607-147, COFFIN OF PORUS PLACED IN VAULT 607-147, BEAR WITH METAL COLLAR 607-147, MAN BALANCES BASIN ON STICK 607-147, PUPPET SHOW 607-147, DIVINUS PATER AND ANTIPATER RECEIVE LETTER 607-148, GAME ON MORRIS BOARD IN LOWER MARGIN 607-148, HUNTING SCENES WITH LADIES 607-149, BATTLE BETWEEN TWO TROOPS OF MOUNTED MEN 607-149, BLIND MEN WITH LEAD DOGS 607-150, DANCING BOYS WITH THREE TRUMPETERS 607-151, BATTLE OF MOUNTED SOLDIERS 607-151, CANDACE SPEAKS TO ALEXANDER AND KNIGHTS 607-152, BOYS BALANCING SWORD AND WHEEL 607-152, CANDEOLUS GIVES MESSAGE TO ALEXANDER'S QUEEN 607-153, DOCTOR AND PATIENT IN LOWER MARGIN 607-153, FRIAR IN PULPIT PREACHES 607-153, ALEXANDER AND QUEEN SPEAK TO YOUTH 607-154, FUNERAL OF FOX IN LOWER MARGIN 607-154, TEXT PAGE WITH BIRDS AND HARE 607-155, ALEXANDER STEPS INTO BASKET SUSPENDED BY CHAINS 607-156, HAWKING SCENE IN LOWER MARGIN 607-156, ALEXANDER SITS IN HOUSE SUSPENDED BY GRIFFINS 607-157, DANCING MONKEYS IN LOWER MARGIN 607-157, ALEXANDER FIGHTS FOUR FLYING GRIFFINS 607-158,HARES CAPTURE HUNTER 607-158, ARMED YOUTH KNEELS BEFORE SEATED MAN 607-159, ALEXANDER AND SIX MOUNTED SOLDIERS GO TO BATTLE 607-159, HORSE HEAVILY PROTECTED BY ARMOUR 607-159, MONKEYS GUIDE BARREL TO OR FROM HOUSE 607-159, ADMIRAL AND MEN EMERGE FROM CASTLE DOOR 607-160, KNIGHTS IN TRAINING IN LOWER MARGIN 607-160, QUINTAIN REVOLVING ON POLE 607-160, BOYS DRAG WOODEN HORSE ON WHEELS 607-160, COOKING SCENE/ BRICK OVEN 607-161, LADY OUTSIDE WOODEN HUT 607-161, ADMIRAL SENDS MESSENGERS TO ALEXANDER TELLING HIM TO LEAVE 607-162, ALEXANDER TOLD TO LEAVE COUNTRY 607-162, WAGON WITH CASK/ BUNDLE/ SHIELDS 607-162, CAULDRON OVER FIRE 607-162, COOKING GEESE OR SWANS ON SPIT 607-162, TENTS/ CASTLE/ KNIGHTS ON BATTLEMENTS 607-162,BATTLE SCENE/ ALEXANDER WITH MOUNTED SOLDIERS 607-163, ALEXANDER WITH MOUNTED SOLDIERS 607-163, LEATHER WORKERS/ MONKEY HAMMERS AT

SADDLE 607-163, BLACKSMITHS WORK AT FORGE 607-163, BATTL
SCENE OF ALEXANDER AND ADMIRAL 607-164, ALEXANDER AND ADMIRA
BATTLE 607-164, MUSICIANS AND DANCERS IN LOWER MARGIN 607-164
ORGAN PLAYED BY LADY IN INITIAL L 607-164, TEXT PAGE WIT
BIRDS AND INITIALS 607-165, ADMIRAL SENDS MESSENGER TO RANSO
PRISONERS 607-166, SOLDIERS MOUNTED FIGHT WITH SPEARS AN
SWORDS 607-167, BOY RECEIVES MONEY FROM OLD MAN 607-167, BO
LIES ON LONG TRESTLE TABLE 607-167, TEXT PAGES WITH BIRD
607/168-171, TOWN SURROUNDS FOUR SCENES 607-172, ADMIRA
ENTHRONED WITH SCEPTRE AND KNEELING PRIEST 607-172, BULL BEIN
LED TO SACRIFICIAL ALTAR BY PRIEST 607-172, MOUNTED ME
607-172, ALEXANDER RECEIVES MESSAGE FROM ADMIRAL 607-172
ARCHERS LOAD AND FIRE CROSSBOWS IN LOWER MARGIN 607-172
CROSSBOWS 607-172, KNIGHTS/ BOYS IN TRAINING 607-173, HOUND
CHASE HARES IN UPPER MARGIN 607-173, TEXT PAGE WITH BIRDS
HOUND AND HARE 607-174, ADMIRAL ENTHRONED TAKES COUNSEL WIT
KING SALIGOR 607-175, CHILDREN PLAY IN LOWER MARGIN 607-175
HARES/ STAG AND DOG IN UPPER MARGIN 607-175, ADMIRAL'S MOUNTE
SOLDIERS EMERGE FROM CITY GATE 607-176, CHILDREN PLAYING GAME
IN LOWER MARGIN 607-176, MAN BENDING OVER PERFORMS RUDE TRIC
607-176, KING IN TENT WITH SOLDIER 607-177, CHILDREN PLAYIN
AND FIGHTING IN LOWER MARGIN 607-177, COCK ON STILTS 607-177
BOYS FIGHT WITH CLUBS AND SHIELDS 607-177, KNIGHTS TILTING I
LEFT COLUMN 607-178, DANCING GOAT AND DRUMMER BOY IN LOWE
MARGIN 607-178, BATTLE BETWEEN TWO MOUNTED TROOPS 607-179
KNIGHTS TILT IN LOWER MARGIN 607-179, ALEXANDER HAS SQUIR
ADJUST HIS BELT 607-180, SQUIRE ADJUSTS BELT OF ARMOURE
ALEXANDER 607-180, CHESS GAME IN LOWER MARGIN 607-180, HUNTIN
SCENE IN LOWER MARGIN 607-180, BATTLE SCENE/ MELEE OF MOUNTE
MEN 607-181, ALEXANDER AND ADMIRAL BATTLE 607-181, CHILDRE
PLAYING IN LOWER MARGIN 607-181, TEXT PAGES WITH BIRDS AN
HARES 607/182-183, BATTLE SCENE/ MELEE OF MOUNTED MEN 607-184
ALEXANDER AND ADMIRAL BATTLE 607-184, TEACHING/ MONKEYS A
SCHOOL 607-184, BATTLE SCENE/ FIGHT BETWEEN ARMOURED TROOP
607-185, ALEXANDER WATCHES AS ONE OF MEN IS SPEARED 607-185
CROSS BOWS IN LOWER MARGIN 607-185, HUNTING SCENE IN LOWE
MARGIN 607-185, ALEXANDER UNHORSES AND KILLS ADMIRAL 607-186
INITIAL L INSET WITH LADY PLAYING TONGS AND JAWBONES 607-186
KNIGHTS/ BANNERS/ SHIELDS/ CASTLE IN LOWER MARGIN 607-186
ADMIRAL'S COFFIN IN SHRINE 607-187, FRUIT GATHERING/ BO
CLIMBS TREE 607-187, MONKEYS READING BOOKS 607-187, ALEXANDE
SEATED ON DOG-HEADED CHAIR 607-188, GROTESQUE AND WILD MAN I
UPPER MARGIN 607-188,HORSE KICKING DRUM IN LOWER MARGI
607-188, QUEEN EUMIXIE'S DREAM INTERPRETED BY WOMAN 607-189
ALEXANDER AS EAGLE CARRIES OFF PEACOCKS 607-189, QUEE
SLEEPING ON BED/ FIVE LADIES WATCH 607-189, QUEEN EUMIXIE O
THRONE WITH DAMSEL 607-190, DANCING IN LOWER MARGIN 607-190
LADIES ON HORSEBACK LED BY MAN 607-191, LADIES ON HORSEBAC
607-191, CHILDREN PLAYING IN LOWER MARGIN 607-191, ALEXANDE
RECEIVES MESSAGE FROM QUEEN 607-192,NUNS CARRIED ON BACKS O
MONKS 607-192, WHEELBARROW WITH COGGED WHEEL 607-192, TEX
PAGE WITH BIRDS 607-193, ALEXANDER AND QUEEN TALK 607-194
COCK FIGHT IN LOWER MARGIN 607-194, ALEXANDER TOLD NOT T
TRUST DIVINUS AND ANTIPATER 607-195, KNIGHTS AS BOYS I
TRAINING IN LOWER MARGIN 607-195, TEXT PAGE WITH BIRDS 607-19

*$ABSTRACT 608
*LIBRARY BODLEIAN
*SLIDE SET TITLE ROMANCE OF ALEXANDER PART 2
*NEGATIVE REFERENCE ROLL 244K
*RENTAL FEE $2.85
*COMMENTS THIS SET, TOGETHER WITH 603-607, REPRODUCES EVER
PAGE IN MS BODLEY 264. THE ILLUMINATIONS CONSIST C
HISTORIATED INITIALS, OFTEN CONTAINING HUMAN FACES, C
PICTORIAL PANELS, AND OF DECORATED MARGINS DEPICTING SCENES C
EVERY-DAY LIFE, SPORTS AND PASTIMES, MUSICAL INSTRUMENTS AN
NUMEROUS BIRDS, HARES, AND GROTESQUES.
*TITLE OF MANUSCRIPT ROMANCE OF ALEXANDER
*SHELFMARK MS BODLEY 264/ FOL 101V 608-1, MS BODLEY 264/ F
102 608-2, MS BODLEY 264/ FOL 102V 608-3, MS BODLEY 264/ F

103 608-4, MS BODLEY 264/ FOL 103V 608-5, MS BODLEY 264/ FOL 104 608-6, MS BODLEY 264/ FOL 104V 608-7, MS BODLEY 264/ FOL 105 608-8, MS BODLEY 264/ FOL 105V 608-9, MS BODLEY 264/ FOL 106 608-10, MS BODLEY 264/ FOL 106V 608-11, MS BODLEY 264/ FOL 107 608-12, MS BODLEY 264/ FOL 107V 608-13, MS BODLEY 264/ FOL 108 608-14, MS BODLEY 264/ FOL 108V 608-15, MS BODLEY 264/ FOL 109 608-16, MS BODLEY 264/ FOL 109V 608-17
*PROVENANCE FLEMISH
*DATE EXECUTED 14TH/1338-44
*LANGUAGE FRENCH
*ARTIST/ SCHOOL DE GRISE/ JEHAN
*TYPE OF MANUSCRIPT ROMANCE
*CONTENTS ROMANCE OF ALEXANDER PART 2 608/1-17, LITERATURE/ ROMANCE OF ALEXANDER 608/1-17, ALEXANDER/ ROMANCE 608/1-17, ALEXANDER ADDRESSES TWO MOUNTED MEN 608-1, KNIGHTS IN ARMOUR TILTING 608-1, KNIGHT BEFORE CITY GATEWAY 608-1, KNIGHTS TILTING WITH BROKEN SPEARS 608-1, MUSICIANS/ TRUMPETS/ BUGLE/ DRUMS 608-1, LADY PRESENTS HELMET TO YOUTH IN LOWER MARGIN 608-1, KNIGHTS TILT IN LOWER MARGIN 608-1, TEXT REFERS TO EPISODE OF DUKE MELCHIO 608-1, CART AND BAGGAGE CARRIERS IN LOWER MARGIN 608-2, LUTE HELD BY LADY IN UPPER MARGIN 608-2, TEXT PAGE 608-3, TEXT PAGE WITH BIRDS 608/4-6, FEAST WITH ALEXANDER AND THREE MEN 608-7, ALEXANDER AT FEAST 608-7, GIRL KNEELING ON BOARD HELD BY YOUTHS 608-7, SWORDS BALANCED ON HILTS 608-7, BAGPIPES AND TABOR 608-7, CITY GATE/ MEN BLOW TRUMPETS FROM WALL 608-8, KNIGHTS IN ARMOUR OUTSIDE TENT 608-8, MARRIAGE PROCESSION 608-8, TEXT PAGE WITH BIRDS 608-9, ALEXANDER ARMS FOR COMBAT 608-10, KNIGHTS AND SQUIRES AT MILITARY CAMP 608-10, DANCING IN LOWER MARGIN 608-10, TEXT PAGE WITH BIRDS 608-11, ALEXANDER FIGHTS LE DUC MALCHYSE 608-12, BATTLE SCENE/ MELEE OF HORSEMEN 608-12, ALEXANDER CHASES MALCHYSE INTO CITY 608-12, BLACKSMITH SHOES HORSE IN LOWER MARGIN 608-12, MUSICIANS IN LEFT COLUMN 608-12, TEXT PAGE WITH BIRDS 608-13, ALEXANDER'S MEN AND EMENIDUS TAKE CITY 608-14, ALEXANDER RECEIVES NEWS FROM KNEELING KNIGHT 608-14, ALEXANDER MEETS DAUGHTER OF MALCHYSE 608-15, CHILDREN PLAYING IN LOWER MARGIN 608-15, ALEXANDER WATCHES MEN FENCING 608-16, FENCING 608-16, CRIPPLES FIGHT IN LOWER MARGIN 608-16, ESCHUIE RECEIVES KEYS FROM KNEELING MAN 608-17, CHESS GAME IN LOWER MARGIN 608-17, INITIAL C INSET WITH LADY PLAYING HARP 608-17

*$ABSTRACT 609
*LIBRARY BODLEIAN
*SLIDE SET TITLE LACTANTIUS
*NEGATIVE REFERENCE ROLL 244L
*RENTAL FEE $3.05
*COMMENTS DETAILS ILLUSTRATE THE MEDIEVAL PRACTICE OF CORRECTION AND ANNOTATION.
*SHELFMARK MS CANON PAT LAT 131/ FOL 1 609-1, MS CANON PAT LAT 131/ FOL 1V-2 609-2, MS CANON PAT LAT 131/ FOL 2V 609-3, MS CANON PAT LAT 131/ FOL 3V-4 609-4, MS CANON PAT LAT 131/ FOL 8V-9 609-5, MS CANON PAT LAT 131/ FOL 13V 609-6, MS CANON PAT LAT 131/ FOL 13 609-7, MS CANON PAT LAT 131/ FOL 43 609-8, MS CANON PAT LAT 131/ FOL 53V 609-9, MS CANON PAT LAT 131/ FOL 73V 609-10, MS CANON PAT LAT 131/ FOL 76 609-11, MS CANON PAT LAT 131/ FOL 81V 609/12-13, MS CANON PAT LAT 131/ FOL 90 609-14, MS CANON PAT LAT 131/ FOL 95 609-15, MS CANON PAT LAT 131/ FOL 107V-108 609-16, MS CANON PAT LAT 131/ FOL 108V 609-17, MS CANON PAT LAT 131/ FOL 128V 609-18, MS CANON PAT LAT 131/ FOL 134 609-19, MS CANON PAT LAT 131/ FOL 135V-136 609-20, MS CANON PAT LAT 131/ FOL 136V 609-21
*PROVENANCE FRENCH
*DATE EXECUTED 13TH
*LANGUAGE LATIN
*AUTHOR LACTANTIUS
*TYPE OF MANUSCRIPT TREATISE
*CONTENTS SCRIBAL PRACTICES OF CORRECTION 609/1-21, WHOLE PAGE 609-1, DOUBLE OPENING 609-2, WHOLE PAGE 609-3, DOUBLE OPENING 609-4, DOUBLE OPENING 609-5, WHOLE PAGE 609-6, WHOLE PAGE 609-7, WHOLE PAGE 609-8, WHOLE PAGE 609-9, WHOLE PAGE 609-10,

WHOLE PAGE 609-11, WHOLE PAGE 609-12, UPPER LEFT COLUMN 609-13, UPPER RIGHT SECTION OF PAGE 609-14, LOWER LEFT HALF OF PAGE 609-15, DOUBLE OPENING 609-16, WHOLE PAGE 609-17, WHOLE PAGE 609-18, WHOLE PAGE 609-19, DOUBLE OPENING 609-20, WHOLE PAGE 609-21

*$ABSTRACT 610
*LIBRARY BODLEIAN
*SLIDE SET TITLE WOODCUTS
*NEGATIVE REFERENCE ROLL 245
*RENTAL FEE $3.15
*SHELFMARK MS RAWL D 403/ FOL 2V-3 610-1, MS RAWL D 403/ FOL 3V 610-2, PR ARCH G F 13 610-3, PR ARCH G F 14 610-4. PR ARCH E 35 610-5, PR ARCH G F 16 610-6, PR ARCH 6 Q I 15 610-7, PR DOUCE 96 610-8, MS DOUCE 133 610-9, PR ARCH G F 5 610-10, PR AUCT 6 Q IV 20 610-11, MS DOUCE 58 610-12, MS BARLOW 47 610-13, PR ARCH G F 7 610/14-15, PR ARCH G F 6 610/16-17, PR ARCH G B 4 610-18, PR ARCH G F 8 610-19, PR GOUGH MISSAL 177/ FOL 17V 610-20, PR AUCT M 3 16 1 610/21-22, MS CANON LITURG 334/ FOL 3V 610-23
*PROVENANCE ENGLISH 610/1-2, ENGLISH? 610-3, ENGLISH 610/4-5, ENGLISH/ LONDON 610-6, GERMAN/ SOUTH 610-7, GERMAN 610/8-9, GERMAN/ SWABIA 610/10-12, GERMAN/ BAVARIA 610/13-17, GERMAN/ MAINZ 610-18, GERMAN/ AUGSBURG 610-19, FRENCH 610-20, DUTCH/ NETHERLANDS 610/21-22, GERMAN/ SOUTH 610-23
*DATE EXECUTED 15TH/1490-95 610-1, 15TH/1498 610-2, 15TH/C1495 610/3-4, 15TH/C1450 610-5, 15TH/C1484 610-6, 15TH/C1487 610-7, 15TH/1460-70? 610-8, 15TH 610-9, 15TH/ 2ND HALF 610-10, 15TH/1470-80 610-11, 15TH/1491? 610-12, 15TH/C1460 610/13-15, 15TH/1460-70 610/16-17, 15TH/1457-58 610-18, 15TH/C1490 610-19, 15TH/C1480-90 610-20, 15TH/1470-80 610/21-22, 15TH/C1440-50 610-23
*CONTENTS WOODCUTS FROM 15TH-CENTURY MSS AND BOOKS 610/1-23, PITY WITH INDULGENCE INSCRIPTION 610-1, INDULGENCE INSCRIPTION 610-1, TRENDLE OF ST GREGORY 610-1, ST GREGORY'S TRENDLE 610-1, LAST JUDGMENT/ INSCRIBED ARMA BEATE BIRGITTE DE SYON 610-2, CHRIST SHOWS FIVE WOUNDS AND PASSION INSTRUMENTS 610-3, PASSION INSTRUMENTS 610-3, CHRIST SHOWS FIVE WOUNDS AND PASSION INSTRUMENTS 610-4, PASSION INSTRUMENTS 610-4, INSCRIPTION/ EX DOMO JHESU DE BETHELEEM 610-4, PITY WITH INDULGENCE INSCRIPTION 610-5, INDULGENCE INSCRIPTION 610-5, MASSACRE OF THE HOLY INNOCENTS 610-6, CRUCIFIXION 610-7, ST FRANCIS RECOVERS THE STIGMATA 610-8, STIGMATA/ ST FRANCIS RECOVERS 610-8, ST BARBARA WITH CHALICE AND HOST 610-9, MADONNA AND CHILD 610-10, ST BARBARA 610-10, ST GREGORY'S MASS 610-10, ST CATHERINE 610-10, ST MARY MAGDALENE CARRIED BY ANGELS 610-11, ST FRANCIS RECEIVES THE STIGMATA 610-12, STIGMATA/ ST FRANCIS RECEIVES 610-12, CHRIST BEFORE PILATE WHO WASHES HANDS 610-13, RESURRECTION OF CHRIST 610-14, CHRIST'S RESURRECTION 610-14, DUPLICATE OF FRAME 14 610-15, LAST SUPPER/ CHRIST WASHES ST PETER'S FEET 610-16, CHRIST WASHES ST PETER'S FEET 610-16, CHRIST IN GARDEN OF GETHSEMENE 610-17, CRUCIFIXION 610-18, VISITATION 610-19, MADONNA AND CHILD/ TWO PORTRAYALS 610-19, ST CATHERINE? 610-19, MONSTRANCE 610-19, CHRIST RISEN APPEARS TO KNEELING PILGRIM 610-20, TOWER OF WISDOM INSCRIBED WITH VIRTUES 610-21,VIRTUES INSCRIBED ON TOWER OF WISDOM 610-21, ST JEROME IN DESERT 610-22, CRUCIFIXION 610-23

*$ABSTRACT 611
*LIBRARY BODLEIAN
*SLIDE SET TITLE TREE OF LIFE AND WATER OF LIFE
*NEGATIVE REFERENCE ROLL 247A
*RENTAL FEE $2.30
*COMMENTS ILLUSTRATIONS OF REV 22/VERSES 1-2 SELECTED FROM SIX ENGLISH 13TH-14TH CENTURY APOCALYPSE MSS.
*SHELFMARK MS AUCT D 4 17/ FOL 22 611-1, MS TANNER 184/ FOL 76 611-2, MS ASHMOLE 753/ FOL 38V 611-3, MS CANON BIBL LAT 62/

FOL 38V 611-4, MS UNIVERSITY COLLEGE 100/ FOL 93V 611-5, MS BODLEY 401/ FOL 68V 611-6
*PROVENANCE ENGLISH 611/1-3, ENGLISH/ PETERBOROUGH 611-4, ENGLISH 611/5-6
*DATE EXECUTED 13TH/C1250-60 611-1, 13TH/ 3RD QUARTER 611-2, 14TH/C1300 611-3, 14TH/ EARLY 611-4, 14TH 611-5, 14TH/ MID 611-6
*LANGUAGE LATIN 611/1-2, FRENCH AND LATIN 611-3, LATIN 611/4-5, FRENCH 611-6
*ARTIST/ SCHOOL SCHOOL OF ST ALBANS/ BASED ON MODEL OF 611-1
*TYPE OF MANUSCRIPT APOCALYPSE
*CONTENTS TREE OF LIFE AND WATER OF LIFE 611/1-6, REV 22/VERSES 1-2/ TREE AND WATER OF LIFE 611/1-6, TREE AND WATER OF LIFE 611-1, WATER OF LIFE 611-2, TREE AND WATER OF LIFE 611-3, WATER OF LIFE 611-4, TREE AND WATER OF LIFE 611-5, TREE AND WATER OF LIFE 611-6

*$ABSTRACT 612
*LIBRARY BODLEIAN
*SLIDE SET TITLE APOCALYPSE/ ENGLISH
*NEGATIVE REFERENCE ROLL 247B
*RENTAL FEE $3.60
*TITLE OF MANUSCRIPT APOCALYPSE
*SHELFMARK MS AUCT D 4 17/ FOL 1 612-1, MS AUCT D 4 17/ FOL 2V 612-2, MS AUCT D 4 17/ FOL 3 612-3, MS AUCT D 4 17/ FOL 3V 612-4, MS AUCT D 4 17/ FOL 7V 612-5, MS AUCT D 4 17/ FOL 8 612-6, MS AUCT D 4 17/ FOL 9 612-7, MS AUCT D 4 17/ FOL 9V 612-8, MS AUCT D 4 17/ FOL 10V 612-9, MS AUCT D 4 17/ FOL 11 612-10, MS AUCT D 4 17/ FOL 11V 612-11, MS AUCT D 4 17/ FOL 12 612-12, MS AUCT D 4 17/ FOL 12V 612-13, MS AUCT D 4 17/ FOL 13 612-14, MS AUCT D 4 17/ FOL 13V 612-15, MS AUCT D 4 17/ FOL 14V 612-16, MS AUCT D 4 17/ FOL 15 612-17, MS AUCT D 4 17/ FOL 15V 612-18, MS AUCT D 4 17/ FOL 16 612-19, MS AUCT D 4 17/ FOL 16V 612-20, MS AUCT D 4 17/ FOL 17 612-21, MS AUCT D 4 17/ FOL 17V 612-22, MS AUCT D 4 17/ FOL 18 612-23, MS AUCT D 4 17/ FOL 18V 612-24, MS AUCT D 4 17/ FOL 19 612-25, MS AUCT D 4 17/ FOL 19V 612-26, MS AUCT D 4 17/ FOL 20V 612-27, MS AUCT D 4 17/ FOL 21V 612-28, MS AUCT D 4 17/ FOL 22 612-29, MS AUCT D 4 17/ FOL 22V 612-30, MS AUCT D 4 17/ FOL 23 612-31, MS AUCT D 4 17/ FOL 23V 612-32
*PROVENANCE ENGLISH
*DATE EXECUTED 13TH/C1250-60
*LANGUAGE LATIN
*ARTIST/ SCHOOL SCHOOL OF ST ALBANS/ BASED ON MODEL OF
*TYPE OF MANUSCRIPT APOCALYPSE
*CONTENTS APOCALYPSE/ ENGLISH/ 13TH 612/1-32, ST JOHN OF PATMOS DISPUTES WITH IDOLATERS 612-1, BAPTISM OF DRUSIANA 612-1, ST JOHN EXILED AT PATMOS 612-2, ST JOHN OF PATMOS IN SHIP AT SEA 612-2, ST JOHN TOLD TO WRITE BOOK 612-3, ST JOHN KNEELS BEFORE CHRIST AMID SEVEN CANDLESTICKS 612-3, CHRIST AMID SEVEN CANDLESTICKS 612-3, SEVEN CANDELSTICKS 612-3, SEVEN CHURCHES 612-3, REV 01/VERSE 11/ ANGEL APPEARS TO ST JOHN 612-3, REV 01/VERSES 1-20/ SEVEN CHURCHES 612-3, ST JOHN'S VISION OF ENTHRONED DEITY 612-4, REV 04/VERSES 1-7/ ST JOHN'S VISION 612-4, SEVEN LAMPS 612-4, ST JOHN'S VISION OF GOD/ LAMB/ 24 ELDERS 612-4, REV 05/VERSE 1/ VISION OF LAMB 612-4, ANTICHRIST GIVES ORDERS TO SERVANT 612-5, EXECUTION OF THE FAITHFUL 612-5, ANTICHRIST'S DEATH BY FIRE FROM HEAVEN 612-5, TRUMPET/ SEVENTH SOUNDED/ 24 ELDERS KNEEL BEFORE GOD 612-6, REV 11/VERSES 15-17/ SEVENTH TRUMPET 612-6, ARK OF THE CONENANT REVEALED 612-6, REV 11/VERSE 19/ ARK OF THE CONVENANT 612-6, DRAGON CAST DOWN BY THREE ANGELS 612-7, REV 12/VERSE 9/ DRAGON CAST DOWN 612-7, ANGELS HOLD SCROLL WITH VERSE OF REV 12 612-9, DRAGON PERSECUTES WOMAN 612-8, REV 12/VERSE 13/ DRAGON PERSECUTES WOMAN 612-8, WOMAN GIVEN WINGS AND FLIES INTO WILDERNESS 612-8, REV 12/VERSE 14/ WOMAN FLIES INTO WILDERNESS 612-8, DRAGON GIVES POWER TO SEVEN-HEADED BEAST 612-9, REV 13/VERSES 2-3/ DRAGON AND SEVEN-HEADED BEAST 612-9, DRAGON WORSHIPPED BY MEN 612-9, REV 13/VERSE 4/ MEN WORSHIP DRAGON 612-9, BEAST WORSHIPPED BY MEN 612-10, REV 13/VERSE 4/ BEAST

WORSHIPPED 612-10, BEAST TRAMPLES CHRISTIAN SOLDIERS AND BLASPHEMES 612-10, REV 13/VERSES 6-10/ BEAST BLASPHEMES 612-10, BEAST/ SECOND EMERGES FROM EARTH 612-11, REV 13/VERSES 11-13/ SECOND BEAST EMERGES 612-11,BEAST/ SECOND ORDERS DEATH OF NONWORSHIPERS 612-11, REV 13/VERSE 15/ SECOND BEAST ORDERS DEATH 612-11, BEAST MARKS FOREHEADS OF BELIEVERS 612-12, REV 13/VERSES 16-18/ BEAST MARKS FOREHEADS 612-12, ST JOHN SEES VISION OF LAMB ON SION 612-12, REV 14/VERSES 1-3/ VISION OF LAMB 612-12, ANGEL FLIES WITH GOSPEL TO PREACH 612-13, REV 14/VERSES 6-7/ ANGEL WITH GOSPEL 612-13, ANGEL ANNOUNCES FALL OF BABYLON 612-13, FALL OF BABYLON ANNOUNCED 612-13, REV 14/VERSE 8/ FALL OF BABYLON 612-13, ANGEL/ THIRD WARNS OF WRATH OF GOD 612-14, REV 14/VERSES 9-10/ THIRD ANGEL WARNS 612-14, SOULS OF BLESSED DEAD RECEIVED INTO HEAVEN 612-14, REV 14/VERSE 13/ SOULS RECEIVED IN HEAVEN 612-14, HARVEST OF THE EARTH 612-15, REV 14/VERSES 14-16/ HARVEST OF THE EARTH 612-15, ANGEL CUTS GRAPES AND DROPS INTO WINEPRESS 612-15, DEMONS TREAD GRAPES AND BLOOD FLOWS 612-15, REV 14/VERSES 17-20/ WINEPRESS 612-15, ANGELS/ SEVEN RECEIVE VIALS OF WRATH 612-16, FIRE FILLS THE TEMPLE 612-16, REV 15/VERSES 6-8/ ANGELS RECEIVE VIALS 612-16, ANGEL/ FIRST POURS VIAL ON EARTH 612-16, REV 16/VERSE 2/ FIRST ANGEL POURS VIAL 612-16, OPENING OF FIFTH SEAL 612-17, SOULS GIVEN WHITE ROBES BY ANGELS 612-17, REV 06/VERSES 9-11/ SOULS GIVEN ROBES 612-17, OPENING OF THE SIXTH SEAL/ GREAT EARTHQUAKE 612-17, REV 06/VERSES 12-17/ FIFTH SEAL 612-17, ANGELS HOLD FOUR WINDS 612-18, REV 07/VERSES 1-3/ ANGELS HOLD WINDS 612-18, ST JOHN'S VISION OF THE MULTITUDE 612-18, REV 07/VERSES 9-17/ VISION OF MULTITUDE 612-18, OPENING OF THE SEVENTH SEAL/ SEVEN TRUMPETS 612-19, REV 08/VERSES 1-2/ SEVENTH SEAL 612-19, ANGEL STANDS BEFORE ALTAR WITH CENSER 612-19, REV 08/VERSES 3-4/ SEVEN TRUMPETS 612-19, ANGEL FILLS CENSER WITH FIRE AND CASTS IT 612-20, EARTHQUAKE/ THUNDER/ LIGHTNING 612-20, TRUMPET FIRST SOUNDED/ HAIL AND FIRE 612-20, REV 08/VERSES 5-7/ FIRST TRUMPET 612-20, TRUMPET/ SECOND AND THIRD SOUNDED 612-20, MOUNTAIN/ BURNING CAST INTO SEA 612-20, STAR/ GREAT FALLS FROM HEAVEN 612-20, REV 08/VERSES 8-11/ SECOND AND THIRD TRUMPETS 612-20, VIALS/ SECOND AND THIRD EMPTIED ON SEAS AND RIVERS 612-21, REV 16/VERSES 3-4/ SECOND AND THIRD VIALS 612-21, ST JOHN HEARS ANGELS PRAISE GOD 612-21, REV 16/VERSES 5-7/ ANGELS PRAISE GOD 612-21, VIAL/ FOURTH EMPTIED ON SEAT OF BEAST 612-22, REV 16/VERSES 10-11/ FOURTH VIAL 612-22, ANGEL PROCLAIMS FALL OF BABYLON 612-23, FALL OF BABYLON 612-23, REV 18/VERSES 1-3 AND 15-18/ FALL OF BABYLON 612-23, ANGEL CASTS MILLSTONE INTO SEA 612-23, MILLSTONE CAST INTO SEA 612-23, REV 18/VERSE 21/ MILLSTONE CAST INTO SEA 612-23, WHORE OF BABYLON LIES IN SMOKE 612-24, GOD ENTHRONED/ ELDERS WORSHIP 612-24, REV 19/VERSES 1-4/ ELDERS WORSHIP GOD 612-24, MARRIAGE SUPPER OF THE LAMB 612-24, REV 19/VERSES 7-8/ MARRIAGE OF THE LAMB 612-24, ANGEL REFUSES ST JOHN'S HOMAGE 612-25, REV 19/VERSES 9-10/ ANGEL AND ST JOHN 612-25, FAITHFUL AND TRUE TREAD WINEPRESS/ WHITE HORSE 612-25, REV 19/VERSES 11-15/ WINEPRESS 612-25, BIRDS CALLED TO EAT FLESH OF MEN 612-26, REV 19/VERSES 17-18/ BIRDS EAT FLESH 612-26, BEAST AND EARTHLY ARMIES MAKE WAR 612-26, REV 19/VERSE 19/ BEAST MAKES WAR 612-26, SOULS OF FAITHFUL ASCEND TO CHRIST 612-27, REV 20/VERSES 4-6/ FAITHFUL SOULS ASCEND 612-27,SATAN AND ARMY ARE DEVOURED BY FIRE FROM GOD 612-27, REV 20/VERSES 7-9/ SATAN DEVOURED BY FIRE 612-27, ST JOHN'S VISION OF NEW JERUSALEM 612-28, REV 21/VERSES 2-6/ VISION OF NEW JERUSALEM 612-28, ST JOHN LED BU ANGEL TO NEW JERUSALEM 612-28, REV 21/VERSE 9/ ST JOHN LED TO NEW JERUSALEM 612-28, WATER OF LIFE FLOWS FROM THRONE OF GOD 612-29, REV 22/VERSES 1-7/ WATER OF LIFE 612-29, ST JOHN'S HOMAGE TO ANGEL REFUSED 612-29, REV 22/VERSES 8-9/ ANGEL REFUSES JOHN'S HOMAGE 612-29, ST JOHN ADDRESSED BY GOD 612-30, ST JOHN RAISES DRUSIANA FROM DEAD 612-30, ST JOHN TELLS BROTHERS THEY ARE UNWORTHY 612-31, FALL OF THE TEMPLE OF DIANA 612-31, TEMPLE OF DIANA/ FALL 612-31, DIANA/ TEMPLE OF 612-31, ST JOHN ACCEPTS CHALLENGE OF ARISTODEMUS 612-32, ARISTODEMUS' CHALLEGE TO ST JOHN 612-32, ST JOHN OF PATMOS DIES/ SOUL CARRIED TO HEAVEN 612-32

*$ABSTRACT 613
*LIBRARY BODLEIAN
*SLIDE SET TITLE BODLEIAN EXHIBITION III
*NEGATIVE REFERENCE ROLL 247C
*RENTAL FEE $2.55
*TITLE OF MANUSCRIPT WHOLE BOOKE OF PSALMES 613/1-2, LIBER AMICORUM 613-3, SONGS OF INNOCENCE AND EXPERIENCE 613/4-8, LETTER TO H S FOX 613/9-10, METAMORPHOSES 613-11
*SHELFMARK PR TANNER 242 613/1-2, MS ENG MISC D 459/ FOL 2 613-3, PR ARCH G E 42/ FOL IV-2 613/4-8, PR NAPIER FAMILY PAPERS 613/9-10, MS CANON CLASS LAT 7/ FOL 1 613-11
*PROVENANCE AMERICAN/ CAMBRIDGE MASS 613/1-2,ENGLISH 613/3-10, ITALIAN/ BOLOGNA 613-11
*DATE EXECUTED 17TH/1640 613/1-2, 18TH/1720-54 613-3, 18TH/1789 613/4-8, 19TH/1835 613/9-10, 14TH/ LATE 613-11
*AUTHOR STUKELEY/ WILLIAM 613-3, BLAKE/ WILLIAM 613/4-8, DARWIN/ CHARLES 613/9-10, OVID 613-11
*TYPE OF MANUSCRIPT PSALM BOOK 613/1-2, POETRY 613/4-8, LETTER 613/9-10, LITERATURE 613-11
*CONTENTS BODLEIAN EXHIBITION III 613/1-11, TITLEPAGE OF FIRST BOOK PRINTED IN ENGLISH AMERICA 613-1, PSALM 1 FROM AMERICAN PSALM BOOK 613-2, PAGE WITH SIGNATURES OF NEWTON/ HALLEY/ WREN 613-3, FRONTISPIECE AND TITLE PAGE 613-4, SPRING BY BLAKE 613-5, LITTLE BLACK BOY BY BLAKE 613-6, CRADLE SONG BY BLAKE 613-7, THE LAMB BY BLAKE 613-8, DARWIN'S LETTER TO H S FOX AD1835 613/9-10, RESURRECTION/ CHRIST STANDS ABOVE SLEEPING SOLDIERS 613-11, CHRIST STANDS ABOVE SLEEPING SOLDIERS 613-11

*$ABSTRACT 614
*LIBRARY BODLEIAN
*NEGATIVE REFERENCE ROLL 247D
*RENTAL FEE $3.50
*TITLE OF MANUSCRIPT MOLDAVIAN GOSPELS
*SHELFMARK MS CANON GREEK 122/ FOL 2 614-1, MS CANON GREEK 122/ FOL 3 614-2, MS CANON GREEK 122/ FOL 6V 614-3, MS CANON GREEK 122/ FOL 7 614-4, MS CANON GREEK 122/ FOL 85V 614-5, MS CANON GREEK 122/ FOL 87 614-6, MS CANON GREEK 122/ FOL 87V 614-7, MS CANON GREEK 122/ FOL 88V 614-8, MS CANON GREEK 122/ FOL 89V 614-9, MS CANON GREEK 122/ FOL 90 614-10, MS CANON GREEK 122/ FOL 141V 614-11, MS CANON GREEK 122/ FOL 142 614-12, MS CANON GREEK 122/ FOL 143 614-13, MS CANON GREEK 122/ FOL 144V 614-14, MS CANON GREEK 122/ FOL 145 614-15, MS CANON GREEK 122/ FOL 231V 614-16, MS CANON GREEK 122/ FOL 232 614-17, MS CANON GREEK 122/ FOL 232V 614-18, MS CANON GREEK 122/ FOL 235V 614-19, MS CANON GREEK 122/ FOL 236 614-20, MS CANON GREEK 122/ FOL 275V 614-21, MS CANON GREEK 122/ FOL 278V 614-22, MS CANON GREEK 122/ FOL 294 614-23, MS CANON GREEK 122/ FOL 299 614-24, MS CANON GREEK 122/ FOL 299V 614-25, MS CANON GREEK 122/ FOL 300 614-26, MS CANON GREEK 122/ FOL 304V 614-27, MS CANON GREEK 122/ FOL 305 614-28, MS CANON GREEK 122/ FOL 310V 614-29, MS CANON GREEK 122/ FOL 312 614-30
*PROVENANCE NEAMTU
*DATE EXECUTED 15TH/1429
*LANGUAGE CYRILLIC AND GREEK
*SCRIBE GAVRIL
*TYPE OF MANUSCRIPT GOSPELS/ MOLDAVIAN
*CONTENTS GOSPELS/ MOLDAVIAN/ 15TH 614/1-30, DECORATED HEAD PIECE AND CYRILLIC TEXT 614-1, DECORATED CYRILLIC INITIAL AND TEXT 614-2, ST MATTHEW 614-3, HEAD PIECE TO OPENING OF ST MATTHEW 614-4, DECORATED PANEL AT END OF ST MATTHEW 614-5, DECORATED HEAD PIECE AND SYNOPSIS ON ST MARK 614-6, DECORATED CYRILLIC INITIAL AND TEXT 614-7, NUMERICAL TABLE IN GREEK 614-8, ST MARK 614-9, HEAD PIECE TO OPENING OF ST MARK 614-10, DECORATED TEXT AT END OF ST MARK 614-11, HEAD PIECE AT BEGINNING OF INDEX 614-12, DECORATED INITIAL AND CYRILLIC TEXT 614-13, ST LUKE 614-14, HEAD PIECE TO OPENING OF ST LUKE 614-15, DECORATED END OF ST LUKE 614-16, DECORATED HEAD PIECE AND INITIAL 614-17, DECORATED INITIAL AND CYRILLIC TEXT 614-18, ST JOHN 614-19, HEAD PIECE TO OPENING OF ST JOHN 614-20, DECORATED INITIAL IN CYRILLIC TEXT 614-21, RED CROSS

DECORATION IN GREEK TEXT 614-22, DECORATED INITIAL IN CYRILLIC TEXT 614-23, TEXT OF ST JOHN'S GOSPEL 614-24, TEXT AND DECORATION AT END OF ST JOHN 614-25, HEAD PIECE TO BEGINNING OF LECTIONARY TEXT 614-26, TABLE/ DECORATED IN RED AND BLUE 614-27, HEAD PIECE TO CYRILLIC INDEX 614-28, RED CROSS IN CYRILLIC TEXT 614-29, COLOPHON WITH DATE 1429 614-30, COLOPHON WITH NAME OF SCRIBE GAVRIL 614-30

*$ABSTRACT 615
*LIBRARY BODLEIAN
*SLIDE SET TITLE BIBLE MORALISEE
*NEGATIVE REFERENCE ROLL 247E
*RENTAL FEE $5.00
*COMMENTS EACH FOLIO CONTAINS EIGHT MINIATURES IN MEDALLIONS. ON EACH FOLIO FOUR MEDALLIONS ILLUSTRATE BIBLICAL PASSAGES ARRANGED IN BIBLICAL ORDER. UNDER EACH OF THESE MEDALLIONS THERE IS AN ACCOMPANYING MEDALLION WHICH EXPLAINS THE INNER MORAL MEANING OF THE BIBLICAL PASSAGE PORTRAYED. COLOR FILMSTRIPS OF THE ENTIRE MANUSCRIPT WITH FULL DESCRIPTIONS OF ALL THE MINIATURES IS AVAILABLE FROM E. P. PRODUCTIONS, LTD., BRADFORD ROAD, EAST ARDSLEY, WAKEFIELD, YORKSHIRE.
*TITLE OF MANUSCRIPT BIBLE MORALISEE
*SHELFMARK MS BODLEY 270B/ FOL 7V 615-1, MS BODLEY 270B/ FOL 1[illegible] 615-2, MS BODLEY 270B/ FOL 15V 615-3, MS BODLEY 270B/ FOL 1[illegible] 615-4, MS BODLEY 270B/ FOL 26 615-5, MS BODLEY 270B/ FOL 3[illegible] 615-6, MS BODLEY 270B/ FOL 37V 615-7, MS BODLEY 270B/ FOL 39[illegible] 615-8, MS BODLEY 270B/ FOL 40 615-9, MS BODLEY 270B/ FOL 4[illegible] 615-10, MS BODLEY 270B/ FOL 45V 615-11, MS BODLEY 270B/ FO[illegible] 47V 615-12, MS BODLEY 270B/ FOL 48 615-13, MS BODLEY 270B/ FO[illegible] 50 615-14, MS BODLEY 270B/ FOL 58 615-15, MS BODLEY 270B/ FO[illegible] 68 615-16, MS BODLEY 270B/ FOL 77V 615-17, MS BODLEY 270B/ FO[illegible] 99 615-18, MS BODLEY 270B/ FOL 100 615-19, MS BODLEY 270B/ FO[illegible] 101 615-20, MS BODLEY 270B/ FOL 105V 615-21, MS BODLEY 270B/ FOL 106 615-22, MS BODLEY 270B/ FOL 112 615-23, MS BODLEY 270B/ FOL 115V 615-24, MS BODLEY 270B/ FOL 116 615-25, MS BODLEY 270B/ FOL 118 615-26, MS BODLEY 270B/ FOL 130 615-27, MS BODLEY 270B/ FOL 131 615-28, MS BODLEY 270B/ FOL 13[illegible] 615-29, MS BODLEY 270B/ FOL 144 615-30, MS BODLEY 270B/ FO[illegible] 146 615-31, MS BODLEY 270B/ FOL 148 615-32, MS BODLEY 270B/ FOL 149V 615-33, MS BODLEY 270B/ FOL 151V 615-34, MS BODLEY 270B/ FOL 152 615-35, MS BODLEY 270B/ FOL 153V 615-36, MS BODLEY 270B/ FOL 155V 615-37, MS BODLEY 270B/ FOL 156 615-38, MS BODLEY 270B/ FOL 158 615-39, MS BODLEY 270B/ FOL 16[illegible] 615-40, MS BODLEY 270B/ FOL 165V 615-41, MS BODLEY 270B/ FO[illegible] 166 615-42, MS BODLEY 270B/ FOL 167V 615-43, MS BODLEY 270B/ FOL 171V 615-44, MS BODLEY 270B/ FOL 173V 615-45, MS BODLEY 270B/ FOL 174 615-46, MS BODLEY 270B/ FOL 176 615-47, MS BODLEY 270B/ FOL 184 615-48, MS BODLEY 270B/ FOL 186 615-49, MS BODLEY 270B/ FOL 190 615-50, MS BODLEY 270B/ FOL 19[illegible] 615-51, MS BODLEY 270B/ FOL 197V 615-52, MS BODLEY 270B/ FO[illegible] 204 615-53, MS BODLEY 270B/ FOL 205V 615-54, MS BODLEY 270B/ FOL 206 615-55, MS BODLEY 270B/ FOL 208 615-56, MS BODLEY 270B/ FOL 216 615-57, MS BODLEY 270B/ FOL 217V 615-58, MS BODLEY 270B/ FOL 218 615-59, MS BODLEY 270B/ FOL 223V 615-60
*PROVENANCE FRENCH/ NORTH
*DATE EXECUTED 13TH/ LAST QUARTER
*LANGUAGE LATIN
*TYPE OF MANUSCRIPT BIBLE MORALISEE
*CONTENTS BIBLE MORALISEE/ FRENCH/ 13TH 615/1-60, BIBLICA[illegible] TYPOLOGY 615/1-60, TYPOLOGY/ BIBLICAL 615/1-60, GENESI[illegible] 03/VERSES 1-6/ TEMPTATION OF ADAM AND EVE 615-1, ADAM AND EV[illegible] TEMPTED 615-1, DEVIL OBEYED BY THOSE WHO TRANSGRESS GOD'S WOR[illegible] 615-1, GENESIS 03/VERSES 9-11/ ADAM BLAMES EVE 615-1, ADA[illegible] BLAMES EVE FOR THE FALL 615-1, GOD THREATENS SINNERS WHO BLAM[illegible] SIN 615-1, GENESIS 03/VERSES 21 AND 23/ EXPULSION 615-1, ADA[illegible] AND EVE EXPULSED FROM EDEN 615-1, CHRIST REPELS THE EVIL FRO[illegible] THE CHURCH 615-1, GENESIS 04/VERSES 1-2/ ADAM PREFERS ABE[illegible] 615-1, ADAM PREFERS ABEL TO CAIN 615-1, CHRIST PREFER[illegible] CHRISTIANS TO WICKED 615-1, GENESIS 17/VERSES 10-12 AND 26-27 GOD AND ABRAHAM 615-2, GOD SPEAKS TO ABRAHAM ABOU[illegible]

CIRCUMCISION 615-2, CIRCUMCISION 615-2, GOOD HOUSEHOLDER CUTS OFF IMPURITY 615-2, GENESIS 18/VERSES 1-8/ ABRAHAM WELCOMES GOD'S ANGELS 615-2, ABRAHAM WELCOMES GOD'S MESSENGERS 615-2, CHRIST REFRESHES HIS FRIENDS WITH GRACE 615-2, GENESIS 18/VERSES 9-10/ SARAH PROMISED SON 615-2, SARAH PROMISED SON BUT SHE LAUGHS 615-2, GOD PROMISES ETERNAL JOY BUT WORLDLY PEOPLE LAUGH 615-2, GENESIS 19/VERSES 1-4/ LOT ENTERTAINS ANGELS 615-2, LOT ENTERTAINS TWO ANGELS IN SODOM 615-2, SODOMITES ARE EVIL MEN AND WOMEN 615-2, GENESIS 19/VERSES 15-17/ LOT LEAVES SODOM 615-3, LOT AND FAMILY LEAVE SODOM 615-3, CHRISTIANS LEAVE THE WORLD 615-3, GENESIS 19/VERSE 26/ LOT'S WIFE 615-3, LOT'S WIFE TURNED TO PILLAR OF SALT 615-3, GENESIS 19/VERSES 33-38/ LOT'S DAUGHTERS 615-3, LOT'S DAUGHTER BEARS SON 615-3, HERMIT TRICKED BY WORLD/ FLESH AND DEVIL 615-3, WORLD/ FLESH AND DEVIL 616-3, GENESIS 22/VERSES 1-2 AND 6/ ABRAHAM AND ISAAC 615-3, ABRAHAM ASKED TO SACRIFICE ISAAC 615-3, CHRIST CARRIES CROSS 615-3, GENESIS 29/VERSES 12-13-AND-17/ JACOB LOVES RACHEL 615-4, JACOB LOVES RACHEL RATHER THAN LEAH 615-4, CHRIST LOVES THE CHURCH 615-4, GENESIS 29/VERSES 30-31/ JACOB AND FAMILY 615-4, JACOB WITH TWO WIVES AND TWELVE CHILDREN 615-4, CHRIST AND TWELVE APOSTLES 615-4, GENESIS 30/VERSE 35/ LABAN AND FLOCK 615-4, LABAN REMOVES GOATS AND SHEEP FROM FLOCK 615-4, CHRIST AND DEVIL 615-4, DEVIL AND CHRIST 615-4, GENESIS 30/VERSES 37-38/ JACOB CHANGES FLOCK 615-4, JACOB CHANGES FLOCK 615-4, CHRIST CHANGES THE FOLK BY PLACING SAINTS BESIDE STREAM 615-4, GENESIS 40/VERSES 1-3/ JOSEPH IN PRISON 615-5, JOSEPH IN PRISON WITH BUTLER AND BAKER 615-5, JOSEPH IN PRISON IS CHRIST IN WORLD 615-5, GENESIS 40/VERSES 16-17/ BAKER'S DREAM 615-5, JOSEPH INTERPRETS BAKER'S DREAM 615-5, BAKER'S DREAM MEANS GREED/ PRIDE/ LUXURY 615-5, GENESIS 40/VERSES 18-19/ BAKER'S DEATH FORETOLD 615-5, JOSEPH FORETELLS BAKER'S DEATH 615-5, BAKER REPRESENTS THE PUNISHED WICKED 615-5, GENESIS 41/VERSES 1-3 AND 5-7/ PHARAOH'S DREAM 615-5, PHARAOH DREAMS OF KINE AND EARS OF CORN 615-5, KINE REPRESENT SEVEN VIRTUES AND VICES 615-5, EXODUS 01/VERSES 8-9/ KING ABHORS CHILDREN OF ISRAEL 615-6, KING OF EGYPT ABHORS CHILDREN OF ISRAEL 615-6,DEVIL TELLS REEVES TO ENSLAVE SONS OF CHRIST 615-6, EXODUS 01/VERSE 11/ BONDAGE OF ISRAELITES 615-6, CHILDREN OF ISRAEL IN BONDAGE 615-6, PHARAOH REPRESENTS THE DEVIL 615-6, DEVIL 615-6, EXODUS 01/VERSE 14/ ISRAELITES FORCED TO WORK 615-6, ISRAELITES FORCED TO BUILD CITIES AND TILL 615-6, DEVIL DESTROYS FOLK WITH SIN 615-6, EXODUS 01/VERSES 15-16/ PHARAOH ORDERS DEATH OF SONS 615-6, PHARAOH ORDERS DEATH OF HEBREW SONS 615-6, DEVIL ORDERS OLD LAW TO KILL VIRILE SONS 615-6, EXODUS 01/VERSE 17/ MIDWIVES SAVE MALE CHILDREN 615-7, MIDWIVES SAVE HEBREW MALES 615-7, HOLY CHURCH NURTURES GOOD CHRISTIANS 615-7, EXODUS 01/VERSE 22/ PHARAOH ORDERS DROWNING 615-7, PHARAOH ORDERS THAT MALE SONS BE DROWNED 615-7, PHARAOH REPRESENTS DEVIL WHO SMOTHERS GOOD WORKS 615-7, EXODUS 02/VERSES 1-2/ MOSES BORN 615-7, MOSES BORN TO DAUGHTER OF LEVI 615-7, NATIVITY OF CHRIST 615-7, CHRIST'S NATIVITY 615-7, EXODUS 02/VERSE 3/ MOSES IN PAPYRUS ARK 615-7, MOSES LEFT IN PAPYRUS ARK 615-7, MOSES IN BASKET REPRESENTS CHRIST IN CRIB 615-7, EXODUS 02/VERSES 11-12/ MOSES HIDES BODY OF EGYPTIAN 615-8, MOSES HIDES BODY OF EGYPTIAN WHOM HE KILLED 615-8, CHRIST HIDES OUR SINS THROUGH PENANCE 615-8, EXODUS 02/VERSE 15/ MOSES ESCAPES TO MIDIAN 615-8, MOSES ESCAPES TO MIDIAN 615-8, CHRIST LEAVES JOYS OF WORLD 615-8, EXODUS 02/VERSE 16/ MOSES BY WELL 615-8, MOSES AT WELL MEETS SEVEN DAUGHTERS 615-8, MOSES IS CHRIST WHO FINDS SEVEN GRACES 615-8, EXODUS 02/VERSE 17/ SHEPHERDS COME TO WELL 615-8, SHEPHERDS PREVENT DAUGHTERS FROM WATERING FLOCK 615-8, DEVIL TRIES TO DRIVE AWAY SEVEN VIRTUES 615-8,EXODUS 02/VERSE 17/ DAUGHTERS GET WATER 615-9, MOSES HELPS SEVEN DAUGHTERS WATER FLOCKS 615-9, CHRIST WATERS THE VIRTUES AT WELL OF DIVINITY 615-9, EXODUS 02/VERSES 21-22/ MARRIAGE OF MOSES 615-9, MOSES MARRIES ONE OF SEVEN DAUGHTERS 615-9, MOSES REPRESENTS CHRIST/ HIS WIFE IS THE CHURCH 615-9, EXODUS 03/VERSES 1-2/ MOSES AND BURNING BUSH 615-9, MOSES AND THE BURNING BUSH 615-9, BURNING BUSH 615-9, LEAVES OF BUSH ARE EVIL 615-9, EXODUS 04/VERSE 9/ WATER CHANGED TO BLOOD 615-10, MOSES CHANGES WATER TO BLOOD 615-10,

GOD SHOWS CHRIST'S BLOOD 615-10, EXODUS 04/VERSE 27/ AARON MEETS MOSES 615-10, AARON MEETS MOSES IN WILDERNESS 615-10, MOSES REPRESENTS LAW/ AARON IS GRACE 615-10, EXODUS 05/VERSE 1/ MOSES AARON AND PHARAOH 615-10, MOSES ASKES PHARAOH TO RELEASE ISRAELITES 615-10, PRELATES TELL DEVIL TO RELEASE CHRIST'S PEOPLE 615-10, DEVIL 615-10, EXODUS 05/VERSES 6-8/ ISRAELITES FORCED TO WORK 615-10, PHARAOH INCREASES TASKS FOR ISRAELITES 615-10, DEVIL WORKS AT CHRISTIANS 615-10, EXODUS 09/VERSE 22/ DOWNPOUR OF HAIL 615-11, GOD CREATES DOWNPOUR OF HAIL TO COVER LAND 615-11, GOD STRIKES DOWN EVIL MEN IN HELL 615-11, HELL SCENE 615-11, DEVIL WITH BELLOWS BLOWS HELL MOUTH 615-11, EXODUS 10/VERSES 4-5/ PLAGUE OF LOCUSTS 615-11, GOD PROMISES TO BRING PLAGUE OF LOCUSTS 615-11, PLAGUE OF LOCUSTS 615-11, LOCUSTS ARE BAD PEOPLE WHO SUBVERT TRUTH 615-11, EXODUS 10/VERSES 21-23/ DARKNESS IN EGYPT 615-11,GOD COMMANDS DARKNESS IN EGYPT AND LIGHT FOR ISRAELITES 615-11, DARKNESS REPRESENTS DARKNESS OF SIN IN HELL 615-11, EXODUS 12/VERSES 3-6/ FEAST OF PASSOVER 615-11, PASSOVER SACRIFICE AND FEAST INSTITUTED 615-11, SACRIFICE OF LAMB REPRESENTS SACRIFICE OF CHRIST 615-11, EXODUS 12/VERSES 35-36/ DEPARTURE OF ISRAELITES 615-12, ISRAELITES RECEIVE GOLD AND RAIMENT FROM EGYPTIANS 615-12, GOOD PEOPLE RECEIVE WISDOM/ ELOQUENCE/ GRACE/ VIRTUE 615-12, EXODUS 13/VERSES 21-22/ PILLARS OF CLOUD AND FIRE 615-12, GOD GUIDES ISRAELITES OUT OF EGYPT 615-12, CHRIST GUARDS HIS DISCIPLES 615-12, EXODUS 14/VERSES 2-AND-7-9/ ISRAELITES PURSUED 615-12, CHARIOTS AND HORSEMEN PURSUE ISRAELITES 615-12, DEVIL PURSUES CHRISTIANS 615-12, EXODUS 14/VERSES 11-14-AND-16/ MOSES DIVIDES WATERS 615-12, MOSES LIFTS ROD AND DIVIDES RED SEA 615-12, MOUNTAINS AND SEA REPRESENT WORLD/ FLESH/ DEVIL 615-12, WORLD/ FLESH AND DEVIL 615-12, EXODUS 14/VERSE 21/ MOSES DIVIDES WATERS 615-13,MOSES PLACES ROD IN SEA AND DRY LAND APPEARS 615-13, PRELATE/ GOOD SEPARATES CHRISTIANS FROM DEVIL 615-13, EXODUS 14/VERSE 22/ CROSSING OF RED SEA 615-13, CROSSING OF RED SEA 615-13, TWELVE SONS OF ISRAEL REPRESENT TWELVE APOSTLES 615-13, EXODUS 14/VERSE 23/ PHARAOH'S CHARIOTS 615-13, CHARIOTS OF PHARAOH FOLLOW ISRAELITES 615-13, PHARAOH IN PURSUIT REPRESENTS DEVIL 615-13, EXODUS 14/VERSES 27-31/ EGYPTIANS DROWN 615-13, EGYPTIANS DROWN IN RED SEA 615-13, MOSES IS CHRIST SAVING SOULS AND DROWNING ENEMIES 615-13, EXODUS 16/VERSES 4-5/ GOD SENDS BREAD 615-14, GOD SENDS BREAD FROM HEAVEN 615-14, CHRIST SENDS GRACE 615-14, EXODUS 16/VERSES 8-AND-19-20/ MOSES REBUKES PEOPLE 615-14, MOSES REBUKES PEOPLE 615-14, JEWS WHO HIDE MANNA ARE AVARICIOUS SCHOLARS 615-14, EXODUS 17/VERSES 5-6/ MOSES STRIKES ROCK 615-14,MOSES STRIKES ROCK TO FIND WATER 615-14, STRIKING ROCK REPRESENTS CRUCIFIXION 615-14, CRUCIFIXION 615-14, EXODUS 17/VERSE 8/ AMALEK COMES TO FIGHT 615-14,AMALEK COMES TO FIGHT ISRAELITES 615-14, MOSES IS CHRIST/ AMALEK IS DEVIL 615-14, DEVIL 615-14, LEVITICUS 01/VERSES 5-AND-13/ BURNT OFFERINGS 615-15, AARON AND SONS SACRIFICE BULLOCK AND LAMB 615-15, SACRIFICES REPRESENT REJECTION OF PRIDE AND TEMPTATION 615-15, DEVIL 615-15, LEVITICUS 01/VERSE 14/ MOSES AND AARON 615-15, MOSES WATCHES AARON AND SON MAKE OBLATIONS 615-15, PEOPLE WHO MAKE OFFERINGS ARE SIMPLE AND PURE 615-15, LEVITICUS 01/VERSE 13/ GOD RECEIVES OFFERING 615-15, AARON AND PRIESTS OFFER ENTRAILS 615-15, OFFERING ENTRAILS IS TO CLEANSE CONSCIENCE 615-15, LEVITICUS 01/VERSES 16-17/ GOD REJECTS OFFERING 615-15, OFFERING OF DOVE WITH BROKEN WING REJECTED 615-15, DOVE WITH BROKEN WING REPRESENTS PRIDEFUL OFFERING 615-15, NUMBERS 01/VERSE 10/ FAMILY OF JOSEPH 615-16, JOSEPH'S FAMILY/ SONS OF TWO HOUSES CHOSEN 615-16, JOSEPH IS CHRIST FATHER OF GENTILES AND JEWS 615-16, NUMBERS 01/VERSE 10/ ELISHAMA THE CHIEF 615-16, ELISHAMA THE CHIEF 615-16, ELISHAMA REPRESENTS CHRIST 615-16, NUMBERS 01/VERSE 10/ GAMALIEL IS CHIEF 615-16, GAMALIEL IS CHIEF OF MANASSEH 615-16, MANASSEH MEANS FORGETFUL 615-16, CHRIST FOUND THE ISRAELITES FORGETFUL 615-16, NUMBERS 01/VERSE 11/ ABIDAN IS CHIEF 615-16, ABIDAN IS CHIEF OF HOUSE OF BENJAMIN 615-16, CHRIST IS JUDGE OF QUICK AND DEAD 615-16, NUMBERS 13/VERSES 30-33/ MOSES AND PRINCES 615-17, MOSES AND PRINCES WHO SPIED OUT LAND OF CANAAN 615-17, CALEB QUIETS DOUBTERS 615-17, CALEB REPRESENTS CHRIST/ DOUBTERS AR

615-24, SAMSON TAKES HONEYCOMBS FROM LION 615-24, CHRIST RESCUES PROPHETS FROM HELL 615-24, HARROWING OF HELL 615-24, JUDGES 14/VERSES 11-14/ SAMSON ASKS RIDDLE 615-24, SAMSON ASKS RIDDLE OF WIFE'S PEOPLE 615-24, EATER IS THE DEVIL/ MEAT IS THE SINNER 615-24, DEVIL 615-24, JUDGES 15/VERSE 1/ SAMSON GOES TO WIFE 615-24, SAMSON WITH KID GOES TO WIFE 615-24, CHRIST COMES TO HIS CHURCH 615-24, JUDGES 15/VERSE 1/ SAMSON'S WIFE 615-25, SAMSON TOLD HIS WIFE GIVEN TO COMPANION 615-25, DEVIL PROMPTS JEWS TO STONE CHRIST 615-25, CHRIST STONED BY JEWS 615-25, JUDGES 15/VERSES 4-5/ SAMSON WITH FOXES 615-25, SAMSON SENDS FOXES WITH BURNING TAILS INTO CORNFIELDS 615-25, FOXES ARE INFIDELS AND PUBLICANS WHO BURN CHRISTIANS 615-25, JUDGES 15/VERSES 12-13/ SAMSON BOUND WITH CORD 615-25, SAMSON BOUND WITH CORD BY FOLLOWERS 615-25, CHRIST LETS HIMSELF BE BOUND AND SCOURGED 615-25, JUDGES 15/VERSES 14-15/ SAMSON SLAYS PHILISTINES 615-25, SAMSON SLAYS PHILISTINES WITH JAWBONE 615-25, RESURRECTION OF CHRIST CONFOUNDS JEWS AND DEVIL 615-25, DEVIL FALLS BACKWARDS TO HELL MOUTH 615-25, JUDGES 16/VERSES 4-7/ DELILAH AND PHILISTINES 615-26, DELILAH ASKED TO FIND SOURCE OF SAMSON'S STRENGTH 615-26, DELILAH REPRESENTS FLESH/ SAMSON THE SPIRIT 615-26, JUDGES 16/VERSE 14/ DELILAH FASTENS HAIR 615-26,DELILAH FASTENS SAMSON'S HAIR TO BEAM 615-26, FLESH DECEIVES THE SPIRIT 615-26, JUDGES 16/VERSE 19/ DELILAH CUTS HAIR 615-26, DELILAH CUTS SAMSON'S HAIR 615-26, SPIRIT SEDUCED BY FLESH 615-26, DEVILS STAND BY CRIMINAL HANGING 615-26, JUDGES 16/VERSE 21/ SAMSON BLINDED 615-26, SAMSON BLINDED AND IMPRISONED 615-26, SINNER LOSES GRACE AND SUFFERS WORLDLY CARES 615-26, KINGS-I 03/VERSE 1/ SAMUEL MINISTERS TO ELI 615-27, SAMUEL MINISTERS TO ELI 615-27, BAD PRIESTS BUSY WITH JOYS OF FLESH 615-27, KINGS-I 03/VERSE 4/ SAMUEL CALLED BY GOD 615-27,SAMUEL CALLED BY GOD 615-27, SAMUEL SHOULD BE LIKE PROPHET/ JUDGE/ PRIEST 615-27, KINGS-I 04/VERSE 4/ ARK OF COVENANT 615-27, ARK OF COVENANT 615-27, PRELATES/ BAD BRING HOLY CHURCH AGAINST DEVIL 615-27, DEVILS 615-27, KINGS-I 04/VERSES 10-11/ JEWS AND PHILISTINES BATTLE 615-27, BATTLE BETWEEN ISRAELITES AND PHILISTINES 615-27, SARACENS ARE DEVILS DEFEATING BAD PRELATES 615-27, DEVILS 615-27, KINGS-I 05/VERSE 2/ PHILISTINES CARRY ARK 615-28, PHILISTINES CARRY ARK TO HOUSE OF DAGON 615-28, DEVILS PLACE HOLY CHURCH NEXT TO BEELZEBUB 615-28, BEELZEBUB 615-28, KINGS-I 05/VERSES 3-6/ IMAGE OF DAGON DESTROYED 615-28, DAGON'S IMAGE DESTROYED 615-28, DEVIL CONQUERED BY CHURCH 615-28, KINGS-I 05/VERSE 9/ PLAGUE OF EMERODS 615-28, PLAGUE OF EMERODS AND MICE 615-28, PHILISTINES BITTEN BY MICE ARE BAD BISHOPS 615-28, KINGS-I 06/VERSE 5/ PHILISTINES PRAISE GOD 615-28, PHILISTINES MAKE IMAGES OF EMERODS AND MICE 615-28, GOD FORGIVES BAD BISHOPS WHO DO PENANCE 615-28, KINGS-I 16/VERSE 23/ DAVID AND SAUL 615-29, DAVID PLAYS HARP BEFORE SAUL 615-29, CHRIST'S CRUCIFIXION EXPELS DEVIL FROM JEWS 615-29, CRUCIFIXION 615-29, KINGS-I 17/VERSES 8-9/ GOLIATH CHALLENGES ISRAELITES 615-29, GOLIATH CHALLENGES ISRAELITES 615-29, DEVIL CHALLENGES GOOD CHRISTIANS 615-29, KINGS-I 17/VERSE 32/ DAVID ACCEPTS CHALLENGE 615-29, DAVID ACCEPTS GOLIATH'S CHALLENGE 615-29, CHRIST WILL FIGHT THE DEVIL 615-29, KINGS-I 17/VERSES 38-41-AND-48-49/ DAVID AND GOLIATH 615-29, DAVID KILLS GOLIATH 615-29, CHRIST DEFEATS DEVIL WITH CROSS 615-29, DEVIL 615-29, KINGS-I 26/VERSES 5-AND-7-12/ ABISHAI AND SAUL 615-30, ABISHAI WANTS TO KILL SLEEPING SAUL 615-30, CHRIST TAKES AWAY POWER OF JEWS 615-30, KINGS-I 27/VERSE 2/ DAVID GOES TO ACHISH 615-30,DAVID WITH 600 MEN GOES TO ACHISH 615-30, GOOD COUNSELORS COME BEFORE KING 615-30, KINGS-I 28/VERSES 11-AND-19/ SAUL AND WITCH 615-30, SAUL CONSULTS WITCH OF ENDOR 615-30, WITCH OF ENDOR RAISES SPIRIT OF SAMUEL 615-30, DEVIL TEMPTS CHRIST 615-30, CHRIST TEMPTED BY DEVIL 615-30, KINGS-I 29/VERSE 3-4/ ACHISH HONORS DAVID 615-30, DAVID HONORED BY ACHISH 615-30, ACHISH IS GOOD PRINCES 615-30, KINGS-I 30/VERSES 17-AND-20/ DAVID SMITES AMALEKITES 615-31, DAVID SMITES AMALEKITES 615-31, HARROWING OF HELL 615-31, KINGS-I 30/VERSE 22/ DAVID AND MEN OF BELIAL 615-31, DAVID REFUSES TO DIVIDE SPOILS 615-31, GOD DIVIDES HIS GRACE ACCORDING TO HIS WILL 615-31, KINGS-I 31/VERSES 1-2/ PHILISTINES SMITE ISRAELITES 615-31, PHILISTINES SMITE

ISRAELITES 615-31, ANTICHRIST'S MESSENGERS SMITE CHRISTIANS 615-31, KINGS-I 31/VERSES 3-5/ DEATH OF SAUL 615-31, SAUL FALLS ON HIS SWORD 615-31, FLATTERS DESTROY THEMSELVES 615-31, KINGS-II 01/VERSES 8-9/ DAVID AND AMALEKITE 615-32, DAVID ORDERS DEATH OF AMALEKITE 615-32, HE WHO DIGS PIT SHALL FALL THEREIN 615-32, KINGS-II 01/VERSE 17/ DAVID AT TOMB 615-32, DAVID LAMENTS OVER TOMB OF SAUL AND JONATHAN 615-32, CHRISTIANS MOURN THOSE WHO LOSE TO DEVIL 615-32, KINGS-II 01/VERSES 20-21/ DAVID WARNS HEARERS 615-32, DAVID AFRAID PHILISTINES WILL HEAR LAMENTATION 615-32, CHRIST BIDS FAITHFUL TO BE WARY 615-32, KINGS-II 01/VERSE 25/ DAVID'S LAMENTATION 615-32, DAVID'S LAMENTATION 615-32, DAVID'S LAMENT MEANS MAN FALLS THRICE 615-32, KINGS-II 01/VERSE 8-AND-10/ HOUSE OF JUDAH 615-33, ISHBOSHETH MADE KING OF ISRAEL 615-33, ERROR OF CONFUSION REIGNS AMONG JEWS 615-33, DEVIL TRANSFORMS HIMSELF INTO ANGEL OF LIGHT 615-33, KINGS-II 04/VERSE 5/ DEATH OF ISHBOSHETH 615-33, ISHBOSHETH KILLED BY TWO ROBBERS 615-33, ROBBERS ATTACK THE SOUL 615-33, KINGS-II 04/VERSE 12/ DAVID ORDERS ROBBERS' DEATH 615-33, ROBBERS ARE DEVIL CAST IN HELL 615-33, DEVIL CAST INTO HELL MOUTH 615-33, HELL MOUTH 615-33, KINGS-II 05/VERSES 6-7/ DAVID ATTACKS JERUSALEM 615-33, DAVID ATTACKS JERUSALEM 615-33, CHRIST DESTROYS UNBELIEVERS 615-33, KINGS-II 09/VERSES 6-7/ DAVID AND MEPHIBOSHETH 615-34, DAVID HAS MEPHIBOSHETH SIT AT TABLE 615-34, CHRIST REFRESHES VIRTUOUS DAILY WITH MASSES 615-34, KINGS-II 09/VERSES 12-13/ MEPHIBOSHETH AND FAMILY 615-34, MEPHIBOSHETH LAME AND HIS FAMILY 615-34, THOSE ONCE DESPISED ARE ADMIRED BY CHURCH 615-34, KINGS-II 10/VERSE 2/ DAVID SENDS HANUN SERVANTS 615-34, DAVID SENDS SERVANTS TO HANUN 615-34, CHRIST SENDS MESSENGERS INTO THE WORLD 615-34,KINGS-II 10/VERSE 4/ HANUN SHAVES MESSENGERS 615-34, HANUN IS DEVIL WHO REMOVES HALF OF REASON 615-34, DEVIL 615-34, KINGS-II 10/VERSE 4/ HANUN CUTS GARMENTS 615-35, HANUN CUTS GARMENTS OF DAVID'S SERVANTS 615-35, DEVIL UNCOVERS WANTONESS OF PRELATES 615-35, KINGS-II 10/VERSE 5/ DAVID AND SERVANTS 615-35, DAVID TELLS SERVANTS TO WAIT IN JERICHO 615-35, CHRIST BIDS FAITHFUL TO BECOME HERMITS 615-35,KINGS-II 10/VERSE 7/ DAVID AND HANUN MUSTER TROOPS 615-35, DAVID AND HANUN MUSTER THEIR TROOPS 615-35, CHRIST SENDS DISCIPLES INTO THE WORLD 615-35, KINGS-II 11/VERSE 2/ DAVID AND BATHSHEBA 615-35, DAVID SEES BATHSHEBA IN BATH 615-35, CHRIST SEES HOLY CHURCH WASH SINNERS 615-35, KINGS-II 11/VERSE 4/ DAVID SENDS FOR BATHSHEBA 615-36, DAVID SENDS FOR BATHSHEBA 615-36, DAVID IS CHRIST WHO LOVED CHURCH 615-36, KINGS-II 11/VERSE 8/ URIAH TOLD TO WASH FEET 615-36, DAVID TELLS URIAH TO WASH HIS FEET 615-36, CHRIST BIDS CHRISTIANS TO BE RECONCILED 615-36, KINGS-II 11/VERSE 11/ FOOD SENT TO URIAH 615-36, DAVID ORDERS URIAH TO EAT AND DRINK 615-36, CHRIST GIVES JEWS OLD LAW 615-36, KINGS-II 11/VERSE 14/ URIAH KILLED IN BATTLE 615-36, URIAH KILLED BY PHILISTINES 615-36, JOAB IS DEVIL WHO TEMPTS MAN 615-36, DEVIL 615-36, KINGS-II 13/VERSES 1-6/ AMMON FEIGNS ILLNESS 615-37, AMMON FEIGNS ILLNESS BECAUSE OF LOVE FOR SISTER 615-37, RICH WANTONS GAIN ENDS BY DECEIT 615-37, KINGS-II 13/VERSES 11-15/ AMMON TAKES TAMAR 615-37, AMMON TAKES TAMAR BY FORCE 615-37, AMMON REPRESENTS RICH RAKE 615-37, KINGS-II 13/VERSE 17/ AMMON EXPELS TAMAR 615-37,AMMON TURNS OUT TAMAR FROM HOUSE 615-37, TAMAR COMPLAINS TO ABSALOM 615-37, WOMAN COMPLAINS TO DEVIL 615-37, DEVIL 615-37, KINGS-II 13/VERSES 17 AND 28/ ABSALOM'S FEAST 615-37, ABSALOM INVITES KING'S SON TO FEAST 615-37, DEVIL GIVES MAN EVIL WORKS TO EAT 615-37, KINGS-II 13/VERSE 29/ AMMON KILLED 615-38, AMMON KILLED BY ABSALOM'S SERVANTS 615-38, DEVIL THRUSTS SINNER INTO HELL 615-38, KINGS-II 13/VERSE 29/ AMMON'S SON FLEES 615-38, AMMON'S SON FLEES ON MULE 615-38, GOOD CHRISTIAN FLEES DEVIL 615-38, DEVIL 615-38, KINGS-II 14/VERSES 2-6/ DAVID AND WISE WOMAN 615-38, DAVID TOLD OF FRATRICIDE 615-38, DEVIL RESISTED BY CONTRITION AND CONFESSION 615-38, KINGS-II 14/VERSE 19/ DAVID AND JOAB 615-38, DAVID TELLS JOAB TO BRING ABSALOM 615-38, PRELATES RECEIVE PENITENTS ON MAUNDY THURSDAY 615-38, KINGS-II 18/VERSE 9/ ABSALOM HUNG BY HAIR 615-39, ABSALOM HUNG FROM TREE BY HIS HAIR 615-39, JEWS HUNG BY ERROR AND CUPIDITY 615-39, KINGS-II 18/VERSE 14/ JOAB KILLS ABSALOM 615-39,ABSALOM KILLED BY JOAB 615-39, DEVIL PIERCES SINNERS

WITH PRIDE/ AVARICE/ WANTONESS 615-39, KINGS-II 18/VERSES 15-17/ BURIAL OF ABSALOM 615-39, ABSALOM BURIED BY JOAB 615-39, DEVIL CAST INTO HELL 615-39, HELL 615-39, KINGS-II 18/VERSE 23/ AHITOPHEL HANGS HIMSELF 615-39, AHITOPHEL HANGS HIMSELF 615-39, JUDAS HANGS HIMSELF 615-39, KINGS-III 09/VERSES 13-18/ SOLOMON PRESENTS TEMPLE 615-40, SOLOMON PRESENTS TEMPLE TO GOD 615-40, CHRIST THANKS GOD 615-40, KINGS-III 10/VERSES 1-2/ SHEBA VISITS SOLOMON 615-40, QUEEN OF SHEBA VISITS SOLOMON 615-40, HOLY CHURCH BRINGS GOOD SOULS TO CHRIST 615-40, KINGS-III 10/VERSES 18-20/ SOLOMON'S THRONE 615-40, SOLOMON'S THRONE 615-40, VIRGIN IS THRONE 615-40, LIONS ARE OLD AND NEW TESTAMENTS 615-40, LIONS/ TWELVE ARE APOSTLES 615-40, SIX STEPS ARE SIX VIRTUES 615-40, KINGS-III 11/VERSES 1-4/ SOLOMON AND IDOLS 615-40, SOLOMON AND WIVES PRAY TO IDOLS 615-40, DEVIL WORSHIPPED BY EVIL SCHOLARS 615-40, KINGS-III 12/VERSE 1/ REHOBOAM MADE KING 615-41, REHOBOAM MADE KING 615-41, WORLDLY PEOPLE MAKE BAD CHOICE OF KING 615-41, KINGS-III 12/VERSES 6-8/ REHOBOAM AND WISE MEN 615-41, REHOBOAM AND WISE MEN 615-41, GOOD COUNSELORS ADVISE KINGS 615-41, KINGS-III 12/VERSES 13-14/ REHOBOAM AND YOUNG MEN 615-41, REHOBOAM CONSULTS YOUNG MEN 615-41, BAD PRINCES OPPRESS THE POOR 615-41, KINGS-III 12/VERSES 17-28/ JEROBOAM AND IDOLS 615-41, JEROBOAM TELLS PEOPLE TO WORSHIP IDOLS 615-41,DEVIL ENCOURAGES IDOLATRY 615-41, KINGS-III 13/VERSES 1-2/ JEROBOAM AT ALTAR 615-42, JEROBOAM ABOUT TO SACRIFICE HARE 615-42, BAD PRINCE DOES FEALTY TO DEVIL 615-42, DEVIL AND BAD PRINCE 615-42, KINGS-III 13/VERSE 4/ ALTAR IS BROKEN 615-42, ALTAR BROKEN AND HARE ESCAPES 615-42, PRAYERS OF GOOD MAKE BAD PRINCES STERILE 615-42, KINGS-III 13/VERSE 8/ JEROBOAM OFFERS REWARD 615-42, JEROBOAM OFFERS REWARDS TO PROPHET 615-42, BAD PRINCES SEEK PARDON WITH PENANCE 615-42, KINGS-III 13/VERSE 15/ JEROBOAM OFFERS FOOD 615-42, JEROBOAM OFFERS FOOD TO PROPHET 615-42, GOOD PRINCES BEG GOOD CLERKS TO STAY 615-42, KINGS-III 13/VERSES 14-15/ MAN OF GOD 615-43, MAN OF GOD REFUSES FALSE PROPHET OF BETHEL 615-43, BAD CLERKS TRY TO SEDUCE GOOD SCHOLARS 615-43, KINGS-III 13/VERSES 18-22/ PROPHET DECEIVES MAN 615-43, PROPHET/ FALSE DECEIVES MAN OF GOD 615-43, DEVIL DECEIVES FOOLISH SCHOLARS 615-43, KINGS-III 13/VERSE 24/ MAN OF GOD SLAIN 615-43, MAN OF GOD SLAIN BY LION 615-43, LION SLAYS MAN OF GOD 615-43, DEVIL TORMENTS BODIES BUT LEAVES SOULS UNHARMED 615-43, KINGS-III 17/VERSE 1/ WARNING OF ELIJAH 615-43, ELIJAH THE TISHBITE WARNS AHAB ABOUT DROUGHT 615-43, JEWS TOLD HOLY SPIRIT WILL NOT COME UNTIL JUDGMENT 615-43, KINGS-III 19/VERSES 20-21/ ELISHA WELCOMES ELIJAH 615-44, ELISHA ENTERTAINS ELIJAH AT FEAST 615-44, ELIJAH IS APOSTLES WHO FIND PREACHERS 615-44, KINGS-III 21/VERSES 1-4/ AHAB COVETS VINEYARD 615-44, AHAB COVETS NABOTH'S VINEYARD 615-44, DEVIL SEEKS TO TAKE AWAY HOLY CHURCH 615-44, KINGS-III 21/VERSES 6-7/ AHAB AND JEZEBEL 615-44, JEZEBEL PROMISES AHAB SHE WILL GET VINEYARD 615-44, DEVIL COMPLAINS TO SYNAGOGUE 615-44, KINGS-III 21/VERSES 12-13/ NABOTH AND FALSE WITNESSES 615-44, NABOTH BETRAYED BY FALSE WITNESSES 615-44, SYNAGOGUE BEARS FALSE WITNESS AGAINST CHRIST 615-44, KINGS-III 22/VERSES 27-34/ MICAIAH IMPRISONED 615-45, MICAIAH IMPRISONED 615-45, AHAB IS HEROD WHO IMPRISONED JOHN THE BAPTIST 615-45, ST JOHN THE BAPTIST IMPRISONED BY HEROD 615-45, KINGS-III 22/VERSES 34-38/ AHAB SHOT 615-45, AHAB SHOT BY ARROW 615-45, HEROD IS SINNER AT DECOLLATION OF JOHN THE BAPTIST 615-45, ST JOHN THE BAPTIST BEHEADED 615-45, KINGS-IV 01/VERSE 2/ AHAZIAH IS ILL 615-45, AHAZIAH FALLS THROUGH LATTICE 615-45, JEW FALLS INTO DESPAIR 615-45, KINGS-IV 01/VERSE 3/ AHAZIAH AND BAAL 615-45, DEVIL AND EVIL PHILOSOPHERS 615-45, KINGS-IV 01/VERSES 9-10/ ELIJAH AND AHAZIAH 615-46, ELIJAH EVOKES FIRE FROM HEAVEN 615-46, JEWS HARDENED BY FIRE OF CUPIDITY 615-46, KINGS-IV 01/VERSE 13/ ELIJAH AND HUMBLE CAPTAIN 615-46, ELIJAH BESEECHED BY HUMBLE MEN 615-46, CHRIST BLESSES THE HUMBLE 615-46, KINGS-IV 01/VERSES 15-16/ ELIJAH SENT TO AHAZIAH 615-46, ELIJAH SENT TO AHAZIAH 615-46, CHRIST TELLS PHARISEES THEY WILL DIE 615-46, KINGS-IV 02/VERSES 11-13/ ELIJAH TAKEN TO HEAVEN 615-46, ELIJAH TAKEN TO HEAVEN IN CHARIOT OF FIRE 615-46, CHARIOT OF FIRE 615-46, CHRIST'S ASCENSION 615-46, ASCENSION OF CHRIST

615-46, KINGS-IV 02/VERSE 24/ BEARS EAT CHILDREN 615-47,BEARS EAT CHILDREN WHO MOCK ELISHA 615-47, BEARS ARE TITUS AND VESPASIAN 615-47, KINGS-IV 04/VERSE 1/ ELISHA AND WOMAN 615-47, ELISHA AND WOMAN WHO LOSES SONS TO CREDITORS 615-47, DEVILS TAKE GOOD AND BAD SONS 615-47, KINGS-IV 04/VERSES 2-3/ WOMAN WITH OIL 615-47, ELISHA TELLS WOMAN TO POUR OIL INTO VESSELS 615-47, VESSELS FILLED WITH OIL OF HOLY SPIRIT 615-47, KINGS-IV 04/VERSES 6-7/ WOMAN SELLS OIL 615-47, ELISHA TELLS WOMAN TO SELL OIL 615-47, SYNAGOGUE FREES ITSELF THROUGH BAPTISMAL WATERS 615-47, KINGS-IV 25/VERSES 1-4/ NEBUCHADNEZZAR BESIEGES JERUSALEM 615-48, NEBUCHADNEZZAR IMPRISONS ZEDEKIAH 615-48, NEBUCHADNEZZAR IS DEVIL/ ZEDEKIAH IS EVIL 615-48, DEVIL 615-48, KINGS-IV 25/VERSE 6/ ZEDEKIAH BLINDED 615-48, ZEDEKIAH BLINDED AND SONS KILLED 615-48, DEVIL BLINDS THOSE WHO PERVERT JUSTICE 615-48,KINGS-IV 25/VERSES 8-9/ NEBUCHADNEZZAR BURNS TEMPLE 615-48, NEBUCHADNEZZAR BURNS TEMPLE 615-48, DEVIL BURNS WORLD WITH GREED AND LUXURY 615-48, EZRA 01/VERSES 1-2/ EZRA REBUILDS TEMPLE 615-48,EZRA REBUILDS TEMPLE 615-48, CYRUS MEANS CHRIST WHO RESCUED FAITHFUL 615-48, NEHEMIAH 02/VERSES 1-3/ NEHEMIAH AND ARTAXERXES 615-49, NEHEMIAH OFFERS WINE TO ARTAXERXES 615-49, CHRIST OFFERS SOUL TO GOD 615-49, NEHEMIAH 04/VERSES 1-3/ SANBALLAT MOCKS JEWS 615-49, SANBALLAT MOCKS JEWS FOR REBUILDING WALLS 615-49, TOBIAH PRAYS TO GOD FOR REVENGE 615-49, TYRANTS TRY TO FORCE CHRISTIANS TO ABANDON FAITH 615-49, NEHEMIAH 04/VERSE 20/ JEWS GUARD WALLS 615-49, NEHEMIAH ORDERS JEWS TO GUARD WALLS 615-49, JUDGMENT DAY WHEN DEAD RISE 615-49, NEHEMIAH 05/VERSES 8-10/ NEHEMIAH REDEEMS JEWS 615-49, NEHEMIAH REDEEMS JEWS 615-49, CHRIST RELEASES CAPTIVES FROM DEVIL 615-49, HARROWING OF HELL 615-49, TOBIT 02/VERSES 3-9/ TOBIT BURIES SLAIN MAN 615-50, TOBIT BURIES SLAIN MAN 615-50, CHRIST BID TO EAT BY DISCIPLES 615-50, TOBIT 02/VERSES 10-19/ TOBIT BLINDED 615-50, TOBIT BLINDED BY SWALLOW DUNG 615-50, PREACHERS TIRE OF LIFE AND ARE BLINDED 615-50, TOBIT 02/VERSES 20-23/ ANNA AND TOBIT 615-50, TOBIT REPROVES ANNA FOR THEFT OF KID 615-50, FLESH HAS DESIRES CONTRARY TO SPIRIT 615-50, TOBIT 03/VERSES 7-10/ SARA REPROVED 615-50, SARA'S SEVEN HUSBANDS KILLED BY DEVIL 615-50, ASMODEUS THE DEVIL KILLS SEVEN HUSBANDS 615-50, SEVEN HUSBANDS ARE GENTILES 615-50, TOBIT 10/VERSE 10/ RAGUEL GIVES SARA TO TOBIT 615-51, RAGUEL GIVES SARA TO TOBIT 615-51, PREACHERS SENT INTO THE WORLD 615-51, TOBIT 11/VERSES 10-11/ TOBIAS WELCOMES TOBIT 615-51, TOBIAS/ BLIND WELCOMES TOBIT 615-51, FAITHFUL WELCOME FAITH OF CHRIST 615-51, TOBIT 11/VERSES 13-16/ TOBIT RESTORES FATHER'S EYES 615-51, TOBIT RESTORES FATHER'S EYES 615-51, CHRIST STRIKES OUT MALICE OF DEVIL 615-51, DEVIL 615-51, TOBIT 12/VERSE 6/ RAPHAEL MAKES HIMSELF KNOWN 615-51, RAPHAEL MAKES HIMSELF KNOWN 615-51, APOSTLES CRY THAT THEY ARE ONLY MORTAL 615-51, TOBIT 14/VERSES 5-12/ DEATH OF TOBIAS 615-52, TOBIAS TELLS TOBIT TO DEPART AFTER HIS DEATH 615-52, HOLY MEN GO FORTH FOR THE LOVE OF CHRIST 615-52, JUDITH 07/VERSES 1-6/ HOLOFERNES ATTACKS BETHULIA 615-52, HOLOFERNES ATTACKS BETHULIA 615-52, DEVIL SLAYS PREACHERS AND TEACHERS 615-52, JUDITH 08/VERSES 9-13/ JUDITH REBUKES JEWS 615-52, JUDITH REBUKES CHABRI AND CHARMI 615-52, WHEN TROUBLED SEEK GOD WITH TEARS/ PRAYERS/ GOOD WORKS 615-52, JUDITH 11/VERSE 1/ JUDITH PRAYS 615-52, JUDITH IN HAIRCLOTH AND ASHES PRAYS 615-52, PREACHERS SHOULD PRACTICE WHAT THEY PREACH 615-52, ESTHER 07/VERSE 10/ HAMAN HANGED 615-53, HAMAN HANGED ON GALLOWS HE PREPARED FOR MORDECAI 615-53, TORTURERS WILL BE TORTURED AT JUDGMENT 615-53,HELL SCENE 615-53, ESTHER 08/VERSES 3-5/ AHASUERUS AND MORDECAI 615-53, AHASUERUS BESTOWS HONORS ON MORDECAI 615-53, OLD LAW RELIEVED BY GOSPELS 615-53, JOB 01/VERSE 2/ JOB WITH SONS AND DAUGHTERS 615-53, JOB WITH SONS AND DAUGHTERS 615-53, JOB'S SONS ARE THE FAITHFUL 615-53, JOB'S DAUGHTERS REPRESENT THREE KINDS OF FAITHFUL 615-53, JOB 01/VERSE 3/ JOB WITH HIS HERDS 615-53, JOB WITH HIS HERDS 615-53, CHRIST WITH HIS FAITHFUL 615-53, JOB 01/VERSES 3-7/ JOB WITH HERDS AND HOUSEHOLD 615-54, JOB WITH HERDS AND HOUSEHOLD 615-54, JEWS WORSHIPPED IDOLS BEFORE CONVERSION 615-54, JOB 01/VERSE 4/ SONS OF JOB FEAST 615-54, FEAST OF SONS AND DAUGHTERS OF JOB 615-54, APOSTLES DISPENSE FEASTS OF THE WORD OF GOD 615-54, JOB 01/VERSE 5/ JOB MAKES

BURNT OFFERING 615-54,JOB SACRIFICES RAM AS OFFERING FOR HIS SONS 615-54, CHRIST WASHES APOSTLES' FEET 615-54, JOB 01/VERSE 7/ DEVIL APPEARS BEFORE CHRIST 615-54, DEVIL APPEARS BEFORE CHRIST 615-54, DEVIL BOASTS HE DECEIVES JEWS AND GENTILES 615-54, JOB 01/VERSES 9-12/ DEVIL AND GOD 615-55, GOD GIVES DEVIL PERMISSION TO DESTROY JOB'S POSSESSIONS 615-55, DEVIL DOUBTS IF CHRIST WAS HUMAN OR DIVINE 615-55, JOB 01/VERSES 14-15/ SABEANS KILL SERVANTS 615-55, SABEANS KILL JOB'S SERVANTS 616-55, PRELATES ARE CORRUPTED BY FLESH 615-55, JOB 01/VERSE 16/ JOB AND MESSENGER 615-55, JOB TOLD THAT FIRE CONSUMED SHEEP 615-55, DEVIL DESTROYS FAITHFUL BY BAD PRELATES 615-55, JOB 01/VERSE 17/ CHALDEANS KILL SERVANTS 615-55,JOB'S CAMELS TAKEN AND SERVANTS KILLED 615-55, VICE/ THREE KINDS 615-55, JOB 01/VERSES 20-21/ JOB'S HEAD SHAVED 615-56, JOB'S HEAD SHAVED 615-56, SHAVING MEANS CHRIST TOOK SACRAMENTS FROM JEWS 615-56, JOB 02/VERSE 3/ GOD AND SATAN 615-56, DEVIL SHOWN HOW JOB RETAINS INTEGRITY 615-56, DEVIL TEMPTS MAN 615-56, JOB 02/VERSES 4-5/ GOD AND SATAN 615-56, GOD AND SATAN 615-56, DEVIL TORMENTS CHRIST'S BODY 615-56, JOB 02/VERSE 7/ SATAN SMITES JOB WITH BOILS 615-56, DEVIL SMITES JOB WITH BOILS 615-56, CHRIST SCOURGED AND CRUCIFIED 615-56, CRUCIFIXION 615-56, JOB 14/VERSES 17-19/ MOUNTAIN BROUGHT TO NOTHING 615-57, JOB'S SIN SEALED UP IN BAG 615-57, GOD IS INDULGENT TOWARD SINNERS 615-57, JOB 15/VERSE 25/ ELIPHAZ THE TEMANITE 615-57, ELIPHAZ THE TEMANITE AND JOB 615-57, JEWS WOULD NOT LISTEN TO MOSES 615-57, MOSES WEARING HORNS AND HOLDING THE LAW 615-57, JOB 15/VERSES 33-34/ WICKED MAN 615-57, WICKED MAN SHALL SHAKE OFF UNRIPE GRAPE 615-57, VINE MEANS THE HYPOCRITE 615-57, JOB 16/VERSES 10-11/ JOB'S ENEMIES 615-57, JOB'S ENEMIES FEAR HIM IN THEIR WRATH 615-57, DEVIL 615-57, CHRIST'S ENEMIES 615-57, DEVIL LEADS CHRISTIANS TO SIN 615-57, JOB 16/VERSE 14/ DEVIL ATTACKS JOB 615-58, DEVIL ATTACKS JOB 615-58, JEWS CRUCIFY CHRIST 615-58, CRUCIFIXION 615-58, JOB 16/VERSES 15-16/ JOB IN SACKCLOTH AND ASHES 615-58, PENITENT IS BIRCHED BY PRIEST 615-58, JOB 17/VERSE 13/ JOB'S GRAVE 615-58, JOB'S GRAVE 615-58, FRIENDS SOON FORGET MAN'S DEATH 615-58, JOB 18/VERSES 1-5 AND 8/ BILDAD 615-58, BILDAD SAYS WICKED ARE CAUGHT IN SNARE 615-58, DEVIL BINDS SINNERS AND CASTS INTO HELL 615-58, HELL SCENE 615-58, JOB 19/VERSES 9-12/ JOB COMPLAINS 615-59, JOB COMPLAINS THAT GOD HAS DESTROYED HIS HOPE 615-59, DEVILS DRAW SINNERS TO HELL 615-59, JOB 19/VERSES 23-24/ JOB COMPLAINS 615-59, JOB WISHES HIS WORDS WERE WRITTEN IN BOOK 615-59, CRUCIFIXION 615-59, JOB 19/VERSES 25-26/ RESURRECTION OF JOB 615-59, JOB TO BE RESURRECTED AT JUDGMENT 615-59, APOSTLES PREACH OF CHRIST'S RESURRECTION 615-59, JOB 20/VERSES 1 AND 15/ WICKED VOMIT RICHES 615-59, GOD MAKES WICKED VOMIT RICHES 615-59, WICKED GO TO HELL WITH SINS 615-59, DEVIL AND WICKED 615-59, JOB 38/VERSE 41/ GOD AND RAVEN 615-60, GOD PROVIDES RAVEN WITH FOOD 615-60, RAVEN IS GENTILE WORLD BLACK WITH SIN 615-60, JOB 39/VERSES 1-4/ GOATS AND DEER 615-60, GOATS AND DEER BRING FORTH YOUNG 615-60, APOSTLES BRING FORTH CHILDREN FOR CHURCH 615-60, JOB 39/VERSE 10/ UNICORN 615-60, UNICORN DRAWS HARROW 615-60, NATIVITY 615-60, JOB 39/VERSES 14-15/ OSTRICH LEAVES EGGS 615-60, OSTRICH LEAVES EGGS TO BE HARMED 615-60, SINNERS FORGET THEY MAY BE DAMNED 615-60

*$ABSTRACT 616
*LIBRARY BODLEIAN
*SLIDE SET TITLE FIFTEENTH CENTURY FLORENTINE PORTRAITS
*NEGATIVE REFERENCE ROLL 248D
*RENTAL FEE $2.35
*COMMENTS SELECTION FROM 7 MANUSCRIPTS.
*TITLE OF MANUSCRIPT SERMONS OF BERNARD OF CLAIRVAUX 616-1, MORALIA IN JOB OF GREGORY THE GREAT 616-2, SUMMA DE CASIBUS CONSCIENTIAE 616-3, IL CANZONIERE OF PETRARCH 616/4-5, WORKS OF CAESAR 616-6, IL CANZONIERE OF PETRARCH 616-7
*SHELFMARK MS CANON PAT LAT 156/ FOL 1 616-1, MS CANON ITAL 187/ FOL 76 616-2, MS CANON MISC 400/ FOL 5 616-3, MS D'ORVILLE 514/ FOL 1 616-4, MS MONTAGU D 33/ FOL 9 616-5, MS

CANON CLASS LAT 266/ FOL 1 616-6, MS CANON ITAL 78/ FOL 1 616-7
*PROVENANCE ITALIAN/ FLORENCE
*DATE EXECUTED 15TH/ 1ST QUARTER 616-1, 15TH/ 1ST QUARTER 616-2, 15TH/ MID 616-3, 15TH/C1450-60 616-4, 15TH/ 3RD QUARTER 616/5-7
*LANGUAGE LATIN 616-1 AND 3 AND 6-7, ITALIAN 616-2 AND 4-5
*ARTIST/ SCHOOL SCHOOL OF THE CONVENT OF S MARIA DEGLI ANGELI 616-1, STROZZI/ ZANOBI 616-3, SCHOOL OF FRANCESCO D'ANTONIO DEL CHERICO 616-6
*AUTHOR BERNARD OF CLAIRVAUX 616-1, GREGORY THE GREAT 616-2, BARTHOLOMAEUS DE SANCTO CONCORDIO 616-3, PETRARCH 616/ 4-5 AND 7 CAESAR 616-6
*TYPE OF MANUSCRIPT SERMONS 616-1, COMMENTARY 616-2, SUMMA 616-3, POETRY 616/4-5 AND 7, HISTORY 616-6
*CONTENTS PORTRAITS/ FLORENTINE 616/1-7, ST BERNARD OF CLAIRVAUX LECTURES TO MONKS 616-1, ST GREGORY THE GREAT 616-2, BARTHOLOMAEUS DE SANCTO CONCORDIO 616-3, PETRARCH 616/4-5 AND 7, CAESAR/ JULIUS 616-6

*$ABSTRACT 617
*LIBRARY BODLEIAN
*SLIDE SET TITLE CREATURES IN A CATENA ON JOB
*NEGATIVE REFERENCE ROLL 248E
*RENTAL FEE $2.65
*COMMENTS THE TEXTS FROM JOB ARE QUOTED ABOVE THE PICTURES IN THE MANUSCRIPT. THE CREATURES ILLUSTRATED ARE NOT MENTIONED IN THE BIBLICAL TEXT.
*TITLE OF MANUSCRIPT CATENA ON JOB
*SHELFMARK MS LAUD GREEK 86/ PAGE 87 617-1, MS LAUD GREEK 86/ PAGE 96 617-2, MS LAUD GREEK 86/ PAGE 164 617-3, MS LAUD GREEK 86/ PAGE 191 617-4, MS LAUD GREEK 86/ PAGE 237 617-5, MS LAUD GREEK 86/ PAGE 320 617-6, MS LAUD GREEK 86/ PAGE 368 617-7, MS LAUD GREEK 86/ PAGE 387 617-8, MS LAUD GREEK 86/ PAGE 389 617-9, MS LAUD GREEK 86/ PAGE 391 617/10-11, MS LAUD GREEK 86/ PAGE 401 617-12, MS LAUD GREEK 86/ PAGE 431 617-13
*PROVENANCE BYZANTINE
*DATE EXECUTED 16TH/ EARLY
*LANGUAGE GREEK
*TYPE OF MANUSCRIPT CATENA
*CONTENTS CREATURES IN A CATENA ON JOB 617/1-13, LIONS/ GREEN DRAGON/ ANT-LION 617-1, EAGLES/ CROWNED FLY UPWARD 617-2, JOB 04/VERSES 10-11 617-1, JOB 05/VERSE 7 617-2, GOD STRETCHES ARMS OVER THE BEASTS/ BIRDS/ FISHES 617-3, JOB ON ASHES SPEAKS TO THREE FRIENDS 617-3, JOB 12/VERSES 7-11 617-3, WICKED MAN WAITS TO DIE/ TWO VULTURES 617-4, JOB 15/VERSES 22-23 617-4, MILKING SHEEP AND COWS/ ROW OF BEE HIVES 617-5, JOB 20/VERSE 17 617-5, FIDDLE AND FOUR LARGE BIRDS 617-6, JOB 30/VERSES 29-31 617-6, BOAR/ RABBIT/ BEASTS RUN FOR SHELTER DURING STORM 617-7, JOB 37/VERSE 8 617-7, RAVENS/ LION/ BEAST 617-8, JOB 38/VERSES 39-41 617-8, ZEBRA/ HIND SUCKLING ITS YOUNG/ TWO OTHER ANIMALS 617-9, JOB 39/VERSES 1-4 617-9, UNICORN AND BIRDS ON NEST OF EGGS 617-10, JOB 39/VERSES 10-14 617-10, HORSE PRANCING 617-11, JOB 39/VERSE 15 617-11, LION AND BEAR EAT GRASS 617-12, JOB 40/VERSE 15 617-12, JOB'S HERD OF SHEEP/ CAMELS/ OXEN/ ASSES 617-13, JOB 42/VERSE 12 617-13

*$ABSTRACT 618
*LIBRARY BODLEIAN
*SLIDE SET TITLE CENTAURS
*NEGATIVE REFERENCE ROLL 248F
*RENTAL FEE $2.45
*COMMENTS SELECTIONS FROM NINE MSS OF 12TH-16TH CENTURIES.
*TITLE OF MANUSCRIPT BOOK OF HOURS 618-1, ASTRONOMICAL AND ASTROLOGICAL TREATISES 618-2, BESTIARY 618-3, DIVINE COMEDY 618-4, ASTRONOMICA 618-5, BIBLE/ NEW TESTAMENT 618-6, BOOK OF HOURS 618-7, EPITRE D'OTHEA A HECTOR 618-8, POEMS WITH GLOSS 618-9

*SHELFMARK MS RAWL LITURG E 17/ FOL 51 618-1, MS LAUD MISC 644/ FOL 10V 618-2, MS DOUCE 88/ FOL 115 618-3, MS CANON ITAL 108/ FOL 11 618-4, MS CANON CLASS LAT 179/ FOL 39 618-5, MS CANON BIBL LAT 1/ FOL 146V 618-6, MS BUCHANAN E 8/ FOL 14 618-7, MS BODLEY 421/ FOL 62V 618-8, MS AUCT T 2 22/ FOL 10 618-9
*PROVENANCE FRENCH/ NORMANDY 618-1, FRENCH/ BAYEUX 618-2, ENGLISH 618-3, ITALIAN/ SOUTH 618-4, ITALIAN/ NORTH? 618-5, ITALIAN 618-6, FRENCH/ PARIS 618-7, FRENCH 618-8, GERMAN? 618-9
*DATE EXECUTED 15TH/ 3RD QUARTER 618-1, 13TH/C1268-74 618-2, 14TH/C1300 618-3, 14TH/ 2ND HALF 618-4, 15TH/ 3RD QUARTER 618-5, 13TH/ 1ST HALF 618-6, 16TH/C1500 618-7, 15TH/ 3RD QUARTER 618-8, 12TH/ 2ND HALF 618-9
*LANGUAGE LATIN 618/1-3, ITALIAN 618-4, LATIN 618/5-6, FRENCH AND LATIN 618-7, FRENCH 618-8, LATIN 618-9
*AUTHOR DANTE 618-4, HYGINUS 618-5, DE PISAN/ CHRISTINE 618-8, PRUDENTIUS 618-9
*TYPE OF MANUSCRIPT BOOK OF HOURS/ USE OF COUTANCES 618-1, ASTRONOMICAL AND ASTROLOGICAL TREATISES 618-2, BESTIARY 618-3, POETRY 618-4, ASTRONOMICAL TREATISE 618-5, BIBLE/ NEW TESTAMENT 618-6, BOOK OF HOURS/ USE OF PARIS 618-7, LITERATURE 618-8, POETRY 618-9
*CONTENTS CENTAURS 618/1-9, MYTHOLOGICAL CREATURES/ CENTAURS 618/1-9, CENTAUR WITH DRAWN BOW AMID FOLIAGE 618-1, CENTAURUS HOLDS BRANCH AND SMALL ANIMAL 618-2, CENTAUR AIMS BOW AT GROTESQUE 618-3, CHIRON AND CENTAURS GUARD RIVER OF BOILING BLOOD 618-4, RIVER OF BOILING BLOOD 618-4, INFERNO/ CANTO 12/ LINES 47FF 618-4, CENTAURUS HOLDS RABBIT BY HIND LEGS 618-5, GROTESQUE RESEMBLES CENTAUR WITH DRAWN BOW 618-6, INITIAL P PAULUS 618-6, CENTAUR WITH DRAWN BOW/ SAGITTARIUS 618-7, SAGITTARIUS/ CENTAUR WITH BOW 618-7, NOVEMBER/ SAGITTARIUS/ MAN COLLECTS ACORNS 618-7, CENTAUR IN BATTLE BETWEEN GREEKS AND TROJANS 618-8, ACHILLES SLAYS HECTOR 618-8, CENTAUR WITH ROUND OBJECTS 618-9

*$ABSTRACT 619
*LIBRARY BODLEIAN
*SLIDE SET TITLE MAPS
*NEGATIVE REFERENCE ROLL 248G
*RENTAL FEE $2.65
*COMMENTS SELECTION FROM THREE MSS OF 15TH-16TH CENTURIES.
*TITLE OF MANUSCRIPT CHRONICLE OF ENGLAND 619/1-3, PORTOLAN CHART 619/4-5, MAP OF LAXTON 619/6-13
*SHELFMARK MS ARCH SELD B 10/ FOL 184 619-1, MS ARCH SELD B 10/ FOL 184V 619-2, MS ARCH SELD B 10/ FOL 185 619-3, MS DOUCE 391/ 3RD OPENING 619/4-5, MS MAPS NOTTS A 2/ SHEET 1 619-6, MS MAPS NOTTS A 2/ SHEET 7 619/7-8, MS MAPS NOTTS A 2/ SHEET 5 619/9-10, MS MAPS NOTTS A 2/ SHEET 4 619/11-12, MS MAPS NOTTS A 2/ SHEET 8 619-13
*PROVENANCE ENGLISH 619/1-3, SPANISH 619/4-5, ENGLISH 619/6-13
*DATE EXECUTED 15TH/C1470-80 619/1-3, 16TH/ 2ND HALF 619/4-5, 17TH/1636 619/6-13
*LANGUAGE FRENCH AND LATIN 619/1-3, ENGLISH 619/6-13
*AUTHOR HARDING/ JOHN 619/1-3,
*ARTIST/ SCHOOL PIERCE/ MARK 619/6-13
*TYPE OF MANUSCRIPT MAPS
*CONTENTS MAPS 619/1-13, MAP OF SCOTLAND WITH PICTURES OF ENNERMETHE/ SEINT JOHNSTON 619-1, MAP OF SCOTLAND/ ABBEY OF LINDORES/ ABBEY OF BALMARINO 619-1, MAP OF SCOTLAND/ ARDISTON/ DON/ FAWKELANDE/ DUNBREYTAYNE 619-1, MAP OF SCOTLAND/ STRYUELYN/ GLASGEWE/ EDENBURGH 619-1, MAP OF SCOTLAND/ DUNBAR/ CARLELE/ WERKWORTH/ NORTH BERWIK 619-1, MAP OF SCOTLAND DIVIDED BY RIVERS/ DYE/ DONE/ SPEY 619-2, HILLS DIVIDE OFF THE WILD SCOTS 619-2, MAP OF SCOTLAND/ WATERS OF SUTHER/ SUTHERLAND/ CAITHNESS 619-3, MAP OF SCOTLAND/ RIVER STYX/ PALACE OF PLUTO 619-3, RIVER STYX 619-3, PLUTO'S PALACE 619-3, MAP OF INDIA/ PERSIA/ ARABIA/ RED SEA/ EAST AFRICA 619-4, PRESTER JOHN AND THE GRAND TURK/ RULERS 619-4,PRESTER JOHN/ RULER OF THE INDIES 619-5, MAP OF LAXTON 619/6-13, PART OF KIRTON LORDSHIP/ ENCLOSURE 3031/ SHEEP 619-6, PART OF RUFFARD

ABBEY FIELDES/ LORDSHIP OF AKERING 619-7, PART OF READ INGE AND OWLD PARK 619-8, EGMONTON/ PLOWING SCENE 619-9, PLOWING 619-9, EGMONTON/ REAPERS/ FARM CART AND CATTLE 619-10, REAPING 619-10, FARM CART AND CATTLE 619-10, PART OF OMPTON LORDSHIP/ ENCLOSURE 1623 619-11, PART OF OMPTON LORDSHIP/ WINDMILL 619-12, PART OF LORDSHIP OF KARS/ ENCLOSURE 1991/ SHEEP 619-13

*$ABSTRACT 620
*LIBRARY BODLEIAN
*SLIDE SET TITLE EARLY SCIENCE II
*NEGATIVE REFERENCE ROLL 248H
*RENTAL FEE $3.05
*COMMENTS SELECTION OF DIAGRAMS FROM SEVEN MSS OF 10TH-13TH CENTURIES.
*TITLE OF MANUSCRIPT DE SOMNIO SCIPIONIS 620/1-2, DE SOMNIO SCIPIONIS 620-3, TIMAEUS 620/4-5, DE SOMNIO SCIPIONIS 620/6-12, DRAGMATICON 620/13-16, DE NATURA RERUM 620/17-21, DE SOMNIO SCIPIONIS 620/17-21
*SHELFMARK MS AUCT T 2 27/ FOL 12V 620-1, MS AUCT T 2 27/ FOL 34V 620-2, MS AUCT T 2 27/ FOL 88V 620-3, MS AUCT F 3 15/ FOL 20 620-4, MS AUCT F 3 15/ FOL 30 620-5, MS SELDEN SUPRA 26/ FOL 33V 620-6, MS SELDEN SUPRA 26/ FOL 74V 620-7, MS SELDEN SUPRA 25/ FOL 199V 620-8, MS SELDEN SUPRA 25/ FOL 203V 620-9, MS SELDEN SUPRA 25/ FOL 204V 620-10, MS SELDEN SUPRA 25/ FOL 205 620-11, MS SELDEN SUPRA 25/ FOL 211V 620-12, MS E MUSAEO 121/ FOL 41V 620-13, MS E MUSAEO 121/ FOL 50V 620-14, MS E MUSAEO 121/ FOL 54 620-15, MS E MUSAEO 121/ FOL 55V-56 620-16, MS AUCT F 2 20/ FOL 4V 620-17, MS AUCT F 2 20/ FOL 5V 620-18, MS AUCT F 2 20/ FOL 6 620-19, MS AUCT F 2 20/ FOL 25V 620-20, MS AUCT F 2 20/ FOL 45 620-21
*PROVENANCE FRENCH 620/1-2, GERMAN/ SOUTH 620-3, IRISH 620/4-5, ENGLISH? 620/6-7, ENGLISH 620/13-16, ENGLISH 620/17-21
*DATE EXECUTED 10TH/ LATE 620/1-2, 11TH/ EARLY 620-3, 12TH? 620/4-5, 12TH/ 2ND HALF 620/6-7, 13TH/ EARLY 620/8-12, 13TH/ 2ND HALF 620/13-16, 11TH/ 2ND HALF 620/17-21
*LANGUAGE LATIN
*AUTHOR MACROBIUS 620/1-3, PLATO'S TIMAEUS BY CHALCIDIUS 620/4-5, MACROBIUS 620/6-12, WILLIAM OF CONCHES 620/13-16, ISIDORE 620/17-21, MACROBIUS 620/17-21
*TYPE OF MANUSCRIPT TREATISES AND COMMENTARIES 620/1-21
*CONTENTS SCIENCE 620/1-21, DIAGRAM/ CIRCULAR DIVIDED INTO QUARTERS 620-1, COMPASS POINTS 620-1, ELEMENTS/ FOUR 620-1, SEASONS/ FOUR 620-1, DIAGRAM/ CIRCULAR/ GREAT RAIN IN BABYLON 620-2, BABYLON/ GREAT RAIN IN 620-2, DIAGRAM/ CIRCULAR/ SIMILAR TO FRAME 2 620-3, DIAGRAM OF MUSICAL INTERVALS 620-4, MUSICAL INTERVALS 620-4, TABULA 620-5, DIAGRAM/ TRIANGULAR 620-6, DIAGRAM/ CIRCULAR 620/7-10, DIAGRAM/ CIRCULAR INSET WITH CONCENTRIC CIRCLE 620-11, DIAGRAM OF THE PLANETS 620-12, PLANETS/ DIAGRAM 620-12, DIAGRAM OF FOUR POSITIONS OF A PLANET 620-13, PLANET/ FOUR POSITIONS 620-13, DIAGRAM/ CIRCULAR LABELLED WITH FOUR ELEMENTS 620-14, ELEMENTS/ FOUR 620-14, DIAGRAM/ RECTANGULAR WITH POSITIONS OF MOON 620-15, MOON/ DIAGRAM SHOWING POSITIONS 620-15, DIAGRAMS OF SUN'S RELATION TO EARTH 620-16, SUN'S RELATION TO THE EARTH 620-16, DIAGRAM/ CIRCULAR OF FOUR SEASONS 620-17, SEASONS/ FOUR 620-17, DIAGRAM/ CIRCULAR OF FOUR ELEMENTS 620-18, ELEMENTS/ FOUR 620-18, DIAGRAM OF FOUR ELEMENTS AND SEASONS 620-19, DIAGRAM OF FOUR ELEMENTS 620-20, RELATIONS OF FOUR ELEMENTS TO DRY/ WARM/ HUMID/ COLD 620-20, DIAGRAM/ CIRCULAR 620-21

*$ABSTRACT 621
*LIBRARY BODLEIAN
*SLIDE SET TITLE BINDINGS
*NEGATIVE REFERENCE ROLL 248I
*RENTAL FEE $2.40
*TITLE OF MANUSCRIPT JUSTINIANUS INSTITUTIONES 621-1, SINGALEESCH GEBEEDE-BOEK 621-2, OPERA REGIA 621-3, HOLY BIBLE 621-4, THE FULNESSE OF CHRIST FOR US 621-5, THE HISTORY OF THE

RENOWN'D DON QUIXOTE 621-6, L'ART DE BIEN VIVRE ET DE BIEN MOURIR 621-7, HORTUS E ITHAMENSIS 621-8
*SHELFMARK PR AUCT IV Q II 1 621-1, PR ARCH B E 6 621-2, PR ARCH A C 3 621-3, PR ARCH A D 14 621-4, PR ARCH A F 108 621-5, PR ARCH A F 116 621-6, PR DOUCE 169 621-7, PR ARCH NAT HIST H 11 621-8
*PROVENANCE GERMAN/ MAINZ 621-1, CEYLON/ COLOMBO 621-2, ENGLISH/ LONDON 621-3, ENGLISH/ CAMBRIDGE 621-4, ENGLISH/ LONDON 621/5-6, FRENCH/ PARIS TEXT 621-7, ENGLISH/ LONDON BINDING 621-7, ENGLISH/ LONDON 621-8
*DATE EXECUTED 15TH/1468 TEXT 621-1, 19TH/1805-18 BINDING 621-1, 18TH/1737 621-2, 17TH/1619 621-3, 17TH/1673 621-4, 17TH/1639 621-5, 18TH/1700 621-6, 15TH/1493 TEXT 621-7, 18TH/1776-89 BINDING 621-7, 18TH/1732 621-8
*AUTHOR KING JAMES I 621-3, PRESTON/ JOHN 621-5, CERVANTES 621-6, DILLENIUS/ JOHANNES JACOBUS 621-8
*TYPE OF MANUSCRIPT INSTITUTIONES 621-1, GEBEEDE-BOEK 621-2, OPERA REGIA 621-3, BIBLE/ OLD TESTAMENT 621-4, RELIGIOUS TREATISE 621-5, LITERATURE 621-6, TREATISE 621-7, NATURAL HISTORY 621-8
*CONTENTS BINDINGS/ 15TH-19TH 621/1-8, BLUE MOROCCO/ ELABORATELY TOOLED IN GILT BY BOZERIAN JEUNE 621-1, BOUND AT NETHERLANDS EAST INDIA COMPANY'S PRESS 621-2, PRESENTATION COPY IN BLUE MOROCCO TO BODLEIAN 621-3, RED MOROCCO BOUND FOR ELIZABETH CHOLMONDELEY 621-4, EMBROIDERED BINDING IN COLORED SILKS 621-5, RED MOROCCO AND GILT TOOLED WITH STRAP ORNAMENT 621-6, RED AND GREEN MOROCCO/ BOUND BY RICHARD DYMOTT 621-7, CRIMSON MOROCCO/ GILT TOOLED/ BLUE INLAYS 621-8

*$ABSTRACT 622
*LIBRARY BODLEIAN
*SLIDE SET TITLE PSALTER/ ENGLISH
*NEGATIVE REFERENCE ROLL 248J
*RENTAL FEE $2.65
*COMMENTS ALL THE ILLUSTRATIONS FROM THE PSALTER.
*SHELFMARK MS DOUCE 131/ FOL 1 622-1, MS DOUCE 131/ FOL 20 622-2, MS DOUCE 131/ FOL 32 622-3, MS DOUCE 131/ FOL 42V 622-4, MS DOUCE 131/ FOL 43 622-5, MS DOUCE 131/ FOL 54 622-6, MS DOUCE 131/ FOL 68V 622-7, MS DOUCE 131/ FOL 81V 622-8, MS DOUCE 131/ FOL 83V 622-9, MS DOUCE 131/ FOL 96V 622-10, MS DOUCE 131/ FOL 97 622-11, MS DOUCE 131/ FOL 110 622-12, MS DOUCE 131/ FOL 126 622-13
*PROVENANCE ENGLISH/ EAST ANGLIA
*DATE EXECUTED 14TH/C1340
*LANGUAGE LATIN
*ARTIST/ SCHOOL ORMESBY PSALTER/ CLOSE TO THE LATEST ADDITIONS
*TYPE OF MANUSCRIPT PSALTER
*CONTENTS PSALTER/ ENGLISH/ 14TH 622/1-13, PSALM 1 INITIAL B BEATUS/ DAVID PLAYS HARP 622-1, INITIAL B BEATUS/ DAVID PLAYS HARP 622-1, DAVID PLAYS HARP 622-1, DAVID AND GOLIATH 622-1, JESSE TREE ABOUND BORDERS 622-1, PSALM 26/27 INITIAL D DOMINUS ILLUMINATIO/ SAMUEL 622-2, INITIAL D DOMINUS ILLUMINATIO/ SAMUEL 622-2, SAMUEL ANOINTING DAVID 622-2, MEN/ TWO FIGHT WITH SWORDS AND SHIELDS 622-2, CAT CHASES RAT 622-2, FIDDLE PLAYED BY GOAT 622-2, TRUMPET PLAYED BY ANIMAL 622-2, PSALM 38/39 INITIAL D DIXI CUSTODIAM/ AMALEKITE KILLED 622-3, INITIAL D DIXI CUSTODIAM/ AMALEKITE KILLED 622-3, DAVID ORDERS SOLDIER TO KILL AMALEKITE 622-3, APE ON GOAT TILTS WITH DOG ON STAG 622-3, PSALM 51/52 INITIAL Q QUID GLORIARIS/ SAUL STABS HIMSELF 622-4, INITIAL Q QUID GLORIARIS/ KING SAUL STABS HIMSELF 622-4, SAUL/ KING STABS HIMSELF 622-4, STRINGED INSTRUMENT PLUCKED BY GROTESQUES 622-4, BAGPIPES PLAYED BY GROTESQUES 622-4, COCK FIGHT BEFORE BATTLEMENTED HENHOUSE 622-4, PSALM 52/53 INITIAL D DIXIT INSIPIENS/ DAVID AND FOOL 622-5, INITIAL D DIXIT INSIPIENS/ DAVID AND FOOL 622-5, DAVID AND FOOL 622-5, PIPE AND TABOR AND TRUMPET PLAYED BY GROTESQUES 622-5, WAGON/ COVERED DRAWN BY HORSES 622-5, PSALM 68/69 INITIAL S SALVUM ME FAC/ JONAH 622-6, INITIAL S SALVUM ME FAC/ JONAH EMERGES FROM WHALE 622-6, JONAH EMERGES FROM MOUTH OF WHALE 622-6, KNIGHTS/ MOUNTED FIGHT AS LADY WATCHES

622-6, PSALM 80/81 INITIAL E EXULTATE DEO/ KING DAVID 622-7, INITIAL E EXULTATE DEO/ DAVID PLAYS BELLS 622-7, DAVID PLAYS BELLS/ TWO DEPICTIONS 622-7, DAVID PLAYS PSALTERY 622-7, DAVID PLAYS HARP 622-7, KNIGHT CHARGES WILD MAN WITH CLUB 622-7, WILD MAN WITH CLUB CHARGED BY MOUNTED KNIGHT 622-7, PSALM 97/98 INITIAL C CANTATE DOMINO/ PRIEST RAISES HOST 622-8, INITIAL C CANTATE DOMINO/ PRIEST RAISES HOST 622-8, PRIEST RAISES HOST BEFORE ALTAR 622-8, KNIGHT LANCES WILD MAN 622-8, WILD MAN LANCED BY KNIGHT/ LADY WATCHES 622-8,PSALM 101/102 INITIAL D DOMINE EXAUDI/ DAVID PRAYS 622-9, INITIAL D DOMINE EXAUDI/ DAVID PRAYS 622-9, DAVID KNEELS IN PRAYER/ GOD ABOVE ALTAR 622-9,JUDGMENT OF SOLOMON 622-10, SOLOMON'S JUDGMENT/ FIVE FIGURES LOOK ON 622-10, PSALM 109/110 INITIAL D DIXIT DOMINUS/ TRINITY 622-11, INITIAL D DIXIT DOMINUS/ TRINITY 622-11, TRINITY 622-11, PSALM 119/120 INITIAL A AD DOMINUM/ VIRGIN AND CHILD 622-12, INITIAL A AD DOMINUM/ OWNER KNEELS BEFORE VIRGIN 622-12, VIRGIN AND CHILD/ OWNER KNEELS BEFORE 622-12, PSALM 137/138 INITIAL C CONFITEBOR TIBI/ CONFESSION 622-13, INITIAL C CONFITEBOR TIBI/ WOMAN CONFESSES TO MONK 622-13, CONFESSION OF WOMAN TO MONK 622-13

*$ABSTRACT 623
*LIBRARY BODLEIAN
*SLIDE SET TITLE HERBAL
*NEGATIVE REFERENCE ROLL 248K
*RENTAL FEE $3.40
*COMMENTS 28 SLIDES SELECTED FROM ENGLISH HERBAL. SEE ALSO BODLEIAN ROLL 175K/ ABSTRACT 139.
*SHELFMARK MS BODLEY 130/ FOL 2 623-1, MS BODLEY 130/ FOL 3 623-2, MS BODLEY 130/ FOL 3V 623-3, MS BODLEY 130/ FOL 4 623-4, MS BODLEY 130/ FOL 4V 623-5, MS BODLEY 130/ FOL 5 623-6, MS BODLEY 130/ FOL 5V 623-7, MS BODLEY 130/ FOL 7 623-8, MS BODLEY 130/ FOL 7V 623-9, MS BODLEY 130/ FOL 9 623-10, MS BODLEY 130/ FOL 10V 623-11, MS BODLEY 130/ FOL 11 623-12, MS BODLEY 130/ FOL 16V 623-13, MS BODLEY 130/ FOL 18V 623-14, MS BODLEY 130/ FOL 24V 623-15, MS BODLEY 130/ FOL 25 623-16, MS BODLEY 130/ FOL 26V 623-17, MS BODLEY 130/ FOL 27 623-18, MS BODLEY 130/ FOL 33 623-19, MS BODLEY 130/ FOL 33V 623-20, MS BODLEY 130/ FOL 34 623-21, MS BODLEY 130/ FOL 38 623-22, MS BODLEY 130/ FOL 41 623-23, MS BODLEY 130/ FOL 41V 623-24, MS BODLEY 130/ FOL 50V 623-25, MS BODLEY 130/ FOL 51 623-26, MS BODLEY 130/ FOL 52V 623-27, MS BODLEY 130/ FOL 56 623-28
*PROVENANCE ENGLISH/ BURY ST EDMUNDS
*DATE EXECUTED 11TH/ LATE
*LANGUAGE LATIN
*AUTHOR PSEUDO APULEIUS
*TYPE OF MANUSCRIPT HERBAL
*CONTENTS HERBAL/ ENGLISH/ 11TH 623/1-28, BOTANICAL ILLUSTRATION 623/1-28, BEET 623-1, STRAWBERRY 623-2, MARSH MALLOW 623-3, HORSETAIL/ FALSE BULLRUSH 623-4, MALVA SYLVESTRIS 623-5, BUGLOSS 623-6, SQUILL/ USE AS INVISIBLE INK 623-7, HOREHOUND 623-8, FOX'S FOOT/ STINKING IRIS/ GLADDEN 623-9, MADDER 623-10, DROPWORT 623-11, NARCISSUS POETICUS 623-12, VERVAIN 623-13, WOAD 623-14, EVERFERN 623-15, ASPARAGUS 623-16, YARROW 623-17, RUE 623-18, WORMWOOD/ HERBA ABSINTHIUM 623-19, SAGE 623-20, BETONY 623-21, IRIS/ YELLOW FLAG 623-22, ORCHIS 623-23, AUTUM GENTIAN 623-24, LILY AND SPURGE 623-25, WILD THISTLE/ SONCHUS 623-26, CUCUMBER 623-27, DILL AND MARJORAM 623-28

*$ABSTRACT 624
*LIBRARY UNIVERSITY COLLEGE OXFORD
*SLIDE SET TITLE APOCALYPSE/ ENGLISH
*NEGATIVE REFERENCE ROLL 248L
*RENTAL FEE $2.70
*COMMENTS SELECTION OF 14 SLIDES FROM ENGLISH APOCALYPSE.
*SHELFMARK MS UNIVERSITY COLLEGE 100/ FOL 25 624-1, MS

UNIVERSITY COLLEGE 100/ FOL 27V 624-2, MS UNIVERSITY COLLEGE 100/ FOL 29 624-3, MS UNIVERSITY COLLEGE 100/ FOL 32V 624-4, MS UNIVERSITY COLLEGE 100/ FOL 34V 624-5, MS UNIVERSITY COLLEGE 100/ FOL 36 624-6, MS UNIVERSITY COLLEGE 100/ FOL 43V 624-7, MS UNIVERSITY COLLEGE 100/ FOL 53 624-8, MS UNIVERSITY COLLEGE 100/ FOL 58 624-9, MS UNIVERSITY COLLEGE 100/ FOL 59 624-10, MS UNIVERSITY COLLEGE 100/ FOL 82 624-11, MS UNIVERSITY COLLEGE 100/ FOL 82V 624-12, MS UNIVERSITY COLLEGE 100/ FOL 84V 624-13, MS UNIVERSITY COLLEGE 100/ FOL 86 624-14
*PROVENANCE ENGLISH
*DATE EXECUTED 14TH
*LANGUAGE LATIN
*TYPE OF MANUSCRIPT APOCALYPSE
*CONTENTS APOCALYPSE/ ENGLISH/ 14TH 624/1-14, OPENING OF SIXTH SEAL/ EARTHQUAKE AND SUN DARK 624-1, REV 06/VERSES 12-15/ SIXTH SEAL 624-1, CHRIST HOLDS AGNUS DEI/ PEOPLE HOLD PALMS 624-2, REV 07/VERSES 9-11/ CHRIST WITH AGNUS DEI 624-2, OPENING OF SEVENTH SEAL/ ANGELS WITH TRUMPETS 624-3, CHRIST IN MANDORLA 624-3, REV 08/VERSES 1-3/ SEVENTH SEAL 624-3, TRUMPET/ FIFTH SOUNDED/ STAR FALLS FROM HEAVEN 624-4, BOTTOMLESS PIT OPENED AND LOCUSTS EMERGE 624-4, LOCUST WITH HUMAN FACE AND CROWN 624-4, REV 09/VERSES 1-10/ FIFTH TRUMPET 624-4, TRUMPET/ SIXTH SOUNDED/ CHRIST IN MANDORLA 624-5, CHRIST IN MANDORLA/ ALTAR BEFORE 624-5, ANGEL LOOSENS FOUR ANGELS BOUND IN EUPHRATES 624-5, REV 09/VERSES 13-14/ SIXTH TRUMPET 624-5, ANGEL WITH ONE FOOT ON SEA/ ONE OF EARTH 624-6, THUNDERS/ SEVEN AS BEAST'S HEADS 624-6, REV 10/VERSES 1-3 624-6, WOMAN CLOTHED WITH SUN OUTSIDE DOORWAY OF HEAVEN 624-7, REV 12/VERSE 1/ WOMAN CLOTHED WITH SUN 624-7, LAMB OF GOD ON SION 624-8, REV 14/VERSE 1/ LAMB OF GOD 624-8, GRAPES CUT FROM VINE OF EARTH/ WINEPRESS 624-9, WINEPRESS OF THE WRATH OF GOD 624-9, REV 14/VERSES 17-20/ GREAT WINEPRESS 624-9, SEVEN ANGELS WITH HARPS 624-10, REV 15/VERSES 1-2/ ANGELS WITH HARPS 624-10, DRAGON PUSHED INTO HELL BY ANGEL WITH KEY 624-11, HELL DOORWAY/ DRAGON PUSHED INTO 624-11, REV 20/VERSES 1-2/ DRAGON PUSHED INTO HELL 624-11, ANGEL DESCENDS TO TAKE RIGHTEOUS TO HEAVEN 624-12, REV 20/VERSES 4-5/ SALVATION OF RIGHTEOUS 624-12, DEAD STAND IN OPEN TOMBS BEFORE CHRIST 624-13, REV 20/VERSE 12/ DEAD RAISED BY CHRIST 624-13, ST JOHN'S VISION OF NEW JERUSALEM 624-14, NEW JERUSALEM 624-14, REV 21/VERSE 2/ VISION OF NEW JERUSALEM 624-14, ANGEL GUIDES JOHN TO NEW JERUSALEM 624-14, REV 21/VERSES 9-10/ JOHN GUIDED TO NEW JERUSALEM 624-14

*$ABSTRACT 625
*LIBRARY BODLEIAN
*SLIDE SET TITLE MARRIAGE OF THE LAMB
*NEGATIVE REFERENCE ROLL 248M
*RENTAL FEE $2.25
*COMMENTS ILLUSTRATIONS OF REV 19 VERSES 7-9, THE MARRIAGE SUPPER OF THE LAMB, SELECTED FROM FIVE ENGLISH 13TH-14TH CENTURY APOCALYPSE MSS.
*SHELFMARK MS AUCT D 4 17/ FOL 18V 625-1, MS ASHMOLE 753/ FOL 32 625-2, MS AUCT D 4 14/ FOL 49V 625-3, MS CANON BIBL LAT 62/ FOL 32 625-4, MS BODLEY 401/ FOL 58 625-5
*PROVENANCE ENGLISH
*DATE EXECUTED 13TH/1250-60 625-1, 14TH/C1300 625-2, 14TH/ EARLY 625/3-4, 14TH/ MID 625-5
*LANGUAGE LATIN
*ARTIST/ SCHOOL SCHOOL OF ST ALBANS/ BASED ON MODEL OF 625-1
*TYPE OF MANUSCRIPT APOCALYPSE
*CONTENTS MARRIAGE OF THE LAMB 625/1-5, APOCALYPSE/ ENGLISH/ 13TH 625/1-5, REV 19/VERSES 7-9/ MARRIAGE OF LAMB 625/1-5, LAMB/ MARRIAGE SUPPER 625/1-5

*$ABSTRACT 626
*LIBRARY CORPUS CHRISTI COLLEGE OXFORD
*SLIDE SET TITLE MAPS FROM CORPUS CHRISTI COLLEGE

*NEGATIVE REFERENCE ROLL 249A
*RENTAL FEE $3.20
*PROVENANCE ENGLISH 626/1-24
*DATE EXECUTED 17TH/1604 626-1, 18TH/1702 626-2, 19TH 626/3-4, 18TH/1741 626-5, 18TH/1705 626-6, 19TH/1822 626-7, 19TH/1850 626-8, 19TH/1812 626-9, 18TH/1777 626/10-12, 19TH/1879 626/13-17, 18TH/1766 626-18, 17TH/1659 626/19-24
*TYPE OF MANUSCRIPT MAPS AND PLANS
*CONTENTS MAPS AND PLANS/ ENGLISH 626/1-24, MAPS OF GLOUCESTERSHIRE 626/1-5, DAGLINGWORTH AND DUNTISBOURNE 1604 626-1, DUNTISBOURNE 1702 626-2, COWCOMBE ESTATE/ MINCHINHAMPTON 19TH-CENTURY 626-3, DETAIL OF COMMON AREA AT TOP RIGHT 626-4, SALPERTON 1741 626-5, MAP OF LINCOLNSHIRE 626-6, LISSINGTON 1705 626-6, MAPS OF OXFORDSHIRE 626/7-17, MARSTON 1822 626-7, HEADINGTON 1850 626-8, EYNSHAM 1812 626-9, TACKLEY 1777 626-10, DETAIL OF UPPER RIGHT SECTION 626-11, DETAIL OF TITLE 626-12, TACKLEY/ WHITES PLAN/ HYDRAULIC RAM 1879 626-13,TACKLEY/ WHITES PLAN/ HYDRAULIC RAM 626-14, HEYFORD/ LARGE PLAN 626-15, DETAIL OF AREA WITH BUILDINGS 626/16-17, MAP OF SOMERSET 626-18, MELSBOROUGH PLAN 1766 626-18, MAPS OF SURREY 626/19-24, MILTON MANOR/ ORIGINAL DRAFT 1659 626-19, DETAIL/ LEFT SECTION 626-20, DETAIL/ CENTER SECTION 626-21, DETAIL/ RIGHT SECTION 626-22, MILTON MANOR NO 1 1659 626-23, MILTON MANOR NO 2 1659 626-24

*$ABSTRACT 627
*LIBRARY BODLEIAN
*SLIDE SET TITLE MAP OF TITTLESHALL AND HEVENINGHAM PEDIGREE ROLL
*NEGATIVE REFERENCE ROLL 249B
*RENTAL FEE $4.20
*TITLE OF MANUSCRIPT TITTLESHALL MAP 627/1-15,HEVENINGHAM PEDIGREE ROLL 627/16-44
*PROVENANCE ENGLISH
*DATE EXECUTED 16TH/1596 627/1-15, 17TH/ LATE 627/16-44
*TYPE OF MANUSCRIPT MAP 627/1-15, PEDIGREE ROLL 627/16-44
*CONTENTS MAP OF TITTLESHALL WITH AUTOGRAPH NOTES 627/1-15, HERALDRIC PEDIGREE/ HEVENINGHAM 627/16-44

*$ABSTRACT 628
*LIBRARY BODLEIAN
*SLIDE SET TITLE IRISH HERALDRY
*NEGATIVE REFERENCE ROLL 250
*RENTAL FEE $4.00
*COMMENTS A COLLECTION OF ARMS OF IRISH FAMILIES OF THE PERIOD OF CHARLES I.
*SHELFMARK MS RAWL B 69/ FOL 4-42
*PROVENANCE IRISH
*DATE EXECUTED 17TH
*TYPE OF MANUSCRIPT HERALDRY
*CONTENTS HERALDRY/ IRISH 628/1-40, COATS OF ARMS/ IRISH 628/1-40, CROKER/ FITZ-ROW/ DUSHED/ FLEMING ORELE/ OROYRKE/ OHANLAN 628-1, OTOOLE OF POWIS/ OTOOLE 628-1, DARLEYS/ CARDIEF/ DARCY/ PHEPOW/ STOKES/ CADDO 628-2, BOYES/ BURHILL/ WEST 628-2, SYNNATTE/ OBURNE/ WATERHOWSE/ PYFOULDE/ BOWCHER 628-3, VELDON/ WARRIN/ FENTON/ CORAN 628-3, BOXFOURD/ FRYERE/ HALL/ BALLE/ GRENE/ BUTLER 628-4, HEWETT/ NAUGH/ SHELTON 628-4, BARNELL/ BATHE/ CANTWELL/ DECYE/ ODRON/ FLALESBURY 628-5, PERTE/ NOTTINGHAM/ WAFFIER 628-5, FOTZ RORYE/ COGAN/ MUSTIAN/ WADDING/ HARROLD 628-6, SILVELNEY/ ST VALLENTYNE BROWNE/ KENLEYE/ PELLETT 628-6, PETTETT/ FELD/ HERPOOLE/ RIDER/ KELLEY/ WHITE 628-7, OCONNER/ BUTLER/ OFARRELL 628-7, CANNAN/ MALONE/ DOBBINS/ AYLMER/ BRADY/ PHIEPOWE 628-8, KERDIFFE/ KENSLEY/ AYLMER OF THE LIONS 628-8, GROGAN/ KETTING/ KELLON/ KERDIFFE/ LAFFEILD 628-9, LACY/ LOVETT/ LOMBERT/ LAKARD 628-9, MACKWILLIAMS/ NEWTERELL/ PLUNKETT/ PLONKETT/ TYRNYES 628-10, SILNELNEY/ SLAYNEY/ STODY ALIAS STOOKES/ TERELL 628-10, SHOURHAM/ TYLNEY/ TUTE/ WAFFER/ WALLING/

WELLESLEY 628-11, WESTON/ WICHE OR WHITE/ WHITBEY 628-11, WYSE/ WOODLOCK/ WITELINCH OF KNOCK/ BRICE 628-12, SHERLEY/ NEWMAN/ RIDER 628-12, HORE/ BEARNES/ JAMES/ MAULTBIE/ STRETT ALIAS STREETE 628-13, HALARAN/ BARON/ CORCKRAN/ WELSH 628-13, MACQUERS/ KELEY/ MONEY/ MARDE/ CRUESSE/ KYRDIFF 628-14, KINSLEY/ KETTYN/ KELLOM 628-14, SEARCHFEILD/ FINNEGLAS/ SCORLOCK/ LYNAM/ LENNON 628-15, WELSHE/ WELSH/ ARCHER/ WELSHE 628-15, HORE/ BENETT/ NEVELL/ DEVOREX/ PYGOTT/ KINGE/ HACKETT 628-16, STANTON/ LUTTERELL 628-16, COSBYE/ BATHE/ FITZ-SYMONS/ HOLLYWOOD/ PRESTON 628-17, LYNCH/ LYNCH/ KYNTE/ SHELINGFORD 628-17, LOCARD/ LONGSPEY/ DOLAFEILD/ UFFORD/ HERBRIGHT 628-18, DERPATRICK/ DRACOTT/ PYGOTT/ DUKE 628-18, FITZ-ALURED/ BELLEW/ BUTLER VISCOUNT MONTGARRETT 628-19, COMYNE/ GYFFORD/ SEDGRAVE/ PEACOCK/ TRAVERS/ BRICE 628-19, OCONNOR/ GENNEVELL/ CROMLYN ALIAS CROMWELL/ FITZWILLIAM 628-20, BRUMINGHAM/ HAMLYN/ SEDGRAVE/ BUTTLER/ POORE 628-20, CARRICK OF THE E OF ORMOND'S HOUSE/ BUTTLER/ SAUADGE 628-21, HANCOCK/ DUNGAIN/ STOUHURST/ ALLEN/ TAYLOR/ RUSSELL 628-21, ELIOTT MACK JONNEN/ BURT/ BURFOURD/ SEXTON/ ARTHUR 628-22, BUTLER/ BUTTLER/ HUSES/ MANUS ALIAS MAUDE 628-22, MACGENNIS/ MACWILLIAM/ DOWDALL/ EVERS/ MOORE/ CRUSE 628-23, BARNWELL/ BARNWELL/ DRAKES 628-23, BARNWELL/ BARNWELL/ ARDERNE/ FITZHENRY/ JAFFE 628-24, WHITTE/ FLATBURY/ DOWDALL/ VALE 628-24, NEWTREWILLE/ MACGILL PATRICK/ BURCH/ BARINGTON 628-25, FITZ EUSTAS/ LACYE/ WHIGHT/ LACY/ ST MICHELL 628-25, CLERKE/ BURTON/ HADLEY/ SWANSHED/ HARNE 628-26, CHARNELL/ TALBOT/ OBRAJAYNE 628-26, ALLEN/ ROCHEFORD/ USHER/ CLYNTON/ GOZ OR GOCHE 628-27, WARING/ BLACKNEY/ OBRYAN/ LD VERNON 628-27, SR HENRY HARRINGTON/ AGARD/ BARKLEY/ NORRIS/ GRACE 628-28, COPENGOY/ LANE/ OKHAMLYN/ PASTELOW 628-28, DELAHIDE/ PARRES/ TYRRELL/ SAVAGE/ MALONE 628-29, SUTTON/ OCONNOR/ WELLES/ PURSELL 628-29, BOXANE/ TIRON ONEALE/ ODONELL/ SHEARLES/ FITZ-PATRICK 628-30, FITZ-GARRETT/ DYLLON/ WHITE/ BLAKES 628-30, UGHAN/ UGHAN/ SMYTHE/ TIPPER/ OMORE/ TALBOTT 628-31, DEVENISH/ RED DOWDALL/ WHITE/ DOWDALL/ COWIKE 628-31, FAGAN/ FALLAN/ ROWNSELL ALIAS ROWNSEVALL/ HAMLYN 628-32, PLUNKETT/ DEVENISH/ CANDELL/ PROWDFOOTE/ PENTNEY 628-32, FAGAN/ WELESLEY/ THROGHGRAM/ HAROLDE/ CAREW 628-33, COLCLOUGH/ COOLEY/ MASTERSOME/ APSLEY 628-33,MCCARTIE OMARGHE/ DANELLS/ MACKWORTH/ ST LEGER/ BLUNT 628-34, WARINE/ BREBAZON/ LOFTUS/ FITZ-STEVINS 628-34, BERNINGHAM/ LD BERNINGHAM/ BERNINGHAM EARLE OF LOWTH 628-35, FITZ-WILLIAM/ COLEMAR/ PILLETT/ MALEPHANT/ FITZ-GERALD 628-35, LOMBERT/ BAGNOLL/ SHERLOCK/ GOGH/ HAMLING/ WARING 628-36, BLACKNE/ BRICE/ RIDNE 628-36, KINGDOM OF IRELAND/ BURGH/ ORMOND/ KILDARE/ FITZGERALD 628-37, DOSMOND FITZGERALD/ BERMINGHAM OF LOUTH 628-37, E OF KLENRICHARD/ E OF KLENRICHARD/ E OF TOOMOND 628-37, E OF TERONE/ PRESTON/ PRINDEGES/ MORTIMER/ CURSEY 628-38, NEWGENT/ ST LAWRENCE/ PLOUNCKETT/ LD POWER 628-38, LD DYLLON/ DAVID LD BARRYE/ LD ROCK/ TYRRELL 628-39, KETTEN/ BUTLER/ OF DON BOYNE/ BUTLER OF CAER 628-39, BARON OF ELINGTON/ OCARRALL 628-39, MACMOROGHE/ OCAHARE/ WYSE/ FITZ-SYMOND/ FOSTER 628-40, TUTE/ CUSSACK/ BROWNE/ MACMAHON 628-40

*$ABSTRACT 629
*LIBRARY BODLEIAN
*SLIDE SET TITLE EAST ANGLIAN MANUSCRIPTS
*NEGATIVE REFERENCE ROLL 251A
*RENTAL FEE $3.25
*COMMENTS MANUSCRIPTS SHOWN AT AN EXHIBITION OF MEDIEVAL ART IN EAST ANGLIA, C1300-1500.
*TITLE OF MANUSCRIPT MISSAL 629/1-14, HISTORY OF RAMSEY ABBEY 629-15, BREVIARY FROM CHERTSEY ABBEY 629-16, PSALTER 629/17-21, ON THE PASSION OF OUR LORD 629/22-23, BOOK OF HOURS 629/24-25
*SHELFMARK MS HATTON 1/ FOL 8V 629-1, MS HATTON 1/ FOL 20V 629-2, MS HATTON 1/ FOL 24V 629-3, MS HATTON 1/ FOL 25V 629-4, MS HATTON 1/ FOL 96V 629-5, MS HATTON 1/ FOL 100V 629-6, MS HATTON 1/ FOL 111V 629-7, MS HATTON 1/ FOL 114V 629-8, MS HATTON 1/ FOL 120V 629-9, MS HATTON 1/ FOL 139V 629-10, MS HATTON 1/ FOL 148V 629-11, MS HATTON 1/ FOL 151V 629-12, MS

HATTON 1/ FOL 169 629-13, MS HATTON 1/ FOL 185V 629-14, MS RAWL B 333/ FOL 1 629-15, MS LAT LITURG E 37/ FOL 1 629-16, MS DOUCE B 4/ FIG 1 629-17, MS DOUCE D 19/ FOL 3/1 629-18, MS DOUCE D 19/ FOL 3/2 629-19, MS DOUCE D 19/ FOL 3/3 629-20, MS DOUCE D 19/ FOL 3/4 629-21, MS BODLEY 758/ FOL 1 629-22, MS BODLEY 758/ FOL 87 629-23, MS JONES 46/ FOL 8 629-24, MS JONES 46/ FOL 69 629-25
*PROVENANCE ENGLISH/ EAST ANGLIA 629/1-14, ENGLISH/ RAMSEY ABBEY 629-15, ENGLISH/ CHERTSEY ABBEY 629-16, ENGLISH/ PETERBOROUGH 629/17-21, ENGLISH/ NORFOLK 629/22-23, ENGLISH/ NORFOLK? 629/24-25
*DATE EXECUTED 14TH/ LATE 629/1-14, 14TH/ EARLY 629/15-21, 15TH/ 1405 629/22-23, 15TH/C1440-50 629/24-25
*AUTHOR DE MESSA/ MICHAEL 629/22-23
*SCRIBE DE MEDYLTON/ RALPH 629/22-23
*TYPE OF MANUSCRIPT MISSAL 629/1-14, HISTORY 629-15, BREVIARY 629-16, PSALTER 629/17-21, RELIGIOUS TREATISE 629/22-23, BOOK OF HOURS 629/24-25
*CONTENTS EAST ANGLIAN MANUSCRIPTS 629/1-25, CHRIST IN RAINBOW SHOWING WOUNDS 629-1, NATIVITY/ MARY SITS ON CANOPIED BED 629-2, CIRCUMCISION OF CHRIST 629-3, CHRIST'S CIRCUMCISION 629-3, ADORATION OF THE MAGI 629-4, PRIEST SAYS MASS 629-5, RESURRECTION/ FOUR SLEEPING GUARDS 629-6, ASCENSION 629-7, PENTECOST/ HOLY SPIRIT DESCENDS AS DOVE AND FIRE 629-8, CORPUS CHRISTI/ ADORATION OF BLESSED SACRAMENT 629-9, PRIESTS CENSE MONSTRANCE CONTAINING HOST 629-9, CHURCH DEDICATION/ BISHOP SPRINKLES HOLY WATER 629-10, BISHOP DEDICATES CHURCH BUILDING 629-10, PRESENTATION OF CHRIST IN TEMPLE 629-11, CHRIST PRESENTED IN TEMPLE 629-11, ANNUNCIATION 629-12, ASSUMPTION OF THE VIRGIN 629-13, VIRGIN'S ASSUMPTION 629-13, VIGIL FOR AN APOSTLE 629-14, INITIAL WITH TWO SHEEP/ RAMS FOR RAMSEY? 629-15, ST PETER RELEASED FROM PRISON BY ANGEL 629-16, DAVID AND FOOL 629-17, DAVID PLAYS BELLS/ COMPANION PLAYS PORTATIVE ORGAN 629-18, PSALTERY PLAYED BY ANGEL 629-19, REBEC PLAYED BY ANGEL 629-20, PORTATIVE ORGAN PLAYED BY ANGEL 629-21, CRUCIFIXION WITH MICHAEL DE MESSA 629-22, AUTHOR PORTRAIT WITH CRUCIFIXION 629-22, SCRIBE/ RALPH DE MEDYLTON AT WORK 629-23, TEXT WITH FULL DECORATED BORDER 629-24, VIGIL FOR THE DEAD/ TEXT WITH DECORATED BORDER 629-25

*$ABSTRACT 630
*LIBRARY BODLEIAN
*SLIDE SET TITLE APOCALYPSE/ ENGLISH
*NEGATIVE REFERENCE ROLL 251B
*RENTAL FEE $5.90
*TITLE OF MANUSCRIPT APOCALYPSE
*SHELFMARK MS CANON BIBL LAT 62/ FOL 1 630-1, MS CANON BIBL LAT 62/ FOL 1V 630-2, MS CANON BIBL LAT 62/ FOL 2 630-3, MS CANON BIBL LAT 62/ FOL 2V 630-4, MS CANON BIBL LAT 62/ FOL 3 630-5, MS CANON BIBL LAT 62/ FOL 3V 630-6, MS CANON BIBL LAT 62/ FOL 4 630-7, MS CANON BIBL LAT 62/ FOL 4V 630-8, MS CANON BIBL LAT 62/ FOL 5 630-9, MS CANON BIBL LAT 62/ FOL 5V 630-10, MS CANON BIBL LAT 62/ FOL 6 630-11, MS CANON BIBL LAT 62/ FOL 6V 630-12, MS CANON BIBL LAT 62/ FOL 7 630-13, MS CANON BIBL LAT 62/ FOL 7V 630-14, MS CANON BIBL LAT 62/ FOL 8 630-15, MS CANON BIBL LAT 62/ FOL 8V 630-16, MS CANON BIBL LAT 62/ FOL 9 630-17, MS CANON BIBL LAT 62/ FOL 9V 630-18, MS CANON BIBL LAT 62/ FOL 10 630-19, MS CANON BIBL LAT 62/ FOL 10V 630-20, MS CANON BIBL LAT 62/ FOL 11 630-21, MS CANON BIBL LAT 62/ FOL 11V 630-22, MS CANON BIBL LAT 62/ FOL 12 630-23, MS CANON BIBL LAT 62/ FOL 12V 630-24, MS CANON BIBL LAT 62/ FOL 13 630-25, MS CANON BIBL LAT 62/ FOL 13V 630-26, MS CANON BIBL LAT 62/ FOL 14 630-27, MS CANON BIBL LAT 62/ FOL 14V 630-28, MS CANON BIBL LAT 62/ FOL 15 630-29, MS CANON BIBL LAT 62/ FOL 15V 630-30, MS CANON BIBL LAT 62/ FOL 16 630-31, MS CANON BIBL LAT 62/ FOL 16V 630-32, MS CANON BIBL LAT 62/ FOL 17 630-33, MS CANON BIBL LAT 62/ FOL 17V 630-34, MS CANON BIBL LAT 62/ FOL 18 630-35, MS CANON BIBL LAT 62/ FOL 18V 630-36, MS CANON BIBL LAT 62/ FOL 19 630-37, MS CANON BIBL LAT 62/ FOL 19V 630-38, MS CANON BIBL LAT 62/ FOL 20 630-39, MS CANON BIBL LAT 62/ FOL

20V 630-40, MS CANON BIBL LAT 62/ FOL 21 630-41, MS CANON BIBL LAT 62/ FOL 21V 630-42, MS CANON BIBL LAT 62/ FOL 22 630-43, MS CANON BIBL LAT 62/ FOL 22V 630-44, MS CANON BIBL LAT 62/ FOL 23 630-45, MS CANON BIBL LAT 62/ FOL 23V 630-46, MS CANON BIBL LAT 62/ FOL 24 630-47, MS CANON BIBL LAT 62/ FOL 24V 630-48, MS CANON BIBL LAT 62/ FOL 25 630-49, MS CANON BIBL LAT 62/ FOL 25V 630-50, MS CANON BIBL LAT 62/ FOL 26 630-51, MS CANON BIBL LAT 62/ FOL 26V 630-52, MS CANON BIBL LAT 62/ FOL 27 630-53, MS CANON BIBL LAT 62/ FOL 27V 630-54, MS CANON BIBL LAT 62/ FOL 28 630-55, MS CANON BIBL LAT 62/ FOL 28V 630-56, MS CANON BIBL LAT 62/ FOL 29 630-57, MS CANON BIBL LAT 62/ FOL 29V 630-58, MS CANON BIBL LAT 62/ FOL 30 630-59, MS CANON BIBL LAT 62/ FOL 60 630-60, MS CANON BIBL LAT 62/ FOL 31 630-61, MS CANON BIBL LAT 62/ FOL 31V 630-62, MS CANON BIBL LAT 62/ FOL 32 630-63, MS CANON BIBL LAT 62/ FOL 32V 630-64, MS CANON BIBL LAT 62/ FOL 33 630-65, MS CANON BIBL LAT 62/ FOL 33V 630-66, MS CANON BIBL LAT 62/ FOL 34 630-67, MS CANON BIBL LAT 62/ FOL 34V 630-68, MS CANON BIBL LAT 62/ FOL 35 630-69, MS CANON BIBL LAT 62/ FOL 35V 630-70, MS CANON BIBL LAT 62/ FOL 36 630-71, MS CANON BIBL LAT 62/ FOL 36V 630-72, MS CANON BIBL LAT 62/ FOL 37 630-73, MS CANON BIBL LAT 62/ FOL 37V 630-74, MS CANON BIBL LAT 62/ FOL 38 630-75, MS CANON BIBL LAT 62/ FOL 38V 630-76, MS CANON BIBL LAT 62/ FOL 39 630-77, MS CANON BIBL LAT 62/ FOL 39V 630-78

*PROVENANCE ENGLISH/ PETERBOROUGH

*DATE EXECUTED 14TH/ EARLY

*LANGUAGE LATIN

*TYPE OF MANUSCRIPT APOCALYPSE

*CONTENTS APOCALYPSE/ ENGLISH/ 14TH 630/1-78, ST JOHN OF PATMOS CALLED 630-1, REV 01/VERSES 1-3/ CALL OF JOHN 630-1, ST JOHN'S VISION OF CHRIST 630-2, REV 01/VERSES 13-17 630-2, VISION OF THE THRONE OF GOD 630-3, REV 06/VERSES 3-8/ VISION OF THRONE OF GOD 630-3, ST JOHN OF PATMOS AND THE ELDERS 630-4, REV 05/VERSE 5/ ST JOHN AND ELDERS 630-4, ADORATION OF THE ELDERS 630-5, REV 04/VERSE 10/ ADORATION OF ELDERS 630-5, VISION OF THE LAMB 630-6, REV 05/VERSE 6/ VISION OF THE LAMB 630-6, LAMB TAKES BOOK 630-7, REV 05/VERSES 7-8/ LAMB TAKES BOOK 630-7, OPENING OF THE FIRST SEAL 630-7, REV 06/VERSE 2/ OPENING OF FIRST SEAL 630-8, OPENING OF SECOND SEAL 630-9, REV 04/VERSE 4/ OPENING OF SECOND SEAL 630-9, OPENING OF THIRD SEAL 630-10, REV 06/VERSE 5/ OPENING OF THIRD SEAL 630-10, OPENING OF FOURTH SEAL 630-11, REV 06/VERSE 8/ OPENING OF FOURTH SEAL 630-11, OPENING OF FIFTH SEAL 630-12, REV 06/VERSES 9-11/ OPENING OF FIFTH SEAL 630-12,OPENING OF SIXTH SEAL 630-13, REV 06/VERSES 12-16/ OPENING OF SIXTH SEAL 630-13, ANGELS AND WINDS 630-14, REV 07/VERSES 1-3/ ANGELS AND WINDS 630-14, MULTITUDE/ GREAT 630-15, REV 07/VERSES 9-17/ GREAT MULTITUDE 630-15, OPENING OF SEVENTH SEAL 630-16, REV 08/VERSES 1-4/ OPENING OF SEVENTH SEAL 630-16, TRUMPET/ FIRST 630-17, REV 08/VERSES 5-7/ FIRST TRUMPET 630-17, TRUMPETS/ SECOND/ THIRD AND FOURTH 630-18, REV 08/VERSES 8-13/ 2ND 3RD AND 4TH TRUMPETS 630-18, TRUMPET/ FIFTH 630-19, REV 08/VERSE 13/ FIFTH TRUMPET 630-19, LOCUSTS 630-20, REV 09/VERSES 7-12 630-20, TRUMPET/ SIXTH 630-21, REV 09/VERSES 13-16/ SIXTH TRUMPET 630-21, HORSEMEN/ FOUR 630-22, REV 09/VERSES 17-21/ FOUR HORSEMEN 630-22, ANGEL/ GREAT 630-23, REV 10/VERSES 1-3/ GREAT ANGEL 630-23, TEMPLE MEASURED 630-24, REV 11/VERSES 1-2, MEASURING THE TEMPLE 630-24, WITNESSES/ TWO 630-25, REV 11/VERSES 3-6/ TWO WITNESSES 630-25, BEAST SLAYS TWO WITNESSES 630-26, REV 11/VERSES 7-8/ BEAST SLAYS WITNESSES 630-26,RESURRECTION AND ASCENSION OF WITNESS 630-27, REV 11/VERSES 11-13/ RESURRECTION OF WITNESS 630-27, TRUMPET/ SEVENTH 630-28, REV 11/VERSES 15-17/ SEVENTH TRUMPET 630-28, WOMAN CLOTHED WITH THE SUN 630-29, REV 11/VERSE 19/ WOMAN CLOTHED WITH SUN 630-29, ST MICHAEL FIGHTS DRAGON 630-30, REV 12/VERSES 7-10/ ST MICHAEL FIGHTS DRAGON 630-30, DRAGON PERSECUTES THE WOMAN 630-31, REV 12/VERSES 13-15/ DRAGON PERSECUTES WOMAN 630-31, DRAGON PERSECUTES THE WOMAN 630-32, REV 12/VERSES 15-17/ DRAGON PERSECUTES WOMAN 630-32, DRAGON AND SEED OF THE WOMAN 630-33, REV 12/VERSE 17/ DRAGON AND SEED OF WOMAN 630-33,DRAGON AND BEAST 630-34, REV 13/VERSES 1-3, DRAGON AND BEAST 630-34, DRAGON AND BEAST WORSHIPPED 630-35,

REV 13/VERSE 4/ DRAGON AND BEAST WORSHIPPED 630-35, BEAST WORSHIPPED 630-36, REV 13/VERSES 4-6/ BEAST WORSHIPPED 630-36, BEAST SLAYS SAINTS 630-37, REV 13/VERSE 7/ BEAST SLAYS SAINTS 630-37, PROPHET/ FALSE 630-38, REV 13/VERSES 11-12/ FALSE PROPHET 630-38, PROPHET/ FALSE EXERCISES POWER 630-39, REV 13/VERSES 13-15/ FALSE PROPHET EXERCISES POWER 630-39, MARK OF THE BEAST 630-40, REV 13/VERSES 16-18/ MARK OF THE BEAST 630-40, LAMB ON MOUNT SION 630-41, REV 14/VERSE 1/ LAMB ON SION 630-41, NEW SONG 630-42, REV 14/VERSES 2-5/ THE NEW SONG 630-42, ANGEL WITH EVERLASTING GOSPEL 630-43, REV 14/VERSES 6-7/ EVERLASTING GOSPEL 630-43, BABYLON'S FALL ANNOUNCED 630-44, REV 14/VERSE 8/ BABYLON'S FALL ANNOUNCED 630-44,WORSHIPPERS OF THE BEAST 630-45, REV 14/VERSES 9-11/ WORSHIPPERS OF BEAST 630-45, BLESSED ARE THE DEAD 630-46, REV 14/VERSE 13/ BLESSED ARE THE DEAD 630-46, HARVEST OF THE EARTH 630-47, REV 14/VERSES 14-16/ HARVEST OF EARTH 630-47, VINTAGE OF THE EARTH 630-48, REV 14/VERSES 17-18/ VINTAGE OF EARTH 630-48, VINTAGE OF THE EARTH/ SECOND SCENE 630-49, REV 14/VERSES 19-20/ VINTAGE OF EARTH 630-49, SONG OF MOSES 630-50, REV 15/VERSES 1-4/ SONG OF MOSES 630-50, SONG OF THE LAMB 630-50, REV 15/VERSES 1-4/ SONG OF THE LAMB 630-50, VIALS GIVEN UP 630-51, REV 15/VERSES 5-8/ VIALS GIVEN UP 630-51, VIAL/ FIRST 630-52, REV 16/VERSE 2/ FIRST VIAL 630-52, VIALS/ SECOND AND THIRD 630-53, REV 16/VERSES 3-7/ 2ND AND 3RD VIALS 630-53, VIAL/ FOURTH 630-54, REV 16/VERSES 8-9/ FOURTH VIAL 630-54, VIALS/ FIFTH AND SIXTH 630-55, REV 16/VERSES 10-12/ 5TH AND 6TH VIALS 630-55, FROGS 630-56, REV 16/VERSES 13-16/ THE FROGS 630-56, VIAL/ SEVENTH 630-57, REV 16/VERSES 17-19/ 7TH VIAL 630-57, WHORE OF BABYLON 630-58, REV 17/VERSES 1-2/ WHORE OF BABYLON 630-58, WHORE OF BABYLON ON THE BEAST 630-59, REV 17/VERSES 3-4/ WHORE ON THE BEAST 630-59, BABYLON/ FALL 630-60, REV 18/VERSES 1-2/ FALL OF BABYLON 630-60, ANGEL WITH MILLSTONE 630-61, MILLSTONE 630-61, REV 18/VERSE 21/ ANGEL WITH MILLSTONE 630-61, WHORE OF BABYLON DRUNK 630-62, REV 17/VERSES 6-12/ DRUNKEN WHORE OF BABYLON 630-62, MARRIAGE OF THE LAMB 630-63, REV 19/VERSES 7-9/ MARRIAGE OF LAMB 630-63, ST JOHN OF PATMOS INSTRUCTED BY ANGEL 630-64, REV 19/VERSES 9-10/ ANGEL INSTRUCTS JOHN 630-64, ARMIES OF GOD 630-65, REV 19/VERSES 11-16/ ARMIES OF GOD 630-65, BIRDS SUMMONED 630-66, BATTLE WITH THE BEAST 630-67, REV 19/VERSES 19-20/ BATTLE WITH THE BEAST 630-67, BEAST DEFEATED 630-68, REV 19/VERSES 20-21/ BEAST DEFEATED 630-68, DRAGON IMPRISONED 630-69, REV 20/VERSES 1-3/ DRAGON IMPRISONED 630-69, RESURRECTION/ FIRST 630-70, REV 20/VERSES 4-5/ FIRST RESURRECTION 630-70, SIEGE OF THE HOLY CITY 630-71, REV 20/VERSE 9/ HOLY CITY UNDER SEIGE 630-71, BEAST AND THE FALSE PROPHET DEFEATED 630-72, REV 20/VERSE 10/ DEFEAT OF BEAST AND FALSE PROPHET 630-72, LAST JUDGMENT 630-73, JUDGMENT/ LAST 630-73, REV 20/VERSES 11-15/ LAST JUDGMENT 630-73, HOLY CITY 630-74, REV 21/VERSES 2-8/ THE HOLY CITY 630-74, TWELVE GATES 630-75, REV 21/VERSE 12/ TWELVE GATES 630-75, RIVER OF LIFE 630-76, REV 22/VERSES 1-3/ RIVER OF LIFE 630-76, ST JOHN OF PATMOS AND ANGEL 630-77, REV 22/VERSES 6-12/ JOHN AND ANGEL 630-77, WORDS OF CHRIST 630-78, REV 22/VERSES 13-15/ WORDS OF CHRIST 630-78

*$ABSTRACT 631
*LIBRARY BODLEIAN
*SLIDE SET TITLE SPRING
*NEGATIVE REFERENCE ROLL 251C
*RENTAL FEE $3.25
*COMMENTS SELECTION FROM 13 15TH-16TH CENTURY MANUSCRIPTS, MAINLY CALENDAR ILLUSTRATIONS.
*TITLE OF MANUSCRIPT BOOK OF HOURS 631/1-3, PRIVATE PRAYERS WITH HYMNS 631-4, BOOK OF HOURS 631/5-8, PSALTER WITH CALENDAR 631/9-10, BOOK OF HOURS 631/11-22, FIRST SECOND AND FOURTH DECADES 631-23, ROMAN DE LA ROSE 631-24, BOOK OF HOURS 631-25
*SHELFMARK MS DOUCE 135/ FOL 3 631-1, MS DOUCE 135/ FOL 4 631-2, MS DOUCE 276/ FOL 16 631-3, MS GOUGH LITURG 7/ FOL 4 631-4, MS CANON LITURG 99/ FOL 8 631-5, MS CANON LITURG 99/ FOL 9 631-6, MS LITURG 41/ FOL 4V-5 631-7, MS LITURG 41/ FOL

5V-6 631-8, MS LITURG 60/ FOL 4 631-9, MS LITURG 60/ FOL 5 631-10, MS RAWL LITURG E 14/ FOL 8 631-11, MS RAWL LITURG E 14/ FOL 9 631-12, MS RAWL LITURG E 20/ FOL 4 631-13, MS RAWL LITURG E 20/ FOL 4V 631-14, MS RAWL LITURG E 20/ FOL 5 631-15, MS RAWL LITURG E 20/ FOL 5V 631-16, MS RAWL LITURG F 14/ FOL 4 631-17, MS RAWL LITURG F 14/ FOL 5 631-18, MS RAWL LITURG F 31/ FOL 2V 631-19, MS RAWL LITURG F 31/ FOL 3V 631-20, MS RAWL LITURG E 36/ FOL 2V 631-21, MS RAWL LITURG E 36/ FOL 3 631-22, MS LAUD LAT 112/ FOL 68 631-23, MS DOUCE 364/ FOL 8V 631-24, MS DOUCE 276/ FOL 1B 631-25

*PROVENANCE FRENCH 631/1-2, FRENCH/ NORTH 631-3, FLEMISH 631-4, FRENCH 631/5-10, FLEMISH 631/11-12, FRENCH 631/13-16, FRENCH 631/17-22, ITALIAN/ VERONA? 631-23, FRENCH 631-24, FRENCH/ NORTH 631-25

*DATE EXECUTED 16TH/ 2ND QUARTER 631/1-2, 16TH/ EARLY 631-3, 16TH/C1500 631/4-6, 15TH/C1470-80 631/7-8, 15TH/ LATE 631/9-10, 15TH/C1440 631/11-12, 15TH/ 2ND HALF 631/13-16, 16TH/ EARLY 631/17-20, 16TH/C1500-25 631/21-22, 15TH/ EARLY 631-23, 15TH/C1460-70 631-24, 16TH/ EARLY 631-25

*LANGUAGE LATIN 631/1-4, FRENCH AND LATIN 631/5-6, LATIN 631/5-6, FRENCH AND LATIN 631/11-18, LATIN 631/19-20, FRENCH AND LATIN 631/21-22, LATIN 631-23, FRENCH 631-24, LATIN 631-25

*AUTHOR LIVY 631-23, DE LORRIS/ GUILLAUME AND JEAN DE MEUNG 631-24

*ARTIST/ SCHOOL GHENT/ BRUGES SCHOOL 631-4, MASTER OF GUILLEBERT DE METZ 631/11-12

*SCRIBE JEAN LORIN 631-24

*TYPE OF MANUSCRIPT BOOK OF HOURS/ USE OF ROME 631/1-3, PRAYERS WITH HYMNS 631-4, BOOK OF HOURS/ USE OF BOURGES 631/5-6, BOOK OF HOURS 631/7-8, PSALTER 631/9-10, BOOK OF HOURS/ USE OF TOURNAI 631/11-12, BOOK OF HOURS/ USE OF EVREUX 631/13-16, BOOK OF HOURS/ USE OF PARIS 631/17-20, BOOK OF HOURS/ USE OF ROME 631/21-22, CLASSICAL LITERATURE 631-23, POETRY 631-24, BOOK OF HOURS/ USE OF ROME 631-25

*CONTENTS SPRING 631/1-25, CALENDAR ILLUSTRATIONS 631/1-25, APRIL/ TAURUS/ MAN HAWKING AND PILGRIMS 631-1, TAURUS 631-1, HAWKING 631-1, PILGRIMS APPROACH CHURCH 631-1, MAY/ GEMINI/ COUPLE ON HORSE/ LOVERS 631-2, GEMINI 631-2, LOVERS BESIDE WOOD 631-2, VIRGIN AND CHILD/ MAN WITH TWO DOGS 631-3, APRIL/ LOVERS SIT IN ARBOUR/ SHEPHERD WITH FLOCK 631-4, LOVERS SIT IN ARBOUR 631-4, SHEPHERD WITH FLOCK 631-4, APRIL/ MAN AND TWO GIRLS PICK FLOWERS 631-5, FLOWER PICKING 631-5, MAY/ TWO HORSEMEN CARRY GREEN BRANCHES 631-6, HORSEMEN CARRY GREEN BRANCHES 631-6, APRIL/ TAURUS/ MEN WITH GREEN BRANCHES 631-7, TAURUS 631-7, MEN WITH GREEN BRANCHES 631-7, MAY/ GEMINI/ MAN AND WOMAN/ HAYMAKING SCENE 631-8, GEMINI 631-8, HAYMAKING 631-8, APRIL/ MAN CARRIES GREEN BRANCH 631-9, MAN CARRIES GREEN BRANCH 631-9, MAY/ GROUP OF HORSEMEN HAWKING 631-10, HAWKING 631-10, APRIL/ MAN CARRIES GREEN BRANCH 631-11, MAN CARRIES GREEN BRANCH 631-11, MAY/ MAN HAWKING ON WHITE HORSE 631-12, HAWKING/ MAN ON WHITE HORSE 631-12, APRIL/ MAN AND WOMAN HOLDING HANDS 631-13, MAN AND WOMAN HOLDING HANDS 631-13, APRIL/ TAURUS 631-14, TAURUS 631-14, MAY/ MAN AND WOMEN ON HORSE 631-15, MAN AND WOMAN ON HORSE 631-15, MAY/ GEMINI/ MAN AND WOMAN 631-16, GEMINI 631-16, APRIL/ TAURUS/ LADY HOLDS FLOWERS 631-17, TAURUS 631-17, LADY HOLDS FLOWERS 631-17, MAY/ GEMINI/ KING HOLDS FLOWER 631-18, GEMINI 631-18, KING HOLDS FLOWER 631-18, APRIL/ TAURUS/ LADY SEATED ON GRASS 631-19, TAURUS 631-19, LADY SEATED ON GRASS 631-19, JUNE/ CANCER/ HAYMAKING 631-20, CANCER 631-20, HAYMAKING 631-20, APRIL/ TAURUS/ GIRLS PICKING FLOWERS 631-21, TAURUS 631-21, FLOWER PICKING 631-21, MAY/ GEMINI/ COUPLE ON WHITE HORSE 631-22, GEMINI 631-22, COUPLE ON WHITE HORSE 631-22, COURTLY MAN AND WOMAN WALK BY WOOD 631-23, GOD OF LOVE AND SWEET LOOKS IN ROSE GARDEN 631-24, GARDEN/ ROSE 631-24, MARCH-APRIL/ GEMINI/ CANCER 631-25, GEMINI 631-25, CANCER 631-25 CANCER 631-25

*$ABSTRACT 632

*LIBRARY JESUS COLLEGE OXFORD

*SLIDE SET TITLE PSALTER WITH CANTICLES
*NEGATIVE REFERENCE ROLL 251D
*RENTAL FEE $2.60
*TITLE OF MANUSCRIPT PSALTER WITH CANTICLES
*SHELFMARK MS JESUS COLLEGE 40/ FOL 8 632-1, MS JESUS COLLEGE 40/ FOL 35V 632-2, MS JESUS COLLEGE 40/ FOL 54 632-3, MS JESUS COLLEGE 40/ FOL 59V 632-4, MS JESUS COLLEGE 40/ FOL 71 632-5, MS JESUS COLLEGE 40/ FOL 71V 632-6, MS JESUS COLLEGE 40/ FOL 78V 632-7, MS JESUS COLLEGE 40/ FOL 110 632-8, MS JESUS COLLEGE 40/ FOL 129V 632-9, MS JESUS COLLEGE 40/ FOL 132 632-10, MS JESUS COLLEGE 40/ FOL 150 632-11, MS JESUS COLLEGE 40/ FOL 171V 632-12
*PROVENANCE ENGLISH
*DATE EXECUTED 14TH/ EARLY
*LANGUAGE LATIN
*TYPE OF MANUSCRIPT PSALTER WITH CANTICLES
*CONTENTS PSALTER/ ENGLISH/ 14TH 632/1-12, INITIAL B BEATUS VIR/ DAVID PLAYS HARP 632-1, DAVID PLAYS HARP 632-1, BATTLE BETWEEN MOUNTED KNIGHTS WITH LANCES 632-1, KNIGHTS/ MOUNTED FIGHT WITH LANCES 632-1, INITIAL D DOMINUS ILLUMINATIO/ DAVID ANOINTED KING 632-2, DAVID ANOINTED KING 632-2, INITIAL D DIXI CUSTODIAM/ DAVID KNEELS BEFORE CHRIST 632-3, DAVID KNEELS BEFORE CHRIST 632-3, REBEC PLAYED BY FIGURE 632-4, INITIAL Q QUID GLORIARIS/ DAVID KILLS GOLIATH 632-5, DAVID KILLS GOLIATH 632-5, KNIGHTS PREPARE FOR TOURNAMENT 632-5, KNIGHT HOISTED ONTO HORSE 632-5, INITIAL D DIXIT INSIPIENS/ DAVID AND THE FOOL 632-6, DAVID AND THE FOOL/ GOD WATCHES 632-6, INITIAL S SALVUM ME FAC/ JONAH EMERGES FROM WHALE 632-7, JONAH EMERGES FROM WHALE/ GOD BLESSES FROM ABOVE 632-7, INITIAL E EXULTATE DEO/ DAVID PLAYS BELLS 632-8, KNIGHT ASSISTED ONTO AND OFF HIS HORSE 632-8, INITIAL C CANTATE DOMINO/ MONKS SING AT LECTERN 632-9, MONKS SING AT LECTERN 632-9, INITIAL D DOMINE EXAUDI/ CHRIST SPEAKS TO DAVID 632-10, DAVID AND CHRIST 632-10, INITIAL D DIXIT DOMINUS/ LAST JUDGMENT 632-11, LAST JUDGMENT 632-11, NAKED FIGURES FIGHT AMONG TOMB STONES 632-11, TAMBOURINE PLAYED BY FIGURE IN RED ROBE 632-12

*$ABSTRACT 633
*LIBRARY BODLEIAN
*SLIDE SET TITLE TWO ENGLISH STYLE MANUSCRIPTS
*NEGATIVE REFERENCE ROLL 251E
*RENTAL FEE $2.65
*TITLE OF MANUSCRIPT COMMENTARY ON THE PSALTER 633/1-12, CANONICAL EPISTLES 633-13
*SHELFMARK MS AUCT E INF 6/ FOL 1 633-1, MS AUCT E INF 6/ FOL 4V 633-2, MS AUCT E INF 6/ FOL 19 633-3, MS AUCT E INF 6/ FOL 21V 633-4, MS AUCT E INF 6/ FOL 22 633-5, MS AUCT E INF 6/ FOL 50 633-6, MS AUCT E INF 6/ FOL 52V 633-7, MS AUCT E INF 6/ FOL 55V 633-8, MS AUCT E INF 6/ FOL 83 633-9, MS AUCT E INF 6/ FOL 84 633-10, MS AUCT E INF 6/ FOL 102 633-11, MS AUCT E INF 6/ FOL 119 633-12, MS DOUCE 110/ FOL 3 633-13
*PROVENANCE ENGLISH OR FRENCH 633/1-12, ENGLISH 633-13
*DATE EXECUTED 12TH/C1170-77 633/1-12, 16TH/1504 633-13
*LANGUAGE LATIN
*AUTHOR LOMBARD/ PETER 633/1-12, HUBERT OF BOSHAM EDITOR 633/1-12
*SCRIBE MEGHEN/ PETER 633-13
*TYPE OF MANUSCRIPT COMMENTARY 633/1-12, RELIGIOUS TREATISE 633-13
*CONTENTS ENGLISH STYLE MSS 633/1-13, TEXT OF PETER LOMBARD WITH DECORATED INITIALS 633-1, TEXTUAL DECORATION INCLUDING WHITE LION GROTESQUES 633-2, DECORATION/ INTRICATE INCLUDING GROTESQUES 633-3, DECORATION INCLUDING GROTESQUES 633-4, MAN/ NAKED SURROUNDED BY FLAMES IN MARGIN 633-4, INSCRIPTION HOMO IN IGNE DEUS IN HOMINE 633-4,GROTESQUE 633-5, GROTESQUE/ WHITE LION 633-6, SERPENTS IN DECORATION 633-7, GROTESQUES IN INTRICATE DECORATION 633-8, TEACHER AND LISTENING PUPIL 633-9, CHRIST AND DOVE IN DECORATION 633-10, MERMAID AND CHILD 633-11, TEXT/ DECORATED 633-12, TEXT/ OPENING OF ST JAMES 633-13

*$ABSTRACT 634
*LIBRARY BODLEIAN
*SLIDE SET TITLE ANGLO-SAXON ILLUMINATION II
*NEGATIVE REFERENCE ROLL 251F
*RENTAL FEE $2.30
*COMMENTS A SUPPLEMENT TO BODLEIAN ROLL 217H/ ABSTRACT 487.
*TITLE OF MANUSCRIPT DIALOGUES BY GREGORY THE GREAT 634-1, PSALTER 634/2-4, AETHELRED TROPER 634-5, BATTLE OF MALDON/ 18TH-CENTURY TRANSCRIPTION 634-6
*SHELFMARK MS TANNER 3/ FOL 1V 634-1, MS DOUCE 296/ FOL 40 634-2, MS DOUCE 296/ FOL 9 634-3, MS DOUCE 296/ FOL 40V 634-4, MS BODLEY 775/ FOL 8 634-5, MS RAWL B 203/ FOL 7 634-6
*PROVENANCE ENGLAND/ WEST? 634-1, ENGLISH/ CROWLAND 634/2-4, ENGLISH/ WINCHESTER 634-5, ENGLISH 634-6
*DATE EXECUTED 11TH/ 2ND HALF 634-1, 11TH/ 2ND QUARTER 634/2-4, 11TH/ MID 634-5, 18TH/ 1724 634-6
*LANGUAGE LATIN 634/1-5, ENGLISH/ OLD ENGLISH 18TH-CENTURY TRANSCRIPTION 634-6
*AUTHOR GREGORY THE GREAT 634-1, ELPHINTONE/ JOHN TRANSCRIBER 634-6
*TYPE OF MANUSCRIPT DIALOGUES 634-1, PSALTER 634/2-4, TROPER 634-5, OLD ENGLISH TEXT/ TRANSCRIPTION 634-6
*CONTENTS ANGLO-SAXON ILLUMINATION 634/1-6, ST GREGORY LECTURES A MONK 634-1, CHRIST TREADING UPON THE BEASTS 634-2, INITIAL B BEATUS WITH LION MASK 634-3, INITIAL Q QUID GLORIARIS/ ARMOURED FIGURE 634-4, ST MICHAEL FIGHTS A DRAGON 634-4, TROPES FOR ADVENT 634-5, BATTLE OF MALDON TEXT 634-6

*$ABSTRACT 635
*LIBRARY BODLEIAN
*SLIDE SET TITLE ST BRENDAN
*NEGATIVE REFERENCE ROLL 251G
*RENTAL FEE $3.10
*TITLE OF MANUSCRIPT LIVES OF SAINTS INCLUDING ST BRENDAN
*SHELFMARK MS LAUD MISC 173/ FOL 115 635-1, MS LAUD MISC 173/ FOL 115V 635-2, MS LAUD MISC 173/ FOL 119 635-3, MS LAUD MISC 173/ FOL 119V 635/4-5, MS LAUD MISC 173/ FOL 120V 635-6, MS LAUD MISC 173/ FOL 121 635/7-8, MS LAUD MISC 173/ FOL 122 635-9, MS LAUD MISC 173/ FOL 123 635/10-11, MS LAUD MISC 173/ FOL 123V 635-12, MS LAUD MISC 173/ FOL 125V 635-13, MS LAUD MISC 173/ FOL 126 635-14, MS LAUD MISC 173/ FOL 126V 635-15, MS LAUD MISC 173/ FOL 127 635-16, MS LAUD MISC 173/ FOL 128V 635-17, MS LAUD MISC 173/ FOL 129 635/18-19, MS LAUD MISC 173/ FOL 129V 635-20, MS LAUD MISC 173/ FOL 131 635-21, MS LAUD MISC 173/ FOL 131V 635-22
*PROVENANCE GERMAN
*DATE EXECUTED 15TH/ EARLY
*LANGUAGE LATIN
*TYPE OF MANUSCRIPT LIVES OF SAINTS
*CONTENTS ST BRENDAN 635/1-22, MONK LANDS ON WHALE WHICH HE MISTAKES FOR ISLAND 635-1, WHALE MISTAKEN FOR ISLAND BY MONK 635-1, ST BRENDAN'S SHIP LANDS AT ISLE OF BIRDS 635-2,ABBEY CHURCH WITH SPIRES AND BURNING LAMPS 635-3, ABBEY CHURCH INTERIOR WITH THREE ALTARS 635-4, ST BRENDAN KNEELS BEFORE ABBOT 635-5, ABBEY CHURCH 635-6, SEA SHORE/ FISH IN SEA 635-7, MONKS HUDDLE TOGETHER 635-8, ST BRENDAN AND MONKS MAKE FIRE ON WHALE'S BACK 635-9, ST BRENDAN'S BOAT ATTACKED BY HUGE FISH 635-10,MONKS ARE SAVED BY SECOND FISH 635-11, FISH CUT INTO THREE PIECES 635-12, BIRD CARRIES BRANCH IN ITS BEAK 635-13, GRYPHON/ HALF LION AND HALF EAGLE 635-14, GRYPHON ATTACKS ST BRENDAN IN HIS BOAT 635-14, MONKS SAVED BY BIRD WHO ATTACKS GRYPHON 636-15, CRYSTAL COLUMN TO WHICH ROPES ARE ATTACHED 635-16, DEMON WITH TONGS HURLS TORCH AT MONK'S BOAT 635-17, MONK IN SEA BELOW CLIFF 635-18, VOLCANO 635-19, DEMON STANDS BEHIND MONK SITTING BY SEA 635-20, HERMITAGE CUT INTO FACE OF CLIFFS 635-21, HERMIT WITH LONG HAIR AND BEARD 635-22

*$ABSTRACT 636
*LIBRARY BODLEIAN
*SLIDE SET TITLE WOODCUTS FROM RUSSIAN MENOLOGION/ CALENDAR
*NEGATIVE REFERENCE ROLL 253B
*RENTAL FEE $2.60
*COMMENTS THE WOODCUTS WERE PRINTED AT THE CELEBRATED MONASTERY OF THE CAVES AT KIEV. SOME OF THE SHEETS ARE DATED 1626-29 AND A FEW ARE SIGNED BY PAMYA BERYNDA OR LEONTI. THE BASIC GREEK CALENDAR IS SUPPLEMENTED BY EFFIGIES AND SCENES RELATING TO RUSSIAN SAINTS.
*TITLE OF MANUSCRIPT MENOLOGION
*SHELFMARK PR ARCH B B 4
*PROVENANCE RUSSIAN/ KIEV
*DATE EXECUTED 17TH/1626-29
*LANGUAGE GREEK
*ARTIST/ SCHOOL PAMYA BERYNDA AND LEONTI
*TYPE OF MANUSCRIPT MENOLOGION
*CONTENTS MENOLOGION/ RUSSIAN/ 17TH 636/1-12, CALENDAR/ RUSSIAN/ 17TH 636/1-12, WOODCUTS/ RUSSIAN 636/1-12, SEPTEMBER 636-1, OCTOBER 636-2, NOVEMBER 636-3, DECEMBER 636-4, JANUARY 636-5, FEBRUARY 636-6, MARCH 636-7, APRIL 636-8, MAY 636-9, JUNE 636-10, JULY 636-11, AUGUST 636-12

*$ABSTRACT 637
*LIBRARY BODLEIAN
*SLIDE SET TITLE WOODCUTS FROM RUSSIAN MENOLOGION/ FEASTS
*NEGATIVE REFERENCE ROLL 253C
*RENTAL FEE $3.15
*TITLE OF MANUSCRIPT MENOLOGION
*SHELFMARK PR ARCH B B 4
*PROVENANCE RUSSIAN/ KIEV
*DATE EXECUTED 17TH/1626-29
*LANGUAGE GREEK
*ARTIST/ SCHOOL PAMYA BERYNDA AND LEONTI
*TYPE OF MANUSCRIPT MENOLOGION
*CONTENTS FEASTS FROM RUSSIAN MENOLOGION 637/1-23, MENOLOGION/ RUSSIAN/ 17TH 637/1-23, WOODCUTS/ RUSSIAN 637/1-23, MIRACLE AT CHONAE/ SEPTEMBER 6 637-1, NATIVITY OF THE MOTHER OF GOD/ SEPTEMBER 8 637-2, EXALTATION OF THE CROSS/ SEPTEMBER 14 637-2, INTERCESSION OF THE MOTHER OF GOD/ OCTOBER 1 637-3, SYNAXIS OF THE ARCHANGELS/ NOVEMBER 8 637-4, SEVENTH COUNCIL/ NICAEA II/ NOVEMBER 11 637-5, ENTRY OF MOTHER OF GOD INTO THE TEMPLE/ NOV 21 637-6, STEPHEN THE NEW/ NOV 28 637-6, ST ANNE'S CONCEPTION / DECEMBER 9 637-7, PETER THE METROPOLITAN/ DEC 21 637-8, NATIVITY OF OUR LORD/ DEC 25 637-9, SYNAXIS OF THE MOTHER OF GOD/ DEC 26 637-10, BAPTISM OF OUR LORD/ JANUARY 6 637-11, SYNAXIS OF JOHN BAPTIST/ JANUARY 7 637-11, CHRIST MEETS SYMEON/ FEBRUARY 2 637-12, ANNUNCIATION AND SYNAXIS OF GABRIEL/ MARCH 25-26 637-13, JOHN CLIMAX WITH THE CRUCIFIXION AND HYPATIUS/ MAR 30-31 637-13, MARY OF EGYPT/ APRIL 1 637-14, MARY OF EGYPT'S MEETING WITH ZOSIMOS 637-14, MARY OF EGYPT AT PRAYER 637-14, MARY OF EGYPT/ COMMUNION AND BURIAL 637-14, THEODORE OF THE CAVES/ BURIAL/ MAY 3 637-15, SIGN OF THE CROSS/ MAY 637-16, CONSTANTINE AT THE BATTLE OF MILVIAN BRIDGE 637-16, JOHN THE BAPTIST'S BIRTH/ JUNE 24 637-17, SS PETER AND PAUL AND 12 APOSTLES/ JUNE 29-30 637-17, ROBE OF THE MOTHER OF GOD/ JULY 2 637-18, MAKRINA AND DIOS/ JULY 19 637-19, CHRISTINA/ BORIS/ GLEB/ JULY 24 637-20, HOLY CROSS AND THE MACCHABEES/ AUGUST 1 637-21,TRANSFIGURATION/ AUGUST 6 637-21, DORMITION OF THE MOTHER OF GOD/ AUGUST 15 637-22, MANDILION AND DIOMEDE/ AUGUST 16 637-22, ADRIAN AND NATALIA WITH ICON OF VIRGIN/ AUG 26 637-23, GIRDLE OF THE MOTHER OF GOD/ AUG 31 637-23

*$ABSTRACT 638
*LIBRARY BODLEIAN
*SLIDE SET TITLE LANCELOT DU LAC
*NEGATIVE REFERENCE ROLL 253D

*RENTAL FEE $2.35
*TITLE OF MANUSCRIPT LANCELOT DU LAC
*SHELFMARK MS DOUCE 215/ FOL 1 638-1, MS DOUCE 215/ FOL 3V 638-2, MS DOUCE 215/ FOL 14 638-3, MS DOUCE 215/ FOL 31V 638-4, MS DOUCE 215/ FOL 32 638-5, MS DOUCE 215/ FOL 35 638-6, MS DOUCE 215/ FOL 39V 638-7
*PROVENANCE FRENCH
*DATE EXECUTED 14TH/C1300 638/1 AND 4 AND 6-7, 15TH/ EARLY 638/2 AND 5
*LANGUAGE FRENCH
*ARTIST/ SCHOOL SCHOOL OF BOUCICAUT MASTER 638/2 AND 5
*TYPE OF MANUSCRIPT ROMANCE/ ARTHURIAN
*CONTENTS LITERATURE/ LANCELOT DU LAC 638/1-7, ROMANCE OF LANCELOT DU LAC 638/1-7, AGRAVAIN APPROACHES PAVILION 638-1, KNIGHT AND DAMSEL BESIDE BIER 638-1, GROTESQUES 638-1, GUERREHES CHARGES KNIGHT THREATENING OLD MAN 638-2, LANCELOT CONFESSES TO HERMIT 638-3, ADAM AND EVE 638-4, ADAM AND EVE/ EXPULSION 638-5, PERCEVAL AND BOHORS IN A SHIP 638-6, PERCEVAL READS SCROLL FOUND IN ALMS-BAG 638-6, GALAHAD AND PERCEVAL RIDE TOWARDS CASTLE OF CARTELOIS 638-7

*$ABSTRACT 639
*LIBRARY BODLEIAN
*SLIDE SET TITLE OCCUPATIONS OF THE MONTHS
*NEGATIVE REFERENCE ROLL 253F
*RENTAL FEE $2.70
*TITLE OF MANUSCRIPT ASTROLOGICAL TREATISES
*SHELFMARK MS RAWL D 1220/ FOL 6 639-1, MS RAWL D 1220/ FOL 7V 639-2, MS RAWL D 1220/ FOL 10V 639-3, MS RAWL D 1220/ FOL 14 639-4, MS RAWL D 1220/ FOL 15V 639-5, MS RAWL D 1220/ FOL 17 630-6, MS RAWL D 1220/ FOL 18V 639-7, MS RAWL D 1220/ FOL 20V 639-8, MS RAWL D 1220/ FOL 22 639-9, MS RAWL D 1220/ FOL 23V 639-10, MS RAWL D 1220/ FOL 24 639-11, MS RAWL D 1220/ FOL 27 639-12, MS RAWL D 1220/ FOL 28V 639-13, MS RAWL D 1220/ FOL 29 639-14
*PROVENANCE ENGLISH
*DATE EXECUTED 15TH/ 3RD QUARTER
*LANGUAGE ENGLISH
*TYPE OF MANUSCRIPT ASTROLOGICAL TREATISES
*CONTENTS OCCUPATIONS OF THE MONTHS 639/1-14, ZODIAC SIGNS 639/1-14, TEACHING/ TWO MEN IN HIGH-BACKED CHAIRS 639-1, ELEMENTS/ FOUR 639-2, MARCH/ ARIES/ TREE PRUNING 639-3, ARIES/ TREE PRUNING 639-3, APRIL/ TAURUS/ MAN HOLDS BUSH 639-4, TAURUS/ MAN HOLDS BUSH 639-4, MAY/ GEMINI/ WOMAN HOLDS FLOWERING BRANCHES 639-5, GEMINI/ WOMAN HOLDS FLOWERING BRANCHES 639-5,JUNE/ CANCER/ WEEDING WITH KNIFE ON STICK 639-6, CANCER/ WEEDING WITH KNIFE 639-6, WEEDING WITH HOOKED KNIFE ON STICK 639-6, JULY/ LEO/ REAPER SHARPENING SCYTHE 639-7, LEO/ REAPER SHARPENING SCYTHE 639-7, REAPER SHARPENING SCYTHE 639-7, SCYTHE BEING SHARPENED 639-7, SEPTEMBER/ LIBRA/ THRESHING 639-8, LIBRA/ THRESHING 639-8, THRESHING 639-8, OCTOBER/ SCORPIO/ SOWING 639-9, SCORPIO/ SOWING 639-9, SOWING 639-9, NOVEMBER/ SAGITTARIUS/ SLAUGHTERING OX 639-10, SAGITTARIUS/ SLAUGHTERING OX 639-10, SLAUGHTERING OX 639-10, AUGUST/ VIRGO/ REAPING CORN 639-11, VIRGO/ REAPING CORN 639-11, REAPING CORN 639-11, DECEMBER/ CAPRICORN/ MAN DRINKING 639-12, CAPRICORN/ MAN DRINKING 639-12, MAN DRINKING 639-12, JANUARY/ AQUARIUS/ MAN WARMS HIMSELF BY FIRE 639-13, AQUARIUS/ MAN WARMS HIMSELF BY FIRE 639-13, MAN WARMS HIMSELF BY FIRE 639-13, FEBRUARY/ PISCES/ MAN HOLDS SPADE 639-14, PISCES/ MAN HOLDS SPADE 639-14, SPADE HELD BY MAN 639-14

*$ABSTRACT 640
*LIBRARY BODLEIAN
*SLIDE SET TITLE LOVE/ LUXURIA
*NEGATIVE REFERENCE ROLL 254A
*RENTAL FEE $2.50
*COMMENTS A SEQUENCE OF DOUBLE-PAGE OPENINGS SHOWING THE QUEST

OF A LOVER FOR HIS BELOVED. THE ILLUMINATIONS REVERSE THE SPIRITUAL MEANING OF THE PSALMS THEY ACCOMPANY. THEY DEPICT LE MONDE RENVERSE, A FALSE SET OF VALUES AND ACTIONS WHICH ARE SEEN AS COMIC AND LAUGHABLE. THE ILLUMINATIONS ARE RATHER CLOSELY LINKED TO THE TEXT OF THE PSALMS AS THOUGH THE DOMINUS/ LORD WERE TURNED INTO THE DOMINA/ LADY.
*TITLE OF MANUSCRIPT PORTABLE PSALTER
*SHELFMARK MS DOUCE 6/ FOL 122V-123 640-1, MS DOUCE 6/ FOL 125V-126 640-2, MS DOUCE 6/ FOL 128V-129 640-3, MS DOUCE 6/ FOL 129V-130 640-4, MS DOUCE 6/ FOL 133V-134 640-5, MS DOUCE 6/ FOL 134V-135 640-6, MS DOUCE 6/ FOL 154V-155 640-7, MS DOUCE 6/ FOL 159V-160 640-8, MS DOUCE 6/ FOL 160V-161 640-9, MS DOUCE 6/ FOL 164V-165 640-10
*PROVENANCE FLEMISH/ GHENT
*DATE EXECUTED 14TH/C1320-30
*LANGUAGE LATIN
*TYPE OF MANUSCRIPT PSALTER/ PORTABLE
*CONTENTS LOVER'S QUEST FOR HIS BELOVED 640/1-10, LOVER'S GOAL 640-1, LOVER SHOOTS ARROW AT RABBIT 640-1, RABBIT REPRESENTS SYMBOL OF DESIRE 640-1, PSALM 126/VERSES 4-5 640-1, LOVER WRAPPED IN COILS OF ROPE BY LADY 640-1, PSALM 127/VERSES 1-3 640-1, LOVER'S HUMILITY 640-2, LOVER SETS OUT TO ACHIEVE THE RABBIT 640-2, LOVER BECOMES SERVANT OF LADY 640-2, PSALM 130/ THE PROPHET'S HUMILITY 640-2, AMOR WITH ARROW AND LION OF LUST 640-2, LION OF LUST 640-2, PETER-I 05/VERSE 8 640-2, PSALM 131/ THE HAPPINESS OF BROTHERLY LOVE 640-2, LOVE WORKS DISCORD 640-3, KNIGHT FIGHTS UNCHIVALROUS KNIGHT 640-3, LOVER WATCHES APE RIDE BEAR 640-3, APE WITH MITRE/ CROZIER/ CLOVEN HOOF 640-3, WAR OF SEXES SYMBOLIZED BY APE AND BEAR 640-3, APE REPRESENTS FEMALE SEXUALITY 640-3, BEAR REPRESENTS MALE SEXUALITY 640-3, STAG DRESSED IN LOVER'S MANTLE 640-3, MAN BUILDS WALL OF DIVISION 640-3, CAIN PLOWS WITH JAWBONE 640-3, CAIN REPRESENTS BROTHERLY DISCORD 640-3, DANCE OF LOVE 640-4, LOVER PLAYS PHALLIC BAGPIPES 640-4, LADY DANCES ON LOVER'S SHOULDERS 640-4, PSALM 134/VERSES 1-3 640-4, MAN WITH WINE-JUGS RIDES HORSE 640-4, LOVER'S INSTRUMENT 640-5, LOVER REACHES INTO GAP IN HIS CLOTHING 640-5, LOVER BLOWS HORN AT CRANE 640-5, PSALM 136/VERSES 1-5 640-5, ASSAULT IN THE NEST 640-6, MAN AND HYBRID HOLDS ROCKS 640-6, PSALM 136/VERSES 8-9 640-6, INITIAL C CONFITEBOR/ LADY WATCHES CHICKS 640-6, LADY WATCHES MAN FEED CHICKS IN NEST 640-6, CHICKS REPRESENT GOOD SOULS AND VIRTUOUS ACTS 640-6, MAN REVEALS BUTTOCKS 640-6, RABBIT RUNS AWAY 640-6, PSALM 137/VERSE 2/ PROFANE VERSION IN ILLUSTRATION 640-6, LADY'S RESTRAINT 640-7, UNICORN BUTTS FOLIAGE OF MARGIN 640-7, PSALM 147/ INITIAL L LAUDA JERUSALEM 640-7, INITIAL L LAUDA JERUSALEM 640-7, APE READS WATCHED BY APE WITH CROZIER 640-7, PSALM 146/VERSE 9 640-7, LADY RIDES BRIDLED LION/ SYMBOL OF LUST 640-7,LION AS SYMBOL OF LUST 640-7, PRESENTATION OF THE LOVER'S HEART 640-8, DOG JUMPS AT SITTING RABBIT 640-8, AMOR HOLDS SPEAR AND WATCHES LOVERS 640-8, AMOR'S SERVANT LEADS LOVER TO LADY 640-8, LOVER PRESENTS HIS PIERCED HEART TO LADY 640-8, ISAIAH 12/VERSES 1-3 640-8, STAG OF DESIRE WEARS LOVER'S MANTLE 640-8, LOVER'S GOAL ACHIEVED 640-9, ISAIAH 38/VERSE 10 640-9, LADY TURNS AWAY FROM LOVER TO FOX 640-9, LOVER PRAYS TO LADY FOR FAVOR OF RABBIT 640-9, ADAM/ OLD WITH LION'S BODY EMBRACES LADY 640-9, LOVER EMBRACES LADY IN BEDROOM 640-9, LADY'S TRIUMPH 640-10, INITIAL C CANTEMUS DOMINO/ BASED ON EXODUS 15 640-10, RABBIT AS HUNTER WITH CAPTURED DOG 640-10, LADY IN INITIAL LOOKS AT OLD MAN 640-10, APE HITS CRANE WITH STICK 640-10

*$ABSTRACT 641
*LIBRARY BODLEIAN
*SLIDE SET TITLE HARROWING OF HELL
*NEGATIVE REFERENCE ROLL 254B
*RENTAL FEE $3.85
*COMMENTS SCENES AND TYPOLOGY FROM 12 MANUSCRIPTS.
*TITLE OF MANUSCRIPT BIBLE MORALISEE 641/1-14,PSALTER WITH NEQUAMS COMMENTARY 641-15, PASSION OF CHRIST AND MIRACLES OF VIRGIN 641-16, LIFE OF THE VIRGIN AND OF CHRIST 641/17-22,

BOOK OF HOURS 641-23, PSALTER 641-24, SPECULUM HUMANAE SALVATIONIS 641/25-27, BOOK OF HOURS 641-28, SPECULUM HUMANAE SALVATIONIS 641-29, PSALTER 641-30, DE CIVITATE DEI OF AUGUSTINE 641-31, PORTABLE PSALTER 641-32, BIBLE MORALISEE 641/33-37

*SHELFMARK MS BODLEY 270B/ FOL25V 641-1, MS BODLEY 270B/ FOL 69V 641-2, MS BODLEY 270B/ FOL 110 641-3, MS BODLEY 270B/ FOL 115V 641/4-6, MS BODLEY 270B/ FOL 117V 641/9-11, MS BODLEY 270B/ FOL 147V 641-12, MS BODLEY 270B/ FOL 177V 641-13, MS BODLEY 270B/ FOL 181V 641-14, MS BODLEY 284/ FOL 223V 641-15, MS CANON ITAL 275/ FOL 30V 641-16, MS CANON ITAL 280/ FOL 203 641-17, MS CANON ITAL 280/ FOL 204 641-18, MS CANON ITAL 280/ FOL 204V 641-19, MS CANON ITAL 280/ FOL 205 641-20, MS CANON ITAL 280/ FOL 206V 641-21, MS CANON ITAL 280/ FOL 250 641-22, MS CANON LITURG 75/ FOL 116 641-23, MS CANON LITURG 393/ FOL 253 641-24, MS CORPUS CHRISTI COLLEGE OXFORD 161/ FOL 121 641-25, MS CORPUS CHRISTI COLLEGE OXFORD 161/ FOL 123 641-26, MS CORPUS CHRISTI COLLEGE OXFORD 161/ FOL 126 641-27, MS DOUCE 29/ FOL 77 641-28, MS DOUCE 204/ FOL 32B 641-29, MS JESUS COLLEGE 40/ FOL 150 641-30, MS LAUD MISC 469/ FOL 7V 641-31, MS LITURG 396/ FOL 105 641-32, MS BODLEY 270B/ FOL 186 641-33, MS BODLEY 270B/ FOL 192 641/34-35, MS BODLEY 270B/ FOL 214 641-36, MS BODLEY 270B/ FOL 218 641-37

*PROVENANCE FRENCH 641/1-14, ENGLISH/ CIRENCESTER? 641-15, ITALIAN/ VENICE? 641-16, ITALIAN/ NORTH 641/17-22, FRENCH 641-23, ITALIAN 641-24, ENGLISH 641/25-27, ITALIAN/ URBINO OR MANTUA 641-28, SPANISH/ CATALONIA/ ROUSSILLON 641-29, ENGLISH 641/30-31, FLEMISH/ GHENT 641-32, FRENCH 641/33-37

*DATE EXECUTED 13TH/ MID 641/1-14, 13TH/ 1ST QUARTER 641-15, 15TH/ 1ST QUARTER 641-16, 15TH/C1400 641/17-22, 15TH/ EARLY 641-23, 13TH/ LATE 641-24, 15TH/ EARLY 641/25-27, 16TH/1530-38 641-28, 15TH/C1440 641-29, 14TH 641-30, 12TH/ 2ND QUARTER 641-31, 13TH/ 3RD QUARTER 641-32, 13TH/ MID 641/33-37

*LANGUAGE LATIN 641/1-15, ITALIAN/ VENETIAN DIALECT 641-16, ITALIAN 641/17-22, FRENCH AND LATIN 641/23-24, LATIN 641/25-37

*ARTIST/ SCHOOL BOUCICAUT MASTER AND EGERTON MASTER 641-23, RAIMONDI/ VINCENZO 641-28, DYAMAS/ LAURENTIUS 641-29

*TYPE OF MANUSCRIPT BIBLE MORALISSE 641/1-14, PSALTER WITH COMMENTARY 641-15, MIRACLES 641-16, LIFE OF VIRGIN 641/17-22, BOOK OF HOURS/ USE OF PARIS 641-23, PSALTER 641-24, SPECULUM 641/25-27, BOOK OF HOURS/ USE OF ROME 641-28, SPECULUM 641-29, PSALTER 641-30, RELIGIOUS TREATISE 641-31, PSALTER 641-32, BIBLE MORALISEE 641-33,

*CONTENTS HARROWING OF HELL 641/1-37, HELL/ HARROWING 641/1-37, TYPOLOGY 641/1-37, CHRIST DESCENDS TO HELL AND RESCUES PATRIARCHS 641-1, PAGIEL AS TYPE OF CHRIST WHO HELPS MANKIND 641-2, HARROWING OF HELL 641-2, CHRIST BREAKS DOORS OF HELL AND RESCUES ADAM 641-3, SAMSON KILLING LION IS TYPE OF CHRIST 641-4, CHRIST'S TEMPTATION 641-5, CHRIST RESCUES PROPHETS FROM HELL 641-6, DEVIL TEMPTS JEWS TO PERSECUTE CHRIST 641-7, RESURRECTION 641-8, HARROWING OF HELL 641-9, ENTOMBMENT OF CHRIST 641-9, SAMSON CARRIES OFF GATES OF GAZA/ TYPE OF CHRIST 641-11, CHRIST IN THE TOMB 641-12, SONS OF SYNAGOGUE WHO WORSHIPPED IDOLS IN HELL 641-13, RESURRECTION OF CHRIST 641-14, SAMSON CARRIES OFF GATES OF GAZA 641-15, HARROWING OF HELL 641-16, CHRIST IN HELL COMMANDS TWO DEVILS 641-17, PATRIARCHS IN HELL/ ISAIAH/ DAVID/ JOSHUA 641-18, CHRIST THROWS OPEN GATES OF HELL 641-19, ADAM AND EVE WATCH CHRIST OPEN HELL GATES 641-19, CHRIST TRAMPLES ON BOUND DEVIL 641-20, DEVIL/ BOUND 641-20, CHRIST LEADS PATRIARCHS AND ADAM AND EVE FROM HELL 641-21, CHRIST DRIVES ADAM AND EVE OUT OF PARADISE 641-22, ADAM AND EVE DRIVEN OUT OF PARADISE BY CHRIST 641-22, CRUCIFIXION/ BONES OF ADAM AT FOOT OF CROSS 641-23, HARROWING OF HELL 641-24, HARROWING OF HELL 641-25, RESURRECTION 641-26, SAMSON CARRIES OFF GATES OF GAZA 641-27, ENTOMBMENT OF CHRIST 641-28, SAMSON CARRIES OFF GATES OF GAZA 641-29, CHRIST AT LAST JUDGMENT 641-30, LAST JUDGMENT 641-30, HARROWING OF HELL, CHRIST AS JUDGE 641-31, VIRGIN AND ANGELS RESCUE SOULS FROM DEVIL 641-31, HARROWING OF HELL 641-32, CHRIST RESCUES SOULS FROM DEVIL 641-33, DEVIL TEMPTS THOSE WHO ARREST CHRIST 641-34, CHRIST/ RISEN BINDS DEVIL 641-35, DEVIL BOUND BY CHRIST 641-35, CHRIST EXPELLS ADAM FROM EDEN 641-36, ADAM

EXPELLED FROM EDEN BY CHRIST 641-36, WICKED LOSE WEALTH AND GLORY AND GO TO HELL 641-37

*$ABSTRACT 642
*LIBRARY BODLEIAN
*SLIDE SET TITLE GOSPELS/ GERMAN
*NEGATIVE REFERENCE ROLL 255A
*RENTAL FEE $2.55
*TITLE OF MANUSCRIPT GOSPELS
*SHELFMARK MS LAUD LAT 102/ FOL 5 642/1-2, MS LAUD LAT 102/ FOL 6 642-3, MS LAUD LAT 102/ FOL 9 642-4, MS LAUD LAT 102/ FOL 12 642-5, MS LAUD LAT 102/ FOL 15 642-6, MS LAUD LAT 102/ FOL 16 642-7, MS LAUD LAT 102/ FOL 20 642-8, MS LAUD LAT 102/ FOL 46 642-9, MS LAUD LAT 102/ FOL 112 642-10, MS LAUD LAT 102/ FOL 174V 642-11
*PROVENANCE GERMAN/ FULDA
*DATE EXECUTED 09TH/ 1ST THIRD
*LANGUAGE LATIN
*SCRIBE ANGLO-SAXON AND CAROLINGIAN
*TYPE OF MANUSCRIPT GOSPELS
*CONTENTS GOSPELS/ GERMAN/ 09TH 642/1-11, CANON TABLES/ DECORATED 642/1-3, INITIAL P PLURES 642-4, INITIAL B BEATO 642-5, INITIAL M MATTHEUS 642-6, INITIAL N NATIVITAS 642-7, ST MATTHEW'S GOSPEL/ BEGINNING OF TEXT 642-8, ST MATTHEW'S GOSPEL/ CHAPTER 16 642-9, ST LUKE'S GOSPEL/ BEGINNING OF TEXT 642-10, ST JOHN'S GOSPEL/ BEGINNING OF TEXT 642-11

*$ABSTRACT 643
*LIBRARY BODLEIAN
*SLIDE SET TITLE MADONNA LACTANS
*NEGATIVE REFERENCE ROLL 255C
*RENTAL FEE $2.50
*COMMENTS FROM 10 MSS OF THE 14TH TO THE 16TH CENTURIES, ILLUSTRATING THE VIRGIN MARY NURSING THE CHRIST CHILD.
*TITLE OF MANUSCRIPT BOOK OF HOURS 643/1-7, GOSPEL LECTIONARY 643-8, VITA GLORIOSISSIME VIRGINIS MARIAE 643-9, LIFE OF THE VIRGIN AND OF CHRIST 643-10
*SHELFMARK MS CANON LITURG 129/ FOL 146V 643-1, MS DOUCE 19/ FOL 140V 643-2, MS RAWL LITURG F 33/ FOL 174V 643-3, MS RAWL LITURG F 20/ FOL 125 643-4, MS RAWL LITURG F 25/ FOL 112 643-5, MS RAWL LITURG F 32/ FOL 79V 643-6, MS RAWL LITURG F 27/ FOL 132 643-7, MS LAT LITURG E 3/ FOL 3V 643-8, MS CANON MISC 476/ FOL 42 643-9, MS CANON ITAL 280/ FOL 53V 543-10
*PROVENANCE FLEMISH 643-1, ITALIAN 643-2, FRENCH 643-3, FRENCH/ PARIS? 643-4, FRENCH/ ROUEN 643-5, FRENCH/ WEST 643-6, FRENCH 643-7, GERMAN/ NORTH-WEST 643-8, ITALIAN/ VENICE 643-9, ITALIAN/ NORTH? 643-10
*DATE EXECUTED 15TH/C1460-70 643-1, 16TH/ 2ND QUARTER 643-2, 16TH/1566 643-3, 15TH/ LATE 643-4, 16TH/C1500 643-5, 15TH/ LATE 643-6, 14TH/C1380-90 643-7, 15TH/ LATE INSERTED MINIATURE 643-8, 14TH/ MID 643-9, 15TH/C1400 643-10
*LANGUAGE LATIN 643/ 1 AND 6-10, FRENCH AND LATIN 643/2-5
*ARTIST/ SCHOOL RAIMONDI/ VINCENZO 643-1, FR ESTIENNE 643-3, RELATED TO GROUP OF LEGENDA AUREA 643-7
*SCRIBE DE BUGNIES/ FR JULIEN 643-3
*TYPE OF MANUSCRIPT BOOK OF HOURS/ USE OF ROME 643/1-3, BOOK OF HOURS/ USE OF PARIS 643-4, BOOK OF HOURS/ USE OF ROUEN 643-5, BOOK OF HOURS 643-6, BOOK OF HOURS/ USE OF PARIS 643-7, GOSPEL LECTIONARY 643-8, LIFE OF THE VIRGIN 643/9-10
*CONTENTS MADONNA LACTANS 643/1-10, VIRGIN MARY NURSING THE CHRIST CHILD 643/1-10, CHRIST CHILD NURSED BY VIRGIN MARY 643/1-10, BREAST FEEDING/ VIRGIN MARY NURSES CHRIST 643/1-10

*$ABSTRACT 644
*LIBRARY BODLEIAN
*SLIDE SET TITLE MIDDLE ENGLISH TEXTS

*NEGATIVE REFERENCE ROLL 255D
*RENTAL FEE $2.35
*TITLE OF MANUSCRIPT TEMPLE OF GLASS BY LYDGATE 644-2, LEGEND OF GOOD WOMEN 644-3, BOOK OF THE DUCHESS 644-4, BALLADS UPON THE CHANCE OF DYCE 644-5, HOUSE OF FAME 644-6, RESON AND SENSUALLYTE BY LYDGATE 644-7
*SHELFMARK MS FAIRFAX 16/ FOL 9 644-1, MS FAIRFAX 16/ FOL 63 644-2, MS FAIRFAX 16/ FOL 83 644-3, MS FAIRFAX 16/ FOL 130 644-4, MS FAIRFAX 16/ FOL 148V-149 644-5, MS FAIRFAX 16/ FOL 154V-155 644-6, MS FAIRFAX 16/ FOL 210V-211 644-7
*PROVENANCE ENGLISH
*DATE EXECUTED 15TH/C1450 AND LATER
*LANGUAGE ENGLISH/ MIDDLE ENGLISH
*ARTIST/ SCHOOL ABELL/ WILLIAM
*AUTHOR LYDGATE/ JOHN 644/2 AND 7, CHAUCER/ GEOFFREY 644/3-4 AND 6
*TYPE OF MANUSCRIPT POETRY/ MIDDLE ENGLISH
*CONTENTS LITERATURE/ MIDDLE ENGLISH TEXTS 644/1-7, LADY/ ELIZABETHAN 644-1, ORRERY WITH MOTTO COR MUNDANUM 644-1, TEXT OF TEMPLE OF GLASS 644-2, PROLOGUE TO LEGEND OF GOOD WOMEN 644-3, TEXT OF BOOK OF THE DUCHESS 644-4, DICE ILLUSTRATED IN MARGIN 644-5, TEXT OF HOUSE OF FAME 644-6, TEXT OF RESON AND SENSUALLYTE 644-7

*$ABSTRACT 645
*LIBRARY BODLEIAN
*SLIDE SET TITLE MS CANON MISC 110
*NEGATIVE REFERENCE ROLL 256A
*RENTAL FEE $2.95
*SHELFMARK MS CANON MISC 110/ FOL 6 645/1-2, MS CANON MISC 110/ FOL 7 645-3, MS CANON MISC 110/ FOL 9 645-4, MS CANON MISC 110/ FOL 123-124 645/5-6, MS CANON MISC 110/ FOL 150-152 645-7, MS CANON MISC 110/ FOL 17V 645-8, MS CANON MISC 110/ FOL 29V 645-9, MS CANON MISC 110/ FOL 41V 645-10, MS CANON MISC 110/ FOL 51V 645-11, MS CANON MISC 110/ FOL 63V 645-12, MS CANON MISC 110/ FOL 86V-88V 645-13, MS CANON MISC 110/ FOL 98V-110V 645-14, MS CANON MISC 110/ FOL 109V-111V 645-15, MS CANON MISC 110/ FOL 119V-120V 645-16, MS CANON MISC 110/ FOL 129V-130V 645-17, MS CANON MISC 110/ FOL 149V-150V 645-18, MS CANON MISC 110/ FOL 161V-163V 645-19
*PROVENANCE ENGLISH/ NORWICH
*DATE EXECUTED 15TH/C1400
*LANGUAGE LATIN
*AUTHOR DE INSULIS/ ALANUS 645/1-19, CAPELLA/ MARTIANUS 645/1-19, SILVESTER/ BERNARDUS 645/1-19
*TYPE OF MANUSCRIPT TREATISE
*CONTENTS INITIAL WITH AUTHOR'S PORTRAIT 645-1, AUTHOR'S PORTRAIT 645-1, DETAIL OF INITIAL WITH AUTHOR'S PORTRAIT 645-2, INITIAL WITH MAN'S FACE 645-3, GROTESQUE MAN IN BORDER 645-3, INITIAL WITH GROTESQUE 645-4, PARROT HOLDS SCROLL 645-4, ANGEL CROWNS MAN AND WOMAN 645-5, MAN PLACES RING ON LADY'S FINGER 645-5, DETAIL OF MAN GIVING RING TO LADY 645-6, INITIAL WITH DOG BITING SWORDSMAN 645-7, DOG BITES SWORDSMAN 645-7, CATCHWORD IN FORM OF DOG 645-8, CATCHWORD IN FORM OF EAGLE 645-9, CATCHWORD IN SCROLL HELD BY HAND 645-10, CATCHWORD IN FORM OF MAN'S HEAD 645-11, CATCHWORD IN FORM OF HEART 645-12, CATCHWORD IN FORM OF LION 645-13, CATCHWORD IN FORM OF GROTESQUE BISHOP 645-14, GROTESQUE BISHOP 645-14, CATCHWORD IN FORM OF ANGEL 645-15, CATCHWORD IN FORM OF HARE 645-16, CATCHWORD IN FORM OF FISH 645-17, MAN'S HEAD WITH SCROLL ISSUING FROM MOUTH 645-18, CATCHWORD IN FORM OF ARM IN FULL SLEEVE 645-19

*$ABSTRACT 646
*LIBRARY BODLEIAN
*SLIDE SET TITLE CHERTSEY ABBEY BREVIARY
*NEGATIVE REFERENCE ROLL 256B
*RENTAL FEE $5.25

*COMMENTS RECONSTRUCTED FROM FOUR MANUSCRIPTS.
*TITLE OF MANUSCRIPT CHERTSEY ABBEY BREVIARY
*SHELFMARK MS LAT LITURG E 6/ FOL 5V-6 646-1, MS LAT LITURG E 6/ FOL 10V-11 646-2, MS LAT LITURG D 42/ FOL 1 646-3, MS LAT LITURG D 42/ FOL 2 646-4, MS LAT LITURG D 42/ FOL 3 646-5, MS LAT LITURG D 42/ FOL 4 646-6, MS LAT LITURG D 42/ FOL 5 646-7, MS LAT LITURG D 42/ FOL 6 646-8, MS LAT LITURG D 42/ FOL 7 646-9, MS LAT LITURG D 42/ FOL 8 646-10, MS LAT LITURG D 42/ FOL 9 646-11, MS LAT LITURG D 42/ FOL 10 646-12, MS LAT LITURG D 42/ FOL 11 646-13, MS LAT LITURG D 42/ FOL 12 646-14, MS LAT LITURG D 42/ FOL 13 646-15, MS LAT LITURG D 42/ FOL 14 646-16, MS LAT LITURG D 42/ FOL 15 646-17, MS LAT LITURG D 42/ FOL 16 646-18, MS LAT LITURG D 42/ FOL 17 646-19, MS LAT LITURG D 42/ FOL 18 646-20, MS LAT LITURG D 42/ FOL 19 646-21, MS LAT LITURG D 42/ FOL 20 646-22, MS LAT LITURG D 42/ FOL 21 646-23, MS LAT LITURG D 42/ FOL 22 646-24, MS LAT LITURG D 42/ FOL 23 646-25, MS LAT LITURG D 42/ FOL 24 646-26, MS LAT LITURG D 42/ FOL 25 646-27, MS LAT LITURG D 42/ FOL 26 646-28, MS LAT LITURG D 42/ FOL 27 646-29, MS LAT LITURG D 42/ FOL 28 646-30, MS LAT LITURG D 42/ FOL 29 646-31, MS LAT LITURG D 42/ FOL 30 646-32, MS LAT LITURG D 42/ FOL 31 646-33, MS LAT LITURG D 42/ FOL 32 646-34, MS LAT LITURG D 42/ FOL 33 646-35, MS LAT LITURG D 42/ FOL 34 646-36, MS LAT LITURG D 42/ FOL 35 646-37, MS LAT LITURG D 42/ FOL 36 646-38, MS LAT LITURG D 42/ FOL 37 646-39, MS LAT LITURG D 42/ FOL 38 646-40, MS LAT LITURG D 42/ FOL 39 646-41, MS LAT LITURG D 42/ FOL 40 646-42, MS LAT LITURG D 42/ FOL 41 646-43, MS LAT LITURG D 42/ FOL 42 646-44, MS LAT LITURG D 42/ FOL 43 646-45, MS LAT LITURG D 42/ FOL 44 646-46, MS LAT LITURG D 42/ FOL 45 646-47, MS LAT LITURG D 42/ FOL 46 646-48, MS LAT LITURG D 42/ FOL 47 646-49, MS LAT LITURG E 39/ FOL 1 646-50, MS LAT LITURG E 39/ FOL 15 646/51-52, MS LAT LITURG E 39/ FOL 42V 646-53, MS LAT LITURG E 39/ FOL 88V 646-54, MS LAT LITURG E 39/ FOL 108V 646-55, MS LAT LITURG E 39/ FOL 118V 646-56, MS LAT LITURG E 39/ FOL 125V 646-57, MS LAT LITURG E 39/ FOL 147V 646-58, MS LAT LITURG E 39/ FOL 156V 646-59, MS LAT LITURG E 37/ FOL 1 646/60-61, MS LAT LITURG E 37/ FOL 89V-90 646-62, MS LAT LITURG E 37/ FOL 91V-92 646-63, MS LAT LITURG E 37/ FOL 185V 646-64, MS LAT LITURG E 37/ FOL 203 646-65
*PROVENANCE ENGLISH
*DATE EXECUTED 14TH/ 2ND QUARTER
*LANGUAGE LATIN
*ARTIST/ SCHOOL MASTER OF THE QUEEN MARY PSALTER
*TYPE OF MANUSCRIPT BREVIARY
*CONTENTS BREVIARY/ ENGLISH/ 14TH 646/1-65, CALENDAR WITH ENTRY FOR ST ERKENWALD 646-1, ST ERKENWALD ENTRY IN CALENDAR 646-1, LITANY IN CALENDAR 646-2, NOAH'S ARK/ SEXAGESIMA 646-3, EVE CREATION/ SEPTUAGESIMA 646-4, CREATION OF EVE 646-4, INITIAL WITH TEMPTATION OF CHRIST 646-5, TEMPTATION OF CHRIST 646-5, CHRIST TEMPTED 646-5, INITIAL WITH JACOB RECEIVING ISAAC'S BLESSING 646-6, JACOB RECEIVES ISAAC'S BLESSING 646-6, ISAAC'S BLESSING OF JACOB 646-6, INITIAL/ JOSEPH PUT INTO CISTERN 646-7, JOSEPH PUT INTO CISTERN BY BROTHERS 646-7, INITIAL/ MOSES FOUND BY PHARAOH'S DAUGHTER 646-8, MOSES FOUND BY PHARAOH'S DAUGHTER 646-8, INITIAL/ CROWD ABOUT TO STONE CHRIST 646-9, CHRIST ABOUT TO BE STONED BY CROWD 646-9, INITIAL/ CHRIST'S ENTRY INTO JERUSALEM 646-10, CHRIST'S ENTRY INTO JERUSALEM 646-10, ENTRY INTO JERUSALEM 646-10, INITIAL/ LAST SUPPER 646-11, LAST SUPPER 646-11, INITIAL/ RISEN CHRIST APPEARS TO APOSTLES 646-12, CHRIST RISEN APPEARS TO APOSTLES 646-12, INITIAL/ ASCENSION 646-13, ASCENSION 646-13, INITIAL/ PENTECOST/ HOLY SPIRIT DESCENDS 646-14, PENTECOST/ HOLY SPIRIT DESCENDS ON APOSTLES 646-14, HOLY SPIRIT DESCENDS ON APOSTLES 646-14, INITIAL/ DIVES AND LAZARUS 646-15, DIVES AND LAZARUS 646-15, LAZARUS AND DIVES 646-15, INITIAL/ ENTHRONED KING CROWNS KNEELING BOY 646-16, KING ENTHRONED CROWNS KNEELING BOY 646-16, INITIAL/ TOBIAS AND THE ANGEL 646-17, TOBIAS AND THE ANGEL 646-17, INITIAL/ JUDITH KILLS HOLOFERNES 646-18, JUDITH KILLS HOLOFERNES 646-18, INITIAL/ HAMAN IS HANGED 646-19, HAMAN HANGED/ ESTHER PLEADS WITH AHASUERUS 646-19, ESTHER PLEADS WITH AHASUERUS 646-19, INITIAL/ MOUNTED SOLDIERS ATTACK CITY 646-20, SOLDIERS MOUNTED ATTACK CITY DEFENDED BY BOWMAN

646-20, CHRIST IN MAJESTY 646-21, INITIAL/ INITIAL B BEATUS VIR/ JESSE TREE 646-22, INITIAL B BEATUS VIR/ JESSE TREE 646-22, JESSE TREE 646-22, KNIGHT KILLS GROTESQUE IN BORDER 646-22, PSALM 26/27 INITIAL D DOMINUS ILLUMINATIO/ DAVID 646-23, INITIAL D DOMINUS ILLUMINATION/ DAVID POINTS TO EYES 646-23, DAVID POINTS TO HIS EYES 646-23, PSALM 38/39 INITIAL D DIXI CUSTODIAM/ DAVID POINTS TO MOUTH 646-24, INITIAL D DIXI CUSTODIAM/ DAVID POINTS TO MOUTH 646-24, DAVID POINTS TO HIS MOUTH 646-24, PSALM 68/69 INITIAL S SALVUM/ JONAH AND WHALE 646-25, INITIAL S SALVUM/ JONAH AND WHALE 646-25, JONAH THROWN OVERBOARD AND CAST UP BY WHALE 646-25, PSALM 80/ 81 INITIAL E EXULTATE/ DAVID PLAYS BELLS 646-26, INITIAL E EXULTATE/ DAVID PLAYS BELLS 646-26, DAVID PLAYS BELLS 646-26, PSALM 97/ 98 INITIAL C CANTATE/ THREE CLERICS SING 646-27, INITIAL C CANTATE/ THREE CLERICS SINGING 646-27, CLERICS SINGING 646-27, PSALM 109/ 110 INITIAL D DIXIT/ TRINITY 646-28, INITIAL D DIXIT/ TRINITY 646-28, TRINITY 646-28, PRESENTATION IN THE TEMPLE 646-29, CHRIST PRESENTED IN TEMPLE 646-29, PURIFICATION 646-29, ST PETER IN CATHEDRA 646-30, ST BENEDICT 646-31, ANNUNCIATION 646-32, ST HELENA FINDS THE TRUE CROSS 646-33, ST JOHN THE BAPTIST NAMED 646-34, SIMON MAGNUS FALLS 646-35, ST MARY MAGDALENE 646-36, ST MARTIN AND THE BEGGAR 646-37, ST EDMUND THE MARTYR 646-38, ST CATHERINE OF ALEXANDRIA 646-39, ST ANDRWEW 646-40, ST NICHOLAS WITH BOYS SAVED FROM BRINE TUB 646-41, JOSCHIM AND ANNA AT THE GOLDEN GATE 646-42, ST THOMAS THE APOSTLE TOUCHES CHRIST'S WOUNDED SIDE 646-43, POPE KNEELS BEFORE GOD 646-44, SAINT IS BEHEADED 646-45, WOMAN CROWNED HOLDS PALM AND BOOK 646-46, MAN READING 646-47, BISHOP OR ABBOT PREACHES TO MONKS 646-48, CHRIST PREACHES TO CROWD 646-49, ST SILVESTER 646-50, ST PAUL CONVERTED 646-51, DETAIL OF HISTORIATED INITIAL OF ST PAUL 646-52, INVENTION OF THE CROSS/ TEXT PAGE 646-53, ST LAWRENCE 646-54, NATIVITY OF THE VIRGIN 646-55, ST MATTHEW WITH ST MARK'S LION 646-56, ST MICHAEL 646-57, TRINITY WITH EVANGELIST SYMBOLS 646-58, TEXT FOR ALL SOULS 646-59, ST PETER DELIVERED FROM PRISON 646-60, DETAIL OF HISTORIATED INITIAL OF ST PETER 646-61, TEXT 646/62-65

*$ABSTRACT 647
*LIBRARY BODLEIAN
*SLIDE SET TITLE MS E MUSAEO 60
*NEGATIVE REFERENCE ROLL 256C
*RENTAL FEE $2.35
*TITLE OF MANUSCRIPT SEXTUS LIBER DECRETALIUM
*SHELFMARK MS E MUSAEO 60/ FOL 2 647-1, MS E MUSAEO E 60/ FOL 37 647-2, MS E MUSAEO 60/ FOL 49 647-3, MS E MUSAEO 60/ FOL 68 647-4, MS E MUSAEO 60/ FOL 71V 647-5, MS E MUSAEO 60/ FOL 78 647-6, MS E MUSAEO 60/ FOL 79 647-7
*PROVENANCE ENGLISH
*DATE EXECUTED 14TH/1320-30
*LANGUAGE LATIN
*AUTHOR BONIFACE VIII
*TYPE OF MANUSCRIPT DECRETALIUM
*CONTENTS POPE BONIFACE VIII 647/1-7, BONIFACE VIII WITH TWO ATTENDANTS 647-1, FIGURE/ SEATED WITH TWO ATTENDANTS 647-2, PRIEST SAYS MASS/ CLERIC TURNS MAN AWAY FROM ALTAR 647-3, TEXT PAGE 647-4, HOUNDS CHASING HARE IN TOP BORDER 647-5, HARE CHASED BY HOUNDS 647-5, MARRIAGE CEREMONY 647-6, BISHOP SPEAKS TO CLERIC 647-7, TRIAL SCENE 647-7

*$ABSTRACT 648
*LIBRARY BODLEIAN
*SLIDE SET TITLE TISCHENDORF MANUSCRIPTS
*NEGATIVE REFERENCE ROLL 256D
*RENTAL FEE $2.35
*COMMENTS GREEK BIBLICAL TEXTS COLLECTED BY TISCHENDORF IN THE EAST IN 1853 AND SOLD TO THE BODLEIAN.
*TITLE OF MANUSCRIPT GOSPELS 648/1-4, GENESIS/ PARTS 648-5,

GOSPELS/6-7
*SHELFMARK MS AUCT T INF 1 1/ FOL 4 648-1, MS AUCT T INF 1 1/ FOL 92V-93 648-2, MS AUCT T INF 1 1/ FOL 94 648-3, MS AUCT T INF 1 1/ FCL 157V 648-4, MS AUCT T INF 2 1/ FOL 6 648-5, MS AUCT T INF 2 2/ FOL 17 648-6, MS AUCT T INF 2 2/ FOL 61 648-7
*DATE EXECUTED 09TH 648/1-4, 09TH? 648-5, 10TH/979? 648/6-7
*LANGUAGE GREEK
*TYPE OF MANUSCRIPT GOSPELS 648/1-4, GENESIS/ PARTS 648-5, GOSPELS 648/6-7
*CONTENTS BIBLICAL TEXTS/ GREEK 648/1-7, ST LUKE'S GOSPEL/ BEGINNING OF TEXT 648-1, ST LUKE'S GOSPEL/ END OF TEXT 648-2, ST JOHN'S GOSPEL/ PREFACE 648-2, ST JOHN'S GOSPEL/ BEGINNING OF TEXT 648-3, ST JOHN'S GOSPEL/ END OF TEXT 648-4, JERUSALEM COLOPHON 648-4, COLOPHON 648-4, GENESIS CHAPTERS 9 AND 10/ NOAH AND DESCENDANTS 648-5, ST MARK'S GOSPEL/ BEGINNING OF TEXT 648-6, ST LUKE'S GOSPEL/ BEGINNING OF TEXT 648-7 ST LUKE'S GOSPEL/ BEGINNING OF TEXT 648-7

*$ABSTRACT 649
*LIBRARY BODLEIAN
*SLIDE SET TITLE MAPS OF WALES
*NEGATIVE REFERENCE ROLL 257C
*RENTAL FEE $2.25
*TITLE OF MANUSCRIPT GOUGH MAP 649-1, MAP OF WALES 649-2, WALES 649-3, ACCURATE MAP OF NORTH WALES 649-4, NEW MAP OF SOUTH WALES 649-5
*SHELFMARK MS GOUGH GEN TOP 16 649-1, PR DOUCE O SUBT 15 649-2, PR GOUGH MAPS 92 649-3, PR E C17 10 27 649-4, PR E C17 10 1 649-5
*PROVENANCE ENGLISH
*DATE EXECUTED 14TH/C1360 649-1, 17TH/1606 649-2, 17TH/1611 649-3, 18TH/1760 649-4, 18TH/1777 649-5
*ARTIST/ SCHOOL ORTELIUS/ ABRAHAM 649-2, SPEED 649-3, BOWEN 649-4, KITCHEN 649-5
*TYPE OF MANUSCRIPT MAPS
*CONTENTS MAPS OF WALES 649/1-5, WALES/ MAPS 649/1-5, DETAIL OF AREA IN SOUTH WEST BRITAIN 649-1, MAP OF WALES 649-2, MAP OF WALES 649-3, MAP OF NORTH WALES 649-4, MAP OF SOUTH WALES 649-5

*$ABSTRACT 650
*LIBRARY BODLEIAN
*SLIDE SET TITLE FLEMISH BOOKS OF HOURS
*NEGATIVE REFERENCE ROLL 257D
*RENTAL FEE $4.00
*TITLE OF MANUSCRIPT BOOK OF HOURS
*SHELFMARK MS RAWL LITURG E 4/ FOL 4 650-1, MS RAWL LITURG E 4/ FCL 13 650-2, MS RAWL LITURG E 4/ FOL 14V 650-3, MS RAWL LITURG E 4/ FOL 16V 650-4, MS RAWL LITURG E 4/ FOL 17 650-5, MS RAWL LITURG E 4/ FOL 24 650-6, MS RAWL LITURG E 4/ FOL 27V 650/7-8, MS RAWL LITURG E 4/ FOL 29V 650-9, MS RAWL LITURG E 4/ FOL 31V 650-10, MS RAWL LITURG E 4/ FOL 35V 650-11, MS RAWL LITURG E 4/ FOL 38V 650-12, MS RAWL LITURG E 4/ FOL 40V 650-13, MS RAWL LITURG E 4/ FOL 49V 650-14, MS RAWL LITURG E 4/ FCL 54V 650-15, MS RAWL LITURG E 4/ FOL 56V 650-16, MS CANON LITURG 183/ FOL 7 650-17, MS CANON LITURG 183/ FOL 7V-8 650-18, MS CANON LITURG 183/ FOL 12 650-19, MS CANON LITURG 183/ FOL 19V 650-20, MS CANON LITURG 183/ FOL 20 650-21, MS CANON LITURG 183/ FOL 20V 650-22, MS CANON LITURG 183/ FOL 21 650-23, MS CANON LITURG 183/ FOL 21V 650-24, MS CANON LITURG 183/ FOL 22 650-25, MS CANON LITURG 183/ FOL 22V 650-26, MS CANON LITURG 183/ FOL 23 650-27, MS CANON LITURG 183/ FOL 24 650-28, MS CANON LITURG 183/ FOL 36V 650-29, MS CANON LITURG 183/ FOL 44 650-30, MS CANON LITURG 183/ FOL 47V 650-31, MS CANON LITURG 183/ FOL 51 650-32, MS CANON LITURG 183/ FOL 54 650-33, MS CANON LITURG 183/ FOL 57V 650-34, MS CANON LITURG 183/ FOL 63 650-35, MS CANON LITURG 183/ FOL 68 650-36, MS CANON LITURG 183/ FOL 81 650-38, MS CANON LITURG 183/ FOL 91

650-39, MS CANON LITURG 183/ FOL 95V 650-40
*PROVENANCE FLEMISH/ NETHERLANDS 650/1-16, FLEMISH 650/17-40
*DATE EXECUTED 15TH/ 3RD QUARTER
*LANGUAGE LATIN 650/1-16, FRENCH AND LATIN 650/17-40
*TYPE OF MANUSCRIPT BOOK OF HOURS/ USE OF SARUM 650/1-16, BOOK OF HOURS/ USE OF ROME 650/17-40
*CONTENTS BOOKS OF HOURS/ FLEMISH/ 15TH 650/1-40, CALENDAR FOR JULY/ TEXT 650-1, JULY CALENDAR/ TEXT 650-1, HOLY SPIRIT AS DOVE 650-2, ST MARGARET 650-3, CHRIST IN GARDEN OF GETHSEMENE 650-4, HOURS OF THE VIRGIN/ BEGINNING OF TEXT 650-5, ST THOMAS A BECKET'S MARTYRDOM 650-6, ST GEORGE 650-7, ST GEORGE/ DUPLICATE OF FRAME 7 650-8, ST CHRISTOPHER 650-9, TRINITY/ CRUCIFIED CHRIST LIES ON GOD'S LAP 650-10, CHRIST CRUCIFIED LIES ON GOD'S LAP 650-10, ST MARY MAGDALENE 650-11, ST BARBARA 650-12, CHRIST TAKEN DOWN FROM CROSS 650-13, DEPOSITION 650-13, ENTOMBMENT 650-14, CHRIST ENTOMBED 650-14, ST JOHN THE BAPTIST 650-15 ST JOHN THE EVANGELIST 650-16, CRUCIFIXION 650-17, TEXT/ DOUBLE OPENING 650-18, PENTECOST 650-19, ST JOHN THE BAPTIST 650-20, ST GEORGE 650-21, ST NICHOLAS 650-22, ST SEBASTIAN 650-23, ST KATHERINE 650-24, ST BARBARA 650-25, ST MARY MAGDALENE 650-26, ST MARGARET 650-27, ANNUNCIATION 650-28, VISITATION 650-29, NATIVITY 650-30, ANNUNCIATION TO THE SHEPHERDS 650-31, ADORATION OF THE MAGI 650-32, PRESENTATION OF CHRIST IN THE TEMPLE 650-33, CHRIST PRESENTED IN THE TEMPLE 650-33, MASSACRE OF HOLY INNOCENTS 650-34, HOLY INNOCENTS MASSACRED 650-34, FLIGHT INTO EGYPT 650-35, PIETA 650-36, CORONATION OF VIRGIN 650-37, LAST JUDGMENT/ CHRIST ON RAINBOW/ MARY AND JOHN 650-38, CHRIST ON RAINBOW 650-38, LITANY/ PART OF THE TEXT 650-39, OFFICE OF THE DEAD/ MOURNERS NEAR COFFIN 650-40, MOURNERS AND CLERGY NEAR DRAPED COFFIN 650-40

*$ABSTRACT 651
*LIBRARY BODLEIAN
*SLIDE SET TITLE FORTUNE'S WHEEL
*NEGATIVE REFERENCE ROLL 257E
*RENTAL FEE $2.30
*TITLE OF MANUSCRIPT BIBLE 651-1, ROMAN DE LA ROSE 651/2 AND 4, MEMORABILIA OF VALERIUS MAXIMUS 651-3, ASTROLOGICAL TABLES 651-5, EPITRE D'OTHEA A HECTOR 651-6
*SHELFMARK MS CANON BIBL LAT 36/ FOL 192V 651-1, MS SELDEN SUPRA 57/ FOL 34 651-2, MS DOUCE 203/ FOL 103V 651-3, MS DOUCE 188/ FOL 45 651-4, MS CANON ITAL 38/ FOL 25 651-5, MS BODLEY 421/ FOL 52V 651-6
*PROVENANCE ITALIAN/ PADUA 651-1, FRENCH 651/2-4, ITALIAN/ FLORENCE 651-5, FRENCH 651-6
*DATE EXECUTED 13TH/ LATE 651-1, 14TH/ 2ND QUARTER 651-2, 15TH/ AFTER 1401 651-3, 15TH/ EARLY 651-4, 15TH/1456 651-5, 15TH/ 1ST QUARTER 651-6
*LANGUAGE LATIN 651-1, FRENCH 651/2-4, ITALIAN 651-5, FRENCH 651-6
*ARTIST/ SCHOOL MASTER OF THE GASTON PHEBUS 651-3
*AUTHOR DE LORRIS/ GUILLAUME AND JEAN DE MEUNG 651/2 AND 4, VALERIUS MAXIMUS 651-3, D'HESDIN/ SIMON TRANSLATOR 651-3, DE PISAN/ CHRISTINE 651-6
*SCRIBE BONIFAZIO 651-5
*TYPE OF MANUSCRIPT BIBLE 651-1, ROMANCE 651/2 AND 4, MEMORABILIA 651-3, ASTROLOGICAL TREATISE 651-5, LITERATURE 651-6
*CONTENTS FORTUNE'S WHEEL 651/1-6, WHEEL OF FORTUNE 651/1-6

*$ABSTRACT 652
*LIBRARY BODLEIAN
*SLIDE SET TITLE MILLER'S TALE
*NEGATIVE REFERENCE ROLL 258
*RENTAL FEE $3.20
*COMMENTS ILLUSTRATIONS SELECTED FROM VARIOUS MSS TO ILLUSTRATE CHAUCER'S TEXT OF THE MILLER'S TALE.

*TITLE OF MANUSCRIPT HOURS OF ANNE OF BOHEMIA 652-1, TREATISE ON ASTRONOMY 652-2, LIBER FORTUNAE 652-3, COMMENTARY ON THE PSALMS 652-4, ROMAN DE LA ROSE 652-5, DE TOPOGRAPHIA HIBERNIAE 652-6, BESTIAIRE D'ARMOUR 652-7, ROMAN DE LA ROSE 652/8-9, BIBLE HISTORIALE 652-10, ROMANCE OF ALEXANDER 652-11, CHOIR PSALTER 652-12, ORMESBY PSALTER 652-13, PSALTER 652-14, INFANCY OF CHRIST 652-15, TO LERNE TO DIE BY HOCCLEVE 652-16, ASTROLOGICAL AND ECCLESIASTICAL CALENDAR 652-17, VERNON MANUSCRIPT 652-18, BIBLE HISTORIALE 652-19, CAEDMON GENESIS 652-20, ROMANCE OF ALEXANDER 652-21, PSALTER 652-22, PRIVATE PRAYERS WITH HYMNS 652-23, ROMANCE OF ALEXANDER 652-24
*SHELFMARK MS LAT LITURG F 3/ FOL 68 652-1, MS BODLEY 614/ FOL 34V-35 652-2, MS DIGBY 46/ FOL 8V 652-3, MS AUCT D 2 8/ FOL 88 652-4, MS DOUCE 195/ FOL 60V 652-5, MS LAUD MISC 720/ FOL 163 652-6, MS DOUCE 308/ FOL 98 652-7, MS DOUCE 195/ FOL 61V 652-8, MS DOUCE 195/ FOL 66V 652-9, MS DOUCE 211/ FOL 172V 652-10, MS BODLEY 264/ FOL 97V 652-11, MS ASHMOLE 1525/ FOL 101 652-12, MS DOUCE 366/ FOL 9V 652-13, MS DOUCE 118/ FOL 140V 652-14, MS SELDEN SUPRA 38/ FOL 2V 652-15, MS SELDEN SUPRA 53/ FOL 118 652-16, MS RAWL D 939/ SECTION 2 652-17, MS ENG POET E 1/ FOL 231 652-18, MS DOUCE 211/ FOL 12V 652-19, MS JUNIUS 11/ PAGE 66 652-20, MS BODLEY 264/ FOL 133 652-21, MS DOUCE 6/ FOL 160V 652-22, MS GOUGH LITURG 7/ FOL 2 652-23, MS BODLEY 264/ FOL 84 652-24
*PROVENANCE FLEMISH 652-1, ENGLISH 652/2-4, FRENCH 652-5, ENGLISH 652-6, FRENCH/ LORRAINE 652-7, FRENCH 652/8-9, FRENCH/ PARIS 652-10, FLEMISH 652-11, ENGLISH/ ST AUGUSTINE'S CANTERBURY 652-12, ENGLISH/ EAST ANGLIA 652-13, FRENCH/ ARTOIS 652-14, ENGLISH 652/15-18, FRENCH/ PARIS 652-19, ENGLISH/ WINCHESTER OR CANTERBURY 652-20, FLEMISH 652-21, FLEMISH/ GHENT 652-22, FLEMISH 652/23-24
*DATE EXECUTED 14TH/1382-94 652-1, 12TH/ MID 652-2, 14TH/ LATE 652-3, 12TH/ LATE 652-4, 15TH/1487-95 652-5, 13TH/ 3RD QUARTER 652-6, 14TH/ 1ST QUARTER 652-7, 15TH/ LATE 652/8-9, 14TH/ EARLY 652-10, 14TH/1388-44 652-11, 13TH/ EARLY 652-12, 13TH/ LATE 14TH/ EARLY 652-13, 13TH/ LATE 652-14, 14TH/C1320-30 652-15, 15TH/C1430 652-16, 14TH/C1370 652-17, 14TH/ AFTER 1382 652-18, 14TH/ 1ST QUARTER 652-19, 11TH/C1000 652-20, 14TH/1338-44 652-21, 14TH/C1320-30 652-22, 16TH/C1500 652-23, 14TH/1338-44 652-24
*LANGUAGE DUTCH AND LATIN 652-1, LATIN 652/2-4 AND 6, FRENCH 652/5 AND 7-11, LATIN 652/12-14, FRENCH 652/15 AND 17 AND 19, ENGLISH 652/16 AND 18, ENGLISH/ OLD ENGLISH 652-20, FRENCH 652/21 AND 24, LATIN 652-22, ENGLISH AND LATIN 652-23
*ARTIST/ SCHOOL TESTARD/ ROBINET 652/5 AND 8-9, DE GRISE/ JEHAN 652/11 AND 21 AND 24
*AUTHOR SILVESTRIS/ BERNARDUS 652-3, LOMBARD/ PETER 652-4, DE LORRIS/ GUILLAUME AND JEAN DE MEUNG 652/5 AND 8-9, CAMBRENSIS/ GIRALDUS 652-6, DE FOURNIVALL/ RICHARD 652-7, DESMOULINS/ GUYART 652-10, HOCCLEVE/ THOMAS 652-16
*TYPE OF MANUSCRIPT BOOK OF HOURS/ USE OF ROME 652-1, ASTRONOMICAL TREATISE 652/2-3, COMMENTARY 652-4, POETRY 652/5 AND 8-9, TREATISE 652-6, LITERATURE 652-7, BIBLE HISTORIALE 652/10 AND 19, ROMANCE 652-11, PSALTER/ CHOIR 652-12, PSALTER 652/13-14, LIFE OF CHRIST 652-15, TREATISE 652-16, CALENDAR/ ASTROLOGICAL 652-17, POETRY 652/18 AND 20, ROMANCE 652/21 AND 24, PSALTER 652-22, PRAYERS 652-23
*CONTENTS CHAUCER'S MILLER'S TALE FROM VARIOUS MSS 652/1-24, LITERATURE/ MILLER'S TALE 652/1-24, MILLER'S TALE FROM VARIOUS MSS 652/1-24, CHRIST BROUGHT BEFORE PILATE 652-1, CIRCLE SHOWING 12 HEADS OF WINDS/ RAINBOW 652-2, EUCLID HOLDS SPHERE AND DIOPTRA 652-3, ASTROLABE HELD BY HERMANUS 652-3, INITIAL D KING DAVID PLAYS PSALTERY 652-4, DAVID PLAYS PSALTERY 652-4, PSALTERY PLAYED BY DAVID 652-4, CHIMEBELLS PLAYED BY MAN 652-4, HUSBAND/ JEALOUS GUARDS HIS WIFE 652-5, WEASEL 652-6, SWALLOW EATS WHILE FLYING 652-7, TARQUINIUS ATTACKS LUCRETIA 652-8, HUSBAND/ SUSPICIOUS MALTREATS HIS WIFE 652-9, ABSALOM ENTANGLED BY HIS HAIR IN TREE 652-10, DANCING LADIES TO ACCOMPANIMENT OF VIOL PLAYER 652-11, INITIAL D MEN PLAY REBEC 652-12, REBEC PLAYED BY MEN 652-12, GITTERN PLAYED BY ANGEL 652-13, PRIEST SWINGS CENSER 652-14, HEROD QUESTIONS THE MAGI 652-15, MAGI QUESTIONED BY HEROD 652-15, DEATH AS SKELETON

ATTENDS DEATHBED 652-16, SAINTS WHOSE FEASTS FALL IN OCTOBER 652-17, ST FRIDESWIDE 652-17, ST LUKE WITH WINGED BULL 652-17, PATER NOSTER TEXT IN THREE COLUMNS 652-18, GOD TELLS NOAH OF FLOOD 652-19, NOAH TOLD OF FLOOD 652-19, NOAH'S ARK/ THREE TIERED VIKING SHIP 652-20, NOAH'S WIFE REFUSES TO BOARD ARK 652-20, WINEMAKING/ MEN TREAD GRAPES 652-21, LOVERS APPROACH BED WHERE THEY MAKE LOVE 652-22, FEBRUARY/ TRIMMING TREES AND GATHERING WOOD 652-23, SMITHS WORK AT A FORGE 652-24

*$ABSTRACT 653
*LIBRARY BODLEIAN
*SLIDE SET TITLE KNIGHT'S TALE
*NEGATIVE REFERENCE ROLL 259
*RENTAL FEE $3.20
*COMMENTS ILLUSTRATIONS SELECTED FROM VARIOUS MSS TO ILLUSTRATE CHAUCER'S TEXT OF THE KNIGHT'S TALE.
*TITLE OF MANUSCRIPT ROMANCE OF ALEXANDER 653/1-2 AND 7 AND 10-11, ROMANCE OF ALEXANDER 653/15-16 AND 19-24, ROMAN DE LA ROSE 653/3 AND 6 AND 8 , ROMAN DE LA ROSE 653/13 AND 17, LI LIVRES DU GRAUNT CAAM 653/4-5 AND 9, ASTROLOGICAL TREATISE 653/12 AND 14 AND 18
*SHELFMARK MS BODLEY 264/FOL 97 653-1, MS BODLEY 264/ FOL 149V 653-2, MS BODLEY 371/ FOL 40V 653-3, MS BODLEY 264/ FOL 222 653-4, MS BODLEY 264/ FOL 252V 653-5, MS DOUCE 371/ FOL 12 653-6, MS BODLEY 264/ FOL 167 653-7, MS DOUCE 371/ FOL 20V 653-8, MS BODLEY 264/ FOL 240V 653-9, MS BODLEY 264/ FOL 109 653-10, MS BODLEY 264/ FOL 145 653-11, MS RAWL D 1220/ FOL 31V 653-12, MS DOUCE 371/ FOL 4V 653-13, MS RAWL D 1220/ FOL 30V 653-14, MS BODLEY 264/ FOL 122V 653-15, MS BODLEY 264/ FOL 188V 653-16, MS DOUCE 371/ FOL 6 653-17, MS RAWL D 1220/ FOL 25V 653-18, MS BODLEY 264/ FOL 121 653-19, MS BODLEY 264/ FOL 113V 653-20, MS BODLEY 264/ FOL 165 653-21, MS BODLEY 264/ FOL 59 653-22, MS BODLEY 264/ FOL 191 653-23, MS BODLEY 264/ FOL 172V 653-24
*PROVENANCE FLEMISH 653/1-2 AND 7 AND 10-11, FLEMISH 653/15-16 AND 19-24, FRENCH/ PARIS 653/3 AND 6 AND 8, FRENCH/ PARIS 653/13 AND 17, ENGLISH 653/4-5 AND 9, ENGLISH 653/12 AND 14 AND 18
*DATE EXECUTED 14TH/1338-44 653/1-2 AND 7 AND 10-11, 14TH/1338-44 653/15-16 AND 19-24, 15TH/C1400 653/3-6 AND 8-9 AND 13 AND 17, 15TH/ 3RD QUARTER 653/12 AND 14 AND 18
*LANGUAGE FRENCH 653/1-11 AND 13, FRENCH 653/15-17 AND 19-24, ENGLISH 653/12 AND 14 AND 18
*ARTIST/ SCHOOL DE GRISE/ JEHAN 653/1-2 AND 7 AND 10-11, DE GRISE/ JEHAN 653/15-16 AND 19-24, JOHANNES 653/4-5 AND 9
*AUTHOR DE LORRIS/ GUILLAUME AND JEAN DE MEUNG 653/3 AND 6, DE LORRIS/ GUILLAUME AND JEAN DE MEUNG 653/8 AND 13 AND 17, POLO/ MARCO 653/4-5 AND 9
*TYPE OF MANUSCRIPT ROMANCE 653/1-3 AND 6-8 AND 10-11 AND 15-17, ROMANCE 653/19-24, TRAVEL 653/4-5 AND 9, ASTROLOGICAL TREATISE 653/12 AND 14 AND 18
*CONTENTS CHAUCER'S KNIGHT'S TALE FROM VARIOUS MSS 653/1-24, LITERATURE/ KNIGHT'S TALE 653/1-24, KNIGHT'S TALE FROM VARIOUS MSS 653/1-24, QUEEN OF FEMINIE DREAMS WHILE HANDMAIDENS LOOK ON 653-1, SIX SEATED ATTENDANTS 653-1, BORDER/ CASTELLATED WITH FOUR LADIES LOOKING OUT 653-1, ALEXANDER AND HIS HOST IN ARMS 653-2, TRUMPETS BLOWN BY TWO MEN/ DRUMMER 653-2, HOUSE OF FORTUNE 653-3, WHEEL OF FORTUNE/ KING SITS ON TOP 653-3, FORTUNE'S WHEEL 653-3, CITY OF BAUDAS STORMED 653-4, CORPSE BURNED OUTSIDE CYANGLU 653-5, GOLDEN CALF IN CITY OF CYANGLU 653-5, GOD OF LOVE SHOOTS ARROW IN DREAMER'S EYE 653-6, KING PHILIP RECEIVES A LETTER 653-7, LADY REASON APPROACHES THE LOVER 653-8, PRISONER LOOKS OUT OF TOWER 653-8, KHAN HUNTS BEAR/ BOAR AND DEER 653-9, HUNTING OF BEAR/ BOAR AND DEER 653-9, ALEXANDER AND ATTENDANT WATCH MEN FIGHT 653-10, ALEXANDER TALKS TO HIS COURTIERS 653-11, VENUS RULES FRIDAY 653-12, WHEEL OF FORTUNE 653-12, VENUS' CHILDREN DISPORT 653-12, DREAMER KNOCKS AT GATE OF GARDEN OF MIRTH 653-13, GARDEN OF MIRTH/ IDLENESS IS DOORKEEPER 653-13, IDLENESS AS DOORKEEPER OF GARDEN OF MIRTH 653-13, MARS RULES OVER TUESDAY

653-14, DIANA URGES ACTEON'S HOUNDS TO TEAR HIM APART 653-15, ALEXANDER AT A FEAST 653-16, MUSICAL INSTRUMENTS/ BAGPIPES/ TABOR/ NAKERS/ PSALTERY 653-16, CAROLE OF LOVE IN GARDEN OF MIRTH 653-17, SATURN WITH SCYTHE RULES OVER SATURDAY 653-18, KNIGHTS JOUSTING 653-19, JOUSTING KNIGHTS 653-19, SWORDSMITH GRINDS SWORD BLADE 653-20, GRINDSTONE IN WOODEN FRAME FOR GRINDING SWORDS 653-20, TOURNMENT HELMET MADE BY SMITH 653-21, SMITH MAKES HELMET WITH BELLOWS AND TONGS 653-21, ALEXANDER AND TROOPS BATTLE ARMY OF PORUS 653-22, ALEXANDER DYING WITH GRIEVING FRIENDS 653-23, PORUS STANDS BETWEEN BRIDE AND GROOM 653-24, MARRIAGE CEREMONY AND FEAST 653-24

*$ABSTRACT 654
*LIBRARY BODLEIAN
*SLIDE SET TITLE MS DOUCE 6/ PART 4
*NEGATIVE REFERENCE ROLL 260A
*RENTAL FEE $4.10
*COMMENTS NUMEROUS GROTESQUES AND ANIMAL HEADS ARE NOT FULLY DESCRIBED.
*TITLE OF MANUSCRIPT PORTABLE PSALTER
*SHELFMARK MS DOUCE 6/ FOL 118V-119 654-1, MS DOUCE 6/ FOL 119V-120 654-2, MS DOUCE 6/ FOL 120V-121 654-3, MS DOUCE 6/ FOL 121V-122 654-4, MS DOUCE 6/ FOL 122V-123 654-5, MS DOUCE 6/ FOL 123V-124 654-6, MS DOUCE 6/ FOL 124V-125 654-7, MS DOUCE 6/ FOL 125V-126 654-8, MS DOUCE 6/ FOL 126V-127 654-9, MS DOUCE 6/ FOL 127V-128 654-10, MS DOUCE 6/ FOL 128V-129 654-11, MS DOUCE 6/ FOL 129V-130 654-12, MS DOUCE 6/ FOL 130V-131 654-13, MS DOUCE 6/ FOL 131V-132 654-14, MS DOUCE 6/ FOL 132V-133 654-15, MS DOUCE 6/ FOL 133V-134 654-16, MS DOUCE 6/ FOL 134V-135 654-17, MS DOUCE 6/ FOL 135V-136 654-18, MS DOUCE 6/ FOL 136V-137 654-19, MS DOUCE 6/ FOL 137V-138 654-20, MS DOUCE 6/ FOL 138V-139 654-21, MS DOUCE 6/ FOL 139V-140 654-22, MS DOUCE 6/ FOL 140V-141 654-23, MS DOUCE 6/ FOL 141V-142 654-24, MS DOUCE 6/ FOL 142V-143 654-25, MS DOUCE 6/ FOL 143V-144 654-26, MS DOUCE 6/ FOL 144V-145 654/27-28, MS DOUCE 6/ FOL 145V-146 654-29, MS DOUCE 6/ FOL 146V-147 654-30, MS DOUCE 6/ FOL 147V-148 654-31, MS DOUCE 6/ FOL 148V-149 654-32, MS DOUCE 6/ FOL 149V-150 654-33, MS DOUCE 6/ FOL 150V-151 654-34, MS DOUCE 6/ FOL 151V-152 654-35, MS DOUCE 6/ FOL 152V-153 654-36, MS DOUCE 6/ FOL 153V-154 654-37, MS DOUCE 6/ FOL 154V-155 654-38, MS DOUCE 6/ FOL 155V-156 654-39, MS DOUCE 6/ FOL 156V-157 654-40, MS DOUCE 6/ FOL 157V-158 654-41, MS DOUCE 6/ FOL 158V-159 654-42
*PROVENANCE FLEMISH/ GHENT
*DATE EXECUTED 14TH/C1320-30
*LANGUAGE LATIN
*TYPE OF MANUSCRIPT PSALTER/ PORTABLE
*CONTENTS PSALTER/ FLEMISH/ 14TH 654/1-42, WOMAN CARRIES BASKET OF EGGS ON HEAD 654-1, HARE/ APE SPINNING/ TRUMPETER 654-1, WOMAN MAKES WAFERS/ MAN CARRIES FISH 654-1, HARE CAUGHT BY TALL MAN 654-2, MONSTER CAUGHT BY MAN 654-2, APE WITH BOW SHOOTS AT APE 654-2, APE SNARES GREAT TIT 654-3, APE SITS OUTSIDE CHAPEL 654-3, MOTHER AND CHILD 654-3, APE/ STAG/ MAN'S HEAD/ MAN PLAYS HORN 654-4, HARE SHOT AT MY MAN 654-5, WOMEN CARRY MAN HIDING IN BASKET TOWARDS CHURCH 654-5, DOUBLE FLUTE PLAYED BY MAN 654-5, ALPEN HORN BLOWN BY MAN IN SHORT CAPE 654-6, APE PRIEST BLESSES TWO APES 654-6, APE BISHOP BLESSES DOG'S HEAD 654-6, STORK PECKS APE 654-7, KNIGHT IN CHAIN MAIL 654-7, UNICORN/ THREE-FACED HEAD 654-7, WATER DRAWN FROM WELL/ MAN CARRIES ON YOKE 654-8, HARE TIED TO POLE CARRIED BY MEN 654-8, GOD OF LOVE SHOOTS ARROW AT WOMAN 654-8, MOON VIEWED THROUGH TELESCOPE 654-9, TELESCOPE USED TO VIEW MOON 654-9, APE HOLDS CROZIER 654-9, MAN WITH TRAY OF BELTS 654-10, KNIGHTS FIGHT/ ONE THROWS STONES 654-11, APE BISHOP RIDES BEAR 654-11, MAN BUILDS WALL 654-11, PLOWING WITH JAWBONE 654-11, STAG WITH SWORD AND SHIELD 654-11, LADY DANCING/ MAN PLAYS BAGPIPES 654-12, HORSE LADEN WITH BOTTLES 654-12, BELLOWS HELD BY MAN 654-12, GROTESQUES/ THREE 654-13, APE CLUBS SWORDSMAN 654-14, GAME WITH STICKS PLAYED BY APES 654-14, LADY WITH

ROSARY/ MAN WITH LONG POLE 654-14, FALCONER WITH LURE/ GAUNTLET/ HAWK 654-15, YOUTH HOLDS LEAFY BRANCH 654-16, TRUMPET BLOWN BY MAN/ STORK WATCHES 654-16, MAN CHEWS HANDLE OF SPOON 654-16, MAN CARRIES BASKET OF FISH 654-16, NETTING A BIRD 654-17, CHICKS FEED IN NEST BY SPOON 654-17, MASON WITH CHISEL AND MALLET 654-18, BEE KEEPER WEARING VEIL HANGS DRUMS NEAR HIVE 654-19, JESTER RIDES IN CART PUSHED BY APES 654-19, MAN CARRIES LAMB 654-19, PIPE PLAYED BY MAN/ MAN AND WOMAN KISS 654-20, SEVEN HEADED LINE ENDINGS/ MAN HOLDS POT 654-21, PRIEST/ MAN READING/ MAN DRINKING 654-22, APE ABOUT TO THROW STONES AT PRIEST 654-22, LINE ENDINGS WITH FACES 654-23, STORK/ TRUMPETER/ MAN SUPPORTS INITIAL 654-24, MAN CLUBS STAG'S HEAD/ APE DANCING 654-25, DULCIMER PLAYED BY MAN 654-25, MAN READING/ SIX HEADED LINE ENDINGS 654-26, KNIGHT FIGHTS MONSTER 654-27, LANTERN HELD BY MAN 654-27, BELL HELD BY MAN 654-27, DUPLICATE OF FRAME 27 654-28, KNIGHT WITH SHIELD AND SCIMITAR 654-29, MAN WITH SWORD/ BLUE TIT/ HARE 654-30, SHINTY OR HOCKEY STICK AND BALL 654-31, PIPE PLAYED BY MAN/ TWO APES/ STORK 654-32, FIVE HEADED LINE ENDINGS 654-33, HORN PLAYED BY MAN 654-34, UNICORN'S HORN HELD BY MAN 654-34, KNIGHT FIGHTS APE 654-35, JESTER CARRIES SWADDLED APE ACROSS RIVER 654-36, GAME OF SKITTLES PLAYED BY APE 654-37, LADY WITH WHIP RIDES ON LION 654-38, APE WITH CROZIER 654-38, FIDDLE PLAYED BY MAN 654-38, UNICORN 654-39, COOKING/ MAN STIRS POT 654-39, MAN THROWS STICK AT DEAD DUCK 654-40, LURING OF SMALL BIRD 654-40, STRINGED INSTRUMENT PLAYED BY MOUSE 654-40, HAND BELLS RUNG BY MAN 654-41, APE KING GIVES LETTER TO APE MESSENGER 654-41, DRILL USED TO PUT HOLES IN DICE 654-41, APE ON STILTS/ TRUMPETER/ MAN SPINNING 654-42

*$ABSTRACT 655
*LIBRARY BODLEIAN
*SLIDE SET TITLE MS DOUCE 6/ PART 5
*NEGATIVE REFERENCE ROLL 260B
*RENTAL FEE $3.20
*COMMENTS NUMEROUS GROTESQUES, HUMAN HEADS AND ANIMAL HEADS ARE NOT FULLY DESCRIBED.
*TITLE OF MANUSCRIPT PORTABLE PSALTER
*SHELFMARK MS DOUCE 6/ FOL 159V-160 655-1, MS DOUCE 6/ FOL 160V-161 655-2, MS DOUCE 6/ FOL 161V-162 655-3, MS DOUCE 6/ FOL 162V-163 655-4, MS DOUCE 6/ FOL 163V-164 655-5, MS DOUCE 6/ FOL 164V-165 655-6, MS DOUCE 6/ FOL 165V-166 655-7, MS DOUCE 6/ FOL 166V-167 655-8, MS DOUCE 6/ FOL 167V-168 655-9, MS DOUCE 6/ FOL 168V-169 655-10, MS DOUCE 6/ FOL 169V-170 655-11, MS DOUCE 6/ FOL 170V-171 655-12, MS DOUCE 6/ FOL 171V-172 655-13, MS DOUCE 6/ FOL 172V-173 655-14, MS DOUCE 6/ FOL 173V-174 655-15, MS DOUCE 6/ FOL 174V-175 655-16, MS DOUCE 6/ FOL 175V-176 655-17, MS DOUCE 6/ FOL 176V-177 655-18, MS DOUCE 6/ FOL 177V-178 655-19, MS DOUCE 6/ FOL 178V-179 655-20, MS DOUCE 6/ FOL 179V-180 655-21, MS DOUCE 6/ FOL 180V-181 655-22, MS DOUCE 6/ FOL 181V-182 655-23, MS DOUCE 6/ FOL 182V-183 655-24
*PROVENANCE FLEMISH/ GHENT
*DATE EXECUTED 14TH/C1320-30
*LANGUAGE LATIN
*TYPE OF MANUSCRIPT PSALTER/ PORTABLE
*CONTENTS PSALTER/ FLEMISH/ 14TH 655/1-24, HARE CHASED BY HOUND 655-1, LOVER OFFERS PIERCED HEART TO LADY 655-1, GOD OF LOVE AS ANGEL ENCOURAGES LOVER 655-1, LOVERS APPROACH HOUSE AND GO TO BED 655-2, PORTATIVE ORGAN 655-3, APE SHOOTS WINGED FACE/ MONSTERS IN INITIAL 655-4, HARE FED FROM DISH 655-5, APE WITH CLUB 655-6, HARE CARRIES DEAD HOUND OVER SHOULDER 655-6, LINE ENDINGS WITH FACES 655-7, LINE ENDINGS WITH FIGURES 655-8, HORN BOOK AND BAG CARRIED BY BOY 655-9, BOYS FIGHT WITH STICKS AND SHIELDS 655-9, GROTESQUES KISSING 655-9, MAN CARRIES CARCASE ON SPIT 655-10, LINE ENDINGS WITH HEADS 655-11, MAN WRITES FIRST LINE OF TEXT 655-12, UNICORN/ GROTESQUE WITH WOMAN'S HEAD 655-13, CANDLES HELD BY WOMAN 655-14, SOLDIER/ SARACEN WITH SCIMITAR AND SHIELD 655-15, OX ABOUT TO BE KILLED WITH AXE 655-16, MAN SPITTING OUT SPOONS FROM HIS MOUTH

655-17, MAN HOLDS CLOTH/ FOUR LINE ENDINGS 655-18, MAN HOLDS DISH AND CAULDRON 655-19, FOX 655-20, MAN WITH CLUB WAITS FOR APES 655-20, LINE ENDINGS WITH FACES 655-21, BAKING LOAVES OF BREAD IN OVEN 655-22, APE ASPERGES HAIRY DEVIL 655-23, DEVIL ASPERGED BY APE 655-23, KNIGHT HOLDS LANCE WITH PENNANT 655-23, TRUMPET BLOWN BY MAN 655-24, LINE ENDINGS WITH HEADS

*$ABSTRACT 656
*LIBRARY BODLEIAN
*SLIDE SET TITLE PETER APIANUS
*NEGATIVE REFERENCE ROLL 260C
*RENTAL FEE $2.35
*TITLE OF MANUSCRIPT ASTRONOMICUM CAESARUM
*SHELFMARK PR ARCH B B 7/ PAGE 21 656-1, PR ARCH B B 7/ PAGE 31 656-2, PR ARCH B B 7/ PAGE 21 656-3, PR ARCH B B 7/ PAGE 35 656-4, PR ARCH B B 7/ PAGE 54 656-5, PR ARCH B B 7/ PAGE 55 656-6, PR ARCH B B 7/ PAGE 59 656-7
*PROVENANCE GERMAN/ INGOLSTADT
*DATE EXECUTED 16TH/1540
*AUTHOR APIANUS/ PETRUS
*TYPE OF MANUSCRIPT ASTRONOMICAL TREATISE
*CONTENTS DIAGRAMS FROM ASTRONOMICAL TREATISE 656/1-7, ASTRONOMICAL TREATISE 656/1-7, DEFERENS SATURNI 656-1, LATITUDO MARTIS 656-2, DUPLICATE OF FRAME 1 656-3, DEFERENS VENTRIS 656-4, CAUTELA OBSERVANDA IN DISPOSICIONE ROTARUM 656/5-6, ARGUMENTUM SOLIS 656-7

*$ABSTRACT 657
*LIBRARY BODLEIAN
*SLIDE SET TITLE BIBLES III
*NEGATIVE REFERENCE ROLL 260D
*RENTAL FEE $2.20
*TITLE OF MANUSCRIPT DOUCE BIBLE 657/1-2, BIBLE 657/3-4
*SHELFMARK PR ENG 1583 B 1 657/1-2, PR BIBL ENG 1602 B 1 657/3-4
*PROVENANCE ENGLISH
*DATE EXECUTED 16TH/1584 657/1-2, 17TH/1602 657/3-4
*TYPE OF MANUSCRIPT BIBLES
*CONTENTS BIBLES/ EARLY PRINTED 657/1-4, BOOK COVER EMBROIDERED WITH PATTERN OF ROSES 657-1, ADAM AND EVE TEMPTED IN GARDEN OF EDEN 657-2, TITLE PAGE/ COLORED AND DECORATED 657-3, GENESIS/ FIRST PAGE OF TEXT 657-4

*$ABSTRACT 658
*LIBRARY BODLEIAN
*SLIDE SET TITLE GOSPELS/ GERMAN
*NEGATIVE REFERENCE ROLL 261
*RENTAL FEE $3.25
*TITLE OF MANUSCRIPT GOSPELS
*SHELFMARK MS LAUD LAT 102/ FOL 1-174V
*PROVENANCE GERMAN/ FULDA
*DATE EXECUTED 09TH/ 1ST THIRD
*LANGUAGE LATIN
*SCRIBE ANGLO-SAXON AND CAROLINGIAN SCRIBES
*TYPE OF MANUSCRIPT GOSPELS
*CONTENTS GOSPELS/ GERMAN/ 9TH 658/1-25, CANON TABLES/ DECORATED 658/1-16, INITIAL P PLURES/ DECORATED 658-17, INITIAL B BEATO/ DECORATED 658-18, INITIAL M MATTHEUS/ DECORATED 658-19, INITIAL N NATIVITAS/ DECORATED 658-20, ST MATTHEW'S GOSPEL/ TITLE INSCRIPTION 658-21, ST MATTHEW'S GOSPEL/ BEGINNING 658-22, ST MARK'S GOSPEL/ BEGINNING 658-23, ST LUKE'S GOSPEL/ BEGINNING 658-24, ST JOHN'S GOSPEL/ BEGINNING 658-25

*$ABSTRACT 659
*LIBRARY VARIOUS OXFORD LIBRARIES
*SLIDE SET TITLE HISTORY OF OXFORD LIBRARIES
*NEGATIVE REFERENCE ROLL 122
*RENTAL FEE $4.50
*COMMENTS 50 SLIDES SELECTED FROM 38 MSS.
*TITLE OF MANUSCRIPT MEMORIALE FRATRIS THOME DE BARNEBY 659/1-2, MORALIA ON JOB 659-3, ON SENTENCES OF PETER LOMBARD 659/4-6, ON EZECHIEL 659-7, WORKS OF RAYMOND LULL 659-8, ON THE SENTENCES 659-9, CONFLATUS ON BOOK 1 OF SENTENCES 659-10, POSTILS 659-11, ON ECCLESIASTICUS 659-12, ON THE PSALTER 659-13, ON ST LUKE 659/14-15, ON METAPHYSICS 659/16-17, TEXTUS ANIMALIUM 659-18, ON METAPHYSICS 659-19, ON LOGIC 659-20, MARTIANUS CAPELLA 659-21, ASSIT EI NUMEN QUI SCRIPSIT TALE VOLUMEN 659/22-23, POSTILS 659/24-25, TEXTUS ETHICORUM 659/26-27, DIGESTUM NOVUM 659/28-29, ON PHYSICS 659-30, ON DE CELO ET MUNDO 659-31, CONFLATUS ON BOOK 1 OF SENTENCES 659-32, ON GALATIANS 659-33, TEXTUS LOGICALIUM 659-34, TEXTUS NATURALIUM 659-35, ON OPTICS 659-36, G FLOWR AND 10 DE SORTE HYLL 659-37, WORKS OF GREGORY 659-38, AMBROSE 659-39, PSEUDO DIONYSIUS 659/41-42, ON BOOK 1 OF THE SENTENCES 659/43-44, BIBLE AND POSTILS 659-45, ESDRAS GLOSSED 659-46, HISTORIA SCHOLASTICA 659-47, PRIMA SECUNDAE OF THE SUMMA 659-48
*SHELFMARK MS MERTON COLLEGE 55 659/1-2, MS MERTON COLLEGE 56 659-3, MS MERTON COLLEGE 62 659/4-6, MS MERTON COLLEGE 81 659-7, MS MERTON COLLEGE 89 659-8, MS MERTON COLLEGE 116 659-9, MS MERTON COLLEGE 133 659-10, MS MERTON COLLEGE 153 659-11, MS MERTON COLLEGE 154 659-12, MS MERTON COLLEGE 167 659-13, MS MERTON COLLEGE 170 659/14-15, MS MERTON COLLEGE 269 659/16-17, MS MERTON COLLEGE 271 659-18, MS MERTON COLLEGE 273 659-19, MS MERTON COLLEGE 280 659-20, MS MERTON COLLEGE 291 659-21, MS MERTON COLLEGE 309 659/22-23, MS EXETER COLLEGE 58 659/24-25, MS ORIEL COLLEGE 25/ FOL 8V 659/26-27, MS ORIEL COLLEGE 27 659/28-29, MS BALLIOL COLLEGE 114 659-30, MS BALLIOL COLLEGE 244 659-31, MS MAGDALEN COLLEGE LAT 103/ FOL 24 659-32, MS MAGDALEN COLLEGE LAT 154/ FOL 5 659-33, MS MAGDALEN COLLEGE 187/ FOL 242 659-34, MS CORPUS CHRISTI COLLEGE OXFORD 111/ FOL 197 659-35, MS CORPUS CHRISTI COLLEGE OXFORD 490/ NO 8 659-36, MS BODLEY 52/ FOL IV-1 659-37, MS BODLEY 688/ FOL 115 659-38, MS BODLEY 752/ FOL 1 659-39, MS LINCOLN COLLEGE LAT 38/ FOL IV 659-40, MS LINCOLN COLLEGE LAT 101 659/41-42, MS LINCOLN COLLEGE LAT 109/ FOL 18 AND 105 659/43-44, MS NEW COLLEGE 10/ FOL 182 659-45, MS NEW COLLEGE 25/ FOL 1V-1 659-46, MS NEW COLLEGE 101/ FOL 1V-2 659-47, MS NEW COLLEGE 122/ FOL 1 659-48, MS UNIVERSITY COLLEGE 1100 659/49-50
*DATE EXECUTED 14TH/C1358? 659-7, 15TH/1427 659-10, 14TH 659/14-15, 12TH 659-21, 14TH 659/28-29, 14TH/1308 659-31, 15TH/1430 659-32, 15TH/1447 659-33, 15TH/C1429 659-37, 12TH 659-39, 15TH/1436-45 659/41-42, 14TH/1355-56 659-47
*CONTENTS HISTORY OF OXFORD LIBRARIES 659/1-50, OXFORD LIBRARIES/ HISTORY OF 659/1-50

*$ABSTRACT 660
*LIBRARY ETON COLLEGE OXFORD
*SLIDE SET TITLE ANTHEMS
*NEGATIVE REFERENCE ROLL 143
*RENTAL FEE $15.15
*COMMENTS WRITTEN FOR ETON IN THE EARLY 16TH CENTURY. THE ARMS OF ETON COLLEGE APPEAR IN SOME OF THE INITIALS. IT INCLUDES AN INDEX OF THE NAMES OF THE COMPOSERS.
*TITLE OF MANUSCRIPT BOOK OF ANTHEMS
*SHELFMARK MS ETON COLLEGE 178
*PROVENANCE ENGLISH
*DATE EXECUTED 16TH/ EARLY
*TYPE OF MANUSCRIPT MUSIC/ ANTHEMS
*CONTENTS MUSIC/ ANTHEMS 660/1-263, ANTHEMS 660/1-263

*$ABSTRACT 661
*LIBRARY BODLEIAN
*SLIDE SET TITLE BELLS
*NEGATIVE REFERENCE ROLL 158A
*RENTAL FEE $4.85
*TITLE OF MANUSCRIPT MEXICAN CHRONICLE 661/1-3 AND 57, LANCELOT DU LAC 661/4-5, HERBAL AND BESTIARY 661-6, ROMANCE OF ALEXANDER 661/12-15, EPITRE D'OTHEA A HECTOR 661/16-17, ORDINAL BENEDICTINE 661/22-25, BIBLE HISTORIALE 661-47, ORMESBY PSALTER 661-49, ARITHMETICAL AND ASTRONOMICAL PIECES 661-54, GLOSSES ON CLEMENTINE CONSTITUTIONS 661-56
*SHELFMARK MS ARCH SELD A 1/ FOL 40 661-1, MS ARCH SELD A 1/ FOL 41 661-2, MS ARCH SELD A 1/ FOL 1 661-3, MS ASHMOLE 828/ FOL 62 661/4-5, MS ASHMOLE 1504/ FOL 4V 661-6, MS AUCT D 2 2/ FOL 94V 661-7, MS AUCT D 3 8/ FOL 235 661-8, MS AUCT D 4 3/ FOL 109 661-9, MS AUCT D 5 17/ FOL 258V 661-10, MS BARLOW 22/ FOL 99 661-11, MS BODLEY 264/ FOL 68V 661-12, MS BODLEY 264/ FOL 76 661-13, MS BODLEY 264/ FOL 90 661-14, MS BODLEY 264/ FOL 130 661-15, MS BODLEY 421/ FOL 4V 661/16-17, MS BODLEY 953/ PAGE 272 661-18, MS CANON BIBL LAT 11/ FOL 244V 661-19, MS CANON BIBL LAT 41/ FOL 223V 661-20, MS CANON LITURG 72/ FOL 77V 661-21, MS CANON LITURG 325/ FOL 23 661-22, MS CANON LITURG 325/ FOL 223V 661-23, MS CANON LITURG 325/ FOL 224 661-24, MS CANON LITURG 325/ FOL 224V 661-25, MS CANON LITURG 105/ FOL 118V 661-26, MS CANON LITURG 378/ FOL 35 661/27-28, MS CORPUS CHRISTI COLLEGE OXFORD 17/ FOL 84 661-29, MS DIGBY 9/ FOL 245V 661-30, MS DOUCE 5/ FOL 2 661-31, MS DOUCE 6/ FOL 1 661-32, MS DOUCE 6/ FOL 10 661/33-34, MS DOUCE 6/ FOL 96V 661-35, MS DOUCE 6/ FOL 145 661-36, MS DOUCE 18/ FOL 142 661-37, MS DOUCE 23/ FOL 169 661-38, MS DOUCE 24/ FOL 1V 661-39, MS DOUCE 48/ FOL 106V 661-40, MS DOUCE 50/ FOL 265 661-41, MS DOUCE 113/ FOL 196V 661-42, MS DOUCE 118/ FOL 34 661-43, MS DOUCE 118/ FOL 35V 661-44, MS DOUCE 118/ FOL 92 661-45, MS DOUCE 131/ FOL 68V 661-46, MS DOUCE 211/ FOL 265 661-47, MS DOUCE 263/ FOL 75V 661-48, MS DOUCE 366/ FOL 109 661-49, MS GOUGH LITURG 18/ FOL 87 661-50, MS LAUD MISC 752/ FOL 236V 661-51, MS LITURG 198/ FOL 76V 661-52, MS RAWL G 126/ FOL 226V 661-53, MS SELDEN SUPRA 25/ FOL 115 661-54, MS TRINITY COLLEGE OXFORD 53/ FOL 206 661-55, MS BODLEY 247/ FOL 289V 661-56, MS ARCH SELDEN A 1/ FOL 2 661-57
*PROVENANCE MEXICAN 661/1-3 AND 57, FRENCH 661/4-5, ENGLISH 661/6-7 AND 11, FRENCH 661/8 AND 10 AND 16-17, FLEMISH 661/9 AND 12-15, ENGLISH 661/18 AND 29-30, FRENCH 661/19-20 AND 26, ITALIAN 661/21 AND 27-28, GERMAN/ SOUTHERN AUSTRIA 661/22-25, FLEMISH 661/31-36, ENGLISH 661-37, FRENCH 661-38, FRENCH/ FRENCH FLANDERS? 661-39, FRENCH/ NORTH 661-40, FRENCH 661-41, ITALIAN 661-42, FRENCH/ ARTOIS 661/43-45, ENGLISH 661-46, FRENCH/ PARIS 661-47, FRENCH 661-48, ENGLISH 661/49-54, FRENCH 661-55, ENGLISH 661-56
*DATE EXECUTED 16TH/ 2ND QUARTER 661/1-3 AND 57, 14TH 661/4-5, 16TH/C1520-30 661-6, 14TH/ 2ND QUARTER 661-7, 13TH 661-8, 14TH/C1300 661-9, 13TH/ LATE 661-10, 14TH/ EARLY 661-11, 14TH/1338-44 661/12-15, 15TH/ 3RD QUARTER 661/16-17, 14TH/ LATE 661-18, 13TH/ 3RD QUARTER 661-19, 13TH/ LATE 661-20, 15TH/C1470-80 661-21, 13TH/C1256 661/22-25, 13TH/C1270-80 661-26, 15TH 661/27-28, 15TH/ EARLY 661-29, 13TH/C1270-80 661-30, 14TH 661/31-36, 15TH/C1433 661-37, 14TH/C1300 661/38-39, 13TH/ 3RD QUARTER 661/40-41, 13TH/ 2ND HALF 661-42, 13TH/ LATE 661/43-45, 14TH 661-46, 14TH/ 1ST QUARTER 661-47, 16TH 661-48, 14TH/C1300 661-49, 14TH 661-50, 12TH-13TH 661-51, 14TH/ 3RD QUARTER 661-52, 13TH/ LATE 661-53, 12TH-15TH 661-54, 13TH 661-55, 14TH/ MID 661-56
*LANGUAGE SPANISH 661/1-3 AND 57, FRENCH 661/4-5, ENGLISH 661-6, LATIN 661/7-11, FRENCH 661/12-17, LATIN 661/18-46 AND 48, FRENCH 661-47, LATIN 661/48-56
*ARTIST/ SCHOOL DE GRISE/ JEHAN 661/12-15, RELATED TO STYLE OF HONORE'S ATELIER 661-26, BY THE ARTIST OF THE MODENA PRAYER BOOK 661/27-28
*AUTHOR DE PISAN/ CHRISTINE 661/16-17, DESMOULINS/ GUYART 661-47, GUILLELMUS DE MONTE LAUDUNS 661-56
*TYPE OF MANUSCRIPT CHRONICLE 661/1-3 AND 57, ROMANCE 661/4-5, HERBAL AND BESTIARY 661-6, PSALTER 661/7-9, BIBLE 661-10,

PSALTER 661-11, ROMANCE 661/12-15, LITERATURE 661/16-17, COMMENTARY ON THE PSALTER 661-18, BIBLE 661/19-20, PSALTER/ CLUNIAC 661-21, ORDINAL/ BENEDICTINE 661/22-25, PSALTER 661/26-29, BIBLE 661-30, PSALTER 661/31-41, BIBLE 661-42, PSALTER 661/43-46, BIBLE HISTORIALE 661-47, CAMPANA LOQUITUR 661-48, PSALTER 661/49-50, BIBLE 661/51 AND 53, PSALTER 661-52, ARITHEMETICAL AND ASTRONOMICAL PIECES 661-54, BIBLE 661-55, GLOSSES 661-56

*CONTENTS BELLS 661/1-57, CROTALS/ FOUR ON A CORD 661-1, CROTALS/ GOLDEN ON A GREAVE 661-2, MEXICAN RECORDS 661-3, BELL WITH TWO APES 661-4, BELL WITH TWO APES 661-5, BELL 661-6, DAVID STRIKING THREE BELLS 661-7, DAVID STRIKING THREE BELLS 661-8, DAVID STRIKING THREE BELLS 661-9, DAVID STRIKING FOUR BELLS 661-10, DAVID STRIKING THREE BELLS 661-11, GROTESQUE WITH HORN AND BELL 661-12, JUGGLING 661/13-15, CLOCK WITH BELL 661-16, CLOCK WITH BELL/ WHOLE PAGE 661-17, BELLS RUNG BY MAN IN SURPLICE 661-18, DAVID RINGS BELLS 661-19, DAVID STRIKES FOUR BELLS 661-20, PRIESTS RING BELLS BY PULLING ROPES 661-21, BELL BLESSING 661/22-25, DAVID STRIKES FOUR BELLS 661-26, BELLS PLAYED BY YOUTH SEATED ON BEAM 661/27-28, DAVID STRIKES FOUR BELLS 661-29, DAVID AT ORGAN STRIKING TWO BELLS 661-30, BELLS PLAYED BY PEOPLE 661-31, DAVID STRIKES FOUR BELLS 661-32, GROTESQUE WITH TWO BELLS 661/33-34, HARE WITH BELL 661-35, GROTESQUE WITH BELL 661-36, DAVID STRIKES FIVE BELLS 661-37, DAVID STRIKES FIVE BELLS ON ROD 661-38, CANDLES MISINTERPRETED AS BELL ROPES 661-39, DAVID STRIKES FIVE BELLS 661-40, HARP AND BELLS 661-41, BELLS ATTACHED TO A WHEEL 661-42, HANDBELLS AND LADY 661-43, MONKEY PLAYS TWO BELLS 661-44, DAVID STRIKES FIVE SILVER BELLS 661-45, DAVID PLAYS BELLS/ TWO SCENES 661-46, BELL IN CURIOUS MUSICAL INSTRUMENT 661-47, CAMPANA LOQUITUR 661-48, DAVID STRIKES BELLS 661-49, DAVID STRIKES THREE BELLS 661-50, DAVID ON THRONE/ TWO MEN SOUND BELLS 661-51, DAVID STRIKING FOUR BELLS 661-52, DAVID STRIKING FOUR BELLS 661-53, BELLS 661-54, DAVID STRIKES THREE BELLS 661-55, ORO DEUM VERUM 661-56, CROTAL ON FOOT 661-57 CROTAL ON FOOT 661-57

*$ABSTRACT 662
*LIBRARY BODLEIAN
*SLIDE SET TITLE FLOWERS FROM A FLEMISH BOOK OF HOURS
*NEGATIVE REFERENCE ROLL 159A
*RENTAL FEE $3.45
*TITLE OF MANUSCRIPT BOOK OF HOURS
*SHELFMARK MS DOUCE 112/ FOL 5-161
*PROVENANCE FLEMISH
*DATE EXECUTED 16TH/ EARLY
*LANGUAGE LATIN
*ARTIST/ SCHOOL MASTER OF THE DAVID SCENES IN GRIMANI BREVIARY
*TYPE OF MANUSCRIPT BOOK OF HOURS/ USE OF ROME
*CONTENTS BOOK OF HOURS/ FLEMISH/ 16TH 662/1-29, FLOWERS FROM A FLEMISH BOOK OF HOURS 662/1-29, BOTANICAL ILLUSTRATION 662/1-29, HEARTSEASE AND STRAWBERRY 662-1, VIOLET AND PINK 662-2, COLUMBINE 662-3, MONKSHOOD 662-4, IRIS 662-5, VIOLET AND STRAWBERRY 662-6, LILY 662-7, DAISY AND HEARTSEASE 662-8, COLUMBINE 662-9, BEANFLOWER AND CORNFLOWER 662-10, PEA 662-11, SNOWDROP AND STOCK 662-12, WOUNDWORT AND FORGET ME NOT 662-13, PROVENCE ROSE 662-14, THISTLE 662-15, FLOWERS/ COLUMBINE/ HEARTSEASE/ DAISY/ PINKS/ SNOWDROPS 662-16, HEARTSEASE AND STOCK 662-17, POPPY AND FORGET ME NOT 662-18, RED OR BLACK BRYONY 662-19, MALLOW AND STRAWBERRY 662-20, STRAWBERRY FLOWER 662-21, STOCK AND SCARLET PIMPERNEL 662-22, STRAWBERRY FLOWER AND FRUIT AND BITTERSWEET 662-23, ROSE AND FORGET ME NOT 662-24, CAMPANULA AND STRAWBERRY GROW ON SAME STALK 662-25, PINKS 662-26, DAISY/ DOUBLE 662-27, ROSE AND SPEEDWELL 662-28, FLOWERS/ HEARTSEASE/ PROVENCE ROSE/ FORGET ME NOT 662-29

*$ABSTRACT 663
*LIBRARY BODLEIAN

*SLIDE SET TITLE WINDMILLS
*NEGATIVE REFERENCE ROLL 169C
*RENTAL FEE $2.45
*COMMENTS 15 SLIDES WITH DETAILS SELECTED FROM 13 MSS.
*TITLE OF MANUSCRIPT ROMANCE OF ALEXANDER 663/1-2, BOOK OF HOURS 663/3-8 AND 10 AND 13, LA VIGNE DE NOSTRE SEIGNEUR 663-9, EPITRE D'OTHEA A HECTOR 663-11, HERBAL 663-12, LAXTON MAP 663/14-15
*SHELFMARK MS BODLEY 264/ FOL 8 663-1, MS BODLEY 264/ FOL 49 663-2, MS DOUCE 144/ FOL 52 663-3, MS LAUD MISC 204/ FOL 18V 663-4, MS AUCT D INF 2 11/ FOL 74V 663-5, MS RAWL LITURG E 12/ FOL 73V 663-6, MS RAWL LITURG E 27/ FOL 81 663-7, MS DOUCE 276/ FOL 33 663-8, MS DOUCE 134/ FOL 6 663-9, MS DOUCE 102/ FOL 41V 663-10, MS BODLEY 421/ FOL 31V 663-11, MS ASHMOLE 1504/ FOL 14V 663-12, MS DOUCE 135/ FOL 47 663-13, MS MAPS C 17 48 9/ SHEET 4 663-14, MS MAPS C 17 48 9/ SHEET 5 663-15
*DATE EXECUTED 14TH/1338-44 663/1-2, 15TH/1407 663-3, 15TH/ EARLY 663-4, 15TH/1430-50 663-5, 15TH/ 1ST HALF 663-6, 15TH 663-7, 16TH/ EARLY 663-8, 15TH/C1450-70 663-9, 15TH/ EARLY 663-10, 15TH/ 3RD QUARTER 663-11, 16TH/C1520-30 663-12, 16TH/ 2ND HALF 663-13, 17TH/1635 663/14-15
*LANGUAGE FRENCH 663/1-2, FRENCH AND LATIN 663-3, LATIN 663-4, FRENCH AND LATIN 663/5-7, LATIN 663-8, FRENCH 663-9, FRENCH AND LATIN 663-10, FRENCH 663-11, ENGLISH 663-12, LATIN 663-13
*ARTIST/ SCHOOL DE GRISE/ JEHAN 663/1-2, MASTER OF SIR JOHN FASTOLF 663-5
*AUTHOR DE PISAN/ CHRISTINE 663-11
*TYPE OF MANUSCRIPT ROMANCE 663/1-2, BOOK OF HOURS/ USE OF PARIS 663-3, BOOK OF HOURS/ USE OF SARUM 663/4-5, BOOK OF HOURS/ USE OF BAYEUX 663-6, BOOK OF HOURS/ USE OF LE MANS 663-7, BOOK OF HOURS/ USE OF ROME 663-8, LIFE OF CHRIST 663-9, BOOK OF HOURS/ USE OF TROYES 663-10, LITERATURE 663-11, HERBAL 663-12, BOOK OF HOURS/ USE OF ROME 663-13, MAP 663/14-15
*CONTENTS WINDMILLS 663/1-15, MAN APPROACHES MILL 663-1, MAN ENTERS MILL 663-2, LANDSCAPE/ ROCKY 663-3, ST CHRISTOPHER 663-4, BETHLEHEM 663-5, BETHLEHEM 663-6, SKY/ STARRY 663-7, TALL POST MILL 663-8, KNIGHTS IN FOREGROUND 663-9, VISITATION 663-10, MAN WITH PACK HORSE 663-11, TIMBER MILL ON STONE BASE 663-12, PUTTI WITH MILL 663-13, DETAIL FROM LAXTON MAP 663-14, DETAIL FROM LAXTON MAP 663-15

*$ABSTRACT 664
*LIBRARY BODLEIAN
*SLIDE SET TITLE LANDSCAPES WITH WINDMILLS
*NEGATIVE REFERENCE ROLL 169F
*RENTAL FEE $2.50
*COMMENTS 10 SLIDES SELECTED FROM 7 NORTH EUROPEAN MSS.
*TITLE OF MANUSCRIPT BOOK OF HOURS 664/1-2, QUEEN MARY'S PSALTER 664/3-4, MIRROURE OF THE WORLD 664-5, EPITRE D'OTHEA A HECTOR 664/6-7, BOOK OF HOURS 664/8-10
*SHELFMARK MS AUCT D INF 2 11/ FOL 48V 664-1, MS RAWL LITURG E 12/ FOL 140 664-2, MS AUCT D INF 2 13/ FOL 62V 664/3-4, MS BODLEY 283/ FOL 38V 664-5, MS BODLEY 421/ FOL 29V 664-6, MS BODLEY 421/ FOL 59V 664-7, MS CANON LITURG 129/ FOL 55V 664-8, MS DOUCE 256/ FOL 78V 664-9, MS DOUCE 256/ FOL 178 664-10
*PROVENANCE FRENCH/ NORMANDY 664-1, FRENCH/ WEST 664-2, DUTCH 664/3-4, ENGLISH 664-5, FRENCH 664/6-7, FLEMISH? 664-8, FLEMISH 664/9-10
*DATE EXECUTED 15TH/C1430-50 664-1, 15TH/ 1ST HALF 664-2, 15TH/ 3RD QUARTER 664/3-7, 15TH/C1460-70 664-8, 16TH/ EARLY 664/9-10
*LANGUAGE FRENCH AND LATIN 664/1-2, LATIN 664/3-4, ENGLISH AND DUTCH 664-5, FRENCH 664/6-7, LATIN 664/8-10
*ARTIST/ SCHOOL MASTER OF SIR JOHN FASTOLF 664-1, MASTER OF GIJS-BRECHT VAN BREDERODE 664/3-4, MASTER OF THE DAVID SCENES IN GRIMANI BREVIARY 664/9-10
*AUTHOR FRERE LORENS 664-5, DE PISAN/ CHRISTINE 664/6-7
*TYPE OF MANUSCRIPT BOOK OF HOURS/ USE OF SARUM 664-1, BOOK OF HOURS/ USE OF BAYEUX 664-2, BOOK OF HOURS AND PSALTER 664/3-4, MIROIR DU MONDE 664-5, LITERATURE 664/6-7, BOOK OF HOURS/ USE OF ROME 664/8-10

*CONTENTS LANDSCAPES WITH WINDMILLS 664/1-10, WINDMILLS WITH LANDSCAPES 664/1-10, ST CHRISTOPHER CARRIES CHRIST ACROSS STREAM 664-1, WINDMILL AND CASTLE IN BACKGROUND 664-1, ST MARGARET WITH MESSENGER FROM OLIBRIUS 664-2, LANDSCAPE WITH WINDMILL 664-2, BETRAYAL OF CHRIST 664-3, WINDMILL AND TOWN IN BACKGROUND 664-3, DESCENT FROM THE CROSS WITH WINDMILL 664-4, ENVY/ MAN RIDING DOG BARRED BY DOG 664-5, LANDSCAPE WITH WINDMILL AND CHURCH TOWERS 664-5, ATROPOS POINTS SPEAR AT POPE/ EMPEROR/ BISHOP AND KING 664-6, WINDMILL ON HILL IN BACKGROUND 664-6, ECHO STANDS WITH HANDS OUTSTRETCHED 664-7, NARCISSUS TURNS AWAY FROM REFLECTION IN WATER 664-7, WINDMILL ON HILL IN BACKGROUND 664-7, NATIVITY WITH COUNTRY LANDSCAPE AND WINDMILL 664-8, ANGELS AND SHEPHERDS/ WINDMILL/ COTTAGE/ TOWN 664-9, ST PHILIP AND ST JAMES WITH WINDMILL ON MOUND 664-10

*$ABSTRACT 665
*LIBRARY BODLEIAN
*SLIDE SET TITLE ENGLISH TOPOGRAPHY/ 18TH CENTURY MANSIONS
*NEGATIVE REFERENCE ROLL 174B
*RENTAL FEE $2.40
*SHELFMARK MS GOUGH DRAWINGS A 3/ FOL 9 665-1, MS GOUGH DRAWINGS A 3/ FOL 15 665-2, MS GOUGH DRAWINGS A 3/ FOL 32 665-3, MS GOUGH DRAWINGS A 4/ FOL 18 665-4, MS GOUGH DRAWINGS A 4/ FOL 20 665-5, MS GOUGH DRAWINGS A 4/ FOL 44 665-6, MS GOUGH DRAWINGS A 4/ FOL 46 665-7, MS GOUGH DRAWINGS A 4/ FOL 63 665-8
*PROVENANCE ENGLISH
*DATE EXECUTED 18TH
*TYPE OF MANUSCRIPT TOPOGRAPHY
*CONTENTS TOPOGRAPHY/ 18TH-CENTURY MANSIONS 665/1-8, ARCHITECTURE/ 18TH-CENTURY MANSIONS 665/1-8, EASTBURY HOUSE/ DORSET 665-1, KENSINGTON PALACE/ LONDON 665-2, AMESBURY HOUSE/ WILTS 665-3, WOLTERTON/ NORFOLK 665-4, WOLTERTON/ NORFOLK 665-5, WIMBLEDON HOUSE/ SURREY 665-6, STOWE HOUSE/ BUCKINGHAMSHIRE 665-7, ROUSHAM/ OXON 665-8

*$ABSTRACT 666
*LIBRARY BODLEIAN
*SLIDE SET TITLE WILLIAM MORRIS
*NEGATIVE REFERENCE ROLL 176B
*RENTAL FEE $3.20
*TITLE OF MANUSCRIPT RUBAIYAT 666-1, DWELLERS AT EYR 666-2, OGIER THE DANE 666/4-6, BEN THORIR 666/7-13, BANDED MEN 666/14-15, TALES OF A MAN NAMED SIGI 666/16-21, THORSTEIN THE SON OF EGIL 666-22, KING HAFBUR 666/23-24
*SHELFMARK MS DON F 3/ FOL 1 666-1, MS ENG MISC C 265/ PAGE 1 666-2, MS ENG MISC C 265/ PAGE 26 666-3, MS ENG MISC D 265/ FOL 1 666-4, MS ENG MISC D 265/ FOL 1V 666-5, MS ENG MISC D 265/ FOL 2 666-6, MS ENG MISC D 266/ PAGE 1 666-7, MS ENG MISC D 266/ PAGE 2 666-8, MS ENG MISC D 266/ PAGE 4 666-9, MS ENG MISC D 266/ PAGE 6 666-10, MS ENG MISC D 266/ PAGE 7 666-11, MS ENG MISC D 266/ PAGE 12 666-12, MS ENG MISC D 266/ PAGE 23 666-13, MS ENG MISC D 267/ PAGE 1 666-14, MS ENG MISC D 267/ PAGE 1 666/14-15, MS ENG MISC D 268/ FOL VII 666/16-17, MS ENG MISC D 268/ FOL 3 666-18, MS ENG MISC D 268/ FOL 5 666-19, MS ENG MISC D 268/ FOL 36V 666-20, MS ENG MISC D 268/ FOL 37 666-21, MS ENG MISC E 233/1 PAGE 1 666-22, MS ENG MISC E 233/2 PAGE 1 666/23-24
*PROVENANCE ENGLISH
*DATE EXECUTED 19TH/1834-96
*LANGUAGE ENGLISH
*ARTIST/ SCHOOL MORRIS/ WILLIAM
*TYPE OF MANUSCRIPT LITERATURE
*CONTENTS BOOK ILLUSTRATIONS BY WILLIAM MORRIS 666/1-24, MORRIS/ WILLIAM BOOK ILLUSTRATIONS 666/1-24

*$ABSTRACT 667
*LIBRARY BODLEIAN
*SLIDE SET TITLE WILLIAM MORRIS' ILLUMINATION OF HORACE
*NEGATIVE REFERENCE ROLL 176C
*RENTAL FEE $3.65
*SHELFMARK MS LAT CLASS E 38/ PAGES 8-149
*PROVENANCE ENGLISH
*DATE EXECUTED 19TH
*ARTIST/ SCHOOL MORRIS/ WILLIAM
*AUTHCR HORACE
*TYPE OF MANUSCRIPT CLASSICAL TEXT
*CONTENTS HORACE ILLUSTRATED BY WILLIAM MORRIS 667/1-33, MORRIS/ WILLIAM BOOK ILLUSTRATIONS 667/1-33

*$ABSTRACT 668
*LIBRARY BODLEIAN
*SLIDE SET TITLE FLOWERS FROM A BOOK OF HOURS
*NEGATIVE REFERENCE ROLL 177B
*RENTAL FEE $2.60
*COMMENTS PRINTED BY JOH SCHONSPERGER AT AUGSBURG.
*TITLE OF MANUSCRIPT BOOK OF HOURS
*SHELFMARK PR DOUCE FF 59/ PAGES 1-218
*PROVENANCE GERMAN/ AUGSBURG
*DATE EXECUTED 16TH/1514
*LANGUAGE LATIN
*TYPE OF MANUSCRIPT BOOK OF HOURS/ USE OF ROME
*CONTENTS BOOK OF HOURS/ GERMAN/ 16TH 668/1-12, BOTANICAL ILLUSTRATION 668/1-12, FLOWERS FROM A BOOK OF HOURS 668/1-12, DIANTHUS/ CORNCOCKLE/ WOODY NIGHTSHADE/ ALPINE STRAWBERRY 668-1, LILY OF THE VALLEY 668-1, STRAWBERRY/ SPEEDWELL/ CAMPANULA/ HEARTSEASE/ HAREBELL 668-2, COLUMBINE/ PEA/ CORNFLOWER 668-3, ALPINE STRAWBERRY/ CRANESBILL/ SPEEDWELL 668-4, CORNFLOWER/ STRAWBERRY 668-4, SCABIOUS/ SPEEDWELL/ REST HARROW 668-5, ALPINE STRAWBERRY/ LILY OF THE VALLEY 668-5, PIMPERNEL/ WHITE CAMPION/ STRAWBERRY 668-6, PANSY/ EVENING PRIMROSE/ BORAGE 668-6, LILY OF THE VALLEY/ SPEEDWELL 668-7, FORGET ME NOT/ WOODY NIGHTSHADE/ TULIP 668-8, MONKSHOOD/ SPEARWORT/ CORNFLOWER/ DIANTHUS 668-9, DIANTHUS/ MONKSHOOD/ STRAWBERRY 668-10, RED CURRANT BERRIES 668-11, DIANTHUS/ POPPY/ STRAWBERRY/ VIOLET/ WALL FLOWER 668-12

*$ABSTRACT 669
*LIBRARY BODLEIAN
*SLIDE SET TITLE GEORGIAN ART 10TH-14TH CENTURIES
*NEGATIVE REFERENCE ROLL 181A/2
*RENTAL FEE $2.45
*COMMENTS 15 SLIDES SELECTED FROM PLATES IN S.Y AMIRANASHVILI, ISTORIYA GRUZINKOY MONUMENTALNOY DJIVOPISI, VOL. 1, 1957.
*PROVENANCE RUSSIAN/ GEORGIA
*DATE EXECUTED 10TH-11TH
*TYPE OF MANUSCRIPT WALL PAINTINGS AND WINDOWS
*CONTENTS GEORGIAN ART 669/1-15, RUSSIAN ART 669/1-15, WALL PAINTINGS/ RUSSIAN 669/1-15, DAVID-GAREDJA/ ANGEL/ UDABNO CATHEDRAL 669-1, LANI BEFORE DAVID-GAREDJA AND LUKIAN/ UDABNO CATHEDRAL 669-2, DAVID-GAREDJA/ ORNAMENT OF CENTRAL REFECTORY/ UDABNO CATH 669-3, ATENI/ ORNAMENT IN SOUTH ASPE 669-3, ASCENSION/ APOSTLE 669-4, ANGEL OF THE ANNUNCIATION 669-5. ANNUNCIATION/ ANGEL OF 669-5, JOSEPH'S DREAM/ ANGEL APPEARS 669-6, BAPTISM/ AXE LAID TO ROOT OF TREE 669-7, ANNUNCIATION/ ANNA IN THE GARDEN 669-8, DECORATIONS IN SOUTH ARCH/ ATENI 669-9, DECORATION OF FRIEZE OF FRESCO OF SOUTH ASPE/ ATENI 669-10, DECORATION OF ARCH OF NORTH WINDOW 669-11, DECORATION OF WINDOW OF SOUTH APSE 669-11, ST MICHAEL/ GELATI 669-12, ST GABRIEL/ GELATI 669-13, VIRGIN MARY 669-14, HOLY CHILD 669-15

*$ABSTRACT 670
*LIBRARY BODLEIAN
*SLIDE SET TITLE WALL PAINTINGS FROM KIEV/ NOVGOROD/ OLD LADOGA
*NEGATIVE REFERENCE ROLL 181A/3
*RENTAL FEE $2.80
*COMMENTS 16 SLIDES SELECTED FROM PLATES IN M.K. KARGHER, DREVNERUSSKAYA DJIVOPIS XI-XIV 1963.
*PROVENANCE RUSSIAN/ KIEV/ NOVGOROD/ OLD LADOGA
*DATE EXECUTED 11TH-12TH
*TYPE OF MANUSCRIPT WALL PAINTINGS
*CONTENTS RUSSIAN ART 670/1-16, WALL PAINTINGS/ RUSSIAN 670/1-16, ANNUNCIATION 670-1, VIRGIN MARY 670-2, ST PAUL 670-3, SAINT 670-4, SAINTS 670-5, BEAR HUNT 670-6, HUNTING BEAR 670-6, SAINTS 670-7, ST MICHAEL 670-8, BEARDED HEADS/ FRAGMENT OF FRESCO 670-9, ST PETER THE APOSTLE 670-10, ST JOHN THE BAPTIST'S HEAD FOUND/ DETAIL 670-11, SALOME/ DETAIL 670-12, ST GEORGE AND THE DRAGON 670-13, ST FEOFAN 670-14, EZEKIEL 670-15, ST SIMON 670-16

*$ABSTRACT 671
*LIBRARY BODLEIAN
*SLIDE SET TITLE UKRAINIAN ART 11TH-18TH
*NEGATIVE REFERENCE ROLL 181A/4
*RENTAL FEE $2.80
*COMMENTS 16 SLIDES OF PLATES FROM G. LOGUIN, UKRAINSKOYE ISKUSSTUO, 1963.
*TITLE OF MANUSCRIPT OSTROMIROV GOSPEL 671-5,PERESOPNITZKI GOSPEL 671-12
*PROVENANCE RUSSIAN/ UKRAIN
*DATE EXECUTED 18TH/1752 671-1, 11TH 671/2-4, 11TH/1056-57 671-5, 12TH/1108 671/6-7, 13TH/C1280 671-8, 15TH 671-9, 16TH/MID 671-10, 16TH/1579 671-11, 16TH/1556-61 671-12, 17TH/1697-99 671-13, 18TH 671-14, 18TH/1752 671-16
*TYPE OF MANUSCRIPT GOSPELS 671/5 AND 12
*CONTENTS RUSSIAN ART 671/1-16, UKRAINIAN ART 671/1-16, FRONT COVER/ DANIEL EFREMOVICH 671-1, ANGEL 671-2, VIRGIN MARY 671-3, SAINT 671-4, ST LUKE 671-5, DMITRI SOLUNSKI 671-6, ARCHDEACON STEPHEN 671-7, VIRGIN AND CHILD/ IKON 671-8, IKON/ VIRGIN AND CHILD 671-8, ST GEORGE KILLS DRAGON 671/9-10, ANNUNCIATION/ IKON 671-11, IKON/ ANNUNCIATION 671-11, ST MARK WRITES/ FLORAL BORDER 671-12, ST MICHAEL 671-13, KAZAK MAMAI/ SEATED MAN WITH MUSICAL INSTRUMENT 671-14, CHRIST BLESSING 671-15, DANIEL EFREMOVICH 671-16

*$ABSTRACT 672
*LIBRARY BODLEIAN
*SLIDE SET TITLE MACROBIUS
*NEGATIVE REFERENCE ROLL 218E
*RENTAL FEE $2.15
*TITLE OF MANUSCRIPT DE SOMNIO SCIPIONIS
*SHELFMARK MS CANON CLASS LAT 257/ FOL 1 672-1, MS CANON CLASS LAT 257/ FOL 1V 672-2, MS CANON CLASS LAT 257/ FOL 2 672-3
*PROVENANCE ITALIAN/ BOLOGNA
*DATE EXECUTED 14TH/1383
*LANGUAGE LATIN
*TYPE OF MANUSCRIPT COMMENTARY ON CICERO'S SOMNIUM SCIPIONIS
*CONTENTS DE SOMNIUM SCIPIONIS 672/1-3, MACROBIUS/ PORTRAIT 672-1, SCIPIO AND KING MASINISSA SURVEY HEAVENLY SPHERES 672-1, HEAVENLY SPHERES 672-1, SCIPIO ASLEEP IN BED 672-2, ROME AND CARTHAGE SHOWN IN CENTER OF HEAVENLY SPHERES 672-2, SCIPIO/ HIS FATHER AND GRANDFATHER IN MILKY WAY 672-2, MACROBIUS WRITING AT DESK WITH OPEN BOOK CUPBOARD 672-3

*$ABSTRACT 673
*LIBRARY BODLEIAN
*SLIDE SET TITLE FIFTEENTH-CENTURY ILLUMINATION

*NEGATIVE REFERENCE ROLL 284A
*RENTAL FEE $2.35
*TITLE OF MANUSCRIPT BOOK OF HOURS 673-1, CHOIR PSALTER 673-3-4, BOOK OF HOURS 673/5-7
*SHELFMARK MS RAWL LITURG D 1/ FOL 29V 673-1, MS RAWL LITURG D 1/ FOL 110V 673-2, MS HATTON 45/ FOL 43 TOP 673-3, MS HATTON 45/ FOL 43 BOTTOM 673-4, MS TRINITY COLLEGE 73/ FOL 68 673-5, MS TRINITY COLLEGE 73/ FOL 86 673-6, MS TRINITY COLLEGE 73/ FOL 148V 673-7
*PROVENANCE ENGLISH/ LONDON 673/1-2, FRENCH/ MADE IN ENGLAND 673/3-4, ENGLISH/ EAST ANGLIA 673/5-7
*DATE EXECUTED 15TH/C1420 673/1-2, 15TH/ MID 673/3-7
*ARTIST/ SCHOOL MASTER OF SIR JOHN FASTOLF 673/3-4
*TYPE OF MANUSCRIPT BOOK OF HOURS/ USE OF SARUM 673/1-2, PSALTER/ CHOIR 673/3-4, BOOK OF HOURS 673/5-7
*CONTENTS FIFTEENTH CENTURY ILLUMINATION 673/1-7, INITIAL D DEUS WITH DEPOSITION 673-1, DEPOSITION 673-1, INITIAL O WITH VIRGIN AND CHILD 673-2, VIRGIN AND CHILD 673-2, INITIAL O WITH ST JOHN THE BAPTIST 673-2, ST JOHN THE BAPTIST 673-2, TEXT WITH DECORATED LINE ENDINGS/ TOP 673-3, TEXT WITH DECORATED LINE ENDINGS/ BOTTOM 673-4, INITIAL C CONVERTE WITH WHITE ROSE 673-5, STRAWBERRY MOTIF IN BORDER 673-5, INITIAL V VIRGO WITH VIRGIN AND CHILD 673-6, VIRGIN AND CHILD 673-6, INITIAL B BEATI WITH CHRIST BLESSING 673-7, CHRIST BLESSING SOUL CARRIED IN CLOTH BY ANGELS 673-7

*$ABSTRACT 674
*LIBRARY BODLEIAN
*SLIDE SET TITLE IKONS IN THE TRETYAKOV GALLERY MOSCOW
*NEGATIVE REFERENCE ROLL 181A/7
*RENTAL FEE $3.45
*COMMENTS REPRODUCED FROM V.I. ANTONEVA, KATALOG DREVNERUSSKOI DJIVOPISI OPITT ISTORIKO KHUDODJEST VENNOI KLASSIFIKATZII, I, MOSCOW, 1963.
*PROVENANCE RUSSIAN 674/1-29
*DATE EXECUTED 15TH/1408 674-1, 12TH/C1113 674/2-3, 12TH/ EARLY 674-4, 12TH/ MID 674-5, 12TH-13TH 674-6, 14TH-15TH 674-7, 15TH 674-8, 15TH/ LAST QUARTER 674-9, 14TH/ 2ND HALF 674-10, 14TH/C1300 674-11, 16TH/ EARLY 674-12, 15TH/ 1ST QUARTER 674-13, 15TH-16TH 674-14, 14TH/ EARLY 674-15, 14TH/1340 674-16, 14TH/C1380 674-17, 14TH/ END 674-18, 14TH/1392 674/19-20, 15TH/1403 674-21, 15TH/1408 674-22, 15TH/C1411 674-23, 15TH/1420 674-24, 15TH/1422-27 674-25, 15TH/ LAST QUARTER 674-26, 16TH/1500 674-27, 16TH/ EARLY 674/28-29
*ARTIST/ SCHOOL RUBLIEV/ ANDREW AND DANIEL THE BLACK 674/1 AND 22, SOLUNSKY/ DIMITRI 674-2, VLADIMIR-SUZDAL SCHOOL 674-5, NOVGOROD SCHOOL 674-9, ROSTOV-SUZDAL SCHOOL 674/11-12, TVER SCHOOL 674/13-14, FEOFAN GREK 674/19-21, RUBLIEV/ ANDREW 674/23-25, DIONYSSIUS AND HIS SONS 674-27, DIONYSSIUS 674-28, DIONYSSIUS SCHOOL 674-29
*TYPE OF MANUSCRIPT IKONS
*CONTENTS IKONS/ RUSSIAN 674/1-29, RUSSIAN ART 674/1-29, VIRGIN FROM DEESIS TIER 674-1, ST DIMITRI SOLUNSKY 674-2, VIRGIN MARY/ HEAD 674-3, VIRGIN OF VLADIMIR 674-4, ADORATION OF CROSS 674-5, CROSS/ ADORATION 674-5, ASSUMPTION OF THE VIRGIN 674-6, VIRGIN'S ASSUMPTION 674-6, SS FLOR/ NICHOLAS/ BLASIUS/ ANASTASE 674-7, SS NICHOLAS/ BLASIUS/ FLOR/ LAURA 674-8, VIRGIN AND CHILD BETWEEN ELIAS AND ST PYATNITZA 674-8, ST PYATNITZA 674-8, THREE MARYS 674-9, MARYS/ THREE 674-9, SS PARASKEVA/ PYATNITZA/ BARBARA/ ULYANA 674-10, ST MICHAEL 674-10, ST GEORGE AND THE DRAGON 674-12, ASSUMPTION OF THE VIRGIN 674-13, VIRGIN'S ASSUMPTION 674-13, ASCENSION 674-14, ST BORIS AND GLEB/ LIFE OF 674-15, ST BORIS AND GLEB ON HORSES 674-16, ST NICHOLAS/ LIFE OF 674-17, ANNUNCIATION 674-18, VIRGIN OF THE DON 674-19, DORMITION OF THE VIRGIN 674-20, VIRGIN'S DORMITION 674-20, TRANSFIGURATION 674-21, ST GREGORY THE THEOLOGIAN FROM DEESIS TIER 674-22, CHRIST IN MAJESTY 674-23, ST PAUL 674-24, TRINITY/ OLD TESTAMENT 674-25, ST JOHN THE BAPTIST FROM DEESIS TIER 674-26, ST DIMITRI SOLUNSKY 674-27, ST ALEXIS THE METROPOLITAN HEALS EMPRESS TAIDULA 674-28, ST JOHN OF PATMOS 674-29

*$ABSTRACT 675
*LIBRARY BODLEIAN
*SLIDE SET TITLE OLD TESTAMENT TRINITY OF ANDREW RUBLIEV
*NEGATIVE REFERENCE ROLL 181A/8
*RENTAL FEE $3.15
*COMMENTS DETAILS FROM THE OLD TESTAMENT TRINITY AND RELATED WORKS INCLUDING THE JETROVO GOSPELS AND FEOFAN GREK, FROM N. DEMINA, TROITZA RUBLIEVA, 1963.
*TITLE OF MANUSCRIPT OLD TESTAMENT TRINITY 675/1 AND 10-17 AND 23, JITROVO GOSPEL 675/2-5, SVENIGOROD ROW OF IKONS 675/6-9, FEOFAN GREK 675/18-20, DEYSIS ROW OF IKONS 675-21
*DATE EXECUTED 14TH/C1390-1427
*ARTIST/ SCHOOL RUBLIEV/ ANDREW AND HIS SCHOOL
*TYPE OF MANUSCRIPT IKONS AND PAINTINGS
*CONTENTS RUSSIAN ART 675/1-23, RUSSIAN IKONS AND PAINTINGS 675/1-23, IKONS AND PAINTINGS 675/1-23, OLD TESTAMENT TRINITY/ THREE ANGELS AT MAMRE 675-1, ORNAMENTED PAGE FROM JITROVO GOSPEL 675-2, DOLPHIN FROM PAGE OF JITROVO GOSPEL 675-3, HERON AND SNAKE FROM JETROVO GOSPEL 675-4, ANGEL FROM JETROVO GOSPEL 675-5, ST MICHAEL FROM SVENIGOROD ROW OF IKONS 675-6, ST PAUL 675-7, CHRIST 675/8-9, TRINITY/ OLD TESTAMENT DETAILS 675/10-17 AND 23, ANGELS 675/10-11, TREE OF LIFE 675/10-11, ANGELS 675-12, ANGEL WITH HORSE/ SYMBOL OF SON 675-13, ANGEL IN CENTER/ SYMBOL OF FATHER 675-14, ANGEL AT RIGHT/ SYMBOL OF HOLY SPIRIT 675-15, HAND OF ANGEL ON RIGHT 675-16, HAND OF ANGEL IN CENTER 675-17, DORMITION OF THE VIRGIN/ GRIEVING APOSTLES 675/18-19, VIRGIN'S DORMITION 675/18-19, CANDLE FROM DORMITION OF VIRGIN 675-20, VIRGIN MARY FROM DEYSIS ROW OF IKONS 675-21, VIRGIN OF VLADIMIR 675-22, PALACES/ DETAIL FROM OLD TESTAMENT TRINITY 675-23

*$ABSTRACT 676
*LIBRARY BODLEIAN
*SLIDE SET TITLE LATER IKONS FROM THE TRETYAKOV GALLERY
*NEGATIVE REFERENCE ROLL 181J/1
*RENTAL FEE $2.80
*COMMENTS PHOTOGRAPHED FROM V.I. ANTONOVA AND N.E. MNEVA, KATALOG DREVNERUSSKOI ISTORIKO KHUDODJESTVENNOI KLASSIFIKATZII, II, MOSCOW, 1963.
*PROVENANCE RUSSIAN
*DATE EXECUTED 16TH/1550 676-1, 16TH/ MID 676-2, 16TH/1530 676-3, 16TH/ 2ND HALF 676-4, 17TH/C1600 676/5-6, 16TH/ 2ND HALF 676-7, 16TH/1565-96 676-8, 17TH 676-9, 16TH/ EARLY 676-10, 16TH/ EARLY 676-11, 17TH/C1645 676-12, 17TH/ AFTER 1668 676-14, 17TH/ MID 676-15, 17TH/ EARLY 676-16
*ARTIST/ SCHOOL ATELIER OF MACARIUS 676/1 AND 3-4, RUBLIEV/ ANDREW 676-2, GODUNOV SCHOOL 676/5-6, MACARIUS 676-7, STROGANOV SCHOOL 676-11, SCHOOL OF IMPERIAL PAINTERS 676-12, SCHOOL OF ARMOURY PALACE 676/13-14
*TYPE OF MANUSCRIPT IKONS/ RUSSIAN
*CONTENTS RUSSIAN ART 676/1-16, IKONS/ RUSSIAN 676/1-16, CHURCH MILITANT AS MOUNTED KNIGHT 676-1, KNIGHT/ MOUNTED AS CHURCH MILITANT 676-1, OLD TESTAMENT TRINITY 676-2, TRINITY/ OLD TESTAMENT 676-2, VIRGIN AND CHILD 676-3, THREE MARYS AT TOMB 676-4, MARYS/ THREE AT TOMB 676-4, ABRAHAM SACRIFICES CALF 676-5, SARAH KNEADS DOUGH 676-6, ELEVATION OF CROSS BY PATRIARCH MACARIUS 676-7, CROSS ELEVATED BY PATRIARCH MACARIUS 676-7, VISION OF BLESSED EULOGIA 676-8, TRANSFIGURATION OF CHRIST 676-9, CHRIST'S TRANSFIGURATION 676-9, CHRIST/ VIRGIN/ JOHN THE BAPTIST IN ROW OF IKONS 676-10, MARTYRS/ FORTY OF SEBASTE 676-11, DEVIL PROMPTS AGRICOLA 676-11, AGRICOLA AND DEVIL 676-11, MARTYRS IN ICY LAKE 676-11, PRINCE GEORGE VSEVOLODICH 676-12, ST MICHAEL TRIUMPHS OVER DEVIL 676-13, THEODORE STRATELATUS WITH EVANGELISTS BEHIND 676-13, CRUCIFIXION WITH MANY OTHER SCENES 676-14, PENITENT THIEF IN PARADISE 676-15, RAKH/ THE PENITENT THIEF 676-15, ST JOHN THE BAPTIST AS ANGEL IN WILDERNESS 676-16, ST JOHN THE BAPTIST/ LIFE OF 676-16

*$ABSTRACT 677
*LIBRARY BODLEIAN
*SLIDE SET TITLE MS GOUGH KENT 16
*NEGATIVE REFERENCE ROLL 283C
*RENTAL FEE $2.20
*COMMENTS A SURVEY OF PORTS BETWEEN DOVER AND LANDS-END, MADE FOR THE ADMIRALTY.
*TITLE OF MANUSCRIPT A SURVEY OF PORTS
*SHELFMARK MS GOUGH KENT 16/ FOL 2 677-1, MS GOUGH KENT 16/ FOL 2V 677-2, MS GOUGH KENT 16/ FOL 27V 677-3, MS GOUGH KENT 16/ FOL 28 677-4
*PROVENANCE ENGLISH
*DATE EXECUTED 17TH/1698
*LANGUAGE ENGLISH
*TYPE OF MANUSCRIPT MAP SURVEY
*CONTENTS TOPOGRAPHY/ ENGLISH/ 17TH 677/1-4, MAP SURVEY OF ENGLISH PORTS 677/1-4, PREFACE TO MAP SURVEY 677/1-2, DESCRIPTION OF POOLE HARBOUR 677-3, MAP OF POOLE HARBOUR 677-4

*$ABSTRACT 678
*LIBRARY BODLEIAN
*SLIDE SET TITLE LETTERS TO QUEEN ELIZABETH I FROM CZAR OF RUSSIA
*NEGATIVE REFERENCE ROLL 283D
*RENTAL FEE $2.30
*SHELFMARK MS ASHMOLE 1763/ FOL 47A 678-1, MS ASHMOLE 1763/ FOL 49A 678-2, MS ASHMOLE 1763/ FOL 51B 678-3, MS ASHMOLE 1763/ FOL 52A 678-4, MS ASHMOLE 1763/ FOL 53A 678-5, MS ASHMOLE 1763/ FOL 54A 678-6
*PROVENANCE RUSSIAN
*DATE EXECUTED 16TH/ END
*AUTHOR CZAR OF RUSSIA
*TYPE OF MANUSCRIPT LETTERS
*CONTENTS LETTERS TO ELIZABETH I FROM CZAR OF RUSSIA 678/1-6, QUEEN ELIZABETH I/ LETTERS TO 678/1-6, LETTER/ WHOLE 678-1, DRAWING FROM WHICH HOLLAR ENGRAVED RUSSIAN SEAL 678-2, LETTER/ TOP HALF 678-3, LETTER/ LOWER HALF 678-4, LETTER/ WHOLE 678-5, LETTER/ WHOLE 678-6

*$ABSTRACT 679
*LIBRARY BODLEIAN
*SLIDE SET TITLE HESPERIDES
*NEGATIVE REFERENCE ROLL 288B
*RENTAL FEE $2.85
*COMMENTS AN EPIC IN PRAISE OF SIGISMONDO MALATESTA.
*TITLE OF MANUSCRIPT HESPERIDES
*SHELFMARK MS CANON CLASS LAT 81
*PROVENANCE ITALIAN/ RIMINI
*DATE EXECUTED 15TH/1457-68
*LANGUAGE LATIN
*ARTIST/ SCHOOL GIOVANNI DE BARTOLO BETTINI DE FANO
*AUTHOR BASINIO DE BASINI OF PARMA
*TYPE OF MANUSCRIPT LITERATURE/ EPIC
*CONTENTS LITERATURE/ ITALIAN 679/1-17, HESPERIDES 679/1-17, ORNAMENTAL FRAME WITH PUTTI 679-1, ARMIES PREPARING FOR BATTLE 679-2, ARMY BESIEGING A CASTLE 679-3, CATAPULT/ TENTS/ CHURCH 679-3, SEA SHORE/ FLEET OF SAILING SHIPS 679-4, SHIPS/ FLEET OF SAILING SHIPS 679-4, CASTLE BESIEGED FROM LAND AND SEA 679-5, SIEGE ENDS/ MEN FROM CASTLE EMERGE 679-6, PEACE NEGOTIATIONS BETWEEN TWO GROUPS OF HORSEMEN 679-7, PROCESSION WITHIN CITY 679-8, SHIP NEAR SHORE/ SHIP IN BACKGROUND 679-9, SHIPWRECK/ PEOPLE AND CARGO FLOAT NEAR WRECK 679-11, SIGISMUND AND PSYCHE ON ISLAND 679-12, PSYCHE/ SIGISMUND/ ZEPHYRUS ON RIGHT 679-13, MYTHOLOGICAL FIGURES ON LEFT 679-13, FIERY PIT/ SACRIFICE OF CHAINED ANIMALS 679-13, ARMY/ MOUNTED/ SNOW STORM IN BAY 679-14, ARMY/ MOUNTED TRAVELS ALONG RIVER VALLEY 679-15, BATTLE BETWEEN MOUNTED TROOPS 679-16, ARMY ENCAMPED NEAR TOWN/ MOUNTED SOLDIERS 679-17

*$ABSTRACT 680
*LIBRARY BODLEIAN
*SLIDE SET TITLE MISCELLANY 3
*NEGATIVE REFERENCE ROLL 271B
*RENTAL FEE $3.20
*TITLE OF MANUSCRIPT BOOK OF HOURS 680/1-2, ORMESBY PSALTER 680/3-4, CHRONICLE OF ENGLAND 680-5, SONGS AND HYMNS 680-6, GREGORIAN SACRAMENTARY 680/7-24
*SHELFMARK MS LAUD MISC 188/ FOL 21 680-1, MS LAUD MISC 188/ FOL 41 680-2, MS DOUCE 366/ FOL 9V 680-3, MS DOUCE 366/ FOL 10 680-4, MS ARCH SELD B 10/ FOL 198V 680-5, MS ARCH SELD B 26/ FOL 19V-20 680-6, MS CANON LITURG 319/ FOL 29V 680-7, MS CANON LITURG 319/ FOL 30V 680-8, MS CANON LITURG 319/ FOL 31V 680-9, MS CANON LITURG 319/ FOL 38V-39 680-10, MS CANON LITURG 319/ FOL 38V 680-11, MS CANON LITURG 319/ FOL 39 680-12, MS CANON LITURG 319/ FOL 95V-96 680-13, MS CANON LITURG 319/ FOL 95V 680-14, MS CANON LITURG 319/ FOL 96 680-15, MS CANON LITURG 319/ FOL 110V-111 680-16, MS CANON LITURG 319/ FOL 110V 680-17, MS CANON LITURG 319/ FOL 111 680-18, MS CANON LITURG 319/ FOL 115V-116 680-19, MS CANON LITURG 319/ FOL 115V 680-20, MS CANON LITURG 319/ FOL 116 680-21, MS CANON LITURG 319/ FCL 123V 680-22, MS CANON LITURG 319/ FOL 126V 680-23, MS CANON LITURG 319/ FOL 155V 680-24
*PROVENANCE ENGLISH 680/1-6, GERMAN 680/7-24
*DATE EXECUTED 14TH/C1380 680/1-2, 13TH-14TH 680/3-4, 15TH/C1470-80 680-5, 15TH/ MID 680-6, 10TH/ LATE 680/7-24
*LANGUAGE LATIN 680/1-5, ENGLISH AND LATIN 680-6, LATIN 680/7-24
*ARTIST/ SCHOOL REICHENAU SCHOOL
*TYPE OF MANUSCRIPT BOOK OF HOURS 680/1-2, PSALTER 680/3-4, CHRONICLE 680-5, SONGS AND HYMNS 680-6, SACRAMENTARY 680/7-24
*CONTENTS ANNUNCIATION 680-1, PRESENTATION OF CHRIST IN TEMPLE 680-2, CHRIST PRESENTED IN TEMPLE 680-2, INITIAL B BEATUS/ JESSE TREE 680-3, JESSE TREE WITH DONERS 680-3, INITIAL B BEATUS/ DAVID HARPING 680-4, DAVID HARPING 680-4, ARMS OF HENRY PERCY 680-5, SONG/ GLAD AND BLYTHE MOTE YE BE 680-6, INTRODUCTION AND INITIAL IN GOLD 680-7, INITIAL IN GOLD 680-7, INITIAL/ VERE DIGNUM 680-8, CRUCIFIXION/ TE IGITUR 680-9, TE IGITUR 680-9, LAY OUT OF FOLIOS 38V-39 680-10, NATIVITY AND SHEPHERDS 680-11, INITIAL C/ FULL PAGE 680-12, LAY OUT OF FOLIOS 95V-96 680-13, ANGEL ADDRESSING THREE MARYS 680-14, THREE MARYS 680-14, INITIAL D/ FULL PAGE 680-15, LAY OUT OF FOLIOS 110V-111 680-16, ASCENSION 680-17, INITIAL C/ FULL PAGE 680-18, LAY OUT OF FOLIOS 115V-116 680-19, PENTECOST 680-20, INITIAL D/ FULL PAGE 680-21, INITIAL D/ PAGE WITH SMALL INITIAL 680-22, INITIAL D/ PAGE WITH SMALL INITIAL 680-23, INITIAL O/ PAGE WITH SMALL INITIAL 680-24 INITIAL O/ PAGE WITH SMALL INITIAL 680-24

*$ABSTRACT 681'
*LIBRARY BODLEIAN
*SLIDE SET TITLE RUSSIAN ILLUMINATED MANUSCRIPTS
*NEGATIVE REFERENCE ROLL 182L
*RENTAL FEE $3.25
*COMMENTS PHOTOGRAPHED FROM COLOR PLATES IN A.N. SVIRIN, ISKUSSTVO KNIGI DREVNEYE RUSI XI-XVII VV, 1964.
*TITLE OF MANUSCRIPT OSTROMIROV GOSPELS 681/1-5, MSTISLAVOV GOSPELS 681-8, KHLUDOV PSALTER 681-9, SIISKY GOSPELS 681-10, PSALTER OF THE TERRIBLE 681-11, KOSNKA GOSPEL 681-12, PSALTER 681/13-14, GOSPELS OF THE ANDRONIEV MONASTERY 681-15, PSALTER WITH ENTHRONEMENT 681/16-17, BOOK OF THE PROPHETS 681/18-19, GOSPEL 681/20-21, GOSPELS 681-22, ANANEVSKY GOSPELS 681/23-24, FESTIAL OF THE VOLKEV ORATORY 681-25
*PROVENANCE RUSSIAN
*DATE EXECUTED 11TH/1056-57 681/1-5, 11TH/1073 681/6-7, 12TH/ BEFORE 1117 681-8, 13TH/ LATE 681-9, 14TH/1339 681-10, 14TH 681-11, 14TH/1392 681-12, 14TH/1397 681/13-14, 15TH/ 1ST HALF 681/15-17, 15TH/1489 681/18-19, 16TH/ EARLY 681/20-21, 16TH/1507 681-22, 16TH 681/23-24, 19TH 681-25
*TYPE OF MANUSCRIPT GOSPELS 681/1-5 AND 8 AND 10 AND 12,

GOSPELS 681/15 AND 20-21 AND 22-24, PSALTER 681/9 AND 11 AND 13-14 AND 16-17, BOOK OF PROPHETS 681/18-19
*CONTENTS RUSSIAN ILLUMINATED MSS 681/1-25, RUSSIAN ART/ ILLUMINATED MSS 681/1-25, ST MARK 681-1, ST JOHN 681-2, ST JOHN'S GOSPEL/ OPENING PAGE 681-3, INITIAL/ DETAIL OF PAGE 681-4, INITIAL/ DETAIL OF PAGE 681-5, PRINCELY FAMILY 681-6, ARCHITECTURAL FRONTISPIECE 681-7, ST LUKE 681-8, DAVID AMONG MUSICIANS 681-9, MUSICIANS WITH KING DAVID 681-9, CHRIST WITH APOSTLES 681-10, ASAPH THE PROPHET 681-11, INITIALS/ ZOOMORPHIC FROM KOSNKA GOSPEL 681-12, PAGE WITH MARGINAL DECORATION/ PEACOCKS 681-13, PEACOCKS 681-13, CREATION OF ADAM? 681-13, ADAM CREATION? 681-13, INITIAL/ FOLIATED 681-14, ANGELS IN MARGIN 681-14, CHRIST IN MAJESTY 681-15, HEAD PIECE/ DECORATED 681-16, HORSEMEN 681-16, HEAD PIECE/ DECORATED 681-17, ACANTHUS ORNAMENT 681-18, ANGELS SIT AMID FOLIAGE 681-19, HEAD PIECE WITH ACANTHUS DECORATION 681-20, HEAD PIECE WITH ZOOMORPHIC DECORATION 681-21, ST JOHN SITS IN ARCHITECTURAL FRAME 681-22, ST MARK WITH SCROLL/ CITY IN BACKGROUND 681-23, HEAD PIECE WITH DECORATION 681-24, HEAD PIECE WITH ARCHITECTURAL FRAME 681-25

*$ABSTRACT 682
*LIBRARY BODLEIAN
*SLIDE SET TITLE MISCELLANY 12
*NEGATIVE REFERENCE ROLL 283A
*RENTAL FEE $2.30
*TITLE OF MANUSCRIPT DE RE MILITARI 682/3-4, HESPERIDES 682/5-6
*SHELFMARK MS ASHMOLE 804/ PP 16-17 682-1, MS CANON CLASS LAT 274/ FOL IV 682-3, MS CANON CLASS LAT 274/ FOL 2 682-4, MS CANON CLASS LAT 81/ FOL 49V 682-5, MS CANON CLASS LAT 81/ FOL 50 682-6
*PROVENANCE ENGLISH 682/1-2, ITALIAN/ NAPLES 682/3-4, ITALIAN/ RIMINI 682/5-6
*DATE EXECUTED 15TH/1442-58 682/3-4, 15TH/1457-68 682/5-6
*LANGUAGE LATIN
*ARTIST/ SCHOOL GIOVANNI DI BARTOLO BETTINI DA FANO 682/5-6
*AUTHOR VEGETIUS/ FLAVIUS 682/3-4, BASINIO DE BASINI OF PARMA 682/5-6
*TYPE OF MANUSCRIPT GENEALOGICAL COLLECTION 682-1, COAT OF ARMS 682-2, MILITARY TREATISE 682/3-4, LITERATURE 682/5-6
*CONTENTS MISCELLANY 12 682/1-6, GENEALOGICAL TEXTS 682-1, TEXTS CONCERNING FAMILIES OF HARINGTON AND LASCELLS 682-1, COAT OF ARMS OF RUTHVEN/ EARL OF GOWRIE 682-2, KNIGHT ON LEFT SIDE OF COAT OF ARMS 682-2, KING ALFONSO I IN ARMOR ON HORSEBACK 682-3, TEXT/ FIRST PAGE WITH DECORATED BORDER 682-4, ARMY AND CAMP 682-5, SOLDIERS/ MOUNTED AND ON FOOT 682-6, TRUMPETS 682-6

*$ABSTRACT 683
*LIBRARY BODLEIAN
*SLIDE SET TITLE MISCELLANY 13
*NEGATIVE REFERENCE ROLL 287A
*RENTAL FEE $2.55
*TITLE OF MANUSCRIPT CODEX MENDOZA 683/1-3, BOOK OF HOURS OF ANNE OF BOHEMIA 683-4, DE MODO SIGNIFICANDI 683-5, PSALTER WITH COMMENTARIES 683-6, CANONES HOROPTRI 683-7, GREGORY NAZIANZENUS 683-8, JOHN CHRYSOSTOM 683-9, ASTROLOGICAL WORKS 683/10-11
*SHELFMARK MS ARCH SELD A 1/ FOL 46 683-1, MS ARCH SELD A 1/ FOL 64 683-2, MS ARCH SELD A 1/ FOL 65 683-3, MS LAT LITURG F3/ FOL 51 683-4, MS BODLEY 643 683-5, MS AUCT D 4 1/ FOL 15V 683-6, MS BODLEY 504/ FOL 1 683-7, MS RAWL A 431/ FOL 3 683-8, MS UNIVERSITY COLLEGE 40/ FOL 1 683-9, MS CORPUS CHRISTI COLLEGE 123/ FOL 29 683-10, MS CORPUS CHRISTI COLLEGE 123/ FOL 30 683-11
*PROVENANCE MEXICAN 683/1-3, FLEMISH 683-4, ENGLISH 683-5, BYZANTINE 683-6, ENGLISH 683/7-11
*DATE EXECUTED 16TH/ 2ND QUARTER 683/1-3, 14TH/1382-94 683-4,

15TH/ 1ST HALF 683-5, 09TH/ LATE 683-6, 16TH 683-7, 16TH/ EARLY 683-8, 16TH 683-9, 14TH-15TH 683/10-11
*LANGUAGE SPANISH 683/1-3, DUTCH AND LATIN 683-4, LATIN 683/5-11
*AUTHOR MAGNUS/ ALBERTUS 683-5, GREGORY OF NAZIANZENUS 683-8, CHRYSOSTOM/ JOHN 683-9
*TYPE OF MANUSCRIPT CHRONICLE 683/1-3, BOOK OF HOURS/ USE OF ROME 683-4, LOGIC TEXTS 683-5, PSALTER WITH COMMENTARIES 683-6, RELIGIOUS TREATISES 683/8-9, ASTROLOGICAL WORKS 683/10-11
*CONTENTS MISCELLANY 13 683/1-11, TRIBUTE PAID TO MONTEZUMA 683-1, MONTEZUMA/ TRIBUTE PAID TO 683-1, WARRIOR IN RED CLOAK 683-2, WARRIOR-PRIEST AND PRISONER 683-3, TEXT AND DECORATED BORDERS 683-4, FOX AND THREE BIRDS 683-4, TEXT OF DE MODO SIGNIFICANDI 683-5, DAVID/ FULL-LENGTH PORTRAIT 683-6, INITIAL E 683-7, INITIAL V AND DECORATIVE FLORAL BORDER 683-8, DECORATIVE FLORAL BORDER 683-8, INITIAL A AND DECORATIVE FLORAL BORDER 683-9, DECORATIVE FLORAL BORDER 683-9, ZODIACAL MAN 683-10, DIAGRAM OF THE PLANETS 683-11, PLANETS/ DIAGRAM OF 683-11

*$ABSTRACT 684
*LIBRARY BODLEIAN
*SLIDE SET TITLE ESTHER INGLIS
*NEGATIVE REFERENCE ROLL 182P
*RENTAL FEE $2.20
*TITLE OF MANUSCRIPT LES PROVERBES DE SALOMON ESCRITES EN DIVERSES SORTES DE LETTRES
*SHELFMARK MS BODLEY 990/ P XV 684-1, MS BODLEY 990/ P 19 684-2, MS BODLEY 990/ P 6 684-3, MS BODLEY 990/ P 44 684-4
*PROVENANCE FRENCH
*DATE EXECUTED 16TH/1599
*LANGUAGE FRENCH
*ARTIST/ SCHOOL INGLIS/ ESTHER
*TYPE OF MANUSCRIPT PROVERBS
*CONTENTS CALLIGRAPHY 684/1-4, ESTHER INGLIS 684/1-4, FRONTISPIECE WITH PORTRAIT OF INGLIS 684-1, PORTRAIT OF ARTIST 684-1, TEXT WITH CALLIGRAPHY 684-2, PORTRAIT OF ARTIST 684-3, TEXT WITH CALLIGRAPHY 684-4

*$ABSTRACT 685
*LIBRARY BODLEIAN
*SLIDE SET TITLE MEDIEVAL FRENCH TOMBS OF THE 11TH-14TH CENTURIES
*NEGATIVE REFERENCE ROLL 185A PARTS 1-7
*RENTAL FEE $6.20
*COMMENTS FROM THE COLLECTION OF DRAWINGS BY GAIGNIERES. MANY OF THE TOMBS ARE NOW LOST. THE DATES REFER TO THE YEAR OF DEATH, IF KNOWN, OF THE PERSON OR PERSONS COMMEMORATED.
*SHELFMARK MS GOUGH DRAWINGS GAIGNIERES VOLS I-XIV
*PROVENANCE FRENCH/ ALENCON 685/1-2, FRENCH/ CORDELIERS PARIS 685/3-4, FRENCH/ JACOBINS PARIS 685-5, FRENCH/ SAINT DENIS 685-6, FRENCH/ JACOBINS PARIS 685/7-12, FRENCH/ POISSY 685-13, FRENCH/ JACOBINS 685-14, FRENCH/ ST GEORGE VENDOSME 685-15, FRENCH/ ABBAYE D'EU 685/16-18, FRENCH/ JACOBINS PARIS 685-19, FRENCH/ NANTES CATHEDRAL 685-20, FRENCH/ ROYAUMONT 685-21, FRENCH/ ST YVED DE BRAINE 685/22 AND 26-27, FRENCH/ BEAUVAIS CATHEDRAL 685-23, FRENCH/ VILLENEUVE LES NANTES 685-28, FRENCH/ SAINT DENIS 685-29, FRENCH/ JUMIEGES 685-30, FRENCH/ SAINT DENIS 685-31, FRENCH/ ROYAUMONT 685/32-33, FRENCH/ POISSY 685-34, FRENCH/ SAINT DENIS 685/35-43, FRENCH/ ROUEN 685-44, FRENCH/ SAINT DENIS 685/45-46, FRENCH/ JACOBINS ROUEN 685-47, FRENCH/ ECOINS 685-48, FRENCH 685/49-50, FRENCH/ JUMIEGES 685/51-61, FRENCH/ ABBAYE DE L'ESTRIE 685-62, FRENCH/ ST YVED DE BRAINE 685/63-64, FRENCH/ ABBAYE DE L'ESTOILE 685-65, FRENCH/ ABBAYE DE LONGPONT 685-66, FRENCH/ LONGPONT 685/67-68, FRENCH/ ABBAYE DE CHALOCHE 685-69, FRENCH/ ABBAYE DE TURPENAY 685-70, FRENCH/ ANGERS CATHEDRAL 685/71-72

FRENCH/ ANGERS JACOBINS 685-73, FRENCH/ ANGERS 685-74, FRENCH/ L'ABBAYE D'EVRON AU MAINE 685-75, FRENCH/ NOTRE DAME DE CHAMPAGNE 685-76, FRENCH/ ABBAYE DE CHALOCHE 685/78-79, FRENCH/ VILLENEUVE LES NANTES 685-80, FRENCH/ ST LUCIEN BEAUVAIS 685-81, FRENCH/ BONNEVAL 685/82-83, FRENCH/ TRINITE DE VENDOME 685-84
*DATE EXECUTED 14TH/C1346-79 685-1, 14TH/C1311-19 685-2, 14TH/C1336 685/3-4, 14TH/C1349-63 685-5, 14TH/C1349 685-6, 14TH/C1317 685-7, 14TH/C1342 685/8-9, 14TH/C1383 685-10, 14TH/C1356 685/11-12, 15TH/C1402 685-13, 15TH/C1404 685-14, 14TH/C1374 685-18, 13TH/C1295 685-19, 14TH/C1399 685-20, 13TH/C1260 685-21, 13TH/C1218 685-22, 13TH/C1217 685-23, 13TH/C1274 685-24, 13TH/C1250 685-27, 13TH/C1221-72 685-28, 13TH/ POSTHUMOUS TOMB 685-29, 13TH/C1295 685-31, 13TH/C1247 685-32, 13TH/C1222 685-33, 13TH 685-34, 14TH/C1300 685-35, 13TH/C1271 685-36, 14TH/C1314 685-47, 14TH/C1315 685-48, 11TH-14TH 685/49-62, 13TH 685/63-65, 13TH/C1271 685-66, 14TH/C1312 685-67, 13TH/C1217 685-68, 13TH 685-69, 12TH/C1170-89 685-70, 12TH/C1149 685/71-72, 13TH/C1260 685-73, 14TH/C1371 685-74, 13TH/C1277 685-75, 13TH/C1260 685-76, 14TH/ MID 685-78, 13TH 685-79, 14TH 685-80, 13TH/C1292 685-81, 12TH 685/82-83, 14TH/C1360 685-84
*CONTENTS MEDIEVAL FRENCH TOMBS 685/1-84, TOMBS/ FRENCH MEDIEVAL 685/1-84, DRAWINGS/ FRENCH 18TH CENTURY 685/1-84, CHARLES DE FRANCE AND MARIE D'ESPAGNE/ TOMB OF 685-1, LOUIS DE FRANCE AND MARGUERITE D'ARTOIS/ TOMB OF 685-2, CHARLES D'EVREUX/ TOMB OF 685/3-4, PHILIPPE DE NAVARRE AND JEANNE DE FRANCE/ TOMB OF 685-5, JEANNE DE FRANCE/ TOMB OF 685-6, ROBERT DE FRANCE/ TOMB OF 685-7, LOUIS I/ TOMB OF 685/8-9, BEATRIX DE BOURBON/ TOMB OF 685-10, PIERRE I/ TOMB OF 685/11-12, MARIE DE BOURBON/ TOMB OF 685-13, LOUIS DE BOURBON/ TOMB OF 685-14, JEAN DE BOURBON AND CATHERINE/ TOMB OF 685-15, JEAN D'ARTOIS AND YSABEL DE MELUN/ TOMB OF 685/16-17, ISABEAU D'ARTOIS/ TOMB OF 685-18, CHARLES I ROI DE SICILE/ TOMB OF 685-19, JEAN V DUC DE BRETAGNE/ TOMB OF 685-20, LOUIS DE FRANCE/ TOMB OF 685-21, ROBERT II COMTE DE DREUX/ TOMB OF 685-22, PHILIPPE DE DREUX/ TOMB OF 685-23, MARIE DE BOURBON/ TOMB OF 685-24, TOMB/ EARLIEST WITH WEEPERS 685/25-26, PIERRE MAUCLERC DUC DE BRETAGNE/ TOMB OF 685-27, ALIX DUCHESSE DE BRETAGNE/ TOMB OF 685-28, YOLANDE COMTESSE DE LA MARCHE/ TOMB OF 685-28, CHARLES THE BALD/ TOMB OF 685-29, LES ENERVES DU JUMIEGES/ TOMB OF 685-30, MARGUERITE DE PROVENCE/ TOMB OF 685-31, JEAN DE FRANCE/ TOMB OF 685-32, PHILIPPE DE FRANCE/ TOMB OF 685-33, ST LOUIS' CHILDREN/ TOMB OF 685-34, PHILIPPE III LE HARDI/ TOMB OF 685-35, ISABELLA OF ARAGON TO PHILIP OF VALOIS/ TOMB OF 685/36-43, CHARLES V HEART/ TOMB OF 685-44, CHARLES V AND JEANNE DE BOURBON/ TOMB OF 685-45, CHARLES VI AND ISABELLA OF BAVARIA/ TOMB OF 685-46, CARDINAL NICOLAS DE FREAUVILLE/ TOMB OF 685-47, ENGUERRAN DE MARIGNY/ TOMB OF 685-48, WILLIAM THE CONQUERER/ TOMB OF 685-49, MATILDA/ TOMB OF 685-50, ABBOTS OF JUMIEGES/ TOMB OF 685/51-61, JEAN DE FLORIGNY/ TOMB OF 685-62, TOMBS FROM ST YVED DE BRAINE 685/63-64, WOMAN WITH WEEPERS 685-65, MARIE DE MONTMIREL/ TOMB OF 685-66, ENGUERRAN IV DE COUCY/ TOMB OF 685-67, JEAN DE MONTMIREL/ TOMB OF 685-68, TOMB FOR THREE CHILDREN 685-69, BARTHELEIM AND N DE L'ISLE BOUCHARD/ TOMB OF 685-70, ULGER BISHOP OF ANGERS/ TOMB OF 685/71-72, MICHEL DE VILLOISEAU/ TOMB OF 685-73, AMAURI DE CRAON/ TOMB OF 685-74, RENARD SIEUR D'EVRON/ TOMB OF 685-75, GUILLAUME ROLAND/ TOMB OF 685-76, KNIGHT/ ANONYMOUS/ TOMB OF 685-77, THIBAUT IV DE MATHEFELON/ TOMB OF 685-78, HAMELIN D'INGERANDE/ TOMB OF 685-79, GAUTIER DE MACHECOUL/ TOMB OF 685-80, CARDINAL CHOLET/ TOMB OF 685-81, COUNT OF DUNOIS/ TOMB OF 685/82-83, GUY BEAUCHAMP/ TOMB OF 685-84

*$ABSTRACT 686
*LIBRARY BODLEIAN
*SLIDE SET TITLE GAIGNIERES DRAWINGS OF FRENCH TOMBS
*NEGATIVE REFERENCE ROLL 189I
*RENTAL FEE $2.45
*COMMENTS PRESENTED TO LOUIS XIV IN 1717.

*SHELFMARK MS GOUGH DRAWINGS GAIGNIERES VOLS 1-14
*PROVENANCE FRENCH
*DATE EXECUTED 18TH/C1700
*ARTIST/ SCHOOL GAIGNIERES
*TYPE OF MANUSCRIPT DRAWINGS
*CONTENTS FRENCH MONUMENTAL TOMBS 686/1-9, TOMBS/ FRENCH MONUMENTAL 686/1-9, DRAWINGS OF FRENCH TOMBS 686/1-9, SIMON DE BEAULIEU/ TOMB OF 686-1, PHILIPPE DE FRANCE/ TOMB OF 686-2, NICHOLAS DE NONANCON/ TOMB OF 686-3, CARDINAL COLET/ TOMB OF 686-4, ROBERT/ ARCHBISHOP OF ROUEN/ TOMB OF 686-5, ANSCULPHE DE PIERREFONDS/ TOMB OF 686-6, TOMB IN ST HILAIRE POITIERS 686-7, TOMB IN ST AUBIN ANGERS 686-8, PIERRE/ BISHOP OF POITIERS/ TOMB OF 686-9

*$ABSTRACT 687
*LIBRARY BODLEIAN
*SLIDE SET TITLE ORACLES OF LEO THE WISE
*NEGATIVE REFERENCE ROLL 190E
*RENTAL FEE $2.55
*COMMENTS IN GREEK WITH LATIN TRANSLATION BY FRANCESCO BAROZZI. DEDICATED TO JACOPO FOSCARI, VENETIAN GOVERNOR OF CRETE.
*SHELFMARK MS BAROCCI 170/ FOL 7V 687-1, MS BAROCCI 170/ FOL 14 687-2, MS BAROCCI 170/ FOL 14V 687-3, MS BAROCCI 170/ FOL 15V 687-4, MS BAROCCI 170/ FOL 16V 687-5, MS BAROCCI 170/ FOL 19V 687-6, MS BAROCCI 170/ FOL 20V 687-7, MS BAROCCI 170/ FOL 23V 687-8, MS BAROCCI 170/ FOL 24V 687-9, MS BAROCCI 170/ FOL 26V 687-10
*PROVENANCE BYZANTINE/ CRETE
*DATE EXECUTED 16TH/1577
*LANGUAGE GREEK WITH LATIN TRANSLATION
*TYPE OF MANUSCRIPT ORACLES
*CONTENTS ORACLES OF LEO THE WISE 687/1-10, EAGLE WITH MALTESE CROSS ON UNICORN 687-1, UNICORN WITH EAGLE ON SHOULDER 687-1, CORPSE OF CHRIST? IN TOMB/ FIERY PILLAR 687-2, FIERY PILLAR 687-2, TOMB OPEN/ MAN PREACHES 687-3, CORONATION OF EMPEROR PERFORMED BY ANGEL 687-4, EMPEROR'S CORONATION 687-4, DEATH OF EMPEROR/ DEATH AS SKELETON 687-5, EMPEROR'S DEATH 687-5, DEATH AS SKELETON 687-5, EMPEROR LEAVES CHURCH RIDING HORSE 687-6, CHURCH PERSONIFIED AS YOUTH WITH CHALICE 687-6, WOMAN/ CROWNED SEATED IN CASTLE 687-7, SHIP APPROACHES ROCKS 687-7, CITY ENGULFED BY SEA 687-8, IKON OF THEOTOKOS 687-8, CHRIST ON CHALICE 687-8, EMPEROR TRAMPLES ON CROSS 687-9, CROSS TRAMPLED BY EMPEROR 687-9, ANTICHRIST ENTHRONED AS EMPEROR 687-10, EMPEROR AS ANTICHRIST 687-10, LAST JUDGMENT 687-11

*$ABSTRACT 688
*LIBRARY BODLEIAN
*SLIDE SET TITLE ARCHITECTURAL DESIGNS ATTRIBUTED TO GERBREI
*NEGATIVE REFERENCE ROLL 190H
*RENTAL FEE $2.15
*SHELFMARK MS GOUGH DRAWINGS A 2
*PROVENANCE ENGLISH
*DATE EXECUTED 17TH-18TH
*ARTIST/ SCHOOL GERBREI/ BALTHAZAR
*TYPE OF MANUSCRIPT ARCHITECTURAL DESIGNS
*CONTENTS ARCHITECTURAL DESIGNS 688/1-3, GATE PIERS AT HAMPSTEAD MARSHALL 688/1-2, FRONT PORTAL AT HAMPSTEAD MARSHALL 688-3

*$ABSTRACT 689
*LIBRARY BODLEIAN
*SLIDE SET TITLE MAPS MID-SUSSEX
*NEGATIVE REFERENCE ROLL 190J
*RENTAL FEE $2.45
*TITLE OF MANUSCRIPT CANTII/ SOUTHSEXIAE/ SURRIAE ET MIDDLESEXIAE COMITAT VERA DESCRIPTIO 689/1-2, SUSSEXIAE SIUE

SOUTHSEX OLIM PARS REGNORUM 689-3, THREATRE 689-4, 56 NEW AND ACCURATE MAPS OF GREAT BRITAIN 689-5, AN ACTUAL SURVEY OF SUSSEX 689-6, GENERAL VIEW OF THE AGRICULTURE OF SUSSEX 689-7, ORDNANCE SURVEY/ FIRST EDITION 689-8, MAP OF HORSHAM 689-9
*PROVENANCE ENGLISH
*DATE EXECUTED 16TH/C1575 689/1-2, 17TH/1607 689-3, 17TH/C1611 689-4, 18TH/C1708 689-5, 18TH/1724 689-6, 18TH/C1793 689-7, 19TH/1832 689-9
*TYPE OF MANUSCRIPT MAPS
*CONTENTS MAPS OF MID-SUSSEX 689/1-9, TOPOGRAPHY/ ENGLISH 689/1-9, MAP OF KENT/ SUSSEX/ SURREY/ MIDDLESEX 689-1, MAP SHOWING FORESTS OF ST LEONARDS AND WORTH 689-2, MAP OF NORTH-CENTRAL SUSSEX 689-3, MAP OF ST LEONARDS AND WORTH FOREST AREAS 689-4, MAP OF SUSSEX 689-5, MAP OF NORTH-CENTRAL SUSSEX 689-6, MAP SHOWING LAND USE AND SOIL DIVISIONS 689-7,MAP DETAIL OF AREA AROUND CRAWLEY 689-8, MAP OF HORSHAM SHOWING BOUNDARY CHANGES 689-9

*$ABSTRACT 690
*LIBRARY BODLEIAN
*SLIDE SET TITLE G W KNORR
*NEGATIVE REFERENCE ROLL 196E
*RENTAL FEE $2.40
*COMMENTS AUGMENTED BY J.E.E WALSH AND TRANSLATED BY J.F. ISENFLAMM.
*TITLE OF MANUSCRIPT DELICES DE LA NATURE
*PROVENANCE GERMAN/ NUREMBERG
*DATE EXECUTED 18TH/1779
*ARTIST/ SCHOOL KNORR/ G W
*TYPE OF MANUSCRIPT NATURAL HISTORY
*CONTENTS NATURAL HISTORY 690/1-8, BUTTERFLIES 690/1-2, MINERALS 690/3-8

*$ABSTRACT 691
*LIBRARY BODLEIAN
*SLIDE SET TITLE ESTATE MAPS OF STONOR AND WOLVERCOTE
*NEGATIVE REFERENCE ROLL 197A
*RENTAL FEE $2.75
*PROVENANCE ENGLISH
*DATE EXECUTED 18TH/1725 691/1-11, 18TH/1765 691/12-15
*TYPE OF MANUSCRIPT MAPS
*CONTENTS MAPS/ ESTATE 691/1-15, TOPOGRAPHY/ ESTATE MAPS 691/1-15, MAPS OF STONOR IN OXFORDSHIRE 691/1-11, MAPS OF WOLVERCOTE IN OXFORDSHIRE 691/12-15

$ABSTRACT 692
*LIBRARY BODLEIAN
*SLIDE SET TITLE DE GOMME MAP OF OXFORD
*NEGATIVE REFERENCE ROLL 198A
*RENTAL FEE $2.25
*TITLE OF MANUSCRIPT DE GOMME MAP
*SHELFMARK MS TOP OXON B 167
*PROVENANCE ENGLISH
*DATE EXECUTED 17TH/1644
*TYPE OF MANUSCRIPT MAP
*CONTENTS MAP OF OXFORD 692/1-5, TOPOGRAPHY/ ESTATE MAPS 692/1-5, OXFORD/ MAP 692/1-5, MAP OF OXFORD/ WHOLE PAGE 692-1, MAP OF OXFORD/ NORTH-EAST 692-2, MAP OF OXFORD/ SOUTH-EAST 692-3, MAP OF OXFORD/ NORTH-WEST 692-4, MAP OF OXFORD/ SOUTH-WEST 692-5

$ABSTRACT 693
*LIBRARY BODLEIAN
*SLIDE SET TITLE BUCKINGHAMSHIRE STAINED GLASS

*NEGATIVE REFERENCE ROLL 199A
*RENTAL FEE $4.90
*COMMENTS COLORED GLASS RECORDED IN BUCKINGHAMSHIRE BY REV. F.G. LESS, 1854-84.
*TITLE OF MANUSCRIPT SCRAPBOOK OF REV F G LEE
*SHELFMARK MS TOP BUCKS C 1 693/1-20, MS TOP BUCKS C 4 693/21-58
*PROVENANCE ENGLISH
*DATE EXECUTED 19TH
*ARTIST/ SCHOOL LEE/ REV F G
*TYPE OF MANUSCRIPT WATERCOLORS OF STAINED GLASS
*CONTENTS STAINED GLASS FROM BUCKINGHAMSHIRE 693/1-58, WATERCOLORS OF STAINED GLASS 693/1-58, BURNHAM 693/1-2, LITTLE KIMBLE 693-3, ICKFORD 693-4, BIERTON 693-5, CHEDDINGTON 693-6, DINTON 693-7, UPPER WINCHENDON 693-8, LOWER WINCHENDON 693/9-10, CHEARSLEY 693-11, CHESHAM BOIS 693-12, CHESHAM BOIS 693/13-14, CHESHAM BOIS 693/15-17, MENTMORE 693-18, ASCOTT HOUSE NEAR WING 693-19, CHENIES 693-20, SHENLEY 693-21, SHENLEY 693-22, SHERRINGTON 693-23, SINGLEBOROUGH 693-24, SIMPSON 693-25, SIMPSON 693-26, TATTENHOE 693-27, TINGEWICK 693-28, TOWERSEY 693-29, WHITCHURCH 693-30, WOODBURN DEYNCOURT 693-31, WADDESDON 693/32-33, CHIPPING WYCOMBE 693/34-35, COTTAGE IN BUCKINGHAM 693-36, NO LOCALITY STATED 693-37, FINGEST AND SAUNDERTON? 693-38, DRAYTON BEAUCHAMP 693-39, EMBERTON 693-40, GREAT LINFORD 693-41, HAMPDON 693-42, HITCHAM 693/43-44, LUFFIELD 693-45, LITTLE BRICKHILL 693-46, MOULSOE 693/47-48, MOULSOE 693-49, GT MISSENDON 693-50, MENTMORE 693-51, NEWTON 693-52, PADBURY 693/53-54, QUAINTON 693/55-57, DODDERSHALL OR LUDGERSHALL 693-55

*$ABSTRACT 694
*LIBRARY BODLEIAN
*SLIDE SET TITLE BUCKINGHAMSHIRE HOUSES
*NEGATIVE REFERENCE ROLL 199B
*RENTAL FEE $2.70
*COMMENTS WATERCOLORS OF BUCKINGHAMSHIRE HOUSES
*TITLE OF MANUSCRIPT SCRAPBOOK OF REV F G LEE
*SHELFMARK MS TOP BUCKS C 1 694/1-3, MS TOP BUCKS C 4 694/4-14
*PROVENANCE ENGLISH
*DATE EXECUTED 19TH
*ARTIST/ SCHOOL LEE/ REV F G
*TYPE OF MANUSCRIPT WATERCOLORS OF HOUSES
*CONTENTS HOUSES FROM BUCKINGHAMSHIRE 694/1-14, WATERCOLORS OF HOUSES 694/1-14, ARCHITECTURE/ WATERCOLORS OF HOUSES 694/1-14, AYLESBURY/ ORIGINAL MARKET HOUSE 694-1, RAYNERS RESIDENCE IN PENN BUCKS 694-2 SALDEN HOUSE IN MURSLEY 694-3, ASTON CLINTON 694-4, HIGH STREET IN BEACONSFIELD 694-5, WALL PAINTINGS AT BURNHAM 694-6, STONE GRAVE-HEAD AT FARNHAM ROYAL 694-7, LITTLE MARLOW NUNNERY 694-8, CHAPEL OF THE MANOR OF HORTON 694-9, CROKE'S MANOR HOUSE IN MARSH GIBBON 694-10, SHORNE'S WELL AT NORTH MARSTON 694-11, PIGOTT'S HOUSE AT DODDERSHALL 694-12, SNELLSHALL PRIORY NEAR WHADDON CHASE 694-13, HOUSE OF JOHN DE GREY AT SHENLEY 694-14

*$ABSTRACT 695
*LIBRARY BODLEIAN
*SLIDE SET TITLE BUCKINGHAMSHIRE CHURCHES
*NEGATIVE REFERENCE ROLL 199C
*RENTAL FEE $2.50
*TITLE OF MANUSCRIPT SCRAPBOOK OF BISHOP WILBERFORCE
*SHELFMARK MS OXFORD DIOC PAPERS B 72
*PROVENANCE ENGLISH
*DATE EXECUTED 19TH
*ARTIST/ SCHOOL WILBERFORCE/ BISHOP
*TYPE OF MANUSCRIPT WATERCOLORS OF CHURCHES
*CONTENTS CHURCHES FROM BUCKINGHAMSHIRE 695/1-10, WATERCOLORS OF CHURCHES 695/1-10, ARCHITECTURE/ WATERCOLORS OF CHURCHES CHURCH OF ASTON ABBOTTS 695-1, CHURCH OF ST MARY AT AYLESBURY

695-2, CUBLINGTON CHURCH 695-3, CHURCH AT GREAT HAMPDEN 695-4, HORSENDEN CHURCH 695-5, ILMER CHURCH 695-6, MAIDSMORETON CHURCH 695-7, CHURCH AT MONKS RISBOROUGH 695-8, CHURCH AT SEER GREEN 695-9, STEWKLEY CHURCH 695-10

*$ABSTRACT 696
*LIBRARY BODLEIAN
*SLIDE SET TITLE BUCKINGHAMSHIRE MAPS
*NEGATIVE REFERENCE ROLL 199D
*RENTAL FEE $2.75
*COMMENTS MAPS FROM SAXTON TO EARLY ORDNANCE SURVEY.
*TITLE OF MANUSCRIPT OXONII BUCKINGHAMIAE 696-1, LE THEATRE DU MONDE 696-3, A MAPP OF BUCKINGHAMSHIRE 696-4, OXFORD BUCKINGHAM 696-5, BUCKINGHAM BY JOHN SPEED 696-6, BUCKINGHAM BY A BRYANT 696-7, CARY'S IMPROVED MAP OF ENGLAND 696-8, ORDNANCE SURVEY 696/9-15
*SHELFMARK PR DOUCE PRINTS B 27/ FOL 11 696-1, PR G MAPS 96R/ FOL 18 696-2, PR GOUGH MAPS 90 696-5, PR C 17 B 2/ FOL 14 696-6, PR C 17 15 7 696-7, PR C 17 A 14/ SHEET 26 696-8, ORDNANCE SURVEY/ 2ND EDITION 696-9, ORDNANCE SURVEY/ 3RD EDITION 696/10-11, ORDNANCE SURVEY/ 3RD EDITION 696-12, ORDNANCE SURVEY 1903/ SHEET 62 696-13, ORDNANCE SURVEY 1906 696-14, ORDNANCE SURVEY/ SHEET 28 696-15
*PROVENANCE ENGLISH 696/1-2 AND 4-15, FRENCH 696-3
*DATE EXECUTED 16TH/1574 696-1, 17TH/1634 696-2, 17TH/1645-48 696-3, 17TH/1673 696-4, 18TH/1720 696-5, 17TH/1666 696-6, 19TH/1823 696-8, 19TH/1898 696-9, 20TH/1905 696-11, 20TH/1907 696-12, 20TH/1903 696-13, 20TH/1906 696-14
*ARTIST/SCHOOL SAXTON 696/1-2, BLAEU/ JEAN 696-3, BLOME/ RICHARD 696-4, SAXTON 696-5, SPEED/ JOHN 696-6, BRYANT/ A 696-7, CARY 698-8
*TYPE OF MANUSCRIPT MAPS
*CONTENTS MAPS OF BUCKINGHAMSHIRE 696/1-15, TOPOGRAPHY/ BUCKINGHAMSHIRE MAPS 696/1-15

*$ABSTRACT 697
*LIBRARY ORIEL COLLEGE
*SLIDE SET TITLE MAP OF SHENNINGTON OXON
*NEGATIVE REFERENCE ROLL 201H
*RENTAL FEE $2.50
*TITLE OF MANUSCRIPT MAP OF SHENNINGTON OXON
*PROVENANCE ENGLISH
*DATE EXECUTED 18TH/1781 697/1-4, 18TH/1732 697/5-10
*TYPE OF MANUSCRIPT MAP
*CONTENTS MAPS OF SHENNINGTON OXON 697/1-10, TOPOGRAPHY/ MAPS OF SHENNINGTON OXON 697/1-10

*$ABSTRACT 698
*LIBRARY BODLEIAN
*SLIDE SET TITLE TRADESCANT'S ORCHARD
*NEGATIVE REFERENCE ROLL 208G
*RENTAL FEE $2.95
*COMMENTS PAINTINGS OF FRUIT
*SHELFMARK MS ASHMOLE 1461/ FOL 13-145
*PROVENANCE ENGLISH
*DATE EXECUTED 17TH/ 1ST HALF
*ARTIST/ SCHOOL TRADESCANT
*TYPE OF MANUSCRIPT BOTANICAL
*CONTENTS BOTANY/ PAINTINGS OF FRUIT 698/1-19,RED GOOSEBERRY 698-1, MAY CHERRY WITH GRASSHOPPER/ FLY/ SNAIL/ BUTTERFLY 698-2, GRASSHOPPER 698-2, FLY 698-2, SNAIL 698-2, BUTTERFLY 698-2, TRADESCANT CHERRY 698-3, WHIGHT CHERRY 698-4, HARTE CHERRY WITH SNAIL 698-5, SNAIL 698-5, QUENE MOTHER PLUM/ ROBIN EATS CATERPILLAR 698-6, ROBIN EATS CATERPILLAR 698-6, GREENE PESIOD PLUM/ SPIDER IN WEB AND FLY 698-7, SPIDER IN WEB AND FLY 698-7, PRUON DAMSON 698-8, WHIGHT DATE/ LADYBIRD/ INSECT/

LIZARD 698-9, LADYBIRD/ FLYING 698-9, INSECT/ WINGED 698-9, LIZARD 698-9, ROUND APRICOCK/ BROWN BIRD CATCHES CATERPILLAR 698-10, BIRD CATCHES CATERPILLAR 698-10, ROMAN REED NECTRION/ PINK AND YELLOW MOTH 698-11, MOTH/ PINK AND YELLOW 698-11, YELLOW NECTRION/ FROG 698-12, FROG 698-12, GRETE EARLY YELLOW PEECH/ FLY AND CATERPILLAR 698-13, FLY AND CATERPILLAR 698-13, WHIGHTE PEECH/ LADYBIRD AND FROG 698-14, LADYBIRD/ FLYING 698-14, FROG 698-14, EARLY RIPE APPLE/ PINK BUTTERFLY AND OWL 698-15, BUTTERFLY/ PINK 698-15, OWL 698-15, JERUSALEM PEERE/ GRASSHOPPER 698-16, GRASSHOPPER 698-16, PORTINEGALE QUINCE/ BIRD EATS SEED 698-17, BIRD EATS SEED 698-17, GREETE ROMAN HASELL NUT/ RED SQUIRREL AND FROG 698-18, SQUIRREL 698-18, FROG 698-18, BLUE GRAPE 698-19

*$ABSTRACT 699
*LIBRARY BODLEIAN
*SLIDE SET TITLE TRADE BINDINGS
*NEGATIVE REFERENCE ROLL 211A
*RENTAL FEE $3.75
*COMMENTS ART NOUVEAU TRADE BINDINGS OF THE 19TH CENTURY.
*TITLE OF MANUSCRIPT EARLY ITALIAN POETS 699-1, ITALIAN HISTORY AND ART OF THE MIDDLE AGES 699-1, GOBLIN MARKET 699-1, ATALANTA IN CALYDON 699-2, SONGS BEFORE SUNRISE 699-2, DANTE'S COMEDY HELL 699-3, PRINCE'S PROGRESS 699-4, POEMS 699-5, BALLADS AND SONNETS 699-6, A SHADOW OF DANTE 699-7, PARABLES AND TALES 699-8, LIFE OF WILLIAM BLAKE 699-9, POEMS 699-10, GABRIEL DENVER 699-11, WOMAN'S VOICES 699-12, LOVE IS ENOUGH 699-13, STORY OF THE VOLSUNGS 699-13, WREN'S CITY CHURCHES 699-14, THE TRAGIC MARY 699-15, HOUSE OF POMEGRANATES 699-16, TESS OF THE D'URBEVILLES 699-17, A GROUP OF NOBLE DAMES 699-17, POEMS 699-18, IN THE KEY OF BLUE 699-19, SILVERPOINTS 699-20, THE SPHINX 699-21, DE PROFUNDIS 699-22, LE MORTE D'ARTHUR 699-23, DECORATIONS 699-24, VERSES 699-24, RAPE OF THE LOCK 699-25, GREEK VASE PAINTINGS 699-26, D G ROSSETTI 699-27, PRACTICAL DESIGNING 699-27, EMMA 699-27, GOBLIN MARKET 699-28, GREEN ARRAS 699-28, POEMS 699-29, SECRET ROSE 699-30, POEMS 699-30, FALSE DAWN 699-31, THE SHEPHERD'S CALENDAR 699-32, WILD HONEY 699-34, THE CRESCENT MOON 699-35, REVERIES 699-35, PER AMICA SILENTIA LUNA 699-35, WILD SWANS AT COOLE 699-35
*PROVENANCE ENGLISH
*DATE EXECUTED 19TH/1861 699-1, 19TH/1863 699-1, 19TH/1862 699-1, 19TH/1865 699-2, 19TH/1871 699-2, 19TH/1865 699-3, 19TH/1866 699-4, 19TH/1870 699-5, 19TH/1881 699-6, 19TH/1871 699-7, 19TH/1872 699-8, 19TH/1880 699-9, 19TH/1882 699-10, 19TH/1873 699-11, 19TH/1887 699-12, 19TH/1873 699-13, 19TH/1870 699-13, 19TH/1883 699-14, 19TH/1890 699-15, 19TH/1891 699-16, 19TH/1891 699-17, 19TH/1892 699-17, 19TH/1892 699-18, 19TH/1893 699-19, 19TH/1893 699-20, 19TH/1894 699-21, 20TH/1905 699-22, 19TH/1893 699-23, 19TH/1899 699-24, 19TH/1896 699-24, 19TH/1896 699-25, 19TH/1894 699-26, 19TH/1870 699-27, 19TH/1893 699-27, 19TH/1898 699-27, 19TH/1893 699-28, 19TH/1896 699-28, 19TH/1895 699-29, 19TH/1897 699-30, 19TH/1899 699-30, 19TH/1897 699-31, 19TH/1898 699-32, 19TH/1898 699-33, 19TH/1899 699-33, 20TH/1908 699-34, 20TH/1913 699-35, 20TH/1916 699-35, 20TH/1918 699-35, 20TH/1919 699-35
*ARTIST/ SCHOOL BOOK COVER DESIGNERS 699/1-35, ROSSETTI/ D G 699/1-8 AND 10, SHIELDS/ F 699-9, BROWN/ F MADOX 699-11, TRAQUAIR/ PHOEBE A 699-12, MORRIS/ WILLIAM 699-13, WEBB/ P 699-13, MCMURDO/ A H 699-14, SELWYN IMAGE 699-15, RICKETTS/ CHARLES 699/16-22 AND 34, BEARDSLEY/ A 699/23-25, MCCOLL/ D S 699-26, ROSSETTI/ D G 699-27, WHITE/ GLEESON 699-27, HOUSMAN/ L 699-28, FELL/ H F 699-29, GYLES/ A 699-30, TURBAYNE/ A A 699-31, CRANE/ W 699-32, MORRIS/ TALWIN 699-33, MOORE/ T STURGE 699-35
*AUTHOR ROSSETTI/ CHRISTINA 699/1 AND 4, SWINBURNE/ A C 699-2, ROSSETTI/ W M TRANSLATOR 699-3, ROSSETTI/ D G 699/5-6, ROSSETTI/ MARIA 699-7, HAKE/ T G 699-8, GILCHRIST/ A 699-9, SHELLEY/ P B 699-10, BROWN/ OLIVER MADOX 699-11, SHARP/ MRS W

699-12, MORRIS/ WILLIAM 699-13, FIELD/ MICHAEL 699-15, WILDE/ O 699/16 AND 18, HARDY/ T 699-17, SYMONDS/ J A 699-19, GRAY/ J 699-20, WILDE/ O 699/21-22, MALORY/ THOMAS 699-23, BEARDSLEY/ A 699-24, DOWSON/ E 699-24, POPE/ ALEXANDER 699-25, MCCOLL/ D S 699-26, ROSSETTI/ D G 699-27, WHITE/ GLEESON 699-27, TURBAYNE/ A A 699-27, ROSSETTI/ CHRISTINA 699-28, HOUSMAN/ L 699-28, YEATS/ W B 699/29-30, PREVOST/ F 699-31, SPENSER/ EDMUND 699-32, FIELD/ MICHAEL 699-34, TAGORE/ RABINDRANATH 699-35, YEATS/ W B 699-35
*TYPE OF MANUSCRIPT BOOK BINDINGS/ TRADE
*CONTENTS BINDINGS/ TRADE 699/1-35, BOOK BINDINGS 699/1-35, ART NOUVEAU BINDINGS 699/1-35, BOOK DESIGNERS 699/1-35, LINE AND DOT STYLE 699-1, JAPANESE EMBLEMATIC CIRCLE STYLE 699-2, EMBLEMATIC STYLE 699-3, LINE AND CIRCLE STYLE 699-4, SPINE BLOCK/ OVER LARGE 699-5, SPINE BLOCK/ MODIFIED SPINE 699-5, TRELLIS DESIGN SPREAD OVER BOTH COVERS 699-6, SYMBOLIC COVER 699-7, SYMBOLIC COVER 699-8, DESIGN ADAPTED FROM SKETCH BY ROBERT BLAKE 699-9, CIRCULAR DESIGN 699-10, JAPANESE STYLE 699-11, COVER FOR WOMEN'S VOICES 699-12, COVERS BY WILLIAM MORRIS AND ASSOCIATE 699-13,EARLY ART NOUVEAU/ FLOWING LINE 699-14, SINUOUS FLORAL DESIGN 699-15, STYLE OF THE NINETIES 699-16, JAPANESE STYLE 699-17, HIGH SINUOUS LINE STYLE 699-18, COVER BY C RICKETTS 699-19, COVER SHOWING ORIGINAL BRASS BINDER'S BLOCK 699-20, DESIGN LOOKING FORWARD TO RECTILINEAR STYLE 699-21, JAPANESE STYLE/ SIMPLE AND SYMBOLIC 699-22, ART NOUVEAU DESIGN 699-23, DESIGNS BY A BEARDSLEY 699/24-25, DESIGN FORESHADOWS MODERN FREE-HAND WORK 699-26, VARIATIONS ON ROSSETTI'S DESIGNS 699-27, REPETITIVE ALL-OVER DESIGN 699-28, PICTORIAL AND SYMBOLIC COVER 699-29, CELTIC REVIVAL WITH MYSTIC AND SYMBOLIC STRAINS 699-30, COVER BY A A TURBAYNE 699-32, COVER BY W CRANE/ HIGHLY INDIVIDUAL STYLE 699-32, GOOD MODERN DESIGN FOR CHEAP PUBLICATIONS 699-33, TRELLIS DESIGN 699-34, RECTILINEAR SYMBOLIC DESIGNS 699-35

*$ABSTRACT 700
*LIBRARY BODLEIAN
*SLIDE SET TITLE STOWE BUCKS
*NEGATIVE REFERENCE ROLL 211B
*RENTAL FEE $2.45
*COMMENTS PLANS OF STOWE HOUSE IN BUCKINGHAMSHIRE.
*SHELFMARK MS GOUGH DRAWINGS A 4/ FOL 46
*PROVENANCE ENGLISH
*DATE EXECUTED 18TH/C1723
*ARTIST/ SCHOOL BRIDGEMAN/ CHARLES
*TYPE OF MANUSCRIPT PLANS
*CONTENTS TOPOGRAPHY/ PLANS OF STOWE HOUSE 700/1-9, ARCHITECTURE/ PLANS OF STOWE HOUSE 700/1-9, STOWE HOUSE/ PLANS 700/1-9

*$ABSTRACT 701
*LIBRARY BODLEIAN
*SLIDE SET TITLE ESTATE MAPS BY T LANGDON
*NEGATIVE REFERENCE ROLL 211F
*RENTAL FEE $3.40
*COMMENTS PROPERTIES BELONGING TO CORPUS CHRISTI COLLEGE OXON IN 1606.
*TITLE OF MANUSCRIPT T LANGDON'S ESTATE MAPS
*PROVENANCE ENGLISH
*DATE EXECUTED 17TH/C1606
*ARTIST/ SCHOOL LANGDON T
*TYPE OF MANUSCRIPT MAPS/ ESTATE
*CONTENTS MAPS/ ESTATE OF BUCKINGHAMSHIRE AND HAMPSHIRE 701/1-28, TOPOGRAPHY/ ENGLISH ESTATE MAPS 701/1-28, MAP OF HENDRED/ DETAIL OF CARTOUCHE 701-1, MAP OF HENDRED/ BLOCK OF STRIPS OF CULTIVATED LAND 701-2, MAP OF HENDRED/ DETAIL OF VILLAGE 701-3, MAP OF WEST AND EAST HENDRED WITH OAKLEY/BRILL 701-4, MAP OF WEST HENDRED WITH KINGSCLERE HANTS 701-5, MAP OF WEST HENDRED 701-6, MAP OF STREATLEY BUCKS 701-7, MAP OF

ASHFORD HILL AND NEWTON IN KINGSCLERE 701-8, MAP OF BENHAM IN KINGSCLERE 701-9, MAP OF BEAR FARM IN WARNFORD HANTS 701-10, MAP OF WARNFORD 701-11, MAP OF CULMISTON IN CHERITON HANTS 701/12-13, MAP OF MAPLEDURWELL HANTS 701-14, MAP OF HOOKLANDS IN MAPLEDURWELL 701-15, MAP OF WALTERS AND ROBJOYES IN ODIHAM HANTS 701-16, MAP OF PILLERS AND MOCKETS IN ODIHAM 701-17, MAP OF HURSLEY HANTS 701-18, MAP OF ROMBRIDGE IN BLING HANTS 701-19, MAP OF NURSLING HANTS 701-20, MAP OF BRACHEFIELD IN MICHAELMAS 701-21, MAP OF WEST WELLOW WILTS AND SHELLEY IN BLING 701-22, MAP OF MARWELL IN OUSELBURY HANTS 701/23-24, MAP OF PLAISTOWES AND BABRIDGE IN OUSELBURY 701-25, MAP OF BANBRIDGE AND HENSTINGE IN OUSELBURY AND TWYFORD 701-26, MAP OF POLHAMPTON AND QUIDHAMPTON IN OVERSTON HANTS 701-27, MAP OF OVERTON HANTS 701-28

*$ABSTRACT 702
*LIBRARY BODLEIAN
*SLIDE SET TITLE DE BRY'S AMERICA
*NEGATIVE REFERENCE ROLL 212E-G-F
*RENTAL FEE $4.85
*COMMENTS A SELECTION FROM THE REMAINS OF WHAT MUST HAVE BEEN A SPLENDID COPY OF DE BRY'S FAMOUS BOOK, PUBLISHED IN FRANKFURT IN 1590. THE ENGRAVINGS HAVE ALL BEEN COLORED BY HAND.
*TITLE OF MANUSCRIPT GRANDS ET PETITS VOYAGES
*PROVENANCE GERMAN/ FRANKFURT
*DATE EXECUTED 16TH/1590-92
*LANGUAGE FRENCH
*AUTHOR DE BRY
*TYPE OF MANUSCRIPT HISTORY
*CONTENTS DE BRY'S AMERICA 702/1-57, ENGRAVINGS/ 16TH CENTURY 702/1-57, PART I VIRGINIA 702/1-19, MAP OF VIRGINIA/ C1590 702-1, VIRGINIA/ MAP 702-1, ENGLISH ARRIVE IN VIRGINIA 702-2, DRESS AND APPEARANCE OF VIRGINIAN CHIEFTAINS 702-3, INDIAN CHIEFTAINS IN VIRGINIA 702-3, DRESS AND APPEARANCE OF WOMEN OF SECOTA 702-4,INDIAN WOMEN 702-4, DRESS AND APPEARANCE OF PRIESTS OF SECOTA 702-5, PRIESTS/ INDIAN 702-5, SECOTA NOBLEWOMEN 702-6, INDIAN NOBLEWOMEN 702-6, DRESS AND APPEARANCE OF ROANOAC CHIEFS 702-7, INDIAN CHIEFS 702-7, DRESS AND APPEARANCE OF POMEIOOC NOBLEWOMEN 702-8, POMEIOOC NOBLEWOMEN 702-8, INDIAN NOBLEWOMEN 702-8, DRESS/ WINTER OF OLD MEN OF POMEIOOC 702-9, OLD MEN OF POMEIOOC 702-9, MAGICIAN OR CONJUROR WITH SYMBOLS OF ART 702-10, INDIAN MAGICIAN OR CONJUROR 702-10, BOAT MAKING BY INDIANS 702-11, FISHING METHODS OF INDIANS 702-12, COOKING METHODS OF INDIANS 702-13, EATING HABITS OF INDIANS 702-14, FIRE FESTIVAL TO CELEBRATE GOOD FORTUNE 702-15, FESTIVAL OF DANCING IN VIRGINIA 702-16, INDIAN VILLAGE OF POMEIOOC 702-17, TEMPLE/ CHIEF'S DWELLING/ WATER SUPPLY LABELLED ABC 702-17, IDOL KIWASA 702-18, PICT WARRIOR FROM BRITAIN 702-19, DE BRY'S FLORIDA 702/20-40, FLORIDA FROM DE BRY'S AMERICA 702/20-40, FRENCH REACH HARBOR NAMED ROYAL HARBOR 702-20,INDIANS HONOR MONUMENT TO FRENCH KING 702-21, FRENCH BUILD THEIR CITADEL 702-22, SATURIOVAN CEREMONIALS BEFORE BATTLE WITH ENEMY 702-23, INDIAN CEREMONY BEFORE BATTLE 702-23, INDIAN RITUAL WITH TROPHIES FROM DEFEATED ENEMY 702-24, HERMAPHRODITES CARRY DEAD TO GRAVES 702-25, INDIAN WIVES MOURN DEAD AND PETITION KING 702-26, SICK INDIANS CARED FOR 702-27, TILLING AND SOWING 702-28, FRUIT GATHERED AND STORED IN HOUSES 702-29, SMOKING FOOD TO PRESERVE IT 702-30, HUNTING DEER 702-31, DEER HUNTING 702-31, HUNTING CROCODILES 702-32, CROCODILE HUNTING 702-32, INDIANS SWIM TO ISLAND 702-33, FEAST PREPARATIONS 702-34, TOWN BUILDING BY INDIANS 702-35, ENEMY TOWN SET FIRE 702-36, GAMES AND SPORT OF INDIAN YOUTHS 702-37, QUEEN BROUGHT TO KING IN PROCESSION 702-38, KING AND QUEEN OF INDIANS TAKE WALK 702-39, GOLD PROSPECTING IN RIVER 702-40, DE BRY'S BRAZIL 702/41-57, BRAZIL FROM DE BRY'S AMERICA 702/41-57, JOANNES STADIUS LEAVES LISBON ON VOYAGE TO BRAZIL 702-41, BATTLE WITH FRENCH SHIP IN BUTTUGAR HARBOR 702-42, SHIP APPROACHES SHORE OF AMERICA 702-43, SAILORS FIND CROSS ERECTED ON MOUND 702-44, SHIPWRECK OFF ST VINCENT ISLAND 702-45, STADIUS CAPTURED BY INDIANS

702-46, PORTUGUESE ATTEMPT TO RESCUE STADIUS 702-47, INDIANS PREPARE TO SACRIFICE 702-48, PORTUGUESE ATTEMPT TO RESCUE STADIUS 702-49, SHIP SENT TO GET STADIUS MEETS COLD RESPONSE 702-50, SICK MAN BROUGHT BACK TO HIS HOUSE 702-51, INDIANS EAT FISH AFTER EATING CAPTIVE 702-52, CANNIBALS COOK VICTIM IN FRONT OF STADIUS 702-53, FRENCH BOAT TOO HEAVY TO CARRY AWAY STADIUS 702-54, BATTLE WITH ANOTHER TRIBE DURING EXPEDITION 702-55, INDIANS MISTREAT CAPTIVES 702-56, RETURN VOYAGE FROM BRAZIL 702-57

*$ABSTRACT 703
*LIBRARY BODLEIAN
*SLIDE SET TITLE FRENCH ROYAL TOMBS
*NEGATIVE REFERENCE ROLL 214G
*RENTAL FEE $2.40
*COMMENTS 18TH-CENTURY DRAWINGS BY GAIGNIERES.
*SHELFMARK MS GOUGH DRAWINGS GAIGNIERES/ VOL 2
*PROVENANCE FRENCH/ ABBEY OF ST GERMAIN 703/1-2, FRENCH/ ABBEY OF ST DENIS 703-3, FRENCH/ ABBEY OF LONCHAMP 703-4, FRENCH/ ABBEY OF ROYAUMONT 703/5-7
*DATE EXECUTED 18TH
*ARTIST/ SCHOOL GAIGNIERES
*TYPE OF MANUSCRIPT DRAWINGS OF FRENCH TOMBS
*CONTENTS FRENCH ROYAL TOMBS 703/1-8, DRAWINGS OF FRENCH ROYAL TOMBS 703/1-8, TOMBS/ DRAWINGS BY GAIGNIERES 703/1-8, TOMB OF CHILPERIC/ D584 703-1, TOMB OF CLOTHAIRE/ D628 703-2, TOMB OF HUGH CAPET AND ODO 703-3, TOMB OF ISABEL OF FRANCE 703-4, TOMB OF JEAN OF FRANCE 703-5, TOMB OF BLANCHE OF FRANCE/ DAUGHTER OF LOUIS 703/6-7, TOMB OF MARGARET OF SCOTLAND/ WIFE OF LOUIS XI 703-8

*$ABSTRACT 704
*LIBRARY ALL SOULS COLLEGE OXFORD
*SLIDE SET TITLE HOVEDEN ATLAS
*NEGATIVE REFERENCE ROLL 231
*RENTAL FEE $6.20
*COMMENTS MAPS OF COLLEGE ESTATES, DRAWN AND COLORED CHIEFLY BY THOMAS LANGDON FROM SURVEYS MADE BY THOMAS CLERK.
*TITLE OF MANUSCRIPT HOVEDEN ATLAS
*PROVENANCE ENGLISH
*DATE EXECUTED 16TH-17TH/ 1588-1605
*ARTIST/ SCHOOL LANGDON/ THOMAS
*TYPE OF MANUSCRIPT MAPS OF COLLEGE ESTATES
*CONTENTS HOVEDEN ATLAS 704/1-84, MAPS OF COLLEGE ESTATES 704/1-84, TOPOGRAPHY/ MAPS OF COLLEGE ESTATES 704/1-84, PORTFOLIO 1 704/1-30, ALL SOULS COLLEGE/ UNDATED 704-1, MAP OF PADBURY BUCKS/ 1591 704-2, MAP OF MAIDS MORTON BUCKS/ 1595 704-3, MAP OF MAIDS MORTON/ NW SECTION/ 1596 704-4, MAP OF MAIDS MORTON/ SW SECTION/ 1596 704-5, MAP OF MAIDS MORTON/ SOUTH SECTION/ 1595 704-6, MAP OF MAIDS MORTON/ NE SECTION/ 1595 704-7, MAP OF MAIDS MORTON/ SE SECTION/ 1595 704-8, MAP OF WEEDON WESTON NORTHANTS/ 1593 704-9, MAP OF WEEDON WESTON/ NW SECTION/ 1593 704-10, MAP OF WEEDON WESTON/ SW SECTION/ 1593 704-11, MAP OF WEEDON WESTON/ SOUTH SECTION/ 1593 704-12, MAP OF WEEDON WESTON/ NORTH SECTION/ 1593 704-13, MAP OF WEEDON WESTON/ NE SECTION 704-14, MAP OF WEEDON WESTON/ EAST SECTION/ 1593 704-15, MAP OF WEEDON WESTON/ LOWER SE SECTION/ 1593 704-16, MAP OF WEEDON WESTON/ UPPER SE SECTION/ 1593 704-17, MAP OF WAPPENHAM WILD AND WOODS NORTHANTS/ 1593 704-18, MAP OF WHADBOROUGH IN LEICESTERSHIRE/ 1586 704-19, MAP OF SANDEWELL FIELD IN BOSYATE NORTHANTS/ 1605 704-20, MAP OF DICHE FIELD IN BOSYATE NORTHANTS/ 1605 704-21, MAP OF WOODE FIELD IN BOSYATE NORTHANTS/ 1605 704-22, MAP OF SALFORD BEDS/ 1595 704-23, MAP OF SALFORD/ NW SECTION/ 1595-96 704-24, MAP OF SALFORD/ NE SECTION/ 1595-96 704-25, MAP OF SALFORD/ SW SECTION/ 1595-96 704-26, MAP OF SALFORD/ SE SECTION/ 1596 704-27, MAP OF HOLCOTE AND RICHMOND BEDS/ 1595 704/28-30, PORTFOLIO 2 704/31-66, MAP OF EDGEWARE MIDDLESEX/ 1599 704-31,

MAP OF EDGEWARE/ SOUTH SECTION /1597 704-32, MAP OF EDGEWARE/ WEST SECTION/ 1597 704-33, MAP OF EDGEWARE/ SE SECTION/ 1597 704-34, MAP OF EDGEWARE/ EAST SECTION/ EARLSBURY/ 1597 704-35, MAP OF EDGEWARE/ NW SECTION/ 1597 704-36, MAP OF EDGEWARE/ NORTH SECTION/ 1597 704-37, MAP OF EDGEWARE/ NE SECTION/ 1597 704-38, MAP OF KINGSBURY MIDDLESEX/ 1597 704-39, MAP OF KINGSBURY/ NW SECTION/ 1597 704-40, MAP OF KINGSBURY/ NE SECTION/ 1597 704-41, MAP OF KINGSBURY/ WEST SECTION/ 1597 704-42, MAP OF KINGSBURY/ EAST SECTION/ 1597 704-43, MAP OF KINGSBURY/ SW SECTION/ 1597 704-44, MAP OF KINGSBURY/ SE SECTION/ 1597 704-45, MAP OF HENDON MIDDLESEX/ 1597 704-46, MAP OF HENDON MIDDLESEX/ 1597 704-47, MAP OF HARLESDEN MIDDLESEX/ 1599 704-48, MAP OF HARLESDEN/ SE SECTION/ CHELSEA/ 1599 704-49, MAP OF HARLESDEN/ SW SECTION/ WILLESDEN/ FULHAM 704-50, MAP OF HARLESDEN/ NE SECTION/ CRICKLEWOOD/ 1599 704-51, MAP OF HARLESDEN/ NW SECTION/ NEASDON/ 1599 704-52, MAP OF HORSHAM KENT/ 1593 704-53, MAP OF BAUOR MARSH IN HORSHAM / 1593 704-54, MAP OF HORSHAM/ 1724 COPY OF LOST ORIGINAL 704-55, MAP OF NEWINGTON IN HORSHAM/ 1593 704-56, MAP OF NEWINGTON AND HARRIETSHAM IN HORSHAM 704-57, MAP OF RAINHAM AND HARTLIP KENT/ 1593 704-58, MAP OF UPCHURCH IN HORSHAM/ 1593 704-59, MAP OF SCOTNEY KENT/ 1588-89 704-60, MAP OF GOOGY HALL KENT/ 1589 704-61, MAP OF NEWLANDS KENT/ 1588-89 704-62, MAP OF ROMNEY MARSH AND HOPE KENT 704-63, MAP OF IVYCHURCH/ BROOKLAND/ APPLEDORE KENT/ 1589 704-64, MAP OF ROMNEY MARSH KENT/ 1592 704-65, MAP OF NORTH AND SOUTH WALLAND AND DENGEMARSH KENT 704-66, PORTFOLIO 3 704/67-87, MAP OF CRENDON BUCKS/ SOUTH SECTION/ 1593 704-67-68, MAP OF CRENDON/ EAST SECTION/ 1593 704-69, MAP OF CRENDON/ NORTH SECTION/ 1593 704-70, MAP OF CRENDON/ NE SECTION/ 1593 704-71, MAP OF LEWKNOR OXON/ 1598 704-72, MAP OF WHEATLEY OXON/ NW SECTION/ 1593 704-73, MAP OF WHEATLEY/ SW SECTION/ 1593 704-74, MAP OF WHEATLEY/ EAST SECTION/ 1593 704-75, MAP OF WHEATLEY/ SE SECTION/ 1593 704-76, MAP OF STANTON HARCOURT OXON 704-77, MAP OF ASTON'S EYT BERKS AND TETHERHILL BUCKS/ 1593-95 704-78, MAP OF LANGLEY MARSH BUCKS/ 1596 704-79, MAP OF LANGLEY MARSH/ WICKHAM/ 1596 704-80, MAP OF SOUTH PETHERTON IN SOMERSETSHIRE/ 1605 704-81, MAP OF SOUTH PETHERTON/ 1605 704-82, MAP OF SOUTH PETHERTON/ 1605 704-83, MAP OF ALBERBURY AND EYTON IN SHROPSHIRE/ 1602 704-84, MAP OF ALBERBURY / 1593 704/85-87

*$ABSTRACT 705
*LIBRARY BODLEIAN
*SLIDE SET TITLE ENGLISH CATS
*NEGATIVE REFERENCE ROLL 247F
*RENTAL FEE $2.50
*COMMENTS SELECTION FROM 10 ENGLISH MSS. OF THE 12TH-15TH CENTURIES.
*TITLE OF MANUSCRIPT CALENDAR/ TREATISE ON ASTRONOMY 705-1, BESTIARY 705-2, PSALTER 705-3, MEDICAL AND HERBAL TEXTS 705-4, BESTIARY 705-5, PORTABLE PSALTER 705-6, BESTIARY 705-7, BESTIARY 705-8, ORMESBY PSALTER 705-10
*SHELFMARK MS BODLEY 614/ FOL 3 705-1, MS ASHMOLE 1511/ FOL 35V 705-2, MS ASHMOLE 1525/ FOL 39 705-3, MS ASHMOLE 1462/ FOL 58V 705-4, MS BODLEY 764/ FOL 51 705-5, MS NEW COLLEGE 358/ FOL XV 705-6, MS UNIVERSITY COLLEGE 120/ P 24 705-7, MS DOUCE 88/ FOL 95 705-8, MS DOUCE 366/ FOL 131 705-9, MS BODLEY 546/ FOL 40V 705-10
*PROVENANCE ENGLISH 705/1 AND 4-5 AND 7-10, ENGLISH/ PETERBOROUGH? 705-2, ENGLISH/ CANTERBURY 705-3, ENGLISH/ ST ALBANS 705-6
*DATE EXECUTED 12TH/ MID 705-1, 13TH/ EARLY 705-2, 13TH/ 1ST QUARTER 705-3, 12TH/ LATE 705-4, 13TH/ 2ND QUARTER 705-5, 13TH/1246-60 705-6, 13TH-14TH 705-7, 14TH/C1300 705-8, 13TH-14TH 705-9, 15TH/ 2ND QUARTER 705-10
*TYPE OF MANUSCRIPT CALENDAR/ TREATISE ON ASTRONOMY 705-1, BESTIARY 705-2, PSALTER 705-3, MEDICAL AND HERBAL TEXTS 705-4, HERBAL 705-4, BESTIARY 705-5, PSALTER/ PORTABLE 705-6, BESTIARY 705/7-8, PSALTER 705-9, TREATISE ON HUNTING 705-10
*CONTENTS CATS ENGLISH 705/1-10, ANIMALS/ CATS 705/1-10,

ZOOLOGY/ CATS 705/1-10, CAT SITS WITH YOUTH BEFORE FIRE 705-1, JANUS FEASTING/ DETAIL OF CAT 705-1, CAT CLEANS ITSELF 705-2, CATS CATCH MICE 705-2, CAT STANDS AT LECTERN/ THREE RAT STUDENTS 705-3, CAT/ WHITE 705-4, CAT SLEEPING 705-5, CAT REACHES INTO BIRD CAGE 705-5, CAT LIFTS MOUSE OFF NEST OF EGGS 705-5, CAT HOLDS MOUSE 705-6, BEATUS PAGE FROM PORTABLE PSALTER 705-6, CAT CLEANS ITSELF 705-7, MOUSE ON NEST OF EGGS 705-7, CAT EATS RAT 705-8, CAT WAITS FOR RAT TO EMERGE FROM HOLE 705-9, CAT/ WILD 705-10

*$ABSTRACT 706

*LIBRARY BODLEIAN

*SLIDE SET TITLE CONTINENTAL CATS

*NEGATIVE REFERENCE ROLL 247G

*RENTAL FEE $2.85

*COMMENTS SELECTION FROM 16 MSS. OF 12TH-17TH CENTURIES.

*TITLE OF MANUSCRIPT PSALTER 706-1, ROMANCE OF REYNARD THE FOX AND ISENGRIN 706-2,BOOK OF HOURS 706-3, BESTIARY 706-4, BOOK OF HOURS 706/5-6, PORTABLE PSALTER 706-7, BOOK OF HOURS 706/8-12, BOOK OF PAPIRIUS 706-13, BOOK OF HOURS 706/14-15, SPECULUM HUMANAE SALVATIONIS 706-16, ALBUM AMICORUM 706-17

*SHELFMARK MS DOUCE 118/ FOL 134V 706-1, MS DOUCE 360/ FOL 6 706-2, MS DOUCE 80/ FOL 106V 706-3, MS BODLEY 533/ FOL 13 706-4, MS DOUCE 276/ FOL 53V 706-5, MS DOUCE 135/ FOL 17V 706-6, MS DOUCE 5/ FOL 44 706-7, MS CANON LITURG 92/ FOL 103 706-8, MS LITURG 58/ FOL 116V 706-9, MS DOUCE 112/ FOL 1V 706-10, MS ASTOR A 24/ FOL 2V 706-11, MS DOUCE 248/ FOL 210 706-12, MS RAWL C 328/ FOL 123V 706-13, MS DOUCE 29/ FOL 23V 706-14, MS DOUCE 29/ FOL 56 706-15, MS DOUCE 204/ FOL 24 706-16, MS ASHMOLE 1/ FOL 137 706-17

*PROVENANCE FRENCH/ ARTOIS 706-1, FRENCH 706/2-3, ENGLISH 706-4, FRENCH/ NORTH 706-5, FRENCH 706-6, FLEMISH/ GHENT 706-7, FLEMISH/ HAINAUT? 706-8, FLEMISH 706/9-10, FLEMISH/ BRUGES 706-11, DUTCH/ DELFT 706-12, ITALIAN/ SOUTH? 706-13, ITALIAN/ URBINO OR MANTUA 706/14-15, SPANISH/ CATALONIA/ ROUSSILLON 706-16, GERMAN 706-17

*DATE EXECUTED 13TH/ LATE 706-1, 14TH/1339 706-2, 15TH/ EARLY 706-3, 13TH/ MID 706-4, 16TH/ EARLY 706-5, 16TH/ 2ND QUARTER 706-6, 14TH/C1320-30 706-7, 15TH/C1430-40 706-8, 15TH/C1480 706-9, 16TH/ EARLY 706-10, 16TH/C1525 706-11, 15TH/ MID 706-12, 14TH/ MID 706-13, 16TH/C1530-38 706/14-15, 15TH/C1430-50 706-16, 17TH/1618-27 706-17

*LANGUAGE LATIN 706/1 AND 4-7, LATIN 706/9-11 AND 13-16, FRENCH 706-2, FRENCH AND LATIN 706/3 AND 8, DUTCH 706-12, GERMAN AND LATIN 706-17

*ARTIST/ SCHOOL BOUCICAUT AND BEDFORD MASTERS 706-3, MASTER OF DAVID SCENES IN GRIMANI BREVIARY 706-10, RAIMONDI/ VINCENZO 706-15, DYAMAS/ LAURENTIUS 706-16

*AUTHOR ALBUCASIS 706-13, LUDOLF VON DEM WERDER 706-17

*SCRIBE DYAMAS/ LAURENTIUS 706-16

*TYPE OF MANUSCRIPT PSALTER 706-1, ROMANCE 706-2, BOOK OF HOURS/ USE OF PARIS 706-3, BESTIARY 706-4, BOOK OF HOURS/ USE OF ROME 706/5-6, PSALTER/ PORTABLE 706-7, BOOK OF HOURS/ USE OF PARIS 706-8, BOOK OF HOURS/ USE OF ROME 706/9-10, BOOK OF HOURS 706/11-12, MEDICAL TREATISES 706-13, BOOK OF HOURS/ USE OF ROME 706/14-15, SPECULUM HUMANAE SALVATIONIS 706-16, ALBUM AMICORUM 706-17

*CONTENTS CATS/ CONTINENTAL 706/1-17, ANIMALS/ CATS 706/1-17, ZOOLOGY/ CATS 706/1-17, CAT WITH RAT IN MOUTH 706-1, TIBART THE CAT WAITS OUTSIDE RENART'S LAIR 706-2, CAT PLAYS ORGAN 706-3, ORGAN PLAYED BY CAT 706-3, CAT FOLLOWED BY SMALLER CAT 706-4, CATS/ TWO CHASE RAT 706-5, CAT/ FOX/ MONKEY FROM CREATION SCENE 706-6, CREATION OF ANIMALS 706-6, CAT WITH MOUSE IN MOUTH 706-7, CAT BEFORE VIRGIN AND CHILD 706-8, VIRGIN AND CHILD/ CAT IN FOREGROUND 706-8, CAT IN BACKGROUND OF VIRGIN AND CHILD SCENE 706-9, VIRGIN AND CHILD WITH CAT IN BACKGROUND 706-9,CAT SEATED ON WALL BEFORE SOLDIER WITH SPEAR 706-10, ST VERONICA LEGEND/ CAT SEATED ON WALL 706-10, CAT WATCHES WOMAN LAY A TABLE 706-11, WOMAN LAYING A TABLE 706-11, CAT HOLDS RAT 706-12, CAT WITH RAT IN MOUTH 706-13, CAT SITS

ON CRADLE OF ST JOHN BAPTIST 706-14, ST JOHN BAPTIST BIRTH SCENE 706-14, CAT AND TWO DOGS IN LAST SUPPER SCENE 706-15, LAST SUPPER/ CAT AND TWO DOGS IN FOREGROUND 706-15, CAT HISSING AT APE 706-16, BIRDS/ RABBIT/ OWL 706-16, FOX WITH COCK IN MOUTH 706-16, NEBUCHADNEZZAR'S DREAM/ DETAIL OF TREE 706-16,CATS ON COAT OF ARMS 706-17, COAT OF ARMS WITH TWO CATS 706-17

*$ABSTRACT 707
*LIBRARY BODLEIAN
*SLIDE SET TITLE DECORATION OF ITALIAN MANUSCRIPTS
*NEGATIVE REFERENCE ROLL 262A
*RENTAL FEE $14.95
*TITLE OF MANUSCRIPT DE AMICITIA/ DE OFFICIIS 707/1-3, PHARSALIA 707/4-5, TRAGEDIES BY SENECA 707/6-7, COMEDIES BY TERENCE 707/8-10, PTOLOMY 707-11, FIRST DECADE BY LIVY 707/12-13, DE IRA DEI 707/14-15, PHILIPPICS 707/16-17, LIVES OF PLUTARCH 707-18, DE INSTITUTIONE ORATORIA 707/19-20, PEREGRINA HISTORIA 707-21, GRAMMATICON 707-21, DE EXCIDIO TROIAE OF DARES PHRYGIUS 707-22, HOMILIES OF BASIL THE GREAT 707-23, INSTITUTIONES DIVINAE OF LACTANTIUS 707/24-26,EPITOME OF POMPEIUS TROGUS BY JUSTIN 707/27-28,COMMENTARY ON AVICENNA 707-29, FRANCISCAN BREVIARY 707/30-31, BOOK OF HOURS 707/32-35, DE BELLO ITALICO 707/36-37, POETICS OF ARISTOTLE 707/38-39, NATURAL HISTORY BY PLINY 707/40-41, DE MYSTICA THEOLOGIA 707-42, DE BELLO TROIANS 707-43, RHETORICA AD HERENNIUM 707/44-45, ANNALS OF TACITUS 707/46-50, TRIONFI BY PETRARCH 707/51-52, MEMORABILIA OF VALERIUS MAXIMUS 707/53-54, CATHOLICON OF JOHANNES DE BALBIS 707/55-57, COMMENTARY ON THE SONG OF SONGS 707/58-59, FIRST DECADE BY LIVY 707-60, DE INSTITUTIONE ORATORIA 707/61-63, COMMENTARY ON ARISTOTLE'S ETHICS 707-64, TRAGEDIES OF SENECA 707/65-66, COMEDIES OF TERENCE 707-67, ECHERINIS OF ALBERTINUS MUSSATUS 707-68, DEVOTIONAL TRACTS 707/69-71, DE INVENTIONE RHETORICA 707-72, LIFE OF ST LOUIS 707/73-74, ALMANSOR OF RHASIS 707-75, DE SIGNIFICATIONE VERBORUM 707/76-77, LETTERS AND TREATISES BY JEROME 707/78-79, RHETORICA AD HERENNIUM 707/80-81, MISSAL 707-82, DE VIRTUTIBUS 707-83, DISSERTATION AGAINST JEWISH ERRORS 707-84, WORKS BY VIRGIL 707-85, EPISTOLAE AD FAMILIARES 707-86, PHILIPPICS OF CICERO 707-87, VERRANIUM DE OPTIMO IMPERATORE 707/88-89, SALLUST 707/90-91, EPITOME OF POMPEIUS TROGUS 707/92-93, RHETORICA AD HERENNIUM 707-94, DE RATIONE BENE MORIENDI 707/95-96, DE MAGISTRATIBUS ROMANORUM 707/97-98, POEMS OF GIOVANNI PONTANS 707-99, WORKS OF VIRGIL 707/100-101, BOOK OF HOURS 707/102-103, EPISTOLAE AD FAMILIARES 707-104, LIVY 707/105-106, PRISCIAN 707-107, TRAGEDIES OF SENECA 707/108-111, HEROIDES OF OVID 707-112, OLD TESTAMENT 707/113-115, EPISTOLAE METRICAE 707/116-117, WORKS OF CLAUDIAN 707/118-119, LETTERS OF JEROME 707/120-124, TIBULLUS 707/125-126, EPISTOLAE AD FAMILIARES 707-127, METAMORPHOSES OF OVID 707/128-129, JUVENAL 707/130-131, LIBER DE INGENUIS MORIBUS 707-132, COMEDIES OF TERENCE 707-133, LIVES OF THE PHILOSOPHERS 707/134-136, LEONARDO BRUNI 707/137-138, ARS AMATORIA OF OVID 707-139, FACETIAE BY POGGIO 707-140, LIFE OF ST ALBAN 707/141-143, FIRST AND THIRD DECADES BY LIVY 707/144-146, SERMONS OF EPHRAIM 707-147, FILOCOLO BY BOCCACCIO 707/148-150, DE RERUM NATURA BY LUCRETIUS 707-151, COMMENTARY ON THE SATIRES OF JUVENAL 707/152-154, LAUS CALVITII BY SINESIUS CYRENENSIS 707/155-156, ASTRONOMICON 707/157-158, TIBULLUS 707-159, TUSCULAN DISPUTATIONS BY CICERO 707/160-161, LIVES OF THE TWELVE CAESARS BY SUETONIUS 707/162-163, DE ORATORE BY CICERO 707-164, TRISTIA BY OVID 707/165-168, EPIGRAMS BY MARTIAL 707/169-170, MARTYROLOGY BY PSEUDO JEROME 707-171, DIALOGUS INTER MICHROTYRUM ET THEOGENIUM 707-172, SATIRES BY JUVENAL 707-173, LA BELLA MANO 707/174-175, ARS COMPENDIOSA INVENIENDI VERITATEM 707-176, EPITOME OF POMPEIUS TROGUS 707-177, NOTITIA DIGNITATUM/ BRIEF ABSTRACT 707/178-179,DE DEVISIONE ORBIS OF ANTONIUS 707/178-179, DE VARIETATE FORTUNAE 707/180-181, DE RE MILITARI 707/182-183, LIBRO DELLE DONNE FAMOSE 707/184-185, WORKS OF VIRGIL

707/186-188, EPITOME OF POMPEIUS TROGUS 707/189-191, RHETORICA AD HERENNIUM 707/192-193, VARIOUS WORKS BY CAESAR 707/194-195, DE RE RUSTICA 707-196, EPISTOLAE AD FAMILIARES 707/197-198, FLORUS 707-199, COMEDIES BY TERENCE 707/200-201, IL CANZONIERE OF PETRARCH 707/202-203, LIVES OF ALEXANDER AND CAESAR 707/204-205, EPISTOLAE AD FAMILIARES 707-206, SATIRES BY PERSIUS 707-207, DE VERBORUM SIGNIFICATIONE BY FESTUS 707-208, BREVIARY 707/209-211, BOOK OF HOURS 707/212-213, THEBAIS BY STATIUS 707-214, METAMORPHOSES OF OVID 707-215, POMERIUM BY GERVASIUS RICCOBALDUS 707-216, COMMENTARY ON INSTITUTIONES OF JUSTINIAN 707-217, EPISTOLAE AD FAMILIARES 707/218-219, DE INVENTIONE RHETORICA BY CICERO 707-220, DE BELLO ITALICO BY LEONARDO BRUNI 707/221-222, SALLUST 707-223, DE RE COQUINARIA OF APICIUS 707-224, DE UTILITATE BY PLUTARCH 707/225-226, BOOK OF HOURS 707-227, HESPERIDES BY BASINIO DE BASINI OF PARMA 707-228, IL CANZONIERE BY PETRARCH 707-229, COMMENTARY ON HOMER 707-230, EPITOME OF LIVY BY FLORUS 707-231, ODES BY HORACE 707-232, INSTITUTIONES DIVINAE BY LACTANTIUS 707/233-234, DE VERBORUM SIGNIFICATIONE LIBER 707-235, INSTITUTIONES DIVINAE BY LACTANTIUS 707/236-238, ORATIONS BY CICERO 707-239, RES RUSTICA BY COLUMELLA 707/240-243, HISTORIA ALEXANDRI MAGNI 707/244-245, HOMILIES ON PROVERBS BY BASIL 707/246-248, DE RE MILITARI BY VEGETIUS 707/249-251, DE INSTRUENDIS ACIEBUS BY AELIAN 707/252-254, PONTIFICAL 707/255-256, AUGUSTINE 707-257, BOOK OF HOURS 707/258-259, DE NATURA DEORUM BY CICERO 707-260

*SHELFMARK MS CANON CLASS LAT 221/ FOL 18 707-1, MS CANON CLASS LAT 221/ FOL 58 707-2, MS CANON CLASS LAT 221/ FOL 71V 707-3, MS CANON CLASS LAT 68/ FOL 1 707-4, MS CANON CLASS LAT 68/ FOL 105V 707-5, MS D'ORVILLE 21/ FOL 41 707-6, MS D'ORVILLE 21/ FOL 118V 707-7, MS CANON CLASS LAT 98/ FOL 37 707-8, MS CANON CLASS LAT 98/ FOL 38 707-9, MS CANON CLASS LAT 98/ FOL 58V 707-10, MS MAGDALEN COLLEGE LAT 37/ FOL 61 707-11, MS DIGBY 224/ FOL 3 707-12, MS DIGBY 224/ FOL 106V 707-13, MS RAWL G 47/ FOL 23 707-14, MS RAWL G 47/ FOL 51 707-15, MS D'ORVILLE 76/ FOL 1 707-16, MS D'ORVILLE 76/ FOL 37V 707-17, MS CANON CLASS LAT 294/ FOL 155V 707-18, MS AUCT F 3 26/ FOL 34V 707-19, MS AUCT F 3 26/ FOL 299 707-20, MS D'ORVILLE 536/ FOL 8V 707-21, MS CANON CLASS LAT 158/ FOL 3 707-22, MS AUCT T 4 16/ FOL 1 707-23, MS CANON PAT LAT 162/ FOL 37 707-24, MS CANON PAT LAT 180/ FOL 1 707-25, MS CANON PAT LAT 180/ FOL 92V 707-26, MS CANON CLASS LAT 148/ FOL 1 707-27, MS CANON CLASS LAT 148/ FOL 96V 707-28, MS DIGBY 135/ FOL 1 707-29, MS CANON LITURG 201/ FOL 175 707-30, MS CANON LITURG 201/ FOL 213V 707-31, MS ASTOR A 6/ FOL 2 707-32, MS ASTOR A 6/ FOL 2 DETAIL 707-33, MS ASTOR A 6/ FOL 119V 707-34, MS ASTOR A 6/ FOL 137V 707-35, MS RAWL G 68/ FOL 2 707-36, MS RAWL G 68/ FOL 35V 707-37, MS CANON CLASS LAT 280/ FOL 2 707-38, MS CANON CLASS LAT 280/ FOL 93V 707-39, MS CANON CLASS LAT 295/ FOL 1 707-40, MS CANON CLASS LAT 295/ FOL 382 707-41, MS CANON MISC 534/ FOL 1 707-42, MS CANON CLASS LAT 267/ FOL 1 707-43, MS CANON CLASS LAT 228/ FOL 1 707-44, MS CANON CLASS LAT 228/ FOL 1 DETAIL 707-45, MS AUCT F 2 24/ PAGE 1 707-46, MS AUCT F 2 24/ PAGE 1 DETAIL TOP 707-47, MS AUCT F 2 24/ PAGE 1 DETAIL BOTTOM 707-48, MS AUCT F 2 24/ PAGE 74 707-49, MS AUCT F 2 24/ PAGE 238 707-50, MS CANON ITAL 72/ FOL 1 707-51, MS CANON ITAL 72/ FOL 19V 707-52, MS CANON CLASS LAT 259/ FOL 1 707-53, MS CANON CLASS LAT 259/ FOL 25V 707-54, MS CANON MISC 576/ FOL 1 707-55, MS CANON MISC 576/ FOL 1 DETAIL 707-56, MS CANON MISC 576/ FOL 246V 707-57, MS LAT TH C 14/ FOL 1 707-58, MS LAT TH C 14/ FOL 5 707-59, MS LAUD LAT 50/ FOL 189V 707-60, MS LAUD LAT 51/ FOL 1 707-61, MS LAUD LAT 51/ FOL 20V 707-62, MS LAUD LAT 51/ FOL 108V 707-63, MS CANON MISC 251/ FOL 2 707-64, MS AUCT F 1 14/ FOL 1 707-65, MS AUCT F 1 14/ FOL 62V 707-66, MS D'ORVILLE 155/ FOL 101 707-67, MS CANON CLASS LAT 110/ FOL 8 707-68, MS HOLKHAM MISC 12/ FOL 1 707-69, MS HOLKHAM MISC 12/ FOL 135V 707-70, MS HOLKHAM MISC 12/ FOL 131 707-71, MS D'ORVILLE 81/ FOL 1 707-72, MS CANON MISC 144/ FOL 75 707-73, MS CANON MISC 144/ FOL 99 707-74, MS CANON MISC 566/ FOL 1 707-75, MS CANON MISC 106/ FOL 61 707-76, MS CANON MISC 106/ FOL 175 707-77, MS CANON PAT LAT 224/ FOL 1 707-78, MS CANON PAT LAT 224/ FOL 14 707-79, MS CANON CLASS LAT 242/ FOL 29V

707-80, MS CANON CLASS LAT 242/ FOL 44V 707-81, MS CANON
LITURG 371/ FOL 7 707-82, MS CANON MISC 519/ FOL 1 707-83, MS
DOUCE 247/ FOL 1 707-84, MS CANON CLASS LAT 51/ FOL 101
707-85, MS CANON CLASS LAT 236/ FOL 1 707-86, MS CANON CLASS
LAT 219/ FOL 1 707-87, MS ADD B 59/ FOL 1V 707-88, MS ADD
59/ FOL 1 707-89, MS CANON CLASS LAT 134/ FOL 1 707-90, MS
CANON CLASS LAT 134/ FOL 15V 707-91, MS CANON CLASS LAT 146/
FOL 1 707/92-93, MS CANON CLASS LAT 249/ FOL 1 707-94, MS
LYELL 81/ FOL 1 707/95-96, MS BUCHANAN E 15/ FOL 1 DETAIL
707-97, MS BUCHANAN E 15/ FOL 1 WHOLE 707-98, MS CANON CLASS
LAT 123/ FOL 1 707-99, MS CANON CLASS LAT 65/ FOL 55 707-100,
MS CANON CLASS LAT 65/ FOL 138 707-101, MS CANON LITURG 140/
FOL 13 707-102, MS CANON LITURG 140/ FOL 132 707-103, PR AUCT
N INF 2 3 707-104, PR AUCT L 1 9 707-105, PR AUCT Q INF 2 2
707-106, PR AUCT O 4 1 707-107, MS CANON CLASS LAT 90/ FOL
WHOLF 707-108, MS CANON CLASS LAT 90/ FOL 1 DETAIL 707-109, MS
CANON CLASS LAT 90/ FOL 50V 707-110, MS CANON CLASS LAT 90/
FOL 63V 707-111, MS LAT CLASS D 8/ FOL 3 707-112, MS CANON
BIBL LAT 58/ FOL 1 707-113, MS CANON BIBL LAT 58/ FOL 5
707-114, MS CANON BIBL LAT 58/ FOL 346V 707-115, MS CANON MISC
101/ FOL 79V 707-116, MS CANON MISC 101/ FOL 120 707-117, MS
RAWL G 134/ FOL 3 707-118, MS RAWL G 134/ FOL 50V 707-119, MS
LAT TH C 31/ FOL 1 707/120-123, MS LAT TH C 31/ FOL 13
707-124, MS D'ORVILLE 166/ FOL 1 707-125, MS D'ORVILLE 166/
FOL 48 707-126, MS LAUD LAT 63/ FOL 1 707-127, MS ADD C 138/
FOL 1 707-128, MS ADD C 138/ FOL 12V 707-129, MS AUCT F 5 6/
FOL 3 707-130, MS AUCT F 5 6/ FOL 67V 707-131, MS CANON MISC
87/ FOL 1 707-132, MS CANON CLASS LAT 101/ FOL 20 707-133, MS
CANON CLASS LAT 186/ FOL 1 707-134, MS CANON CLASS LAT 186/
FOL 76V 707-135, MS CANON CLASS LAT 186/ FOL 206V 707-136, MS
CANON MISC 354/ FOL 1 707-137, MS CANON MISC 354/ FOL 1V
707-138, MS CANON CLASS LAT 22/ FOL 19V 707-139, MS RAWL C
567/ FOL 1 707-140, MS CANON PAT LAT 17/ FOL 1 707-141, MS
CANON PAT LAT 17/ FOL 19V 707-142, MS CANON PAT LAT 17/ FOL
43V 707-143, MS CANON CLASS LAT 298/ FOL 1 707-144, MS CANON
CLASS LAT 298/ FOL 97 707-145, MS CANON CLASS LAT 298/ FOL 14
707-146, MS CANON PAT LAT 211/ FOL 3 707-147, MS CANON ITAL
85/ FOL 10V 707-148, MS CANON ITAL 85/ FOL 43 707-149, MS
CANON ITAL 85/ FOL 50V 707-150, MS AUCT F 1 13/ FOL 4 707-151
MS ARCH SELD B 50/ FOL 3 707-152, MS ARCH SELD B 50/ FOL 13
707-153, MS ARCH SELD B 50/ FOL 47V 707-154, MS BODLEY 80/ FOL
4V-5 707-155, MS BODLEY 80/ FOL 8V 707-156, MS BODLEY 646/ FOL
1 707-157, MS BODLEY 646/ FOL 1V 707-158, MS LAUD LAT 78/ FOL
39 707-159, MS AUCT F 2 19/ FOL 1 707-160, MS AUCT F 2 19/ FOL
37V 707-161, MS CANON CLASS LAT 133/ FOL 1 707-162, MS CANON
CLASS LAT 133/ FOL 29 707-163, MS CANON CLASS LAT 247/ FOL 10
707-164, MS DCUCE 146/ FOL 1 707-165, MS DOUCE 146/ FOL 7
707-167, MS DOUCE 146/ FOL 138 707-168, MS AUCT F 4 33/ FOL
707-169, MS CANON CLASS LAT 85/ FOL 110V 707-170, MS CANON
LITURG 301/ FOL 1 707-171, MS CANON CLASS LAT 19/ FOL 7
707-172, MS CANON CLASS LAT 40/ FOL 2 707-173, MS CANON ITAL
56/ FOL 1 707-174, MS CANON ITAL 57/ FOL 1 707-175, MS CANON
MISC 123/ FOL 4V-5 707-176, MS D'ORVILLE 91/ FOL 99V 707-177
MS D'ORVILLE 147/ FOL 14 707-178, MS D'ORVILLE 147/ FOL 20
707-179, MS CANON MISC 557/ FOL 3 707-180, MS CANON MISC 557/
FOL 68 707-181, PR DOUCE 289 707/182-183, MS CANON ITAL 86/
FOL 3 WHOLE 707-184, MS CANON ITAL 86/ FOL 3 DETAIL 707-185
MS CANON CLASS LAT 61/ FOL 62 707-186, MS CANON CLASS LAT 61/
FOL 131V 707-187, MS CANON CLASS LAT 61/ FOL 132 707-188, MS
ADD C 283/ FOL 3V 707-189, MS ADD C 283/ FOL 32 707-190, MS
ADD C 283/ FOL 54V 707-191, MS D'ORVILLE 80/ FOL
707/192-193, MS CANON CLASS LAT 265/ FOL 1 707-194, MS CANO
CLASS LAT 265/ FOL 47V 707-195, MS LAT CLASS D 2/ FOL
707-196, MS CANON CLASS LAT 225/ FOL 1 WHOLE 707-197, MS CANON
CLASS LAT 225/ FOL 1 DETAIL 707-198, MS CANON CLASS LAT 194
FOL 2 707-199, MS CANON CLASS LAT 100/ FOL 3V 707-200, M
CANON CLASS LAT 100/ FOL 79 707-201, MS CANON ITAL 70/ FOL
707-202, MS CANCN ITAL 70/ FOL 144 707-203, MS RAWL G 87/ FO
2 707-204, MS RAWL G 87/ FOL 70V 707-205, MS D'ORVILLE 75/ FO
1 707-206, MS CANON CLASS LAT 45/ FOL 1 707-207, MS CANON MIS
158/ FOL 1 707-208, MS CANON LITURG 383/ FOL 7 WHOLE 707-209
MS CANON LITURG 383/ FOL 7 DETAIL 707-210, MS CANON LITUR

383/ FOL 12 707-211, MS CANON LITURG 131/ FOL 14 707-212, MS CANON LITURG 131/ FOL 142 707-213, MS CANON CLASS LAT 74/ FOL 1 707-214, MS CANON CLASS LAT 7/ FOL 1 707-215, MS CANON MISC 415/ FOL 14V 707-216, MS CANON MISC 477/ FOL 1 707-217, MS E D CLARKE 24/ FOL 1 707-218, MS E D CLARKE 24/ FOL 197V 707-219, MS CANON CLASS LAT 207/ FOL 1 707-220, MS LAT CLASS D 27/ FOL 1 WHOLE 707-221, MS LAT CLASS D 27/ FOL 1 DETAIL 707-222, MS D'ORVILLE 150/ FOL 1 707-223, MS CANON CLASS LAT 168/ FOL 1 707-224, MS CANON CLASS LAT 167/ FOL 1 707-225, MS CANON CLASS LAT 167/ FOL 38V 707-226, MS CANON LITURG 287/ FOL 62V-63 707-227, MS CANON CLASS LAT 81/ FOL 70V 707-228, MS DIGBY 141/ FOL 1 707-229, MS RAWL A 402/ FOL 2V 707-230, MS LAUD LAT 58/ FOL 1 707-231, MS CANON CLASS LAT 26/ FOL 1 707-232, MS AUCT F 2 27/ FOL 1 707-233, MS AUCT F 2 27/ FOL 73V 707-234, MS LYELL 74/ FOL 1 707-235, MS CANON PAT LAT 139/ FOL 1 WHOLE 707-236, MS CANON PAT LAT 139/ FOL 1 DETAIL 707-237, MS CANON PAT LAT 139/ FOL 81V 707-238, MS RAWL G 138/ FOL 67 707-239, MS CANON CLASS LAT 305/ FOL 1 WHOLE 707-240, MS CANON CLASS LAT 305/ FOL 1 DETAIL 707-241, MS CANON CLASS LAT 305/ FOL 3V 707-242, MS CANON CLASS LAT 305/ FOL 134V 707-243, MS CANON CLASS LAT 136/ FOL 1 707-244, MS CANON CLASS LAT 136/ FOL 141V 707-245, MS CANON GREEK 108/ FOL 2 707-246, MS CANON GREEK 108/ FOL 3V 707-247, MS CANON GREEK 108/ FOL 26 707-248, MS CANON CLASS LAT 274/ FOL 1V 707-249, MS CANON CLASS LAT 274/ FOL 37V 707-250, MS CANON CLASS LAT 274/ FOL 106V 707-251, MS LAT CLASS D 38/ FOL 1 WHOLE 707-252, MS LAT CLASS D 38/ FOL 1 DETAIL 707-253, MS LAT CLASS D 38/ FOL 6V 707-254, MS CANON LITURG 375/ FOL 1 WHOLE 707-255, MS CANON LITURG 375/ FOL 1 DETAIL 707-256, MS CANON PAT LAT 33/ FOL 1 707-257, MS CANON LITURG 263/ FOL 1 707-258, MS CANON LITURG 263/ FOL 81 707-259, PR AUCT L 3 5A 707-260

*PROVENANCE ITALIAN/ LOMBARDY 707/1-5, ITALIAN/ MILAN 707/6-7, ITALIAN/ LOMBARDY 707/8-11, ITALIAN/ MILAN 707/12-17, ITALIAN/ LOMBARDY 707/18-35, ITALIAN/ MILAN 707/36-37, ITALIAN/ VENICE? 707/38-39, ITALIAN/ LOMBARDY 707/40-41, ITALIAN/ MILAN 707-42, ITALIAN/ GENOA? 707-43, ITALIAN/ MILAN 707/44-45, ITALIAN/ GENOA 707/46-50, ITALIAN/ VENICE? 707/51-52, ITALIAN/ VENICE? 707-53-54, ITALIAN/ VENICE 707/55-57, ITALIAN/ VENICE? 707/58-59, ITALIAN/ BOLOGNA? 707-60, ITALIAN/ VENICE? 707/61-63, ITALIAN/ VENICE 707/64-68, ITALIAN/ VENICE? 707/69-71, ITALIAN/ NORTH-EAST 707-72, ITALIAN/ VENICE? 707/73-77, ITALIAN/ VENICE 707/78-79, ITALIAN/ NORTH-EAST 707/80-81, ITALIAN/ VENICE 707/82-83, ITALIAN/ VENICE OR VERONA 707-84, ITALIAN/ VENICE? 707-85, ITALIAN/ VENICE 707-86, ITALIAN/ VENICE? 707-87, ITALIAN/ VENICE 707/88-89, ITALIAN/ VENICE? 707/90-91, ITALIAN/ VENICE 707/92-93, ITALIAN/ VENICE? 707-94, ITALIAN/ VENICE 707/95-98, ITALIAN/ VENETO 707/99-101, ITALIAN/ VENICE 707/102-107, ITALIAN/ PADUA 707/108-112, ITALIAN/ PADUA OR VENICE 707/113-115, ITALIAN/ PADUA 707/116-117, ITALIAN/ MANTUA 707/118-119, ITALIAN/ PADUA 707/120-126, ITALIAN/ PADUA? 707-127, ITALIAN/ FERRARA? 707/128-129, ITALIAN 707/130-131, ITALIAN/ PADUA 707-132, ITALIAN/ FERRARA 707/133-138, ITALIAN/ NORTH-EAST 707-139, ITALIAN/ PADUA 707-140, ITALIAN/ FERRARA 707/141-143, ITALIAN/ MANTUA OR FERRARA 707/144-146, ITALIAN/ FERRARA OR PADUA 707-147, ITALIAN/ MANTUA OR FERRARA 707/148-150, ITALIAN/ PADUA 707/151-163, ITALIAN/ NORTH-EAST 707-164, ITALIAN/ PADUA OR ROME 707/165-169, ITALIAN/ VENICE 707-170, ITALIAN/ PADUA OR VENICE 707-171, ITALIAN/ VERONA? 707-172, ITALIAN/ VERONA 707/173-174, ITALIAN/ VERONA? 707/175-177, ITALIAN/ CREMONA-BOLOGNA 707/178-179, ITALIAN/ NORTH 707/180-181, ITALIAN/ VERONA 707/182-183, ITALIAN/ FERRARA? 707/184-191, ITALIAN/ FERRARA 707/192-205, ITALIAN/ FERRARA? 707/206-208, ITALIAN/ FERRARA 707/209-213, ITALIAN/ BOLOGNA 707/214-220, ITALIAN/ BOLOGNA? 707/221-222, ITALIAN/ BOLOGNA 707/223-227, ITALIAN/ RIMINI 707-228, ITALIAN/ ROME OR NAPLES 707-229, ITALIAN/ ROME? 707-230, ITALIAN/ CENTRAL 707-231, ITALIAN/ ROME 707-232, ITALIAN/ CENTRAL 707/233-234, ITALIAN/ ROME? 707-235, ITALIAN/ ROME 707/236-243, ITALIAN/ ROME? 707/244-245, ITALIAN/ ROME 707/246-248, ITALIAN/ NAPLES 707/249-254, ITALIAN/ NAPLES? 707/255-257, ITALIAN/ NAPLES 707/258-259, ITALIAN/ ROME? 707-260

*DATE EXECUTED 15TH/ MID 707/18-21, 15TH/ 3RD QUARTER 707-22, 15TH/ MID 707-23, 15TH/1461 707-24, 15TH/ MID 707/25-26, 15TH/1468 707/27-28, 14TH 707/1-3, 14TH/ LATE 707/4-5, 15TH/EARLY 707/6-10, 15TH/C1432 707/12-13, 15TH/144 707/14-15, 15TH/ 2ND QUARTER 707/16-17, 15TH/1458-64 707-29, 15TH/ MID 707/30-31, 15TH 707/32-35, 15TH/ 3RD QUARTER 707/36-37, 15TH/ 3RD QUARTER 707/38-39, 15TH/1479 707/40-41, 16TH/1500 707-42, 15TH/3RD QUARTER 707-43, 15TH/ MID 707/44-45, 15TH/1463 707/46-50, 15TH/ END 707/51-52, 15TH/C1400 707/53-54, 15TH/ EARLY 707/55-57, 15TH/ EARLY 707/58-59, 15TH/ EARLY 707-60, 15TH/ 1ST QUARTER 707/61-63, 15TH/1424 707-64, 15TH/ EARLY 707/65-66, 15TH/ 2ND QUARTER 707-67, 15TH/C1416 707-68, 15TH/1440 707/69-71, 15TH/ 2ND QUARTER 707-72, 15TH/ 3RD QUARTER 707/73-74, 15TH/1443-44 707-75, 15TH/ 3RD QUARTER 707/76-77, 15TH/1420 707/78-79, 15TH/ MID 707/80-81, 15TH/ 3RD QUARTER 707/82-86, 15TH/C1480 707-87, 15TH/1457-62 707/88-89, 15TH/ 3RD QUARTER 707/90-93, 15TH/C1470-80 707-94, 15TH/1471-87 707/95-96, 15TH/C1470-80 707/97-98, 15TH/ LATE 707/99-103, 15TH/1469 707-104, 15TH/1470 707-105, 15TH/1481 707/106-107, 14TH/ LATE 707/108-111, 15TH/C1400 707-112, 15TH/C1420-40 113-115, 15TH/1414-3 707/116-117, 15TH/ EARLY 707/118-119, 15TH/C1450-6 707/120-124, 15TH/ MID 707/125-126, 15TH/ 1455 707-127, 15TH/3RD QUARTER 707/128-129, 15TH 707/130-131, 15TH/147 707-132, 15TH/1446 707-133, 15TH/3RD QUARTER 707/134-136, 15TH/ MID 707/137-139, 15TH/1460 707-140, 15TH/146 707/141-143, 15TH/C1470-80 707/144-146, 15TH/ 3RD QUARTER 707-147, 15TH/C1463-64 707/148-150, 15TH/C1460 707/151-154, 15TH/C1461 707/155-156, 15TH/C1460 707/157-158, 15TH/ 3RD QUARTER 707/159-164, 15TH/ LATE 707/165-170, 15TH/1486-9 707-171, 15TH/ 3RD QUARTER 707-172, 15TH/1468 707-173, 15TH/1465 707-174, 15TH/ 3RD QUARTER 707/175-177, 15TH/1460-6 707/178-179, 15TH/ 3RD QUARTER 707/180-181, 15TH/147 707/182-183, 15TH/1418-24 707/184-185, 15TH/ 2ND QUARTER 707/186-191, 15TH/ 3RD QUARTER 707/192-193, 15TH/145 707/194-196, 15TH/1462 707/197-198, 15TH/ 3RD QUARTER 707/199-208, 15TH/1470 707/209-211, 15TH/ LATE 707/212-215, 15TH/ EARLY 707-216, 18TH/1720 707-217, 15TH/1449 707/218-219, 15TH/ MID 707-220, 15TH/ 3RD QUARTER 707/221-223, 15TH/149 707-224, 15TH/ LATE 707/225-227, 15TH/1457-68 707-228, 15TH/1465 707-229, 15TH/ MID 707-230, 15TH/1453 707-231, 15TH/ MID 707/232-235, 15TH/ 3RD QUARTER 707/236-245, 15TH/147 707/246-248, 15TH/1442-58 707/249-251, 15TH/C1455 707/252-254, 15TH/ 3RD QUARTER 707/255-256, 15TH/1457 707-257, 15TH/C1470-80 707/258-259, 15TH/1471 707-60

*LANGUAGE LATIN 707/1-11, ITALIAN 707/12-13, LATIN 707/14-22, GREEK 707-23, LATIN 707/24-50, ITALIAN 707/51-52, LATI 707/53-147, ITALIAN 707/148-150, LATIN 707/151-171, ITALIA 707-172 AND 174, LATIN 707/173 AND 175-183, ITALIA 707/184-185, LATIN 707/186-201, ITALIAN 707/202-203, LATI 707/204-228, ITALIAN 707-229, LATIN 707/230-245, LATIN AN GREEK 707/246-248, LATIN 707/249-260

*ARTIST/ SCHOOL PIETRO DA PAVIA/ CLOSE IN STYLE TO 707/1-3, MASTER OF THE VITAE IMPERATORUM 707/12-17, MASTER OF THE VITA IMPERATORUM/ RELATED TO 707-18, IPPOLYTA MASTER/ RELATED T 707/36-37, CORTESE/ CRISTOFORO 707/64-66, CORTESE/ CRISTOFORO, RELATED TO 707-67, BELLINI/ LEONARDO/ RELATED TO 707-82, MAESTRO DEI PUTTI/ RELATED TO 707/97-98, LODOVICO SANBONIFAZI OF PADUA 707/116-117, NICHOLAUS GERMINE DE CRIPIS 707/118-119, BENEDETTO BORDONE OF PADUA 707-171, FELICIANO/ FELICE 707/172-176, FELICIANO/ FELICE/ RELATED TO 707-177, FOUQUET, JEAN 707/209-211, SCHOOL OF NICCOLO DI GIACOMO DA BOLOGN 707-215, GIOVANNI DI BARTOLO BETTINI DA FANO 707-228, JOACHINUS DE GIGANTIBUS/ RELATED TO 707-229 AND 244-245, JOACHINUS DE GIGANTIBUS/ SCHOOL OF 707/258-259

*AUTHOR CICERO 707/1-3, LUCAN 707/4-5, TERENCE 707/8-10, PTOLOMY 707-11, LIVY 707/12-13, LACTANTIUS 707/14-15, CICER 707/16-17, PLUTARCH 707-18, QUINTILIAN 707/19-20, DECEMBRIO, PIERCANDIDO 707-21, PHRYGIUS/ DARES 707-22, BASIL THE GREA 707-23, LACTANTIUS 707/24-26, JUSTIN 707/27-28, GIOVANMATTE DE GRADI OF MILAN 707-29, BRUNI/ LEONARDO 707/36-37 ARISTOTLE/ TRANSLATED BY LEONARDO BRUNI 707/38-39, PLIN

707/40-41, HUGO DE BALMA 707-42, DICTYS CRETENSIS 707-43, BOETHIUS 707/44-45, TACITUS 707/46-50, PETRARCH 707/51-52, VALERIUS MAXIMUS 707/53-54, JOHANNES DE BALBIS 707/55-57, HONORIUS AUGUSTODUNENSIS 707/58-59, LIVY 707-60, QUINTILIAN 707/61-63, BURLEY/ WALTER 707-64, SENECA 707/65-66, TERENCE 707-67, MUSSATUS/ ALBERTINUS 707-68, BONAVENTURE 707/69-71, CICERO 707-72, RHASIS 707-75, FESTUS/ POMPEIUS 707/76-77, JEROME 707/78-79, PEYRAUT/ GUILLAUME 707-83, SAMUEL OF MOROCCO 707-84, VIRGIL 707-85, CICERO 707/86-87, ONOSANDER 707/88-89, SALLUST 707/90-91, JUSTIN 707/92-93, BAROZZI/ PIETRO 707/95-96, FENESTELLA/ LUCIUS 707/97-98, PONTANO/ GIOVANNI 707-99, VIRGIL 707/100-101, CICERO 707-104, LIVY 707/105-106, PRISCIAN 707-107, SENECA 707/108-111, OVID 707-112, PETRARCH 707/116-117, CLAUDIAN 707/118-119, JEROME 707/120-124, TIBULLUS 707/125-126, CICERO 707-127, OVID 707/128-129, JUVENAL 707/130-131, VERGERIO/ PP 707-132, TERENCE 707-133, LAERTIUS/ DIOGENES 707/134-136, BRUNI/ LEONARDO 707/137-138, OVID 707-139, POGGIO 707-140, LIVY 707/144-146, EPHRAIM 707-147, BOCCACCIO 707/148-150, LUCRETIUS 707-151, DA LONIGO/ OGNIBENE 707/152-154, SINESIUS CYRENENSIS 707/155-156, BASINIO DE BASINI OF PARMA 707/157-158, TIBULLUS 707-159, CICERO 707/160-161, SUETONIUS 707/162-163, CICERO 707-164, OVID 707/165-168, MARTIAL 707/169-170, JEROME/ PSEUDO 707-171, ALBERTI/ LB 707-172, JUVENAL 707-173, GUISTO DE CONTI 707/174-175, SIMONIDES 707-176, JUSTIN 707-177, ANTONIUS 707/178-179, POGGIO 707/180-181, VALTURIO/ R 707/182-183, BOCCACCIO 707/184-185, VIRGIL 707/186-188, JUSTIN 707/189-191, CAESAR 707/194-195, VARRO 707-196, CICERO 707/197-198, FLORUS 707-199, TERENCE 707/200-201, PETRARCH 707/202-203, PLUTARCH 707/204-205, CICERO 707-206, PERSIUS 707-207, FESTUS 707-208, STATIUS 707-214, OVID 707-215, RICCOBALDUS/ GERVASIUS 707-216, JOHANNES BAPTISTA CETTI OF BERGAMO 707-217, CICERO 707/218-220, BRUNI/ LEONARDO 707/221-222, SALLUST 707-223, APICIUS 707-224, PLUTARCH 707/225-226, BASINIO DE BASINI OF PARMA 707-228, PETRARCH 707-229, MARSUPPINI/ CARLO 707-230, FLORUS 707-231, HORACE 707-232, LACTANTIUS 707/233-234, VEGIO/ MAFFEO 707-235, LACTANTIUS 707/236-238, CICERO 707-239, COLUMELLA 707/240-243, RUFUS/ Q CURTIUS 707/244-245, BASIL 707/246-248, VEGETIUS 707/249-251, AELIAN 707/252-254, AUGUSTINE 707-257, CICERO 707-260

*SCRIBE JOHANNES/ SON OF GUIDO DE MALZINZELIS 707/6-7, DECEMBRIO/ PIERCANDIDO 707-18, GUARIMBERTIS/ THOMAS 707-21, THEODORE OF GAZA 707-23, UBERTUS DE GHIRINGHELIS 707-24, GULIELMUS BASCIERA DE CAMPO 707-29, HIERONIMUS BALIOCUS OF NOVARA 707/40-41, ZEBO DA FIRENZE/ RELATED TO 707-60, GODEFRIDUS JOHANNES DE JUTFAES 707-64, MAGISTER ANTONIUS 707-75, CATALDO/ ROGERIS 707/78-79, GRADENIGO/ GIOVANNI 707/90-91, MASTER OF THE MORGAN ARISTOTLE/ FOLLOWER OF 707-107, NIOLAUS PRESBYTER 707/108-111, BATTISTA SANSONE OF PADUA 707-112, NICHOLAUS GERMINE DE CRISPIS 707/118-119, SQUARA/ BART 707-132, JOP R 707-140, ANGELO AQUILANO 707/157-158, BARTOLOMEO SANVITO OF PADUA 707/165-169, SALLANDO/ PIERANTONIO 707-171, JOHANNES MICHAELIS CARAVAZIENSIS DE SPERONIS 707-173, FELICIANO/ FELICE 707/174-177, GEORGIUS/ CL 707/192-193, GERARDUS DE CAMPIS 707/194-195, ANTONIUS FARINA 707/197-198, FRATER HIE 707/202-203, JO ANTONIUS BONA 707-217, GENTILIS POETA CIVIS ET BONIS NOTARIUS 707/218-219, PIERANTONIO SALLANDO OF REGGIO 707/224-227, ANDREOCCIUS GERARDI OF SIENA 707-229, GUILIANO AMEDEI/ ATTRIBUTED TO 707/240-243, RHOSOS/ JOHANNES 707/246-248, CURLUS/ JACOBUS 707/249-251, PARUTA/ BARTHOLOMAEUS 707-257

*TYPE OF MANUSCRIPT CLASSICAL TEXT 707/1-20, RELIGIOUS TEXT 707-21, CLASSICAL TEXT 707-22, HOMILIES 707-23, CLASSICAL TEXT 707/24-28, COMMENTARY 707-29, BREVIARY/ USE OF ROME 707/30-31, BOOK OF HOURS 707/32-35, RELIGIOUS TEXT 707/36-37, POETICS 707/38-39, NATURAL HISTORY 707/40-41, RELIGIOUS TEXT 707-42, HISTORY 707-43, RHETORICAL TREATISE 707/44-45, ANNALS 707/46-50, LITERATURE 707/51-52, MEMORABILIA 707/53-54, RELIGIOUS TEXT 707/55-57, COMMENTARY 707/58-59, CLASSICAL TEXT 707/60-63, COMMENTARY 707-64, CLASSICAL TEXT 707/65-67, TREATISE 707-68, DEVOTIONAL TRACTS 707/69-71, CLASSICAL TEXT

707-72, SAINT'S LIFE 707/73-74, MEDICAL TEXTS 707-75, TREATISE 707/76-77, LETTERS AND TREATISES 707/78-79, RHETORICAL TREATISE 707/80-81, MISSAL/ USE OF ROME 707-82, RELIGIOUS TREATISE 707/83-84, CLASSICAL TEXT 707/85-87, TREATISE 707/88-89, CLASSICAL TEXT 707/90-91, EPITOME 707/92-93, RHETORICAL TREATISE 707-94, RELIGIOUS TREATISE 707/95-96, TREATISE 707/97-98, POETRY 707-99, CLASSICAL TEXT 707/100-101, BOOK OF HOURS/ USE OF VENICE 707/102-103, CLASSICAL TEXT 707/104-112, BIBLE/ OLD TESTAMENT 707/113-115, METRICAL TREATISE 707/116-117, CLASSICAL TEXT 707/118-119, LETTERS 707/120-124, CLASSICAL TEXT 707/125-131, RELIGIOUS TREATISE 707-132, CLASSICAL LITERATURE 707-133, LIVES OF PHILOSOPHERS 707/134-136, WORKS OF LEONARDO BRUNI 707/137-138, CLASSICAL TEXT 707-139, WORK BY POGGIO 707-140, SAINT'S LIFE 707/141-143, CLASSICAL LITERATURE 707/144-146, SERMONS 707-147, LITERATURE 707/148-150, CLASSICAL TEXT 707-151, COMMENTARY 707/152-154, TREATISE 707/155-156, TREATISE 707/157-158, CLASSICAL TEXT 707/159-170, MARTYROLOGY 707-171, TREATISE 707-172, CLASSICAL LITERATURE 707-173, LITERATURE 707/174-175, TREATISE 707-176, CLASSICAL TEXT 707-177, MISCELLANY 707/178-179, TREATISE 707/180-183, LITERATURE 707/184-185, CLASSICAL LITERATURE 707/186-191, RHETORICAL TREATISE 707/192-193, CLASSICAL TEXT 707/194-195, TREATISE 707-196, CLASSICAL TEXT 707/197-198, WORK BY FLORUS 707-199, CLASSICAL LITERATURE 707/200-201, LITERATURE 707/202-203, CLASSICAL LITERATURE 707/204-205, CLASSICAL TEXT 707-206, CLASSICAL LITERATURE 707-207, CLASSICAL TEXT 707-208, BREVIARY/ USE OF ROME 707/209-211, BOOK OF HOURS/ USE OF ROME 707/212-213, CLASSICAL LITERATURE 707/214-215, TREATISE 707-216, COMMENTARY 707-217, CLASSICAL TEXT 707/218-219, RHETORICAL TREATISE 707-220, TREATISE 707/221-222, CLASSICAL TEXT 707/223-226, BOOK OF HOURS/ USE OF ROME 707-227, LITERATURE 707-228, LITERATURE 707-229, COMMENTARY 707-230, EPITOME 707-231, CLASSICAL LITERATURE 707-232, CLASSICAL TEXT 707/233-234, TREATISE 707-235, CLASSICAL TEXT 707/236-243, HISTORY 707/244-245, HOMILIES 707/246-248, CLASSICAL TEXT 707/249-254, PONTIFICAL 707/255-256, CLASSICAL TEXT 707-257, BOOK OF HOURS/ USE OF ROME 707/258-259, CLASSICAL TEXT 707-260
*CONTENTS DECORATION OF ITALIAN MSS 707/1-260, ITALIAN MANUSCRIPTS 707/1-260, INITIALS FROM ITALIAN MSS 707/1-260, CAPITALS FROM ITALIAN MSS 707/1-260, INITIAL O AND PAGE WITH BORDER 707-1, INITIAL P AND TEXT PAGE 707-2, INITIAL S 707-3, INITIAL B WITH HISTORIATED FIGURE 707-4, INITIAL E 707-5, INITIAL C WITH HISTORIATED FIGURE 707-6, INITIAL WITH TONSURED MAN 707-7, INITIAL H AND RUBRICATED TEXT 707-8, INITIAL Q AND RUBRICATED TEXT 707-9, INITIAL S 707-10, INITIAL A 707-11, INITIAL I WITH HISTORIATED FIGURE 707-12, INITIAL I WITH HISTORIATED FIGURE 707-13, INITIAL Q 707-14, INITIAL F 707-15, INITIAL A WITH HISTORIATED SCENE 707-16, COAT OF ARMS 707-16, INITIAL N 707-17, INITIAL P 707-18, INITIAL T 707-19, INITIAL S 707-20, INITIAL P 707-21, INITIAL P WITH COAT OF ARMS 707-22, INITIAL M WITH COAT OF ARMS 707-23, INITIAL Q 707-24, INITIAL M 707-25, INITIAL U 707-26, INITIAL C 707-27, INITIAL P 707-28, INITIAL D 707/29-30, INITIAL D WITH HISTORIATED SKELETON 707-31, INITIAL D/ FULL PAGE WITH ANGELS/ COAT OF ARMS 707/32-33, COAT OF ARMS 707/32-33, INITIAL D 707-34, INITIAL D WITH VIRGIN AND CHILD 707-35, VIRGIN AND CHILD 707-35, INITIAL E/ FULL PAGE WITH FRUIT IN BORDERS 707-36, INITIAL C/ DETAIL 707-37, INITIAL I/ COAT OF ARMS IN INTERLACED BORDER 707-38, COAT OF ARMS 707-38, INITIAL Q 707-39, INITIAL L 707-40, INITIAL N 707-41, INITIAL A 707-42, INITIAL C/ COAT OF ARMS 707-43, COAT OF ARMS 707-43, INITIAL E 707-44, INITIAL E/ DETAIL 707-45, INITIAL N WITH HISTORIATED FIGURE 707-46, INITIAL N WITH HISTORIATED FIGURE/ DETAIL 707-47, BAGPIPES 707-48, INITIAL C/ DETAIL 707-49, INITIAL M 707-50, INITIAL N 707-51, INITIAL L 707-52, INITIAL A 707-53, INITIAL A 707-54, INITIAL P/ WHOLE PAGE 707-55, INITIAL P/ DETAIL 707-56, INITIAL N 707-57, INITIAL I 707-58, INITIAL O/ CROWNED VIRGIN PRAYS 707-59, VIRGIN? PRAYS 707-59, TEXT PAGE FROM LIVY 707-60, INITIAL Q 707-61, INITIAL T 707-62, INITIAL H 707-63, INITIAL U 707-64, INITIAL S WITH HISTORIATED FIGURE 707-65, INITIAL I 707-66, INITIAL A 707-67, INITIAL Q 707-68,

INITIAL S 707-69, SAINT KNEELING 707-70, VIRGIN AND CHILD 707-70, INITIAL F 707-71, INITIAL D 707-72, INITIAL I 707-73, INITIAL G 707-74, INITIAL I 707-75, INITIAL E WITH WOMAN'S HEAD 707-76, INITIAL U WITH GARLANDED HEAD 707-77, INITIAL P 707-78, INITIAL I 707-79, INITIAL A 707-80, INITIAL Q 707-81, INITIAL E/ BIRDS AND FLOWERS IN BORDER 707-82, INITIAL D/ FLORAL BORDER 707-83, INITIAL R WITH CLERICS 707-84, INITIAL A 707-85, INITIAL F 707-86, INITIAL A 707-87, FRONTISPIECE 707-88, INITIAL E 707-89, INITIAL O 707-90, INITIAL F 707-91, INITIAL P 707/92-93, INITIAL E 707-94, INITIAL M 707-95, PUTTI WITH COAT OF ARMS 707-96, COAT OF ARMS 707-96, INITIAL O 707/97-98, INITIAL I 707-99, INITIAL A 707-100, INITIAL T 707-101, INITIAL O WITH VIRGIN AND CHILD 707-102, VIRGIN AND CHILD 707-102, INITIAL D 707-103, INITIAL E 707-104, INITIAL I 707/105-106, INITIAL C WITH FIGURE WRITING 707-107, INITIAL S 707/108-109, INITIAL O 707-110, INITIAL I 707-111, INITIAL A 707-112, INITIAL A WITH SEATED FIGURE 707-113, INITIAL U WITH STANDING FIGURES 707-114, INITIAL S 707-115, INITIAL Q WITH COAT OF ARMS 707-116, COAT OF ARMS 707-116, INITIAL P 707/117-118, INITIAL Q 707-119, INITIAL C 707/120-122, BORDER DETAIL/ ST JOHN AS EAGLE? 707-123, INITIAL N 707-124, INITIAL D 707-125, INITIAL N 707-126, INITIAL Q 707-127, INITIAL I 707-128, INITIAL R 707-129, INITIAL S 707-130, INITIAL E 707-131, INITIAL F/ PUTTI WITH ARMS 707-132, COAT OF ARMS WITH PUTTI 707-132, INITIAL M 707-133, INITIAL V 707-134, INITIAL Q 707-135, INITIAL E 707-136, INITIAL V 707-137, INITIAL O 707-138, INITIAL D 707-139, INITIAL M 707-140, INITIAL E 707-141, INITIAL G 707-142, INITIAL A 707-143, INITIAL F 707-144, INITIAL H 707-145, INITIAL Q 707-146, INITIAL D 707-147, INITIAL S 707-148, INITIAL P 707-149, INITIAL A 707-150, INITIAL A 707-151, INITIAL Q 707-152, INITIAL U 707-153, INITIAL C 707-154, INITIAL S 707-155, INITIAL D 707-156, FRONTISPIECE 707-157, INITIAL A 707-158, INITIAL C 707-159, INITIAL C 707-160, INITIAL N 707-161, INITIAL I 707-162, INITIAL G 707-163, INITIAL I 707-164, INITIAL P 707-165, INITIAL M 707-166, INITIAL N 707-167, INITIAL V 707-168, INITIAL M 707-169, INITIAL N 707-170, INITIAL V 707/171-172, INITIAL S 707-173, INITIAL A 707/174-175, INITIAL H 707-176, INITIAL M 707-177, INITIAL I 707-178, PAGE WITH DATE 707-179, INITIAL M WITH COAT OF ARMS 707-180, COAT OF ARMS 707-180, INITIAL Q 707-181, INITIAL C 707-182, INITIAL M 707-183, COAT OF ARMS 707/184-185, INITIAL E AND A 707-186, INITIAL Q 707-187, INITIAL S 707-188, INITIAL P 707-189, INITIAL L 707-190, INITIAL A 707-191, INITIAL E 707-192, INITIAL O 707-193, INITIAL G 707-194, INITIAL Q 707-195, INITIAL S 707-196, INITIAL E WITH COAT OF ARMS 707-197, COAT OF ARMS 707-197, INITIAL E 707-198, INITIAL P 707-199, INITIAL V WITH HISTORIATED FIGURE 707-200, INITIAL A 707-201, INITIAL V WITH HISTORIATED FIGURE 707-202, INITIAL N 707-203, INITIAL R 707-204, INITIAL C 707-205, INITIAL E 707-206, INITIAL N 707-207, INITIAL A 707-208, INITIAL P 707/209-210, INITIAL D 707-211, INITIAL D WITH VIRGIN AND CHILD 707-212, VIRGIN AND CHILD 707-212, INITIAL D 707-213, INITIAL F 707-214, INITIAL I/ FIGURE CARRIES BANNER 707-215, INITIAL A 707-216, INITIAL Q WITH HISTORIATED FIGURE 707-217, INITIAL E 707-218, INITIAL F 707-219, INITIAL S 707-220, INITIAL F WITH COAT OF ARMS 707-221, COAT OF ARMS 707-221, INITIAL O 707-223, INITIAL C WITH COAT OF ARMS 707-224, COAT OF ARMS 707-224, INITIAL V 707-225, INITIAL I 707-226, TEXT PAGE/ PURPLE WITH GOLD LETTERS 707-227, INITIAL I/ PUTTI IN INTERLACED BORDER 707-228, INITIAL V/ INHABITED INTERLACE 707-229, INITIAL R 707-230, INITIAL P WITH COAT OF ARMS 707-231, COAT OF ARMS 707-231, INITIAL M WITH COAT OF ARMS 707-232, COAT OF ARMS 707-232, INITIAL M 707-233, INITIAL V 707-234, INITIAL A 707-235, INITIAL M WITH COAT OF ARMS 707-236, COAT OF ARMS 707-237, INITIAL C 707/238-239, INITIAL S WITH COAT OF ARMS 707-240, COAT OF ARMS 707-240, COAT OF ARMS 707-241, INITIAL Q 707-242, INITIAL C 707-243, INITIAL I 707-244, INITIAL A 707-245, INITIAL Q 707-246, INITIAL B 707-247, INITIAL A 707-248, KNIGHT ON HORSEBACK/ COAT OF ARMS 707-249, COAT OF ARMS 707-249, INITIAL S 707-250, INITIAL D 707-251, INITIAL C WITH COAT OF ARMS 707-252, COAT OF ARMS 707-253, INITIAL S

707-254, INITIAL P 707-255, COAT OF ARMS 707-256, INITIAL A WITH COAT OF ARMS 707-257, COAT OF ARMS 707-257, INITIAL D WITH VIRGIN AND CHILD 707-258, VIRGIN AND CHILD 707-258, INITIAL D WITH FIGURE 707-259, INITIAL Q 707-60

*$ABSTRACT 708
*LIBRARY BODLEIAN
*SLIDE SET TITLE MARTYROLOGY
*NEGATIVE REFERENCE ROLL 262B
*RENTAL FEE $2.90
*COMMENTS FRAGMENT OF A ROMAN MARTYROLOGY WITH FEASTS FOR PARTS OF JUNE, JULY, AND AUGUST. MARGINAL NOTES OF OBITS OF ABBOTS AND BENEFACTORS.
*TITLE OF MANUSCRIPT MARTYROLOGY
*SHELFMARK MS RAWL B 486/ FOLS 16-22V
*PROVENANCE IRISH/ ABBEY OF ST MARY/ NAVAN CO
*DATE EXECUTED 14TH
*LANGUAGE LATIN
*TYPE OF MANUSCRIPT MARTYROLOGY
*CONTENTS MARTYROLOGY/ IRISH / TEXT WITH OBITS 708/1-18, IRISH MARTYROLOGY 708/1-18, OBIT OF PATRITIUS CANTWELL 708-3, OBIT OF BARABAE DE ANGULO 708-16, OBIT OF PATRITIUS CANTWELL 708-17

*$ABSTRACT 709
*LIBRARY BODLEIAN
*SLIDE SET TITLE FIFTEENTH-CENTURY ENGLISH MINIATURES
*NEGATIVE REFERENCE ROLL 262C
*RENTAL FEE $3.65
*TITLE OF MANUSCRIPT PSALTER 709/1-2, SIEGE OF TROY BY JOHN LYDGATE 709/3-6, REGISTRUM BREVIUM 709-7, MISSAL 709/8-10, INDEX TO STATUTES OF ENGLAND 1444-45 709-11, BRIDGETTINE BREVIARY 709/12-15, PSALTER 709/16-20, ALCHEMICAL ROLL 709-21, GENEALOGY OF KINGS OF ENGLAND C1469-70 709-22, GENEALOGY OF KINGS OF ENGLAND C1467-69 709/23-24, GENEALOGY OF KINGS OF ENGLAND 709-25, MISSAL 709/26-27, ROMANCE OF ALEXANDER 709/28-29, ASTRONOMICAL CALENDAR 709-30, POEMS OF JOHN GOWER 709-31, ASTRONOMICAL CALENDAR 709-32, COMPENDIUM HISTORIAE IN GENEALOGIA CHRISTI 709-33
*SHELFMARK MS LAUD LAT 114/ FOL 7V 709-1, MS LAUD LAT 114/ FOL 127V 709-2, MS DIGBY 232/ FOL 1A 709-3, MS DIGBY 232/ FOL 3B 709-4, MS RAWL C 446/ FOL 1 709-5, MS RAWL C 446/ FOL 115 709-6, MS RAWL A 386/ FOL 83 709-7, MS TRINITY COLLEGE 8/ FOL 44V 709-8, MS TRINITY COLLEGE 8/ FOL 131V 709-9, MS TRINITY COLLEGE 8/ FOL 150 709-10, MS DOUCE 159/ FOL 1 709-11, MS AUCT D 4 7/ FOL 1 709-12, MS AUCT D 4 7/ FOL 73 709/13-14, MS AUCT D 4 7/ FOL 150 709-15, MS LITURG 153/ FOL 25 709-16, MS LITURG 153/ FOL 37V 709-17, MS LITURG 153/ FOL 49V 709-18, MS LITURG 153/ FOL 88 709-19, MS LITURG 153/ FOL 102 709-20, MS BODLEY ROLLS 1 709-21, MS LYELL 33/ FOL 1V 709-22, MS E MUSAEO 42/ FOL 1V 709/23-24, MS CORPUS CHRISTI COLLEGE OXFORD 207/ FOL 3V 709-25, MS ORIEL COLLEGE 75/ FOL 141 709-26, MS ORIEL COLLEGE 75/ FOL 143 709-27, MS BODLEY 264/ FOL 1 709-28, MS BODLEY 264/ FOL 2V 709-29, MS ASHMOLE 370/ FOL 27V 709-30, MS LAUD MISC 719/ FOL 21 709-31, MS SELDEN SUPRA 90/ FOL 11V 709-32, MS BARLOW 53 ROLL 709-33
*PROVENANCE ENGLISH
*DATE EXECUTED 13TH/MID 709/1-2, 15TH/ AFTER 1420 709/3-4, 15TH/ 2ND QUARTER 709/5-6, 15TH/ MID 709-7, 14TH/ BEFORE 1388 709/8-10, 15TH/ MID 709-11, 15TH/ 2ND QUARTER 709/12-15, 15TH/ EARLY 709/16-20, 15TH/ MID 709-21, 15TH/C1469 709-22, 15TH/C1467-69 709/23-24, 15TH/ MID 709-25, 15TH/ EARLY 709/26-27, 15TH/C1400 709/28-29, 15TH/C1424 709-30, 15TH 709-31, 15TH/C1434 709-32, 15TH/C1420-30 709-33
*LANGUAGE LATIN 709/1-2, ENGLISH 709/3-6, LATIN 709/5-10, FRENCH 709-11, LATIN 709/12-20, ENGLISH AND LATIN 709-21, ENGLISH 709/22-25, LATIN 709/26-27, ENGLISH 709/28-29, ENGLISH AND LATIN 709-30, ENGLISH 709-31, ENGLISH AND LATIN 709-32, ENGLISH 709-33

*AUTHOR LYDGATE/ JOHN 709/3-6, RIPLEY/ GEORGE 709-21, NICHOLAS OF LYNN 709-30, GOWER/ JOHN 709-31, SOMER/ JOHN 709-32, PETER OF POITIERS 709-33
*TYPE OF MANUSCRIPT PSALTER 709/1-2, LITERATURE 709/3-6, REGISTER 709-7, MISSAL/ USE OF SARUM 709/8-10, INDEX TO STATUTES 709-11, BREVIARY 709/12-15, PSALTER 709/16-20, ALCHEMICAL TEXT 709-21, GENEALOGY 709/22-25, MISSAL/ USE OF SARUM 709/26-27, ROMANCE 709/28-29, ASTRONOMICAL CALENDAR 709/30 AND 32, POETRY 709-31, RELIGIOUS TREATISE 709-33
*CONTENTS ENGLISH MINIATURES AND INITIALS 709/1-33, FIFTEENTH CENTURY ILLUMINATION 709/1-33, INITIAL B/ DAVID PLAYS HARP 709-1, DAVID PLAYS HARP 709-1, HARP PLAYED BY DAVID 709-1, INITIAL C/ DAVID WITH CHOIR 709-2, DAVID WITH CHOIR 709-2, CHOIR WITH DAVID 709-2, LYDGATE PRESENTS BOOK TO KING HENRY V 709-3, AUTHOR PORTRAIT OF JOHN LYDGATE 709-3, PELEUS PRAYS/ PLAGUE STRIKES THESSALY/ ANTS 709-4, PLAGUE STRIKES THESSALY 709-4, LYDGATE PRESENTS BOOK TO KING HENRY VI 709-5, AUTHOR PORTRAIT OF JOHN LYDGATE 709-5, AGAMEMNON AND THE WOUNDED ACHILLES 709-6, KING ENTHRONED SPEAKING TO LAWYERS 709-7, ADORATION OF MAGI 709-8, RESURRECTION 709-9, PENTECOST 709-10, LAWYERS DEBATING 709-11, GOD BLESSING 709-12, BEATUS PAGE/ DAVID PLAYS HARP 709-13, DAVID PLAYS HARP 709-13, HARP PLAYED BY DAVID 709-13, BEATUS PAGE/ DAVID PLAYS HARP 709-14, DAVID PLAYS HARP 709-14, HOLY GHOST AS DOVE 709-15, DOVE AS HOLY GHOST 709-15, INITIAL D DOMINUS ILLUMINATIO/ DAVID POINTS TO EYE 709-16, DAVID POINTS TO HIS EYES 709-16, INITIAL D DIXI CUSTODIAM/ DAVID ENTHRONED 709-17, DAVID ENTHRONED 709-17, INITIAL D DIXIT INSIPIENS/ FOOL 709-18, FOOL WITH JESTER'S COSTUME AND WAND 709-18, INITIAL C CANTATE DOMINO/ MONKS SINGING 709-19, MONKS SINGING 709-19, INITIAL D DIXIT DOMINUS/ TWO GOD-LIKE FIGURES CONVERSE 709-20, GOD-LIKE FIGURES CONVERSE 709-20, ALCHEMICAL SCENES IN ROUNDELS FORM A WHEEL 709-21, ADAM AND EVE TEMPTED BY SERPENT WITH WOMAN'S FACE 709/22-25, SERPENT WITH WOMAN'S FACE TEMPTS ADAM AND EVE 709/22-25, ABRAHAM PREPARES TO SACRIFICE ISAAC 709-26, ABRAHAM MEETS WITH MELCHIZEDEK 709-27, NECTANEBOR'S PALACE/ TOWN BY RIVER/ SHIPS 709-28, LIFE OF ALEXANDER/ FOUR SCENES 709-29, ZODIACAL MAN 709-30, ARCHER DRAWS BOW 709-31, ZODIACAL MAN 709-32, ADAM AND EVE TEMPTED BY SERPENT WITH WOMAN'S FACE 709-33

*$ABSTRACT 710
*LIBRARY BODLEIAN
*SLIDE SET TITLE OWLS
*NEGATIVE REFERENCE ROLL 262D
*RENTAL FEE $2.80
*COMMENTS SELECTED FROM TWELVE MSS. OF THE 13TH-17TH CENTURIES.
*TITLE OF MANUSCRIPT ALBUM AMICORUM 710-1, BESTIARY 710/2-5, BOOK OF HOURS 710-6, CHOIR BREVIARY 710-7, ACTS OF QUEEN ELIZABETH 710-8, BOOK OF HOURS 710/9-16
*SHELFMARK MS AUTOGR G 3/ FOL 5V 710-1, MS BODLEY 533/ FOL 18 710-2, MS BODLEY 602/ FOL 64 710-3, MS BODLEY 602/ FOL 64V 710-4, MS BODLEY 764/ FOL 73V 710-5, MS BUCHANAN E 4/ FOL 166V 710-6, MS CANON LITURG 383/ FOL 65V 710-7, MS ENG HIST E 198/ FOL 43 710-8, MS DOUCE 77/ FOL 63V 710-9, MS DOUCE 152/ FOL 21 710-10, MS DOUCE 152/ FOL 53 710-11, MS DOUCE 152/ FOL 70 710-12, MS DOUCE 253/ FOL 100 710-13, MS DOUCE 276/ FOL 2V 710-14, MS DOUCE 311/ FOL 22 710/15-16
*PROVENANCE GERMAN/ BAVARIA 710-1, ENGLISH 710/2-5, FRENCH 710-6, ITALIAN/ NORTH 710-7, ENGLISH 710-8, FRENCH 710/9-14, FLEMISH 710/15-16
*DATE EXECUTED 17TH/1631-33 710-1, 13TH/ MID 710-2, 13TH/ 2ND QUARTER 710/3-5, 15TH/ LATE 710-6, 15TH/C1470 710-7, 17TH/C1600 710-8, 15TH/1450-70 710-9, 15TH/ LATE 710/10-12, 15TH/C1480 710-13, 16TH/ EARLY 710-14, 15TH/ AFTER 1488 710/15-16
*LANGUAGE LATIN 710/1-5, FRENCH AND LATIN 710-6, LATIN 710-7, ENGLISH 710-8, FRENCH AND LATIN 710-9, LATIN 710/10-12, FRENCH AND LATIN 710-13, LATIN 710/14-16

*ARTIST/ SCHOOL SCHOOL OF MATTHEW PARIS 710/3-4, SCHOOL OF MAITRE FRANCOIS 710-6, SCHOOL OF BOURDICHON 710-6
*AUTHOR SPEIDL/ G F 710-1, WOODWALL/ WILLIAM 710-8
*TYPE OF MANUSCRIPT ALBUM AMICORUM 710-1, BESTIARY 710/2-5, BOOK OF HOURS/ USE OF ROME 710-6, BREVIARY 710-7, ACTS OF QUEEN ELIZABETH 710-8, BOOK OF HOURS 710-9, BOOK OF HOURS/ USE OF AMIENS 710/10-12, BOOK OF HOURS/ USE OF ROUEN 710-13, BOOK OF HOURS/ USE OF ROME 710/14-16
*CONTENTS OWLS 710/1-16, ANIMALS/ OWLS 710/1-16, ZOOLOGY/ OWLS 710/1-16

*$ABSTRACT 711
*LIBRARY BODLEIAN
*SLIDE SET TITLE ENGLISH BOOK PRODUCTION
*NEGATIVE REFERENCE ROLL 262E
*RENTAL FEE $2.55
*COMMENTS SELECTED FROM FOUR MSS. OF 13TH-14TH CENTURIES.
*TITLE OF MANUSCRIPT ORMESBY PSALTER 711/1-2, BIBLE 711/3-5, BIBLE 711/6-7, PSALTER 711/8-11
*SHELFMARK MS DOUCE 366/ FOL 9V 711-1, MS DOUCE 366/ FOL 10 711-2, MS AUCT D 3 2/ FOL 156 711-3, MS AUCT D 3 2/ FOL 198 711-4, MS AUCT D 3 2/ FOL 360 711-5, MS AUCT D 4 8/ FOL 333 711-6, MS AUCT D 4 8/ FOL 333V 711-7, MS BARLOW 22/ FRONT COVER 711-8, MS BARLOW 22/ FOL 4V-5 711-9, MS BARLOW 22/ FOL 13 711-10, MS BARLOW 22/ FOL 53 711-11
*PROVENANCE ENGLISH/ EAST ANGLIA 711/1-2, ENGLISH 711/3-7, ENGLISH/ PETERBOROUGH 711/8-11
*DATE EXECUTED 14TH/C1310 711-1, 14TH/C1320-30 711-2, 13TH/ END 711/3-5, 13TH/ 3RD QUARTER 711/6-7, 14TH/C1321-41 711/8-11
*LANGUAGE LATIN
*TYPE OF MANUSCRIPT PSALTER 711/1-2, BIBLE 711/3-7, PSALTER 711/8-11
*CONTENTS BOOK PRODUCTION 711/1-11, BEATUS PAGE WITH JESSE TREE 711-1, JESSE TREE 711-1, FOLIOT AND BARDOLF/ OWNER PORTRAIT 711-1, BISHOP OF NORWICH AND ROBERT OF ORMESBY 711-1,BEATUS PAGE WITH INITIAL OF DAVID PLAYING HARP 711-2, DAVID PLAYS HARP 711-2, HARP PLAYED BY DAVID 711-2, INITIAL I/ RED AND BLUE DECORATION 711-3, BEATUS PAGE 711-4, DAVID PLAYS HARP 711-4, VIRGIN AND CHILD 711-4, DAVID AND GOLIATH 711-4, INITIAL L/ RED AND BLUE DECORATION 711-5, ANGEL IN BORDER 711-5, PSALM 80/ INITIAL L LAUDATE/ DAVID PLAYS FIDDLE 711-6, INITIAL L LAUDATE/ DAVID PLAYS FIDDLE 711-6, DAVID PLAYS FIDDLE 711-6, FIDDLE PLAYED BY DAVID 711-6, PSALM 83 AND 84/ DECORATED INITIALS 711-7, BOOK COVER SHOWING BINDING THONGS 711-8, CALENDAR PAGE FROM PSALTER 711-9, CHRIST PREACHING SERMON ON THE MOUNT 711-10, CHRIST ARRESTED 711-10, CHRIST SCOURGED 711-10, CHRIST CARRIES CROSS 711-10, INITIAL D DIXI CUSTODIAM/ DAVID PRAYS 711-11, DAVID PRAYS 711-11

*$ABSTRACT 712
*LIBRARY BODLEIAN
*SLIDE SET TITLE ORMESBY PSALTER
*NEGATIVE REFERENCE ROLL 262F
*RENTAL FEE $3.10
*TITLE OF MANUSCRIPT ORMESBY PSALTER
*SHELFMARK MS DOUCE 366/ FOL 9V-10 712-1, MS DOUCE 366/ FOL 55V 712/2-4, MS DOUCE 366/ FOL 71V 712/5-6, MS DOUCE 366/ FOL 72 712/7-8, MS DOUCE 366/ FOL 89 712/9-11, MS DOUCE 366/ FOL 109 712/12-15, MS DOUCE 366/ FOL 128 712/16-19, MS DOUCE 366/ FOL 131 712/20-22
*PROVENANCE ENGLISH/ EAST ANGLIA
*DATE EXECUTED 13TH/ LATE TO C1300
*LANGUAGE LATIN
*TYPE OF MANUSCRIPT PSALTER
*CONTENTS ORMESBY PSALTER 712/1-22, PSALTER/ ENGLISH/ 13TH 712/1-22, BEATUS PAGES/ DOUBLE OPENING 712-1, JESSE TREE WITH DONER AND OTHER FIGURES 712-1,DAVID PLAYS HARP 712-1, HARP PLAYED BY DAVID 712-1, PSALM 38/39 INITIAL D DIXI CUSTODIAM/

TRIAL OF CHRIST 712-2, INITIAL D DIXI CUSTODIAM/ TRIAL OF CHRIST 712-2, CHRIST'S TRIAL 712/2-3, UNICORN IN VIRGIN'S LAP SPEARED BY HUNTER 712-4, PSALM 51/52 INITIAL Q QUID GLORIARIS/ STOLEN COCK 712-5, INITIAL Q QUID GLORIARIS / STOLEN COCK 712-5, COCK STOLEN 712/5-6, PSALM 52/53 INITIAL D DIXIT INSIPIENS/ RIDDLE 712-7, INITIAL D DIXIT INSIPIENS/ RIDDLE 712-7, RIDDLE OF WHO COMES NEITHER DRIVING NOR WALKING 712-8, PSALM 68/69 INITIAL S SALVUM ME FAC/ JONAH 712-9, INITIAL S SALVUM ME FAC/ JONAH AND WHALE 712-9, JONAH AND THE WHALE 712/9-10, RIDDLE OF LAMB/ WOLF AND GREEN FOOD 712-11, PSALM 80/81 INITIAL E EXULTATE DEO/ DAVID AND MUSICIANS 712-12, INITIAL E EXULTATE DEO/ DAVID AND MUSICIANS 712-12, DAVID AND MUSICIANS 712/12-13, MUSICIANS WITH BELLS/ HORN AND HARP 712-13, WRESTLERS IN BORDER 712-14, MAN FRIGHTENED BY SNAIL 712-15, SNAIL FRIGHTENS MAN 712-15, PSALM 97/98 INITIAL C CANTATE DOMINO/ CHOIR SINGS 712-16, INITIAL C CANTATE DOMINO/ CHOIR SINGS 712-16, CHOIR SINGS 712/16-17, KNIGHT FIGHTS BEAST 712-18, PRUNING VINES 712-19, PSALM 101/102 INITIAL D DOMINE EXAUDI/ CHRIST AND DAVID 712-20, INITIAL D DOMINE EXAUDI/ CHRIST AND DAVID 712-20, CHRIST AND DAVID 712/20-21, GIFT OF A RING 712-22, CAT WATCHING RAT HOLE 712-22

*$ABSTRACT 713
*LIBRARY UTRECHT UNIVERSITY LIBRARY
*SLIDE SET TITLE UTRECHT PSALTER
*NEGATIVE REFERENCE ROLL 263A
*RENTAL FEE $3.55
*COMMENTS REPHOTOGRAPHED IN BLACK AND WHITE FROM FACSIMILE PUBLISHED IN 1873.
*TITLE OF MANUSCRIPT UTRECHT PSALTER
*PROVENANCE GERMAN/ UTRECHT
*DATE EXECUTED 09TH/ EARLY
*LANGUAGE LATIN
*ARTIST/ SCHOOL SCHOOL OF RHEIMS
*TYPE OF MANUSCRIPT PSALTER
*CONTENTS UTRECHT PSALTER 713/1-31, PSALTER/ GERMAN/ 9TH 713/1-31, PSALM 1/ THE BLESSED MAN 713-1, PSALM 2/ POTTER'S WHEEL 713-2, PSALM 3/ IMPRESSIONISTIC TREES 713-3, PSALM 19/20 BEEHIVE 713-4, PSALM 22/23 STILL WATERS/ HORN OF OIL 713-5, PSALM 25/26 AQUEDUCT/ FOUNTAIN/ BUILDINGS 713-6, PSALM 26/27 BATTLE/ TENTS/ BUILDINGS 713-7, PSALM 47/48 VIKING BOATS/ DANCERS 713-8, PSALM 51/52 DOEG 713-9, DOEG 713-9, PSALM 63/64 SHARPENING SWORDS/ ANGEL PROTECTS PSALMIST 713-10, SWORD SHARPENING 713-10, ANGEL PROTECTS PSALMIST 713-10, PSALM 72/73 MARE AND COLT/ IDOL/ SINNERS 713-11, MARE AND COLT 713-11, IDOL 713-11, SINNERS 713-11, PSALM 74/74 NATIVITY/ MIDWIVES/ DRAGONS 713-12, NATIVITY 713-12, MIDWIVES 713-12, DRAGONS 713-12, PSALM 77/78 CROWD/ THE LAW/ DAVID/ UNICORN 713-13, DAVID 713-13, UNICORN 713-13, PSALM 79/80 SHADOW/ WALL BROKEN/ BOAR SPOILS WINE 713-14, PSALM 80/81 HARP/ TRUMPET/ WHEAT/ HONEY 713-15, HARP 713-15, TRUMPET 713-15, PSALM 83/84 SIEGE/ NESTLINGS FED 713-16, SIEGE 713-16, NESTLINGS FED 713-16, PSALM 84/85 OXEN/ PLOUGH/ REAPING/ SICKLES 713-17, OXEN AND PLOUGH 713-17, REAPING 713-17, SICKLES 713-17, PSALM 92/93 RIVER/ GOD/ THRONE 713-18, PSALM 107/108 PSALTERY/ HARP/ MEASURING ROD 713-19, PSALTERY AND HARP 713-19, PSALM 110/111 LANDSCAPE/ TABLE/ FOOD VESSALS 713-20, PSALM 111/112 PALACE/ THE POOR/ THE WICKED 713-21, PSALM 112/113 CITY/ FURNITURE/ PRINCES/ MOTHER 713-22, PSALM 115/116 CRUCIFIXION/ CHALACE/ MARTYRS 713-23, CRUCIFIXION 713-23, CHALICE 713-23, MARTYRS 713-23, PSALM 124/125 MOUNTAINS 713-24, PSALM 125/126 CAPTIVITY/ SOWING IN TEARS/ REAPING 713-24, CAPTIVITY 713-24, SOWING IN TEARS 713-24, REAPING 713-24, PSALM 126/127 ENEMIES IN THE GATE 713-25, ENEMIES IN THE GATE 713-25, PSALM 127/128 VINE/ CHILDREN AT TABLE 713-25, PSALM 128/129 MOWING/ SCYTHES/ SHEAVES 713-26, MOWING 713-26, SCYTHES 713-26, SHEAVES 713-26, PSALM 147/148 SUN AND MOON/ FIRE/ HILLS/ TREES/ BEASTS 713-27, SUN AND MOON 713-27, SERPENT/ FOWLS/ KINGS/ YOUTHS/ MAIDENS 713-27, PSALM 149/150 SINGING/ SWORDS/ STOCKS/ CHAINS 713-28, PSALM 150/151 PSALTERY/ HARP/ ORGAN 713-28, PSALTERY/ HARP/

ORGAN 713-28, ISAIAH XVVVIII VERSES 10-20/ CANTICLE EGO DIXI 713-29, LUKE 01/VERSES 68-79/ CANTICLE BENEDICTUS 713-30, NATIVITY 713-30, STAR OVER HOUSE OF DAVID 713-30, FIDES CATHOLICA 713-31, PSALM 151 APOCRYPHAL/ SAUL/ DAVID AND GOLIATH 713-32, SAUL 713-32, DAVID AND GOLIATH 713-32

*$ABSTRACT 714
*LIBRARY BODLEIAN
*SLIDE SET TITLE ALBUM AMICORUM
*NEGATIVE REFERENCE ROLL 263B AND C
*RENTAL FEE $3.40
*TITLE OF MANUSCRIPT ALBUM AMICORUM OF PAUL VAN DALE 714/1-14, ALBUM AMICORUM OF FRIEDRICH RECHLINGER 714/15-28
*SHELFMARK MS DOUCE D 11/ FOL 2 714-1, MS DOUCE D 11/ FOL 5 714-2, MS DOUCE D 11/ FOL 9 714-3, MS DOUCE D 11/ FOL 10 714-4, MS DOUCE D 11/ FOL 12 714-5, MS DOUCE D 11/ FOL 15 714-6, MS DOUCE D 11/ FOL 16 714-7, MS DOUCE D 11/ FOL 19 714-8, MS DOUCE D 11/ FOL 29 714-9, MS DOUCE D 11/ FOL 30 714-10, MS DOUCE D 11/ FOL 32 714-11, MS DOUCE D 11/ FOL 33 714-12, MS DOUCE D 11/ FOL 36 714-13, MS DOUCE D 11/ FOL 43 714-14, MS DOUCE 244/ FOL 34 714-15, MS DOUCE 244/ FOL 35 714-16, MS DOUCE 244/ FOL 36 714-17, MS DOUCE 244/ FOL 37 714-18, MS DOUCE 244/ FOL 39 714-19, MS DOUCE 244/ FOL 40A 714-20, MS DOUCE 244/ FOL 40B 714-21, MS DOUCE 244/ FOL 41 714-22, MS DOUCE 244/ FOL 42 714-23, MS DOUCE 244/ FOL 43 714-24, MS DOUCE 244/ FOL 44 714-25, MS DOUCE 244/ FOL 46 714-26, MS DOUCE 244/ FOL 47 714-27, MS DOUCE 244/ FOL 49 714-28
*PROVENANCE FLEMISH 714/1-14, GERMAN/ SOUTH 714/15-28
*DATE EXECUTED 16TH/C1569-78 714/1-14, 16TH-17TH/C1598-1610 714/15-28
*LANGUAGE ITALIAN AND LATIN 714/1-14, LATIN 714/15-28
*AUTHOR VAN DALE/ PAUL 714/1-14, RECHLINGER/ FRIEDRICH 714/15-28
*TYPE OF MANUSCRIPT ALBUM AMICORUM
*CONTENTS ALBUM ANICORUM/ TWO MSS 714/1-28, PORTRAIT 714-1, DOGE OF VENICE 714-2, GENERALE DEL MARE/ VENETO 714-3, PROCURADOR DE SAN MARCO 714-4, MAGN RETTORE DI PADOVE 714-5, NOBLEMAN AND SERVANT 714-6, SENATORS OF VENICE 714-7, DOGARESSA 714-8, LADY OF PADUA 714-9, LADY OF NAPLES 714-10, COUNTRYWOMAN OF PADUA 714-11, CORTEGIANA VENETIANA 714-12, GENTLEWOMAN OF CREMONA 714-13, POOR MEN 714-14, GENTLEMAN IN BLACK AND SILVER SUIT 714-15, JUDGE/ ENGLISH ON HORSEBACK 714-16, WATER CARRIER 714-17, PEASANTS 714-18, LADY MAYORESS AND ATTENDANTS 714-19, YEOMAN OF THE GUARD 714-20, KNIGHT OF THE GARTER 714-21, FISH WIFE RIDING 714-22, CITIZEN OF LONDON'S WIFE 714-23, LADY FROM ANTWERP 714-24, LADY/ ENGLISH 714-25, NOBLEWOMAN/ ENGLISH 714-26, GIRL/ GERMAN 714-27, BOAT ON THAMES 714-28

*$ABSTRACT 715
*LIBRARY BODLEIAN
*SLIDE SET TITLE FOURTEENTH CENTURY ILLUMINATIONS
*NEGATIVE REFERENCE ROLL 263D
*RENTAL FEE $2.60
*TITLE OF MANUSCRIPT BOOK OF HOURS 715/1-5, HOURS OF ANNE OF BOHEMIA 715-6, ASTROLOGICAL AND ECCLESIASTICAL CALENDAR 715-7, LIBELLUS GEOMANCIE 715/8-12
*SHELFMARK MS DOUCE 62/ FOL 31V 715-1, MS DOUCE 62/ FOL 43V 715-2, MS DOUCE 62/ FOL 43 715-3, MS DOUCE 62/ FOL 46V 715-4, MS DOUCE 62/ FOL 82 715-5, MS LAT LITURG F 3/ FOL 50V 715-6, MS RAWL D 939 715-7, MS BODLEY 581/ FOL 1 715-8, MS BODLEY 581/ FOL 5V 715-9, MS BODLEY 581/ FOL 9 715-10, MS BODLEY 581/ FOL 15V 715-11, MS BODLEY 581/ FOL 17V 715-12
*PROVENANCE FRENCH 715/1-5, FLEMISH 715-6, ENGLISH 715/7-12
*DATE EXECUTED 15TH/C1400 715/1-5, 14TH/1381-82 715-6, 14TH/C1370 715-7, 14TH/ AFTER 1391 715/8-12
*LANGUAGE FRENCH AND LATIN 715/1-5, DUTCH AND LATIN 715-6,

ENGLISH AND LATIN 715-7, LATIN 715/8-12
*ARTIST/ SCHOOL ZENOBI DA FIRENZE 715/1-5, RELATED TO EARLIER STYLE OF CARMELITE MISSAL 715/8-12
*TYPE OF MANUSCRIPT BOOK OF HOURS/ USE OF PARIS 715/1-5, BOOK OF HOURS/ USE OF ROME 715-6, ASTROLOGICAL CALENDAR 715-7, GEOMANCY TEXT 715/8-12
*CONTENTS FOURTEENTH CENTURY ILLUMINATION 715/1-12, HOUND CHASING DEER 715-1, SQUIRREL/ GROTESQUE/ DRAGON IN MARGIN 715-1, GROTESQUE BEGGARS AND BISHOP 715-2, HERMIT AND NAKED WOMAN 715-3, GROTESQUE AND MAN IN MARGIN 715-3, REYNARD THE FOX 715-4, GROTESQUE IN MARGIN 715-4, REYNARD THE FOX CHASED BY WOMAN 715-5, GROTESQUE WITH TRUMPET 715-5, HENS AND BUTTERFLY IN MARGIN 715-6, HUNTER WITH HORN AND DOG 715-7, TEXT/ OPENING WITH DECORATED BORDERS 715-8, TEXT OF FOLIO 5V 715-9, INITIAL WITH KING/ PERHAPS RICHARD II 715-10, ASTROLOGICAL FIGURES/ BEARDED MAN AND MAN ON HORSE 715-11, ASTROLOGICAL FIGURES/ KING AND YOUTH 715-12

*$ABSTRACT 716
*LIBRARY BODLEIAN
*SLIDE SET TITLE ILLUMINATIONS FROM SIX MSS
*NEGATIVE REFERENCE ROLL 263E AND 264A
*RENTAL FEE $2.40
*TITLE OF MANUSCRIPT ROMAN DE LA ROSE 716/1-2, LE SONGE DU VERGIER 716-3, AZZO 716-4, VARIOUS WRITINGS OF HUGH OF ST VICTOR 716-5, DOUCE APOCALYPSE 716-6, LE LIVRE DU TRESOR OF BRUNETTO LATINI 716/7-8
*SHELFMARK MS DOUCE 371/ FOL 127V 716-1, MS DOUCE 371/ FOL 129 716-2, MS E MUSAEO 43/ FOL 230V 716-3, MS CANON MISC 411/ FOL 1 716-4, MS LAUD MISC 409/ FOL 3V 716-5, MS DOUCE 180/ PAGE 1 716-6, MS DOUCE 319/ FOL 9 716-7, MS DOUCE 319/ FOL 86 716-8
*PROVENANCE FRENCH/ PARIS 716/1-2, FRENCH 716-3, ITALIAN/ BOLOGNA 716-4, ENGLISH/ ST ALBANS 716-5, ENGLISH 716-6, ITALIAN 716/7-8
*DATE EXECUTED 15TH/C1400 716/1-3, 14TH 716-4, 12TH/ 2ND HALF 716-5, 13TH/ PRE 1272 716-6, 14TH/ EARLY 716/7-8
*LANGUAGE FRENCH 716/1-3, LATIN 716/4-5, FRENCH AND LATIN 716-6, FRENCH 716/7-8
*ARTIST/ SCHOOL ZENOBI DA FIRENZE 716-3
*AUTHOR DE LORRIS/ GUILLAUME AND JEAN DE MEUNG 716/1-2, DE MAISIERES/ PHILIP 716-3, AZZO 716-4, HUGH OF ST VICTOR 716-5, BRUNETTO LATINI 716/7-8
*TYPE OF MANUSCRIPT ROMANCE 716/1-2, LITERATURE 716-3, TREATISE 716-4, VARIOUS WRITINGS 716-5, APOCALYPSE 716-6, LITERATURE 716/7-8
*CONTENTS ILLUMINATIONS FROM SIX MSS 716/1-8, GENIUS AS BISHOP PREACHING 716-1, COURTESY/ PITY/ FRANKNESS SPEAK TO FAIR WELCOME 716-2, FAIR WELCOME 716-2, BOOK PRESENTED TO CHARLES V 716-3, CHARLES V 716-3, TEACHER LECTURES TO EIGHT STUDENTS 716-4, HUGH OF ST VICTOR TEACHES MONKS 716-5, LORD EDWARD AND ELEANOR OF CASTILE KNEEL BEFORE TRINITY 716-6, ELEANOR OF CASTILE AND LORD EDWARD 716-6, TRINITY WITH EDWARD AND ELEANOR OF CASTILE 716-6, TEACHER AND PUPIL 716-7, TEACHER TEACHES A CLASS 716-8

*$ABSTRACT 717
*LIBRARY BODLEIAN
*SLIDE SET TITLE COLOR IN ANTIQUITY
*NEGATIVE REFERENCE ROLL 264B
*RENTAL FEE $2.35
*COMMENTS MOSAICS REPHOTOGRAPHED FROM L. FENGER, DORISCHE POLYCHROMIE, AND M. KORKUTI, ARCHAEOLOGICAL ALBANIA.
*CONTENTS COLOR IN ANTIQUITY/ MOSTLY MOSAICS 717/1-7, MOSAICS 717/2-7, STATUE OF AUGUSTUS FROM PRIMA PORTA 717-1, AUGUSTUS STATUE 717-1, MOSAIC/ POLYCHROME IN GEOMETRIC PATTERN 717-2, GEOMETRIC PATTERN IN MOSAIC 717-2, ACHILLES HOLDS QUEEN OF AMAZONS 717-3, MOSAIC SHOWING HEAD OF WOMAN 717-4, MOSAIC WITH WATER BIRDS 717-5, BIRDS ON MOSAIC 717-5, MOSAIC/ DETAILS 717-6, VINE AND BIRDS ON MOSAIC 717-7

*$ABSTRACT 718
*LIBRARY BODLEIAN
*SLIDE SET TITLE GREEK PAPYRI
*NEGATIVE REFERENCE ROLL 264C
*RENTAL FEE $2.35
*COMMENTS MANUSCRIPTS SELECTED FROM EXHIBITION OF MAINLY GREEK PAPYRI FOR THE XIV INTERNATIONAL CONGRESS OF PAPYROLOGISTS IN 1974.
*TITLE OF MANUSCRIPT LACHES OF PLATO 718/1-2, POST-EURIPIDEAN TRAGIC VERSE 718-3, CARBONIZED ROLL FROM HERCULANEUM 718/4-5, HERCULANEUM PAPYRI 718-6, HAWARA HOMER 718-7
*SHELFMARK MS GREEK CLASS D 22P 718-1, MS GREEK CLASS D 23P 718-2, MS GREEK CLASS F 113P 718-3, MS GREEK CLASS B 1 P2 718-4, MS GREEK CLASS B 1 P12 718-5, MS GREEK CLASS C 1/ FOL 37R 718-6, MS GREEK CLASS A 1 P8 718-7
*PROVENANCE GREEK EMPIRE
*DATE EXECUTED 03RD BC 718/1-2, 01ST AD 718-3, 01ST/79 AD/ BEFORE 718/4-5, 02ND AD 718-7
*LANGUAGE GREEK
*AUTHOR PLATO 718-1, HOMER 718-7
*TYPE OF MANUSCRIPT PAPYRI
*CONTENTS GREEK PAPYRI 718/1-7, PLATO'S LACHES/ WHITE DEPOSIT FROM MUMMY CASE 718/1-2, VERSE ON DEATH OF HECTOR AND FALL OF TROY 718-3, CARBONIZED ROLL FROM HERCULANEUM 718/4-5, PENCIL FACSIMILES BY OFFICINA DEI PAPIRI 718-6, TEXT OF HOMER'S ILIAD II 718-7

*$ABSTRACT 719
*LIBRARY BODLEIAN
*SLIDE SET TITLE FIFTEENTH CENTURY ILLUMINATION
*NEGATIVE REFERENCE ROLL 264D
*RENTAL FEE $2.35
*TITLE OF MANUSCRIPT BOOK OF HOURS 719-1, SOMNIUM VIRIDARII 719/2-4, GENEALOGY OF KINGS OF ENGLAND 719-5, POEMS OF JOHN GOWER 719/6-7
*SHELFMARK MS GOUGH LITURG 9/ PAGE 8 719-1, MS BODLEY 338/ FOL 1 719-2, MS BODLEY 338/ FOL 3 719-3, MS BODLEY 338/ FOL 67V 719-4, MS ALL SOULS COLLEGE 40/ FOL 2 719-5, MS ALL SOULS COLLEGE 98/ FOL 1V DETAIL 719-6, MS ALL SOULS COLLEGE 98/ FOL 1V WHOLE 719-7
*PROVENANCE ENGLISH/ KENT? 719-1, FRENCH 719/2-4, ENGLISH 719/5-7
*DATE EXECUTED 15TH/C1430 719-1, 15TH/ MID 719/2-4, 15TH/ 3RD QUARTER 719-5, 15TH 719/6-7
*LANGUAGE LATIN 719/1-4, ENGLISH 719/6-7
*AUTHOR GOWER/ JOHN 719/6-7
*TYPE OF MANUSCRIPT BOOK OF HOURS/ USE OF SARUM 719-1, TREATISE 719/2-4, GENEALOGY 719-5, POETRY 719/6-7
*CONTENTS FIFTEENTH CENTURY ILLUMINATION 719/1-7, INITIAL AND BORDER 719-1, MATINS 719-1, VIRIDARIUS' DREAM/ KING AND TWO QUEENS IN GARDEN 719-2, KING AND TWO QUEENS TALK IN GARDEN 719-2, VIRIDARIUS ADDRESSES LISTENER 719/3-4, ADAM AND EVE IN ROUNDEL 719-5, ARCHBISHOP ARUNDEL 719/6-7

*$ABSTRACT 720
*LIBRARY BODLEIAN
*SLIDE SET TITLE FACSIMILES OF LATE 11TH-CENTURY ANGLO-NORMAN MANUSCRIPTS
*NEGATIVE REFERENCE ROLL 264E
*RENTAL FEE $2.80
*COMMENTS THE FACSIMILES ARE BY D.M. CALLARD. THE FOLIO NUMBERS ARE GIVEN ON THE FACSIMILES AND AS THERE ARE OFTEN SEVERAL TO ONE PAGE THEY ARE OMITTED IN THE CONTENTS FIELD.
*TITLE OF MANUSCRIPT HOMILIES ON THE GOSPEL OF ST JOHN 720/1-2, CURA PASTORALIS BY GREGORY 720/3-6, COMMENTARY ON ISAIAH BY JEROME 720/7-16
*SHELFMARK MS BODLEY 301 720/1-2, MS BODLEY 783 720/3-6, MS BODLEY 717 720/7-16

*PROVENANCE FRENCH/ NORMANDY
*DATE EXECUTED 11TH/ LATE
*LANGUAGE LATIN
*ARTIST/ SCHOOL FACSIMILES OF ANGLO-NORMAN MSS BY D M CALLARD
*AUTHOR AUGUSTINE 720/1-2, GREGORY 720/3-6, JEROME 720/7-16
*TYPE OF MANUSCRIPT HOMILIES 720/1-2, RELIGIOUS TREATISE 720/3-6, COMMENTARY 720/7-16
*CONTENTS FACSIMILES OF ANGLO-NORMAN MSS 720/1-16, ANGLO-NORMAN MANUSCRIPTS 720/1-16

*$ABSTRACT 721
*LIBRARY CHRIST CHURCH OXFORD
*SLIDE SET TITLE ESTATE MAP OF HILLESDEN BUCKS
*NEGATIVE REFERENCE ROLL 264F
*RENTAL FEE $2.40
*TITLE OF MANUSCRIPT ESTATE MAP OF HILLESDEN
*PROVENANCE ENGLISH
*DATE EXECUTED 18TH/1763
*TYPE OF MANUSCRIPT MAP/ ESTATE
*CONTENTS MAP OF ESTATE AT HILLESDEN BUCKINGHAMSHIRE 721/1-8, TOPOGRAPHY/ ESTATE MAP 721/1-8

*$ABSTRACT 722
*LIBRARY BODLEIAN
*SLIDE SET TITLE PORTRAITS OF SCOTTISH MONARCHS
*NEGATIVE REFERENCE ROLL 265A
*RENTAL FEE $2.30
*TITLE OF MANUSCRIPT ARMS OF THE NOBILITY OF SCOTLAND
*SHELFMARK MS WOOD C 9/ FOL 4 722-1, MS WOOD C 9/ FOL 8 722-2, MS WOOD C 9/ FOL 11 722-3, MS WOOD C 9/ FOL 13 722-4, MS WOOD C 9/ FOL 18 722-5, MS WOOD C 9/ FOL 19 722-6
*PROVENANCE SCOTTISH
*DATE EXECUTED 16TH/1588
*LANGUAGE ENGLISH
*TYPE OF MANUSCRIPT ARMS OF NOBILITY
*CONTENTS SCOTTISH MONARCHS 722/1-6, MALCOLM CANMORE AD1058-1093 AND ST MARGARET 722-1, ST MARGARET 722-1, ROBERT THE BRUCE AD1306-1329 AND HIS WIFE 722-2, JAMES I OF SCOTLAND AD1406-1437 WITH QUEEN 722-3, QUEEN JOAN BEAUFORT 722-3, JAMES IV AD1488-1513 AND QUEEN MARGARET 722-4, MARY QUEEN OF SCOTS AD1542-1567 AND DARNLEY 722-5,JAMES VI OF SCOTLAND AD1567-1625 722-6

*$ABSTRACT 723
*LIBRARY BODLEIAN
*SLIDE SET TITLE MISCELLANY 1
*NEGATIVE REFERENCE ROLL 265B
*RENTAL FEE $2.95
*TITLE OF MANUSCRIPT COLLATIONS OF JOHN CASSIAN 723/1-3, ENCHIRIDION BY AUGUSTINE 723-4, PSALTER WITH GLOSS 723/5-6, HAVELOK THE DANE 723/7-8, NOTITIA DIGNITATUM 723/9-11, BOOK OF HOURS 723-12, OFFICES FOR A LADY 723-13, BOOK OF HOURS 723-14, VALE ROYAL OF ENGLAND 723-15, ROMANCE OF ALEXANDER 723/16-19
*SHELFMARK MS HATTON 23/ FOL 1V 723-1, MS HATTON 23/ FOL 3V 723-2, MS HATTON 23/ FOL 18V 723-3, MS LAT TH D 33/ FOL 1 723-4, MS BODLEY 862/ FOL 1 723-5, MS BODLEY 862/ FOL 67 723-6, MS LAUD MISC 108/ FOL 207V 723-7, MS LAUD MISC 108/ FOL 219V 723-8, MS CANON LITURG 178/ FOL 57V-58 723-12, MS DOUCE 12/ FOL 96V-97 723-13, MS LAUD MISC 7/ FOL 27V 723-14, MS ASHMOLE 765/ FOL 110V 723-15, MS BODLEY 264/ FOL 82 723-16, MS BODLEY 264/ FCL 84 723-17, MS BODLEY 264/ FOL 76 723-18, MS BODLEY 264/ FOL 77 723-19
*PROVENANCE ENGLISH/ WORCESTER 723/1-6, ENGLISH 723/7-8, FRENCH/ ANJOU 723-12, FLEMISH/ BRUGES? 723-13, FLEMISH/ GHENT? 723-14, ENGLISH 723-15, FLEMISH 723/16-19
*DATE EXECUTED 11TH/ LATE 723/1-4, 12TH 723/5-6, 14TH/ LATE

723/7-8, 16TH/ EARLY 723-12, 15TH/ LATE 723/13-14, 16TH/1585 723-15, 14TH/1338-44 723/16-19
*LANGUAGE LATIN 723/1-6, ENGLISH 723/7-8, LATIN 723/9-12 AND 14, ITALIAN AND LATIN 723-13, ENGLISH 723-15, FRENCH 723/16-19
*ARTIST/ SCHOOL MASTER OF THE CROY BOOK OF HOURS 723-14, DE GRISE/ JEHAN 723/16-19
*AUTHOR CASSIAN/ JOHN 723/1-3, AUGUSTINE 723-4
*TYPE OF MANUSCRIPT RELIGIOUS TREATISE 723/1-4, PSALTER 723/5-6, LITERATURE 723/7-8, MILITARY TREATISE 723/9-11, BOOK OF HOURS/ USE OF ROME-ANGERS 723-12, PRAYERS 723-13, BOOK OF HOURS/ USE OF ROME 723-14, ROMANCE 723/16-19
*CONTENTS MISCELLANY 1 723/1-19, INITIAL D DEBITUM/ DRAGCN 723-1, DRAGON 723-1, INITIAL C CUM/ MAN CARRYING BASKET 723-2, MAN CARRYING BASKET 723-2, INITIAL D/ MEN STANDING IN FOLIAGE PATTERN 723-3, MEN STAND IN FOLIAGE PATTERN 723-3, INITIAL D/ DRAGON AND FOLIAGE PATTERN 723-4, DRAGON AND FOLIAGE PATTERN 723-4, INITIAL B BEATUS/ WHITE LIONS ON FOLIAGE PATTERN 723-5, LIONS ON FOLIAGE PATTERN 723-5, INITIAL D DIXIT/ LIONS FIGHTING 723-6, LIONS FIGHT 723-6, TEXT IN DOUBLE COLUMNS WITH RUBRICATED INITIALS 723-7, INITIALS/ RUBRICATED 723-7, INITIAL A/ DECORATED 723-8, FACSIMILES OF FRAGMENTS/ 19TH CENTURY 723/9-11,BATHSHEBA 723-12, DAVID IN PRAYER 723-13, VIRGIN AND CHILD IN CRESCENT MOON 723-14, ARMS OF VARDREY OF CHESHIRE 723-15, RABBIT OR HARE 723-16, BULL FINCH 723-17, MEN TALKING 723-18, BATTLE SCENE 723-19

*$ABSTRACT 724
*LIBRARY BODLEIAN
*SLIDE SET TITLE MISCELLANY 2
*NEGATIVE REFERENCE ROLL 267A
*RENTAL FEE $3.15
*TITLE OF MANUSCRIPT ASTRONOMICAL CALENDAR 724/1-3, SACRAMENTARY 724-4, OFFICE OF THE HOLY GHOST 724-5, LIFE OF ST ELOI 724/6-9, LANCELOT DU LAC 724/10-13, PSALTER 724-14, DECRETALS OF GREGORY IX 724/15-20, POLYCRATICUS 724/22-23
*SHELFMARK MS ASHMOLE 789/ FOL 365 724-1, MS ASHMOLE 370/ FOL 27V 724-2, MS ASHMOLE 5/ FOL 34V 724-3, MS CANON LITURG 354/ FOL 67 724-4, MS LAT LITURG G 5/ PAGE 98 724-5, MS DOUCE 94/ FOL 11 724-6, MS DOUCE 94/ FOL 119 724-7, MS DOUCE 94/ FOL 142V 724-8, MS DOUCE 94/ FOL 158V 724-9, MS RAWL Q B 6/ FOL 6V 724-10, MS RAWL Q B 6/ FOL 187V 724-11, MS RAWL Q B 6/ FOL 240 724/12-13, MS DOUCE 118/ FOL 7 724-14, MS CANON MISC 492/ FOL 1 724-15, MS CANON MISC 492/ FOL 94V 724-16, MS CANON MISC 492/ FOL 235 724-17, MS CANON MISC 492/ FOL 259 724-18, MS CANGN MISC 492/ FOL 315V 724-19, MS CANON MISC 492/ FOL 316 724-20, MS DOUCE CHARTERS 62 724-21, MS BARLOW 6/ FOL 4V 724-22, MS BARLOW 6/ FOL 155 724-23
*PROVENANCE ENGLISH 724/1-3, GERMAN/ AUGSBURG? 724-4, FLEMISH/ MADE IN ENGLAND 724-5, FRENCH/ NOYON 724/6-9, FRENCH/ NORTH 724/10-13, FRENCH/ ARTOIS 724-14 ITALIAN/ BOLOGNA 724/15-20, ENGLISH 724-21, ENGLISH/ MALMESBURY 724/22-23
*DATE EXECUTED 14TH/ AFTER 1387 724/1 AND 3, 15TH/C1424 724-2, 12TH/ LATE 724-4, 16TH/C1500 724-5, 13TH/1294 724/6-9, 14TH/ EARLY 724/10-13, 13TH/ LATE 724-14, 14TH/ LATE 724/15-20, 15TH/C1450 724-21, 13TH/ 2ND QUARTER 724/22-23
*LANGUAGE LATIN 724/1 AND 3-5, ENGLISH AND LATIN 724-2, FRENCH 724/6-13, LATIN 724/14-20 AND 22-23, ENGLISH 724-21
*ARTIST/ SCHOOL NICCOLO DI GIACOMO 724/15-20
*AUTHOR NICHOLAS OF LYNN 724/1-3, JOHN OF SALISBURY 724/22-23
*SCRIBE DE MONSTERUEL/ GERARS 724/6-9, ERNOULS OF AMIENS 724/10-13
*TYPE OF MANUSCRIPT ASTRONOMICAL CALENDARS 724/1-3, SACRAMENTARY 724-4, OFFICE OF THE HOLY GHOST 724-5, SAINT'S LIFE 724/6-9, LITERATURE 724/10-13, PSALTER 724-14, RELIGIOUS TREATISE 724/15-20, CHARTER 724-21, RELIGIOUS TREATISE 724/22-23
*CONTENTS MISCELLANY 2 724/1-23, BLOOD LETTING FIGURE 724-1, ZODIACAL MAN 724/2-3, CRUCIFIXION/ EARLY 13TH/ PERHAPS REPAINTED 724-4, ST MARGARET EMERGES FROM DRAGON 724-5, MARGUERITE IN BORDER 724-5, INITIAL WITH HEAD OF KING CLOVIS

724-6, CLOVIS IN INITIAL 724-6, INITIAL/ ST ELOI CURES MAN NEAR NOYON 724-7, ST ELOI CURES MAN 724-7, INITIAL WITH MAN'S FACE 724-8, INITIAL/ ST ELOI AND ANOTHER MAN 724-9, ST ELOI AND ANOTHER MAN 724-9, INITIAL/ FULL PAGE/ KING SPEAKS TO TWO MEN 724-10, KING SPEAKS TO TWO MEN 724-10, TEXT PAGE 724-11, LYONELL AND TEBICAN 724-12, HECTOR MEETS LADY WEEPING FOR LYONELL 724-13, BEATUS PAGE WITH FOUR SCENES 724-14, DAVID WITH HARP 724-14, DAVID AND GOLIATH 724-14, CRUCIFIXION 724-14, VIRGIN AND CHILD 724-14, POPE AND HIS COURT/ PARTLY ERASED 724-15, INITIAL SHOWS POPE GREGORY IX 724-15, GREGORY IX 724-15, BISHOP RECEIVES PETITIONS FROM MEN 724-16, MARRIAGE SCENE 724-17, COURT/ ECCLESIASTICAL 724-18, CARDINAL PRESENTED SCROLL BY TWO LAYMEN 724-18, LAWYERS 724-18, TABLE OF AFFINITY 724/19-20, TABLE FOR FIXING THE PRICE OF BREAD 724-21, INITIAL I INTER/ ARMED MEN KILL BEASTS 724-22, BEASTS KILLED BY FOUR ARMED MEN 724-22, INITIAL S SOLENT/ MEN IN SAILING SHIP 724-23, SHIP/ SAILING 724-23

*$ABSTRACT 725
*LIBRARY BODLEIAN
*SLIDE SET TITLE MS DOUCE 253
*NEGATIVE REFERENCE ROLL 268A
*RENTAL FEE $2.30
*TITLE OF MANUSCRIPT BOOK OF HOURS
*SHELFMARK MS DOUCE 253/ FOL 13 725-1, MS DOUCE 253/ FOL 28 725-2, MS DOUCE 253/ FOL 58 725-3, MS DOUCE 253/ FOL 75 725-4, MS DOUCE 253/ FOL 82 725-5, MS DOUCE 253/ FOL 134 725-6
*PROVENANCE FRENCH/ NORMANDY
*DATE EXECUTED 15TH/C1480
*LANGUAGE FRENCH AND LATIN
*ARTIST/ SCHOOL JACOB TEN EYKEN/ ATTRIBUTED TO
*TYPE OF MANUSCRIPT BOOK OF HOURS/ USE OF ROUEN
*CONTENTS BOOK OF HOURS/ FRENCH/ 15TH 725/1-6, EVANGELISTS/ FOUR WITH SYMBOLS 725-1, ANNUNCIATION 725-2, FOUNTAIN AND BIRD IN BORDER 725-2, ADORATION OF THE MAGI 725-3, CRUCIFIXION 725-4, DAVID KNEELS IN PRAYER/ GOD IN CLOUD 725-5, GOD IN CLOUD 725-5, OWNER/ WOMAN KNEELS BEFORE VIRGIN AND CHILD 725-6, VIRGIN AND CHILD 725-6

*$ABSTRACT 726
*LIBRARY BODLEIAN
*SLIDE SET TITLE MANUSCRIPTS ASSOCIATED WITH LESNES ABBEY
*NEGATIVE REFERENCE ROLL 270B
*RENTAL FEE $2.35
*TITLE OF MANUSCRIPT AURORA BY PETER RIGA 726-1
*SHELFMARK MS BODLEY 656/ FOL 1V-2 726-1, MS DOUCE 287/ FOL IV 726-2, MS DOUCE 287/ FOL 2V-3 726-3, MS DOUCE 330/ FOL 1 726-4, MS DOUCE 330/ FOL 2V 726-5, MS DOUCE 330/ FOL 129 726-6, MS DOUCE 330/ FACSIMILES OF 16 INITIALS 726-7
*PROVENANCE ENGLISH/ ASSOCIATED WITH LESNES ABBEY KENT
*DATE EXECUTED 13TH/ 1ST QUARTER 726-1, 13TH 726/2-3, 12TH 726/4-7
*LANGUAGE LATIN
*AUTHOR RIGA/ PETER 726-1, BERENGAUDUS 726/4-7
*TYPE OF MANUSCRIPT TREATISES
*CONTENTS MANUSCRIPTS ASSOCIATED WITH LESNES ABBEY 726/1-7, TEXT PAGE WITH MARK OF OWNERSHIP 726-1, OWNERSHIP NOTE 726-2, TEXT OPENING ABOUT THOMAS BECKET 726-3, BECKET/ THOMAS MENTIONED IN TEXT 726-3, OWNERSHIP MARK 726-4, INITIAL A 726-4, INITIAL B 726-5, INITIAL D 726-6, INITIAL FACSIMILES 726-7

*$ABSTRACT 727
*LIBRARY BODLEIAN
*SLIDE SET TITLE MS MARSHALL 21
*NEGATIVE REFERENCE ROLL 270C

*RENTAL FEE $2.50
*COMMENTS SELECTED PAGES AND DETAILS OF INITIALS
*TITLE OF MANUSCRIPT COMMENTARY ON ST MATTHEW 727/1-2 AND 4-6, DE SEPTEM REGULIS 727/3 AND 7-10
*SHELFMARK MS MARSHALL 21/ FOL 1V 727-1, MS MARSHALL 21/ FOL 20V 727-2, MS MARSHALL 21/ FOL 70V 727-3, MS MARSHALL 21/ FOL 33V 727-4, MS MARSHALL 21/ 38V 727-5 MS MARSHALL 21/ FOL 63V 727-6, MS MARSHALL 21/ FOL 81 727-7, MS MARSHALL 21/ FOL 89 727-8, MS MARSHALL 21/ FOL 93V 727-9, MS MARSHALL 21/ FOL 95 727-10
*PROVENANCE FLEMISH/ ST PETER'S GHENT
*DATE EXECUTED 12TH/ 3RD QUARTER
*LANGUAGE LATIN
*AUTHOR HILARY OF POITIERS 727/1-2 AND 4-6, TYCONIUS 727/3 AND 7-10
*TYPE OF MANUSCRIPT COMMENTARY 727/1-2 AND 4-6,TREATISE 727/3 AND 7-10
*CONTENTS INITIALS AND TEXT PAGES 727/1-10, INITIAL G GRESSUS/ FIRST PAGE OF HILARY'S COMMENTARY 727-1, TEXT PAGE WITH THREE COLORED INITIALS 727-2, INITIAL N/ LARGE 727-3, INITIAL D 727-3, INITIAL S AND I 727-4, INITIAL I 727-5, INITIAL C 727-6, INITIAL D 727-7, INITIAL T 727-8, INITIAL R 727-9, INITIAL D 727-10

*$ABSTRACT 728
*LIBRARY BODLEIAN
*SLIDE SET TITLE MS DOUCE 381
*NEGATIVE REFERENCE ROLL 270D
*RENTAL FEE $2.80
*COMMENTS FRAGMENTS AND CUTTINGS FROM TWO BOOKS OF HOURS.
*TITLE OF MANUSCRIPT BOOK OF HOURS/ FRAGMENTS 728/1-12, BOOK OF HOURS?/ CUTTINGS 728/13-16
*SHELFMARK MS DOUCE 381/ FOL 78 728-1, MS DOUCE 381/ FOL 79 728-2, MS DOUCE 381/ FOL 80 728/3-4, MS DOUCE 381/ FOL 81 728-5, MS DOUCE 381/ FOL 82 728-6, MS DOUCE 381/ FOL 83 728-7, MS DOUCE 381/ FOL 84 728-8, MS DOUCE 381/ FOL 85 728-9, MS DOUCE 381/ FOL 86 728-10, MS DOUCE 381/ FOL 87 728-11, MS DOUCE 381/ FOL 88 728-12, MS DOUCE 381/ FOL 164-165 TOP 728-13, MS DOUCE 381/ FOL 164-165 BOTTOM 728-14, MS DOUCE 381/ FOL 166 TOP 728-15, MS DOUCE 381/ FOL 166 BOTTOM 728-16
*PROVENANCE FLEMISH 728/1-12, FLEMISH/ GHENT 728/13-16
*DATE EXECUTED 15TH/ 3RD QUARTER 728/1-12, 15TH/ LATE 728/13-16
*LANGUAGE DUTCH AND LATIN 728/1-12, LATIN 728/13-16
*ARTIST/ SCHOOL LIEVIN VAN LATHEM 728/1-12, MASTER OF THE DRESDEN HOURS 728/13-16
*TYPE OF MANUSCRIPT BOOK OF HOURS/ FRAGMENTS 728/1-12, BOOK OF HOURS?/ CUTTINGS 728/13-16
*CONTENTS BOOKS OF HOURS/ FRAGMENTS AND CUTTINGS 728/1-16, INITIAL CUT OUT 728-1, MEN FIGHT/ BIRD/ FLOWERS IN BORDER 728-1, INITIAL CUT OUT 728-2, MEN TALKING/ MAN ON HORSEBACK FIGHTS WITH SAGITTARIUS 728-2, SAGITTARIUS FIGHTS WITH MAN ON HORSEBACK 728-2, INITIAL CUT OUT 728-3, SNAIL/ MAN WITH CLUB/ FLOWERS IN BORDER 728-3,INITIAL CUT OUT 728-4, ANGELS/ PEACOCK/ COLUMBINES IN BORDER 728-4, ST CHRISTOPHER CARRIES CHRIST CHILD 728-5, HERMIT WITH LANTERN 728-5, ST CHRISTOPHER MARTYRED 728-5, ST ADRIAN TREADS ON LION 728-6, COCKS AND HENS IN BORDER 728-6, ST JAMES THE GREAT/ PILGRIMS IN BORDER 728-7, ST ANTHONY ABBOT WITH PIG 728-8, ST ANTHONY TEMPTED BY DEVILS IN BORDER 728-8, ST BARBARA 728-9, ST BARBARA MARTYRED IN BORDER 728-9, INITIAL CUT OUT 728-10, GRAPEVINE AND MAN IN BORDER 728-10, INITIAL CUT OUT 728-11, CHRIST AND ST VERONICA/ MAN HOLDS THREE NAILS 728-11, ST VERONICA AND CHRIST 728-11, INITIAL CUT OUT 728-12, SNAIL/ HORSEMAN/ BIRD/ GRAPEVINE IN BORDER 728-12, VISITATION/ FOOL IN LOWER BORDER 728-13, FOOL IN LOWER BORDER 728-13, NATIVITY/ APE/ FOOL AND DOG IN BORDER 728-14, ADORATION OF THE MAGI/ APE AND FOOL IN BORDER 728-15, FLIGHT INTO EGYPT/ APE AND FOOL WITH FIDDLE IN BORDER 728-16, FOOL WITH FIDDLE RIDES CAT 728-16

*$ABSTRACT 729
*LIBRARY BODLEIAN
*SLIDE SET TITLE MS GOUGH LITURG 15
*NEGATIVE REFERENCE ROLL 270E
*RENTAL FEE $2.85
*TITLE OF MANUSCRIPT BOOK OF HOURS
*SHELFMARK MS GOUGH LITURG 15/ FOL 14 729-1, MS GOUGH LITURG 15/ FOL 23 729-2, MS GOUGH LITURG 15/ FOL 39V 729-3, MS GOUGH LITURG 15/ FOL 43V 729-4, MS GOUGH LITURG 15/ FOL 47 729-5, MS GOUGH LITURG 15/ FOL 53 729-6, MS GOUGH LITURG 15/ FOL 59 729-7, MS GOUGH LITURG 15/ FOL 63V 729-8, MS GOUGH LITURG 15/ FOL 64V 729-9, MS GOUGH LITURG 15/ FOL 65V 729-10, MS GOUGH LITURG 15/ FOL 66V 729-11, MS GOUGH LITURG 15/ FOL 67 729-12, MS GOUGH LITURG 15/ FOL 68 729-13, MS GOUGH LITURG 15/ FOL 68V 729-14, MS GOUGH LITURG 15/ FOL 70V 729-15, MS GOUGH LITURG 15/ FOL 78 729-16, MS GOUGH LITURG 15/ FOL 94 729-17
*PROVENANCE FLEMISH/ GHENT?
*DATE EXECUTED 15TH/1470-80
*LANGUAGE LATIN
*ARTIST/ SCHOOL RELATED TO LIEVIN VAN LATHEM
*TYPE OF MANUSCRIPT BOOK OF HOURS/ USE OF ROME
*CONTENTS BOOK OF HOURS/ FLEMISH/ 15TH 729/1-17, CRUCIFIXION/ BEAR AND APE IN BORDER 729-1, BEAR AND APE IN BORDER 729-1, ANNUNCIATION 729-2, VISITATION IN BORDER 729-2, NATIVITY 729-3, ANNUNCIATION TO SHEPHERDS IN BORDER 729-3, CIRCUMCISION OF CHRIST 729-4, CHRIST'S CIRCUMCISION 729-4, HUNTING SCENE IN BORDER 729-4, ADORATION OF THE MAGI 729-5, ORGANIST/ ANGELIC IN BORDER 729-5, MASSACRE OF THE INNOCENTS 729-6, BAGPIPER/ APE 729-6, FLIGHT INTO EGYPT/ APE TRAPS BIRDS IN BORDER 729-7, BIRD TRAPPING IN BORDER 729-7, ST CHRISTOPHER 729-8, ST SEBASTIAN 729-9, ST ADRIAN 729-10, ST ANTHONY ABBOT 729-11, ST APOLLONIA 729-12, ST CATHERINE 729-13, ST BARBARA 729-14, VIRGIN AND CHILD 729-15, INITIAL TO PRAYER OBSECRO TE 729-15, DAVID PRAYS TO GOD 729-16, MUSICIAN/ GROTESQUE 729-16, FUNERAL PROCESSION LEAVES CHURCH 729-17, APE WITH BIRD'S NEST IN BORDER 729-17

*$ABSTRACT 730
*LIBRARY BODLEIAN
*SLIDE SET TITLE MS LITURG 396
*NEGATIVE REFERENCE ROLL 270F
*RENTAL FEE $3.90
*TITLE OF MANUSCRIPT PSALTER
*SHELFMARK MS LITURG 396/ FOL 1 730-1, MS LITURG 396/ FOL 1V 730-2, MS LITURG 396/ FOL 2 730-3, MS LITURG 396/ FOL 2V 730-4, MS LITURG 396/ FOL 3 730-5, MS LITURG 396/ FOL 3V 730-6, MS LITURG 396/ FOL 4 730-7, MS LITURG 396/ FOL 4V 730-8, MS LITURG 396/ FOL 5 730-9, MS LITURG 396/ FOL 5V 730-10, MS LITURG 396/ FOL 6 730-11, MS LITURG 396/ FOL 6V 730-12, MS LITURG 396/ FOL 7V 730-13, MS LITURG 396/ FOL 8V 730-14, MS LITURG 396/ FOL 9V 730-15, MS LITURG 396/ FOL 10V 730-16, MS LITURG 396/ FOL 11V 730-17, MS LITURG 396/ FOL 12V 730-18, MS LITURG 396/ FOL 13V 730-19, MS LITURG 396/ FOL 14V 730-20, MS LITURG 396/ FOL 15V 730-21, MS LITURG 396/ FOL 34V 730-22, MS LITURG 396/ FOL 35 730-23, MS LITURG 396/ FOL 47V 730-24, MS LITURG 396/ FOL 48 730-25, MS LITURG 396/ FOL 59V 730-26, MS LITURG 396/ FOL 60 730-27, MS LITURG 396/ FOL 61 730-28, MS LITURG 396/ FOL 73V 730-29, MS LITURG 396/ FOL 74 730-30, MS LITURG 396/ FOL 88V 730-31, MS LITURG 396/ FOL 89 730-32, MS LITURG 396/ FOL 102 730-33, MS LITURG 396/ FOL 103 730-34, MS LITURG 396/ FOL 104V 730-35, MS LITURG 396/ FOL 105 730-36, MS LITURG 396/ FOL 117V 730-37, MS LITURG 396/ FOL 118 730-38
*PROVENANCE FLEMISH/ GHENT
*DATE EXECUTED 13TH/ 3RD QUARTER
*LANGUAGE LATIN
*TYPE OF MANUSCRIPT PSALTER WITH CALENDAR
*CONTENTS PSALTER/ FLEMISH/ 13TH 730/1-38, CALENDAR 730/1-12, JANUARY/ MAN FEASTING AND WARMING HIMSELF BY FIRE 730-1, MAN FEASTING AND WARMING HIMSELF BY FIRE 730-1, FEBRUARY/ GIRL

CARRIES CANDLE 730-2, GIRL CARRIES CANDLE 730-2, MARCH/ MAN PRUNING TREE 730-3, PRUNING TREE 730-3, APRIL/ GIRL DANCING HOLDING FLOWERS 730-4, DANCING GIRL HOLDS FLOWERS 730-4, MAY/ MAN WITH HAWK ON WRIST 730-5, HAWKING 730-5, JUNE/ MAN CARRIES WOOD OR RUSHES 730-6, MAN CARRIES WOOD OR RUSHES 730-6, JULY/ MAN SCYTHING HAY 730-7, SCYTHING HAY 730-7, AUGUST/ MAN REAPING WITH SICKLE 730-8, REAPING WITH SICKLE 730-8, SEPTEMBER/ MAN SOWING SEED 730-9, SOWING SEED 730-9, OCTOBER/ MAN GATHERING FRUIT 730-10, FRUIT GATHERING 730-10, NOVEMBER/ MAN FEEDING PIGS 730-11, PIG FEEDING 730-11, DECEMBER/ MAN KILLING PIGS 730-12, PIG SLAUGHTERED 730-12, ANNUNCIATION TO THE SHEPHERDS 730-15, PRESENTATION 730-16, ADORATION OF THE MAGI 730-17, CHRIST PREACHING 730-18, BAPTISM OF CHRIST 730-19, CHRIST'S BAPTISM 730-19, LAST JUDGEMENT 730-20, BEATUS INITIAL/ JESSE TREE/ ECCLESIA OR VIRGIN 730-21, JESSE TREE 730-21, ECCLESIA OR VIRGIN MARY 730-21, TEMPTATION OF CHRIST/ SATAN SPEAKS TO CHRIST 730-22, CHRIST TEMPTED 730-22, SATAN SPEAKS TO CHRIST 730-22, TEMPTATION OF CHRIST / SATAN CARRIES CHRIST 730-23, CHRIST TEMPTED 730-23, SATAN CARRIES CHRIST TO TEMPLE 730-23, TEMPTATION OF CHRIST/ CHRIST REFUSES TO WORSHIP SATAN 730-24, CHRIST TEMPTED 730-24, CHRIST REFUSES TO WORSHIP SATAN 730-24, ST MARY MAGDALENE WASHES CHRIST'S FEET 730-25, CHRIST'S FEET WASHED BY MARY MAGDALENE 730-25, CHRIST'S ENTRY INTO JERUSALEM 730-26, ENTRY INTO JERUSALEM 730-26, CHRIST PREACHES TO APOSTLES 730-27, LAST SUPPER 730-28, CHRIST GIVES SOP TO JUDAS 730-28, CHRIST WASHES ST PETER'S FEET 730-29, ST PETER'S FEET WASHED BY CHRIST 730-29, AGONY IN THE GARDEN 730-30, ARREST OF CHRIST 730-31, CHRIST ARRESTED 730-31, JUDAS TAKES BACK THE THIRTY PIECES OF SILVER 730-32, CHRIST CARRIES THE CROSS 730-33, SCOURGING OF CHRIST 730-34, CHRIST SCOURGED 730-34, CRUCIFIXION 730-35, HARROWING OF HELL 730-36, CRUCIFIXION 730-37, ST MARY MAGDALENE SEES THE RISEN CHRIST 730-38, ASCENSION 730-38

*$ABSTRACT 731
*LIBRARY BODLEIAN
*SLIDE SET TITLE DOUCE APOCALYPSE
*NEGATIVE REFERENCE ROLL 270G
*RENTAL FEE $3.80
*COMMENTS A SELECTION OF 36 MINIATURES FROM ONE OF THE FINEST APOCALYPSE MANUSCRIPTS OF THE 13TH CENTURY. FOR A MORE DETAILED DISCUSSION OF THE MANUSCRIPT, SEE A.G. AND W.O. HASSALL'S TREASURES FROM THE BODLEIAN LIBRARY, PAGES 89-92.
*TITLE OF MANUSCRIPT DOUCE APOCALYPSE
*SHELFMARK MS DOUCE 180/ PAGE 1 731-1, MS DOUCE 180/ PAGE 4 731-2, MS DOUCE 180/ PAGE 6 731-3, MS DOUCE 180/ PAGE 7 731-4, MS DOUCE 180/ PAGE 8 731-5, MS DOUCE 180/ PAGE 17 731-6, MS DOUCE 180/ PAGE 18 731-7, MS DOUCE 180/ PAGE 20 731-8, MS DOUCE 180/ PAGE 22 731-9, MS DOUCE 180/ PAGE 23 731-10, MS DOUCE 180/ PAGE 25 731-11, MS DOUCE 180/ PAGE 27 731-12, MS DOUCE 180/ PAGE 32 731-13, MS DOUCE 180/ PAGE 33 731-14, MS DOUCE 180/ PAGE 36 731-15, MS DOUCE 180/ PAGE 38 731-16, MS DOUCE 180/ PAGE 39 731-17, MS DOUCE 180/ PAGE 41 731-18, MS DOUCE 180/ PAGE 48 731-19, MS DOUCE 180/ PAGE 49 731-20, MS DOUCE 180/ PAGE 59 731-21, MS DOUCE 180/ PAGE 64 731-22, MS DOUCE 180/ PAGE 65 731-23, MS DOUCE 180/ PAGE 66 731-24, MS DOUCE 180/ PAGE 68 731-25, MS DOUCE 180/ PAGE 69 731-26, MS DOUCE 180/ PAGE 70 731-27, MS DOUCE 180/ PAGE 72 731-28, MS DOUCE 180/ PAGE 73 731-29, MS DOUCE 180/ PAGE 74 731-30, MS DOUCE 180/ PAGE 78 731-31, MS DOUCE 180/ PAGE 79 731-32, MS DOUCE 180/ PAGE 86 731-33, MS DOUCE 180/ PAGE 90 731-34, MS DOUCE 180/ PAGE 93 731-35, MS DOUCE 180/ PAGE 95 731-36
*PROVENANCE ENGLISH/ WINCHESTER?
*DATE EXECUTED 13TH/ BEFORE 1272
*LANGUAGE FRENCH AND LATIN
*TYPE OF MANUSCRIPT APOCALYPSE WITH COMMENTARY
*CONTENTS DOUCE APOCALYPSE 731/1-36, APOCALYPSE/ ENGLISH/ 13TH 731/1-36, REV 01/VERSES 1-3/ CALL OF JOHN 731-1, ST JOHN ON PATMOS CALLED 731-1, REV 02/VERSES 1-7/ LETTER TO EPHESUS 731-2, LETTER TO EPHESUS 731-2, REV 02/VERSES 12-17/ LETTER TO

PERGAMUM 731-3, LETTER TO PERGAMUM 731-3, REV 02/VERSES 27-29/ LETTER TO THYATIRA 731-4, LETTER TO THYATIRA 731-4, REV 03/VERSES 1-6/ LETTER TO SARDIS 731-5, LETTER TO SARDIS 731-5, REV 06/VERSES 9-11/ OPENING OF FIFTH SEAL 731-6, OPENING OF FIFTH SEAL 731-6, REV 06/VERSES 12-17/ OPENING OF SIXTH SEAL 731-7, OPENING OF SIXTH SEAL 731-7, REV 07/VERSES 9-17/ GREAT MULTITUDE 731-8, MULTITUDE/ GREAT 731-8, REV 08/VERSES 3-5/ CENSER 731-9, CENSER 731-9, FIRE POURS ON EARTH 731-9, REV 08/VERSES 6-7/ FIRST TRUMPET 731-10, TRUMPET/ FIRST 731-10, STORM CLOUDS SCATTER HAIL AND FIRE ON EARTH 731-10, REV 08/VERSES 10-11/ THIRD TRUMPET 731-11, TRUMPET/ THIRD 731-11, STAR FALLS FROM HEAVEN 731-11, REV 13/VERSE 13/ EAGLE FLIES TO JOHN 731-12, EAGLE FLIES TO ST JOHN OF PATMOS 731-12, REV 10/VERSES 1-7/ GREAT ANGEL 731-13, ST JOHN OF PATMOS RECEIVES BOOK FROM EAGLE 731-13, REV 10/VERSES 8-11/ JOHN RECEIVES BOOK 731-14, ST JOHN OF PATMOS RECEIVES BOOK FROM ANGEL 731-14, REV 11/VERSES 7-8/ DEATH OF TWO WITNESSES 731-15, BEAST KILLS TWO WITNESSES 731-15, REV 11/VERSES 11-13/ RESURRECTION OF WITNESSES 731-16, RESURRECTION AND ASCENSION OF TWO WITNESSES 731-16, REV 11/VERSES 15-17/ SEVENTH TRUMPET 731-17, TRUMPET/ SEVENTH 731-17, CHRIST SEATED ON RAINBOW 731-17, REV 11/VERSE 19/ TEMPLE IN HEAVEN OPENED 731-18, TEMPLE IN HEAVEN OPENED 731-18, REV 13/VERSES 1-2/ WOMAN AND DRAGON 731-19, DRAGON AND WOMAN CLOTHED WITH SUN 731-19, WOMAN CLOTHED WITH SUN 731-19, REV 13/VERSES 11-13/ BEAST WORSHIPPED 731-20, BEAST WORSHIPPED BY THRONG OF PEOPLE 731-20, REV 15/VERSES 1-4/ SONG OF MOSES AND LAMB 731-21, MOSES GESTURES TOWARDS LAMB 731-21, REV 16/VERSES 4-7/ THIRD FLASK 731-22, ANGEL/ THIRD EMPTIES FLASK INTO SPRINGS 731-22, REV 16/VERSES 8-9/ FOURTH FLASK 731-23, ANGEL/ FOURTH EMPTIES FLASK ON SUN 731-23, REV 16/VERSES 10-11/ FIFTH FLASK 731-24, ANGEL/ FIFTH POURS FLASK ON BEAST'S THRONE 731-24, BEAST'S THRONE 731-24, REV 16/VERSES 13-16/ FROGS 731-25, FROGS EMERGE FROM MOUTHS OF DRAGON/ BEAST/ FALSE PROPHET 731-25, DRAGON/ BEAST/ FALSE PROPHET 731-25, REV 16/VERSES 17-21/ SEVENTH FLASK 731-26, ANGEL/ SEVENTH EMPTIES FLASK 731-26, BEAST HEADS VOMIT LIGHTNING AND THUNDER 731-26, REV 17/VERSES 1-2/ GREAT WHORE OF BABYLON 731-27, WHORE OF BABYLON 731-27, REV 17/VERSES 6-12/ DRUNKEN WHORE 731-28, WHORE OF BABYLON/ DRUNK 731-28, REV 18/VERSES 1-2/ FALL OF BABYLON 731-29, BABYLON/ FALL 731-29, REV 18/VERSES 4-11/ PEOPLE ISSUE FROM BABYLON 731-30, BABYLON EXITED BY PEOPLE 731-30, REV 19/VERSES 1-5/ TRIUMPH OF HEAVEN 731-31, TRIUMPH OF HEAVEN OVER WHORE OF BABYLON 731-31, CHRIST IN MAJESTY WITH WHORE IN FLAMES 731-31, REV 19/VERSES 6-8/ MARRIAGE OF LAMB 731-32, MARRIAGE OF THE LAMB 731-32, TEMPLE IN HEAVEN AS GOTHIC STRUCTURE 731-32, REV 20/VERSES 4-5/ RESURRECTION OF DEAD 731-33, RESURRECTION OF DEAD 731-33, REV 21/VERSES 2-8/ VISION OF NEW JERUSALEM 731-34, VISION OF NEW JERUSALEM 731-34, NEW JERUSALEM 731-34, REV 21/VERSES 15-21/ MEASURING THE CITY 731-35, ANGEL MEASURES CITY 731-35, REV 22/VERSES 6-12/ JOHN AND ANGEL 731-36, ST JOHN OF PATMOS WORSHIPS ANGEL 731-36

*$ABSTRACT 732
*LIBRARY BODLEIAN
*SLIDE SET TITLE NUN'S PRIEST'S TALE BY CHAUCER
*NEGATIVE REFERENCE ROLL 276
*RENTAL FEE $3.90
*COMMENTS ILLUSTRATIONS SELECTED FROM VARIOUS NON-CHAUCERIAN MSS TO ILLUSTRATE SELECTED SCENES IN CHAUCER'S NUN'S PRIEST'S TALE. LINE REFERENCES ARE TO THE WORKS OF GEOFFREY CHAUCER, 2ND EDITION, EDITED BY F. N. ROBINSON.
*TITLE OF MANUSCRIPT ROMAN DE LA ROSE 732-1, BESTIARY 732-2, HOURS OF THE VIRGIN 732-3, BESTIARY 732-4, BOOK OF HOURS 732-5, EPITRE D'OTHEA A HECTOR 732-6, MASTER OF GAME 732-7, DE NATURA RERUM 732-8, LIVRE DE LA VIGNE NOSTRE SEIGNEUR 732-9, HERBAL 732-10, HERBAL 732-11, HERBAL OF PSEUDO-APULEIUS BARBARUS 732-12, SPECULUM HUMANAE SALVATIONIS 732-13, ROMAN DE LA ROSE 732-14, DE SOMNIO SCIPIONIS 732-15, PSALTER 732-16, HISTOIRE ANCIENNE JUSQU A CESAR 732-17, BIBLE 732-18, GOSPELS

732-19, MIROIR DU MONDE 732-20, DE SOMNIO SCIPIONIS 732-21, CALENDAR 732/22-23, ROMANCE OF ALEXANDER 732-24, LE VIEULX ROMAN DE LANCELOT DU LAKE 732-25, BESTIARY 732/26-28, DE CONSOLATIONE PHILOSOPHIAE 732-29, BOKE OFF ASTRONOMY AND OFF PHILOSOPHYE 732-30, HISTOIRE ANCIENNE JUSQU A CESAR 732-31, ORMESBY PSALTER 732-32, ASTROLOGICAL AND ECCLESIASTICAL CALENDAR 732-33, ROMANCE OF ALEXANDER 732-34, DOUCE APOCALYPSE 732-35, LINCOLN APOCALYPSE 732-36, ROMAN DE LA ROSE 732-37, ROMANCE OF RENART THE FOX AND ISENGRIN 732-38

*SHELFMARK MS DOUCE 364/ FOL 5V 732-1, MS BODLEY 764/ FOL 41V 732-2, MS ASTOR A 24/ FOL 7V 732-3, MS BODLEY 764/ FOL 85V 732-4, MS DOUCE 267/ FOL 7V 732-5, MS LAUD MISC 570/ FOL 28V 732-6, MS DOUCE 335/ FOL 25 732-7, MS AUCT F 2 20/ FOL 6 732-8, MS DOUCE 134/ FOL 100 732-9, MS ASHMOLE 1462/ FOL 23 732-10, MS ASHMOLE 1504/ FOL 15 732-11, MS BODLEY 130/ FOL 50V 732-12, MS DOUCE 204/ FOL 24 732-13, MS DOUCE 195/ FOL 1 732-14, MS CANON CLASS LAT 257/ FOL 1 732-15, MS DOUCE 48/ FOL 17 732-16, MS DOUCE 353/ FOL 117 732-17, MS LAUD MISC 752/ FOL 5V 732-18, MS CANON BIBL LAT 60/ FOL 11 732-19, MS DOUCE 336-37/ FOL 6 732-20, MS AUCT F 2 20/ FOL 42V 732-21, MS BODLEY 614/ FOL 18V 732-22, MS BODLEY 614/ FOL 17V 732-23, MS BODLEY 264/ FOL 59 732-24, MS ASHMOLE 828/ FOL 76 732-25, MS BODLEY 764/ FOL 26 732-26, MS DOUCE 88/ FOL 29V 732-27, MS BODLEY 764/ FOL 74V 732-28, MS AUCT F 6 5/ FOL 1V 732-29, MS RAWL D 1220/ FOL 31V 732-30, MS DOUCE 353/ FOL 173 732-31, MS DOUCE 366/ FOL 71V 732-32, MS RAWL D 939/ SECTION 1 732-33, MS BODLEY 264/ FOL 78 732-34, MS DOUCE 180/ PAGE 25 732-35, MS LINCOLN COLLEGE LAT 16/ FOL 150 732-36, MS DOUCE 332/ FOL 58 732-37, MS DOUCE 360/ FOL 21 732-38

*PROVENANCE FRENCH 732-1, ENGLISH 732-2, FLEMISH/ BRUGES 732-3, ENGLISH 732-4, FRENCH/ BESANCON 732-5, FRENCH 732-6, ENGLISH 732/7-8, FRENCH 732-9, ENGLISH 732/10-11, ENGLISH/ BURY ST EDMUNDS 732-12, SPANISH/ CATALONIA ROUSSILLON 732-13, FRENCH 732-14, ITALIAN/ BOLOGNA 732-15, FRENCH/ NORTH? 732-16, FRENCH 732-17, ENGLISH 732-18, GERMAN/ SALZBURG 732-19, FRENCH 732/20-21, ENGLISH 732/22-23, FLEMISH 732-24, FRENCH 732-25, ENGLISH 732/26-28, ENGLISH/ WINCHESTER OR HEREFORD? 732-29, ENGLISH 732-30, FRENCH 732-31, ENGLISH/ EAST ANGLIA 732-32, ENGLISH 732-33, FLEMISH 732-34, ENGLISH 732/35-36, FRENCH 732/37-38

*DATE EXECUTED 15TH/C1460-70 732-1, 13TH 732-2, 16TH/C1525 732-3, 13TH 732-4, 15TH/C1470 732-5, 15TH/1450 732-6, 15TH/ MID 732-7, 11TH/ 2ND QUARTER 732-8, 15TH/C1450-70 732-9, 12TH/ LATE 732-10, 16TH/1520-30 732-11, 11TH/ LATE 732-12, 15TH/C1430-50 732-13, 15TH/ LATE 732-14, 14TH/1383 732-15, 13TH/ 3RD QUARTER 732-16, 15TH/ LATE 732-17, 12TH/ LATE 732-18, 12TH/1178 732-19, 15TH/ BEFORE 1463? 732-20, 11TH/ 1ST HALF 732-21, 12TH/ MID 732/22-23, 14TH/1338-44 732-24, 14TH/ EARLY 732-25, 13TH/ 2ND QUARTER 732-26, 13TH/ LATE 732-27, 13TH/ 2ND QUARTER 732-28, 12TH/ 2ND QUARTER 732-29, 15TH/ 3RD QUARTER 732/30-31, 14TH/ EARLY 732-32, 14TH/ 2ND HALF 732-33, 14TH/1338-44 732-34, 13TH 732-35, 14TH 732-36, 14TH/ LATE 732-37, 14TH/1339 732-38

*LANGUAGE FRENCH 732-1, LATIN 732/2-4, FRENCH AND LATIN 732-5, FRENCH 732-6, ENGLISH 732-7, LATIN 732-8, FRENCH 732-9, LATIN 732/10-13, FRENCH 732-14, LATIN 732/15-16, FRENCH 732-17, LATIN 732/18-19, FRENCH 732-20, LATIN 732/21-23, FRENCH 732/24-25, LATIN 732/26-29, ENGLISH 732-30, FRENCH 732-31, LATIN 732-32, ENGLISH AND LATIN 732-33, FRENCH 732-34, FRENCH AND LATIN 732-35, LATIN 732-36, FRENCH 732/37-38

*ARTIST/ SCHOOL MASTER OF SIR JOHN FASTOLF 732-6, DYAMAS/ LAURENTIUS 732-13, TESTARD/ ROBINET 732-14, DE GRISE/ JEHAN 732/24 AND 34

*AUTHOR DE LORRIS/ GUILLAUME AND JEAN DE MEUNG 732-1, DE PISAN/ CHRISTINE 732-6, EDWARD DUKE OF YORK 732-7, ISIDORE OF SEVILLE 732-8, PSEUDO APULEIUS BARBARUS 732-12, DE LORRIS/ GUILLAUME AND JEAN DE MEUNG 732/14 AND 37 MACROBIUS 732/15 AND 21, BOETHIUS 732-29

*TYPE OF MANUSCRIPT ROMANCE 732-1, BESTIARY 732-2, BOOK OF HOURS 732-3, BESTIARY 732-4, BOOK OF HOURS/ USE OF BESANCON 732-5, LITERATURE 732-6, TREATISE ON HUNTING 732-7, TREATISE 732-8, LIFE OF THE VIRGIN 732-9, HERBAL 732-10, PATTERN BOOK

732-11, HERBAL 732-12, RELIGIOUS TREATISE 732-13, ROMANCE 732-14, TREATISE 732-15, PSALTER 732-16, HISTORY 732-17, BIBLE 732-18, GOSPELS 732-19, TREATISE 732-20, TREATISE 732-21, CALENDAR 732-22, CALENDAR 732-23, ROMANCE 732/24-25, BESTIARY 732/26-28, PHILOSOPHY 732-29, ASTRONOMY 732-30, HISTORY 732-31, PSALTER 732-32, CALENDAR 732-33, ROMANCE 732-34, APOCALYPSE 732/35-36, ROMANCE 732/37-38
*CONTENTS CHAUCER/ ILLUSTRATIONS OF NUN'S PRIEST'S TALE 732/1-38, LITERATURE/ NUN'S PRIEST'S TALE BY CHAUCER 732/1-38, POVERTY/ LINE 2821 732-1, COW MILKED BY WOMAN/ LINE 2846 732-2, TAURUS THE BULL/ POULTRY/ MILKING/ LINE 2847-48 732-3, ROOSTER/ LINE 2849 732-4, ORGAN PORTATIVE/ LINE 2851 732-5, ATTEMPANCE WINDS CLOCK/ LINE 2854 732-6, CLOCK WITH VISIBLE WHEELWORK 732-6, FOX/ LINE 2899-900 732-7, HUMOURS OF THE SEASON/ LINE 2923 732-8, DEVIL BITES AND CLAWS DAMNED/ LINE 2936 732-9, CHIRON HOLDS SPRIG OF CENTAURIA MAIOR/ LINE 2962 732-10, HELLEBORE AND IRIS/ LINE 2964 732-11, KATAPUCE OR EUPHORBIA LATHYRIS/ LINE 2865 732-12, NEBUCHADNEZZAR'S DREAM TREE/ DETAIL 732-13, OWLS AND APES/ LINE 3092 732-13, DREAMER FALLS ASLEEP/ LINE 3094 732-14, MACROBIUS WITH SCIPIO AND KING MASINISSA/ LINE 3123-24 732-15, PHARAOH JUDGES HIS BUTLER AND BAKER/ LINE 3133-35 732-16, ACHILLES KILLS HECTOR/ LINE 3141-48 732-17, INITIAL I/ LINE 3163 732-18, CREATION SCENES 732-18, INITIAL I/ LINE 3163 732-19, ADAM AND EVE CREATED/ LINE 3187-88 732-20, ZODIAC SIGNS/ PLANETS/ EARTH/ LINE 3193-95 732-21, TAURUS THE BULL/ LINE 3194 732-22, CHARIOT OF THE SUN GOD/ LINE 3198-99 732-23, LADY OFFERS HER HEART TO YOUTH/ LINE 3200 732-24, LANCELOT BESIDE LADY OF MALEHAUT/ LINE 3211-13 732-25, FOX FEIGNS DEATH TO CATCH BIRDS/ LINE 3215 732-26, ADAM AND EVE EXPELLED FROM EDEN/ LINE 3257-58 732-27, SIRENS PUT SAILORS TO SLEEP WITH SONGS/ LINE 3269-72 732-28, BOETHIUS IN PRISON/ LINE 3293-94 732-29, VENUS HOLDS WHEEL OF FORTUNE/ LINE 3341-46 732-30, WHEEL OF FORTUNE 732-30, PIRRHUS KILLS PRIAM AT PRAYER/ LINE 3355-59 732-31, FOX RUNS AWAY WITH COCK/ LINE 3375-81 732-32, HARRY YE HAYWARDE AND DOG/ LINE 3383 732-33, TRUMPETS BLOWN BY MEN/ LINE 3398-99 732-34, STAR FALLS FROM HEAVEN/ LINE 3401 732-35, EARTHQUAKE/ LINE 3401 732-36, FORTUNE TURNS HER WHEEL/ LINE 3403-04 732-37, WHEEL OF FORTUNE 732-37, RENART CHASED BY WOMAN WITH DISTAFF/ LINE 3515-17 732-38

*$ABSTRACT 733
*LIBRARY BODLEIAN
*SLIDE SET TITLE HORACE
*NEGATIVE REFERENCE ROLL 277B
*RENTAL FEE $3.50
*COMMENTS MANUSCRIPT WRITTEN AND ILLUMINATED BY A. FAIRBANK AND LOUISE POWELL.
*TITLE OF MANUSCRIPT CARMINA BY HORACE
*PROVENANCE ENGLISH
*DATE EXECUTED 20TH
*ARTIST/ SCHOOL FAIRBANK/ A AND LOUISE POWELL
*AUTHOR HORACE
*TYPE OF MANUSCRIPT FACSIMILE OF HORACE MS
*CONTENTS HORACE FACSIMILE 733/1-30, CARMINA BY HORACE 733/1-30, TEXT OPENING OF CARMINA BOOK I 733-1, TEXT PAGES 733/2-3, DETAILS OF LETTERING 733/4-5, MINIATURE IN BOTTOM BORDER 733-6, MINIATURE IN RIGHT HAND BORDER 733-7, TEXT OPENING OF CARMINA BOOK II 733-8, DETAIL OF LETTERING 733-9, MINIATURE IN LEFT HAND BORDER 733-10, MINIATURE IN TOP BORDER 733-11, MINIATURE IN RIGHT HAND BORDER 733-12, MINIATURE IN BOTTOM BORDER 733-13, TEXT PAGES 733-14, TEXT OPENING OF CARMINA BOOK III 733-15, DETAIL OF LETTERING 733-16, MINIATURE IN BOTTOM BORDER 733-17, MINIATURE IN LEFT HAND BORDER 733-18, HORACE/ PORTRAIT 733-19, TEXT PAGE 733-20, TEXT OPENING OF CARMINA BOOK IV 733-21, TEXT PAGE/ TOP HALF 733-22, TEXT PAGE/ BOTTOM HALF 733-23, TEXT PAGE OF EPODE I 733-24, DETAIL OF LETTERING 733-25, DETAIL OF BOTTOM BORDER 733-26, DETAIL OF RIGHT HAND BORDER 733-27, DETAIL OF TOP BORDER 733-28, COLOPHON OF A FAIRBANK 733-29, COLOPHON OF LOUISE POWELL 733-30

*$ABSTRACT 734
*LIBRARY BODLEIAN
*SLIDE SET TITLE VIRGIL'S BUCOLICS AND GEORGICS
*NEGATIVE REFERENCE ROLL 277C
*RENTAL FEE $3.05
*COMMENTS MANUSCRIPT WRITTEN AND ILLUMINATED BY A. FAIRBANK
AND LOUISE POWELL.
*TITLE OF MANUSCRIPT BUCOLICS AND GEORGICS BY VIRGIL
*PROVENANCE ENGLISH
*DATE EXECUTED 20TH
*ARTIST/ SCHOOL FAIRBANK/ A AND LOUISE POWELL
*AUTHOR VIRGIL
*TYPE OF MANUSCRIPT FACSIMILE OF VIRGIL MS
*CONTENTS BUCOLICS AND GEORGICS BY VIRGIL 734/1-21, VIRGI
FACSIMILE 734/1-21, TITLE PAGE TO BUCOLICS AND GEORGICS 734-1,
CALENDAR SCENES AND ZODIAC SIGNS 734-1, ZODIAC SIGNS 734-1,
ARIES TO VIRGO 734-2, LIBRA TO PISCES 734-3, ECOLOGUE I FRO
BUCOLICS 734-4, INITIAL T TITYRE 734-5, INITIAL F FORMOSU
734-6, ECOLOGUE II FROM BUCOLICS 734-6, INITIAL D DIC 734-7,
ECOLOGUE III FROM BUCOLICS 734-7, INITIAL S SICELIDES 734-8,
ECOLOGUE IV FROM BUCOLICS 734-8, INITIAL C CUR 734-9, ECOLOGU
V FROM BUCOLICS 734-9, INITIAL P PRIMA 734-10, ECOLOGUE V
FROM BUCOLICS 734-10, INITIAL F FORTE 734-11, ECOLOGUE VI
FROM BUCOLICS 734-11, INITIAL P PASTORUM 734-12, ECOLOGUE VIII
FROM BUCOLICS 734-12, INITIAL Q QUO 734-13, ECOLOGUE IX FRO
BUCOLICS 734-13, INITIAL E EXTREMUM 734-14, ECOLOGUE X FRO
BUCOLICS 734-14, GEORGICS BOOK I 734-15, INITIAL Q QUI
734-16, GEORGICS BOOK I 734-16, GEORGICS BOOK II 734-17,
INITIAL H HACTENUS 734-18, GEORGICS BOOK III 734-18, INITIAL
TE 734-19, GEORGICS BOOK III 734-19, INITIAL P PROTINU
734-20, GEORGICS BOOK IV 734-20, COLOPHON 734-21

*$ABSTRACT 735
*LIBRARY BODLEIAN
*SLIDE SET TITLE CARTOGRAPHIC TREASURES EXHIBITION I
*NEGATIVE REFERENCE ROLL 279A
*RENTAL FEE $3.85
*COMMENTS PHOTOGRAPHED FROM THE EXHIBITION ARRANGED I
CONNECTION WITH THE SIXTH INTERNATIONAL CONFERENCE ON TH
HISTORY OF CARTOGRAPHY HELD AT THE NATIONAL MARITIME MUSEUM I
SEPTEMBER 1975.
*TITLE OF MANUSCRIPT BODLEIAN EXHIBITION POSTER 735-1, CHART O
THE GLOBE 735-2, TRUE HYDROGRAPHICAL DESCRIPTION OF SO MUCH O
THE WORLD 735-3, MAPPA MUNDI 735/4-7, MAP OF RHODES 735-8, MA
OF CRETE 735-9, MAPS OF ENGLAND AND IRELAND 735-10, MAP O
SOUTHERN EUROPE AND NORTH AFRICA 735/11-12, MAP OF WESTER
EUROPE AND NORTH AFRICA 735-13, MAP OF THE BRITISH ISLE
735-14, MAP OF THE WORLD 735/15-16, MAP OF THE BRITISH ISLE
735-17, MAP OF THE NEW WORLD 735-20, APHRICA 735-21, HAMBUR
735-22, HAMBURG 735-23, AMERICAE PARS MUNC VIRGINIA DICT
735-24, VIRGINIA 735-25, MAP OF THE MOON 735/26-27, MAP OF TH
CONSTELLATIONS IN SOUTHERN HEMISPHERE 735-28, AMERICAE SIV
NOVI ORBIS NOVA DESCRIPTIO 735-29, FOOLS CAP MAP OF THE WORL
735-30, LOMBARDARDIAE ALPESTRIS 735-31, SALTZBUR
ARCHIEPISCOPATUS 735-32, THE CARDE OF THE NORTH COAST O
ENGLAND 735-33,CARTA QUINTA GENERALE DI EUROPA 735-34, MAP O
THE THAMES ESTUARY 735-35, BOLOGNA 735/36-37
*SHELFMARK MS CANON CLASS LAT 257 735-4, MS CANON MISC 56
735-5, MS TANNER 190 735-6, MS TANNER 170 735-7, PR AUCT Q
29 735-8, MS RAWL D 589 735-9, MS ASHMOLE 1352 735-10, M
CANON ITAL 143 735/11-12, MS DOUCE 391 735-13, PR AUCT K 1 1
735-14, PR AUCT P 1 4 735-15, PR BYW H 5 9 735-16, PR SAVILE
5 735-17, PR TANNER 818 2 735-18, PR B 26 14 LINC 735-19, P
DOUCE MM 417 735-20, PR B 2 10 TH SELD 735-22, PR E II 2
735-23, PR J MAPS 230 1A 735-24, MS ASHMOLE 1758 735-25, P
SAVILE B 15 735-26, PR SAVILE F 3 735-27, PR BUCHANAN E 8
735-28, PR DOUCE O SUBT 15 735-29, PR DOUCE PORTFOLIO 142 9
735-30, PR B6 20 ART 735-31, PR J MAPS 230 21 735-32, PR MASO
Q 233 735-33, PR MASON BB 104 735-34, PR MASON S 160 735-35
PR J MAPS 267 47 735/36-37

*DATE EXECUTED 17TH/1610 735-2, 17TH/1600 735-3, 14TH/1383? 735-4, 11TH/C1055-74 735-5, 14TH/1316-21 735-6, 14TH/1347 735-7, 15TH/1485 735-8, 16TH 735-9, 16TH/1546 735-10, 16TH/1559 735/11-12, 16TH 735-13, 15TH/1462 735-14, 15TH/1482 735-15, 16TH/1564 735-16, 16TH/1578 735-17, 16TH/1545 735-18, 16TH/1597 735-19, 16TH/1556 735-20, 17TH/1600 735-21, 16TH-17TH/1572-1618 735-22, 17TH/1653 735-23, 16TH/1590 735-24, 17TH/1612 735-25, 17TH/1647 735-26, 17TH/1665 735-27, 17TH/1693 735-28, 17TH/1606 735-29, 16TH/C1580 735-30, 16TH/1595 735-31, 17TH/1630 735-32, 16TH/1588 735-33, 17TH/1646-47 735-34, 17TH/1639 735-35, 17TH/1663 735/36-37
*AUTHOR WRIGHT/ EDWARD 735-2, HAKLUYT/ RICHARD 735-3, MACROBIUS 735-4, BEDE 735-5, SANUDO 735-6, HIGDEN/ RANULF 735-7, BARTOLOMMEO DALLI SONETTI 735-8, BROUSCON/ G 735-10, BARTOLOMES OLIVES 735/11-12, MARTINES/ JOAN 735-13, PTOLEMY 735/14-17, APIAN/ PETER 735-18, DANFRIE/ PHILIPPE 735-19, MUNSTER/ SEBASTIAN 735-20, MATTHIAS QUAD 735-21, BRAUN AND HOGENBERG 735-22, MERIAN/ MATTHIAS 735-23, DE BRY/ THEODORE 735-24, SMITH/ JOHN 735-25, HEVELIUS/ JOHANNES 735-26, RICCIOLI/ GIOVANNI 735-27, CORONELLI/ VINCENZO 735-28, ORTELIUS/ ABRAHAM 735-29, MERCATOR/ GERARD 735-31, MERCATOR-HONDIUS 735-32, WAGHENAER 735-33, DUDLEY/ ROBERT 735-34, BLEU/ W J 735-35, BLAEU/ J 735/36-37
*TYPE OF MANUSCRIPT MAPS
*CONTENTS CARTOGRAPHY 735/1-37, MAPS 735/1-37, BODLEIAN EXHIBITION POSTER 735-1, CHART OF THE GLOBE 735-2, MAP OF THE WORLD 735-3, MAPPA MUNDI 735/4-7, MAP OF RHODES 735-8, MAP OF CRETE 735-9, MAPS OF ENGLAND AND IRELAND 735-10, MAP OF SOUTHERN EUROPE AND NORTH AFRICA 735-11, MAP OF VENICE/ DETAIL 735-12, MAP OF WESTERN EUROPE AND NORTH AFRICA 735-13, MAP OF THE BRITISH ISLES 735-14, MAP OF THE WORLD 735-15, MAP OF THE WORLD 735-16, MAP OF THE BRITISH ISLES 735-17, ASTROLABE AND CLIMATIC ZONES 735-18, SURVEYORS TAKING SIGHTINGS 735-19, MAP OF THE NEW WORLD 735-20, MAP OF AFRICA 735-21, MAP OF HAMBURG 735/22-23, MAP OF VIRGINIA 735/24-25, MAP OF THE MOON 735/26-27, MAP OF THE CONSTELLATIONS IN SOUTHERN HEMISPHERE 735-28, MAP OF THE NEW WORLD 735-29, MAP OF THE WORLD 735-30, MAP OF LOMBARDIAE ALPESTRIS 735-31, MAP OF SALTZBURG ARCHIEPISCOPATUS 735-32, MAP OF THE NORTH COAST OF ENGLAND 735-33, MAP OF EUROPE 735-34, MAP OF THE THAMES ESTUARY 735-35, MAP OF BOLOGNA 735/36-37

*$ABSTRACT 736
*LIBRARY BODLEIAN
*SLIDE SET TITLE CARTOGRAPHIC TREASURES EXHIBITION II
*NEGATIVE REFERENCE ROLL 279B
*RENTAL FEE $3.75
*COMMENTS PHOTOGRAPHED FROM THE EXHIBITION ARRANGED IN CONNECTION WITH THE SIXTH INTERNATIONAL CONFERENCE ON THE HISTORY OF CARTOGRAPHY HELD AT THE NATIONAL MARITIME MUSEUM IN GREENWICH IN SEPTEMBER 1975.
*TITLE OF MANUSCRIPT MAP OF BUCKINGHAMSHIRE 736-1, OXFORDSHIRE BUCKINGHAMSHIRE BERKSHIRE 736-2,MAP OF CHESHIRE 736-3, NORTHAMPTONSHIRE 736-4, CAMDEN'S BRITANNIA 736-5, OXFORDSHIRE BUCKINGHAMSHIRE BERKSHIRE 736-6,OXFORDSHIRE 736-7, OXFORDSHIRE BERKSHIRE BUCKINGHAMSHIRE 736-8,BERKSHIRE 736-9, THE ROAD FROM LONDON TO ABERISTWITH 736-10, THE ROAD FROM OXFORD TO SALISBURY 736-11, OXFORDSHIRE 736/12-14, MAP OF TWENTY MILES ROUND THE CITY OF OXFORD 736-15, BERKSHIRE 736-16, OXFORDSHIRE AND THE ROAD FROM BRISTOL TO BANBURY 736-17, BUCKINGHAMSHIRE 736-18, OXFORDSHIRE 736-19, ENGLISH ATLAS 736/20-21, ROYAL ENGLISH ATLAS 736-22, BLENHEIM PALACE 736-23, MAP OF PORT MEADOW 736-24, TOPOGRAPHICAL MAP OF THE COUNTY OF BERKS 736-25, OXFORDSHIRE 736/26-27, BERKSHIRE 736-28, OXFORD 736-29, OXFORDSHIRE 736/30-32, ORDNANCE SURVEY 1801 736-33, ORDNANCE SURVEY 1887 736-34, ORDNANCE SURVEY 1875 736-35
*SHELFMARK PR 2027 A46 736-1, PR FOL BS 45 736-2, MS RAWL B 282 736-3, PR E C17 46 14 736-4, PR GOUGH GEN TOP 50 736-5, PR VET B 2 F22 736-6, PR J MAPS 224 10 736-7, PR WOOD 403 736-8, PR ANTIQ F E 11 736-9, PR VET A 3 B10 736-10, PR GOUGH MAPS 112

736-11, PR DOUCE P19 736-13, PR J MAPS 224 17 736-14, PR GOUGH MAPS OXFORDSHIRE 8 736-15, PR GOUGH MAPS BERKSHIRE 2 736-16, PR G A ENG RDS 8 92 736-17, PR GOUGH GEN TOP 220 736-18, PR C17 F3 736-19, PR GOUGH MAPS BERKS 5 736/20-21, PR J MAPS 224 31 736-22, PR G A OXON 8 246 736-23, PR E C17 70 OXFORD 40 736-24, PR GOUGH MAPS BERKS 6 736-25, PR C17 49 A1 736-26, PR J MAPS 224 5 736-27, PR J MAPS 224 14 736-28, PR J MAPS 224 22 736-29, PR E 17 49 4 736-30, PR J MAPS 251 1 736-31, PR J MAPS 224 16 736-32, PR GOUGH MAPS KENT 48 736-33
*PROVENANCE ENGLISH
*DATE EXECUTED 17TH/1648 736-1, 16TH/1579 736-2, 16TH/1588 736-3, 17TH/1602-03 736-4, 17TH/1610 736-5, 17TH/1617 736-6, 17TH/1611 736-7, 17TH/1612 736-8, 17TH/1626 736-9, 17TH/1675 736-10, 18TH/1719 736-11, 17TH/1673 736-12, 17TH/1677 736-13, 17TH/1693 736-14, 18TH/1705 736-15, 18TH/1720 736-16, 18TH/1720 736-17, 18TH/1724 736-18, 18TH/1724 736-19, 18TH/1760 736/20-21, 18TH/1777 736-22, 19TH/1803 736-23, 18TH/1710 736-24, 18TH/1761 736/25-26, 19TH/1801 736-27, 19TH/1805 736-28, 19TH/1832 736-29, 19TH/1824 736-30, 19TH/1834 736-31, 19TH/1852 736-32, 19TH/1801 736-33, 19TH/1887 736-34, 19TH/1875 736-35
*AUTHOR BLAEU/ J 736-1, SAXTON/ CHRISTOPHER 736-2, SMITH/ WILLIAM 736/3-4, CAMDEN 736-5, PIETER VAN DEN KEER 736-6, SPEED/ JOHN 736-7, DRAYTON/ MICHAEL 736-8, BILL/ JOHN 736-9, OGILBY/ JOHN 736-10, GARDNER/ THOMAS 736-11, BLOME/ RICHARD 736-12, PLOT/ ROBERT 736-13, MORDEN/ ROBERT 736-14, COLE/ BENJAMIN 736-15, HOLLAR/ WENCESLAUS 736-16, OWEN/ JOHN AND EMANUEL BROWN 736-17, MOLL/ HERMAN 736-18, BADESLADE/ THOMAS 736-19, BOWEN/ EMANUEL AND THOMAS KITCHIN 736/20-22, PRIDE/ THOMAS 736-23, COLE/ BENJAMIN 736-24, ROCQUE/ JOHN 736-25, DAVIS/ RICHARD 736-26, SMITH/ CHARLES 736-27, CARY/ JOHN 736-28, DAWSON/ ROBERT 736-29, BRYANT/ ANDREW 736-30, GREENWOOD/ C AND J 736-31
*TYPE OF MANUSCRIPT MAPS
*CONTENTS CARTOGRAPHY EXHIBITION II 736/1-35, MAP OF BUCKINGHAMSHIRE 736-1, MAP OF OXFORDSHIRE/ BUCKINGHAMSHIRE/ BERKSHIRE 736-2, MAP OF CHESHIRE 736-3, MAP OF NORTHAMPTONSHIRE 736-4, MAP OF OXFORDSHIRE FROM CAMDEN'S BRITANNIA 736-5, MAP OF OXFORDSHIRE/ BUCKINGHAMSHIRE/ BERKSHIRE 736-6, MAP OF OXFORDSHIRE 736-7, MAP OF OXFORDSHIRE/ BERKSHIRE/ BUCKINGHAMSHIRE 736-8, MAP OF BERKSHIRE 736-9, MAP OF ROAD FROM LONDON TO ABERISTWITH 736-10, MAP OF ROAD FROM OXFORD TO SALISBURY 736-11, MAP OF OXFORDSHIRE 736/12-14, MAP OF TWENTY MILES AROUND OXFORD 736-15, MAP OF BERKSHIRE 736-16, MAP OF OXFORDSHIRE AND ROAD TO BANBURY 736-17, MAP OF BUCKINGHAMSHIRE 736-18, MAP OF OXFORDSHIRE 736-19, MAP OF BERKSHIRE 736/20-21, MAP OF OXFORDSHIRE 736-22, MAP OF BLENHEIM PALACE/ GARDENS/ PARK 736-23, MAP OF PORT MEADOW 736-24, MAP OF BERKSHIRE 736-25, MAP OF WOODSTOCK AREA IN OXFORDSHIRE 736-26, MAP OF OXFORDSHIRE 736-27, MAP OF BERKSHIRE 736-28, MAP OF OXFORD 736-29, MAP OF AREA BETWEEN OXFORD AND WATLINGTON 736-30, MAP OF OXFORDSHIRE 736/31-32, MAP OF KENT FROM ORDNANCE SURVEY OF 1801 736-33, MAP OF OXFORD FROM ORDNANCE SURVEY OF 1887 736-34, MAP OF ABINGDON FROM ORDNANCE SURVEY OF 1875 736-35

*$ABSTRACT 737
*LIBRARY BODLEIAN
*SLIDE SET TITLE GOLD-TOOLED RENAISSANCE BINDINGS
*NEGATIVE REFERENCE ROLL 269
*RENTAL FEE $2.65
*TITLE OF MANUSCRIPT DE RATIONE EXAMINANDAE ORATIONIS 737-4, GRAMMATICA 737-5, HOMILIAE 737-7, FLORILEGIUM 737-13
*SHELFMARK MS AUCT E 1 11 737-1, MS AUCT E 1 16 737-2, MS BAROCCI 31 737-3, MS BAROCCI 53 737-4, MS BAROCCI 80 737-5, MS BAROCCI 103 737-6, MS BAROCCI 208 737-7, MS CANON GREEK 78 737-8, MS LAUD GREEK 5 737-9, MS LAUD GREEK 18 737-10, MS NEW COLLEGE 146 737-11, MS NEW COLLEGE 245 737-12, MS NEW COLLEGE 270 737-13
*DATE EXECUTED 16TH

*AUTHOR EUSEBIUS 737-1, ACOMINATUS/ NICETAS 737-2, EVANGELIA 737-3, MOSCHOPOULOS 737-4, LASCARIS 737-5, MOSCHOPOULOS 737-6, CHRYSOSTOM 737-7, STRABO 737-8, DEMOSTHENES 737-9, PROCLUS 737-10, ORIGEN 737-11, SIMPLICIUS 737-12, STOBAEUS 737-13
*TYPE OF MANUSCRIPT BOOK BINDINGS/ RENAISSANCE
*CONTENTS BOOK BINDINGS/ RENAISSANCE 737/1-13

*$ABSTRACT 738
*LIBRARY BODLEIAN
*SLIDE SET TITLE MISCELLANY 4
*NEGATIVE REFERENCE ROLL 272A
*RENTAL FEE $2.45
*COMMENTS SELECTED FROM 3 MSS OF 15TH AND 16TH CENTURIES.
*TITLE OF MANUSCRIPT FERIAL PSALTER 738/1-4, GOLDEN LEGEND 738-9
*SHELFMARK MS DON D 85/ FOL 1V 738-1, MS DON D 85/ FOL 35V 738-2, MS DON D 85/ FOL 58 738-3, MS DON D 85/ FOL 129V-130 738-4, MS MUS SCH E 420/ FOL 55V 738-5, MS MUS SCH E 421/ FOL 56V 738-6, MS MUS SCH E 421/ FOL 57 738-7, MS MUS SCH E 422/ FOL 55 738-8, MS QUEENS COLLEGE 305/ FOL 84 738-9
*PROVENANCE ENGLISH 738/1-8, FRENCH 738-9
*DATE EXECUTED 15TH/ EARLY 738/1-4, 16TH/ MID 738/5-8, 15TH/ LATE 738-9
*ARTIST/ SCHOOL JOHANNES 738/1-4
*AUTHOR DE VORAGINE/ JACOB 738-9
*TYPE OF MANUSCRIPT PSALTER/ FERIAL 738/1-4, MUSICAL TEXTS 738/5-8, LITERATURE 738-9
*CONTENTS MISCELLANY 4 738/1-9, ST CHRISTOPHER 738-1, INITIAL D DIXIT INSIPIENS/ DAVID WITH FOOL 738-2, DAVID WITH FOOL 738-2, INITIAL C CANTATE DOMINO/ CLERICS SING 738-3, CLERICS SING AT LECTERN 738-3, ST GEORGE KILLS DRAGON 738-4, MUSICAL TEXT/ IF YE LOVE ME KEEP MY COMMANDMENTS 738/5-8, ST HIPPOLYTUS MARTYRED 738-9

*$ABSTRACT 739
*LIBRARY BODLEIAN
*SLIDE SET TITLE FIFTEENTH CENTURY ILLUMINATION
*NEGATIVE REFERENCE ROLL 273A
*RENTAL FEE $5.05
*TITLE OF MANUSCRIPT DICTS AND SAYINGS OF THE PHILOSOPHERS 739/1-5, STATUTES OF ENGLAND TO 1495 739/6-7, ABINGDON MISSAL/ SUMMER PART 739/8-14, ABINGDON MISSAL/ WINTER PART 739/15-19, CONFESSIO AMANTIS 739/20-23, STATUES AND ORDINAUNCES OF THE GARDER 739-26, FERIAL PSALTER 739/27-29, CHOIR PSALTER 739/30-32, BOOK OF HOURS 739-33, LAPWORTH MISSAL 739-34, MISSAL 739/35-43, MASTER OF GAME 739/44-52, QUADRILOGUE 739/53-54, BOOK OF HOURS 739/59-61
*SHELFMARK MS BODLEY 943/ FOL 42V 739-1, MS BODLEY 943/ FOL 70 739-2, MS BODLEY 943/ FOL 73 739-3, MS BODLEY 943/ FOL 78 739-4, MS BODLEY 943/ FOL 84V 739-5, MS HATTON 10/ FOL 290 739-6, MS HATTON 10/ FOL 336V 739-7, MS DIGBY 227/ FOL 10 739-8, MS DIGBY 227/ FOL 86 739-9, MS DIGBY 227/ FOL 146V 739-10, MS DIGBY 227/ FOL 188 739-11, MS DIGBY 227/ FOL 207V 739-12, MS DIGBY 227/ FOL 209 739-13, MS DIGBY 227/ FOL 237 739-14, MS TRINITY COLLEGE 75/ FOL 21V 739-15, MS TRINITY COLLEGE 75/ FOL 33 739-16, MS TRINITY COLLEGE 75/ FOL 183 739-17, MS TRINITY COLLEGE 75/ FOL 199 739-18, MS TRINITY COLLEGE 75/ FOL 224 739-19, MS NEW COLLEGE 266/ FOL 117V 739-20, MS NEW COLLEGE 266/ FOL 124 739-21, MS MAGDALEN COLLEGE 153/ FOL 8V 739-22, MS MAGDALEN COLLEGE 153/ FOL 74V 739-23, MS MAGDALEN COLLEGE 213/ FOL 54 739-24, MS MAGDALEN COLLEGE 213/ FOL 169 739-25, MS BODLEY 609/ FOL 10 739-26, MS DON D 85/ FOL 29 639-27, MS DON D 85/ FOL 35V 739-28, MS DON D 85/ FOL 35V 739-29, MS HATTON 45/ FOL 1 739-30, MS HATTON 45/ FOL 26 739-31, MS HATTON 45/ FOL 69 739-32, MS CORPUS CHRISTI COLLEGE OXFORD/ FOL 7 739-33,MS CORPUS CHRISTI COLLEGE OXFORD/ FOL 102V 739-34, MS ORIEL COLLEGE 75/ FOL 7 739-35, MS ORIEL COLLEGE 75/ FOL 10 739-36, MS ORIEL COLLEGE 75/ FOL 37 739-37,

MS ORIEL COLLEGE 75/ FOL 40V 739-38, MS ORIEL COLLEGE 75/ FOL 150V 739-39, MS ORIEL COLLEGE 75/ FOL 221V 739-40, MS ORIEL COLLEGE 75/ FOL 225V 739-41, MS ORIEL COLLEGE 75/ FOL 270 739-42, MS ORIEL COLLEGE 75/ FOL 142V 739-43, MS DOUCE 335/ FOL 1 739-44, MS DOUCE 335/ FOL 7 739-45, MS DOUCE 335/ FOL 10V 739-46, MS DOUCE 335/ FOL 18V 739-47, MS DOUCE 335/ FOL 28 739-48, MS DOUCE 335/ FOL 39V 739-49, MS DOUCE 335/ FOL 45V 739-50, MS DOUCE 335/ FOL 46V 739-51, MS DOUCE 335/ FOL 50 739-52, MS UNIVERSITY COLLEGE 85/ FOL 1 739-53, MS UNIVERSITY COLLEGE 85/ FOL 70 739-54, MS CANON MISC 110/ FOL 7 739-55, MS CANON MISC 110/ FOL 29V 739-56, MS CANON MISC 110/ FOL 123 739-57, MS CANON MISC 110/ FOL 123 739-58, MS DOUCE 144/ FOL 105 739-59, MS DOUCE 144/ FOL 108V 739-60, MS DOUCE 144/ FOL 109 739-61

*PROVENANCE ENGLISH 739/1-5, ENGLISH/ LONDON 739/6-7, ENGLISH 739/8-29, FRENCH/ MADE IN ENGLAND 739/30-32, ENGLISH 739/33-54, ENGLISH/ NORWICH 739/55-58, FRENCH/ PARIS 739/59-61

*DATE EXECUTED 15TH/ 3RD QUARTER 739/1-5, 15TH/C1475-1500 739/6-7, 15TH/1461 739/8-19, 15TH 739/20-25, 16TH/C1572 739-26, 15TH 739/27-29, 15TH/ MID 739/30-32, 15TH 739-33, 14TH/1398 739-34, 15TH 739/35-43, 15TH/ MID 739/44-54, 15TH/C1400 739/55-58, 15TH/1407 739/59-61

*LANGUAGE ENGLISH 739/1-5, LATIN/ FRENCH/ ENGLISH 739/6-7, LATIN 739/8-19, ENGLISH 739/20-21, LATIN 739/22-23, ENGLISH 739/24-26, LATIN 739/27-43, ENGLISH 739/44-54, LATIN 739/55-58, FRENCH AND LATIN 739/59-61

*ARTIST/ SCHOOL ABELL/ WILLIAM STYLE OF 739/1-5, ABELL/ WILLIAM 739/8-19, MASTER OF SIR JOHN FASTOLF 739/30-32, LIMBOURG BROTHER 739/59-61

*AUTHOR SCROPE/ STEPHEN TRANSLATOR 739/1-5, GOWER/ JOHN 739/20-21, WALDEN/ THOMAS 739/22-23, GOWER/ JOHN 739/24-25, EDWARD DUKE OF YORK 739/44-52, CHARTIER/ ALAIN 739/53-54, DE INSULIS/ ALAN 739/55-58

*TYPE OF MANUSCRIPT TREATISE 739/1-5, STATUTES 739/6-7, MISSAL/ BENEDICTINE USE 739/8-19, LITERATURE 739/20-21, TREATISE 739/22-23, LITERATURE 739/24-25, STATUTES 739-26, PSALTER/ USE OF SARUM 739/27-29, PSALTER/ CHOIR 739/30-32, BOOK OF HOURS 739-33, MISSAL 739/34-43, TREATISE ON HUNTING 739/44-52, TREATISE 739/53-58, BOOK OF HOURS/ USE OF PARIS 739/59-61

*CONTENTS MANUSCRIPT ILLUMINATION/ 15TH CENTURY 739/1-61, FIFTEENTH CENTURY ILLUMINATION 739/1-61, PLATO 739-1, ALEXANDER THE GREAT 739-2, OLYMPIAS 739-3, ALEXANDER THE GREAT 739-4, PTOLEMY 739-5, EDWARD IV ENTHRONED WITH ATTENDANTS 739-6, HENRY VII ENTHRONED WITH ATTENDANTS 739-7, INITIAL/ GOLD ON CALENDAR PAGE 739-8, TEXT WITH COLOURED INITIALS 739-9, ST PETER HOLDS BOOK AND KEY 739-10, OFFICE FOR DEDICATION OF CHURCH 739-11, INITIAL T TERRIBILIS INSET WITH CHURCH 739-11,ST BARTHOLOMEW WITH BOOK AND KNIFE 739-12, ST JAMES THE LESS WITH FULLER'S CLUB 739-13, TRINITY 739-14, CHRIST AS INFANT 739-15, ADORATION OF THE MAGI 739-16, GLORIA WITH MUSICAL NOTATION 739-17, MUSICAL NOTATION 739-17, INITIAL G WITH ANGEL 739-17, ST ANDREW ON CROSS 739-18, INITIAL E WITH APOSTLE 739-19, BARDUS RESCUES ADRIAN FROM PIT 739-20, DIANA/ CALLISTO/ NYMPHS BATHING 739-21, NYMPHS BATHING 739-21, POPE MARTIN V RECEIVES BOOK FROM THOMAS WALDEN 739-22, AUTHOR PORTRAIT 739-22, INITIAL B DECORATED 739-23, INITIAL H AND BORDER 739-24, INITIAL F AND BORDER 739-25, INITIAL I IDEM WITH DATE 1571 739-26, INITIAL D DIXI/ DAVID POINTS TO MOUTH 739-27, DAVID POINTS TO HIS MOUTH 739-27, INITIAL D DIXIT/ DAVID AND FOOL 739-28, DAVID AND FOOL 739/28-29, INITIAL B BEATUS/ DAVID PRAYS 739-30, DAVID PRAYS TO GOD 739-30, INITIAL D DIXI/ DECORATED BORDER 739-31, INITIAL C CANTATE/ DECORATED BORDER 739-32, INITIAL D DOMINE/ VIRGIN AND CHILD 739-33, VIRGIN AND CHILD WITH LADY OWNER 739-33, SCROLL WITH PRAYER FILI DEI MISERERE MEI 739-33, CRUCIFIXION 739-34, INITIAL O/ BLESSING HOLY WATER 739-35, BLESSING HOLY WATER 739-35, INITIAL A/ ANNUNCIATION 739-36, ANNUNCIATION 739-36, INITIAL I/ ST JOHN WITH POISON CUP 739-37, ST JOHN WITH POISON CUP 739-37, INITIAL E/ ADORATION OF THE MAGI 739-38, ADORATION OF THE MAGI 739-38, INITIAL R/ RESURRECTION 739-39, RESURRECTION 739-39, INITIAL S/ PRESENTATION IN THE TEMPLE 739-40, PRESENTATION IN THE TEMPLE 739-40, INITIAL D/ ANNUNCIATION

739-41, ANNUNCIATION 739-41, INITIAL E/ GOD? POINTS TO TREE 739-42, GOD? POINTS TO TREE 739-42, CRUCIFIXION PRECEDES CANON OF MASS 739-43, INITIAL H/ HUNTSMAN 739-44, HUNTSMAN 739-44, INITIAL H/ HARE 739-45, HARE 739-45, INITIAL H/ HART 739-46, HART 739-46, INITIAL A/ WILD BOAR 739-47, BOAR 739-47, INITIAL A/ HOUNDS 739-48, HOUNDS 739-48, INITIAL A/ HOUND 739-49, HOUND 739-49, INITIAL S/ MASTER INSTRUCTS HUNTSMAN 739-50, HUNTSMAN INSTRUCTED BY MASTER 739-50, INITIAL I/ MAN GROOMS HOUNDS 739-51, GROOMING OF HOUNDS 739-51, INITIAL F/ MASTER INSTRUCTS HIS MEN 739-52, MASTER OF HUNT INSTRUCTS MEN 739-52, AUTHOR PORTRAIT WITH PEASANT/ QUEEN/ KNIGHT 739-53, KING AND DOCTOR DISCUSS ARISTOTLE 739-54, INITIAL WITH MAN'S FACE/ JESTER IN BORDER 739-55, JESTER IN BORDER 739-55, CATCH WORD IN FORM OF EAGLE 739-56, MERCY AND PHILOGIA MARRY 739/57-58 POPE GREGORY'S PROCESSION OF LITANIES 739-59, POPE GREGORY'S PROCESSION FOR TRANSLATION OF RELICS 739/60-61

*$ABSTRACT 740
*LIBRARY BODLEIAN
*SLIDE SET TITLE MISCELLANY 5
*NEGATIVE REFERENCE ROLL 273B
*RENTAL FEE $2.45
*TITLE OF MANUSCRIPT PSALTER WITH COMMENTARY 740-1, ENGLISH AND LATIN HYMNS AND SONGS 740-2, ALBUM AMICORUM 740-3, MISCELLANY 740-4, DE INVENTIONE RHETORICA 740-5, WORKS OF CAESAR 740-6, POVERTY AND ITS VICIOUS CIRCLES 740-8, KARTE VON MYKENAE 740-9
*SHELFMARK MS AUCT D 4 1/ FOL 15V 740-1, MS ARCH SELD B 26/ FOL 19V 740-2, MS ASHMOLE 1/ FOL 133 740-3, MS DIGBY 88/ FOL 15 740-4, MS BARLOW 40/ FOL 1 740-5, MS E D CLARKE 25/ FOL 169V 740-6
*DATE EXECUTED 09TH/ LATE 740-1, 15TH/ MID 740-2, 17TH/1618-27 740-3, 15TH-16TH 740-4, 12TH/ 2ND QUARTER 740-5, 15TH/ 3RD QUARTER 740-6, 15TH 740-7, 20TH/1921 740-8, 19TH/1884 740-9
*LANGUAGE GREEK 740-1, ENGLISH AND LATIN 740-2, GERMAN AND LATIN 740-3, ENGLISH AND LATIN 740-4, LATIN 740/5-6
*ARTIST/ SCHOOL JACAPO FILIPPO D'ARGENTA 740-6, LORENZO DI PIETRO 740-7
*AUTHOR LUDOLF VON DEM WARDEN 740-3, CICERO 740-5, CAESAR 740-6, HURRY/ J B 740-8
*TYPE OF MANUSCRIPT PSALTER 740-1, HYMNS AND SONGS 740-2, ALBUM AMICORUM 740-3, MISCELLANY 740-4, RHETORICAL TREATISE 740-5, WORKS 740-6, PAINTING 740-7, MAP 740-9
*CONTENTS MISCELLANY 5 740/1-9, DAVID IN BYZANTINE PSALTER 740-1, GLAD AND BLYTHE MOTE YE BE 740-2, FORTUNA STANDS ON WINGED WHEEL 740-3, DIAGRAM/ CIRCULAR FOR FORTUNE TELLING 740-4, FORTUNE TELLING DIAGRAM 740-4, CICERO FLANKED BY CATO AND CAESAR 740-5, PORTRAIT OF LUDOVICO CARBONE 740-6, GRAIN GIVEN TO HOSPITAL OF S MARIA DELLA SCALA 740-7, POVERTY AND ITS VICIOUS CIRCLES 740-8, MAP OF MYCENAE DISTRICT 740-9

*$ABSTRACT 741
*LIBRARY BODLEIAN
*SLIDE SET TITLE MISCELLANY 6
*NEGATIVE REFERENCE ROLL 274A
*RENTAL FEE $2.30
*TITLE OF MANUSCRIPT DE CIVITATE DEI 741/1-2, COMMENTARY ON PSALMS 51 TO 100 741/3-5, PSALTER AND NEW TESTAMENT 741-6, GLOSS ON THE GOSPELS 741-7, ANNALS OF INNISFALLEN 741-8, FOOLS CAP MAP OF THE WORLD 741-9, MAP OF VIRGINIA 741-10, MAP OF THE WORLD 741-11, THE BATTLE OF PINKIE 741/22-26
*SHELFMARK MS LAUD MISC 469/ FOL 8 741-1, MS LAUD MISC 469/ FOL 198V 741-2, MS LAUD MISC 470/ FOL 12V 741-3, MS LAUD MISC 470/ FOL 64 741-4, MS LAUD MISC 470/ FOL 3 741-5, MS CANON BIBL LAT 76/ FOL 85 741-6, MS MERTON COLLEGE 212/ FOL 10V 741-7, MS RAWL B 503 741-8, MS ASHMOLE 1758 741-10, MS ENG MISC C 13R 741/22-26
*PROVENANCE ENGLISH 741/1-2, ENGLISH/ BURY ST EDMUNDS 741/3-5, GERMAN/ SALZBURG 741-6, ENGLISH OR FRENCH/ OXFORD OR PARIS

741-7, IRISH 741-8, ENGLAND 741/22-26
*DATE EXECUTED 12TH/ 2ND QUARTER 741/1-2, 12TH/ 3RD QUARTER 741/3-5, 12TH/ LATE 741-6, 13TH/ 1ST HALF 741-7, 14TH 741-8, 16TH/C1580 741-9, 17TH/1612 741-10, 15TH/1482 741-11, 16TH/1547 741/22-26
*AUTHOR AUGUSTINE 741/1-5, CANTOR/ PETER 741-7, SMITH/ JOHN 741-10, PTOLEMY 741-11
*TYPE OF MANUSCRIPT RELIGIOUS TREATISE 741/1-2, COMMENTARY 741/3-5, PSALTER AND NEW TESTAMENT 741-6, GLOSS ON GOSPELS 741-7, ANNALS 741-8, MAP 741/9-11, WRAPPERS AND LABELS 741/12-21, DRAWINGS 741/22-26
*CONTENTS MISCELLANY 6 741/1-26, INITIAL G/ DECORATIVE MOTIF WITH MONSTERS 741-1, MONSTERS IN DECORATIVE MOTIF 741-1, INITIAL C CUM/ MAN SPEARS ANOTHER MAN 741-2, INITIAL P PSALMI 741-3, INITIAL A AGNOSCENDA 741-4, INITIAL P 741-5, INITIAL I/ ST JOHN WITH EAGLE HEAD 741-6, ST JOHN WITH EAGLE HEAD 741-6, TEXT PAGE OF GLOSS ON GOSPELS 741-7, OGHAM LETTERS READ NEMO HONORATUR SINE NUMMO NULLUS AMATUR 741-8, MAP OF THE WORLD 741-9, MAP OF VIRGINIA 741-10, MAP OF THE WORLD 741-11, FRUIT WRAPPERS AND LABELS 741/12-21, BATTLE OF PINKIE/ COLOURED DRAWINGS 741/22-26

*$ABSTRACT 742
*LIBRARY BODLEIAN
*SLIDE SET TITLE ENGLISH DRAWINGS
*NEGATIVE REFERENCE ROLL 274B
*RENTAL FEE $2.25
*TITLE OF MANUSCRIPT LEOFRIC MISSAL 742/1-4, CALENDAR AND COMPUTISTICAL TABLES 742-5
*SHELFMARK MS BODLEY 579/ FOL 49 742-1, MS BODLEY 579/ FOL 49V 742/2-4, MS DIGBY 56/ FOL 165V 742-5
*PROVENANCE ENGLISH/ GLASTONBURY 742/1-4, ENGLISH 742-5
*DATE EXECUTED 10TH/C966-76 742/1-4, 12TH/C1164-68 742-5
*LANGUAGE LATIN
*ARTIST/ SCHOOL WINCHESTER SCHOOL 742/1-4
*TYPE OF MANUSCRIPT MISSAL 742/1-4, CALENDAR AND COMPUTISTICAL TABLES 742-5
*CONTENTS ENGLISH DRAWINGS OF THE 10TH AND 12TH CENTURIES 742/1-5, PASCHAL HAND/ DETAIL OF FIGURE ON LOWER LEFT 742-1, VITA FIGURE FROM LEOFRIC MISSAL 742/2-3, VITA FIGURE/ DETAIL OF DRAPERY 742-4, PASCHAL HAND 742-5

*$ABSTRACT 743
*LIBRARY BODLEIAN
*SLIDE SET TITLE MISCELLANY 7
*NEGATIVE REFERENCE ROLL 275
*RENTAL FEE $2.55
*TITLE OF MANUSCRIPT APPARATUS ON THE DECRETALS 743/1-2, MEDICAL TREATISES 743-3, BOOK OF HOURS 743/4-6, WORKS OF AUGUSTINE AND ISIDORE 743-7, BIBLE 743-8, EXPOSITIO IN TEMPLUM DOMINI 743/9-10, JOURNAL OF MAJOR D'ARCY BACON 743-11
*SHELFMARK MS E MUSAEO 19/ FOL V 743-1, MS E MUSAEO 19/ FOL VV 743-2, MS E MUSAEO 19/ FOL 165V 743-3, MS ASTOR A 18/ FOL 65 743-4, MS RAWL LITURG E 20/ FOL 9V 743-5, MS RAWL LITURG F 13/ FOL 80V 743-6, MS DOUCE 198/ FOL 53V 743-7, MS AUCT E INF 2 6/ FOL 155V 743-8, MS LAUD MISC 257/ FOL 143 743-9, MS LAUD MISC 257/ FOL 191 743-10, MS DON E 13/ FOL 104 743-11
*PROVENANCE ITALIAN/ CENTRAL 743/1-2, ITALIAN 743-3, FRENCH 743-4, FRENCH/ EVREUX 743-5, FRENCH/ BAYEUX 743-6, FRENCH/ LIESSIES 743-7, ENGLISH/ WINCHESTER 743-8, ITALIAN/ SICILY 743/9-10, ENGLISH 743-11
*DATE EXECUTED 13TH/ LATE 743/1-3, 15TH/ LATE 743-4, 16TH/C1500 743-5, 15TH/ 3RD QUARTER 743-6, 12TH/ 3RD QUARTER 743-7, 12TH/ LATE 743/8-10
*LANGUAGE LATIN 743/1-10, ENGLISH 743-11
*AUTHOR AUGUSTINE AND ISIDORE 743-7, BEDE 743/9-10, BACON/ MAJOR D'ARCY 743-11
*TYPE OF MANUSCRIPT DECRETALS 743/1-2, MEDICAL TREATISE 743-3

BOOK OF HOURS 743/4-6, CLASSICAL TEXT 743-7, BIBLE 743-8, TREATISE 743/9-10, JOURNAL 743-11
*CONTENTS MISCELLANY 7 743/1-11, ANNUNCIATION 743/1-2, NATIVITY 743/1-2, PRESENTATION OF CHRIST 743/1-2, BAPTISM 743/1-2, FIGURES/ FOUR SHOWING SYSTEMS OF THE BODY 743-3, OFFICE OF THE DEAD/ CLERICS BESIDE CORPSE 743-4, CLERICS BESIDE CORPSE 743-4, LIVING/ THREE MEET THREE DEAD BY WAYSIDE CROSS 743-5, LIVING/ THREE MEET THREE DEAD BY WAYSIDE CROSS 743-6, INITIAL M MODUS 743-7, INITIAL T TOBIAS 743-8, INITIAL P 743-9, INITIALS E AND V 743-10, ODYSSEUS' CAVE IN PARNASSUS 743-11

*$ABSTRACT 744
*LIBRARY TRINITY COLLEGE
*SLIDE SET TITLE MS TRINITY COLLEGE 78
*NEGATIVE REFERENCE ROLL 278A
*RENTAL FEE $2.35
*TITLE OF MANUSCRIPT PSALTER
*SHELFMARK MS TRINITY COLLEGE 78/ FOL 3 744-1, MS TRINITY COLLEGE 78/ FOL 3V 744-2, MS TRINITY COLLEGE 78/ FOL 4 744-3, MS TRINITY COLLEGE 78/ FOL 4V 744-4, MS TRINITY COLLEGE 78/ FOL 5 744-5, MS TRINITY COLLEGE 78/ FOL 111 744-6, MS TRINITY COLLEGE 78/ FOL 144V 744-7
*PROVENANCE BYZANTINE
*DATE EXECUTED 12TH
*LANGUAGE GREEK
*TYPE OF MANUSCRIPT PSALTER
*CONTENTS PSALTER/ BYZANTINE/ 12TH 744/1-7, FIGURES SEATED 744-1, SOLDIER ATTACKS MAN/ DAVID AND GOLIATH? 744-2, DAVID AND GOLIATH? 744-2, DAVID WRITES PSALMS/ GOD BLESSES 744-3, KING WITH HALO CROWNS YOUNG PERSON 744-4, DECORATED HEADPIECES 744/5-7

*$ABSTRACT 745
*LIBRARY BODLEIAN
*SLIDE SET TITLE MISCELLANY 9
*NEGATIVE REFERENCE ROLL 278B
*RENTAL FEE $2.25
*TITLE OF MANUSCRIPT LANCELOT CYCLE 745-1, MISSAL 745-2, BOOK OF HOURS 745-3, PSALTER 745-4, ORMESBY PSALTER 745-5
*SHELFMARK MS DOUCE 303/ FOL 53 745-1, MS CANON LITURG 352/ FOL 144V 745-2, MS DOUCE 62/ FOL 51 745-3, MS DOUCE 118/ FOL 9 745-4, MS DOUCE 366/ FOL 29 745-5
*PROVENANCE FRENCH 745-1, ITALIAN/ TODI 745-2, FRENCH 745-3, FRENCH/ ARTOIS 745-4, ENGLISH/ EAST ANGLIA 745-5
*DATE EXECUTED 14TH/C1300 745-1, 14TH/ 3RD QUARTER 745-2, 15TH/C1400 745-3, 13TH/ LATE 745-4, 13TH/ LATE TO C1300 745-5
*LANGUAGE FRENCH 745-1, LATIN 745-2, FRENCH AND LATIN 745-3, LATIN 745/4-5
*ARTIST/ SCHOOL ZENOBI DA FIRENZE 745-3
*TYPE OF MANUSCRIPT LITERATURE 745-1, MISSAL/ USE OF ROME 745-2, BOOK OF HOURS/ USE OF PARIS 745-3, PSALTER 745/4-5
*CONTENTS MISCELLANY 9 745/1-5, TREE OF LIFE 745-1, CAIN KILLS ABEL 745-1, CRUCIFIXION 745-2, ARMS OF MONTE OLIVETO 745-2, MERMAID OR SIREN WITH COMB AND MIRROR 745/3-4, SIREN GROTESQUE WITH COMB AND MIRROR 745-5

*$ABSTRACT 746
*LIBRARY BODLEIAN
*SLIDE SET TITLE MISCELLANY 10
*NEGATIVE REFERENCE ROLL 280A
*RENTAL FEE $2.90
*TITLE OF MANUSCRIPT DEMETIAN CODE 746/1-2, SOPHIST BY PHILOSTRATUS 746/3-10, SECRETA SECRETORUM 746/11-13, GRANT OF KNIGHTHOOD AND ARMS 746-14, ATLAS MAJOR VOLUME II 746/15-16, ROCK LORDSHIP 746-17, CIVITATES ORBIS TERRARUM 746-18
*SHELFMARK MS RAWL C 821/ FOL IIV 746-1, MS RAWL C 821/ PAGE

173 746-2, MS BAROCCI 50/ FOL 362V-363 746-3, MS BAROCCI 50/ FOL 363V-364 746-4, MS BAROCCI 50/ FOL 364V-365 746-5, MS BAROCCI 50/ FOL 365V-366 746-6, MS BAROCCI 50/ FOL 366V-367 746-7, MS BAROCCI 50/ FOL 367V-368 746-8, MS BAROCCI 50/ FOL 368V-369 746-9, MS BAROCCI 50/ FOL 369V-370 746-10, MS HERTFORD COLLEGE D2/ FOL 1 746/11-13, MS RAWL D 552/ FOL 4 746-14, MS ROLLS NORTHUMBERLAND 746-17
*PROVENANCE WELSH 746/1-2, GREEK 746/3-10, HUNGARY 746/11-13, AUSTRIAN/ VIENNA 746-14, DUTCH/ AMSTERDAM 746/15-16, ENGLISH 746-17, GERMAN/ COLOGNE 746-18
*DATE EXECUTED 13TH-14TH 746/1-2, 11TH/ PROBABLY 746/3-10, 14TH/ 2ND HALF 746/11-13, 17TH/1620 746-14, 17TH/1663 746/15-16, 16TH/1599 746/17-18
*LANGUAGE LATIN 746/1-2, GREEK 746/3-10, LATIN 746/11-16 AND 18
*AUTHOR PHILOSTRATUS 746/3-10, BLEAU/ JAN 746/15-16, BRAUN G AND F HOGENBURG 746-18
*TYPE OF MANUSCRIPT CODE 746/1-2, CLASSICAL TEXT 746/3-10, TREATISE 746/11-13, GRANT OF ARMS 746-14, ATLAS 746/15-16, PLAN 746-17, TREATISE 746-18
*CONTENTS MISCELLANY 10 746/1-18, SCROLL PATTERNS INCORPORATING BEAST MASK 746-1, GREEK MOTTO BY JOHN SELDEN AT TOP OF PAGE 746-1, CRUCIFIXION WITH VIRGIN AND ST JOHN 746-2, TEXT PAGES IN GREEK 746/3-10, INITIAL H HIC/ KING LOUIS D'ANJOU 746-11, KING LOUIS D'ANJOU OF HUNGARY AND POLAND 746-11, ARMS OF HUNGARY/ FRANCE/ AND THE EMPIRE 746-11, INITIAL H HIC/ DETAIL 746-12, ARMS OF HUNGARY/ FRANCE/ AND THE EMPIRE/ DETAIL 746-13, EMPEROR FERDINAND II GRANTS ARMS TO ROBERT ELIOT 746-14, MAP OF HUNGARY/ DETAIL OF TITLE 746-15, MAP OF HUNGARY 746-16, PLAN OF MANOR AND LORDSHIP 746-17, KONIGSBURG AND RIGA PRUSSIA 746-18

*$ABSTRACT 747
*LIBRARY BODLEIAN
*SLIDE SET TITLE FIFTEENTH CENTURY ILLUMINATION
*NEGATIVE REFERENCE ROLL 283E
*RENTAL FEE $4.65
*TITLE OF MANUSCRIPT FERIAL PSALTER 747-1, MISSAL 747/2-13, CHRONICLE 747-14, GENEALOGY OF KINGS OF ENGLAND TO HENRY V 747/15-39, MISSAL/ CUTTINGS 747/40-41, COMPENDIUM MORALE 747-42, BOOK OF HOURS 747-43, CONFESSIO AMANTIS 747-44, NORTHERN PASSION 747-45, BOOK OF HOURS 747/46-52, MISSAL 747-53
*SHELFMARK MS DON D 85/ FOL 65 747-1, MS TRINITY COLLEGE 8/ FOL 9 747-2, MS TRINITY COLLEGE 8/ FOL 12 747-3, MS TRINITY COLLEGE 8/ FOL 37 747-4, MS TRINITY COLLEGE 8/ FOL 146V 747-5, MS TRINITY COLLEGE 8/ FOL 157V 747-6, MS TRINITY COLLEGE 8/ FOL 186 747-7, MS TRINITY COLLEGE 8/ FOL 189 747-8, MS TRINITY COLLEGE 8/ FOL 214V 747-9, MS TRINITY COLLEGE 8/ FOL 230 747-10, MS TRINITY COLLEGE 8/ FOL 9 747-11, MS TRINITY COLLEGE 8/ FOL 146V 747-12, MS TRINITY COLLEGE 8/ FOL 189 747-13, MS ASHMOLE 34/ FOL 1 747-14, MS BODLEY ROLLS 6/ MEMBRANES 1-24 747/15-39, MS DOUCE D 19/ FOL 5A 747-40, MS DOUCE D 19/ FOL 5B 747-41, MS FAIRFAX 4/ FOL 1 747-42, MS LAT LITURG F 21/ FOL 68V 747-43, MS LAUD MISC 609/ FOL 10 747-44, MS RAWL C 86/ FOL 1V 747-45, MS RAWL LITURG D 1/ FOL 101 747-46, MS RAWL LITURG D 1/ FOL 102V 747-47, MS RAWL LITURG D 1/ FOL 104V 747-48, MS RAWL LITURG D 1/ FOL 105 747-49, MS RAWL LITURG D 1/ FOL 62V 747-50, MS RAWL LITURG D 1/ FOL 20 747-51, MS RAWL LITURG D 1/ FOL 59 747-52, MS ORIEL COLLEGE 75 747-53
*PROVENANCE ENGLISH
*DATE EXECUTED 15TH/ 1ST QUARTER 747-1, 14TH/ BEFORE 1388 747/2-13, 15TH/ AFTER 1464 747-14, 15TH/ 2ND QUARTER 747/15-39, 15TH/C1400 747/40-41, 15TH/ 3RD QUARTER 747-42, 15TH/ MID 747-43, 15TH/ EARLY 747-44, 15TH/ MID 747-45, 15TH/C1420 747/46-52, 15TH/ EARLY 747-53
*LANGUAGE LATIN 747/1-13, ENGLISH 747-14, FRENCH AND LATIN 747/15-39, LATIN 747/40-43, ENGLISH 747/44-45, LATIN 747/46-53
*ARTIST/ SCHOOL JOHANNES 747-1
*AUTHOR HARDING/ JOHN 747-14, ROGER OF WALTHAM 747/42-43, GOWER/ JOHN 747-44,

*TYPE OF MANUSCRIPT PSALTER/ USE OF SARUM 747-1, MISSAL/ USE OF SARUM 747/2-13, CHRONICLE 747-14, CHRONICLE 747/15-39, MISSAL/ CUTTINGS 747/40-41, COMPENDIUM 747-42, BOOK OF HOURS 747-43, LITERATURE 747-44, RELIGIOUS TREATISE 747-45, BOOK OF HOURS/ USE OF SARUM 747/46-52, MISSAL 747-53
*CONTENTS ILLUMINATION/ 15TH CENTURY 747/1-53, FIFTEENTH CENTURY ILLUMINATION 747/1-53, INITIAL D DIXIT/ TRINITY 747-1, TRINITY 747-1, INITIAL O OMNIBUS/ BLESSING WATER 747-2, BLESSING WATER 747-2, INITIAL A AD/ INTROIT 747-3, PRIEST AND SERVER AT ALTAR 747-3, INITIAL P PUER/ NATIVITY OF CHRIST 747-4, NATIVITY 747-4, INITIAL V VIRI/ ASCENSION 747-5, ASCENSION 747-5, INITIAL B BENEDICTUS/ TRINITY 747-6, TRINITY 747-6, INITIAL T TERRIBILIS/ DEDICATION OF CHURCH 747-7, DEDICATION OF CHURCH 747-7, BISHOP BLESSES EXTERIOR OF CHURCH 747-7, INITIAL D DOMINUS/ MARTYRDOM OF ST ANDREW 747-8, ST ANDREW MARTYRED 747-8, INITIAL D DE/ NATIVITY OF JOHN THE BAPTIST 747-9, ST JOHN THE BAPTIST'S NATIVITY 747-9, INITIAL C CAUDEAMUS/ ASSUMPTION OF VIRGIN 747-10, ASSUMPTION OF VIRGIN 747-10, BLESSING WATER 747-11, ASCENSION 747-12, ST ANDREW'S VIGIL 747-13, TEXT PAGE WITH DECORATED BORDER 747-14, GOD THE CREATOR 747-15, ADAM AND EVE TEMPTED 747-15, NAMES OF EARLY KINGS 747-15, ADAM AND EVE TEMPTED 747-16, NOAH AND ARK 747-16, BRUTUS' SHIELD 747-17, ANCESTORS BEFORE CHRIST 747-18, NATIVITY 747-19, ARMS OF CONSTANTINE 747-20, ARMS OF ARTHUR 747/20-21, WODEN AND FREYA 747-21, SAXON KINGS/ LIST OF NAMES 747-22, ST AUGUSTINE 747-23, SAXON KINGS/ LIST OF NAMES 747-24, KINGS OF LATE SAXON PERIOD 747-25, KINGS DOWN TO WILLIAM II 747-26, THOMAS A BECKET AND HENRY II 747-27, KINGS DOWN TO EDWARD I 747-28, ARMS OF DESCENDANTS OF EDWARD I 747-29, ARMS OF ENGLISH ROYALTY 747-30, ARMS OF ENGLISH AND FRENCH ROYAL LINES 747/31-33, TEXT PAGE 747-34, ARMS OF RICHARD II 747-35, ARMS 747-36, HENRY V PORTRAIT 747-37, TEXT PAGE 747/38-39, INITIAL P/ NATIVITY 747-40, NATIVITY 747-40, INITIAL E/ ADORATION OF MAGI 747-41, ADORATION OF THE MAGI 747-41, TEXT PAGE WITH DECORATED BORDER 747-42, INITIAL B BEATI/ ANGELS LIFT SOUL TO GOD 747-43, ANGELS LIFT SOUL TO GOD 747-43, LOVER'S CONFESSION 747-44, CRUCIFIXION WITH EVANGELIST SYMBOLS 747-45, INITIAL G GAUDE/ VIRGIN AND CHILD 747-46, VIRGIN AND CHILD 747-46, INITIAL G GAUDE/ ST MICHAEL 747-47, ST MICHAEL 747-47, INITIAL G GAUDE/ ST THOMAS A BECKET 747-48, ST THOMAS A BECKET 747-48, INITIAL G GAUDE/ ST KATHERINE 747-49, ST KATHERINE 747-49, INITIAL D DEUS/ DECORATIVE FOLIAGE 747-50, INITIALS/ DECORATED 747-51, OFFICE OF THE DEAD 747-52, INITIAL D DILEXI/ CLERICS PRAY BY COFFIN 747-52, CLERICS PRAY BY DRAPED COFFIN 747-52, INITIAL D DEUS/ CIRCUMCISION OF CHRIST 747-53,CIRCUMCISION OF CHRIST 747-53

*$ABSTRACT 748
*LIBRARY BODLEIAN
*SLIDE SET TITLE GREEK BINDINGS
*NEGATIVE REFERENCE ROLL 281A
*RENTAL FEE $2.10
*TITLE OF MANUSCRIPT COMMENTARY ON HERMOGENES 748-1, COMMENTARY ON JOHN DAMASCENE 748-2
*SHELFMARK MS BAROCCI 175 748-1, MS LAUD GREEK 63 748-2
*PROVENANCE GREEK
*DATE EXECUTED 15TH/ LATE TO EARLY 16TH
*LANGUAGE GREEK
*AUTHOR JOHN THE SICILIAN 748-1, ZONARAS/ JOHN 748-2
*TYPE OF MANUSCRIPT COMMENTARIES
*CONTENTS BINDINGS/ GREEK 748/1-2

*$ABSTRACT 749
*LIBRARY BODLEIAN
*SLIDE SET TITLE MS DOUCE 6/ PART 6
*NEGATIVE REFERENCE ROLL 281B
*RENTAL FEE $3.00
*TITLE OF MANUSCRIPT PORTABLE PSALTER

*SHELFMARK MS DOUCE 6/ FOL 183V-184 749-1, MS DOUCE 6/ FOL 184V-185 749-2, MS DOUCE 6/ FOL 185V-186 749-3, MS DOUCE 6/ FOL 186V-187 749-4, MS DOUCE 6/ FOL 187V-188 749-5, MS DOUCE 6/ FOL 188V-189 749-6, MS DOUCE 6/ FOL 189V-190 749-7, MS DOUCE 6/ FOL 190V-191 749-8, MS DOUCE 6/ FOL 191V-192 749-9, MS DOUCE 6/ FOL 192V-193 749-10, MS DOUCE 6/ FOL 193V-194 749-11, MS DOUCE 6/ FOL 194V-195 749-12, MS DOUCE 6/ FOL 195V-196 749-13, MS DOUCE 6/ FOL 196V-197 749-14, MS DOUCE 6/ FOL 197V-198 749-15, MS DOUCE 6/ FOL 198V-199 749-16, MS DOUCE 6/ FOL 199V-200 749-17, MS DOUCE 6/ FOL 200V-201 749-18, MS DOUCE 6/ FOL 201V-202 749-19, MS DOUCE 6/ FOL 202V-203 749-20
*PROVENANCE FLEMISH/ GHENT
*DATE EXECUTED 14TH/C1320-30
*LANGUAGE LATIN
*TYPE OF MANUSCRIPT PSALTER/ PORTABLE
*CONTENTS PSALTER/ FLEMISH/ 14TH 749/1-20, BATTLE BETWEEN TWO APES 749-1, TRUMPETER 749-1, FIGURE HOLDS DOG SKULL 749-2, LINE ENDINGS WITH HEADS 749-2, UNICORN 749-3, BAGPIPER 749-3, LINE ENDINGS WITH FACES 749-3, LINE ENDINGS/ FIVE WITH FACES 749-4, MAN PLAYS GRIDIRON WITH FLESH HOOK FOR BOW 749-5, LINE ENDINGS WITH HEADS 749-6, KNIGHT IN MAIL WITH SWORD AND SHIELD 749-7, MAN SHOOTS ARROW AT GROTESQUE HEAD 749-8, BIRD EATS DEAD FOX 749-8, BAGPIPES PLAYED BY APE 749-9, DOG HOLDS STAFF 749-9, WINCH WORKED BY MEN 749-9, MAN WITH BIRCH 749-10, TRUMPETER 749-10, MAN PUTS HANDS IN LION'S MOUTH 749-10, SAINT WITH SWORD 749-10, SS PAUL/ ANDREW/ STEPHEN AND BARTHOLOMEW 749-11, SAINTS WITH KNIFE/ SPEAR AND LARGE BIRD 749-12, LINE ENDINGS WITH HEADS/ BEASTS/ GROTESQUES 749-12, CHEQUER BOARD 749-13, SS ELIZABETH OF HUNGARY AND CATHERINE 749-13, LINE ENDINGS WITH HEADS/ BEASTS/ GROTESQUES 749-13, MAN DRINKS FROM DISH 749-14, MAN HAMMERS NAIL IN HEAD OF GROTESQUE 749-14, APE BISHOP 749-14, LINE ENDINGS WITH FACES 749-15, CLUB AND BUCKLER 749-16, HARE BLOWS TRUMPET 749-17, APE SINGS FROM BOOK 749-17, HUNTING SCENE 749-17, INITIAL WITH TWO MONSTERS 749-17, CARRIAGE WITH APE PASSENGERS 749-18, KNIGHT FIGHTS DRAGON 749-18, BAGPIPES PLAYED BY STAG 749-19, HARE/ DOG/ THREE BIRDS 749-19, MAN WITH AXE ATTACKS APE 749-20, INITIALS WITH MONSTERS 749-20

*$ABSTRACT 750
*LIBRARY BODLEIAN
*SLIDE SET TITLE MISCELLANY 15
*NEGATIVE REFERENCE ROLL 292
*RENTAL FEE $2.80
*TITLE OF MANUSCRIPT EPITRE D'OTHEA A HECTOR 750/1-12, RAGEMON LE BON 750-13, CHAUNCUN DE SECLE 750/13-16, NOTITIA DIGNITATUM 750-17, SIEGE OF TROY 750-18
*SHELFMARK MS LAUD MISC 570/ FOL 24 750-1, MS LAUD MISC 570/ FOL 24V 750-2, MS LAUD MISC 570/ FOL 25 750-3, MS LAUD MISC 570/ FOL 25V 750-4, MS LAUD MISC 570/ FOL 26 750-5, MS LAUD MISC 570/ FOL 26V 750-6, MS LAUD MISC 570/ FOL 27 750-7, MS LAUD MISC 570/ FOL 27V 750-8, MS LAUD MISC 570/ FOL 28 750-9, MS LAUD MISC 570/ FOL 28V 750-10, MS LAUD MISC 570/ FOL 29 750-11, MS LAUD MISC 570/ FOL 29V 750-12, MS DIGBY 86/ FOL 163V 750/13-14, MS DIGBY 86/ FOL 164 750/15-16, MS LAUD MISC 595/ FOL 1A 750-18
*PROVENANCE FRENCH 750/1-12, ENGLISH/ WORCESTERSHIRE 750/13-16, ENGLISH 750-18
*DATE EXECUTED 15TH/1450 750/1-12, 13TH/ LATE 750/13-16, 15TH/1436 750-17, 15TH/ EARLY 750-18
*LANGUAGE FRENCH 750/1-12, ENGLISH AND ANGLO-NORMAN 750/13-16, LATIN 750-17, ENGLISH 750-18
*ARTIST/ SCHOOL MASTER OF SIR JOHN FASTOLF 750/1-12
*AUTHOR DE PISAN/ CHRISTINE 750/1-12, DE COLUMNIS/ GUIDO 750-18
*TYPE OF MANUSCRIPT LITERATURE 750/1-16, MILITARY TREATISE 750-17, LITERATURE 750-18
*CONTENTS MISCELLANY 15 750/1-18, CHRISTINE DE PISAN PRESENTS BOOK TO DUC DE BERRY 750-1, AUTHOR PRESENTS HER BOOK 750-1, DUC DE BERRY RECEIVES BOOK 750-1, TEXT PAGES 750/2-3, HECTOR RECEIVES OTHEA'S EPISTLE 750-4, TEXT PAGES 750/5-9, ATTEMPANCE

WINDS CLOCK 750-10, TEXT PAGES 750/11-12, END OF RAGEMON LE BON 750/13-14, TEXT OF CHAUCUN DEL SECLE 750/15-16, TEXT OF NOTITIA DIGNITATUM 750-17, TEXT PAGE OF THE SIEGE OF TROY 750-18

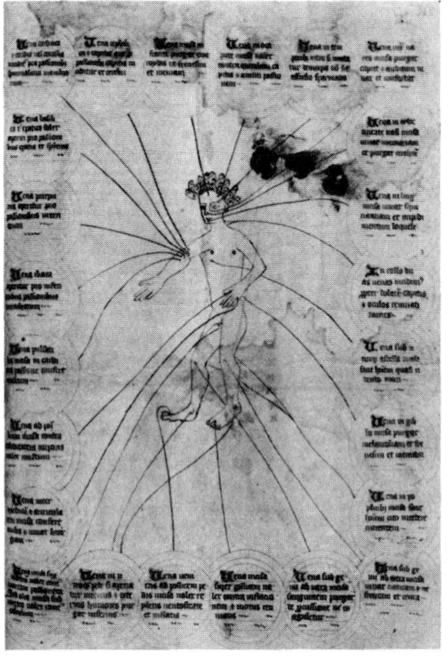

a

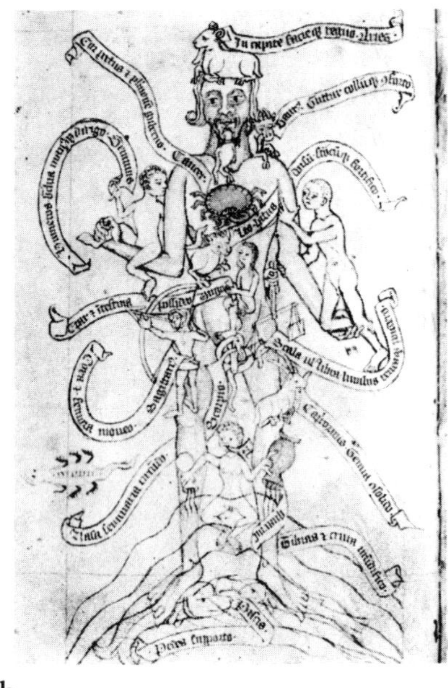

b

c

Plate III

# INDEX TO LIBRARIES

# INDEX TO SLIDE SET TITLES

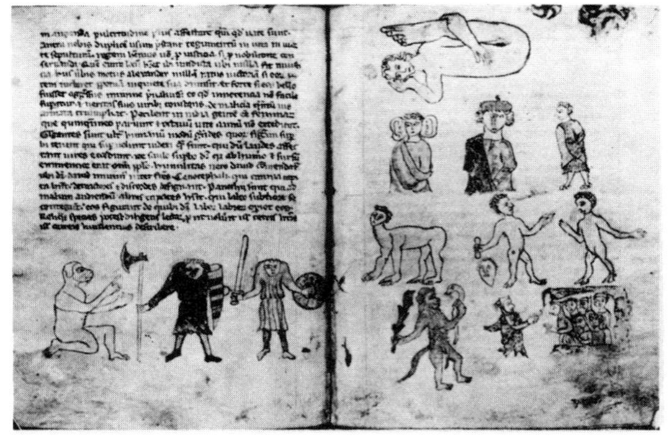

a

b

c

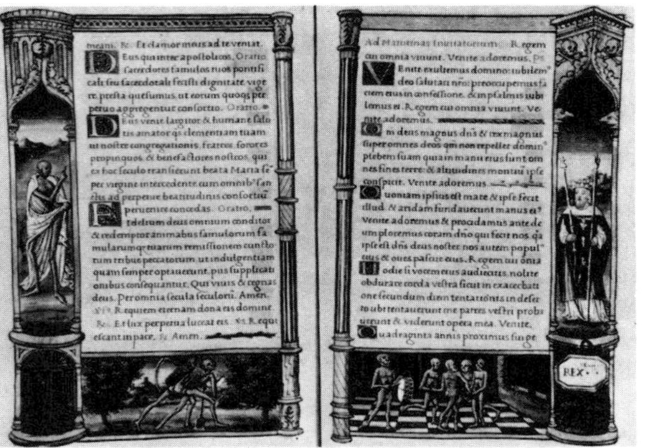

d

Plate IV

(SLIDE SET TITLE)

(SLIDE SET TITLE)

(SLIDE SET TITLE)

Plate V

# INDEX TO NEGATIVE REFERENCES

(NEGATIVE REFERENCE)

(NEGATIVE REFERENCE)

(NEGATIVE REFERENCE)

(NEGATIVE REFERENCE)

(NEGATIVE REFERENCE)

# INDEX TO
# TITLES OF MANUSCRIPTS

a

b

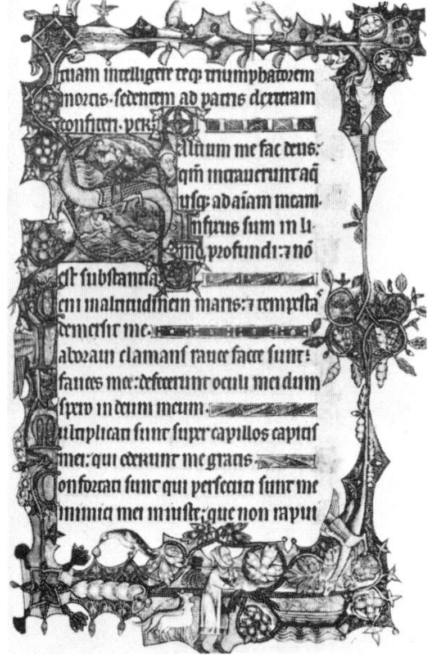
Quam intelligere tecp triumphatorem
mortis. sedentem ad patris dexteram
confiteri. per.
Salvum me fac deus:
qm intraverunt aq
usque ad animam meam.
Infixus sum in li-
mo profundi: et nō
est substantia.
Veni in altitudinem maris: et tempesta
demersit me.
Laboravi clamans rauce facte sunt:
fauces mee: defecerunt oculi mei dum
spero in deum meum.
Multiplicati sunt super capillos capitis
mei: qui oderunt me gratis.
Confortati sunt qui persecuti sunt me
inimici mei iniuste: que non rapui

c

ensamble
aventures
Or dist li contes que qu[a]nt
me sires Gauuains se fu
partis de ses compaing
nons q'il chevaucha
maintes iournee lonc &
pres sans aventure trouver qui fa

d

Plate VI

TITLE OF MANUSCRIPT)

(TITLE OF MANUSCRIPT)

(TITLE OF MANUSCRIPT)

(TITLE OF MANUSCRIPT)

(TITLE OF MANUSCRIPT)

(TITLE OF MANUSCRIPT)

(TITLE OF MANUSCRIPT)

(TITLE OF MANUSCRIPT)

(TITLE OF MANUSCRIPT)

(TITLE OF MANUSCRIPT)

(TITLE OF MANUSCRIPT)

(TITLE OF MANUSCRIPT)

(TITLE OF MANUSCRIPT)

(TITLE OF MANUSCRIPT)

(TITLE OF MANUSCRIPT)

a

b

c

d

Plate VII

# INDEX TO SHELFMARKS

(SHELFMARK)

(SHELFMARK)

(SHELFMARK)

(SHELFMARK)

(SHELFMARK)

(SHELFMARK)

(SHELFMARK)

(SHELFMARK)

(SHELFMARK)

(SHELFMARK)

SHELFMARK)

(SHELFMARK)

(SHELFMARK)

(SHELFMARK)

(SHELFMARK)

SHELFMARK)

(SHELFMARK)

(SHELFMARK)

(SHELFMARK)

(SHELFMARK)

(SHELFMARK)

(SHELFMARK)

(SHELFMARK)

(SHELFMARK)

(SHELFMARK)

(SHELFMARK)

(SHELFMARK)

(SHELFMARK)

(SHELFMARK)

(SHELFMARK)

(SHELFMARK)

(SHELFMARK)

(SHELFMARK)

(SHELFMARK)

(SHELFMARK)

(SHELFMARK)

(SHELFMARK)

(SHELFMARK)

(SHELFMARK)

(SHELFMARK)

(SHELFMARK)

(SHELFMARK)

(SHELFMARK)

(SHELFMARK)

(SHELFMARK)

(SHELFMARK)

(SHELFMARK)

(SHELFMARK)

(SHELFMARK)

(SHELFMARK)

(SHELFMARK)

(SHELFMARK)

(SHELFMARK)

(SHELFMARK)

(SHELFMARK)

(SHELFMARK)

(SHELFMARK)

(SHELFMARK)

a

b

c

d

Plate VIII

# INDEX TO PROVENANCE

(PROVENANCE)

(PROVENANCE)

(PROVENANCE)

Plate IX

a

b

c

d

# INDEX TO DATES EXECUTED

(DATE EXECUTED)

(DATE EXECUTED)

DATE EXECUTED)

DATE EXECUTED)

(DATE EXECUTED)

(DATE EXECUTED)

(DATE EXECUTED)

(DATE EXECUTED)

(DATE EXECUTED)

(DATE EXECUTED)

(DATE EXECUTED)

# INDEX TO LANGUAGES OF TEXTS

a

b

c

In youthe sende me aduersytie
And not when I am olde
The angell toke from thence hys flyght
And lefte alone that carefull knyghte
From hym he wente hys waye
When the angell was paste hys sight
Hys stronge steede that was so wyghte
Deadde vnder hym he laye
Hys hawkes and houndes that he fedde

d

Plate X

(LANGUAGE)

(LANGUAGE)

(LANGUAGE)

a

b

c

d

Plate XI

# INDEX TO
# ARTISTS OR SCHOOLS OF ILLUMINATION

a

b

c

d

Plate XII

# INDEX TO AUTHORS OF TEXTS

(AUTHOR)

(AUTHOR)

(AUTHOR)

(AUTHOR)

(AUTHOR)

(AUTHOR)

(AUTHOR)

# INDEX TO SCRIBES

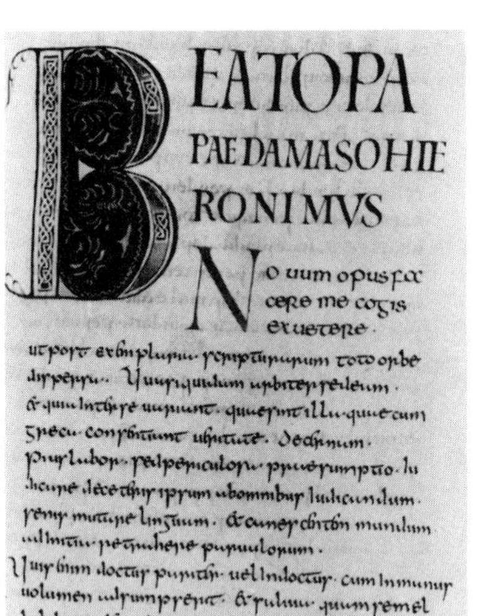

BEATO PAPAE DAMASO HIERONIMVS

Novum opus facere me cogis ex uetere

a

de hac disceptatione iudices
tu senseris: et ego sentire u
tiri. Vale et mei me
kl Novembris.

POGGIVS
baro uiro c
pernultas
publicas ti
mu tempor
debo tamen
pellare paululu atq: auocar
tias quasdam ridiculas
tissimu an mea culpa con
in re solutam tua
intelligas potius culpandu
uiuius desumpsit, neq:
gruens amicitie nre. Eg
scribendi ductus edidi epl

b

QVAN
falsas e
varios:
terram
sione su
vita: di
tamen
secundu
errorum
decepti homines: et primitus de
persuasione inueterata in suscep
ueraverint. Gestio enim conu
vanitate detecta: singularis dei c
vtilius et maius officium reuoca
et in gratiam secum ipsos reducenc
tantopere despiciant. ne ve se in

c

KING HAFBUR AND KING SIWARD,

They needs must stir up strife
All about the swerling Signy,
Who was so fair a wife
O wilt thou win me then
or as fair a maid as I be?

II

It was the kings son Hafbur
Awoke amidst the night,
And fell to talk of a dream of dread
In wise words nowise light.

III

Methought I was in heaven
Amidst that fair abode,

d

Plate XIII

a

b

c

d

Plate XIV

# INDEX TO
# TYPES OF MANUSCRIPTS

(TYPE OF MANUSCRIPT)

(TYPE OF MANUSCRIPT)

(TYPE OF MANUSCRIPT)

(TYPE OF MANUSCRIPT)

# INDEX TO CONTENTS

a

b

c

d

Plate XV

(CONTENTS)

(CONTENTS)

(CONTENTS)

(CONTENTS)

(CONTENTS)

(CONTENTS)

CONTENTS)

(CONTENTS)

(CONTENTS)

(CONTENTS)

(CONTENTS)

(CONTENTS)

(CONTENTS)

(CONTENTS)

(CONTENTS)

(CONTENTS)

(CONTENTS)

(CONTENTS)

(CONTENTS)

(CONTENTS)

(CONTENTS)

(CONTENTS)

(CONTENTS)

(CONTENTS)

(CONTENTS)

(CONTENTS)

(CONTENTS)

(CONTENTS)

(CONTENTS)

(CONTENTS)

(CONTENTS)

(CONTENTS)

CONTENTS)

(CONTENTS)

(CONTENTS)

(CONTENTS)

(CONTENTS)

(CONTENTS)

(CONTENTS)

(CONTENTS)

(CONTENTS)

(CONTENTS)

(CONTENTS)

(CONTENTS)

(CONTENTS)

(CONTENTS)

(CONTENTS)

(CONTENTS)

(CONTENTS)

(CONTENTS)

(CONTENTS)

(CONTENTS)

(CONTENTS)

(CONTENTS)

(CONTENTS)

(CONTENTS)

(CONTENTS)

(CONTENTS)

(CONTENTS)

(CONTENTS)

(CONTENTS)

(CONTENTS)

(CONTENTS)

(CONTENTS)

CONTENTS)

(CONTENTS)

(CONTENTS)

(CONTENTS)

(CONTENTS)

(CONTENTS)

(CONTENTS)

(CONTENTS)

(CONTENTS)

(CONTENTS)

(CONTENTS)

(CONTENTS)

(CONTENTS)

(CONTENTS)

(CONTENTS)

(CONTENTS)

(CONTENTS)

(CONTENTS)

(CONTENTS)

(CONTENTS)

(CONTENTS)

(CONTENTS)

(CONTENTS)

(CONTENTS)

(CONTENTS)

(CONTENTS)

(CONTENTS)

(CONTENTS)

(CONTENTS)

(CONTENTS)

(CONTENTS)

(CONTENTS)

CONTENTS)

(CONTENTS)

(CONTENTS)

(CONTENTS)

(CONTENTS)

(CONTENTS)

CONTENTS)

(CONTENTS)

CONTENTS)

(CONTENTS)

(CONTENTS)

(CONTENTS)

(CONTENTS)

(CONTENTS)

(CONTENTS)

(CONTENTS)

(CONTENTS)

(CONTENTS)

(CONTENTS)

(CONTENTS)

(CONTENTS)

(CONTENTS)

(CONTENTS)

(CONTENTS)

(CONTENTS)

(CONTENTS)

(CONTENTS)

(CONTENTS)

(CONTENTS)

CONTENTS)

(CONTENTS)

CONTENTS)

(CONTENTS)

(CONTENTS)

(CONTENTS)

(CONTENTS)

(CONTENTS)

(CONTENTS)

(CONTENTS)

(CONTENTS)

(CONTENTS)

(CONTENTS)

(CONTENTS)

CONTENTS)

(CONTENTS)

CONTENTS)

(CONTENTS)

(CONTENTS)

CONTENTS)

(CONTENTS)

(CONTENTS)

(CONTENTS)

(CONTENTS)

(CONTENTS)

(CONTENTS)

CONTENTS)

(CONTENTS)

(CONTENTS)

(CONTENTS)

(CONTENTS)

(CONTENTS)

(CONTENTS)

(CONTENTS)

(CONTENTS)

CONTENTS)

(CONTENTS)

CONTENTS)

(CONTENTS)

CONTENTS)

(CONTENTS)

CONTENTS)

(CONTENTS)

(CONTENTS)

(CONTENTS)

(CONTENTS)

(CONTENTS)

(CONTENTS)

(CONTENTS)

(CONTENTS)

(CONTENTS)

(CONTENTS)

(CONTENTS)

(CONTENTS)

(CONTENTS)

(CONTENTS)

(CONTENTS)

(CONTENTS)

(CONTENTS)

(CONTENTS)

(CONTENTS)

(CONTENTS)

(CONTENTS)

(CONTENTS)

(CONTENTS)